Food Addiction and Disorder: Challenges and Concerns

Editor: Ellie Morrison

AMERICAN
MEDICAL PUBLISHERS
www.americanmedicalpublishers.com

AMERICAN
MEDICAL PUBLISHERS
www.americanmedicalpublishers.com

Cataloging-in-Publication Data

Food addiction and disorder : challenges and concerns / edited by Ellie Morrison.
p. cm.
Includes bibliographical references and index.
ISBN 979-8-88740-125-6
1. Compulsive eating. 2. Eating disorders. 3. Compulsive eating--Diagnosis.
4. Compulsive eating--Treatment. 5. Eating disorders--Diagnosis.
6. Eating disorders--Treatment. I. Morrison, Ellie.
RC552.C65 F66 2023
616.852 6--dc23

American Medical Publishers,
41 Flatbush Avenue,
1st Floor, New York,
NY 11217, USA

ISBN 979-8-88740-125-6 (Hardback)

Contents

Preface

This book aims to highlight the current researches and provides a platform to further the scope of innovations in this area. This book is a product of the combined efforts of many researchers and scientists, after going through thorough studies and analysis from different parts of the world. The objective of this book is to provide the readers with the latest information of the field.

Food addiction refers to compulsive overeating, where a person engages in frequent episodes of uncontrolled eating. Food disorders are associated with persistent behaviors of eating which affect the individual's health, their emotions and capability to function in their life. Binge eating is a food disorder characterized by a loss of control over eating. It is one of the most common chronic illnesses among adolescents. Individuals suffering from this disorder eat unusually large amount of food in relatively short periods of time. Some common symptoms of binge eating are feelings of distress, such as shame, disgust, or guilt. Purging behaviors, such as calorie restriction, vomiting, excessive exercise, or laxative or diuretic use are some other symptoms. There are several medical complications associated with binge eating disorders, including heart disease, stroke, type 2 diabetes, severe dehydration and constipation. It can be treated with the help of nutritional assistance and medication. This book explores the challenges and concerns of food addiction and disorders. Researchers and students in this field will be assisted by it.

I would like to express my sincere thanks to the authors for their dedicated efforts in the completion of this book. I acknowledge the efforts of the publisher for providing constant support. Lastly, I would like to thank my family for their support in all academic endeavors.

Editor

1

Longitudinal Changes in Food Addiction Symptoms and Body Weight among Adults in a Behavioral Weight-Loss Program

Eliza L. Gordon [1,2,*], Lisa J. Merlo [3], Patricia E. Durning [1] and Michael G. Perri [1]

1 Department of Clinical and Health Psychology, University of Florida, P.O. Box 100165, Gainesville, FL 32610, USA; pdurning@phhp.ufl.edu (P.E.D.); mperri@phhp.ufl.edu (M.G.P.)

2 Division of Physical Medicine & Rehabilitation, University of Utah, 30 N 1900 E (Rm 1B620), Salt Lake City, UT 84132, USA

3 Department of Psychiatry, McKnight Brain Institute, University of Florida College of Medicine, L4-100K, P.O. Box 100256, Gainesville, FL 32611, USA; lmerlo@ufl.edu

* Correspondence: elwarren.22@phhp.ufl.edu

Abstract: Interest in food addiction (FA) has increased, but little is known about its clinical implications or potential treatments. Using secondary analyses from a randomized controlled trial, we evaluated the associations between changes in FA, body weight, and "problem food" consumption during a 22-month behavioral weight-loss program consisting of an initial four-month in-person intervention, 12-month extended-care, and six-month follow-up (n = 182). Food addiction was measured using the Yale Food Addiction Scale. "Problem foods" were identified from the literature and self-reporting. Multilevel modeling was used as the primary method of analysis. We hypothesized that reductions in problem food consumption during the initial treatment phase would be associated with long-term (22-month) FA reductions. As expected, we found that reductions in problem foods were associated with greater initial reductions in FA symptoms; however, they were also associated with a sharper rebound in symptoms over time ($p = 0.016$), resulting in no significant difference at Month 22 ($p = 0.856$). Next, we hypothesized that long-term changes in FA would be associated with long-term changes in body weight. Although both FA and weight decreased over time ($ps < 0.05$), month-to-month changes in FA were not associated with month-to-month changes in weight ($p = 0.706$). Instead, higher overall FA (i.e., mean scores over the course of the study) were associated with less weight loss ($p = 0.008$) over time. Finally, we hypothesized that initial reductions in problem food consumption would be associated with long-term reductions in weight, but this relationship was not significant ($ps > 0.05$). Given the complexity of the findings, more research is needed to identify interventions for long-term changes in FA and to elucidate the associations between problem foods, FA, and weight.

Keywords: obesity; food addiction; weight loss; treatment; food

1. Introduction

Prior research has suggested that certain foods (e.g., processed foods high in fat and/or sugar) and eating behaviors (e.g., binge eating) can be associated with addiction-like symptoms. Neurological, genetic, and psychological similarities have been observed between problematic eating behaviors and symptoms of substance use disorders (e.g., excessive consumption, cravings, preoccupation, unsuccessful attempts to limit use of the substance) [1–10]. High-fat and/or high-sugar processed foods, such as ice cream, pizza, potato chips, or chocolate, are most commonly associated with addiction-like changes both behaviorally and neurobiologically [9,11,12]. For example, Gearhardt et al. [12] found that individuals who reported experiencing DSM-IV substance dependence symptoms toward food had greater activation in the anterior cingulate cortex, medial orbitofrontal cortex, and amygdala (brain areas implicated in substance dependence) in response to a chocolate milkshake.

In 2009, Gearhardt et al. [13] published the Yale Food Addiction Scale (YFAS), a validated self-report questionnaire that adapts the DSM-IV substance dependence criteria toward "certain foods" for which respondents may have difficulty controlling their intake. Using this scale, Schulte and Gearhardt [14] estimated that approximately 15% of adults in the United States met the YFAS criteria for food addiction (FA; ≥3 symptoms, plus distress/impairment), with higher prevalence among adults with obesity (19%). In addition to obesity, FA symptoms have been associated with increased risk for disordered eating [8,15–17], depression [15–18], emotional eating [15,17], impulsivity [16], lower self-esteem [16], and poorer quality of life [19].

Despite increased empirical interest in FA, research toward evidence-based treatment is inchoate. A systematic review by Cassin et al. [20] found only eight studies related to FA treatment and concluded that there is not sufficient evidence to support any specific intervention. There is a clear need for research toward evidence-based interventions if FA continues to present as a unique problem [21–23]. Potential treatments could draw on successful approaches used in the substance use disorder and obesity treatment literature. For example, Vella and Pai [24] proposed that techniques commonly used in substance use disorder and obesity treatment—such as problem solving, stimulus control, and cognitive behavioral approaches—could help treat FA by reducing impulsivity, building positive coping skills, and improving distress tolerance.

Behavioral weight-loss treatments represent a logical next step toward identifying evidence-based treatments for FA due to their strong theoretical base, effectiveness in treating obesity, and similarity to substance use disorder treatment. Grounded in cognitive-behavioral theory, these interventions aim to produce healthy weight loss primarily by decreasing caloric consumption, improving diet quality, and increasing physical activity [25]. Often provided in a group setting, these interventions can be a source of health-behavior-specific social support, which is vital to long-term recovery from drug addiction [26], and possibly FA [27].

To our knowledge, only two studies have evaluated changes in FA symptoms among adults participating in behavioral weight-loss programs. In a sample of 90 women, Sawamoto et al. [28] found that "successful" participants (i.e., those who maintained a 10% weight loss at 12- and 24-month follow-ups) in a seven-month behavioral weight-loss program reported fewer symptoms of FA post-treatment compared to "unsuccessful" participants, despite no differences in symptoms at baseline. However, the authors did not report whether changes in FA were statistically significant. Chao et al. [29] analyzed changes in weight and FA symptoms among a sample of 178 adults participating in a 14-week behavioral weight-loss program. They found that, although overall YFAS scores significantly decreased from pre- to post-intervention, neither changes in YFAS scores nor baseline YFAS "diagnosis" significantly predicted weight loss. Taken together, findings from these studies appear to suggest that FA symptoms may decrease in behavioral weight-loss programs.

The current study aimed to describe the associations between early changes in "problem food" consumption, long-term changes in FA symptoms, and long-term weight change. Analyses were conducted using data collected from a multi-site behavioral weight-loss randomized control trial that consisted of a four-month in-person treatment phase (Phase 1; Months 0–4), followed by a 12-month extended-care phase (Phase 2; Months 4–16) and a six-month follow-up phase (Phase 3; Months 16–22). Specifically, we aimed (1) to identify associations between initial (Phase 1) changes in "problem food" consumption (e.g., high-sugar/high-fat processed foods recorded in participant dietary logs) and long-term changes in FA symptoms, and (2) to identify the associations between initial changes in "problem food" consumption, long-term FA symptoms, and long-term weight loss. We hypothesized that (a) Phase 1 reductions in "problem foods" would be associated with a long-term reduction in FA symptoms (Months 0–22), (b) long-term changes in FA symptoms would be associated with long-term changes in body weight, and (c) Phase 1 reductions in problem food consumption would be associated with long-term reductions in body weight.

2. Materials and Methods

The current paper describes a secondary data analysis of data from the Rural Lifestyle Eating and Activity Program (Rural LEAP) [30]. The Rural LEAP project was a randomized controlled trial comparing the effects of three strategies for long-term weight management among 528 women and men (ages 21–75; body mass indexes (BMIs) between 30–45) living in rural north Florida. Approval was obtained from the University of Florida Institutional Review Board (IRB), and all participants gave written informed consent. Participants attended a weekly, in-person behavioral weight-loss program for the first four months of treatment (Phase 1). Those who completed Phase 1 with ≥50% attendance were randomly assigned to 12 months of extended care (Phase 2) delivered via individual or group telephone counseling or an education control program delivered via email. All participants received 18 modules with recommendations for maintaining lost weight. In the phone-based conditions, health coaches provided participants with 18 individual or group sessions focused on problem solving of obstacles to the maintenance of weight loss. Phase 3 (Months 16–22) was a no-contact follow-up period for participants to practice the strategies on their own. Assessments were conducted at baseline (Month 0), post-treatment (Month 4), halfway through the extended-care phase (Month 10), post-extended care (Month 16), and after the final no-contact phase (Month 22).

2.1. Participants

The sample included adult men and women with BMIs between 30–45 kg/m^2 and without medical contraindications for weight loss (see prior publications [30,31] for specific inclusion and exclusion criteria). Although four cohorts ("waves") of volunteers participated in the Rural LEAP program, the YFAS was not added to the study until the third and fourth cohorts; thus, the current study only included participants who completed the program during Waves 3 and 4 (n = 196). In addition, the current study excluded participants if they failed to complete eligible dietary records at the end of Month 4 (i.e., ≥3 days recorded per week; complete information on food types/amounts) or if they did not complete the 22-month assessment. This resulted in a sample size of 182 participants for the current study (see Figure 1 for a flow diagram).

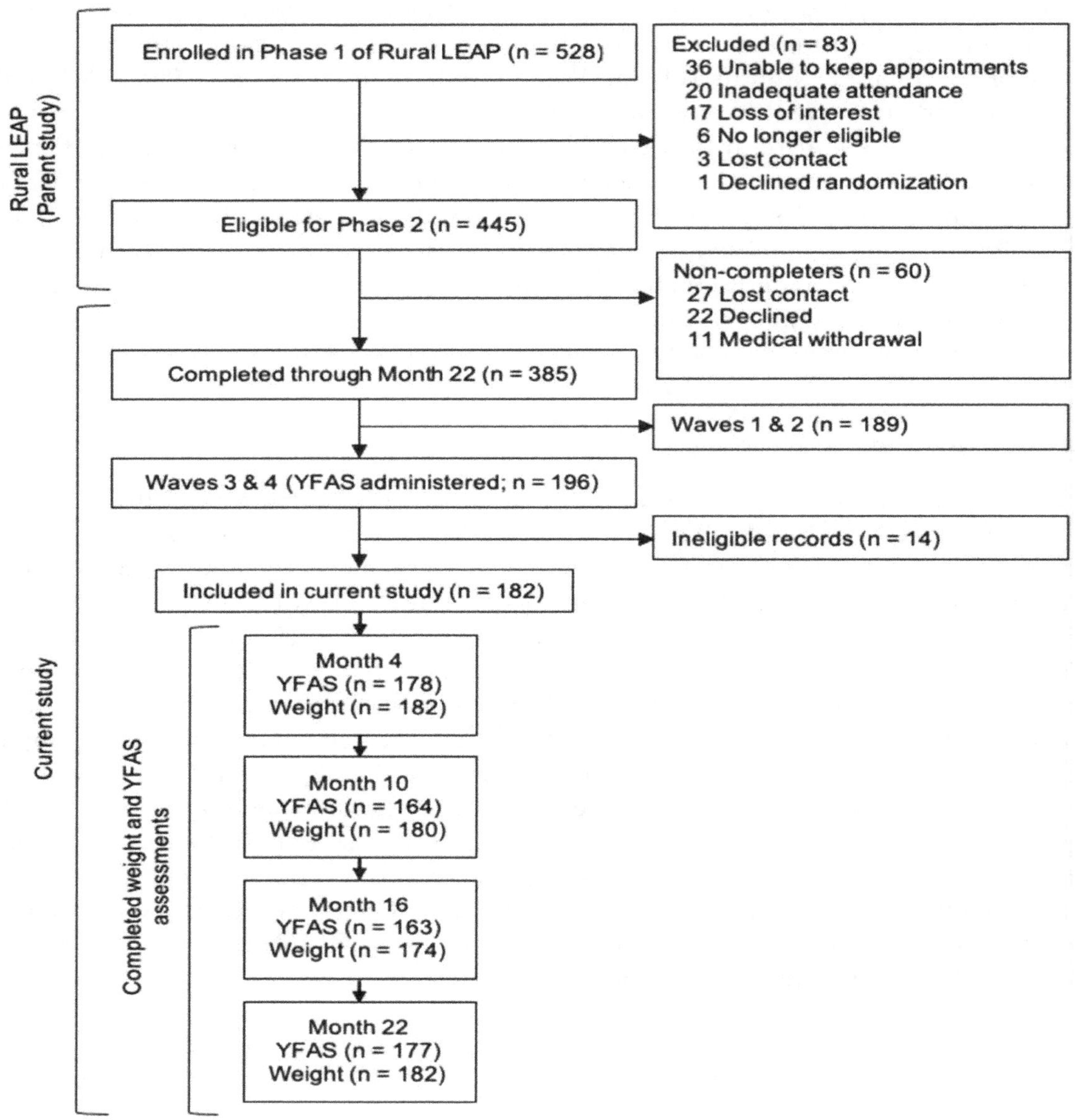

Figure 1. Flow diagram of participants.

2.2. *Main Variables*

2.2.1. Problem foods

"Problem foods" (i.e., foods more likely to be associated with addiction-like symptoms) were self-identified at baseline using participants' responses to the YFAS. Combined with information from prior literature (e.g., [9,11,32–34]), these responses were used to create a combined "problem foods" variable, which included the following food categories from the USDA's "What We Eat In America" survey [35]: pizza, burgers, savory snacks, sweet bakery products, chocolate, candy, ice cream and frozen desserts, fried potatoes, diet soda, sweetened beverages, sugars, and sugar substitutes. A "problem food consumption" score was calculated for each participant based on the average number of times per day he or she consumed a food item from this list. This was calculated by summing the total number of times participants consumed any item from the "problem food" list in a week (e.g., first week of Month 0; last week of Month 16) and dividing this sum by the number of days recorded that week (e.g., average daily frequency of problem food consumption = total number of times "problem food" consumed that week/number of days recorded that week). Data on food consumption was extracted from participants' dietary records, which they were instructed to keep daily during the course of the intervention. Due to low food record completion rates during Phase 2 (approximately 50%), only food logs from Phase 1 were used for the current study. Data extracted from the logs were entered into the secure Research Electronic Data Capture (REDCap) tool [36], and entries were randomly checked for accuracy and consistency. Food records were excluded if they failed to include accurate or complete information (e.g., no quantities or caloric values), if there were less than three complete days recorded per week, or if the participant had abnormal circumstances that week (i.e., severe illness).

2.2.2. Food Addiction Symptoms

The Yale Food Addiction Scale (YFAS) [13] is a validated self-report instrument, and is currently the most frequently used measure of addiction-like eating behaviors. The original version of this scale was used in the current study. It includes 25 questions, with most presented in either Likert or "yes/no" format. Respondents are instructed to answer questions while keeping in mind "certain foods" for which they have difficulty controlling their intake. Each question contributes to one of seven symptoms (e.g., craving, failure to fulfill major role obligations) or clinical criteria (i.e., distress or impairment). The scale's "diagnostic" threshold is based on the DSM-IV criteria for substance dependence (≥3 symptoms, plus distress or impairment). The questionnaire produces two metrics: a dichotomous "diagnosis" score (meets criteria vs. does not meet criteria) and a continuous "symptom" score (0–7 symptoms). The current study used the symptom score for analyses in order to better quantify the degree of change in symptoms.

The YFAS was administered at all five assessment points (Months 0, 4, 10, 16, and 22). While the original questionnaire asks participants to report on symptoms experienced in the past year, we modified the instructions to read "the past four months" at the Month 4 assessment and "the past six months" at Months 10, 16, and 22 in order to reflect the amount of time between assessments.

2.2.3. Body Weight

Body weight was measured to the nearest 0.1 kg using a calibrated digital scale at all five assessments. Participants wore light indoor clothing and emptied pockets prior to weighing.

2.3. Recruitment and Initial Assessment

Recruitment to the parent study (Rural LEAP) primarily used mailed fliers and brochures presented at community and healthcare organizations. Screening occurred first via telephone and then in person at local county extension offices. At the in-person assessment, participants completed measurements of weight and height, psychosocial questionnaires (e.g., YFAS), and other health-/fitness-related assessments, such as a walking test [30]. Data collection occurred primarily through REDCap [36], which was approved by the University of Florida IRB for HIPAA compliance.

2.4. Intervention

Participants were taught strategies to increase physical activity and reduce caloric intake. Each weekly in-person session consisted of a private weigh-in, reviewing progress, problem-solving challenges, a skills-based lesson, and setting of eating and activity goals. Lessons included topics such as basic nutrition education, physical activity, problem solving, managing cravings, seeking social support, and substituting high-calorie foods for low-calorie foods. All participants were instructed to continue self-monitoring during Phase 2. Details on the study and intervention content have been described in prior publications [30,31].

2.5. Statistical Analyses

Analyses were performed in SPSS version 26 and significance levels were set to $p < 0.05$. Multilevel modeling tests used the full sample ($n = 182$); other tests (e.g., descriptive analyses) did not include participants with missing data (see Figure 1 for sample sizes at each timepoint). One-way analyses of variance (ANOVAs), chi-squared tests, and Kruskal–Wallis tests were used for descriptive and supplementary analyses involving categorical variables. Pearson correlations and related-samples Wilcoxon signed-rank tests were used for analyses involving continuous variables. Bootstrapping to 5000 samples was used to correct for non-normal variables in parametric tests. Bootstrapping is a robust and effective resampling technique for non-parametric and/or smaller samples that does not make parametric assumptions on the distribution [37,38].

Multilevel modeling was used for Aims 1 and 2. The Aim 1 model included FA symptoms at each time point (Level 1) nested within 182 participants (Level 2). The model included the following Level 2 predictors: age, BMI, baseline problem food consumption (PFBaseline), Phase 1 changes in problem food consumption (PFChange), linear time slope (MonthLinear), quadratic time slope (MonthQuad), and the interactions between PFChange and each time slope. Level 1 predictors included: linear time slope (MonthLinear), quadratic time slope (MonthQuad), and BMI. Multilevel modeling also controls for the baseline value of the dependent variable (FA symptoms). In the equation below (Equation (1)), "FA" represents the dependent variable (FA symptoms) for person "i" at timepoint "j". Terms marked with γ represent Level 2 intercepts as labeled after the underscore (e.g., γ_{01}_Age represents the Level 2 intercept for age). The residual is represented by the symbol "ζ_{0i}", and subsequent terms marked with ζ represent individual differences in Level 1 parameters not explained by Level 2 predictors. Age was included as a control variable in Aim 1 due to prior literature suggesting differences in food addiction symptoms by age group [8]. We originally added Phase 2 group randomization as a control variable in our multi-level models because it was significantly related to weight loss in the parent study ($n = 445$) [30]. However, it was ultimately removed from the current study due to worsened fit and no significant effects.

$$\begin{aligned} FA_{ij} = [&\gamma_{00}\_Intercept + \gamma_{01}\_Age + \gamma_{02}\_BMI + \gamma_{03}\_PFBaseline + \gamma_{04}\_PFChange + \gamma_{10}\_MonthLinear + \\ &\gamma_{11}\_(MonthLinear*PFChange) + \gamma_{20}\_MonthQuad + \gamma_{21}\_(MonthQuad*PFChange)] + [\zeta_{0i} + \\ &\zeta_{1i}\_MonthLinear + \zeta_{2i}\_MonthQuad + \zeta_{3i}\_BMI + \varepsilon_{ij}] \end{aligned} \tag{1}$$

The Aim 2 model included body weight at each time point (Level 1) nested within 182 participants (Level 2). The model included the following Level 2 predictors: height, race, baseline problem food consumption (PFBaseline), Phase 1 changes in problem food consumption (PFChange), mean between-person FA symptoms (FAMean), centered within-person FA symptoms (FACent), linear time slope (MonthLinear), quadratic time slope (MonthQuad), and the interactions between PFChange, FAMean, and each time slope. The Level 1 predictors included: linear time slope (MonthLinear), quadratic time slope (MonthQuad), and centered within-person FA symptoms (FACent). Symbol definitions for Equation (2) are the same as for Equation (1). FA was split into Level 1 and Level 2 variables in order to test both within- and between-subject effects. Level 2 effects of FA symptoms were calculated by computing person-means (i.e., averaging each participant's YFAS score across all timepoints). Level 1 effects were calculated by computing person-mean centered values (i.e., subtracting participants' scores at each timepoint from their person-mean). Race was included as a control variable in Aim 2 due to prior literature showing differences in body weight by race [39].

$$\begin{aligned} Weight_{ij} = [&\gamma_{00}\_Intercept + \gamma_{01}\_Height + \gamma_{02}\_Race + \gamma_{03}\_PFBaseline + \gamma_{04}\_PFChange + \gamma_{05}\_FAMean + \\ &\gamma_{06}\_FACent + \gamma_{10}\_MonthLinear + \gamma_{11}\_(MonthLinear*PFChange) + \gamma_{12}\_(MonthLinear*FAMean) + \\ &\gamma_{20}\_MonthQuad + \gamma_{21}\_(MonthQuad*PFChange) + \gamma_{22}\_(MonthQuad*FAMean)] + [\zeta_{0i} + \\ &\zeta_{1i}\_MonthLinear + \zeta_{2i}\_MonthQuad + \zeta_{3i}\_FACent + \varepsilon_{ij}] \end{aligned} \tag{2}$$

One-way ANOVA and Bonferroni post-hoc tests were used to evaluate differences between mean values and change scores in FA symptoms and weight (respectively) at each timepoint. Median split graphs were also created to assist in interpreting significant quadratic time interactions.

3. Results

3.1. Demographics

The final study sample included 182 participants (84.6% female) with a mean age of 55.4 ± 9.9 years. Demographic characteristics and YFAS scores are presented in Table 1. At baseline, 24 (13.2%) participants met the YFAS "diagnostic" criteria for FA, and the mean symptom score for the full sample was 2.38 ± 1.58. Non-white participants were more likely to have higher BMIs by about 1.5 kg/m^2 ($p = 0.031$) compared to white participants. No other demographic variables were significantly related to YFAS scores or BMI. YFAS scores were not significantly related to BMI at baseline ($r = 0.061$; $p = 0.410$). There were no significant differences in demographic variables between Waves 1 and 2 (enrolled in the parent study before the YFAS was administered; $n = 215$) and Waves 3 and 4 (from which the current sample was drawn; $n = 230$, $ps > 0.05$). Additionally, there were no significant differences between our sample ($n = 182$) and participants in Waves 3 and 4 who were not eligible for the current study ($n = 48$; $ps > 0.05$).

Table 1. Baseline sample characteristics ($N = 182$).

Characteristic	M (SD)	*n* (%)
Age (years)	55.4 (9.9)	
Weight (kg)	99.6 (13.9)	
BMI (kg/m^2)	36.6 (3.6)	
YFAS symptom score	2.38 (1.58)	
YFAS clinical cutoff		
≥3 symptoms + distress/impairment		24 (13.2)
<3 symptoms or no distress/impairment		158 (86.8)
Gender		
Female		154 (84.6)
Male		28 (15.4)
Ethnicity		
Non-Hispanic		175 (96.2)
Hispanic		7 (3.8)
Race		
White		146 (80.2)
Black or African American		35 (19.2)
Hispanic or Latino		7 (3.8)
American Indian or Alaskan Native		6 (3.3)
Asian		1 (0.5)
Native Hawaiian or Other Pacific Islander		0 (0.0)
Highest level of education		
<High school		4 (2.2)
High school or GED		89 (48.9)
Associate's degree		21 (11.5)
Bachelor's degree		45 (24.7)
Advanced degree		23 (12.6)
Annual household income		
<$20,000		14 (7.7)
$20,000–$34,999		41 (22.5)
$35,000–$49,999		31 (17.0)
$50,000–$74,999		39 (21.4)
>$75,000		45 (24.7)
Unknown		12 (6.6)

3.2. Phase 1 Problem Food Consumption

Baseline problem food consumption was significantly associated with baseline FA symptoms ($r = 0.230$, $p = 0.002$). During Phase 1, the mean frequency of problem food consumption dropped from 2.5 ± 1.2 times/day to 1.5 ± 0.9 times/day ($p < 0.001$). Decreases in problem food consumption were significantly associated with Phase 1 reductions in FA symptoms ($r = 0.165$, $p = 0.028$), but not weight ($r = 0.119$, $p = 0.115$). However, correlation effect sizes were small. Phase 1 changes in FA symptoms were not significantly associated with weight change ($r = 0.082$, $p = 0.277$).

3.3. *Aim 1: Long-Term Changes in Food Addiction Symptoms*

Five models (A–E) were tested using YFAS symptoms as the dependent variable and changes in Phase 1 problem food consumption as the independent variable. Body mass index, age, and baseline problem food consumption were included as covariates. Model A tested the unconditional means model, which included only the intercept. Model B tested the unconditional growth model, which added both linear and quadratic time slopes as predictors, both of which were significant (quadratic time, $p = 0.012$; linear time, $p = 0.010$). Model C tested for the fixed effects of baseline problem food consumption (covariate) and Phase 1 changes in problem food consumption (independent variable) on FA symptoms over time. Fixed effects test the association of a predictor with the intercept (in this study, baseline value) of the dependent variable. Neither predictor had a significant fixed effect.

Model D added the interaction of changes in problem food consumption with both linear and quadratic time, respectively. A variable's interaction effect with time looks at its association with subsequent changes in the dependent variable across time (as opposed to at the intercept only). We found that the quadratic time interaction with problem food change was significant ($p = 0.012$), suggesting that Phase 1 decreases in problem food consumption were initially associated with a slightly sharper decline in FA symptoms, followed by a slightly sharper rebound. The interaction between problem food changes and linear time was not significant, indicating that Phase 1 problem food changes were not associated with long-term changes in FA scores. Model E included our remaining control variables (BMI and age), both of which had significant fixed effects ($p < 0.001$ and $p = 0.043$, respectively). The random effect of BMI was not significant ($p = 0.321$; see Figures 2 and 3 and Table 2).

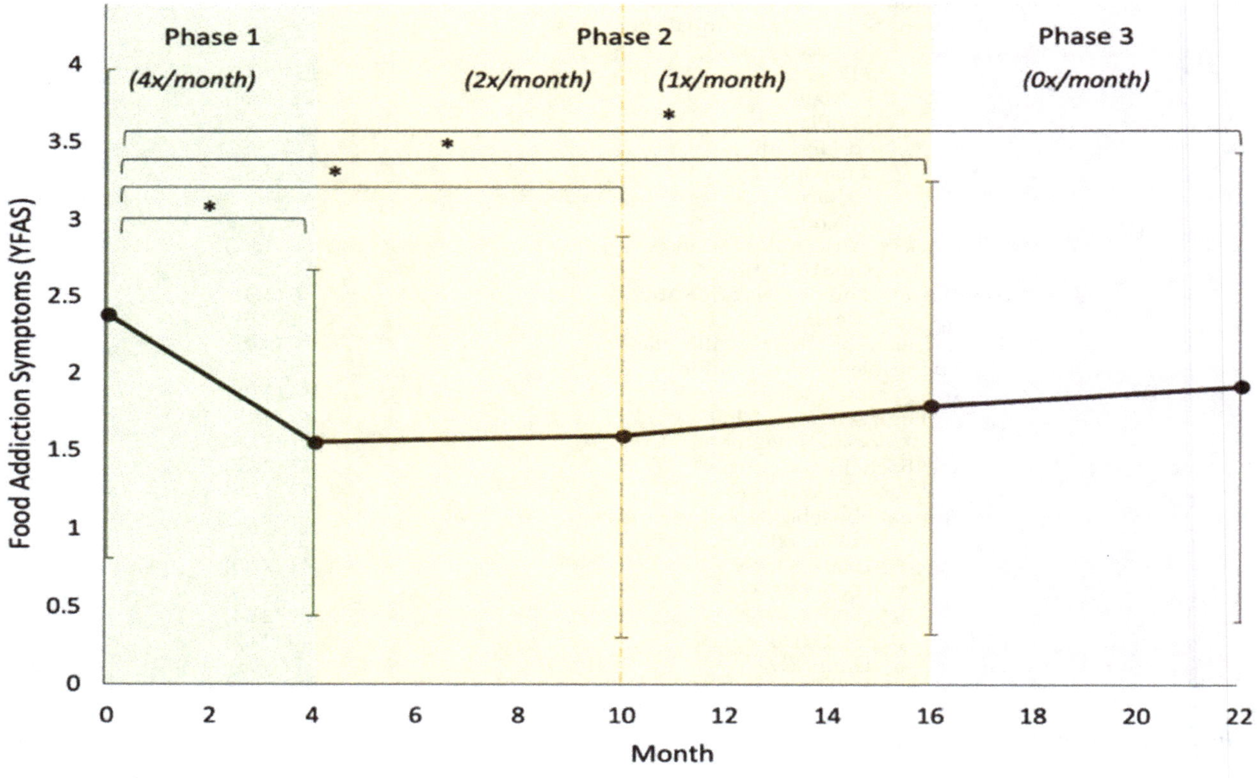

Figure 2. Model-implied trend of food addiction symptoms over time. Shaded areas mark Phases 1, 2, and 3 of the study, with the frequency of intervention sessions noted in italics. * = $p < 0.05$.

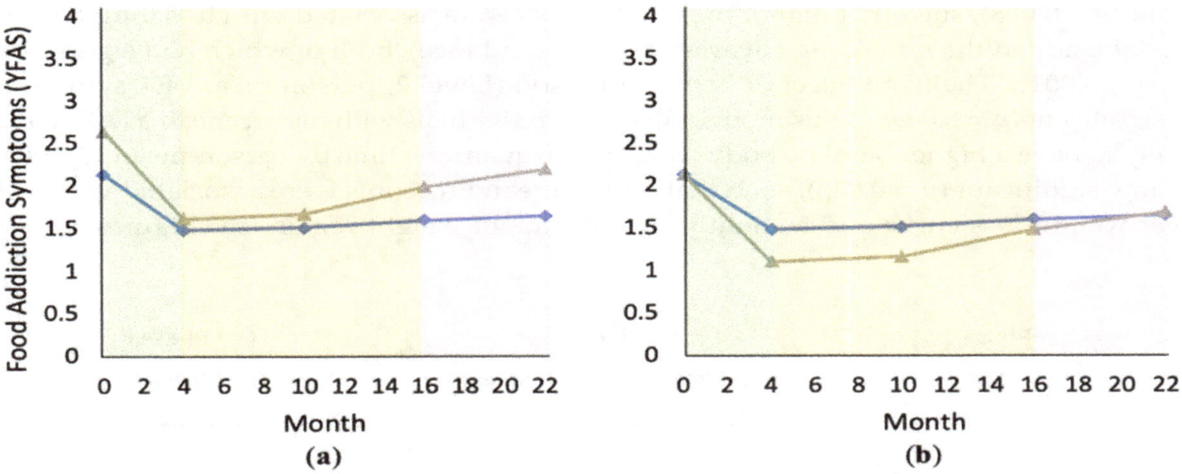

Figure 3. Changes in food addiction (FA) symptoms over time, comparing subjects with greater versus smaller Phase 1 reductions in problem food consumption (based on median split: greater reduction = gray triangles, smaller reduction = blue diamonds): (**a**) graph using original data; (**b**) graph correcting for baseline differences in Yale Food Addiction Scale (YFAS) scores for comparison.

Table 2. Aim 1 results of the model tests (food addiction symptoms as outcome).

	Par	Model A	Model B	Model C	Model D	Model E
Fixed effects						
Initial status						
Intercept	γ_{00}	0.007 (0.058)	−0.216 ** (0.062)	−0.217 *** (0.061)	−0.135 * (0.062)	−0.134 * (0.062)
PF Change	γ_{04}			−0.117 (0.080)	−0.026 (0.084)	−0.026 (0.085)
PF Baseline	γ_{03}			0.088 (0.080)	0.098 (0.080)	0.088 (0.080)
BMI	γ_{02}					0.262 *** (0.049)
Baseline Age	γ_{01}					−0.113 * (0.056)
Rate of change						
Time (linear)	γ_{10}		−0.082 ** (0.026)	−0.083 ** (0.026)	−0.040 (0.026)	−0.039 (0.026)
X PF Change	γ_{11}				−0.003 (0.025)	−0.005 (0.025)
Time (quad)	γ_{20}		0.214 *** (0.031)	0.215 *** (0.031)	0.135 *** (0.034)	0.135 *** (0.033)
X PF Change	γ_{21}				−0.078 * (0.031)	−0.074 * (0.031)
Random effects						
Level 1						
Residual	ε_{ij}	0.496 *** (0.027)	0.385 *** (0.028)	0.389 *** (0.028)	0.360 *** (0.026)	0.352 *** (0.028)
BMI	ζ_{3i}					0.041 (0.042)
Level 2						
Intercept	ζ_{0i}	0.503 *** (0.064)	0.468 *** (0.063)	0.437 *** (0.059)	0.443 *** (0.060)	0.420 *** (0.059)
Time (linear)	ζ_{1i}		0.034 * (0.013)	0.034 * (0.013)	0.034 ** (0.013)	0.033 ** (0.013)
Time (quad)	ζ_{2i}		0.042 * (0.017)	0.036 * (0.016)	0.041 * (0.016)	0.036 * (0.016)
Fit Statistics						
Deviance		2165.464	2099.093	2087.688	2046.568	2041.203
AIC		2171.464	2113.093	2105.688	2070.568	2069.203
BIC		2185.749	2146.424	2148.542	2127.693	2135.849

Estimates are presented with standard errors between parentheses. * $p < 0.05$, ** $p < 0.01$, *** $p < 0.001$. PF = problem foods; BMI = body mass index; AIC = Akaike information criterion; BIC = Bayesian information criterion.

3.4. Aim 2: Long-Term Changes in Body Weight

Five models (A–E) were tested using body weight as the dependent variable and both FA symptoms and changes in Phase 1 problem food consumption as independent variables. Height, race (white vs. not white), and baseline problem food consumption were covariates Model A was the unconditional means model and Model B was the unconditional growth model. In Model B, both linear and quadratic time slopes were significant (*ps* < 0.001).

Model C included the fixed effects of both FA symptoms and problem food consumption (baseline values and change scores); of these, only the fixed effects of within-person (Level 1, person-mean centered) FA symptoms were significant in Model C ($p < 0.001$). Model D added four interaction terms: Phase 1 changes in problem food consumption by time and person-mean (between-subject) FA symptoms by time. Of these, only the interaction between FA symptoms and linear time was significant ($p = 0.008$), such that higher mean FA scores were associated with less long-term weight loss. Model E added the remaining covariates (height and race), both of which had significant fixed effects ($ps \leq 0.001$). The fixed effect of between-person (Level 2, person-mean) FA symptoms also became significant ($p = 0.009$) in this model, such that individuals with higher mean YFAS scores were more likely to have a higher baseline body weight. The quadratic time by person-mean FA interaction also became significant ($p = 0.045$), such that higher mean FA scores were associated with a slightly shallower weight-loss curve and a slightly steeper rate of weight regain (see Figures 4 and 5 and Table 3).

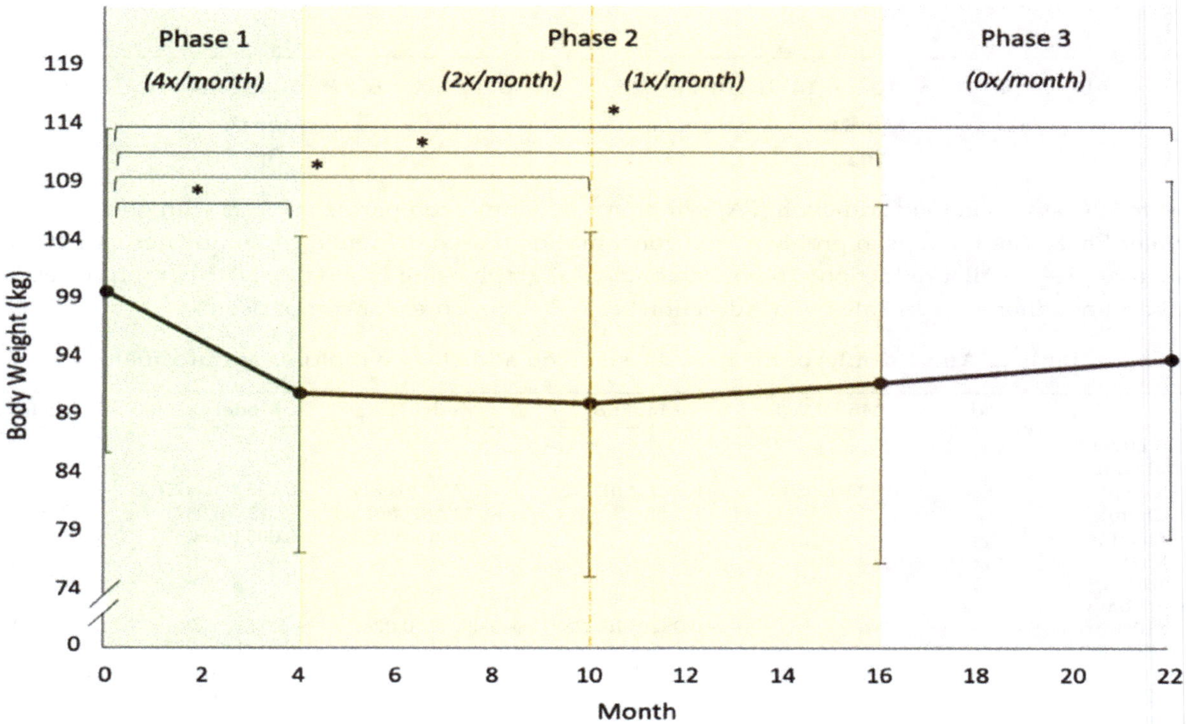

Figure 4. Model-implied trend of body weight over time. Shaded areas mark Phases 1, 2, and 3 of the study, with the frequency of intervention sessions noted in italics. * = $p < 0.05$.

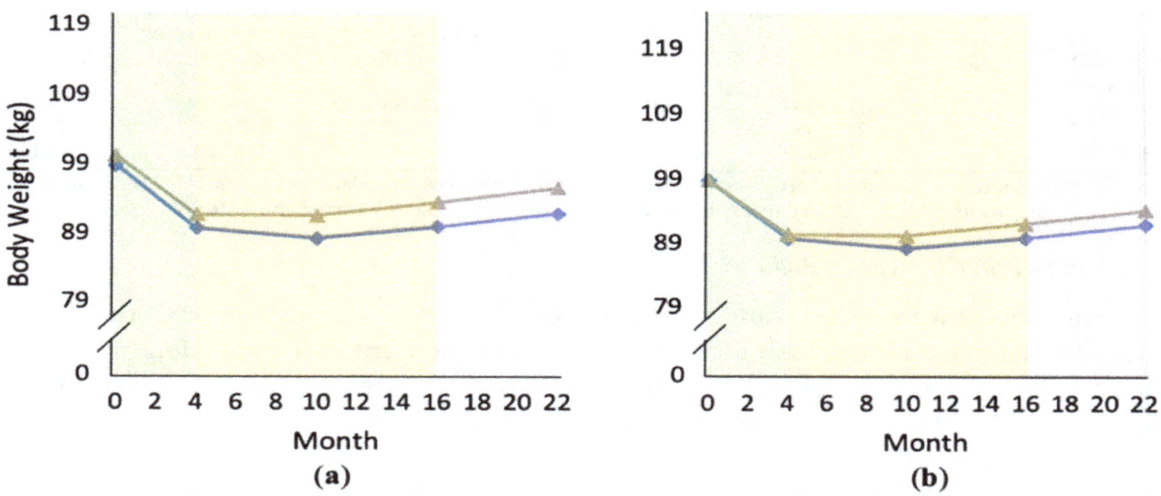

Figure 5. Changes in body weight over time, comparing subjects with higher versus lower person-mean YFAS scores (based on median split: higher YFAS scores = gray triangles; lower YFAS scores = blue diamonds): (**a**) graph using original data; (**b**) graph correcting for baseline differences in body weight for comparison.

Table 3. Aim 2 results of the model tests (body weight as outcome).

	Par	Model A	Model B	Model C	Model D	Model E
Fixed effects						
Initial status						
Intercept	γ_{00}	0.003 (0.069)	−0.235 ** (0.070)	−0.228 ** (0.070)	−0.228 ** (0.070)	−0.230 *** (0.052)
FA (M)	γ_{05}			0.083 (0.091)	0.105 (0.092)	0.181 ** (0.069)
FA (C)	γ_{06}			0.101 *** (0.016)	0.101 *** (0.015)	0.101 *** (0.016)
PF Change	γ_{04}			−0.107 (0.101)	−0.104 (0.101)	−0.063 (0.075)
PF Baseline	γ_{03}			0.005 (0.100)	0.005 (0.100)	−0.015 (0.075)
Height	γ_{01}					0.610 *** (0.052)
White race	γ_{02}					−0.170 ** (0.052)
Rate of change						
Time (linear)	γ_{10}		−0.123 *** (0.015)	−0.121 *** (0.015)	−0.120 *** (0.014)	−0.120 *** (0.014)
X FA (M)	γ_{12}				0.051 ** (0.019)	0.050 ** (0.019)
X PF Change	γ_{11}				0.002 (0.015)	0.002 (0.015)
Time (quad)	γ_{20}		0.238 *** (0.013)	0.224 *** (0.013)	0.224 *** (0.013)	0.224 *** (0.013)
X FA (M)	γ_{22}				−0.033 (0.017)	−0.033 * (0.016)
X PF Change	γ_{21}				−0.005 (0.014)	−0.005 (0.013)
Random effects						
Level 1						
Residual	ε_{ij}	0.147 *** (0.008)	0.049 *** (0.004)	0.044 *** (0.004)	0.044 *** (0.004)	0.046 *** (0.004)
FA (C)	ζ_{3i}			0.002 (0.004)	0.001 (0.003)	0.001 (0.004)
Level 2						
Intercept	ζ_{0i}	0.846 *** (0.092)	0.874 *** (0.093)	0.843 *** (0.090)	0.844 *** (0.090)	0.457 *** (0.050)
Time (linear)	ζ_{1i}		0.030 *** (0.004)	0.028 *** (0.004)	0.027 *** (0.004)	0.026 *** (0.004)
Time (quad)	ζ_{2i}		0.013 *** (0.003)	0.013 *** (0.003)	0.013 *** (0.003)	0.010 ** (0.003)
Fit Statistics						
Deviance		1443.129	1013.281	944.070	933.623	825.881
AIC		1449.129	1027.281	968.070	965.623	861.881
BIC		1463.536	1060.898	1025.195	1041.790	947.569

Estimates are presented with standard errors between parentheses. * $p < 0.05$, ** $p < 0.01$, *** $p < 0.001$. FA = food addiction symptoms; M = mean; C = centered; PF = Problem foods; AIC = Akaike information criterion; BIC = Bayesian information criterion.

3.5. *ANOVAs and Bonferroni Post-Hocs: Food Addiction Symptoms and Body Weight*

3.5.1. Food Addiction

Finally, one-way ANOVA and Bonferroni tests detected statistically significant differences between baseline (Month 0) FA symptoms and each subsequent timepoint, respectively (all *ps* < 0.05). Months 4–22 were not significantly different from each other. Changes in FA symptoms between Months 0–4 (Phase 1) were significantly different from Months 4–10, 10–16, and 16–22 (first half of Phase 2, second half of Phase 2, and Phase 3, respectively; *ps* < 0.001). None of the subsequent phases were significantly different from each other (*ps* > 0.05).

3.5.2. Body Weight

There were statistically significant differences between baseline (Month 0) body weight and each subsequent timepoint (all *ps* < 0.05). Months 4–22 were not significantly different from each other. Phase 1 changes in body weight were significantly different from all other timepoints (*ps* < 0.001), as were the changes during the first half of Phase 2 (Months 4–10; *ps* < 0.001; see Table 4).

Table 4. Means and change slopes for main variables by timepoint.

Timepoint M ± SD	YFAS Score	Body Weight (kg)	Timepoint M ± SD	Change in YFAS Score	Change in Weight (kg)
Month 0	2.39 ± 1.58 ^{b,c,d,e} *N = 182*	99.57 ± 13.95 ^{b,c,d,e} *N = 182*	Months 0–4 (Phase 1)	−0.882 ± 1.47 ^{g,h,i} *N = 178*	−8.83 ± 4.75 ^{g,h,i} *N = 182*
Month 4	1.56 ± 1.1 ^{a} *N = 178*	90.74 ± 13.56 ^{a} *N = 182*	Months 4–10 (Phase 2, 1st half)	0.044 ± 1.23 ^{f} *N = 161*	−0.789 ± 4.51 ^{f,h,i} *N = 180*
Month 10	1.60 ± 1.29 ^{a} *N = 164*	89.90 ± 14.8 ^{a} *N = 180*	Months 10–16 (Phase 2, 2nd half)	0.252 ± 1.10 ^{f} *N = 153*	1.93 ± 3.08 ^{f,g} *N = 174*
Month 16	1.79 ± 1.46 ^{a} *N = 163*	91.65 ± 15.38 ^{a} *N = 174*	Months 16–22 (Phase 3)	0.073 ± 1.11 ^{f} *N = 161*	1.80 ± 3.79 ^{f,b} *N = 174*
Month 22	1.92 ± 1.51 ^{a} *N = 177*	93.67 ± 15.38 ^{a} *N = 182*	-	-	-

Significance evaluated at $p < 0.05$ using One-way analysis of variance (ANOVA) and bootstrapped T-tests. Key: ^{a} = significantly different from Month 0, ^{b} = significantly different from Month 4, ^{c} = significantly different from Month 10, ^{d} = significantly different from Month 16, ^{e} = significantly different from Month 22; ^{f} = significantly different from Months 0–4, ^{g} = significantly different from Months 4–10, ^{h} = significantly different from Months 10–16, ^{i} = significantly different from Months 16–22.

4. Discussion

The primary goal of this study was to evaluate long-term changes in food addiction (FA) symptoms and weight loss among a sample of adults participating in a behavioral weight-loss program. We hypothesized that reductions in problem food consumption during the initial phase of treatment would be associated with long-term reductions in FA symptoms, that long-term changes in FA would be associated with long-term changes in body weight, and that initial reductions in problem food consumption would be associated with long-term reductions in body weight.

4.1. Food Addiction and Problem Foods

We found that changes in problem food consumption during the initial in-person treatment phase were not associated with changes in FA symptoms from the baseline to Month 22. Rather, reductions in problem food consumption were associated with a different pattern of change, suggesting sharper initial reductions in FA symptoms followed by a sharper rebound after the in-person phase. While future research is needed to clarify the relationship between problem food consumption and FA symptoms, our findings suggest that decreasing problem food consumption (in the context of a behavioral weight loss program) may be associated with improvements in FA symptoms in the short term, but that these changes may not last in the long term.

Many have proposed that, similarly to drug addiction treatment models, the goal of FA treatment should be either abstinence [40], moderation [23], or harm reduction [41] in regard to problem food consumption. Others have implied that non-dieting approaches may be beneficial [42–45]. However, few studies have tested the efficacy of any FA treatment. The FA studies identified by Cassin et al. [20] examined a variety of different approaches, including abstinence, cognitive-behavioral therapy, exposure and response prevention, intuitive eating, and mindfulness. However, only two of the included studies specifically targeted FA as a primary outcome. The authors concluded that more research is needed to compare the effects of potential interventions, particularly those drawn from evidence-based treatments for substance use or eating disorders [20].

4.2. Food Addiction and Weight

We found that both FA symptoms and body weight decreased over time, and that higher average YFAS scores over the course of the study were associated with less weight loss. These findings are consistent with several studies that have shown an association between FA symptoms and body weight both cross-sectionally and across time [8,15,28]. However, others have failed to find an association [29,46,47]. Despite some inconsistency, most prior research has shown significant reductions in FA symptoms following weight-loss treatment [28,29,46,48,49]. These findings require further exploration, but it is possible that the connection between FA symptoms and weight may become more apparent over periods of time that extend beyond the length of typical intervention studies (i.e., 4–6 months), and/or that both FA and body weight are influenced or caused by an external factor.

4.3. Problem Foods and Weight

We did not find a significant association between early changes in problem food consumption and long-term changes in weight. This finding was contrary to our hypotheses, and also contrary to some prior cross-sectional and behavioral weight-loss studies [50–54]. One possible explanation could be that participants in our intervention were instructed to reduce calories rather than reduce problem foods specifically; the results may have been different had problem food consumption been directly targeted. Another possible explanation could be that our measure of problem food consumption (number of times consumed per day) did not provide enough power given its seemingly restricted range. However, at least one other study has reported a similarly unexpected finding: Nikiforova and associates [55] found that, among their sample of 300 laparoscopic sleeve gastrectomy patients, there was a 12.9% increase in the number of patients who reported a diet rich in "sweets" and an 8.9% increase in the number of patients who reported a diet rich in "snacks" three years after surgery, despite a significant reduction in BMI. They concluded that while consumption of these foods increased post-surgery, they did not appear to have a negative effect on BMI. Further research is required to clarify the association between high-fat and/or high-sugar foods and body weight, especially while controlling for caloric consumption.

4.4. Implications and Future Directions

Some have proposed that FA causes weight gain through the overconsumption of high-calorie foods (e.g., [56]), while others have suggested that obesity may cause FA symptoms via brain chemistry changes that lead to overeating (e.g., [57]). An additional question to consider is whether FA and obesity may both be symptoms of an external factor. For example, it has been well established that both obesity and FA symptoms are associated with increased depression and anxiety, lower self-esteem, and poorer quality of life [16,19,58–62]. In addition to psychosocial factors, biological contributors, such as gut microbiota and genetics, have also been associated with weight and addiction-like eating [63–66]. Future studies should prospectively analyze the relationships between neurobiological and psychosocial factors, body weight, and FA in order to predict which factors may put individuals at risk of developing either or both of these conditions.

If FA leads to weight gain through the overconsumption of high-calorie, highly palatable foods, reducing consumption of these foods should lead to weight loss. However, the current study's findings did not support an association between changes in problem food consumption and either concurrent (Phase 1) or subsequent (long-term) changes in body weight. Future studies should evaluate long-term changes in problem food consumption simultaneously with both FA symptoms and weight in order to elucidate these relationships. Future studies should also evaluate the long-term effects of problem food consumption on both body weight and FA symptoms by specifically targeting problem food consumption without caloric restriction.

4.5. Strengths and Limitations

The results should be interpreted in light of this study's limitations. First, the analyses conducted cannot demonstrate causal relationships between the variables, nor determine the direction of the association between FA and body weight. Second, the study sample was primarily female and had sociodemographic characteristics similar to adults in the rural southeastern United States, which may limit generalizability to other populations. Additionally, the proportion of participants in the current study who met YFAS criteria for FA (13.2%) was less than the estimated prevalence for adults with overweight/obesity (approximately 25%) [8]. This may be due to the fact that ours was a treatment-seeking sample, as other behavioral weight-loss studies have also reported relatively low

FA prevalence rates (e.g., 19% [15]; 6.7% [29]; 15.2% [47]). Third, dietary records were based on self-reporting and were not independently verified, and problem food consumption was coded post hoc for secondary data analyses. Additionally, we were unable to evaluate long-term changes in problem food consumption due to the low rates of self-monitoring after Phase 1. Fourth, the current sample size may have been insufficient to detect certain differences, such as the effects of Phase 2 group randomization and problem food consumption on weight change. Finally, the present results were consistent with previous research regarding the direction of change in problem food consumption [52,53,67,68]; however, differences in methodology (i.e., using measures of quantity vs. frequency) precluded our ability to compare the clinical significance of the change with that observed in prior studies e.g., [52,53,67,68]. Nevertheless, this is the first study to our knowledge that has evaluated long-term changes in FA symptoms in the context of a behavioral weight-loss program. The above findings regarding the associations between problem food consumption, FA symptoms, and body weight over time have important implications for future research.

5. Conclusions

Despite increased interest in the concept of food addiction, there is a dearth of research regarding its clinical implications and potential treatments. The current study examined long-term (two-year) changes in food addiction symptoms and their association with changes in body weight and "problem food" (i.e., highly palatable food) consumption among adults in a behavioral weight-loss program. The findings suggest that food addiction symptoms improve during behavioral weight-loss treatment and that reducing problem food consumption is associated with short-term improvements in FA symptoms. Despite some evidence for a negative association between food addiction symptoms and weight loss, more research is needed to elucidate the complex interplay of food addiction symptoms, body weight, and problem food consumption. A greater understanding of these relationships may inform the development of effective interventions for long-term changes in FA.

Author Contributions: Conceptualization, data curation, data analysis, and writing—original draft preparation and review/editing, E.L.G.; writing—review/editing, L.J.M.; data curation and writing—review/editing, P.E.D.; supervision, project administration, funding acquisition, and writing—review/editing, M.G.P. All authors have read and agreed to the published version of the manuscript.

References

1. Avena, N.M.; Rada, P.; Hoebel, B.G. Evidence for sugar addiction: Behavioral and neurochemical effects of intermittent, excessive sugar intake. *Neurosci. Biobehav. Rev.* **2008**, *32*, 20–39. [CrossRef] [PubMed]
2. Carter, A.; Hendrikse, J.; Lee, N.; Yücel, M.; Verdejo-Garcia, A.; Andrews, Z.B.; Hall, W. The neurobiology of "food addiction" and its implications for obesity treatment and policy. *Annu. Rev. Nutr.* **2016**, *36*, 105–128. [CrossRef] [PubMed]
3. Gordon, E.L.; Ariel-Donges, A.H.; Bauman, V.; Merlo, L.J. What Is the Evidence for "Food Addiction?" A Systematic Review. *Nutrients* **2018**, *10*, 477. [CrossRef] [PubMed]
4. Gordon, E.L.; Lent, M.R.; Merlo, L.J. The Effect of Food Composition and Behavior on Neurobiological Response to Food: A Review of Recent Research. *Curr. Nutr. Rep.* **2020**, *9*, 75–82. [CrossRef] [PubMed]
5. Ifland, J.R.; Preuss, H.G.; Marcus, M.T.; Rourke, K.M.; Taylor, W.C.; Burau, K.; Jacobs, W.S.; Kadish, W.; Manso, G. Refined food addiction: A classic substance use disorder. *Med. Hypotheses* **2009**, *72*, 518–526. [CrossRef]
6. Meule, A.; Gearhardt, A.N. Food addiction in the light of DSM-5. *Nutrients* **2014**, *6*, 3653–3671. [CrossRef] [PubMed]
7. Olsen, C.M. Natural rewards, neuroplasticity, and non-drug addictions. *Neuropharmacology* **2011**, *61*, 1109–1122. [CrossRef]
8. Pursey, K.M.; Stanwell, P.; Gearhardt, A.N.; Collins, C.E.; Burrows, T.L. The prevalence of food addiction as assessed by the Yale Food Addiction Scale: A systematic review. *Nutrients* **2014**, *6*, 4552–4590. [CrossRef]
9. Pursey, K.M.; Davis, C.; Burrows, T.L. Nutritional Aspects of Food Addiction. *Curr. Addict. Rep.* **2017**, *4*, 142–150. [CrossRef]

10. Ruffle, J.K. Molecular neurobiology of addiction: What's all the (Δ) FosB about? *Am. J. Drug Alcohol Abus.* **2014**, *40*, 428–437. [CrossRef]
11. Schulte, E.M.; Avena, N.M.; Gearhardt, A.N. Which foods may be addictive? The roles of processing, fat content, and glycemic load. *PLoS ONE* **2015**, *10*, e0117959. [CrossRef] [PubMed]
12. Gearhardt, A.N.; Yokum, S.; Orr, P.T.; Stice, E.; Corbin, W.R.; Brownell, K.D. Neural correlates of food addiction. *Arch. Gen. Psychiatry* **2011**, *68*, 808–816. [CrossRef] [PubMed]
13. Gearhardt, A.N.; Corbin, W.R.; Brownell, K.D. Preliminary validation of the Yale food addiction scale. *Appetite* **2009**, *52*, 430–436. [CrossRef] [PubMed]
14. Schulte, E.M.; Gearhardt, A.N. Associations of Food Addiction in a Sample Recruited to Be Nationally Representative of the United States. *Eur. Eat. Disord. Rev.* **2017**, *26*, 112–119. [CrossRef] [PubMed]
15. Burmeister, J.M.; Hinman, N.; Koball, A.; Hoffmann, D.A.; Carels, R.A. Food addiction in adults seeking weight loss treatment. Implications for psychosocial health and weight loss. *Appetite* **2013**, *60*, 103–110. [CrossRef]
16. Gearhardt, A.N.; White, M.A.; Masheb, R.M.; Morgan, P.T.; Crosby, R.D.; Grilo, C.M. An examination of the food addiction construct in obese patients with binge eating disorder. *Int. J. Eat. Disord.* **2012**, *45*, 657–663. [CrossRef]
17. Masheb, R.M.; Ruser, C.B.; Min, K.M.; Bullock, A.J.; Dorflinger, L.M. Does food addiction contribute to excess weight among clinic patients seeking weight reduction? Examination of the Modified Yale Food Addiction Survey. *Compr. Psychiatry* **2018**, *84*, 1–6. [CrossRef]
18. Long, C.G.; Blundell, J.E.; Finlayson, G. A systematic review of the application and correlates of YFAS-diagnosed 'food addiction' in humans: Are eating-related 'addictions' a cause for concern or empty concepts? *Obes. Facts* **2015**, *8*, 386–401. [CrossRef]
19. Brunault, P.; Ducluzeau, P.H.; Bourbao-Tournois, C.; Delbachian, I.; Couet, C.; Réveillère, C.; Ballon, N. Food addiction in bariatric surgery candidates: Prevalence and risk factors. *Obes. Surg.* **2016**, *26*, 1650–1653. [CrossRef]
20. Cassin, S.E.; Sijercic, I.; Montemarano, V. Psychosocial Interventions for Food Addiction: A Systematic Review. *Curr. Addict. Rep.* **2020**, *7*, 9–19. [CrossRef]
21. Davis, C. A commentary on the associations among 'food addiction', binge eating disorder, and obesity: Overlapping conditions with idiosyncratic clinical features. *Appetite* **2017**, *115*, 3–8. [CrossRef] [PubMed]
22. McKenna, R.A.; Rollo, M.E.; Skinner, J.A.; Burrows, T.L. Food Addiction Support: Website Content Analysis. *JMIR Cardio* **2018**, *2*, e10. [CrossRef] [PubMed]
23. Schulte, E.M.; Joyner, M.A.; Potenza, M.N.; Grilo, C.M.; Gearhardt, A.N. Current considerations regarding food addiction. *Curr. Psychiatry Rep.* **2015**, *17*, 19. [CrossRef] [PubMed]
24. Vella, S.L.C.; Pai, N.B. A narrative review of potential treatment strategies for food addiction. *Eat. Weight Disord.-Stud. Anorex. Bulim. Obes.* **2017**, *22*, 387–393. [CrossRef] [PubMed]
25. Foster, G.D.; Makris, A.P.; Bailer, B.A. Behavioral treatment of obesity. *Am. J. Clin. Nutr.* **2005**, *82*, 230S–235S. [CrossRef] [PubMed]
26. Laudet, A.B.; Savage, R.; Mahmood, D. Pathways to long-term recovery: A preliminary investigation. *J. Psychoact. Drugs* **2002**, *34*, 305–311. [CrossRef]
27. Farrow, C.; Tarrant, M.; Khan, S. Using social identity to promote health. In *Addiction, Behavioral Change and Social Identity: The Path to Resilience and Recovery*; Buckingham, S.A., Best, D., Eds.; Routledge: New York, NY, USA; Abington, UK, 2016.
28. Sawamoto, R.; Nozaki, T.; Nishihara, T.; Furukawa, T.; Hata, T.; Komaki, G.; Sudo, N. Predictors of successful long-term weight loss maintenance: A two-year follow-up. *Biopsychosoc. Med.* **2017**, *11*, 14. [CrossRef]
29. Chao, A.M.; Wadden, T.A.; Tronieri, J.S.; Pearl, R.L.; Alamuddin, N.; Bakizada, Z.M.; Pinkasavage, E.; Leonard, S.M.; Alfaris, N.; Berkowitz, R.I. Effects of addictive-like eating behaviors on weight loss with behavioral obesity treatment. *J. Behav. Med.* **2019**, *42*, 246–255. [CrossRef]
30. Perri, M.G.; Shankar, M.N.; Daniels, M.J.; Durning, P.E.; Ross, K.M.; Limacher, M.C.; Janicke, D.M.; Martin, A.D.; Dhara, K.; Bobroff, L.B.; et al. Effect of Telehealth Extended Care for Maintenance of Weight Loss in Rural US Communities: A Randomized Clinical Trial. *JAMA Netw. Open* **2020**, *3*, e206764. [CrossRef]

31. Perri, M.G.; Ariel-Donges, A.H.; Shankar, M.N.; Limacher, M.C.; Daniels, M.J.; Janicke, D.M.; Ross, K.M.; Bobroff, L.B.; Martin, D.; Radcliff, T.A.; et al. Design of the Rural LEAP randomized trial: An evaluation of extended-care programs for weight management delivered via group or individual telephone counseling. *Contemp. Clin. Trials* **2019**, *76*, 55–63. [CrossRef]
32. Burrows, T.; Hides, L.; Brown, R.; Dayas, C.V.; Kay-Lambkin, F. Differences in dietary preferences, personality and mental health in Australian adults with and without food addiction. *Nutrients* **2017**, *9*, 285. [CrossRef] [PubMed]
33. Lemeshow, A.R.; Rimm, E.B.; Hasin, D.S.; Gearhardt, A.N.; Flint, A.J.; Field, A.E.; Genkinger, J.M. Food and beverage consumption and food addiction among women in the Nurses' Health Studies. *Appetite* **2018**, *121*, 186–197. [CrossRef] [PubMed]
34. Pursey, K.M.; Collins, C.E.; Stanwell, P.; Burrows, T.L. Foods and dietary profiles associated with 'food addiction' in young adults. *Addict. Behav. Rep.* **2015**, *2*, 41–48. [CrossRef] [PubMed]
35. USDA Agricultural Research Service. Available online: https://www.ars.usda.gov/northeast-area/beltsville-md-bhnrc/beltsville-human-nutrition-research-center/food-surveys-research-group/docs/dmr-food-categories/ (accessed on 27 July 2020).
36. Harris, P.A.; Taylor, R.; Thielke, R.; Payne, J.; Gonzalez, N.; Conde, J.G. Research electronic data capture (REDCap)—A metadata-driven methodology and workflow process for providing translational research informatics support. *J. Biomed. Inform.* **2009**, *42*, 377–381. [CrossRef] [PubMed]
37. Preacher, K.J.; Hayes, A.F. SPSS and SAS procedures for estimating indirect effects in simple mediation models. *Behav. Res. MethodsInstrum. Comput.* **2004**, *36*, 717–731. [CrossRef] [PubMed]
38. Preacher, K.J.; Hayes, A.F. Asymptotic and resampling strategies for assessing and comparing indirect effects in multiple mediator models. *Behav. Res. Methods* **2008**, *40*, 879–891. [CrossRef]
39. Petersen, R.; Pan, L.; Blanck, H.M. Racial and ethnic disparities in adult obesity in the United States: CDC's tracking to inform state and local action. *Prev. Chronic Dis.* **2019**, *16*, 1–6. [CrossRef]
40. Meule, A. A critical examination of the practical implications derived from the food addiction concept. *Curr. Obes. Rep.* **2019**, *8*, 11–17. [CrossRef]
41. Schulte, E.M.; Joyner, M.A.; Schiestl, E.T.; Gearhardt, A.N. Future directions in "food addiction": Next steps and treatment implications. *Curr. Addict. Rep.* **2017**, *4*, 165–171. [CrossRef]
42. Corwin, R.L. The Face of Uncertainty Eats. *Curr. Drug Abus. Rev.* **2011**, *4*, 174–181. [CrossRef]
43. Corwin, R.L.; Babbs, R.K. Rodent models of binge eating: Are they models of addiction? *ILAR J.* **2012**, *53*, 23–34. [CrossRef] [PubMed]
44. Fletcher, P.C.; Kenny, P.J. Food addiction: A valid concept? *Neuropsychopharmacology* **2018**, *43*, 2506–2513. [CrossRef] [PubMed]
45. Webber, K.H.; Mellin, L.; Mayes, L.; Mitrovic, I.; Saulnier, M. Pilot Investigation of 2 Nondiet Approaches to Improve Weight and Health. *Altern. Ther. Health Med.* **2018**, *24*, 16–20. [PubMed]
46. Sevinçer, G.M.; Konuk, N.; Bozkurt, S.; Coşkun, H. Food addiction and the outcome of bariatric surgery at 1-year: Prospective observational study. *Psychiatry Res.* **2016**, *244*, 159–164. [CrossRef] [PubMed]
47. Lent, M.R.; Eichen, D.M.; Goldbacher, E.; Wadden, T.A.; Foster, G.D. Relationship of food addiction to weight loss and attrition during obesity treatment. *Obesity* **2014**, *22*, 52–55. [CrossRef] [PubMed]
48. Murray, S.M.; Tweardy, S.; Geliebter, A.; Avena, N.M. A Longitudinal Preliminary Study of Addiction-Like Responses to Food and Alcohol Consumption Among Individuals Undergoing Weight Loss Surgery. *Obes. Surg.* **2019**, *29*, 2700–2703. [CrossRef]
49. Pepino, M.Y.; Stein, R.I.; Eagon, J.C.; Klein, S. Bariatric surgery-induced weight loss causes remission of food addiction in extreme obesity. *Obesity* **2014**, *22*, 1792–1798. [CrossRef]
50. Wing, R.R.; Hill, J.O. Successful weight loss maintenance. *Annu. Rev. Nutr.* **2001**, *21*, 323–341. [CrossRef]
51. San-Cristobal, R.; Navas-Carretero, S.; Celis-Morales, C.; Brennan, L.; Walsh, M.; Lovegrove, J.A.; Daniel, H.; Saris, W.H.; Traczyk, I.; Manios, Y.; et al. Analysis of dietary pattern impact on weight status for personalised nutrition through on-line advice: The Food4Me Spanish cohort. *Nutrients* **2015**, *7*, 9523–9537. [CrossRef]
52. Hutchesson, M.J.; Collins, C.E.; Morgan, P.J.; Watson, J.F.; Guest, M.; Callister, R. Changes to dietary intake during a 12-week commercial web-based weight loss program: A randomized controlled trial. *Eur. J. Clin. Nutr.* **2014**, *68*, 64–70. [CrossRef]

53. Kong, A.; Beresford, S.A.; Alfano, C.M.; Foster-Schubert, K.E.; Neuhouser, M.L.; Johnson, D.B.; Duggan, C.; Wang, C.Y.; Xiao, L.; Jeffery, R.W.; et al. Self-monitoring and eating-related behaviors are associated with 12-month weight loss in postmenopausal overweight-to-obese women. *J. Acad. Nutr. Diet.* **2012**, *112*, 1428–1435. [CrossRef] [PubMed]
54. Vidmar, A.P.; Pretlow, R.; Borzutzky, C.; Wee, C.P.; Fox, D.S.; Fink, C.; Mittelman, S.D. An addiction model-based mobile health weight loss intervention in adolescents with obesity. *Pediatric Obes.* **2019**, *14*, e12464. [CrossRef] [PubMed]
55. Nikiforova, I.; Barnea, R.; Azulai, S.; Susmallian, S. Analysis of the Association between Eating Behaviors and Weight Loss after Laparoscopic Sleeve Gastrectomy. *Obes. Facts* **2019**, *12*, 618–631. [CrossRef] [PubMed]
56. Lennerz, B.; Lennerz, J.K. Food addiction, high-glycemic-index carbohydrates, and obesity. *Clin. Chem.* **2018**, *64*, 64–71. [CrossRef] [PubMed]
57. Cope, E.C.; Gould, E. New evidence linking obesity and food addiction. *Biol. Psychiatry* **2017**, *81*, 734–736. [CrossRef]
58. Burrows, T.; Kay-Lambkin, F.; Pursey, K.; Skinner, J.; Dayas, C. Food addiction and associations with mental health symptoms: A systematic review with meta-analysis. *J. Hum. Nutr. Diet.* **2018**, *31*, 544–572. [CrossRef]
59. Chu, D.T.; Nguyet, N.T.M.; Nga, V.T.; Lien, N.V.T.; Vo, D.D.; Lien, N.; Ngoc, V.T.N.; Le, D.H.; Nga, V.B.; Van Tu, P.; et al. An update on obesity: Mental consequences and psychological interventions. *Diabetes Metab. Syndr. Clin. Res. Rev.* **2019**, *13*, 155–160. [CrossRef]
60. Jorm, A.F.; Korten, A.E.; Christensen, H.; Jacomb, P.A.; Rodgers, B.; Parslow, R.A. Association of obesity with anxiety, depression and emotional well-being: A community survey. *Aust. N. Z. J. Public Health* **2003**, *27*, 434–440. [CrossRef]
61. Kamody, R.C.; Thurston, I.B.; Decker, K.M.; Kaufman, C.C.; Sonneville, K.R.; Richmond, T.K. Relating shape/weight based self-esteem, depression, and anxiety with weight and perceived physical health among young adults. *Body Image* **2018**, *25*, 168–176. [CrossRef]
62. Strine, T.W.; Mokdad, A.H.; Dube, S.R.; Balluz, L.S.; Gonzalez, O.; Berry, J.T.; Manderscheid, R.; Kroenke, K. The association of depression and anxiety with obesity and unhealthy behaviors among community-dwelling US adults. *Gen. Hosp. Psychiatry* **2008**, *30*, 127–137. [CrossRef]
63. Bell, C.G.; Walley, A.J.; Froguel, P. The genetics of human obesity. *Nat. Rev. Genet.* **2005**, *6*, 221–234. [CrossRef] [PubMed]
64. Davis, C.; Loxton, N.J.; Levitan, R.D.; Kaplan, A.S.; Carter, J.C.; Kennedy, J.L. Food addiction' and its association with a dopaminergic multilocus genetic profile. *Physiol. Behav.* **2013**, *118*, 63–69. [CrossRef] [PubMed]
65. Osadchiy, V.; Labus, J.S.; Gupta, A.; Jacobs, J.; Ashe-McNalley, C.; Hsiao, E.Y.; Mayer, E.A. Correlation of tryptophan metabolites with connectivity of extended central reward network in healthy subjects. *PLoS ONE* **2018**, *13*, e0201772. [CrossRef] [PubMed]
66. Santacruz, A.; Marcos, A.; Wärnberg, J.; Martí, A.; Martin-Matillas, M.; Campoy, C.; Moreno, L.A.; Veiga, O.; Redondo-Figuero, C.; Garagorri, J.M.; et al. Interplay between weight loss and gut microbiota composition in overweight adolescents. *Obesity* **2009**, *17*, 1906–1915. [CrossRef]
67. Huseinovic, E.; Winkvist, A.; Bertz, F.; Brekke, H.K. Changes in food choice during a successful weight loss trial in overweight and obese postpartum women. *Obesity* **2014**, *22*, 2517–2523. [CrossRef]
68. Assunção, M.C.F.; Gigante, D.P.; Cardoso, M.A.; Sartorelli, D.S.; Santos, I.S. Randomized, controlled trial promotes physical activity and reduces consumption of sweets and sodium among overweight and obese adults. *Nutr. Res.* **2010**, *30*, 541–549. [CrossRef]

2

Prevalence and Associated Factors of Nocturnal Eating Behavior and Sleep-Related Eating Disorder-Like Behavior in Japanese Young Adults: Results of an Internet Survey Using Munich Parasomnia Screening

Kentaro Matsui [1,2,3,4], Yoko Komada [5], Katsuji Nishimura [2], Kenichi Kuriyama [4] and Yuichi Inoue [1,6,*]

1 Japan Somnology Center, Neuropsychiatric Research Institute, Tokyo 1510053, Japan; matsui.kentaro@ncnp.go.jp

2 Department of Psychiatry, Tokyo Women's Medical University, Tokyo 1628666, Japan; nishimura.katsuji@twmu.ac.jp

3 Clinical Laboratory, National Institute of Mental Health, National Center of Neurology and Psychiatry, Tokyo 1878551, Japan

4 Department of Sleep-Wake Disorders, National Institute of Mental Health, National Center of Neurology and Psychiatry, Tokyo 1878551, Japan; kenichik@ncnp.go.jp

5 Liberal Arts, Meiji Pharmaceutical University, Tokyo 2048588, Japan; yoko.komada@gmail.com

6 Department of Somnology, Tokyo Medical University, Tokyo 1608402, Japan

* Correspondence: inoue@somnology.com

Abstract: Nocturnal (night) eating syndrome and sleep-related eating disorder have common characteristics, but are considered to differ in their level of consciousness during eating behavior and recallability. To date, there have been no large population-based studies determining their similarities and differences. We conducted a cross-sectional web-based survey for Japanese young adults aged 19–25 years to identify factors associated with nocturnal eating behavior and sleep-related eating disorder-like behavior using Munich Parasomnia Screening and logistic regression. Of the 3347 participants, 160 (4.8%) reported experiencing nocturnal eating behavior and 73 (2.2%) reported experiencing sleep-related eating disorder-like behavior. Smoking ($p < 0.05$), use of hypnotic medications ($p < 0.01$), and previous and/or current sleepwalking ($p < 0.001$) were associated with both nocturnal eating behavior and sleep-related eating disorder-like behavior. A delayed sleep-wake schedule ($p < 0.05$) and sleep disturbance ($p < 0.01$) were associated with nocturnal eating behavior but not with sleep-related eating disorder-like behavior. Both nocturnal eating behavior and sleep-related eating disorder-like behavior had features consistent with eating disorders or parasomnias. Nocturnal eating behavior but not sleep-related eating disorder-like behavior was characterized by a sleep-awake phase delay, perhaps representing an underlying pathophysiology of nocturnal eating syndrome.

Keywords: nocturnal eating syndrome; sleep-related eating disorder; eating disorder; parasomnia; delayed sleep-wake phase; MUPS

---

1. Introduction

Nocturnal (night) eating syndrome (NES) is characterized by recurrent episodes of eating after the evening meal or after awakening from sleep [1,2]. NES has been described as "other specified feeding or eating disorder" in the Diagnostic and Statistical Manual of Mental Disorders, Fifth Edition [1], but its criteria are relatively unclear. Therefore, the diagnostic criteria proposed by Allison and colleagues [2] have been also used. Similar eating behaviors, but with total amnesia or partial unawareness of eating or drinking, are seen in sleep-related eating disorder (SRED) [3–5]. SRED can be distinguished from NES by its unconscious eating behavior and its inability to recall, which was emphasized in the diagnostic criteria for SRED in the International Classification of Sleep Disorders, Third Edition (ICSD-3) [6]. However, since NES and SRED share several features, the distinction between the two is still controversial [7,8]. NES has been considered an eating disorder with evening hyperphagia, eating episodes occurring upon awakening during the night and resultant morning anorexia [9,10]; the pathology of NES is believed to be a delayed circadian pattern of food intake [11,12]. SRED is classified as parasomnia in the ICSD-3 [6] and characterized by eating while "half-awake, half-asleep" or "asleep" [4,6]. SRED patients often experience sleepwalking [3,4], which is rare in NES patients [13]. To date, no large population-based studies have been conducted on NES and SRED [8], and only a few studies have addressed their similarities and differences in clinical characteristics and pathophysiology [7,13].

Munich Parasomnia Screening (MUPS) is a self-assessment questionnaire consisting of 21 items and is used to evaluate parasomnias and sleep-related movement disorders, including NES and SRED [14]. The questionnaire covers past history and current frequency of abnormal nighttime behaviors and their sensitivity and specificity [14]. Our group previously translated and validated a Japanese version of MUPS [15]. With this questionnaire, we conducted an internet survey for Japanese young adults from the general population and estimated the prevalence of NES and SRED in this cohort. We then analyzed factors related to nocturnal eating behavior and SRED-like behavior in this population to determine similarities and differences in these two disorders.

2. Experimental Section

The present study was conducted as part of a comprehensive research project on the influence of sleep schedule on daytime functioning and depression among young adults [16,17]. This cross-sectional web-based questionnaire for Japanese individuals aged 19–25 years was conducted in February 2012. At that time, ICSD-3 [6] had not been published. The participants were already registered as members of the established internet survey company's research panel and resided throughout Japan. The study protocol was approved by the ethics committee of the Neuropsychiatric Research Institute, Tokyo, Japan (no. 64/2011). Informed consent was obtained from all participants via the survey website.

The questionnaire included demographic information: sex, age, body mass index, residential status (living alone or with family), smoking status, and alcohol consumption. Sleep habits were evaluated as sleep duration (obtained from the Pittsburgh Sleep Quality Index [PSQI], described below), weekday bedtime, and weekday wake-up time. The questionnaire also included the Japanese version of the PSQI for assessing sleep disturbances [18,19], the Japanese version of MUPS for identifying the lifetime incidence of sleepwalking (i.e., walking or sitting up while still asleep), and current episodes of nocturnal eating behavior (i.e., waking again after falling asleep to eat) and SRED-like behavior (i.e., while asleep, eating something or preparing a meal that contains unusual or inedible ingredients, such as a combination of ice cream and cheese or dishwashing detergent instead of butter) [14,15].

Of 3904 participants who accessed the survey website, 3613 responded to the questionnaire. Participants who did not complete the questionnaire (n = 219) or who provided invalid answers (n = 47) were excluded. The responses of the remaining 3347 participants (92.6%) were included in the analyses of the present study (Figure 1).

To investigate factors associated with nocturnal eating behavior and SRED-like behavior [14,15]), we conducted logistic regression analyses for age, sex, body mass index, living alone, hypnotic medication use (three or more times per week) [18,19]), smoking status, alcohol consumption, previous and/or current sleepwalking [14,15]), typical sleep duration (categorized; see below), sleep-wake schedule (delayed/not delayed; phase delay was defined using the midpoint between sleep onset and sleep offset; 4:00 AM [20]), and subjective sleep quality (categorized; see below). Typical sleep duration and sleep-wake schedule were derived from the PSQI [18,19]. Body mass index was categorized as < 25 kg/m^2, 25–29 kg/m^2, and ≥ 30 kg/m^2 [21]. Typical sleep duration was categorized as < 6 and ≥ 6 hours [22,23]. PSQI scores were grouped as < 6 and ≥ 6 points [18,19]. All variables were examined initially with univariate models, and multivariate logistic regression was conducted for all variables that were significantly correlated in univariate models to determine the main correlates controlling for confounding factors. Wald statistics were used to test the significance of odds ratios (ORs) calculated from the regression analysis. SPSS version 22 (IBM SPSS, Armonk, NY, USA) was used for analysis. Statistical significance was set at $p < 0.05$.

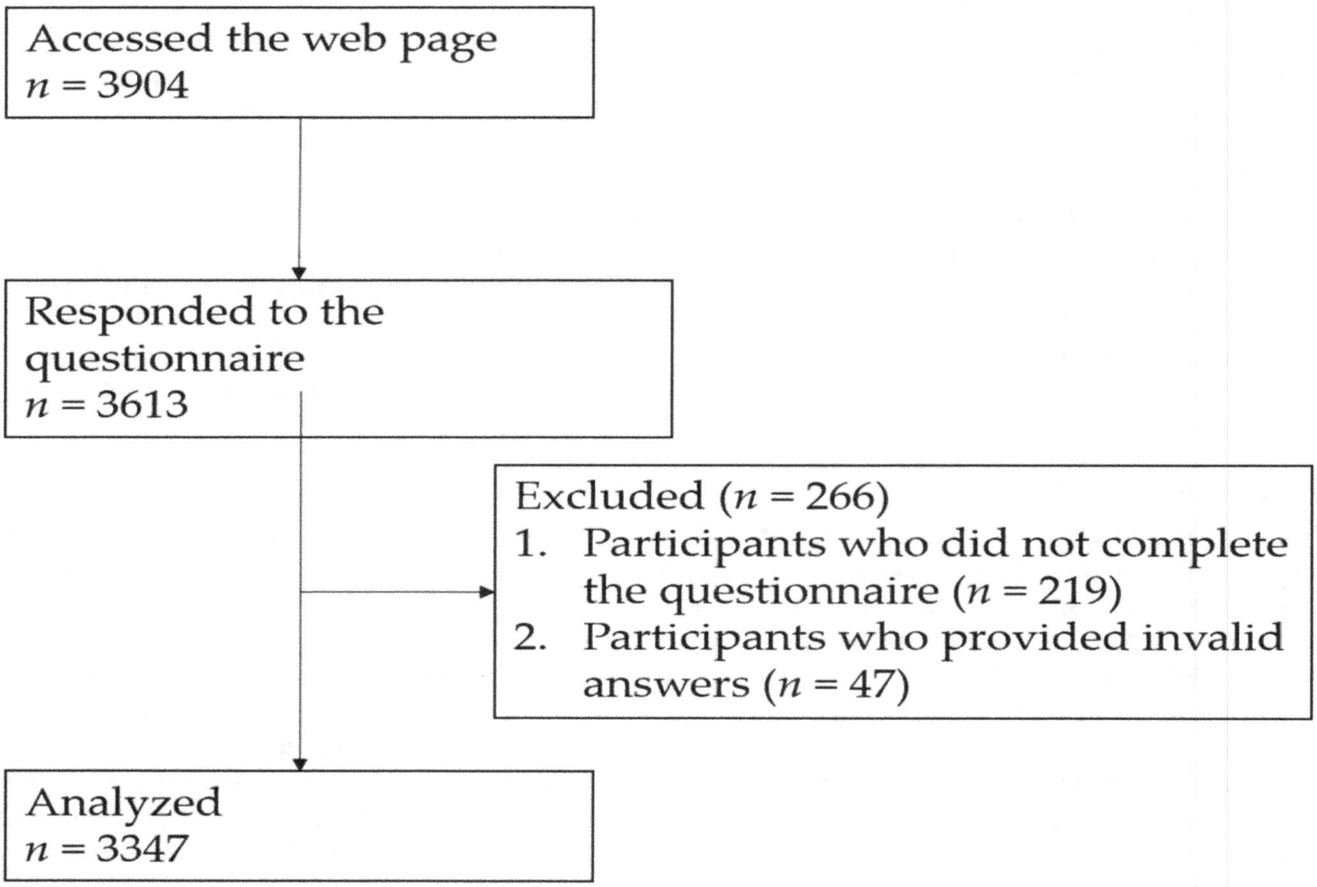

Figure 1. Subject flow diagram.

3. Results

Among the 3347 participants, 160 (4.8%) reported nocturnal eating behavior and 73 (2.2%) reported SRED-like behavior one or more times per year. Nocturnal eating behavior and SRED-like behavior were concomitant in 45 participants, but 72% of participants reporting nocturnal eating behavior and 38% of participants reporting SRED-like behavior did not overlap. Table 1 lists the characteristics of study participants.

Eight factors were significantly associated with nocturnal eating behavior in univariate logistic regression analyses: female sex, body mass index ≥ 30 kg/m^2, current smoking, use of hypnotic medication, previous and/or current sleepwalking, sleeping < 6 hours, delayed sleep-wake schedule, and higher PSQI scores (≥ 6 points). In the multiple logistic regression model, female sex, current smoking, use of hypnotic medication, previous and/or current sleepwalking, delayed sleep-wake schedule, and higher PSQI scores (≥ 6 points) were associated (Table 2).

Table 1. Characteristics of study participants.

Characteristic	Total (n = 3347)	Nocturnal Eating Behavior (n = 160)	Sleep-Related Eating Disorder-Like Behavior (n = 73)
Age, mean (SD), year	22.9 (1.8)	22.9 (1.8)	22.8 (1.7)
Sex (percent male)	45.3	36.3	46.6
Body mass index, mean (SD), kg/m^2	21.1 (3.6)	21.5 (4.4)	22.2 (4.4)
Current smoker (%)	10.5	20.0	21.9
Regular alcohol consumption (%)	35.1	34.4	47.9
Living alone (%)	34.1	35.0	35.6
Use of hypnotic medication (three or more times per week) (%)	2.8	13.1	12.3
Previous and/or current sleepwalking (%)	8.5	35.0	71.2
Typical sleep duration, mean (SD), hours	6.8 (1.4)	6.9 (1.6)	7.0 (1.7)
Midpoint on weekdays, mean (SD), time	4:22 (1:40)	4:41 (1:51)	4:17 (1:33)
Pittsburgh Sleep Quality Index score, mean (SD), points	5.5 (2.7)	7.6 (3.1)	7.2 (3.3)

Nocturnal eating behavior and sleep-related eating disorder-like behavior were defined as occurring at least once per year. SD, standard deviation.

Table 2. Factors associated with nocturnal eating behavior one or more times per year.

Predictor		Univariate Relative Risk (95% Confidence Interval) [1]	p	Multivariate Relative Risk (95% Confidence Interval) [1]	p
Age (years)	3347		n.s.		n.s.
Sex					
Male	1517				
Female	1830	1.485 (1.068–2.065)	<0.05	1.560 (1.103–2.206)	<0.05
Body mass index (kg/m^2)					
<25	3016				
25–29	247		n.s.		n.s.
≥30	84	2.484 (1.219–5.062)	<0.05		n.s.
Living alone					
No	2204				
Yes	1143		n.s.		n.s.
Current smoker					
No	2995				
Yes	352	2.240 (1.495–3.356)	<0.001	1.980 (1.286–3.047)	<0.01
Regular alcohol consumption					
No	2172				
Yes	1175		n.s.		n.s.
Use of hypnotic medication (three or more times per week)					
No	3253				
Yes	94	6.445 (3.854–10.778)	<0.001	4.054 (2.306–7.129)	<0.001
Previous and/or current sleepwalking					
No	3062				
Yes	285	6.955 (4.894–9.886)	<0.001	6.249 (4.335–9.009)	<0.001
Typical sleep duration (hours)					
≥6	2723				
<6	624	1.539 (1.067–2.219)	<0.05		n.s.
Sleep-wake schedule[2]					
Not delayed	1438				
Delayed	1909	1.507 (1.078–2.107)	<0.05	1.478 (1.042–2.096)	<0.05
Pittsburgh Sleep Quality Index score (points)					
<6	1827				
≥6	1520	2.690 (1.915–3.779)	<0.001	1.871 (1.304–2.684)	<0.01

[1] Relative risks approximated to odds ratios. [2] Phase delay was defined using 4:00 AM as the midpoint. n.s., not significant.

Five factors were associated with SRED-like behavior in univariate logistic regression analyses: body mass index of 25–29 kg/m^2, current smoking, regular alcohol consumption, previous and/or current sleepwalking, and higher PSQI scores (≥ 6 points). In the multiple logistic regression model, current smoking, use of hypnotic medication, and previous and/or current sleepwalking were associated (Table 3).

Table 3. Factors associated with sleep-related eating disorder-like behavior one or more times per year.

Predictor		Univariate Relative Risk (95% Confidence Interval) [1]	*p*	Multivariate Relative Risk (95% Confidence interval) [1]	*p*
Age (years)	3347		n.s.		n.s.
Sex					
Male	1517				
Female	1830		n.s.		n.s.
Body mass index (kg/m^2)					
<25	3016				
25–29	247	2.115 (1.068–4.188)	<0.05		n.s.
≥30	84		n.s.		n.s.
Living alone					
No	2204				
Yes	1143		n.s.		n.s.
Current smoker					
No	2995				
Yes	352	2.454 (1.394–4.322)	<0.01	1.998 (1.072–3.724)	<0.05
Regular alcohol consumption					
No	2172				
Yes	1175	1.724 (1.083–2.744)	<0.05		n.s.
Use of hypnotic medication (three or more times per week)					
No	3253				
Yes	94	5.276 (2.542–10.951)	<0.001	3.750 (1.606–8.755)	<0.01
Previous and/or current sleepwalking					
No	3062				
Yes	285	32.318 (19.137–54.576)	<0.001	30.113 (17.764–51.044)	<0.001
Typical sleep duration (hours)					
≥6	2723				
<6	624		n.s.		n.s.
Sleep-wake schedule[2]					
Not delayed	1438				
Delayed	1909		n.s.		n.s.
Pittsburgh Sleep Quality Index (points)					
<6	1827				
≥6	1520	1.848 (1.151–2.969)	<0.05		n.s.

[1] Relative risks approximated to odds ratios. [2] Phase delay was defined using 4:00 AM as the midpoint. n.s., not significant.

4. Discussion

Thus far, sleepwalking has been considered rare in NES subjects [13]. However, we found a relatively strong association between sleepwalking and nocturnal eating behavior, although it was not as strong as the association with SRED-like behavior. This may be attributable to nocturnal eating behavior in the present study being defined as eating behavior after falling asleep or to the overlap reported by some participants between the two conditions. Of note, in this study, both nocturnal eating behavior and SRED-like behavior were associated with the use of hypnotic medication, with relatively high odds ratios. Multiple studies have reported SRED induced by hypnotic medication [24–28], but the evidence for hypnotic medication-induced NES is scarce [29]. but both benzodiazepines and Z-drugs can cause behavioral disinhibition [30,31], which may underlie the association between the use of hypnotic medication and nocturnal eating behavior. In addition, we found that nocturnal eating behavior but not SRED-like behavior was correlated with higher PSQI scores. Although the causal relationship is unclear, an association between insomnia and NES [7,10,32,33] should be considered.

Current smoking was also associated with both nocturnal eating behavior and SRED-like behavior. Smoking is common in eating disorders [34], and especially in bulimia and/or binge eating rather than anorexia [35–37]. Interestingly, NES has been reported to be more frequent in populations with bulimia and/or binge eating disorder rather than anorexia [38]. Thus, nocturnal eating behavior and binge eating may possibly be related to the pathology of addiction, including smoking. As for SRED, several cases in which smoking cessation resulted in SRED have been reported [5,39]. In addition, sleep-related smoking concomitant with NES and/or SRED has been reported [40]. Although Yahia and colleagues did not find a relationship between smoking and NES [32], smoking, as an addiction, may offer an opportunity for studying the pathology of NES and SRED.

Nocturnal eating behavior was associated in our study with the female sex. Just as eating disorders typically affect females [41–43], NES has been reported to be more common in females [10]. However, in both NES and SRED, sex differences in the prevalence are still controversial [5,33,44–50]; some studies have reported that NES was more common in males [44,45]. Thus, our findings should be confirmed in larger studies.

This is the first epidemiological study to indicate a relationship between a delay in the sleep-wake rhythm and nocturnal eating behavior. One study in mice suggested that feeding behavior affects the sleep-wake rhythm via the dopaminergic system [51]. It is still unclear whether delayed eating rhythm results in a delay in the sleep-wake rhythm or vice versa. However, nocturnal secretion of melatonin has been reported to decrease in NES [9]. Moreover, some preliminary studies have suggested that therapeutic interventions that act to consolidate the circadian rhythm, such as bright light therapy [52] and treatment with agomelatine [53,54], are effective for NES. Although these circadian-focused treatments require validation, the findings of the present study indicate that a delay in the sleep-wake rhythm possibly underlies the pathophysiology of NES.

This study has some limitations. First, the study was based on self-rating without face-to-face interviews. A further very important limiting factor is that the MUPS [14] had been developed before the publication of the ICSD-3 [6], and does not include "partial or complete loss of conscious awareness during the eating episode". However, nocturnal eating behavior and SRED-like behavior, which were expressed as "nocturnal eating" and "sleep related eating" in MUPS, respectively, were clearly distinguished by the presence/absence of consciousness [14]. This implication emphasizes the significance of focusing on the differences between nocturnal eating behavior and SRED-like behavior in this study. As this study was an analysis of self-reported data, there is a possibility that we underestimated the prevalence of subjects with SRED-like behavior who could not recall eating behavior at night. In contrast, we may have overestimated the prevalence since we required only one incident over the preceding year. Therefore, the present study should be considered preliminary in assessing the pathophysiology of NES and SRED. The second limitation is a possible sampling bias. Generally, internet users have been reported to experience more sleep problems or shorter sleep durations [55,56]. Third, this study did not confirm any questionnaires or severity scales specific to NES for affected subjects classified only by MUPs. Lastly, we identified the use of hypnotic medication in the survey [18,19], but did not record the type or amount. Similarly, the lack of information on the quantity of alcohol consumed and number of cigarettes smoked is also a limitation.

5. Conclusions

The present study using MUPS suggested that a considerable number of Japanese young adults may have NES, SRED, or both. Factors associated with both nocturnal eating behavior and SRED-like behavior were smoking, sleepwalking, and use of hypnotic medication. Nocturnal eating behavior but not SRED-like behavior was associated with a delayed sleep-wake schedule and sleep disturbances, as well as with the female sex. Confirmation of the reproducibility of these findings and prospective research that includes face-to-face interviews are warranted.

Author Contributions: Conceptualization, Y.K. and Y.I.; investigation, Y.K.; data curation, K.M. and Y.K.; formal analysis, K.M. and Y.I.; supervision, K.N. and K.K..; validation, K.N. and K.K.; original draft writing, K.M.; review and editing, Y.K. and Y.I. All authors have read and agreed to the published version of the manuscript.

Acknowledgments: We thank Dean Meyer, ELS from Edanz Group (www.edanzediting.com/ac) for editing a draft of this manuscript.

References

1. American Psychiatric Association. *Diagnostic and Statistical Manual of Mental Disorders (DSM-5)*, 5th ed.; American Psychiatric Pub: Washington, DC, USA, 2013.
2. Allison, K.C.; Lundgren, J.D.; O'Reardon, J.P.; Geliebter, A.; Gluck, M.E.; Vinai, P.; Mitchell, J.E.; Schenck, C.H.; Howell, M.J.; Crow, S.J.; et al. Proposed diagnostic criteria for night eating syndrome. *Int. J. Eat. Disord.* **2010**, *43*, 241–247. [CrossRef] [PubMed]
3. Schenck, C.H.; Mahowald, M.W. Review of nocturnal sleep-related eating disorders. *Int. J. Eat. Disord.* **1994**, *15*, 343–356. [CrossRef] [PubMed]
4. Winkelman, J.W. Clinical and polysomnographic features of sleep-related eating disorder. *J. Clin. Psychiatry* **1998**, *59*, 14–19. [CrossRef] [PubMed]
5. Schenck, C.H.; Hurwitz, T.D.; O'Connor, K.A.; Mahowald, M.W. Additional Categories of Sleep-Related Eating Disorders and the Current Status of Treatment. *Sleep* **1993**, *16*, 457–466. [CrossRef] [PubMed]
6. American Academy of Sleep Medicine. *International Classification of Sleep Disorders (ICSD-3)*, 3rd ed.; American Academy of Sleep Medicine: Darien, IL, USA, 2014.
7. Vinai, P.; Ferri, R.; Ferini-Strambi, L.; Cardetti, S.; Anelli, M.; Vallauri, P.; Ferrato, N.; Zucconi, M.; Carpegna, G.; Manconi, M. Defining the borders between Sleep-Related Eating Disorder and Night Eating Syndrome. *Sleep Med.* **2012**, *13*, 686–690. [CrossRef] [PubMed]
8. Inoue, Y. Sleep-related eating disorder and its associated conditions. *Psychiatry Clin. Neurosci.* **2015**, *69*, 309–320. [CrossRef]
9. Birketvedt, G.S.; Florholmen, J.; Sundsfjord, J.; Østerud, B.; Dinges, D.; Bilker, W.; Stunkard, A. Behavioral and neuroendocrine characteristics of the night-eating syndrome. *JAMA* **1999**, *282*, 657–663. [CrossRef]
10. Stunkard, A.J.; Grace, W.J.; Wolff, H.G. The night-eating syndrome; a pattern of food intake among certain obese patients. *Am. J. Med.* **1955**, *19*, 78–86. [CrossRef]
11. Boston, R.C.; Moate, P.; Allison, K.C.; Lundgren, J.D.; Stunkard, A.J. Modeling circadian rhythms of food intake by means of parametric deconvolution: Results from studies of the night eating syndrome. *Am. J. Clin. Nutr.* **2008**, *87*, 1672–1677. [CrossRef]
12. Goel, N.; Stunkard, A.J.; Rogers, N.; Van Dongen, H.P.; Allison, K.C.; O'Reardon, J.P.; Ahima, R.S.; Cummings, D.E.; Heo, M.; Dinges, D.F. Circadian rhythm profiles in women with night eating syndrome. *J. Boil. Rhythm.* **2009**, *24*, 85–94. [CrossRef]
13. Vetrugno, R.; Manconi, M.; Ferini-Strambi, L.; Provini, F.; Plazzi, G.; Montagna, P. Nocturnal eating: Sleep-related eating disorder or night eating syndrome? A videopolysomnographic study. *Sleep* **2006**, *29*, 949–954. [CrossRef] [PubMed]
14. Fulda, S.; Hornyak, M.; Muller, K.; Černý, L.; Beitinger, P.A.; Wetter, T.C. Development and validation of the Munich Parasomnia Screening (MUPS). *Somnologie Schlafforsch. Schlafmed.* **2008**, *12*, 56–65. [CrossRef]
15. Komada, Y.; Breugelmans, R.; Fulda, S.; Nakano, S.; Watanabe, A.; Noda, C.; Nishida, S.; Inoue, Y. Japanese version of the Munich Parasomnia Screening: Translation and linguistic validation of a screening instrument for parasomnias and nocturnal behaviors. *Neuropsychiatr. Dis. Treat.* **2015**, *11*, 2953–2958. [CrossRef] [PubMed]
16. Morita, Y.; Sasai-Sakuma, T.; Asaoka, S.; Inoue, Y. The impact of a delayed sleep-wake schedule on depression is greater in women-A web-based cross-sectional study in Japanese young adults. *Chrono Int.* **2015**, *32*, 952–958.
17. Asaoka, S.; Komada, Y.; Aritake, S.; Morita, Y.; Fukuda, K.; Inoue, Y. Effect of delayed sleep phase during university life on the daytime functioning in work life after graduation. *Sleep Med.* **2014**, *15*, 1155–1158. [CrossRef] [PubMed]

18. Buysse, D.J.; Reynolds, C.F.; Monk, T.H.; Berman, S.R.; Kupfer, D.J. The Pittsburgh sleep quality index: A new instrument for psychiatric practice and research. *Psychiatry Res. Neuroimaging* **1989**, *28*, 193–213. [CrossRef]
19. Doi, Y.; Minowa, M.; Uchiyama, M.; Okawa, M.; Kim, K.; Shibui, K.; Kamei, Y. Psychometric assessment of subjective sleep quality using the Japanese version of the Pittsburgh Sleep Quality Index (PSQI-J) in psychiatric disordered and control subjects. *Psychiatry Res. Neuroimaging* **2000**, *97*, 165–172. [CrossRef]
20. Simonelli, G.; Dudley, K.A.; Weng, J.; Gallo, L.C.; Perreira, K.; Shah, N.A.; Alcantara, C.; Zee, P.C.; Ramos, A.R.; Llabre, M.M.; et al. Neighborhood Factors as Predictors of Poor Sleep in the Sueño Ancillary Study of the Hispanic Community Health Study/Study of Latinos (HCHS/SOL). *Sleep* **2016**, *40*, 025.
21. Milano, W.; De Rosa, M.; Milano, L.; Capasso, A. Night eating syndrome An overview. *J. Pharm. Pharmacol.* **2011**, *64*, 2–10. [CrossRef]
22. Petrov, M.E.; Howard, G.; Grandner, M.A.; Kleindorfer, D.; Molano, J.R.; Howard, V.J. Sleep duration and risk of incident stroke by age, sex, and race. *Neurol.* **2018**, *91*, 1702–1709. [CrossRef]
23. Kaneita, Y.; Ohida, T.; Uchiyama, M.; Takemura, S.; Kawahara, K.; Yokoyama, E.; Miyake, T.; Harano, S.; Suzuki, K.; Fujita, T. The relationship between depression and sleep disturbances: A Japanese nationwide general population survey. *J. Clin. Psychiatry* **2006**, *67*, 196–203. [CrossRef] [PubMed]
24. Molina, S.M.; Joshi, K.G. A Case of Zaleplon-Induced Amnestic Sleep-Related Eating Disorder. *J. Clin. Psychiatry* **2010**, *71*, 210–211. [CrossRef] [PubMed]
25. Najjar, M. Zolpidem and Amnestic Sleep Related Eating Disorder. *J. Clin. Sleep Med.* **2007**, *3*, 637–638. [CrossRef] [PubMed]
26. Nzwalo, H.; Ferreira, L.; Peralta, R.; Bentes, C. Sleep-related eating disorder secondary to zolpidem. *BMJ Case Rep.* **2013**, *2013*. [CrossRef] [PubMed]
27. Park, Y.M.; Shin, H.W. Zolpidem Induced Sleep-related Eating and Complex Behaviors in a Patient with Obstructive Sleep Apnea and Restless Legs Syndrome. *Clin. Psychopharmacol. Neurosci.* **2016**, *14*, 299–301. [CrossRef] [PubMed]
28. Yun, C.H.; Ji, K.H. Zolpidem-induced sleep-related eating disorder. *J. Neurol. Sci.* **2010**, *288*, 200–201. [CrossRef]
29. Kim, H.K.; Kwon, J.T.; Baek, J.; Park, D.S.; Yang, K.I. Zolpidem-Induced Compulsive Evening Eating Behavior. *Clin. Neuropharmacol.* **2013**, *36*, 173–174. [CrossRef]
30. Paton, C. Benzodiazepines and disinhibition: A review. *Psychiatr. Bull.* **2002**, *26*, 460–462. [CrossRef]
31. Olson, L.G. Hypnotic hazards: Adverse effects of zolpidem and other z-drugs. *Aust. Prescr.* **2008**, *31*, 146–149. [CrossRef]
32. Yahia, N.; Brown, C.; Potter, S.; Szymanski, H.; Smith, K.; Pringle, L.; Herman, C.P.; Uribe, M.; Fu, Z.; Chung, M.; et al. Night eating syndrome and its association with weight status, physical activity, eating habits, smoking status, and sleep patterns among college students. *Eat. Weight. Disord. Stud. Anorexia Bulim. Obes.* **2017**, *22*, 421–433. [CrossRef]
33. Ceru-Bjork, C.; Andersson, I.; Rossner, S. Night eating and nocturnal eating-two different or similar syndromes among obese patients? *J. Int. Assoc. Study Obes.* **2001**, *25*, 365–372. [CrossRef] [PubMed]
34. Wiseman, C.V.; Turco, R.M.; Sunday, S.R.; Halmi, K.A. Smoking and body image concerns in adolescent girls. *Int. J. Eat. Disord.* **1998**, *24*, 429–433. [CrossRef]
35. Bulik, C.M.; Epstein, L.H.; McKee, M.; Kaye, W. Drug use in women with bulimia and anorexia nervosa. *NIDA Res. Monogr.* **1990**, *105*, 462–463. [CrossRef]
36. Haug, N.A.; Heinberg, L.J.; Guarda, A.S. Cigarette smoking and its relationship to other substance use among eating disordered inpatients. *Eat. Weight. Disord. Stud. Anorexia, Bulim. Obes.* **2001**, *6*, 130–139. [CrossRef] [PubMed]
37. Anzengruber, D.; Klump, K.L.; Thornton, L.; Brandt, H.; Crawford, S.; Fichter, M.; Halmi, K.A.; Johnson, C.; Kaplan, A.; LaVia, M.; et al. Smoking in eating disorders. *Eat. Behav.* **2006**, *7*, 291–299. [CrossRef] [PubMed]
38. Tu, C.Y.; Tseng, M.C.M.; Chang, C.H. Night eating syndrome in patients with eating disorders: Is night eating syndrome distinct from bulimia nervosa? *J. Formos. Med Assoc.* **2019**, *118*, 1038–1046. [CrossRef]
39. Varghese, R.; De Castro, J.R.; Liendo, C.; Schenck, C.H. Two Cases of Sleep-Related Eating Disorder Responding Promptly to Low-Dose Sertraline Therapy. *J. Clin. Sleep Med.* **2018**, *14*, 1805–1808. [CrossRef]
40. Provini, F.; Vetrugno, R.; Montagna, P. Sleep-related smoking syndrome. *Sleep Med.* **2008**, *9*, 903–905. [CrossRef]

41. Striegel-Moore, R.H.; Bulik, C.M.; Weissman, R.S. Risk factors for eating disorders. *Am. Psychol.* **2007**, *62*, 181–198. [CrossRef]
42. Hoek, H.W. Incidence, prevalence and mortality of anorexia nervosa and other eating disorders. *Curr. Opin. Psychiatry* **2006**, *19*, 389–394. [CrossRef]
43. Hudson, J.I.; Hiripi, E.; Pope, H.G.; Kessler, R.C. The prevalence and correlates of eating disorders in the National Comorbidity Survey Replication. *Boil. Psychiatry* **2006**, *61*, 348–358. [CrossRef] [PubMed]
44. Aronoff, N.J.; Geliebter, A.; Zammit, G. Gender and Body Mass Index as Related to the Night-Eating Syndrome in Obese Outpatients. *J. Am. Diet. Assoc.* **2001**, *101*, 102–104. [CrossRef]
45. Tholin, S.; Lindroos, A.; Tynelius, P.; Åkerstedt, T.; Stunkard, A.J.; Bulik, C.M.; Rasmussen, F. Prevalence of Night Eating in Obese and Nonobese Twins. *Obes.* **2009**, *17*, 1050–1055. [CrossRef] [PubMed]
46. Striegel-Moore, R.H.; Franko, D.L.; Thompson, D.; Affenito, S.; Kraemer, H.C.; Weissman, R.S. Night Eating: Prevalence and Demographic Correlates*. *Obes.* **2006**, *14*, 139–147. [CrossRef]
47. Grilo, C.M.; Masheb, R.M. Night-time eating in men and women with binge eating disorder. *Behav. Res. Ther.* **2004**, *42*, 397–407. [CrossRef]
48. Winkelman, J.W. Efficacy and tolerability of open-label topiramate in the treatment of sleep-related eating disorder: A retrospective case series. *J. Clin. Psychiatry* **2006**, *67*, 1729–1734. [CrossRef]
49. Schenck, C.H.; Hurwitz, T.D.; Bundlie, S.R.; Mahowald, M.W. Sleep-Related Eating Disorders: Polysomnographic Correlates of a Heterogeneous Syndrome Distinct from Daytime Eating Disorders. *Sleep* **1991**, *14*, 419–431. [CrossRef]
50. O'Reardon, J.P.; Ringel, B.L.; Dinges, D.F.; Allison, K.C.; Rogers, N.; Martino, N.S.; Stunkard, A.J. Circadian Eating and Sleeping Patterns in the Night Eating Syndrome. *Obes. Res.* **2004**, *12*, 1789–1796. [CrossRef]
51. Mendoza, J.; Clesse, D.; Pévet, P.; Challet, E. Food-reward signalling in the suprachiasmatic clock. *J. Neurochem.* **2010**, *112*, 1489–1499. [CrossRef]
52. McCune, A.M.; Lundgren, J.D. Bright light therapy for the treatment of night eating syndrome: A pilot study. *Psychiatry Res. Neuroimaging* **2015**, *229*, 577–579. [CrossRef]
53. Milano, W.; De Rosa, M.; Milano, L.; Capasso, A. Agomelatine Efficacy in the Night Eating Syndrome. *Case Rep. Med.* **2013**, *2013*, 1–5. [CrossRef] [PubMed]
54. Milano, W.; De Rosa, M.; Milano, L.; Riccio, A.; Sanseverino, B.; Capasso, A. Successful Treatment with Agomelatine in NES: A Series of Five Cases. *Open Neurol. J.* **2013**, *7*, 32–37. [CrossRef] [PubMed]
55. Cain, N.; Gradisar, M. Electronic media use and sleep in school-aged children and adolescents: A review. *Sleep Med.* **2010**, *11*, 735–742. [CrossRef] [PubMed]
56. Do, Y.K.; Shin, E.; Bautista, M.A.; Foo, K. The associations between self-reported sleep duration and adolescent health outcomes: What is the role of time spent on Internet use? *Sleep Med.* **2013**, *14*, 195–200. [CrossRef] [PubMed]

3

Food Addiction in Eating Disorders and Obesity: Analysis of Clusters and Implications for Treatment

Susana Jiménez-Murcia [1,2,3,*], Zaida Agüera [1,2,4], Georgios Paslakis [5,6], Lucero Munguia [3], Roser Granero [2,7], Jéssica Sánchez-González [1], Isabel Sánchez [1,2], Nadine Riesco [1,2], Ashley N Gearhardt [8], Carlos Dieguez [2,9], Gilda Fazia [10,11], Cristina Segura-García [11,12], Isabel Baenas [1], José M Menchón [1,3,13] and Fernando Fernández-Aranda [1,2,3,*]

1 Department of Psychiatry, University Hospital of Bellvitge-IDIBELL, L'Hospitalet de Llobregat, 08907 Barcelona, Spain; zaguera@bellvitgehospital.cat (Z.A.); jsanchezg@bellvitgehospital.cat (J.S.-G.); isasanchez@bellvitgehospital.cat (I.S.); nriesco@bellvitgehospital.cat (N.R.); ibaenas@bellvitgehospital.cat (I.B.); jmenchon@bellvitgehospital.cat (J.M.M.)
2 CIBER Fisiopatología Obesidad y Nutrición (CIBERobn), Instituto de Salud Carlos III, L'Hospitalet de Llobregat, 08907 Barcelona, Spain; roser.granero@uab.cat (R.G.); carlos.dieguez@usc.es (C.D.)
3 Clinical Sciences Department, School of Medicine, University of Barcelona, 08907 L'Hospitalet de Llobregat, Spain; laarcreed_lm@hotmail.com
4 Department of Public Health, Mental Health and Maternal-Child Nursing, School of Nursing, University of Barcelona, 08907 L'Hospitalet de Llobregat, Spain
5 Toronto General Hospital, University Health Network, Toronto, ON M5G 2C4, Canada; paslakis@outlook.de
6 Department of Psychiatry, University of Toronto, Toronto, ON M5T 1R8, Canada
7 Department of Psychobiology and Methodology, Autonomous University of Barcelona, 08193 Barcelona, Spain
8 Department of Psychology, University of Michigan, Ann Arbor, MI 48109, USA; agearhar@umich.edu
9 Department Physiology, Center for Research in Molecular Medicine and Chronic Diseases (CIMUS), Health Research Institute of Santiago USC-IDIS, University Santiago de Compostela, 15705 Santiago de Compostela, Spain
10 Department of Health Sciences, University "Magna Graecia" of Catanzaro, Viale Europa, 88100 Catanzaro, Italy; gildafazia@gmail.com
11 Center for Clinical Research and Treatment of Eating Disorders, Azienda Ospedaliera Universitaria Mater Domini, 88100 Catanzaro, Italy; segura@unicz.it
12 Department of Medical and Surgical Sciences, University "Magna Graecia" of Catanzaro, 88100 Catanzaro, Italy
13 CIBER de Salud Mental (CIBERSAM), Instituto de Salud Carlos III, L'Hospitalet de Llobregat, 08907 Barcelona, Spain
* Correspondence: sjimenez@bellvitgehospital.cat (S.J.-M.); ffernandez@bellvitgehospital.cat (F.F.-A.)

Abstract: Food addiction (FA) has been associated with greater psychopathology in individuals with eating disorders (ED) and obesity (OBE). The current study aims to provide a better phenotypic characterization of the FA construct by conducting a clustering analysis of FA in both conditions (ED and OBE). The total sample was comprised of 234 participants that scored positive on the Yale Food Addiction Scale 2.0. (YFAS-2) (119 bulimia nervosa (BN), 50 binge eating disorder (BED), 49 other specified feeding or eating disorder (OSFED) and 16 OBE). All participants completed a comprehensive battery of questionnaires. Three clusters of FA participants were identified. Cluster 1 (dysfunctional) was characterized by the highest prevalence of OSFED and BN, the highest ED severity and psychopathology, and more dysfunctional personality traits. Cluster 2 (moderate) showed a high prevalence of BN and BED and moderate levels of ED psychopathology. Finally, cluster 3 (adaptive) was characterized by a high prevalence of OBE and BED, low levels of ED psychopathology, and more functional personality traits. In conclusion, this study identified three distinct clusters of ED-OBE patients with FA and provides some insight into a better phenotypic characterization of the FA construct when considering psychopathology, personality and ED pathology. Future studies should address whether these three food addiction categories are indicative of therapy outcome.

Keywords: food addiction; eating disorders; bulimia nervosa; binge eating disorders; obesity; other specified feeding or eating disorders; cluster analysis

1. Introduction

Food addiction (FA) is a concept that has been of increasing scientific interest and debate. An immense body of literature within the field of eating disorder (ED) research has emerged, with whole special issues of scientific journals being dedicated to its characterization [1,2]. In addition to obvious phenomenological similarities between addiction and ED (e.g., loss of control, continued use despite negative consequences, cravings), a great number of neurobiological findings have emerged to additionally support the new concept, not only in preclinical studies, but also in humans [3–6].

Still, not all controversies have yet been resolved. Starting off as a concept to explain a potential subtype of obesity (OBE) [7–10], FA has also been associated with ED, such as bulimia nervosa (BN) [11–13], binge eating disorder (BED) [14–16], and even anorexia nervosa (AN) [17]. In a systematic review of studies on FA in non-clinical and clinical cohorts, it was especially BED that was associated with the most severe FA symptoms [15]. FA also seems to be prevalent in individuals with OBE waiting for bariatric surgery [18,19] and predicts less effective weight reduction throughout dietary intervention before surgery [20]. Interestingly, surgery-induced weight loss may lead to remission of FA [21,22].

The Yale Food Addiction Scale (YFAS) is the main instrument for the assessment of FA and has been developed to assess FA based on the known criteria used for the assessment of substance dependence, but applied for high palatable foods [23,24]. Higher scores on the YFAS have been associated with higher body mass index (BMI), binge eating episodes, impulsivity, and cravings for highly palatable food [25], as well as with neural responses similar to those found in substance use disorders [26–29].

There is scarce evidence with regard to the identification of key determinants of FA based on personality traits or ED-related symptoms and most of what is known is derived from non-clinical cohorts. In a non-clinical sample, negative urgency (irrational acting in aversive affective states) and low levels of task persistence (lack of perseverance) were shown to be significantly and directly associated with FA and FA mediated their association to BMI [30]. In another study in undergraduates, negative urgency, impulsivity when under distress, and emotion dysregulation positively predicted symptom count on the YFAS [31]. Similar findings were shown in a clinical ED cohort, although negative urgency appeared to be the only independent predictor for FA, while self-directedness and emotion dysregulation predicted negative urgency and were highly related to ED-related symptomatology, but not to food addiction itself [32,33]. In individuals with OBE awaiting bariatric surgery, FA was associated with personality traits such as neuroticism, impulsivity, and alexithymia [34], but also more emotion dysregulation, more harm avoidance, and less self-directedness [35].

FA has also been associated with a positive screen for more severe variants of ED-related psychopathology [7] as well as with a positive screen for major mental health symptoms, major depressive episode, anxiety, early life adversities, such as psychological and sexual abuse, and an overall reduced quality of life [36–38]. Finally, female gender was a predictor of severe food addiction [36] and high reward sensitivity was significantly associated with more severe FA symptoms in females [39].

Due to these meaningful interrelationships in the literature between FA and personality traits, as well as psychopathology, it is important to consider the association of FA with these factors in an integrated way (rather than looking at each construct in isolation). Evaluating how personality and psychopathology cluster within the FA construct could lead to a better understanding of potential distinct phenotypes within FA that could have different clinical profiles.

Based on this premise, the aim of the present paper was to explore empirically the severity of clusters of FA-positive (FA+) participants based on psychopathological symptomatology (namely ED-related psychopathology and general psychopathology) and personality traits, and to investigate how the clinical features and diagnosis of ED and OBE were distributed among them. This is the first study that attempts this type of analysis in order to identify subgroups among participants with positive FA in order to provide a better phenotypic characterization of the FA construct. We hypothesized that, despite overlaps, patients with ED would predominantly fit into a cluster characterized by a more severe ED-related psychopathology that would be different than the cluster predominantly found among individuals with OBE. We then evaluated whether there were differences by ED subtypes, with a subgroup of patients (basically BED, but also BN) who are more similar to participants with OBE. We also hypothesized that, among others, ED-related severity, general psychopathology, and personality traits would be important determinants of the FA phenotypes. The rationale for performing this kind of analysis was to gain insight into the possibility of different FA clusters that would ideally translate into future symptom-targeted treatments for FA phenotypes in individuals with OBE and for those suffering from ED.

2. Materials and Methods

2.1. Participants

From an initial sample of 395, the final participants of the current study were 234 females who scored positive for the FA (based on YFAS 2.) and who also had a diagnosis of ED or OBE (119 with BN, 50 with BED, 49 with other specified feeding or eating disorder (OSFED), and 16 with OBE). All participants in the OBE group ($n = 16$) as well as $n = 42$ participants in the BED group (84.0%), $n = 27$ in the BN group (22.7%), and $n = 2$ in the OSFED group (4.1%) had a BMI higher than 30. All participants included in the study were consecutively referred for assessment and treatment at the Unit of Eating Disorders of the Department of Psychiatry of the University Hospital of Bellvitge in Barcelona, between May of 2016 and November 2018, diagnosed according to the DSM-5 [40] criteria, and were between 18 and 60 years old.

Male participants referred for the Unit in that time period were excluded from the study, as the number of them in our sample was too small for meaningful statistical comparisons ($n = 21$; four with BN, eight with BED, two with OSFED, and seven with OBE). Considering the controversial results of the presence of FA in AN [17], as well as the characteristic fears and cognitive distortions about food and weight involved in AN that may influence patients understanding of what is considered excessive food intake or abnormal eating behavior [41], patients diagnosed with AN were excluded from the study as well. Likewise, due to the different reported prevalence of FA in OBE patients [20] compared to OBE with a comorbid ED [14,15,17], the homogeneity of the sample was preserved by only inducing patients with OBE without ED ($n = 53$), and only those with positive FA were included ($n = 16$).

According to the Declaration of Helsinki, the present study was approved by the Clinical Research Ethics Committee (CEIC) of Bellvitge University Hospital (ethic approval code: PR205/17), and written informed consent was obtained from all participants. All the assessments were conducted by experienced psychologist and psychiatrists.

2.2. Assessment

For the assessment, anthropometric measures such as weight and height (without the participants wearing clothes or shoes) were taken to calculate the BMI (i.e., weight (kg)/height (m^2)). In addition to clinically relevant variables (like age of onset or duration of the disorder) and sociodemographical characteristics, a battery of the Spanish-validated versions of the following instruments was used.

2.2.1. Eating Disorders Inventory 2 (EDI-2)

The Eating Disorders Inventory 2 (EDI-2) [42] is a 91-item multidimensional self-report questionnaire answered on a 6-point Likert scale that assesses different cognitive and behavioral characteristics typical for ED: Drive for Thinness, Bulimia, Body Dissatisfaction, Ineffectiveness, Perfectionism, Interpersonal Distrust, Interoceptive Awareness, Maturity Fears, Asceticism, Impulse Regulation, and Social Insecurity. The validated version for the Spanish population was developed by Garner, 1998 [43], with a mean internal consistency of 0.63 (coefficient alpha).

2.2.2. Symptom Checklist-90-Revised (SCL-90-R)

The Symptom Checklist-90-Revised (SCL-90-R) [44] is used to evaluate a broad range of psychological problems and symptoms of psychopathology. It consist of a 90-item questionnaire that measures nine primary symptom dimensions: Somatization, Obsession-Compulsion, Interpersonal Sensitivity, Depression, Anxiety, Hostility, Phobic Anxiety, Paranoid Ideation, and Psychoticism; and includes three global indices: global severity index (overall psychological distress), positive symptom distress index (the intensity of symptoms), and a positive symptom total (self-reported symptoms). The global severity index can be used as a summary of the test. The validation of the scale in a Spanish population [45], obtained a mean internal consistency of 0.75 (coefficient alpha).

2.2.3. Yale Food Addiction Scale 2.0 (YFAS-2)

The Yale Food Addiction Scale 2.0 (YFAS-2) [24] is a 35-item self-report questionnaire for measuring FA during the previous 12 months. This original instrument (YFAS) was based on the Diagnostic and Statistical Manual of Mental Disorders (DSM-IV-TR) criteria for substance dependence and was adapted to the context of food consumption. The newer version of the instrument, YFAS-2, is based on DSM-5 Criteria and evaluates 11 symptoms. The scale produces two measurements: (a) a continuous symptom count score that reflects the number of fulfilled diagnostic criteria (ranging from 0 to 11), and (b) a food addiction threshold based on the number of symptoms (at least 2) and self-reported clinically significant impairment or distress. This final measurement allows for the binary classification of food addiction (present versus absent). Additionally, based on the revised DSM-5 taxonomy, is possible to establish severity cut-offs: mild (2–3 symptoms), moderate (4–5 symptoms), and severe (6–11 symptoms). The translation and validation of the YFAS-2 for Spanish speaking samples with ED was carried out by Granero et al. (2018) [13], showing excellent internal reliability coefficient ($\alpha = 0.94$), as well as an excellent accuracy in discriminating between healthy controls and ED subsamples ($\kappa = 0.75$).

2.2.4. Temperament and Character Inventory-Revised (TCI-R)

The Temperament and Character Inventory-Revised (TCI-R) [46] is a 240-item, 5-point Likert scale, questionnaire that measures four temperament dimensions (Harm Avoidance, Novelty Seeking, Reward Dependence, and Persistence) and three character dimensions (Self-Directedness, Cooperativeness, and Self-Transcendence) of personality. The Spanish validation in an adult population was carried out by Gutiérrez-Zotes et al. [47]; the internal consistency (coefficient alpha) of the scales was 0.87.

2.3. Statistical Analysis

Statistical analysis was carried out with SPSS23 for Windows. Empirical clusters were explored with the two-step-cluster procedure, using as indicators the ED severity level (EDI-2 scores), the global psychopathological state (SCL-90-R scores), the personality profile (TCI-R scores), and the DSM-5 diagnostic subtype. Two-step-cluster used the log-likelihood distance measure through a multinomial probability mass function for categorical variables and a normal density function for continuous variables. This clustering technique has desirable features which makes it different from traditional grouping and latent class techniques [48,49]: (a) scalability, which allows analysis of large data files by constructing a cluster-features-tree which is used as a summary of the records; (b) automatic selection of the number of clusters-classes; and (c) handling of categorical and quantitative variables. Criteria for the final model selected in this study were adequate goodness-of-fit (based on a cohesion and separation index) and adequate clinical interpretability [50]. In this study, the Silhouettes coefficient was used as a measure of the goodness of the final cluster solution. This coefficient estimates the cohesion of the elements within a cluster and the separation between the clusters, and it ranges from –1 to +1 (being the values lower than 0.30 interpreted as poor fitting, between 0.30 and 0.50 as fair fitting, and higher than 0.50 as good fitting [51]).

Comparison between clusters was based on chi-square tests (χ^2) for categorical variables and analysis of variance (ANOVA) for quantitative criteria. Effect size was measured through Cohen's-d coefficient for mean and proportion comparisons (low effect size was considered for $|d| > 0.2$, moderate for $|d| > 0.5$, and large for $|d| > 0.8$; [52]). The Finner's method was used to control Type-I error due to multiple statistical comparisons (this procedure is included into the Familywise error rate stepwise procedures and offers a more powerful test than the classical Bonferroni correction) [53].

3. Results

3.1. Characteristics of the Sample

All the participants in the analyses were women who met criteria for FA positive screening score based on the YFAS-2 questionnaire $n = 234$. The distribution of the whole sample according to diagnostic group was 16 OBE (without ED) (6.8%), 50 BED (21.4%), 119 BN (50.9%), and 49 OSFED (20.9%). Most of the participants were single (62.0%, compared to 24.8% married or living with a stable partner and 13.2% separated or divorced) and achieved primary (40.6%) or secondary (44.9%) education levels. Table A1 (Appendix A) includes the distribution of the clinical profiles stratified and compared by the diagnostic subtype.

3.2. Cluster Composition

The best grouping structure selected for the sample of the study was the three-cluster solution, which coincided with the most optimal solution chosen by the two-step-cluster procedure. This solution obtained a Silhouettes index (0.30) into the fair range, suggesting mild-moderate evidence of the cluster structure in the data. The comparison between the largest cluster size ($n = 90$, 38.5%) and the smallest ($n = 60$, 25.6%) yielded a ratio of 1.50.

Figure 1 summarizes the results of the clustering procedure: the bar-graph with the indicator relevance for each variable (which reports how good each variable was for the grouping and can differentiate between the derived clusters: the higher the importance of the measure, the less likely it is that the variation for the variable between clusters is due to chance and the more likely it is due to underlying differences) and the centroids (which summarizes the cluster patterns for the set of variables and allows clinical interpretation of the empirical clusters). The indicator variables with the highest contribution into the clustering were SCL-90-R scales measuring the symptom levels (concretely psychotic, depressive, interpersonal sensitivity, anxiety, paranoia), followed by the EDI-2 scales measuring ED severity (impulse regulation, social insecurity, and ineffectiveness). The personality traits measured with the TCI-R obtained low relevance for the clustering, except for harm avoidance (which achieved moderate-low capacity), as well as the diagnostic subtype (which achieved poor capacity for the differentiation between the groups).

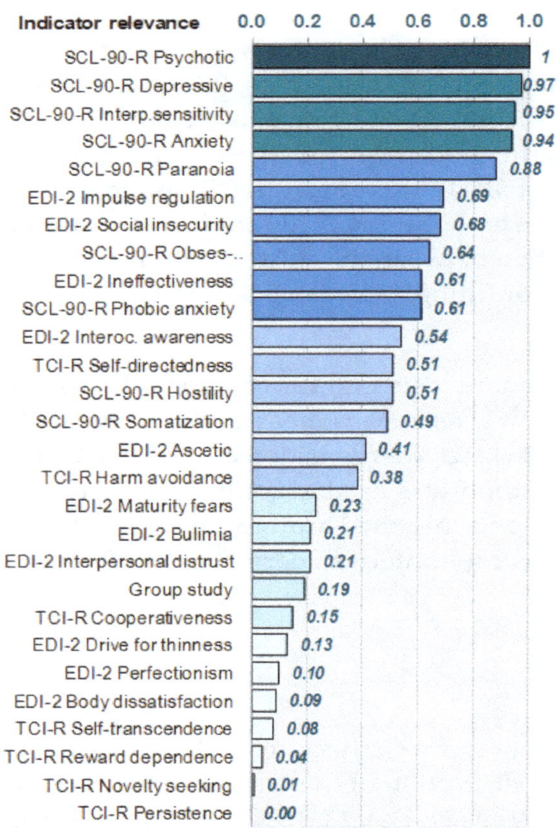

Silouettes' index: 0.30 (mild-moderate)

Centroids	C1 n=60	C2 n=90	C3 n=84	Total n=233
SCL-90-R: Psychotic	2.31	1.56	0.85	1.50
SCL-90-R: Depressive	3.24	2.68	1.67	2.46
SCL-90-R: Interpersonal-sensit.	3.03	2.50	1.38	2.23
SCL-90-R: Anxiety	2.76	1.96	1.08	1.85
SCL-90-R: Paranoia	2.48	1.57	0.87	1.55
EDI-2: Impulse regulation	13.63	7.50	3.27	7.56
EDI-2: Social Insecurity	13.40	9.60	4.51	8.75
SCL-90-R: obsess-comp.	2.83	2.34	1.53	2.18
EDI-2: Ineffectiveness	18.73	15.27	7.08	13.22
SCL-90-R: phobic anxiety	2.04	1.32	0.51	1.21
EDI-2: Interoceptive awareness	18.25	15.54	8.19	13.60
TCI-R: Self-directedness	96.0	104.4	124.7	109.5
SCL-90-R: Hostility	2.32	1.43	0.87	1.46
SCL-90-R: Somatization	2.75	2.13	1.46	2.05
EDI-2: Ascetic	10.45	8.88	5.69	8.14
TCI-R: Harm avoidance	133.2	126.9	109.6	122.3
EDI-2: Maturity fears	12.70	9.03	6.19	8.95
EDI-2: Bulimia	8.68	11.67	6.92	9.20
EDI-2: Interpersonal distrust	9.35	7.08	4.12	6.60
TCI-R: Cooperativeness	124.4	133.4	139.3	133.2
EDI-2: Drive for thinness	17.67	15.60	13.77	15.47
EDI-2: Perfectionism	7.67	6.53	4.52	6.10
EDI-2: Body dissatisfaction	21.60	20.44	17.18	19.57
TCI-R: Self-transcendence	73.35	63.43	63.73	66.08
TCI-R: Reward-dependence	95.83	98.68	103.3	99.59
TCI-R: Novelty seeking	103.3	99.00	100.8	100.7
TCI-R: Persistence	103.4	102.8	107.3	104.6

Figure 1. Results of the clustering procedure. Note. EDI-2: Eating disorders Inventory 2. SCL-90-R: Symptom Checklist-90-Revised. SCL-90-R Obsess-comp.: Obsession-Compulsion SCL-90-R subscale. TCI-R: Temperament and Character Inventory-Revised.

3.3. Comparison between the Empirical Clusters

The first part of Table 1 contains the comparison between the three empirical clusters for the civil status and the education levels. Differences between the groups only were found for the civil status: compared with the other two groups, cluster 1 had the highest proportion of single participants.

The second block of Table 1 contains the comparison between the clusters for the clinical profile. As a whole, clusters were ordered by the psychopathological state and personality profiles. Cluster 1 (n = 60, 25.6%) included the youngest participants (mean 28.8 years-old), with the lowest age of onset (mean 18.5 years-old), the shortest duration of the eating problems (mean 10.5 years), and the lowest BMI (mean 27.6 kg/m^2), but with the highest severity in eating problems (the highest means in the EDI-2), the worst psychopathological state (the highest means in the SCL-90R), the highest levels in the personality traits of harm avoidance and self-transcendence, and the lowest levels in self-directedness and cooperativeness. Cluster 1 was labeled in this study as the "dysfunctional cluster".

Table 1. Comparison between clusters for variables of the study.

	Cluster 1 $n = 60$ (25.6%)		Cluster 2 $n = 90$ (38.5%)		Cluster 3 $n = 84$ (35.9%)		Pairwise Comparisons Cl1-Cl2		Cl1-Cl3		Cl2-Cl3	
	n	%	*n*	%	*n*	%	*p*	|*d*|	*p*	|*d*|	*p*	|*d*|
Civil status—Single	46	76.7%	53	58.9%	46	54.8%	**0.049 ***	0.39	**0.026 ***	**0.51 †**	0.620	0.08
Married—Couple	10	16.7%	22	24.4%	26	31.0%		0.19		0.34		0.15
Separated—divorced	4	6.7%	15	16.7%	12	14.3%		0.32		0.25		0.07
Education Primary	29	48.3%	33	36.7%	33	39.3%	0.164	0.24	0.083	0.18	0.688	0.05
Secondary	27	45.0%	43	47.8%	35	41.7%		0.06		0.07		0.12
University	4	6.7%	14	15.6%	16	19.0%		0.29		0.38		0.09
	Mean	*SD*	*Mean*	*SD*	*Mean*	*SD*	*p*	|*d*|	*p*	|*d*|	*p*	|*d*|
Age (years-old)	28.77	11.05	35.66	12.99	34.54	12.13	**0.001 ***	**0.57 †**	**0.006 ***	**0.50 †**	0.546	0.09
Age of onset (years-old)	18.50	9.17	21.97	10.71	21.66	9.10	**0.034 ***	0.35	0.057	0.35	0.837	0.03
Duration (years)	10.49	9.10	14.30	10.20	12.64	8.72	**0.016 ***	0.39	0.177	0.24	0.246	0.17
YFAS-2: total criteria	8.22	2.66	9.59	1.80	7.55	2.77	**0.001 ***	**0.61 †**	0.102	0.25	**0.001 ***	**0.87 †**
BMI (kg/m^2)	27.55	11.13	30.29	9.08	31.48	10.99	0.114	0.27	**0.025 ***	0.36	0.447	0.12
EDI-2: Drive for thinness	17.67	2.84	15.60	4.82	13.77	4.83	**0.005 ***	**0.52 †**	**0.001 ***	**0.98 †**	**0.007 ***	0.38
EDI-2: Body dissatisfaction	21.60	5.61	20.44	6.52	17.18	7.06	0.288	0.19	**0.001 ***	**0.69 †**	**0.001 ***	**0.51 †**
EDI-2: Interoceptive awar.	18.25	5.77	15.54	5.33	8.19	5.12	**0.003 ***	**0.52 †**	**0.001 ***	**1.84 †**	**0.001 ***	**1.41 †**
EDI-2: Bulimia	8.68	5.30	11.67	3.85	6.92	4.69	**0.001 ***	**0.64 †**	**0.023**	0.35	**0.001 ***	**1.11 †**
EDI-2: Interpers.distrust	9.35	5.23	7.08	4.76	4.12	3.89	**0.003 ***	**0.52 †**	**0.001 ***	**1.14 †**	**0.001 ***	**0.68 †**
EDI-2: Ineffectiveness	18.73	6.57	15.27	6.06	7.08	4.50	**0.001 ***	**0.55 †**	**0.001 ***	**2.07 †**	**0.001 ***	**1.53 †**
EDI-2: Maturity fears	12.70	5.69	9.03	5.37	6.19	5.18	**0.001 ***	**0.66 †**	**0.001 ***	**1.20 †**	**0.001 ***	**0.54 †**
EDI-2: Perfectionism	7.67	4.63	6.53	4.21	4.52	3.65	0.101	0.26	**0.001 ***	**0.75 †**	**0.002 ***	**0.51 †**
EDI-2: Impulse regulation	13.63	5.46	7.50	4.38	3.27	3.41	**0.001 ***	**1.24 †**	**0.001 ***	**2.27 †**	**0.001 ***	**1.08 †**
EDI-2: Ascetism	10.45	3.18	8.88	2.78	5.69	2.91	**0.001 ***	**0.53 †**	**0.001 ***	**1.56 †**	**0.001 ***	**1.12 †**
EDI-2: Social Insecurity	13.40	4.54	9.60	4.10	4.51	3.03	**0.001 ***	**0.88 †**	**0.001 ***	**2.30 †**	**0.001 ***	**1.41 †**
EDI-2: Total	152.13	27.03	127.14	20.64	81.45	22.16	**0.001 ***	**1.04 †**	**0.001 ***	**2.86 †**	**0.001 ***	**2.13 †**
SCL-90-R: somatization	2.75	0.63	2.13	0.71	1.46	0.72	**0.001 ***	**0.93 †**	**0.001 ***	**1.92 †**	**0.001 ***	**0.94 †**
SCL-90-R: obsess-comp.	2.83	0.59	2.34	0.57	1.53	0.64	**0.001 ***	**0.84 †**	**0.001 ***	**2.11 †**	**0.001 ***	**1.34 †**
SCL-90-R: interpers.sens.	3.03	0.53	2.50	0.54	1.38	0.67	**0.001 ***	**1.00 †**	**0.001 ***	**2.73 †**	**0.001 ***	**1.84 †**
SCL-90-R: depressive	3.24	0.43	2.68	0.53	1.67	0.62	**0.001 ***	**1.17 †**	**0.001 ***	**2.93 †**	**0.001 ***	**1.74 †**
SCL-90-R: anxiety	2.76	0.55	1.96	0.64	1.08	0.54	**0.001 ***	**1.36 †**	**0.001 ***	**3.09 †**	**0.001 ***	**1.49 †**
SCL-90-R: hostility	2.32	0.88	1.43	0.73	0.87	0.67	**0.001 ***	**1.10 †**	**0.001 ***	**1.86 †**	**0.001 ***	**0.81 †**
SCL-90-R: phobic anxiety	2.04	0.83	1.32	0.79	0.51	0.52	**0.001 ***	**0.89 †**	**0.001 ***	**2.22 †**	**0.001 ***	**1.21 †**
SCL-90-R: paranoia	2.48	0.62	1.57	0.59	0.87	0.53	**0.001 ***	**1.50 †**	**0.001 ***	**2.77 †**	**0.001 ***	**1.25 †**
SCL-90-R: psychotic	2.31	0.52	1.56	0.45	0.85	0.48	**0.001 ***	**1.55 †**	**0.001 ***	**2.92 †**	**0.001 ***	**1.53 †**
SCL-90-R: GSI index	2.73	0.36	2.06	0.33	1.26	0.38	**0.001 ***	**1.90 †**	**0.001 ***	**3.96 †**	**0.001 ***	**2.26 †**
SCL-90-R: PST index	81.63	6.60	71.93	8.36	55.42	13.26	**0.001 ***	**1.29 †**	**0.001 ***	**2.50 †**	**0.001 ***	**1.49 †**
SCL-90-R: PSDI index	3.01	0.34	2.60	0.36	2.03	0.36	**0.001 ***	**1.20 †**	**0.001 ***	**2.81 †**	**0.001 ***	**1.57 †**
TCI-R: Novelty seeking	103.32	16.27	99.00	16.77	100.79	14.63	0.105	0.25	0.347	0.16	0.460	0.11
TCI-R: Harm avoidance	133.15	13.32	126.94	16.59	109.63	16.15	**0.018 ***	0.41	**0.001 ***	**1.59 †**	**0.001 ***	**1.06 †**
TCI-R: Reward-depend.	95.83	17.43	98.68	15.33	103.25	15.83	0.289	0.17	**0.007 ***	0.45	0.062	0.29
TCI-R: Persistence	103.42	22.25	102.77	20.58	107.33	19.98	0.852	0.03	0.267	0.19	0.149	0.23
TCI-R: Self-directedness	96.03	13.89	104.39	15.30	124.70	17.28	**0.002 ***	**0.57 †**	**0.001 ***	**1.83 †**	**0.001 ***	**1.24 †**
TCI-R: Cooperativeness	124.40	19.00	133.38	16.53	139.31	11.39	**0.001 ***	**0.50 †**	**0.001 ***	**0.95 †**	**0.013 ***	0.42
TCI-R: Self-transcendence	73.35	13.87	63.43	15.43	63.73	17.46	**0.001 ***	**0.68 †**	**0.001 ***	**0.61 †**	0.903	0.02

Note. SD: standard deviation. * Bold: significant comparison (0.05 level). † Bold: effect size into the moderate ($|d| > 0.50$) to high range ($|d| > 0.80$). YFAS-2: Yale food addiction scale 2.0. BMI: Body mass index. EDI-2: Eating disorders Inventory 2. SCL-90-R: Symptom Checklist-90-Revised. TCI-R: Temperament and Character Inventory-Revised.

Cluster 2 ($n = 90$, 38.5%) included the participants with the longest duration of the eating problems (mean 14.3 years) and the highest level of food addiction (mean 9.6). The mean for BMI (30.3 kg/m2) was higher than in cluster 1, but similar to that obtained in cluster 3. The mean scores in the EDI-2 and the SCL-90R were high for participants into cluster 2, but clearly lower than values registered for cluster 1. Cluster 2 was labeled in this study as the "moderate cluster".

Cluster 3 ($n = 84$, 35.9%) was characterized by similar mean scores in age (34.5 years-old), onset of eating problems (21.7 years) and duration of the disorder (12.6 years) than cluster 2. The most adaptive scores in the clinical profile was registered for cluster 3 (the lowest scores in the EDI-2 and the SCL-90R), as well as the highest means in the personality traits of persistence, self-directedness and cooperativeness. Cluster 3 was labeled in this study as the "functional cluster".

Figure 2 includes the 100%-stacked bar chart with the distribution of the DSM-5 ED diagnostic subtype into each empirical cluster. OBE patients were primary included into cluster 3 (68.85), while BED patients were mostly distributed into clusters 3 and 2 (48.0% and 44.0%, respectively). Approximately half of the BN patients were into cluster 2 (52.1%), and the remaining participants into this group were distributed between cluster 1 (27.7%) and cluster 3 (20.2%). A little more than half of the OSFED patients were in cluster 3 (51%), and almost 41% in cluster 1.

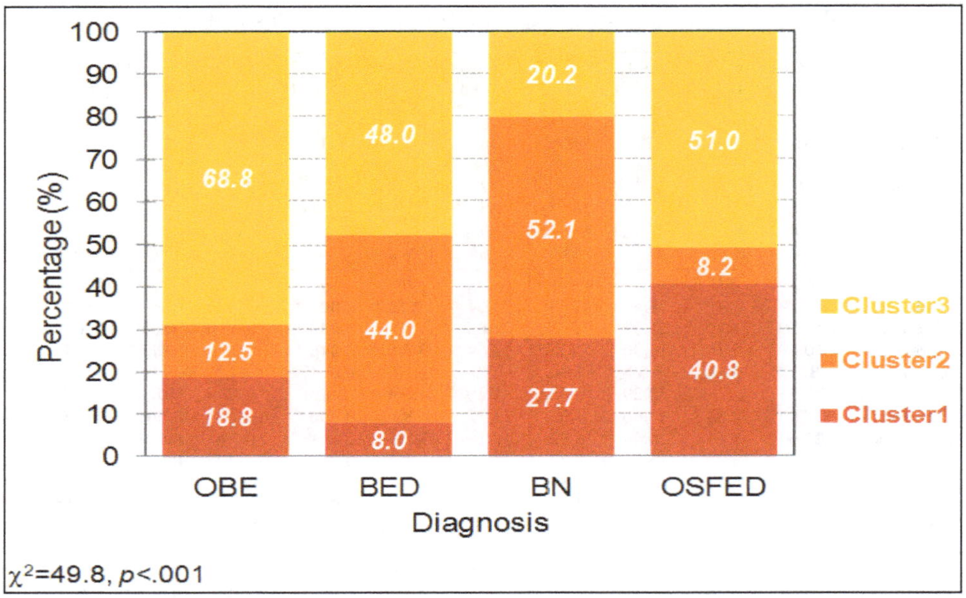

Figure 2. Distribution of the diagnostic subtype and the food addiction (FA) severity group within the empirical clusters. Note. OBE: obesity. BED: binge eating disorder. BN: bulimia nervosa. OSFED: other specified feeding eating disorder.

As a synthesis of the results, Figure 3 contains the radar-chart comparing the empirical clusters for the main clinical variables of the study. To allow adequate interpretability, z-standardized scores were plotted.

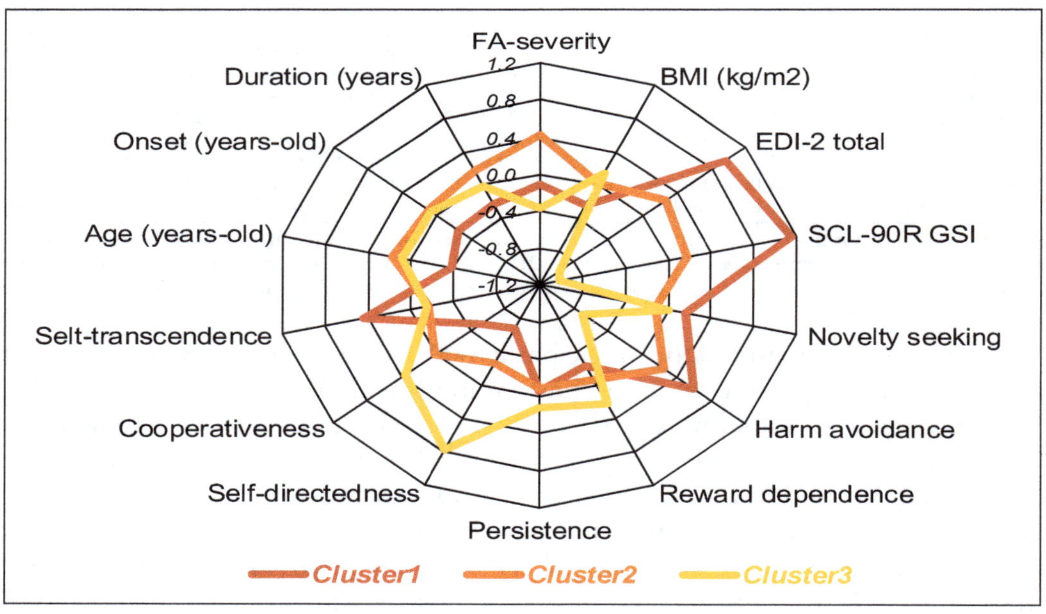

Figure 3. Radar-chart comparing the z-standardized mean scores between the empirical clusters Note. FA: Food addiction. BMI: Body mass index. EDI-2: Eating disorders Inventory 2. SCL-90-R GSI: Global Severity Index of the Symptom Checklist-90-Revised.

4. Discussion

The aim of the present study was to explore empirical severity clusters with FA-positive (FA+) females, and to investigate whether these FA clusters differed by ED and OBE. A three-cluster structure was detected based on general psychopathology, ED severity, and personality traits. These clusters ranged from a more functional cluster, to moderate and highly dysfunctional group.

Although high FA has previously been associated with high eating psychopathology and more dysfunctional personality traits, [32], this is the first study that analyzes a potential heterogeneity within patients with FA. Although all the participants in the current study were FA+, we found that the identified clusters followed a linearity with respect to FA severity with the most dysfunctional clusters (1 and 2) having the highest FA symptoms level, and the most functional one, the lowest. For the "dysfunctional cluster", we found a higher prevalence of OSFED and BN, both ED conditions characterized by more dysfunctional personality traits, greater impulsivity, and more general psychopathology, [54–57], as well by their worse prognosis [56]. Consistent with this literature, the cluster with more OFED and BN had the worst psychopathological state and highest severity in ED symptomatology.

Personality traits that were elevated in the most dysfunction cluster were greater difficulties in establishing goals and objectives to guide their lives (self-directedness), the highest levels of anxiety, worry, fear (harm avoidance), and being a more self-centered person (lower cooperativeness). All of these characteristics have not only been associated with FA [32,35], but also with BN, substance use disorders (SUD), and comorbidity between BN and SUD [58,59]. This cluster was also associated with higher levels of novelty seeking, which is a predictor of risky behaviors and associated with SUD and ED pathologies [59–64]. Therefore, the commonality of these extreme personality features in addictive profiles, suggests it could be important in the etiology and maintenance of FA and could be the focus of intervention efforts. Additionally, the aforementioned characteristics have been related to higher risk of dropout and poor outcome in OSFED patients with purging behaviors [56], suggesting important clinical relevance. Although the association of FA and treatment outcome was not the aim of this study, prior research suggests that higher initial FA scores have been associated with a worse prognosis in BN [65].

In sum, the severity of this dysfunctional cluster may be driven by the comorbid ED provided and characteristics associated with these disorders. Thus, in order to be successful, the treatment aimed at patients who are in this cluster should target its principal psychological and psychiatric characteristics, in addition to factors that may maintain FA. As previous literature has reported, changes in personality traits are related to an overall improvement in eating pathology [66], and interventions that could target the personality factors elevated in this cluster would likely be of benefit. Additionally, due to the severity of the psychopathological state in this cluster, pharmacological approaches to address comorbid psychiatric conditions could be also considered if it is needed.

The second cluster, the moderate cluster, was the one that presented the highest level of FA, although functioning was more adaptive than cluster 1 (i.e., lower ED severity, intermediate psychopathology levels). Therefore, we hypothesize that it is FA which mostly determines the characteristics of this cluster. Regarding the personality traits, high levels of harm avoidance and low self-directedness were present in this cluster, but at moderate levels compared to cluster 1 (the dysfunctional). Related to the ED pathology, there was a high presence of patients with BN followed by patients with BED within this cluster. Higher FA scores have been already associated with bingeing ED-subtype patients [13,14,17,67], given the tendency to consume more high-fat/high-sugar caloric food during binges episodes, which may result in a higher number of FA symptoms [17] given the similar neural responses in reward pathways modulated by dopamine by those types of food and addictive drugs [6,16,29,68–70]. In fact, new maintenance models of BN and BED have emerged, that take into consideration the addictive response to palatable foods [71]. Related studies have also found that similar patterns of neural underpinning of tolerance and dependence observed in SUD appear to be related to binge-type eating disorders as well [72,73]. This is consistent with the high comorbidity between SUD and binge-type ED [74,75]. Finally, another important aspect to mention is that it has been shown that individuals with BN or BED experience more frequent and more intense food cravings than persons without binge eating [76–79] and that both conditions show significantly larger food cue reactivity (self-reported craving) [80]. This intense desire or urge to eat a particular type of food also, at a neural level, resembles responses to drug cues in SUD [26]. Therefore, it could be suggested that the treatment directed to patients in this cluster should target the reward related neural processes that maintain addictive disorders. In this regard, it has been suggested that previously developed interventions for addictions could be applied to binge eating behaviors [71], such as training in the reduction of food cue reactivity in order to reduce craving [81,82] and a reduction in the intake of high-fat/high-sugar caloric food which hyper-activate reward systems.

The "adaptative" cluster presents with more functional personality traits and low levels of general psychopathology, as well as the lowest levels of FA. Thus, the FA in this cluster may be the result of different factors than patients in clusters 1 and 2, which could have important implications in the treatment. First, it is important to mention that within this cluster, there was the highest presence of patients with OBE without ED. This is consistent with prior findings that patients with OBE with a comorbid ED have a higher level of psychopathology than OBE patients without ED [83–86]. Second, this cluster presents the most functional personality traits, the lowest levels of harm avoidance and self-transcendence, and the highest in cooperativeness and self-directedness. Similar results have been found in healthy control groups when comparing them with ED and behavioral addiction patients [87,88]. Thus, BMI could be playing an important role in this cluster, considering that in our sample there are statistically significant differences between cluster 1 (the dysfunctional) and 3 (the adaptative) in BMI. It has been suggested that visceral adiposity levels could be a mediator of the relationship between middle-dorsal insula network connectivity (insula region relevant for eating behavior) and food craving [28], being that visceral fat disrupts insula coding of bodily homeostatic signals, which may boost externally driven food cravings, and also, there are positive associations between food craving and excessive overeating [89,90]. Given the characteristics of this cluster, for which no dysfunctional personality traits of severe ED symptomology or psychopathology must be addressed, it could be hypothesized that nutritional changes that would have a positive impact on a reduction of BMI could be also be beneficial for the reducing FA, through reducing craving episodes. This is consistent with previous studies that find that FA decreases significantly after bariatric surgery [91], and that the induced weight loss by the surgery resulted in the remission of FA in 93% of patients [22]. Finally, there is a moderate representation of patients with BED in this cluster, which may be due to the common co-occurrence between both conditions (OBE-BED). This may be due to the association of features such as grazing [92], craving [93–95], or hedonic [96] and emotional eating [97,98] with OBE and BED. Addressing these factors (and their negative consequences) could be an important focus of treatment in this FA cluster, as grazing is associated with poorer weight loss treatment outcomes in OBE [92] and craving and the use of food to regulate mood are potential triggers for overeating [41,99,100].

The results of this study should take into account the following limitations. First, the sample only included women, so the results cannot be generalized to males; for future studies, it will be important to explore if the FA cluster structure found in this study is replicated in males. Another limitation is that the size of some of the participant groups, divided by ED subtype and OBE, is small. Finally that, due to the fact that the participants were recruited in the same geographical area, the results may not be generalizable to other samples

5. Conclusions

The findings in the present study describe a three-cluster structure of FA-positive (FA+) participants that differ by ED and OBE profile. The clusters range from more to less functional, depending on psychopathology and personality traits. The identification of phenotypes in FA will not only increase knowledge of each cluster's characteristics, but may allow for better individualization of treatment by identifying novel intervention targets and improving treatment outcomes. Likewise, the present study identifies future lines of research, as longitudinal studies that could analyze the predictive validity of this cluster structure on treatment outcome could be of importance.

Author Contributions: The authors had the following roles in this paper: conceptualization, S.J.-M., R.G., A.N.G., C.D., F.F.-A. and R.G.; methodology, F.F.-A, S.J.-M., Z.A. and R.G.; formal statistical analysis, R.G.; data collection and assessment: Z.A., G.P., L.M., J.S.-G., I.S. and N.R.; writing—original draft preparation, Z.A., G.P., L.M., J.S.-G., R.G., A.N.G., F.F.-A. and S.J.-M.; writing—review and editing, Z.A., G.P., L.M., J.S.-G., I.B., J.M.M., A.N.G., C.D., G.F., C.S.-G., F.F.-A., S.J.-M. and R.G.; supervision, F.F.-A. and S.J.-M.; funding acquisition, F.F.-A., J.M.M., C.D. and S.J.-M.; Investigation, S.J.-M., Z.A., G.P., L.M., J.S.-G., G.F. and F.F.-A.; Project administration, S.J.-M. and F.F.-A.; Resources, S.J.-M. and F.F.-A.

Appendix A

Table A1. Clinical profiles in the ED-subtypes.

		Obesity $n = 16$		BED $n = 119$		BN $n = 50$		OSFED $n = 49$		
	α	Mean	SD	Mean	SD	Mean	SD	Mean	SD	p
Age (years-old)		44.13	11.89	40.90	12.62	31.31	11.23	27.73	9.94	**<0.001 ***
Age of onset (years-old)		26.06	11.44	25.90	11.18	19.32	9.14	18.29	6.91	**<0.001 ***
Duration (years)		18.75	9.94	14.79	9.79	12.26	9.24	9.81	8.53	**0.003**
YFAS2.0: total criteria	0.943	8.19	2.51	9.54	1.68	9.00	2.18	6.35	2.97	**<0.001 ***
BMI (kg/m^2)		44.64	8.33	40.46	10.06	26.72	6.85	22.59	4.13	**<0.001 ***
EDI-2: Drive for thinness	0.736	12.31	3.32	12.82	5.19	16.44	4.23	16.88	3.81	**<0.001 ***
EDI-2: Body dissatisfaction	0.842	20.19	6.47	21.74	5.63	19.40	6.85	17.55	7.06	**0.019**
EDI-2: Interoceptive awareness	0.785	11.56	7.12	12.30	6.96	14.69	6.65	12.94	6.58	0.078
EDI-2: Bulimia	0.710	6.13	4.67	10.08	3.72	10.91	4.53	5.14	4.63	**<0.001 ***
EDI-2: Interpersonal distrust	0.802	5.38	4.53	6.52	5.30	7.28	5.09	5.43	4.55	0.121
EDI-2: Ineffectiveness	0.860	12.25	7.84	11.72	6.45	14.78	7.52	11.27	7.41	**0.011 ***
EDI-2: Maturity fears	0.784	8.06	6.92	7.06	5.95	9.79	5.65	9.14	5.95	**0.048 ***
EDI-2: Perfectionism	0.697	5.75	4.16	5.84	3.91	6.69	4.45	5.06	4.26	0.146
EDI-2: Impulse regulation	0.757	4.50	4.47	5.74	5.36	8.56	6.15	7.96	5.73	**0.005 ***
EDI-2: Ascetic	0.717	8.00	3.76	7.24	3.35	8.70	3.53	7.73	3.21	0.071
EDI-2: Social Insecurity	0.770	6.19	5.39	7.76	4.76	9.90	5.33	7.80	4.62	**0.004 ***
EDI-2: Total	0.928	100.31	34.62	108.82	33.40	127.13	34.96	106.90	38.03	**<0.001 ***
SCL-90-R: somatization	0.875	2.07	0.93	2.02	0.75	2.13	0.83	1.88	0.98	0.408
SCL-90-R: obsess-comp.	0.818	1.88	0.94	2.06	0.80	2.29	0.72	2.10	0.85	0.094
SCL-90-R: interpers.sens.	0.854	1.91	1.13	2.02	0.93	2.40	0.83	2.14	0.87	**0.024 ***
SCL-90-R: depressive	0.878	2.12	1.06	2.30	0.88	2.60	0.75	2.40	0.84	**0.044 ***
SCL-90-R: anxiety	0.865	1.36	0.86	1.62	0.87	1.98	0.84	1.92	0.90	**0.008 ***
SCL-90-R: hostility	0.840	0.99	0.71	1.26	0.81	1.59	0.93	1.49	0.94	**0.035 ***
SCL-90-R: phobic anxiety	0.800	1.13	0.93	0.97	0.86	1.31	0.94	1.25	0.96	0.179
SCL-90-R: paranoia	0.745	1.63	0.97	1.42	0.85	1.64	0.83	1.46	0.85	0.355
SCL-90-R: psychotic	0.788	1.21	0.67	1.25	0.73	1.61	0.70	1.59	0.80	**0.009 ***
SCL-90-R: GSI index	0.971	1.69	0.80	1.77	0.67	2.06	0.64	1.91	0.71	**0.025 ***
SCL-90-R: PST index	0.971	60.81	20.65	65.24	15.58	71.10	12.26	67.98	15.03	**0.012 ***
SCL-90-R: PSDI index	0.971	2.44	0.59	2.38	0.55	2.57	0.50	2.48	0.53	0.162
TCI-R: Novelty seeking	0.782	94.69	14.06	100.80	15.70	101.85	17.34	100.00	12.76	0.394
TCI-R: Harm avoidance	0.873	117.69	19.22	120.28	17.00	124.04	18.74	121.73	18.85	0.440
TCI-R: Reward-depend.	0.834	108.94	17.06	99.20	16.70	97.74	15.58	101.43	16.48	0.057
TCI-R: Persistence	0.893	103.94	15.64	97.26	20.19	104.36	21.44	112.76	18.92	**0.003 ***
TCI-R: Self-directedness	0.844	115.31	23.31	108.64	20.65	106.87	18.25	115.06	19.58	0.054
TCI-R: Cooperativeness	0.844	139.88	11.85	131.56	20.63	132.02	16.52	135.59	12.66	0.195
TCI-R: Self-transcendence	0.863	72.38	21.29	66.14	16.53	65.84	14.92	64.55	17.63	0.420

Note. α: Cronbach's alpha in the sample. BED: binge eating disorder; BN: bulimia nervosa; OSFED: other specified feeding eating disorder. SD: standard deviation. * Bold: significant comparison (.05 level). YFAS: Yale food addiction scale 2.0. BMI: Body mass index. EDI-2: Eating disorders Inventory 2. SCL-90-R: Symptom Checklist-90-Revised. TCI-R: Temperament and Character Inventory-Revised.

References

1. Schulte, E.M.; Joyner, M.A.; Potenza, M.N.; Grilo, C.M.; Gearhardt, A.N. Current Considerations Regarding Food Addiction. *Curr. Psychiatry Rep.* **2015**, *17*, 17–19. [CrossRef] [PubMed]
2. Fernandez-Aranda, F.; Karwautz, A.; Treasure, J. Food addiction: A transdiagnostic construct of increasing interest. *Eur. Eat. Disord. Rev.* **2018**, *26*, 536–540. [CrossRef] [PubMed]
3. Avena, N.M.; Rada, P.; Hoebel, B.G. Evidence for sugar addiction: Behavioral and neurochemical effects of intermittent, excessive sugar intake. *Neurosci. Biobehav. Rev.* **2008**, *32*, 20–39. [CrossRef] [PubMed]

4. Volkow, N.D.; Wang, G.J.; Fowler, J.S.; Tomasi, D.; Baler, R. Food and Drug Reward: Overlapping Circuits in Human Obesity and Addiction Inhibitory control. *Curr. Top. Behav. Neurosci.* **2011**, *11*, 1–24.
5. Tang, D.W.; Fellows, L.K.; Small, D.M.; Dagher, A. Food and drug cues activate similar brain regions: A meta-analysis of functional MRI studies. *Physiol. Behav.* **2012**, *106*, 317–324. [CrossRef] [PubMed]
6. Michaud, A.; Vainik, U.; Garcia-Garcia, I.; Dagher, A. Overlapping Neural Endophenotypes in Addiction and Obesity. *Front. Endocrinol.* **2017**, *8*, 127. [CrossRef] [PubMed]
7. Gearhardt, A.N.; Boswell, R.G.; White, M.A. The association of "food addiction" with disordered eating and body mass index. *Eat. Behav.* **2014**, *15*, 427–433. [CrossRef]
8. Ferrario, C.R. Food Addiction and Obesity. *Neuropsychopharmacol. Rev.* **2017**, *42*, 361–362. [CrossRef]
9. Cope, E.C.; Gould, E. New Evidence Linking Obesity and Food Addiction. *Biol. Psychiatry* **2017**, *81*, 734–736. [CrossRef]
10. Sinha, R. Role of addiction and stress neurobiology on food intake and obesity. *Biol. Psychol.* **2018**, *131*, 5–13. [CrossRef]
11. Meule, A.; Von Rezori, V.; Blechert, J. Food Addiction and Bulimia Nervosa. *Eur. Eat. Disord. Rev.* **2014**, *22*, 331–337. [CrossRef] [PubMed]
12. De Vries, S.-K.; Meule, A. Food Addiction and Bulimia Nervosa: New Data Based on the Yale Food Addiction Scale 2.0. *Eur. Eat. Disord. Rev.* **2016**, *24*, 518–522. [CrossRef] [PubMed]
13. Granero, R.; Jiménez-Murcia, S.; Gearhardt, A.N.; Agüera, Z.; Aymamí, N.; Gómez-Peña, M.; Lozano-Madrid, M.; Mallorquí-Bagué, N.; Mestre-Bach, G.; Neto-Antao, M.I.; et al. Validation of the Spanish Version of the Yale Food Addiction Scale 2.0 (YFAS 2.0) and Clinical Correlates in a Sample of Eating Disorder, Gambling Disorder, and Healthy Control Participants. *Front. Psychiatry* **2018**, *9*, 208. [CrossRef] [PubMed]
14. Gearhardt, A.N.; White, M.A.; Masheb, R.M.; Morgan, P.T.; Crosby, R.D.; Grilo, C.M. An Examination of the Food Addiction Construct in Obese Patients with Binge Eating Disorder. *Int. J. Eat. Disord.* **2012**, *45*, 657–663. [CrossRef]
15. Penzenstadler, L.; Soares, C.; Karila, L.; Khazaal, Y. Systematic Review of Food Addiction as Measured with the Yale Food Addiction Scale: Implications for the Food Addiction Construct. *Curr. Neuropharmacol.* **2019**, *17*, 1–13. [CrossRef]
16. Smith, D.G.; Robbins, T.W. The Neurobiological Underpinnings of Obesity and Binge Eating: A Rationale for Adopting the Food Addiction Model. *Biol. Psychiatry* **2013**, *73*, 804–810. [CrossRef]
17. Granero, R.; Hilker, I.; Agüera, Z.; Jiménez-Murcia, S.; Sauchelli, S.; Islam, M.A.; Fagundo, A.B.; Sánchez, I.; Riesco, N.; Dieguez, C.; et al. Food Addiction in a Spanish Sample of Eating Disorders: DSM-5 Diagnostic Subtype Differentiation and Validation Data. *Eur. Eat. Disord. Rev.* **2014**, *22*, 389–396. [CrossRef]
18. Ivezaj, V.; Wiedemann, A.A.; Grilo, C.M. Food Addiction and Bariatric Surgery: A Systematic Review of the Literature. *Obes. Rev.* **2017**, *18*, 1386–1397. [CrossRef]
19. Müller, A.; Leukefeld, C.; Hase, C.; Gruner, K.; Mall, J.W.; Köhler, H.; Zwaan, M. De Food addiction and other addictive behaviours in bariatric surgery candidates. *Eur. Eat. Disord.* **2018**, *26*, 1–12.
20. Guerrero Pérez, F.; Sánchez-González, J.; Sánchez, I.; Jiménez-Murcia, S.; Granero, R.; Simó-Servat, A.; Ruiz, A.; Virgili, N.; López-Urdiales, R.; Montserrat-Gil de Bernabe, M.; et al. Food addiction and preoperative weight loss achievement in patients seeking bariatric surgery. *Eur. Eat. Disord. Rev.* **2018**, *26*, 645–656. [CrossRef]
21. Murray, S.M.; Tweardy, S.; Geliebter, A.; Avena, N.M. A Longitudinal Preliminary Study of Addiction-Like Responses to Food and Alcohol Consumption Among Individuals Undergoing Weight Loss Surgery. *Obes. Surg.* **2019**. [CrossRef] [PubMed]
22. Pepino, M.Y.; Stein, R.I.; Eagon, J.C.; Klein, S. Bariatric surgery-induced weight loss causes remission of food addiction in extreme obesity. *Obesity* **2014**, *22*, 1792–1798. [CrossRef] [PubMed]
23. Gearhardt, A.N.; Corbin, W.R.; Brownell, K.D. Food addiction: an examination of the diagnostic criteria for dependence. *J. Addict. Med.* **2009**, *3*, 1–7. [CrossRef] [PubMed]
24. Gearhardt, A.N.; Corbin, W.R.; Brownell, K.D. Development of the Yale Food Addiction Scale Version 2.0. *Psychol. Addict. Behav.* **2016**, *30*, 113–121. [CrossRef] [PubMed]
25. Meule, A.; Gearhardt, A.N. Food addiction in the light of DSM-5. *Nutrients* **2014**, *6*, 3653–3671. [CrossRef] [PubMed]

26. Gearhardt, A.N.; Yokum, S.; Orr, P.T.; Stice, E.; Corbin, W.R.; Brownell, K.D. The Neural Correlates of "Food Addiction". *Arch. Gen. Psychiatry* **2011**, *68*, 808–816. [CrossRef] [PubMed]
27. Davis, C.; Loxton, N.J.; Levitan, R.D.; Kaplan, A.S.; Carter, J.C.; Kennedy, J.L. "Food addiction" and its association with a dopaminergic multilocus genetic profile. *Physiol. Behav.* **2013**, *118*, 63–69. [CrossRef]
28. Contreras-Rodriguez, O.; Burrows, T.; Pursey, K.M.; Stanwell, P.; Parkes, L.; Soriano-Mas, C.; Verdejo-Garcia, A. Food addiction linked to changes in ventral striatum functional connectivity between fasting and satiety. *Appetite* **2019**, *133*, 18–23. [CrossRef]
29. Schulte, E.M.; Yokum, S.; Potenza, M.N.; Gearhardt, A.N. Neural systems implicated in obesity as an addictive disorder: from biological to behavioral mechanisms. *Prog. Brain Res.* **2016**, *223*, 329–346.
30. Murphy, C.M.; Stojek, M.K.; MacKillop, J. Interrelationships among impulsive personality traits, food addiction, and Body Mass Index. *Appetite* **2014**, *73*, 45–50. [CrossRef]
31. Pivarunas, B.; Conner, B.T. Impulsivity and emotion dysregulation as predictors of food addiction. *Eat. Behav.* **2015**, *19*, 9–14. [CrossRef] [PubMed]
32. Wolz, I.; Hilker, I.; Granero, R.; Jiménez-Murcia, S.; Gearhardt, A.N.; Dieguez, C.; Casanueva, F.F.; Crujeiras, A.B.; Menchón, J.M.; Fernández-Aranda, F. "Food Addiction" in Patients with Eating Disorders is Associated with Negative Urgency and Difficulties to Focus on Long-Term Goals. *Front. Psychol.* **2016**, *7*, 61. [CrossRef] [PubMed]
33. Wolz, I.; Granero, R.; Fernández-aranda, F. A comprehensive model of food addiction in patients with binge-eating symptomatology: The essential role of negative urgency. *Compr. Psychiatry* **2017**, *74*, 118–124. [CrossRef] [PubMed]
34. Brunault, P.; Ducluzeau, P.H.; Courtois, R.; Bourbao-Tournois, C.; Delbachian, I.; Réveillère, C.; Ballon, N. Food Addiction is Associated with Higher Neuroticism, Lower Conscientiousness, Higher Impulsivity, but Lower Extraversion in Obese Patient Candidates for Bariatric Surgery. *Subst. Use Misuse* **2018**, *53*, 1919–1923. [CrossRef] [PubMed]
35. Ouellette, A.-S.; Rodrigue, C.; Lemieux, S.; Tchernof, A.; Biertho, L.; Bégin, C. An examination of the mechanisms and personality traits underlying food addiction among individuals with severe obesity awaiting bariatric surgery. *Eat. Weight Disord. Stud. Anorexia, Bulim. Obes.* **2017**, *22*, 633–640. [CrossRef]
36. Burrows, T.; Skinner, J.; McKenna, R.; Rollo, M. Food Addiction, Binge Eating Disorder, and Obesity: Is There a Relationship? *Behav. Sci.* **2017**, *7*, 54. [CrossRef]
37. Burrows, T.; Kay-Lambkin, F.; Pursey, K.; Skinner, J.; Dayas, C. Food addiction and associations with mental health symptoms: A systematic review with meta-analysis. *J. Hum. Nutr. Diet.* **2018**, *31*, 544–572. [CrossRef]
38. Nunes-neto, P.R.; Köhler, C.A.; Schuch, F.B.; Solmi, M.; Quevedo, J.; Maes, M.; Murru, A.; Vieta, E.; Mcintyre, R.S.; Mcelroy, S.L.; et al. Food addiction: Prevalence, psychopathological correlates and associations with quality of life in a large sample. *J. Psychiatr. Res.* **2018**, *96*, 145–152. [CrossRef]
39. Loxton, N.J.; Tipman, R.J. Reward sensitivity and food addiction in women. *Appetite* **2017**, *115*, 28–35. [CrossRef]
40. American Psychiatric Association. *Diagnostic and Statistical Manual of Mental Disorders (DSM-5)*; American Psychiatric Association: Arlington, VA, USA, 2013; ISBN 0-89042-555-8.
41. Gendall, K.A.; Joyce, P.R.; Sullivan, P.F.; Bulik, C.M. Food cravers: Characteristics of those who binge. *Int. J. Eat. Disord.* **1998**, *23*, 353–360. [CrossRef]
42. Garner, D. *Eating Disorder Inventory-2*; Psychological Assessment Resources: Odessa, Ukraine, 1991.
43. Garner, D. *Inventario de Trastornos de la Conducta Alimentaria (EDI-2)—Manual*; TEA Ediciones: Madrid, Spain, 1998.
44. Derogatis, L. *SCL-90-R. Administration, Scoring and Procedures Manual—II for the Revised Version. Clinical Psychometric Research*; Clinical Psychometric Research: Baltimore, MD, USA, 1990.
45. Derogatis, L. *SCL-90-R. Cuestionario de 90 Síntomas-Manual*; TEA Ediciones: Madrid, Spain, 2002.
46. Cloninger, C.R. *The Temperament and Character Inventory–Revised*; Washington University, Center for Psychobiology of Personality: St. Louis, MO, USA, 1999.
47. Gutiérrez-Zotes, J.A.; Bayón, C.; Montserrat, C.; Valero, J.; Labad, A.; Cloninger, C.R.; Fernández-Aranda, F. Temperament and Character Inventory—Revised (TCI-R). Standardization and normative data in a general population sample. *ACTAS Esp. Psiquiatr.* **2004**, *32*, 8–15. [PubMed]
48. Bacher, J. A Probabilistic Clustering Model for Variables of Mixed Type. *Qual. Quant.* **2000**, *34*, 223–235. [CrossRef]

49. Huang, Z. Extensions to the k-Means Algorithm for Clustering Large Data Sets with Categorical Values. *Data Mining Knowl. Discov.* **1998**, *2*, 283–304. [CrossRef]
50. Nylund, K.L.; Asparouhov, T.; Muthén, B.O. Deciding on the Number of Classes in Latent Class Analysis and Growth Mixture Modeling: A Monte Carlo Simulation Study. *Struct. Equ. Model. A Multidiscip. J.* **2007**, *14*, 535–569. [CrossRef]
51. Rousseeuw, P.J. Silhouettes: A graphical aid to the interpretation and validation of cluster analysis. *J. Comput. Appl. Math.* **1987**, *20*, 53–65. [CrossRef]
52. Kelley, K.; Preacher, K.J. On Effect Size. *Association* **2012**, *17*, 137–152. [CrossRef]
53. Finner, H. On a Monotonicity Problem in Step-Down Multiple Test Procedures. *J. Am. Stat. Assoc.* **1993**, *88*, 920. [CrossRef]
54. Fontenelle, L.F.; Mendlowicz, M.V.; Moreira, R.O.; Appolinario, J.C. An empirical comparison of atypical bulimia nervosa and binge eating disorder. *Braz. J. Med. Biol. Res.* **2005**, *38*, 1663–1667. [CrossRef]
55. Mustelin, L.; Lehtokari, V.-L.; Keski-Rahkonen, A. Other specified and unspecified feeding or eating disorders among women in the community. *Int. J. Eat. Disord.* **2016**, *49*, 1010–1017. [CrossRef]
56. Riesco, N.; Agüera, Z.; Granero, R.; Jiménez-Murcia, S.; Menchón, J.M.; Fernández-Aranda, F. Other Specified Feeding or Eating Disorders (OSFED): Clinical heterogeneity and cognitive-behavioral therapy outcome. *Eur. Psychiatry* **2018**, *54*, 109–116. [CrossRef]
57. Van Hanswijck de Jonge, P.; van Furth, E.F.; Hubert Lacey, J.; Waller, G. The prevalence of DSM-IV personality pathology among individuals with bulimia nervosa, binge eating disorder and obesity. *Psychol. Med.* **2003**, *33*, 1311–1317. [CrossRef] [PubMed]
58. Del Pino-Gutiérrez, A.; Jiménez-Murcia, S.; Fernández-Aranda, F.; Agüera, Z.; Granero, R.; Hakansson, A.; Fagundo, A.B.; Bolao, F.; Valdepérez, A.; Mestre-Bach, G.; et al. The relevance of personality traits in impulsivity-related disorders: From substance use disorders and gambling disorder to bulimia nervosa. *J. Behav. Addict.* **2017**, *6*, 396–405. [CrossRef] [PubMed]
59. Janiri, L.; Martinotti, G.; Dario, T.; Schifano, F.; Bria, P. The gamblers' Temperament and Character Inventory (TCI) personality profile. *Subst. Use Misuse* **2007**, *42*, 975–984. [CrossRef] [PubMed]
60. Wang, Y.; Liu, Y.; Yang, L.; Gu, F.; Li, X.; Zha, R.; Wei, Z.; Pei, Y.; Zhang, P.; Zhou, Y.; et al. Novelty seeking is related to individual risk preference and brain activation associated with risk prediction during decision making. *Sci. Rep.* **2015**, *5*, 10534. [CrossRef] [PubMed]
61. Stansfield, K.H.; Kirstein, C.L. Effects of novelty on behavior in the adolescent and adult rat. *Dev. Psychobiol.* **2006**, *48*, 10–15. [CrossRef] [PubMed]
62. Grucza, R.A.; Robert Cloninger, C.; Bucholz, K.K.; Constantino, J.N.; Schuckit, M.I.; Dick, D.M.; Bierut, L.J. Novelty seeking as a moderator of familial risk for alcohol dependence. *Alcohol. Clin. Exp. Res.* **2006**, *30*, 1176–1183. [CrossRef] [PubMed]
63. Krug, I.; Pinheiro, A.P.; Bulik, C.; Jiménez-Murcia, S.; Granero, R.; Penelo, E.; Masuet, C.; Agüera, Z.; Fernández-Aranda, F. Lifetime substance abuse, family history of alcohol abuse/dependence and novelty seeking in eating disorders: Comparison study of eating disorder subgroups. *Psychiatry Clin. Neurosci.* **2009**, *63*, 82–87. [CrossRef] [PubMed]
64. Angres, D.; Nielsen, A. The role of the TCI-R (Temperament Character Inventory) in individualized treatment plannning in a population of addicted professionals. *J. Addict. Dis.* **2007**, *26* (Suppl. 1), 51–64. [CrossRef]
65. Hilker, I.; Sánchez, I.; Steward, T.; Jiménez-Murcia, S.; Granero, R.; Gearhardt, A.N.; Rodríguez-Muñoz, R.C.; Dieguez, C.; Crujeiras, A.B.; Tolosa-Sola, I.; et al. Food Addiction in Bulimia Nervosa: Clinical Correlates and Association with Response to a Brief Psychoeducational Intervention. *Eur. Eat. Disord. Rev.* **2016**, *24*, 482–488. [CrossRef]
66. Agüera, Z.; Krug, I.; Sánchez, I.; Granero, R.; Penelo, E.; Peñas-Lledó, E.; Jiménez-Murcia, S.; Menchón, J.M.; Fernández-Aranda, F. Personality Changes in Bulimia Nervosa after a Cognitive Behaviour Therapy. *Eur. Eat. Disord. Rev.* **2012**, *20*, 379–385. [CrossRef]
67. Davis, C.; Curtis, C.; Levitan, R.D.; Carter, J.C.; Kaplan, A.S.; Kennedy, J.L. Evidence that "food addiction" is a valid phenotype of obesity. *Appetite* **2011**, *57*, 711–717. [CrossRef] [PubMed]
68. Gearhardt, A.N.; Davis, C.; Kuschner, R.; Brownell, K.D. The addiction potential of hyperpalatable foods. *Curr. Drug Abuse Rev.* **2011**, *4*, 140–145. [CrossRef] [PubMed]

69. Schulte, E.M.; Avena, N.M.; Gearhardt, A.N. Which Foods May Be Addictive? The Roles of Processing, Fat Content, and Glycemic Load. *PLoS ONE* **2015**, *10*, 117959. [CrossRef] [PubMed]
70. Wiss, D.A.; Criscitelli, K.; Gold, M.; Avena, N. Preclinical evidence for the addiction potential of highly palatable foods: Current developments related to maternal influence. *Appetite* **2017**, *115*, 19–27. [CrossRef] [PubMed]
71. Treasure, J.; Leslie, M.; Chami, R.; Fernández-Aranda, F. Are trans diagnostic models of eating disorders fit for purpose? A consideration of the evidence for food addiction. *Eur. Eat. Disord. Rev.* **2018**, *26*, 83–91. [CrossRef]
72. Berridge, K.C. "Liking" and "wanting" food rewards: Brain substrates and roles in eating disorders. *Physiol. Behav.* **2009**, *97*, 537–550. [CrossRef]
73. Kessler, R.M.; Hutson, P.H.; Herman, B.K.; Potenza, M.N. The neurobiological basis of binge-eating disorder. *Neurosci. Biobehav. Rev.* **2016**, *63*, 223–238. [CrossRef]
74. Gregorowski, C.; Seedat, S.; Jordaan, G. A clinical approach to the assessment and management of co-morbid eating disorders and substance use disorders. *BMC Psychiatry* **2013**, *13*, 289. [CrossRef]
75. Fernández-Aranda, F.; Steward, T.; Jimenez-Murcia, S. Substance-Related Disorders in Eating Disorders. In *Encyclopedia of Feeding and Eating Disorders*; Wade, T., Ed.; Springer: Singapore, 2016; pp. 1–5.
76. Innamorati, M.; Imperatori, C.; Balsamo, M.; Tamburello, S.; Belvederi Murri, M.; Contardi, A.; Tamburello, A.; Fabbricatore, M. Food cravings questionnaire-trait (FCQ-T) discriminates between obese and overweight patients with and without binge eating tendencies: The italian version of the FCQ-T. *J. Pers. Assess.* **2014**, *96*, 632–639. [CrossRef]
77. Moreno, S.; Rodríguez, S.; Fernandez, M.C.; Tamez, J.; Cepeda-Benito, A. Clinical validation of the trait and state versions of the food craving questionnaire. *Assessment* **2008**, *15*, 375–387. [CrossRef]
78. Ferrer-Garcia, M.; Pla-Sanjuanelo, J.; Dakanalis, A.; Vilalta-Abella, F.; Riva, G.; Fernandez-Aranda, F.; Sánchez, I.; Ribas-Sabaté, J.; Andreu-Gracia, A.; Escandón-Nagel, N.; et al. Eating behavior style predicts craving and anxiety experienced in food-related virtual environments by patients with eating disorders and healthy controls. *Appetite* **2017**, *117*, 284–293. [CrossRef] [PubMed]
79. Van den Eynde, F.; Koskina, A.; Syrad, H.; Guillaume, S.; Broadbent, H.; Campbell, I.C.; Schmidt, U. State and trait food craving in people with bulimic eating disorders. *Eat. Behav.* **2012**, *13*, 414–417. [CrossRef] [PubMed]
80. Meule, A.; Küppers, C.; Harms, L.; Friederich, H.C.; Schmidt, U.; Blechert, J.; Brockmeyer, T. Food cue-induced craving in individuals with bulimia nervosa and binge-eating disorder. *PLoS ONE* **2018**, *13*, e0204151. [CrossRef] [PubMed]
81. Giel, K.E.; Speer, E.; Schag, K.; Leehr, E.J.; Zipfel, S. Effects of a food-specific inhibition training in individuals with binge eating disorder—Findings from a randomized controlled proof-of-concept study. *Eat. Weight Disord.* **2017**, *22*, 345–351. [CrossRef]
82. Turton, R.; Nazar, B.P.; Burgess, E.E.; Lawrence, N.S.; Cardi, V.; Treasure, J.; Hirsch, C.R. To Go or Not to Go: A Proof of Concept Study Testing Food-Specific Inhibition Training for Women with Eating and Weight Disorders. *Eur. Eat. Disord. Rev.* **2018**, *26*, 11–21. [CrossRef]
83. Arias Horcajadas, F.; Sánchez Romero, S.; Gorgojo Martínez, J.J.; Almódovar Ruiz, F.; Fernández Rojo, S.; Llorente Martin, F. Clinical differences between morbid obese patients with and without binge eating. *Actas españolas Psiquiatr.* **2006**, *34*, 362–370.
84. Fandiño, J.; Moreira, R.O.; Preissler, C.; Gaya, C.W.; Papelbaum, M.; Coutinho, W.F.; Appolinario, J.C. Impact of binge eating disorder in the psychopathological profile of obese women. *Compr. Psychiatry* **2010**, *51*, 110–114. [CrossRef]
85. Fichter, M.M.; Quadflieg, N.; Brandl, B. Recurrent overeating: An empirical comparison of binge eating disorder, bulimia nervosa, and obesity. *Int. J. Eat. Disord.* **1993**, *14*, 1–16. [CrossRef]
86. Villarejo, C.; Jiménez-Murcia, S.; Álvarez-Moya, E.; Granero, R.; Penelo, E.; Treasure, J.; Vilarrasa, N.; Gil-Montserrat de Bernabé, M.; Casanueva, F.F.; Tinahones, F.J.; et al. Loss of Control over Eating: A Description of the Eating Disorder/Obesity Spectrum in Women. *Eur. Eat. Disord. Rev.* **2014**, *22*, 25–31. [CrossRef]
87. Álvarez-Moya, E.M.; Jiménez-Murcia, S.; Granero, R.; Vallejo, J.; Krug, I.; Bulik, C.M.; Fernández-Aranda, F. Comparison of personality risk factors in bulimia nervosa and pathological gambling. *Compr. Psychiatry* **2007**, *48*, 452–457. [CrossRef]

88. Fassino, S.; Daga, G.A.; Pierò, A.; Leombruni, P.; Rovera, G.G. Anger and personality in eating disorders. *J. Psychosom. Res.* **2001**, *51*, 757–764. [CrossRef]
89. Brockmeyer, T.; Hahn, C.; Reetz, C.; Schmidt, U.; Friederich, H.C. Approach bias and cue reactivity towards food in people with high versus low levels of food craving. *Appetite* **2015**, *95*, 197–202. [CrossRef] [PubMed]
90. Hetherington, M.M.; Macdiarmid, J.I. Pleasure and excess: Liking for and overconsumption of chocolate. *Physiol. Behav.* **1995**, *57*, 27–35. [CrossRef]
91. Sevinçer, G.M.; Konuk, N.; Bozkurt, S.; Coşkun, H. Food addiction and the outcome of bariatric surgery at 1-year: Prospective observational study. *Psychiatry Res.* **2016**, *244*, 159–164. [CrossRef]
92. Heriseanu, A.I.; Hay, P.; Corbit, L.; Touyz, S. Grazing in adults with obesity and eating disorders: A systematic review of associated clinical features and meta-analysis of prevalence. *Clin. Psychol. Rev.* **2017**, *58*, 16–32. [CrossRef]
93. White, M.A.; Grilo, C.M. Psychometric properties of the Food Craving Inventory among obese patients with binge eating disorder. *Eat. Behav.* **2005**, *6*, 239–245. [CrossRef]
94. Grilo, C.M. The assessment and treatment of binge eating disorder. *J. Pract. Psychiatry Behav. Health* **1998**, *4*, 191–201. [CrossRef]
95. Ng, L.; Davis, C. Cravings and food consumption in binge eating disorder. *Eat. Behav.* **2013**, *14*, 472–475. [CrossRef]
96. Davis, C.A.; Levitan, R.D.; Reid, C.; Carter, J.C.; Kaplan, A.S.; Patte, K.A.; King, N.; Curtis, C.; Kennedy, J.L. Dopamine for "wanting" and opioids for liking: A comparison of obese adults with and without binge eating. *Obesity* **2009**, *17*, 1220–1225. [CrossRef]
97. Eldredge, K.L.; Agras, W.S. Weight and shape overconcern and emotional eating in binge eating disorder. *Int. J. Eat. Disord.* **1996**, *19*, 73–82. [CrossRef]
98. Geliebter, A.; Aversa, A. Emotional eating in overweight, normal weight, and underweight individuals. *Eat. Behav.* **2003**, *3*, 341–347. [CrossRef]
99. Polivy, K.; Herman, C. Etiology of binge eating: Psychological mechanisms. In *Binge Eating: Nature, Assessment, and Treatment*; Fairburn, C., Wilson, G., Eds.; Guilford Press: New York, NY, USA, 1993; pp. 173–205.
100. Greeno, C.G.; Wing, R.R.; Shiffman, S. Binge antecedents in obese women with and without binge eating disorder. *J. Consult. Clin. Psychol.* **2000**, *68*, 95–102. [CrossRef] [PubMed]

4

Ultra-processed Food: Addictive, Toxic and Ready for Regulation

Robert H. Lustig [1,2,3]

[1] Department of Pediatrics, University of California, San Francisco, CA 94143, USA; Robert.Lustig@ucsf.edu
[2] Institute for Health Policy Studies, University of California, San Francisco, CA 94143, USA
[3] Department of Research, Touro University-California, Vallejo, CA 94592, USA

Abstract: Past public health crises (e.g., tobacco, alcohol, opioids, cholera, human immunodeficiency virus (HIV), lead, pollution, venereal disease, even coronavirus (COVID-19) have been met with interventions targeted both at the individual and all of society. While the healthcare community is very aware that the global pandemic of non-communicable diseases (NCDs) has its origins in our Western ultraprocessed food diet, society has been slow to initiate any interventions other than public education, which has been ineffective, in part due to food industry interference. This article provides the rationale for such public health interventions, by compiling the evidence that added sugar, and by proxy the ultraprocessed food category, meets the four criteria set by the public health community as necessary and sufficient for regulation—abuse, toxicity, ubiquity, and externalities (How does your consumption affect me?). To their credit, some countries have recently heeded this science and have instituted sugar taxation policies to help ameliorate NCDs within their borders. This article also supplies scientific counters to food industry talking points, and sample intervention strategies, in order to guide both scientists and policy makers in instituting further appropriate public health measures to quell this pandemic.

Keywords: processed food; nutrition; non-communicable disease; metabolic syndrome; diabetes; addiction; policy

---

1. Introduction: Pandemics and Public Health

We are in the midst of two pandemics. The COVID-19 pandemic had an identifiable start in January 2020. Yet despite media attention and warnings from scientists, many countries are experiencing a "second wave"; here in the United States, we never even cleared the first wave. There is no cure, at least not yet; all we have to mitigate this pandemic are public health efforts—social distancing, handwashing, and face masks—which do not seem to work very well voluntarily, unless made mandatory by authorities. The second pandemic, of non-communicable diseases (NCDs; type 2 diabetes, cardiovascular disease, fatty liver disease, hypertension, heart disease, stroke, cancer, and dementia), has been more insidious, slowly building over a 50-year time frame [1]. There is also no cure for this pandemic; all we have are educational efforts such as voluntary "diet and exercise", which do not seem to work very well either.

NCDs now account for 72% of deaths [2] and 75% of health care dollars in the United States [3] and globally [2]; and the morbidity, mortality, and economic costs continue to climb. In the U.S., Medicare is expected to be insolvent by 2026, and Social Security will be broke by 2034 [4], due to both the loss of economic productivity combined with increased healthcare expenditures. Without young and healthy people paying into the system, old and infirm people cannot take out. The cost of these diseases is not limited to the U.S. [5], and NCDs have been declared a global health crisis by the United Nations (U.N.) [6]. Thus, NCDs pose an existential threat to the survival of each country, and indeed the entire planet. Identifying the cause(s) of NCDs, and upstream policy initiatives to mitigate them is of paramount importance.

Nonetheless, the world has recently faced down two other chronic disease pandemics, tobacco and ethanol; both caused by hedonic substances readily available for purchase, and both responsive to public health regulatory interventions. It was not until the U.S.'s Master Settlement Agreement and the World Health Organization (WHO) Framework Convention on Tobacco Control that we saw a reduction in cigarette consumption and reduction in lung cancer [7]. For alcohol, individual countries have passed their own public health ethanol regulatory efforts, with clear improvements [8].

2. Criteria for Public Health Regulation

The question for public health officials is whether there is something specific and identifiable that could be regulated on a global scale that could help to mitigate the pandemic of NCDs. While some behaviors can be mandated (e.g., mask-wearing), most are left up to each individual (e.g., exercise). Rather, targeting a substance or class of causative substances would be more effective, as predicted by the *Iron Law of Public Health*, which states that reducing availability of a substance reduces consumption, which reduces health harms [9]. Public health officials have identified the four criteria which must be met in order to be considered for public health regulation [10]:

- Abuse (why can't you stop?)
- Toxicity (why do you get sick?)
- Ubiquity (why can't you escape it?)
- Externalities (why does your consumption harm me?)

To generate enthusiasm for any public health regulatory effort, the science and the logic of each of these criteria must be obvious and inescapable. The goal of this treatise is to provide the science that ultraprocessed food in general, and sugar in particular, meet all four criteria, and should be considered as targets for regulation of the NCD pandemic by the public health community and by policymakers.

However, first we must deal with the "elephant in the room"; the mythology that calories are the cause of obesity, and obesity is the cause of NCDs. If this were the case, then the processed food industry can use the mantra that "any calorie can be part of a balanced diet", and thus deflect criticisms of their products. In order to provide evidence for the specific roles of sugar and ultraprocessed food in the pandemic of NCDs, we must first confront and dispel this mythology, by demonstrating that obesity is not a cause of NCDs because normal-weight individuals get NCDs as well. We must also demonstrate that the effects of sugar and ultraprocessed food on NCD prevalence and severity are exclusive of inherent calories, and independent of effects on obesity [11].

3. Obesity Is a 'Marker', Not a Cause of Non-Communicable Diseases (NCDs)

Most clinicians mistakenly attribute the growing rise of NCDs to growing prevalence of obesity because of the *quantity of the food* ingested. This is untrue, for five separate reasons. (a) While obesity prevalence and diabetes prevalence correlate, they are not concordant [12]. There are countries that are obese without being diabetic (such as Iceland, Mongolia, and Micronesia), and there are countries that are diabetic without being obese, such as India, Pakistan, and China (they manifest a 12% diabetes rate). This is further elaborated looking at years of life lost from diabetes vs. obesity [13]. (b) Twenty percent of individuals with obesity are metabolically healthy and have normal life spans [14–16], while up to 40% of normal weight adults harbor metabolic perturbations similar to those in obesity, including type 2 diabetes mellitus (T2DM), dyslipidemia, non-alcoholic fatty liver disease (NAFLD), and cardiovascular disease (CVD) [17,18]. Indeed, in the U.S. 88% of adults exhibit metabolic dysfunction [19], while only 65% are overweight or obese—some normal weight people are metabolically ill as well. (c) The "Little Women of Loja" are a founder-effect cohort in Ecuador who are growth hormone-receptor deficient, and who become markedly obese yet are protected from chronic metabolic disease such as diabetes and heart disease [20]. (d) The secular trend of diabetes in the U.S.

from 1988 to 2012 has demonstrated a 25% increase in prevalence in both the obese *and* the normal weight population [21]. (e) The aging process does not explain T2DM, as children as young as the first decade now manifest these same biochemical processes [22,23]. Now children get two diseases that were never seen before in this age group—T2DM and fatty liver disease. These two diseases used to be prevalent only in the elderly, or in those who abused ethanol.

These five lines of reasoning argue that obesity is a "marker" for the pathophysiology of NCDs (e.g., insulin resistance), but not a primary cause—because a percentage of normal weight people get NCDs as well, while a percentage of people with obesity are metabolically healthy. If obesity was a cause of NCDs, then one could by extension make the case that "eating is addictive"—but clearly neither are true. That young and normal weight people can contract these diseases suggests an exposure, rather than a behavior, at the root of the NCD pandemic, and that the *quantity of the food is not the cause.*

4. Ultraprocessed Food Is the Cause of NCDs

Rather, *the quality of the food is the cause.* Ultraprocessed food, defined as industrial formulations typically with 5 or more ingredients [24], is the category of food that drives NCDs [25], such as obesity [26,27], diabetes [28], heart disease [29], and cancer [30]. In particular, added sugar (i.e., any fructose-containing sweetener; sucrose, high-fructose corn syrup, maple syrup, honey, agave) is the prevalent, insidious, and egregious component of ultraprocessed food that drives that risk.

In this article, using scientific and legal evidence, I will elaborate three related arguments. First, I will demonstrate that ultraprocessed food is addictive because of the sugar that is added to it, and that the food industry specifically adds sugar because of its addictive properties. Second, I will highlight the specific mechanisms by which sugar is toxic to the liver, which leads to NCDs. Lastly, I will argue that added sugar is more appropriately defined as a *food additive* rather than as a *food.* In so doing, I will argue that added sugar, and by extension the entire ultraprocessed food category, meets these criteria established by the public health community for regulation of a substance (abuse, toxicity, ubiquity, externalities) [9].

5. Added Sugar Is Abused

The seminal role of the Western Diet in the pandemic of NCDs is unchallenged [31]. For instance, ultraprocessed food consumption correlates with body mass index (BMI) in the U.S. [26] and in 19 European countries [27]. As market deregulation policies of the 1990s took hold, fast food sales increased incrementally in all countries and cultures to which it has been introduced, along with commensurate increases in BMI [32]. Indeed, every country that has adopted the Western diet is burdened with the development of NCDs and their resultant costs [33]. However, the food industry continues to promulgate the argument that it is the quantity, not the quality of the foods that are to blame. This is not a semantic argument. Quantity is determined by the end user, a personal responsibility issue; while quality is determined by manufacturers, a public health issue. But what if the quality altered the quantity? Those that favored either view over the other would thus appear to be justified within their own stance. Indeed, this debate seems to have drawn to an academic stalemate [34–36]. This must be answered before any form of societal intervention can be contemplated.

5.1. 'Food Addiction' versus 'Eating Addiction'

Recent revelations in the popular literature have alluded to the addictiveness of the Western diet [37,38], driving excessive consumption. Physiologic [39,40] and neuroanatomic [41] overlap between obesity and addiction pathways have been elucidated. Some investigators have argued that specific components of processed food, and in particular those in "fast food", are addictive in a manner similar to cocaine and heroin [42,43]. The Yale Food Addiction Scale (YFAS) logs specific foods as having addictive properties [44], and a children's YFAS also reveals that food addiction is common, especially in obese youth [45].

However, not everyone subscribes to this expanded view of specific foods having addicting properties. For instance, a group of academics in Europe called NeuroFAST does not accept the concept of food addiction, rather calling it "eating addiction" [46]. This group has proffered its own "eating addiction scale" in which all foods are treated similarly [47], and it is the behavior that distinguishes the phenomenon. These investigators state that even though specific foods can generate a reward signal, they cannot be addicting because they are essential to survival. In their own words:

"In humans, there is no evidence that a specific food, food ingredient or food additive causes a substance-based type of addiction (the only currently known exception is caffeine which via specific mechanisms can potentially be addictive). Within this context we specifically point out that we do not consider alcoholic beverages as food, despite the fact that one gram of ethanol has an energy density of 7 kcal [48]".

NeuroFAST recognizes caffeine as addictive, but gives it a pass. Xanthine alkaloids are present naturally in many foods, yet caffeine is classified by the U.S. Food and Drug Administration (FDA) as a food additive. It is also a drug; we give it to premature newborns with underdeveloped nervous systems to stimulate the central nervous system (CNS) to prevent apnea. NeuroFAST also recognizes ethanol as addictive, and also gives it a pass. Natural yeasts constantly ferment fruit while still on the vine or tree, causing it to ripen [49], yet NeuroFAST acknowledges that purified ethanol is not a food. Rather, ethanol is a drug; we used to give it to pregnant women to stop premature labor.

Recently, another European group with food industry ties assessed the effects of specific foodstuffs on "eating dependence" in a cohort of university students, using weight gain as the metric of food addiction. In their study, they found no difference between fats and sugars as cause for weight gain [50]. However, as stated earlier, using weight gain as the metric of food addiction is inherently flawed.

In order to assess mechanism of effects of food on the addiction pathway in the brain, our group at UCSF studied a cohort of postmenopausal women with obesity who received orally the mu-opioid receptor antagonist naltrexone as a probe of the brain's reward system. We found that the amplitude of cortisol responses and nausea generation in response to naltrexone correlated with symptoms of craving for sweet palatable foods in these women. These data suggest that naltrexone interfered with endogenous opioid peptide (EOP) tone that mediated these cravings. In so doing, we have discerned a phenomenon of "Reward Eating Drive" (RED), which belies those individuals with obesity who appear to respond excessively to hedonic food cues [51–53], and which is tied to the opioidergic component of the reward system in the brain, which is driven by sweet foods. Furthermore, using functional magnetic resonance imaging (fMRI) studies, other investigators have defined the prefrontal cortex as responsible for the response of sweet tastes as being "attractive" or "unattractive" [54].

5.2. Addictive Potential of Food Components

If there was a class of consumables that was uniquely addictive, it would have to be "fast food". But is it just the calories, or is there something specific about fast food that generates an addictive response? Fast food contains four components whose hedonic properties have been examined: salt, fat, caffeine, and sugar [37,42].

5.2.1. Salt

In humans, salt intake has traditionally been conceived as a learned preference [55] rather than as an addiction. The preference for salty foods is likely learned early in life. Four- to six-month-old infants establish a salt preference based on the sodium content of breast milk, water used to mix formula, and diet [56]. Because energy-dense fast foods are relatively high in salt [57], in part as a preservative to reduce depreciation, the preference for salty foods is associated with higher calorie intake. For example, a study in Korean teens showed a correlation between frequent fast food intake and preference for saltier versions of traditional foods [58]. Another study examined 27 subjects undergoing opiate (mostly oxycodone) withdrawal and showed significant increases in fast food intake and weight gain over 60 days [59], suggesting "addiction transfer". On the other hand, studies show that people can 'reset' their preference for less salty items. This has been demonstrated in adolescents deprived of salty pizza on their school lunch menu, and hypertensive adults who were retrained to consume a lower sodium diet over 8 to 12 weeks [55]. Furthermore, at low levels, salt intake is well known to be tightly regulated. For example, patients with salt-losing congenital adrenal hyperplasia who lack the mineralocorticoid aldosterone modulate have an obligatory salt loss, which modulates their salt intake [60], until appropriate doses of fludrocortisone are supplemented. The notion that human sodium intake is "physiologically fixed" had been used to criticize recent public health efforts to reduce sodium intake so drastically [61]. Nonetheless, the U.K. government engaged in a secret mass campaign to reduce public salt consumption by 30%, and saw a 40% reduction in hypertension and stroke without signs of withdrawal [62].

5.2.2. Fat

The high fat content of fast food is vital to its rewarding properties. Indeed, there may be a "high-fat phenotype" among human subjects, characterized by a preference for high-fat foods and weak satiety in response to them, which acts as a risk factor for obesity [63]. However, so-called "high-fat foods" preferred by people are almost always also high in carbohydrate (e.g., potato chips, pizza, or cookies). Indeed, adding sugar significantly enhances preference for high-fat foods among normal weight human subjects; yet there was no limit for preference with increasing fat content [64]. Thus, the synergy of high fat along with high sugar is likely to be more effective at stimulating addictive overeating than fat alone. However, these rewarding properties of fat appear to be strictly dependent on simultaneous ingestion of carbohydrate, as low-carbohydrate high-fat (LCHF) [65] and ketogenic diets [66] consistently result in reduced caloric intake, significant weight loss, and resolution of metabolic syndrome. In other words, fat increases the salience of fast food, but does not appear to be addictive in and of itself.

5.2.3. Caffeine

Caffeine is a "model drug" of dependence in humans [67], meeting the DSM-IV and DSM-5 criteria for tolerance, physiologic withdrawal, and psychological dependence in children [68], adolescents [69], and adults [70]. Headache [70], fatigue, and impaired task performance [68] have been demonstrated during withdrawal. While adolescents and children get their caffeine from soft drinks and hot chocolate, adults get most of their caffeine from coffee and tea [71]. These drinks average 239 calories and provide high amounts of sugar [72]. Soft drink manufacturers identify caffeine as a flavoring agent in their beverages, but only 8% of frequent soda drinkers can detect the difference in a blinded comparison of a caffeine-containing and caffeine-free cola [73]. Thus, the most likely function of the caffeine in soda is to increase the salience of an already highly rewarding (high sugar) beverage. These drinks may be acting as a gateway for caffeine-dependent customers to visit a fast food restaurant and purchase fast food [74].

5.2.4. Sugar

Other than caffeine, the component with the highest score on the YFAS is sugar [44]. Adding a soft drink to a fast food meal increases the sugar content 10-fold. Multivariate analysis of fast food transactions demonstrate that only soft drink intake is correlated with changes in BMI; not animal fat products [32]. While soda intake has been shown to be independently related to obesity and the diseases of metabolic syndrome [75,76], fast food eaters clearly consume more soft drinks. Sugar has been used for its analgesic effect in neonatal circumcision [77], suggesting a link between sugar and EOP tone. Indeed, anecdotal reports from self-identified food addicts describe sugar withdrawal as feeling "irritable", "shaky", "anxious" and "depressed" [78]; symptoms also seen in opiate withdrawal. Other studies demonstrate the use of sugar to treat psychological dependence [79]. Sugar craving can vary widely by age, menstrual cycle and time of day [80].

Sugar is added to food either as sucrose, high-fructose corn syrup (HFCS), honey, maple syrup, or agave. In general, each are assumed to consist of half fructose, half glucose; although this percentage has recently come into question when an analysis of store-bought sodas in Los Angeles revealed a fructose content as high as 65% [81]. This difference may be relevant, as fructose appears to generate a greater reward response and more toxicity than does glucose (see below).

5.3. Correlates of Addiction in Animals Exposed to Sucrose

In rodents, oral sucrose administration uniquely induces the acute reactant *c-fos* in the ventral tegmental area, implying activation of the reward pathway [82]. Furthermore, sucrose infusion directly into the nucleus accumbens reduces dopamine and μ-opioid receptors similar to morphine [83], and fMRI studies demonstrate the establishment of hard-wired pathways for craving [84]. Furthermore, sucrose administration to rodents induces behavioral alterations consistent with dependence; i.e., bingeing, withdrawal, craving, and cross-sensitization to other drugs of abuse [85]. Indeed, in one oft-quoted rat study, sweetness surpassed cocaine as reward [86].

5.4. Differential Effects of Fructose vs. Glucose vs. Fat on the Human Brain

Despite being calorically equivalent (4.1 kcal/gm), fructose and glucose are metabolized differently. Glucose is the energy of life. Glucose is so important that if you do not consume it, your liver makes it from amino acids and fatty acids (gluconeogenesis). Conversely fructose, while an energy source, is otherwise vestigial; there is no biochemical reaction in any eukaryote that requires it. Our research has shown that when provided in excess of the liver's capacity to metabolize fructose via the tricarboxylic acid cycle, the rest is turned into liver fat, promoting insulin resistance, and resultant NCDs [87–89].

Physiologically, chronic fructose administration promotes fasting hyperinsulinemia and hypertriglyceridemia [90], which blocks leptin's ability to cross the blood brain barrier [91], and attenuates leptin's ability to extinguish mesolimbic dopamine signaling in rodents [92] and humans [93], thus promoting tolerance and withdrawal [94]. Furthermore, fructose does not suppress the stomach-derived hunger hormone ghrelin [95]. Through these pathways, fructose fosters overconsumption independent of energy need [96]. A comparison of the two monosaccharides demonstrates increased risk for bingeing with fructose (similar to sucrose) as opposed to glucose [97], suggesting the fructose molecule is the moiety that generates both reward and addiction responses.

Neuroanatomically, human fMRI studies show that acute glucose vs. fructose administration exert effects on different sites in the brain. One study infused each monosaccharide intravenously, and measured blood oxygenation level-dependent (BOLD) fMRI signal in cortical areas of the brain; glucose increased the BOLD signal in cortical executive control areas, whereas fructose suppressed the signal coming from those same areas [98]. Another study examined regional cerebral blood flow (rCBF) after oral glucose vs. fructose. With glucose, rCBF within the hypothalamus, thalamus, insula, anterior cingulate, and striatum (appetite and reward regions) was reduced, while fructose reduced rCBF in the thalamus, hippocampus, posterior cingulate cortex, fusiform, and visual cortex [99]. Consistent with other studies, fructose demonstrated lack of satiety or fullness in comparison to glucose. Furthermore, glucose increased "functional connectivity" of the caudate, putamen, precuneus, and lingual gyrus (basal ganglia) more than fructose; whereas fructose increased functional connectivity of the amygdala, hippocampus, parahippocampus, orbitofrontal cortex and precentral gyrus (limbic system) more than glucose [100]. In obese youth, the effects of oral fructose on dopamine activation of the nucleus accumbens is severely attenuated, suggesting down-regulation of dopamine receptors [101]. Lastly, the effects of fat and sugar both separately and together (adjusting for calories) on fMRI signaling have been assessed [102]. High-fat milkshakes increased brain activity in the caudate and oral somatosensory areas (postcentral gyrus, hippocampus, inferior frontal gyrus); while sugar increased activity in the insula extending into the putamen, the Rolandic operculum, and thalamus (gustatory regions). Furthermore, increasing sugar caused greater activity in those regions, but increasing fat content did not alter this activation. In other words, the fat increases the salience of the sugar, but it is the sugar that effectively recruits reward and gustatory circuits.

To summarize, added sugar (and specifically the fructose moiety) is unique in activating reward circuitry; fructose works both directly and indirectly to increase consumption; and that both obesity and chronic fructose exposure down-regulate dopamine receptors, requiring greater and greater stimuli to enact a reward-signaling effect (tolerance), a primary component of addiction.

5.5. 'Food' Addiction Is Really 'Food Additive' Addiction, and 'Added Sugar' Is a Food Additive

In the past, the concept of food addiction was not embraced by psychiatrists. For instance, the DSM-IV published in 1993 listed "substance use disorder" as requiring both tolerance and withdrawal as necessary criteria for the definition of addiction, and (apart from caffeine and ethanol) no foodstuff elicited withdrawal. However, as the public health difficulties stemming from addiction expanded, the definition, of necessity, expanded. The DSM-5 published in 2013 reclassified the field so as to include "behavioral addictions", such as gambling (internet gaming was included in the Appendix as "requiring further study"). Thus, a revised set of criteria related to psychological dependence was proffered [103], including:

1. Craving or a strong desire to use;
2. Recurrent use resulting in a failure to fulfill major role obligations (work, school, home);
3. Recurrent use in physically hazardous situations (e.g., driving);
4. Use despite social or interpersonal problems caused or exacerbated by use;
5. Taking the substance or engaging in the behavior in larger amounts or over a longer period than intended;
6. Attempts to quit or cut down;
7. Time spent seeking or recovering from use;
8. Interference with life activities;
9. Use despite negative consequences.

However, food addiction was not codified in the DSM-5. Nonetheless, systematic reviews of the literature demonstrate that ultraprocessed foods have the highest addictive potential due to their added sugar content [104]. While sugar itself does not exhibit the DSM-IV criteria of classic tolerance and withdrawal, sugar clearly meets the DSM-5 requirements of tolerance and dependence (use despite conscious knowledge and recognition of their detriment).

Coca leaves are medicinal in Bolivia, yet cocaine is a drug, and regulated. Opium poppies are also medicinal, but morphine is a drug, and regulated. Caffeine is found in coffee (medicinal for many), yet concentrated caffeine is a drug, and regulated. In ancient times, sugar was a spice. Through the Industrial Revolution it was a condiment. Now it is purified, and it is a drug. Refined sucrose is the same compound found in fruit, but the fiber has been removed, and it has been crystallized for purity. This process of purification has turned sugar from "food" into "drug" [105]. Like these other addictive consumables, it can be present in low dose in nature and not exert toxic effects; but when purified and added to food, it becomes addictive.

Drugs are a luxury, food is a necessity. NeuroFAST asks how can foods that are necessary to survival also be addicting? Because certain "foods" are *not* necessary for survival. Of the hedonic substances found in food, only alcohol, caffeine, and sugar are addictive. But these are food additives, not foods. Some form of sugar has been added to 74% of the food supply [106], because the food industry knows that when they add it, we buy more [107]. For instance, the tobacco industry manipulated nicotine levels in cigarettes specifically to keep users consuming, and to convert as many as possible into "heavy users" [108]. The food industry has engaged in similar practices, which has increased the percent of calories as added sugar (58%) in ultraprocessed foods [27]. In fact, sugar's allure is a big reason why the processed food industry's current profit margin is 5% (it used to be 1%) [109]. The addictive nature of sugar is also revealed in its economics. For instance, coffee is price-inelastic, i.e., increasing price does not reduce consumption much. When prices jumped in 2014 due to decreased supply, Starbuck's sales remained constant, owing to its hedonic effects [110]. As consumables go, soft drinks are the second most price-inelastic, just below fast food [107]. When the price is raised by 10% (e.g., with taxes), consumption dropped only 7.6%, mostly among the poor, as was seen in Mexico [111]. Thus, sugar consumption is only minimally responsive to either its economic or caloric value, consistent with its addictive properties.

6. Added Sugar Is Toxic

Toxicity is defined as "the degree to which a substance can damage an organism". Such detrimental effects must be exclusive of caloric equivalence, or else *all* calories are toxic, which is clearly not true. Just because a substance is an energy source does not mean that it is not toxic. For instance, alcohol possesses a caloric equivalence (7 kcal/gm), yet we humans have an upper limit of hepatic and brain metabolism, beyond which toxicity becomes manifest, either acute (mental status changes) or chronic (fatty liver disease progressing to cirrhosis, insulin resistance). Alcohol is not dangerous because of its calories or its effects on weight. Alcohol is dangerous because it is alcohol [112]; the biochemistry of the molecule in the liver confers its toxicity. Alcohol exerts its negative effects on liver metabolism through two mechanisms: (1) liver mitochondrial overload with diversion of substrate to the process of *de novo* lipogenesis (DNL; new fat-making), with subsequent hepatic fat accumulation and insulin resistance [113]; and (2) the non-enzymatic binding of the intermediate metabolite acetaldehyde to liver proteins, known as the Maillard or "aging" reaction, with subsequent "carbonyl" stress (see Section 6.1.2), protein denaturation, subsequent inflammation, and cell death.

6.1. Detrimental Effects of Fructose on Liver Metabolism

The metabolic perturbations associated with fructose consumption exclusive of its caloric equivalence are well documented by numerous investigators [114,115]. There are no biochemical reactions that require dietary fructose. The same two primary molecular mechanisms of alcohol delineate the toxicity of fructose apart from its caloric equivalence [105].

6.1.1. *De Novo* Lipogenesis

Only the liver metabolizes fructose for energy, and a fructose bolus (e.g., a soft drink) absorbed across the intestinal lining delivers the majority of the fructose via the portal vein to the liver. Fructose is particularly lipogenic, as the glycolytic intermediate acetyl-CoA is delivered to the liver mitochondria in an unregulated fashion, driving hepatic DNL, which will either be exported as triglyceride (which contributes to heart disease); or possibly overwhelming the liver's lipid export capacity, leading to intrahepatic lipid deposition and hepatic steatosis, resulting in liver insulin resistance, which is a driving force behind all the NCDs [89]. The intermediate metabolic pathways have been elucidated elsewhere [116].

6.1.2. Carbonyl Stress—The Maillard Reaction

Carbonyl stress occurs when the reactive aldehyde or keto-group of a carbohydrate molecule binds non-enzymatically to the amino-group of a protein, leading to the Maillard or the "browning reaction" [117]. This is why bananas brown as they age. This is also why humans get wrinkles as they age. This is also why patients with diabetes check their hemoglobin A1c measurement (which is a carbohydrate molecule bound to position 1 of the globin chain), to determine if their diabetes is out of control. Every time this reaction occurs, the protein becomes less flexible (leading to cell dysfunction), and an oxygen radical is produced, which if not quenched by an antioxidant, can lead to protein or lipid peroxidation, cell damage, and death.

Due to its unique stereochemistry, the ring form of fructose (a five-membered furan with axial hydroxymethyl groups) is under a great deal of ionic strain, which favors the linear form of the molecule, exposing the reactive 2-keto position, which engages in the fructosylation of exposed amino-moieties of proteins via the Maillard reaction, and 7 times faster than the 1-aldehyde position of glucose reacts with those same proteins. Each Maillard reaction generates one oxygen radical, which must be quenched by an antioxidant, or else cellular damage can ensue. Thus, due to its chemical makeup, fructose leads to increased cellular damage [118] and disease progression compared to glucose, and unrelated to its caloric equivalence.

6.1.3. Tying Two Pathophysiologic Mechanisms Together—Methylglyoxal

Recently, our UCSF/Touro research group has determined that methylglyoxal, a specific intermediate in the glycolytic pathway, is likely the nidus of both of these toxic phenomena within the liver [119]. Methylglyoxal is a transient metabolic intermediate of the process of anaerobic glycolysis, whose production is dependent on the availability of excess substrate (either glucose or fructose) in the liver; but, because virtually 100% fructose load is handled by the liver, compared to only 20% of glucose, then fructose is the primary driver of its formation. Methylglyoxal is an alpha-dicarbonyl; it is both a reactive aldehyde (like glucose) and a reactive ketone (like fructose) at the same time. Therefore, it engages in the Maillard reaction 35 times faster than fructose, and 250 times faster than glucose, generating 250 times the oxygen radicals. Methylglyoxal is detoxified to the byproduct D-lactate, which can be measured in the blood, and serves as a proxy of the rate of methylglyoxal formation. D-lactate levels are higher in obese adolescents [120], and reductions in D-lactate levels by fructose restriction in obese children correlate with improvements in DNL, liver fat content, and insulin sensitivity [121], all unrelated to caloric equivalence or obesity. These findings argue that fructose is a chronic, dose-dependent hepatotoxin, which drives progression of NCDs.

6.2. Dissociating Added Sugar from Its Calories and Effects on Weight

The food industry often tries to divert the public health conversation toward obesity [50,122]. Sugar ranks below potato chips and French fries as a cause of weight gain [123]; the data correlating sugar consumption to obesity are weak, accounting for only about 10% of the observed effect [124]. If sugar is only one of many causes of weight gain, it can iterate its mantra, 'a calorie is a calorie'. However, a new study demonstrates that the correlation between added sugar consumption and population obesity obeys a slightly more complex function, taking into account both current and previous consumption of added sugar [125]. This model predicts the effects of added sugar on obesity quite accurately.

But, as stated before, obesity is the wrong metric. Obesity and diabetes are discordant; there are countries where diabetes rates are high yet obesity rates are low, such as India, Pakistan, and China; while their sugar consumption has increased by 15% in the past 6 years alone [126]. When weight and calories are factored out, the correlation between sugar consumption and type 2 diabetes is even stronger [12,127]. To date, the food industry refuses to engage in a discussion on the role of added sugar in chronic metabolic diseases, exclusive of obesity.

There are many case-control studies (reviewed in [128,129]) which point to dietary fructose consumption as a primary cause of T2DM, but such studies are not controlled for calories or weight. In order to prove that fructose (and, therefore, added sugar) is specifically toxic, the molecule must be dissociated from its inherent calories and its effects on weight. Furthermore, standard cross-sectional or correlational studies without a time-factor analysis component are not acceptable, as they cannot distinguish reverse or intermediate causality; it is like the snapshot rather than the movie. Lastly, the food industry is quick to point out that most fructose studies are done in rodents, with large doses over a short period of time. In defense, a recent study in rats shows that sugar at normal levels of consumption can cause morbidity and mortality [130], and a primate study demonstrates similar detrimental effects [131]. Nonetheless, in order to prove toxicity, this section will be limited to human studies using doses of added sugar routinely consumed.

6.2.1. Prospective Association Studies

Three recent studies, all controlled for calories and adiposity and with a time analysis, support sugar as a specific and direct causative agent in T2DM. First, a prospective cohort analysis of the European EPIC-Interact study found that sugar-sweetened beverage (SSB) consumption increased risk for development of diabetes over a 10-year period. The multivariate modeling, which adjusted for both energy intake (EI) and for adiposity (BMI), demonstrated that each SSB consumed increased the hazard risk (HR) ratio by 1.29 (95% CI 1.02, 1.63) exclusive of energy intake (calories) or BMI (obesity) [132]. In the U.S., we are currently consuming the equivalent of 2.5 servings of SSB's per day; so our HR ratio is 1.68.

Second, a meta-analysis of studies isolated consumption of soda (n = 17) and fruit juice (n = 13) separately, while controlling for calories and adjusting for adiposity [76]. This meta-analysis showed that both soda and fruit juice significantly increased the relative risk (RR) ratio for diabetes (1.27, 1.10, respectively) over time. Furthermore, this study specifically took into account the fact that food industry-sponsored studies frequently demonstrate publication and information bias, and calibrated for these biases.

Third, our UCSF group evaluated the National Health and Nutrition Examination Survey (NHANES) adolescent database across three cycles 2005–2012, to determine nutritional consumption and any changes within the American diet within that interval. We then binned subjects into quintiles based on added sugar consumption, and after controlling for caloric intake and BMI, determined what aspects of the diet predicted the prevalence of metabolic syndrome [133]. We set the HR ratio for metabolic syndrome in the 1st quintile (median added sugar consumption = 30 gm/day) at 1.0; by the 4th quintile (median added sugar consumption = 125 gm/day), the HR ratio for metabolic syndrome had increased to 9.7.

6.2.2. Econometric Analyses

One econometric analysis [134] of 156 countries over the period 1995–2014 demonstrated that global availability of sugar and sweeteners was correlated with diabetes prevalence, health care costs per diabetic, and health care costs per capita; demonstrating both personal and societal harm related to added sugar consumption. This analysis also showed that this correlation occurred in both developed and developing countries. However, this study did not account for calories or obesity, and could not account for other aspects of the diet.

Our UCSF/Stanford group performed an econometric analysis to assess what foods were specifically implicated in altered diabetes rates over time [12]. We melded three freely available databases together; (1) the Food and Agriculture Organization statistics database (FAOSTAT; a branch of the World Health Organization), which lists by food availability per person by country, by year 2000–2010, and by line item (total calories, fruits excluding wine, meats, oils, cereals, fiber-containing foods, and sugar/sweeteners); (2) the International Diabetes Federation (IDF) database which lists diabetes prevalence by country by year 2000–2010; and (3) the World Bank World Development Indicators Database for the years 2000–2010, in which Gross Domestic Product is expressed in purchasing power parity in 2005 US dollars for comparability among countries to control for poverty. It also controls for urbanization, aging, physical activity, and obesity. We asked what food(s) availability predict change in diabetes prevalence country by country over the decade? We performed this analysis using generalized estimating equations with a conservative fixed-effects approach (Hausman test), a hazard model to control for selection bias (Heckman selection test), and period effects controlled for secular trends that may have occurred as a result of changes diabetes detection capacity or importation policies. Most importantly, we examined longitudinal data between 2000 and 2010, which allowed us to determine what dietary changes preceded the changes in diabetes prevalence (Granger causality test).

We demonstrated that retrospective changes in sugar availability predicted the prevalence of diabetes during the decade 2000–2010, exclusive of total calories, other foodstuffs, aging, obesity, physical activity, or income. For every 150 calories per day in excess, diabetes prevalence increased

0.1%, but if those 150 calories happened to be a can of soda, diabetes prevalence increased 11-fold, by 1.1% [12]. These data meet the Bradford Hill criteria for "causal medical inference", because we demonstrate dose (more sugar, more diabetes), duration (longer sugar exposure, more diabetes), directionality (the few countries where sugar availability went down experienced a reduction in diabetes), and precedence (we noted a three-year lag between increase in sugar availability and increase in diabetes prevalence; in a prospective modeling study we noticed a three-year lag between sugar reduction and decrease in diabetes prevalence [3]).

This econometric analysis has been criticized for two reasons. First, it is an "ecological study", which by convention is hierarchically considered of low quality. Rather, this econometric analysis is more rigorous and of higher quality than all studies except randomized controlled trials [135], as it assesses multiple points in time, discerns complex relationships between internal and external motivating factors (adjusted over time), and allows for determination of causation (Granger causality test). Second, the FAOSTAT database assesses country-specific food availability rather than consumption, and waste is not taken into account. Rather, assessing availability is a positive feature rather than a negative, as availability is more accurate, easily quantifiable, not subject to the vicissitudes of individual recall, and independent of food wastage.

6.2.3. Interventional Starch-for-Sugar Exchange

Our UCSF/Touro research group documented the effects of isocaloric substitution of sugar with starch in 43 Latino and African-American children with metabolic syndrome over a 10-day period [87–89]. We performed food questionnaires and interviews using sophisticated software to assess their total caloric consumption, as well as specific macronutrient and fiber intake. On Day 0, we assessed their metabolic health on their home diet using: (1) baseline analyte levels; (2) oral glucose tolerance testing; and (3) dual-emission X-ray absorptiometry (DEXA) scanning. Then, for the next 9 days, we catered their meals, to provide the same caloric content, the same fat, protein, and fiber content, and the same amount of total carbohydrate; but we reduced the percent calories from dietary sugar from a mean of 28% to 10%, and the percent calories from fructose from 12% to 4%. They were allowed fruit, but not fruit juice. We gave them a scale to take home and called them every day. If their weight was declining, we made them eat more, and they were given extra snacks to prevent weight loss. Then we studied them again 10 days later.

Every aspect of their metabolic health improved, with essentially no change in weight. Blood pressure reduced by 5 mmHg, triglycerides by 33 mg/dL, low-density lipoproteins (LDL) by 10 mg/dL, glucose levels reduced by 5 mg/dL, glucose area under the curve dropped by 8%, fasting insulin dropped by 10 mU/L, insulin area under the curve dropped 25%, on the same number of calories and without weight loss, just by removing the added sugar and substituting with starch. Furthermore, subcutaneous fat did not change (as there was no weight loss), but visceral fat reduced by 7%, and most importantly liver fat was reduced by 22%. We also showed that insulin dynamics improved markedly, thus reversing their predisposition to T2DM.

Taken together with the aforementioned studies [12,136,137], Koch's Postulates for causation of NCDs by added sugar are fulfilled. Sugar is a chronic, dose-dependent liver toxin unrelated to calories or obesity, similar to ethanol, because fructose and ethanol exert similar effects on the liver and the brain [112].

7. Added Sugar Is Ubiquitous

Sugar has become ubiquitous in the Western diet, increasing from 15 gm/day at the beginning of the 20th century to 94 gm/day at the beginning of the 21st century [138,139]. In the U.S. 56% of the diet is now ultra-processed food, 62% of sugar in the American diet is in this category [28], and some form of sugar has been added to 74% of the items in the American grocery store [106], because the food industry knows that when they add it, we buy more. Similarly, world sugar consumption tripled 1960–2010 while the world population doubled over the same time [140], arguing that most of the world's population has experienced a significant increase in added sugar consumption in the 50 years that NCDs have become prominent [140]. For instance, changes in consumption of Coca-Cola over the interval 1993–2006 correlated with changes in diabetes prevalence in both China and Mexico. During this interval, the consumer price index for sugared beverages increased 50% vs. food, and 25% vs. fruits and vegetables [141]. The introduction of high-fructose corn syrup in 1975 reduced cost the cost of sugar by 50%, which allowed serving size to rise, and sugar to be added to foods that previously did not contain it. For instance, 50% of milk sales in elementary and middle schools are for flavored milk (chocolate, strawberry). Furthermore, in most developing nations, soda is cheaper than water, which has increased consumption of added sugar around the world. Processed foods and sugared beverages are marketed heavily as they are extremely profitable; in 2006, food marketers spent USD $1.05 billion on marketing to children and adolescents; half of which were for sugared beverages [142].

Marketing practices by tobacco and food companies are highly congruent [143]. Big Tobacco in the past, and Big Food currently, have used "commercial speech" provided by the First Amendment to cull favor with the public through advertising and sponsorships. For instance, both have in the past engaged in vigorous advertising campaigns to recruit new users that was defused only by regulatory agency action [144,145]. For decades Big Tobacco provided corporate sponsorship of various public events around the world, such as the Olympics, baseball and football games, and sporting events around the world. The fast food and beverage industries engage in similar marketing practices, sponsoring global events around the world. Big Tobacco shamelessly marketed their products to children (e.g., Joe Camel); while the food and beverage industries have followed suit (e.g., Ronald McDonald). Both have used deceptive business practices to maintain increased use of their product among "heavy users" [146,147].

8. Added Sugar Exerts Externalities

Substances that produce societal harms impact even the non-user. Second-hand smoke and drinking-driving provided strong arguments for tobacco and alcohol control, respectively. The above data demonstrate that the long-term healthcare, human, and economic costs of NCDs place the chronic effects of fructose overconsumption in the same category [148].

Sugared beverages alone kill 184,000 people per year globally [149]. The U.S. wastes $65 billion in work productivity and $150 billion in health care resources, and experiences a 50% increase in absenteeism and health insurance premiums, all to care for the co-morbidities of metabolic syndrome [150]. Currently, 75% of all health care dollars are spent on treating these diseases or resultant disabilities. Rising global NCD rates yield an annual mortality of 35 million people, with a disproportionate 80% of these deaths occurring in low- and middle-income countries, wasting precious medical resources [151]. Lastly, the past three Surgeons General and the Chairman of the Joint Chiefs of Staff have declared obesity a "threat to national security". The original Pentagon report from 2012 has been updated in 2018, and 33% of recruits are now deemed "Still Too Fat To Fight" [152]. Even among those recruited, 43% cannot be deployed into the field due to Stage 3 dental caries due to sugar consumption [153].

Population-wide sugar reduction would prevent premature death, save economies billions and improve quality of life for millions across the globe. Our UCSF group used advanced Markov modeling (using fatty liver disease as the sentinel disease) to demonstrate that reduction of added sugar consumption of just 20% (e.g., a tax) could reduce obesity, type 2 diabetes, heart disease, death rates, and medical expenditures within three years in the United States, and save $10 billion annually, while a 50% reduction (e.g., adhering to U.S. Dept. of Agriculture (USDA) guidelines) could save $31.8 billion annually [3]. On the productivity side, Morgan Stanley modeled global economic growth rates from 2015 to 2035 in low-sugar and high-sugar simulations [154], and showed that using a low-sugar case, economic growth would be maintained at 2.9%, while using a high-sugar case (e.g., the present), economic growth would slowly decline to 0.0%. Thus, the externalities of added sugar consumption are direct and affect everyone.

9. Food Industry Counters

9.1. *Personal Responsibility*

Education of the public through emphasis on "personal responsibility" over the last 30 years have not been effective in stemming the tide of obesity and metabolic syndrome. This should not be surprising, as educational efforts have been unsuccessful in reducing the consumption of other substances of abuse [9,155]. Add to this the fact that 74% of the items in the food supply are spiked with added sugar by the food industry [106]; thus it is virtually impossible for most individuals to disabuse sugar, and to be able to go "cold turkey" in order to reduce toxicity and dependence. This is especially true of the poor, who have limited access to healthy food, and are often limited in their purchases to high-sugar processed food on the Supplemental Nutrition Assistance Program (aka Food Stamps). The ostensible reason that the food industry has added more and more sugar to processed food is for "palatability". Indeed, when they do, we buy more; which reinforces the practice by increasing profits. Indeed, efforts to reduce the negative health impact of "junk food" by former Pepsi CEO Indra Nooyi by introducing a "good for you" category (to offset their "fun for you" category) have met with rancor by her own Board of Directors due to a $349 million reduction in profits [156].

The personal responsibility strategy was first deployed by tobacco companies in 1962 as a reason to keep on smoking [157]. This ideology requires four pre-requisites:

9.1.1. Knowledge

Information labelling is not easily understandable by the regular consumer buying food products in the supermarket. Many will trust and buy a product on the way it is promoted, rather than on its nutritional value. Until recently, the US Institute of Medicine, and in the UK and the rest of Europe for the past 15 years, guideline daily amounts on labels have suggested that daily consumption of up to 22 teaspoons of sugar is healthful [158].

9.1.2. Access

Over 70% of foods in the supermarket contain added sugar—it has become almost unavoidable. Processed sugary food and drinks have permeated workplaces, gyms, and schools. Several American hospitals (including UCSF), and the British National Health Service (NHS) have instituted a ban on sugary drinks sold in hospitals, in order to provide a role model for the public. Our UCSF group has documented the metabolic health benefits of a workplace ban on sugared beverages [159].

9.1.3. Affordability

One should be able to afford their choice, and society has to afford it too. Healthy food was twice as expensive as processed food in 2002, and its cost increased by the equivalent of US $0.22 per year over the next 10 years, compared with processed food, which increased by the equivalent of US $0.09 per year [160].

9.1.4. *Non-Anarchy*

The medical costs of chronic metabolic disease due to sugar consumption will cause a doubling of Medicare costs in the next decade [161], bankrupting health care systems around the world [162,163], and the NHS is under an ever-tighter squeeze, resulting in lengthier waiting times [164]. The argument that your actions cannot harm anyone else ignores the diet-related harm experienced by children who are especially vulnerable to poor diet at critical development stages.

Americans currently consume an average of 19.5 tsp/day of added sugar. The American Heart Association has recommended a reduction in added sugar consumption to 6 tsp/day for women and 9 tsp/day for men, a reduction by $^2/_3$ to $\frac{3}{4}$ in amount. Of these 22 tsp, $^1/_3$ can be found in beverages, and 1/6 in desserts. This means that fully $\frac{1}{2}$ of the added sugar in our diet is in foods that we did not know contained sugar, such as salad dressing, bread, tomato sauce, ketchup, and many other common food items. Thus, even if we removed all the soft drinks and desserts from our diet, we would still be over our "sugar limit", which has been set so high by the food industry. Thus, "personal responsibility" alone cannot be expected to confer any relief. Indeed, our food supply has been "adulterated" by the addition of added sugar by the food industry. Furthermore, there are 262 names for sugar, most of which are unknown to the population at large [165]. As the Nutrition Labeling and Education Act of 1990 [166] requires listing food ingredients by mass, the food industry can hide added sugar by using various forms of sugar and thus moving each form further down the label, so that the consumer does not know that the food they are purchasing is laden with added sugar [167]. Furthermore, while each disease within metabolic syndrome can be temporized, there is no pharmacologic "fix" for metabolic syndrome itself. Paracelsus said in 1537: "The dose determines the poison". Added sugar has an upper limit of 25–37.5 gm/day for adults and 12 gm/day for children; and we have been placed over our limit by the food industry.

The reduction of added sugar from the American diet must become the top priority to reverse the prevalence and severity of NCDs. Prevention strategies of necessity must occur through public health interventions to alter the food environment. But how? Food is a personal choice, most consider sugar as just "empty" calories, and if individuals want to consume their discretionary calories as sugar, why should they not be allowed to do so? Yet, tobacco and alcohol similarly pose significant societal threats due to their abuse, toxicity, ubiquity, and externalities (negative impact on society) [155,168], and they are regulated [169].

9.2. *Is Added Sugar 'Food'?*

The food industry will debate any argument for regulating added sugar with two talking points. First, they will point out that sugar is a primary component of fruit, and fruit has been shown to be preventive against NCDs [170]. In contradistinction, fruit juice has been shown to be correlated with these same diseases [76,171]. The reason is that the fiber prevents intestinal absorption, thus reducing the systemic burden of the sugar in whole fruit [172]. Second, the industry argues that dietary sugar is on the FDA's Generally Recognized as Safe (GRAS) list, which gives the food industry license to use any amount of sugar in any foods they wish. Fructose was grandfathered into the first GRAS list in 1958, as it was "natural" and had been used for generations without any obvious ill effects—although sugar was known to be associated with gout as early as the 17th century [173], and known to raise serum uric acid levels (the mechanism of gout) in 1967 [174]. It should be noted that inclusion on the GRAS list prior to 1 January 1958 was through either scientific procedures or experience based on common use in food (requiring a substantial history of consumption for food use by a significant number of consumers) and thought there is reasonable certainty that the substance is not harmful under the intended conditions of use (Food, Drugs, and Cosmetics Act (FDCA) 321(s), 21 CFR 170.30(c), 170.3(f)). However, in 1958 our consumption of added sugar averaged 2 ounces per day, and currently it averages 6.5 ounces per day. Thus, GRAS determinations in 1958 do not hold for today's food supply. The issue of GRAS outliving its intentions is seen for trans-fats and salt; both used by the processed food industry, both proven to be detrimental at doses above what were thought to be safe, and now both under scrutiny by the FDA (although not removed from the GRAS list).

Trans-fats used to be "food", but subsequent research showed they cause heart disease and other metabolic diseases. Nitrates used to be "food", yet research showed they cause colon cancer. Both were eventually removed from the GRAS list, and are now regulated as food additives. Ethanol has always been a food additive, and caffeine dosage above 0.02% (in cola drinks) is similarly regulated.

The question is, does added sugar legally qualify as food? It depends on how you define the word "food". The Food, Drug, and Cosmetics Act (FDCA, 1938) 321.201(f) defines the term "food" as: *(1) articles used for food or drink for man or other animals, (2) chewing gum, and (3) articles used for components of any such article*. The first rule of vocabulary is that you are not allowed to use the word in the definition. The Merriam-Webster Dictionary defines "food" as: *a material consisting essentially of protein, carbohydrate, and fat used in the body of an organism to sustain growth, repair, and vital processes and to furnish energy*. Fructose supplies energy, so that should make it a food. Or does it? Ethanol supplies energy (7 kcal/gm), but it is clearly not a food. There is no biochemical reaction in any eukaryote that requires it. When consumed chronically and in high dose, ethanol is toxic, unrelated to its calories or effects on weight. Not everyone who is exposed becomes addicted, but enough do to warrant public health intervention [175]. Clearly, ethanol is NOT a food, it is a food additive. Similarly, *added sugar is a food additive*—like ethanol, it is not essential for life, it is toxic in chronically high dosage, and a good percentage of the population is addicted. Indeed, the petitioning for removal of fructose from the GRAS list is being currently being entertained by public health non-governmental organizations (NGOs).

10. Possible Societal Interventions

In the last 30 years, there have been four global cultural tectonic shifts in behavior to ameliorate four public health problems: (a) smoking in public places; (b) drunk driving; (c) bicycle helmets and seat belts; (d) condoms in public bathrooms. In each case, public education was necessary but not sufficient, and some form of regulatory policy also had to be enacted to insure compliance. There are many lessons from alcohol and tobacco control policies that can be brought to bear on sugar and ultraprocessed food.

10.1. Public Education

One the most important things we have learned from tobacco and alcohol policy research is that public education, despite being the most popular and a necessary component of prevention, does not work alone [168,176]. Evidence from the U.S. suggests that government labels warning consumers about the health effects of excessive drinking have no effect on alcohol consumption, but might have had some limited effect on risky drinking patterns, such as drunk driving [177]. The most popular approaches–school-based health education, public information campaigns, product labeling, and government guidelines—do not work in isolation [178,179]. It should be noted that education *alone* has not solved any substance of abuse. Nonetheless, education softens the playing field, so that societal policy interventions can become acceptable and take hold.

We must take a look as to what works to reduce the consumption of addictive substances. Research on alcohol policy demonstrates that regulatory controls on the pricing, marketing, and distribution of alcohol are highly effective worldwide in reducing the negative impacts of alcohol consumption [10,168,176]. This strategy has also been effective with tobacco [180]. There are three ways to reduce availability: pricing strategies (e.g., taxation), restriction of access (e.g., blue laws), and interdiction (e.g., banning). No one thinks interdiction is a good idea—alcohol prohibition was tried, and was singularly unsuccessful.

10.2. Pricing Strategies-Taxation

Society accepts taxation because taxes affect only those who use those products. While tobacco and ethanol are significant burdens to society, sugar is by far and away the most expensive burden. The question is, what is the real goal? Making money for the state, or reduction in consumption? Because if you reduce consumption, you limit revenue generation. For a tax on a hedonic substance to work, it has to hurt. Most soda taxes are 10%, but an Oxford group modeled that a soda tax would have to be at least 20% to reduce general consumption [181].

The good news is that due to the emergence of the science around sugar and the inability of education to stop the diabetes pandemic, six American cities and 28 countries globally have enacted sugar taxes, and others are considering some form of legislation [182].

10.3. Pricing Strategies-Subsidies

Agricultural subsidies are payments and other kinds of support extended by the U.S. federal government to certain farmers and agribusinesses. They are a holdover from the original Farm Bill of

1933, when it was necessary to provide cheap food to a destitute population across the country. In the U.S., currently seven states are awarded 45% of the subsidies: Texas 9.6%; Iowa 8.4%; Illinois 6.9%; Minnesota 5.8%; Nebraska 5.7%; Kansas 5.5%; and North Dakota 5.3% [183]; and these are the states that that are the largest producers of corn, soybeans, wheat, and rice—the basics for ultraprocessed food production. There is no economist on the planet who believes in food subsidies, because they distort the market. They make available the wrong stuff while making the right stuff harder to afford. As long as commodities are cheap, real food will stay out of reach for much of the population.

What would happen if subsidies ended? The Giannini group at UC Berkeley modeled what food would actually cost; and the only two items that would increase in price are sugar and corn [184], which is just what we would want to happen. Not surprisingly, these are two of the major industries fighting to maintain the status quo. Still, people will argue, the overall price of food will go up. Well maybe it should, The U.S. spends the least percentage of GDP on food of all nations at 7%—that is because all the food is commodity crop-based and processed. The next two are the UK at 9% and Australia at 11%, the three fattest nations [185].

10.4. Restriction of Access-Workplace Bans

The workplace presents an educational moment and venue. At UCSF, all sugared beverage sales—soda and flavored coffee drinks—were banned from sale in the cafeterias, vanished from patients' meal trays, and disappeared from the menus of any vendors bringing food onto campus. We studied a subgroup of 214 employees who regularly drank sugared beverages before and one year after the ban was put in place [159]. They reported a daily intake of 35 ounces at baseline and 18 ounces at follow-up—a 17-ounce decrease, a cut by almost half. In addition, waist circumference reduced by 2.1 cm. Reductions in sugared beverage intake correlated with improvements in waist circumference, insulin sensitivity, and a pattern of reduction in blood lipids. Some employers may face challenges in implementing a workplace culture where SSB sales bans are perceived as paternalistic. Nevertheless, this proves the *Iron Law* does indeed work.

10.5. Restriction of Access-Stipends

The U.K. provides people with a monthly stipend—which can only be exchanged for real food [186]. This allows each person to use their stipends to vote on local food policy, and in so doing, promote local farmers and organic practices.

10.6. Combination Strategies-Differential Subsidization

Differential subsidization combines the "carrot and stick" approach—the inducement with the punishment [187]. Differential subsidization was employed in 1977 in the Nordic countries, including Sweden, Denmark and Norway, to curb the increasing number of alcoholics in their respective countries. The three countries collectively adopted two pieces of legislation: first, they nationalized the liquor stores resulting in the same products sold at the same amount everywhere; second, they taxed high-alcohol spirits, and then used the money from the tax to subsidize low-alcohol beer. In doing so, they were able to nudge the public away from hard spirits and toward the low-alcohol beer, thus, reducing alcohol consumption. In the process, hospitalizations decreased, car accidents reduced, cirrhosis of the liver declined, and economic productivity improved [188].

This could easily be used to cut sugared beverage consumption—tax soda, and use the revenue generated from the tax to subsidize water. The beverage makers will not care, because they are also selling the water. It is just a straight up exchange, nudging people to a healthier option with a zero-sum scheme. In so doing, you can "nudge" people into doing the right thing, and they won't complain—and most of the time, they will not even notice they have been nudged.

11. Conclusions

When it comes to public health, personal intervention (read: rehab) must be balanced with societal intervention (read: laws). For tobacco, alcohol, opioids, cholera, HIV, lead, pollution, and venereal disease, invoking "personal responsibility" and railing against the "nanny state" was ultimately unsuccessful, and both forms of intervention were ultimately deemed necessary. For added sugar and NCDs, we currently have nothing. The argument for societal intervention in NCDs has been lacking because the food industry has convinced the public that "a calorie is a calorie", that sugar are just "empty calories", and that "personal responsibility" is the answer. While public educational efforts are necessary to warn about the hazards of chronic excessive sugar consumption, they will not be sufficient, as has been seen for every other hedonic substance.

Added sugar, like tobacco, alcohol, cocaine, and opioids, meets public health criteria for societal intervention, i.e., regulation. The roadmap to successful intervention is complex, but we have templates based on how tobacco and alcohol regulation were enacted. As with tobacco and alcohol, the *Iron Law of Public Health* is in force, which states that reduction in availability results in reduction in consumption, which results in reduction in health harms [10]. Policies that target availability, affordability or acceptability (e.g., the Mexico sugar tax) are effective in curbing sugar consumption [111]. But similar to what occurred with the tobacco industry (e.g., *Merchants of Doubt*), the sugar industry, their legislative partners, and their political allies have utilized numerous instruments to deflect culpability and derail policy changes. Some involve influencing science, some involve influencing public opinion, and yet others influence legislatures directly [189]. These activities must be understood and countered before any specific and meaningful policy measures can be proffered.

In this article, I have provided evidence that: (1) sugar is addictive and toxic unrelated to calories; (2) sugar reduction confers health and societal benefits; (3) added sugar, and by inference ultraprocessed food, meets criteria for regulation; (4) sugar reduction is not only possible but required to save health and healthcare, and (5) societal interventions to reduce consumption of processed foods containing added sugar are achievable and necessary. Those interventions (administrative, legislative, judicial) will likely be geographically, politically, and culturally specific; and certain policy interventions will not work in certain venues.

Author Contributions: Along with informal consultations with those mentioned above, R.H.L. researched, designed, drafted, and authored this article. All authors have read and agreed to the published version of the manuscript.

Acknowledgments: I wish to thank my fellow UCSF/Touro University research team members, especially Alejandro Gugliucci, Jean-Marc Schwarz, Kathy Mulligan, Sue Noworolski, Grace Jones, and Ayca Erkin-Cakmak. I need to thank my UCSF policy colleagues, Laura Schmidt, Claire Brindis, and Elissa Epel. Lastly, I thank my legal colleagues, David Faigman and Marsha Cohen at UC Hastings College of the Law, and Michael Roberts and Diana Winters at the UCLA Resnick Center for Food Policy and Obesity, who have also been instrumental in the policy analysis.

References

1. Benziger, C.P.; Roth, G.A.; Moran, A.E. The Global Burden of Disease Study and the Preventable Burden of NCD. *Glob. Heart* **2016**, *11*, 393–397. [CrossRef] [PubMed]
2. Global Burden of Disease Causes of Death Collaborators. Global, regional, and national age-sex specific mortality for 264 causes of death, 1980–2016: A systematic analysis for the Global Burden of Disease Study 2016. *Lancet* **2017**, *390*, 1151–1210. [CrossRef]
3. Vreman, R.A.; Goodell, A.J.; Rodriguez, L.A.; Porco, T.C.; Lustig, R.H.; Kahn, J.G. Health and economic benefits of reducing sugar intake in the United States, including effects via non-alcoholic fatty liver disease: A microsimulation model. *BMJ Open* **2017**, *7*, e103543. [CrossRef] [PubMed]
4. Press, A. Medicare will Become Insolvent in 2026, U.S. Government Says. *Los Angeles Times*. 5 June 2018. Available online: https://www.latimes.com/nation/nationnow/la-na-pol-medicare-finances-20180605-story.html (accessed on 27 September 2020).

5. Yach, D.; Hawkes, C.; Gould, C.L.; Hofman, K.J. The global burden of chronic diseases: Overcoming impediments to prevention and control. *JAMA* **2004**, *291*, 2616–2622. [CrossRef]
6. U.N. General Assembly. Prevention and control of non-communicable diseases. In *U.N. General Assembly*; U.N. General Assembly: New York, NY, USA, 2010.
7. Johnston, L.D.; Miech, R.A.; O'Malley, P.M.; Bachman, J.G.; Schulenberg, J.E.; Patrick, M.E. *Monitoring the Future National Survey Results on Drug Use 1975–2018: Overview, Key Findings on Adolescent Drug Use*; University of Michigan: Ann Arbor, MI, USA, 2019.
8. Room, R. International control of alcohol: Alternative paths forward. *Drug Alcohol Rev.* **2006**, *25*, 581–595. [CrossRef]
9. Room, R.; Babor, T.; Rehm, J. Alcohol and public health. *Lancet* **2005**, *365*, 519–530. [CrossRef]
10. Room, R.; Schmidt, L.A.; Rehm, J.; Mäkela, P. International regulation of alcohol. *Br. Med. J.* **2008**, *337*, a2364. [CrossRef]
11. Lustig, R.H. Sickeningly sweet: Does sugar cause diabetes? Yes. *Can. J. Diabetes* **2016**, *40*, 282–287. [CrossRef]
12. Basu, S.; Yoffe, P.; Hills, N.; Lustig, R.H. The relationship of sugar to population-level diabetes prevalence: An econometric analysis of repeated cross-sectional data. *PLoS ONE* **2013**, *8*, e57873. [CrossRef] [PubMed]
13. Sepúlveda, J.; Murray, C. The state of global health in 2014. *Science* **2014**, *345*, 1275–1278. [CrossRef]
14. Chan, J.M.; Rimm, E.B.; Colditz, G.A.; Stampfer, M.J.; Willett, W.C. Obesity, fat distribution, and weight gain as risk factors for clinical diabetes in men. *Diabetes Care* **1994**, *17*, 961–969. [CrossRef]
15. McLaughlin, T.; Abbasi, F.; Cheal, K.; Chu, J.; Lamendola, C.; Reaven, G.M. Use of metabolic markers to identify overweight individuals who are insulin resistant. *Ann. Int. Med.* **2003**, *139*, 802–809. [CrossRef]
16. Chen, D.L.; Liess, C.; Poljak, A.; Xu, A.; Zhang, J.; Thoma, C.; Trenell, M.; Milner, B.; Jenkins, A.B.; Chisholm, D.J.; et al. Phenotypic characterization of insulin-resistant and insulin-sensitive obesity. *J. Clin. Endocrinol. Metab.* **2015**, *100*, 4082–4091. [CrossRef] [PubMed]
17. Abbasi, F.; Chu, J.W.; Lamendola, C.; McLaughlin, T.; Hayden, J.; Reaven, G.M.; Reaven, P.D. Discrimination between obesity and insulin resistance in the relationship with adiponectin. *Diabetes* **2004**, *53*, 585–590. [CrossRef]
18. Voulgari, C.; Tentolouris, N.; Dilaveris, P.; Tousoulis, D.; Katsilambros, N.; Stefanadis, C. Increased heart failure risk in normal-weight people with metabolic syndrome compared with metabolically healthy obese individuals. *J. Am. Coll. Cardiol.* **2011**, *58*, 1343–1350. [CrossRef]
19. Araújo, J.; Cai, J.; Stevens, J. Prevalence of Optimal Metabolic Health in American Adults: National Health and Nutrition Examination Survey 2009–2016. *Metab. Syndr. Relat. Disord.* **2019**, *17*, 46–52. [CrossRef] [PubMed]
20. Rosenbloom, A.L.; Guevara Aguirre, J.; Rosenfeld, R.G.; Fielder, P.J. The little women of Loja-growth hormone-receptor deficiency in an inbred population of southern Ecuador. *N. Engl. J. Med.* **1990**, *323*, 1367–1374. [CrossRef]
21. Menke, A.; Casagrande, S.; Geiss, L.; Cowie, C.C. Prevalence of and trends in diabetes among adults in the United States, 1988–2012. *JAMA* **2015**, *314*, 1052–1062. [CrossRef]
22. Wiegand, S.; Maikowski, U.; Blankenstein, O.; Biebermann, H.; Tarnow, P.; Gruters, A. Type 2 diabetes and impaired glucose tolerance in European children and adolescents with obesity—A problem that is no longer restricted to minority groups. *Eur. J. Endocrinol.* **2004**, *151*, 199–206. [CrossRef]
23. Biltoft, C.A.; Muir, A. The metabolic syndrome in children and adolescents: A clinician's guide. *Adolesc. Med. State Art Rev.* **2009**, *20*, 109–120.
24. Gibney, M.J. Ultra-Processed Foods: Definitions and Policy Issues. *Curr. Dev. Nutr.* **2019**, *3*, nzy077. [CrossRef]
25. Moubarac, J.C.; Parra, D.; Cannon, G.; Monteiro, C.A. Food classification systems based on food processing: Significance and implications for policies and actions. A systematic literature review and assessment. *Curr. Obes. Rep.* **2014**, *3*, 256–272. [CrossRef]
26. Juul, F.; Martinez-Steele, E.; Parekh, N.; Monteiro, C.A.; Chang, V.W. Ultra-processed food consumption and excess weight among US adults. *Br. J. Nutr.* **2018**, *120*, 90–100. [CrossRef]
27. Monteiro, C.A.; Moubarac, J.C.; Levy, R.B.; Canella, D.S.; Louzada, M.L.D.C.; Cannon, G. Household availability of ultra-processed foods and obesity in nineteen European countries. *Public Health Nutr.* **2018**, *21*, 18–26. [CrossRef]

28. Srour, B.; Fezeu, L.K.; Kesse-Guyot, E.; Allès, B.; Debras, C.; Druesne-Pecollo, N.; Chazelas, E.; Deschasaux, M.; Hercberg, S.; Galan, P.; et al. Ultraprocessed Food Consumption and Risk of Type 2 Diabetes Among Participants of the NutriNet-Santé Prospective Cohort. *JAMA Intern. Med.* **2020**, *180*, 283–291. [CrossRef]
29. Srour, B.; Fezeu, L.K.; Kesse-Guyot, E.; Allès, B.; Méjean, C.; Andrianasolo, R.M.; Chazelas, E.; Deschasaux, M.; Hercberg, S.; Galan, P.; et al. Ultra-processed food intake and risk of cardiovascular disease: Prospective cohort study (NutriNet-Santé). *BMJ* **2019**, *365*, l1451. [CrossRef]
30. Fiolet, T.; Srour, B.; Sellem, L.; Kesse-Guyot, E.; Allès, B.; Méjean, C.; Deschasaux, M.; Fassier, P.; Latino-Martel, P.; Beslay, M.; et al. Consumption of ultra-processed foods and cancer risk: Results from NutriNet-Santé prospective cohort. *BMJ* **2018**, *360*, k322. [CrossRef]
31. Popkin, B.M.; Adair, L.S.; Ng, S.W. Global nutrition transition and the pandemic of obesity in developing countries. *Nutr. Rev.* **2012**, *70*, 3–21. [CrossRef]
32. De Vogli, R.; Kouvonen, A.; Gimeno, D. The influence of market deregulation on fast food consumption and body mass index: A cross-national time series analysis. *Bull. World Health Organ.* **2014**, *92*, 99–107. [CrossRef] [PubMed]
33. GBD Diet Collaborators. Health effects of dietary risks in 195 countries, 1990–2017: A systematic analysis for the Global Burden of Disease Study 2017. *Lancet* **2019**, *393*, 1958–1972. [CrossRef]
34. Ziauddeen, H.; Farooqi, I.S.; Fletcher, P.C. Obesity and the brain: How convincing is the addiction model? *Nat. Rev. Neurosci.* **2012**, *13*, 279–286. [CrossRef]
35. Avena, N.M.; Gearhardt, A.N.; Gold, M.S.; Wang, G.J.; Potenza, M.N. Tossing the baby out with the bathwater after a brief rinse? The potential downside of dismissing food addiction based on limited data. *Nat. Rev. Neurosci.* **2012**, *13*, 514. [CrossRef]
36. Ziauddeen, H.; Farooqi, I.S.; Fletcher, P.C. Food addiction: Is there a baby in the bathwater? *Nat. Rev. Neurosci.* **2012**, *13*, 514. [CrossRef]
37. Moss, M. *Salt, Sugar, Fat: How the Food Giants Hooked Us*; Random House: New York, NY, USA, 2013.
38. Kessler, D.A. *The End of Overeating: Taking Control of the Insatiable American Appetite*; Rodale: New York, NY, USA, 2010.
39. Volkow, N.D.; Wise, R.A. How can drug addiction help us understand obesity? *Nat. Neurosci.* **2005**, *8*, 555–560. [CrossRef] [PubMed]
40. Fortuna, J.L. The obesity epidemic and food addiction: Clinical similarities to drug dependence. *J. Psychoact. Drugs* **2012**, *44*, 56–63. [CrossRef]
41. Wang, G.J.; Volkow, N.D.; Thanos, P.K.; Fowler, J.S. Similarity between obesity and drug addiction as assessed by neurofunctional imaging: A concept review. *J. Addict. Res.* **2004**, *23*, 39–53. [CrossRef] [PubMed]
42. Garber, A.K.; Lustig, R.H. Is fast food addictive? *Curr. Drug Abuse Rev.* **2011**, *4*, 146–162. [CrossRef]
43. Avena, N.M.; Bocarsly, M.E.; Hoebel, B.G.; Gold, M.S. Overlaps in the nosology of substance abuse and overeating: The translational implications of "food addiction". *Curr. Drug Abuse Rev.* **2011**, *4*, 133–139. [CrossRef]
44. Schulte, E.M.; Avena, N.M.; Gearhardt, A.N. Which foods may be addictive? The roles of processing, fat content, and glycemic load. *PLoS ONE* **2015**, *10*, e0117959. [CrossRef] [PubMed]
45. Richmond, R.L.; Roberto, C.A.; Gearhardt, A.N. The association of addictive-like eating with food intake in children. *Appetite* **2017**, *117*, 82–90. [CrossRef]
46. Hebebrand, J.; Albayrak, O.; Adan, R.; Antel, J.; Dieguez, C.; de Jong, J.; Leng, G.; Menzies, J.; Mercer, J.G.; Murphy, M.; et al. "Eating addiction", rather than "food addiction", better captures addictive-like eating behavior. *Neurosci. Biobehav. Rev.* **2014**, *47*, 295–300. [CrossRef]
47. Ruddock, H.K.; Christiansen, P.; Halford, J.C.G.; Hardman, C.A. The development and validation of the Addiction-like Eating Behaviour Scale. *Int. J. Obes.* **2017**, *41*, 1710–1717. [CrossRef]
48. NeuroFAST. NeuroFAST Consensus Opinion on Food Addiction. 2014. Available online: http://www.neurofast.eu/consensus (accessed on 27 September 2020).
49. Pesis, E. The role of the anaerobic metabolites, acetaldehyde and ethanol, in fruit ripening, enhancement of fruit quality and fruit deterioration. *Postharvest Biol. Technol.* **2005**, *37*, 1–19. [CrossRef]
50. Markus, C.R.; Rogers, P.J.; Brouns, F.; Schepers, R. Eating dependence and weight gain; no human evidence for a 'sugar-addiction' model of overweight. *Appetite* **2017**, *114*, 64–72. [CrossRef]
51. Mason, A.E.; Lustig, R.H.; Brown, R.R.; Acree, M.; Bacchetti, P.; Moran, P.J.; Dallman, M.; Laraia, B.; Adler, N.; Hecht, F.M.; et al. Acute responses to opioidergic blockade as a biomarker of hedonic eating among obese women enrolled in a mindfulness-based weight loss intervention trial. *Appetite* **2015**, *91*, 311–320. [CrossRef]

52. Mason, A.E.; Laraia, B.; Daubenmier, J.; Hecht, F.M.; Lustig, R.H.; Puterman, E.; Adler, N.; Dallman, M.; Kiernan, M.; Gearhardt, A.N.; et al. Putting the brakes on the "drive to eat": Pilot effects of naltrexone and reward-based eating on food cravings among obese women. *Eat Behav.* **2015**, *19*, 53–56. [CrossRef]
53. Mason, A.E.; Epel, E.S.; Aschbacher, K.; Lustig, R.H.; Acree, M.; Kristeller, J.; Cohn, M.; Dallman, M.; Moran, P.J.; Bacchetti, P.; et al. Reduced reward-driven eating accounts for the impact of a mindfulness-based diet and exercise intervention on weight loss: Data from the SHINE randomized controlled trial. *Appetite* **2016**, *100*, 86–93. [CrossRef]
54. Rudenga, K.J.; Small, D.M. Ventromedial prefrontal cortex response to concentrated sucrose reflects liking rather than sweet quality coding. *Chem. Senses* **2013**, *38*, 585–594. [CrossRef]
55. Mattes, R.D. The taste for salt in humans. *Am. J. Clin. Nutr.* **1997**, *65*, 692S–697S. [CrossRef]
56. Harris, G.; Booth, D.A. Infants' preference for salt in food: Its dependence upon recent dietary experience. *J. Reprod. Infant Psychol.* **1987**, *5*, 94–104. [CrossRef]
57. Dietary Guidelines Advisory Committee. *Report of the Dietary Guidelines Advisory Committee on the Dietary Guidelines for Americans, 2015*; Agricultural Research Division, U.S. Department of Agriculture: Washington, DC, USA, 2016. Available online: http://www.cnpp.usda.gov/DGAs2010-DGACReport.htm (accessed on 27 September 2020).
58. Kim, G.H.; Lee, H.M. Frequent consumption of certain fast foods may be associated with an enhanced preference for salt taste. *J. Hum. Nutr. Diet.* **2009**, *22*, 475–480. [CrossRef]
59. Cocores, J.A.; Gold, M.S. The salted food addiction hypothesis may explain overeating and the obesity epidemic. *Med. Hypotheses* **2009**, *73*, 892–899. [CrossRef]
60. Kochli, A.; Tenenbaum-Rakover, Y.; Leshem, M. Increased salt appetite in patients with congenital adrenal hyperplasia 21-hydroxylase deficiency. *Am. J. Physiol. Reg. Integr. Comp. Physiol.* **2005**, *288*, R1673–R1681. [CrossRef]
61. McCarron, D.A.; Geerling, J.C.; Kazaks, A.G.; Stern, J.S. Can dietary sodium intake be modified by public policy? *Clin. J. Am. Soc. Nephrol.* **2009**, *4*, 1878–1882. [CrossRef]
62. He, F.J.; Pombo-Rodrigues, S.; Macgregor, G.A. Salt reduction in England from 2003 to 2011: Its relationship to blood pressure, stroke and ischaemic heart disease mortality. *BMJ Open* **2014**, *4*, e004549. [CrossRef]
63. Blundell, J.E.; Stubbs, R.J.; Golding, C.; Croden, F.; Alam, R.; Whybrow, S.; Le Noury, J.; Lawton, C.L. Resistance and susceptibility to weight gain: Individual variability in response to a high-fat diet. *Physiol. Behav.* **2005**, *86*, 614–622. [CrossRef]
64. Drewnowski, A.; Greewood, M.R. Cream and sugar: Human preferences for high-fat foods. *Physiol. Behav.* **1983**, *30*, 629–633. [CrossRef]
65. Hu, T.; Mills, K.T.; Yao, L.; Demanelis, K.; Eloustaz, M.; Yancy, W.S.; Kelly, T.N.; He, J.; Bazzano, L.A. Effects of low-carbohydrate diets versus low-fat diets on metabolic risk factors: A meta-analysis of randomized controlled clinical trials. *Am. J. Epidemiol.* **2012**, *176* (Suppl. 7), S44–S54. [CrossRef]
66. Paoli, A.; Rubini, A.; Volek, J.S.; Grimaldi, K.A. Beyond weight loss: A review of the therapeutic uses of very-low-carbohydrate (ketogenic) diets. *Eur. J. Clin. Nutr.* **2013**, *67*, 789–796. [CrossRef]
67. Griffiths, R.R.; Chausmer, A.L. Caffeine as a model drug of dependence: Recent developments in understanding caffeine withdrawal, the caffeine dependence syndrome, and caffeine negative reinforcement. *Nihon Shinkei Seishin Yakurigaku Zasshi* **2000**, *20*, 223–231.
68. Bernstein, G.A.; Carroll, M.E.; Walters, D.N.; Crosby, R.D.; Perwien, A.R.; Benowitz, N.L. Caffeine withdrawal in normal school-age children. *J. Am. Acad. Child Adolesc. Psychiatry* **1998**, *37*, 858–865. [CrossRef]
69. Bernstein, G.A.; Carroll, M.E.; Thuras, P.D.; Cosgrove, K.P.; Roth, M.E. Caffeine dependence in teenagers. *Drug Alcohol Depend.* **2002**, *66*, 1–6. [CrossRef]
70. Couturier, E.G.; Laman, D.M.; van Duijn, M.A.; van Duijn, H. Influence of caffeine and caffeine withdrawal on headache and cerebral blood flow velocities. *Cephalalgia* **1997**, *17*, 188–190. [CrossRef]
71. Nawrot, P.; Jordan, S.; Eastwood, J.; Rotstein, J.; Hugenholtz, A.; Feeley, M. Effects of caffeine on human health. *Food Addit. Contam.* **2003**, *20*, 1–30. [CrossRef]
72. Huang, C.; Dumanovsky, T.; Silver, L.D.; Nonas, C.; Bassett, M.T. Calories from beverages purchased at 2 major coffee chains in New York City, 2007. *Prev. Chronic Dis.* **2009**, *6*, A118. [PubMed]
73. Griffiths, R.R.; Vernotica, E.M. Is caffeine a flavoring agent in cola soft drinks? *Arch. Fam. Med.* **2000**, *9*, 727–734. [CrossRef]

116. Lim, J.S.; Mietus-Snyder, M.; Valente, A.; Schwarz, J.M.; Lustig, R.H. The role of fructose in the pathogenesis of NAFLD and the metabolic syndrome. *Nat. Rev. Gastroenterol. Hepatol.* **2010**, *7*, 251–264. [CrossRef]
117. Dills, W.L. Protein fructosylation: Fructose and the Maillard reaction. *Am. J. Clin. Nutr.* **1993**, *58*, 779S–787S. [CrossRef] [PubMed]
118. Bremer, A.A.; Mietus-Snyder, M.L.; Lustig, R.H. Toward a unifying hypothesis of metabolic syndrome. *Pediatrics* **2012**, *129*, 557–570. [CrossRef]
119. Mortera, R.R.; Bains, Y.; Gugliucci, A. Fructose at the crossroads of the metabolic syndrome and obesity epidemics. *Front. Biosci.* **2019**, *24*, 186–211.
120. Rodríguez-Mortera, R.; Luevano-Contreras, C.; Solorio-Meza, S.; Caccavello, R.; Bains, Y.; Garay-Sevilla, M.E.; Gugliucci, A. Higher D-lactate levels are associated with higher prevalence of small dense low-density lipoprotein in obese adolescents. *Clin. Chem. Lab. Med.* **2018**, *56*, 1100–1108. [CrossRef]
121. Erkin-Cakmak, A.; Bains, Y.; Caccavello, R.; Noworolski, S.M.; Schwarz, J.M.; Mulligan, K.; Lustig, R.H.; Gugliucci, A. Isocaloric Fructose Restriction Reduces Serum d-Lactate Concentration in Children With Obesity and Metabolic Syndrome. *J. Clin. Endocrinol. Metab.* **2019**, *104*, 3003–3011. [CrossRef] [PubMed]
122. van Buul, V.J.; Tappy, L.; Brouns, F.J. Misconceptions about fructose-containing sugars and their role in the obesity epidemic. *Nutr. Res. Rev.* **2014**, *27*, 119–130. [CrossRef]
123. Mozaffarian, D.; Hao, T.; Rimm, E.B.; Willett, W.C.; Hu, F.B. Changes in diet and lifestyle and long-term weight gain in women and men. *N. Engl. J. Med.* **2011**, *364*, 2392–2404. [CrossRef]
124. Te Morenga, L.; Mallard, S.; Mann, J. Dietary sugars and body weight: Systematic review and meta-analyses of randomised controlled trials and cohort studies. *BMJ* **2013**, *346*, e7492. [CrossRef]
125. Bentley, R.A.; Ruck, D.J.; Fouts, H.N. U.S. obesity as delayed effect of excess sugar. *Econ. Hum. Biol.* **2020**, *36*, 100818. [CrossRef]
126. Gulati, S.; Misra, A. Sugar intake, obesity, and diabetes in India. *Nutrients* **2014**, *6*, 5955–5974. [CrossRef]
127. Deshpande, G.; Mapanga, R.F.; Essop, M.F. Frequent sugar-sweetened beverage consumption and the onset of cardiometabolic diseases: Cause for concern? *J. Endocr. Soc.* **2017**, *1*, 1372–1385. [CrossRef] [PubMed]
128. Malik, V.S.; Popkin, B.M.; Bray, G.A.; Despres, J.P.; Hu, F.B. Sugar-sweetened beverages, obesity, type 2 diabetes mellitus, and cardiovascular disease risk. *Circulation* **2010**, *121*, 1356–1364. [CrossRef]
129. Bray, G.A. Energy and fructose from beverages sweetened with sugar or high-fructose corn syrup pose a health risk for some people. *Adv. Nutr.* **2013**, *4*, 220–225. [CrossRef]
130. Ruff, J.S.; Suchy, A.K.; Hugentobler, S.A.; Sosa, M.M.; Schwartz, B.L.; Morrison, L.C.; Gieng, S.H.; Shigenaga, M.K.; Potts, W.K. Human-relevant levels of added sugar consumption increase female mortality and lower male fitness in mice. *Nat. Commun.* **2013**, *4*, 2245. [CrossRef] [PubMed]
131. Bremer, A.A.; Stanhope, K.L.; Graham, J.L.; Cummings, B.P.; Wang, W.; Saville, B.R.; Havel, P.J. Fructose-fed rhesus monkeys: A nonhuman primate model of insulin resistance, metabolic syndrome, and type 2 diabetes. *Clin. Transl. Sci.* **2011**, *4*, 243–252. [CrossRef]
132. EPIC-Interact Consortium. Consumption of sweet beverages and type 2 diabetes incidence in European adults: Results from EPIC-InterAct. *Diabetologia* **2013**, *56*, 1520–1530. [CrossRef]
133. Rodriguez, L.A.; Madsen, K.A.; Cotterman, C.; Lustig, R.H. Added sugar intake and metabolic syndrome in US adolescents: Cross-sectional analysis of NHANES 2005–2012. *Public Health Nutr.* **2016**, *19*, 2424–2434. [CrossRef]
134. Castro, V. Pure, white and deadly ... expensive: A bitter sweetness in health care expenditure. *Health Econ.* **2017**, *26*, 1644–1666. [CrossRef]
135. Barker, F.G. What is medical evidence? *Clin. Neurosurg.* **2009**, *56*, 24–33.
136. Stanhope, K.L.; Schwarz, J.M.; Keim, N.L.; Griffen, S.C.; Bremer, A.A.; Graham, J.L.; Hatcher, B.; Cox, C.L.; Dyachenko, A.; Zhang, W.; et al. Consuming fructose-, not glucose-sweetened beverages increases visceral adiposity and lipids and decreases insulin sensitivity in overweight/obese humans. *J. Clin. Investig.* **2009**, *119*, 1322–1334. [CrossRef]
137. Maersk, M.; Belza, A.; Stødkilde-Jørgensen, H.; Ringgaard, S.; Chabanova, E.; Thomsen, H.; Pedersen, S.B.; Astrup, A.; Richelsen, B. Sucrose-sweetened beverages increase fat storage in the liver, muscle, and visceral fat depot: A 6-mo randomized intervention study. *Am. J. Clin. Nutr.* **2012**, *95*, 283–289. [CrossRef]
138. Bray, G.A. How bad is fructose? *Am. J. Clin. Nutr.* **2007**, *86*, 895–896. [CrossRef]
139. Vos, M.B.; Kimmons, J.E.; Gillespie, C.; Welsh, J.; Blanck, H.M. Dietary fructose consumption among US children and adults: The Third National Health and Nutrition Examination Survey. *Medscape J. Med.* **2008**, *10*, 160.

140. Popkin, B.M.; Hawkes, C. Sweetening of the global diet, particularly beverages: Patterns, trends, and policy responses. *Lancet Diabetes Endccrinol.* **2016**, *4*, 174–186. [CrossRef]
141. Kuchler, F.; Stewart, H. *Price Trends Are Similar for Fruits, Vegetables, and Snack Foods*; U.S. Department of Agriculture: Washington, DC, USA, 2008. Available online: https://www.ers.usda.gov/webdocs/publications/45951/12368_err55.pdf?v=7164.8 (accessed on 27 September 2020).
142. Food and Nutrition Board, Institute of Medicine. *Food Marketing to Children and Youth: Threat or Opportunity?* National Academies Press: Washington, DC, USA, 2006; Available online: https://www.nap.edu/catalog/11514/food-marketing-to-children-and-youth-threat-or-opportunity (accessed on 27 September 2020).
143. Moodie, R.; Stuckler, D.; Monteiro, C.; Sheron, N.; Neal, B.; Thamarangsi, T.; Lincoln, P.; Casswell, S.; Lancet NCD Action Group. Profits and pandemics: Prevention of harmful effects of tobacco, alcohol, and ultra-processed food and drink industries. *Lancet* **2013**, *381*, 670–679. [CrossRef]
144. *Altria Group Inc. v. Good. 555 U.S. 70*; 2008; pp. 70–71. Available online: https://en.wikipedia.org/wiki/Altria_Group,_Inc._v._Good (accessed on 27 September 2020).
145. *FTC v. Sugar Information, Inc.*; 1972; Volume 81, F.T.C. 711; Available online: https://en.wikipedia.org/wiki/Altria_Group,_Inc._v._Good (accessed on 27 September 2020).
146. *Small v. Lorillard Tobacco Co. 94 N.Y.2d 43, 894*; 1999; pp. 894–895. Available online: https://en.wikipedia.org/wiki/Altria_Group,_Inc._v._Good (accessed on 27 September 2020).
147. *Pelman ex rel. Pelman v. McDonald's Corp. 396 F.3d 508*; 2005; pp. 508–509. Available online: https://en.wikipedia.org/wiki/Altria_Group,_Inc._v._Good (accessed on 27 September 2020).
148. Jarl, J.; Johansson, P.; Eriksson, A.; Eriksson, M.; Gerdtham, U.G.; Hemström, O.; Selin, K.H.; Lenke, L.; Ramstedt, M.; Room, R. The societal cost of alcohol consumption: An estimation of the economic and human cost including health effects in Sweden, 2002. *Eur. J. Health Econ.* **2008**, *9*, 351–360. [CrossRef] [PubMed]
149. Singh, G.M.; Micha, R.; Khatibzadeh, S.; Lim, S.; Ezzati, M.; Mozaffarian, D.; Global Burden of Diseases Nutrition and Chronic Diseases Expert Group (NutriCoDE). Estimated global, regional, and national disease burdens related to sugar-sweetened beverage consumption in 2010. *Circulation* **2015**, *132*, 639–666. [CrossRef]
150. Finkelstein, E.A.; DiBonaventura, M.; Burgess, S.M.; Hale, B.C. The costs of obesity in the workplace. *J. Occup. Environ. Med.* **2010**, *52*, 971–976. [CrossRef]
151. Strong, K.; Mathers, C.; Leeder, S.; Beaglehole, R. Preventing chronic diseases: How many lives can we save? *Lancet* **2005**, *366*, 1578–1582. [CrossRef]
152. Christeson, W.; Taggart, A.D.; Messner-Zidell, S.; Kiernan, M.; Cusick, J.; Day, R. Still too Fat to Fight. 2018. Available online: https://en.wikipedia.org/wiki/Altria_Group,_Inc._v._Good (accessed on 27 September 2020).
153. Mongeau, S.W. USAF Dental readiness classifications and caries-risk assessment. *Mil. Med.* **2008**, *173*, 42–47. [CrossRef]
154. Morgan Stanley Research. The Bittersweet Aftertaste of Sugar. 2015. Available online: http://static.latribune.fr/463077/etude-morgan-stanley-impact-diabete-sur-l-economie-mondiale.pdf (accessed on 27 September 2020).
155. Engelhard, C.L.; Garson, A.; Dorn, S. *Reducing Obesity: Policy Strategies from the Tobacco Wars*; Urban Institute: Washington, DC, USA, 2009.
156. Seabrook, J. Snacks for a fat planet. *New Yorker*, 16 May 2011.
157. Proctor, R.N. *Golden Holocaust: Origins of the Cigarette Catastrophe and the Case for Abolition*; University of California Press: Berkeley, CA, USA, 2011.
158. Pomeranz, J.L. The bittersweet truth about sugar labeling regulations: They are achievable and overdue. *Am. J. Public Health* **2012**, *102*, e14–e20. [CrossRef]
159. Epel, E.S.; Hartman, A.; Jacobs, L.M.; Leung, C.; Cohn, M.A.; Jensen, L.; Ishkanian, L.; Wojcicki, J.; Mason, A.E.; Lustig, R.H.; et al. Association of a workplace sales ban on sugar-sweetened beverages with employee consumption of sugar sweetened beverages and health. *JAMA Int. Med.* **2020**, *180*, 1–8. [CrossRef]
160. Jones, N.R.; Conklin, A.I.; Suhrcke, M.; Monsivais, P. The growing price gap between more and less healthy foods: Analysis of a novel longitudinal UK dataset. *PLoS ONE* **2014**, *9*, e109343. [CrossRef]
161. Cubanski, J.; Neuman, T. *The Facts on Medicare Spending and Financing*; Henry, J., Ed.; Kaiser Family Foundation: Washington, DC, USA, 2017; Available online: https://www.kff.org/medicare/issue-brief/the-facts-on-medicare-spending-and-financing/ (accessed on 27 September 2020).
162. Credit Suisse Research Institute. *Sugar: Consumption at a Crossroads*; Credit Suisse Research Institute: New York, NY, USA, 2013; Available online: http://wphna.org/wp-content/uploads/2014/01/13-09_Credit_Suisse_Sugar_crossroads.pdf (accessed on 27 September 2020).

163. Global Burden of Metabolic Risk Factors for Chronic Diseases Collaboration. Cardiovascular disease, chronic kidney disease, and diabetes mortality burden of cardiometabolic risk factors from 1980 to 2010: A comparative risk assessment. *Lancet Diabetes Endocrinol.* **2014**, *2*, 634–647. [CrossRef]
164. Triggle, N. NHS Ranked 'Number One' Health System. Available online: http://www.bbc.com/news/health-40608253 (accessed on 27 September 2020).
165. Hypoglycemia Support Foundation. Added Sugar Repository. Available online: https://hypoglycemia.org/added-sugar-repository/ (accessed on 27 September 2020).
166. U.S. Congress. Nutrition Labeling and Education Act. In *Public Law 101–535*; U.S. Congress: Washington, DC, USA, 1990. Available online: http://thomas.loc.gov/cgi-bin/bdquery/z?d101:H.R.3562 (accessed on 27 September 2020).
167. Lustig, R.H. Defusing the healthcare time bomb. *San Francisco Chronicle*. 6 January 2013. Available online: http://www.sfgate.com/opinion/article/Defusing-the-health-care-time-bomb-4168827.php (accessed on 27 September 2020).
168. Babor, T.; Caetano, R.; Casswell, S.; Edwards, G.; Giesbrecht, N.; Graham, K.; Grube, J.; Gruenewald, P.; Hill, L.; Holder, H.; et al. *Alcohol: No Ordinary Commodity—Research and Public Policy*; Oxford University Press: Oxford, UK, 2003.
169. Lustig, R.H.; Schmidt, L.A.; Brindis, C.D. The toxic truth about sugar. *Nature* **2012**, *487*, 27–29. [CrossRef] [PubMed]
170. Gan, Y.; Tong, X.; Li, L.; Cao, S.; Yin, X.; Gao, C.; Herath, C.; Li, W.; Jin, Z.; Chen, Y.; et al. Consumption of fruit and vegetable and risk of coronary heart disease: A meta-analysis of prospective cohort studies. *Int. J. Cardiol.* **2015**, *183*, 129–137. [CrossRef]
171. Schulze, M.B.; Manson, J.E.; Ludwig, D.S.; Colditz, G.A.; Stampfer, M.J.; Willett, W.C.; Hu, F.B. Sugar-sweetened beverages, weight gain, and incidence of type 2 diabetes in young and middle-aged women. *JAMA* **2004**, *292*, 927–934. [CrossRef]
172. Reynolds, A.; Mann, J.; Cummings, J.; Winter, N.; Mete, E.; Te Morenga, L. Carbohydrate quality and human health: A series of systematic reviews and meta-analyses. *Lancet* **2019**, *393*, 434–445. [CrossRef]
173. Mintz, S. *Sweetness and Power, The Place of Sugar in Modern History*; Penguin: New York, NY, USA, 1985.
174. Perheentupa, J.; Raivio, K. Fructose-induced hyperuricaemia. *Lancet* **1967**, *2*, 528–531. [CrossRef]
175. Tupala, E.; Tiihonen, J. Dopamine and alcoholism: Neurobiological basis of ethanol abuse. *Prog. Neuropsychopharmacol. Biol. Psychiatry* **2004**, *28*, 1221–1247. [CrossRef] [PubMed]
176. Edwards, G.; Anderson, P.; Babor, T.F.; Casswell, S.; Ferrence, R.; Giesbrecht, N.; Godfrey, C.; Holder, H.D.; Lemmens, P.H.; Mäkelä, K.; et al. Retail price influences on alcohol consumption, and taxation on alcohol as a prevention strategy. In *Alcohol Policy and the Public Good*; Edwards, G., Ed.; Oxford University Press: New York, NY, USA, 1994; pp. 109–213.
177. Greenfield, T.K.; Graves, K.L.; Kaskutas, L.A. Alcohol warning labels for prevention: National survey results. *Alcohol Health Res. World* **1993**, *17*, 67–75.
178. Walls, H.L.; Peeters, A.; Proietto, J.; McNeil, J.J. Public health campaigns and obesity—A critique. *BMC Public Health* **2011**, *11*, 136. [CrossRef]
179. Gonzalez-Suarez, C.; Worley, A.; Grimmer-Somers, K.; Dones, V. School-based interventions on childhood obesity: A meta-analysis. *Am. J. Prev. Med.* **2009**, *37*, 418–427. [CrossRef]
180. Siegel, R.L.; Miller, K.D.; Iemal, A. Cancer statistics, 2020. *CA* **2020**, *70*, 7–30. [CrossRef] [PubMed]
181. Briggs, A.D.M.; Mytton, O.T.; Kehlbacher, A.; Tiffin, R.; Elhussein, A.; Rayner, M.; Jebb, S.A.; Blakely, T.; Scarborough, P. Health impact assessment of the UK soft drinks industry levy: A comparative risk assessment modelling study. *Lancet Public Health* **2016**, *2*, e15–e22. [CrossRef]
182. Lee, Y.; Mozaffarian, D.; Sy, S.; Liu, J.; Wilde, P.E.; Marklund, M.; Abrahams-Gessel, S.; Gaziano, T.A.; Micha, R. Health Impact and Cost-Effectiveness of Volume, Tiered, and Absolute Sugar Content Sugar-Sweetened Beverage Tax Policies in the United States: A Microsimulation Study. *Circulation* **2020**, *142*, 523–534. [CrossRef]
183. Amadeo, K. Farm Subsidies with Pros, Cons, and Impact How Farm Subsidies Affect You. Available online: https://www.thebalance.com/farm-subsidies-4173885 (accessed on 4 July 2019).
184. Alston, J.M.; Sumner, D.A.; Vosti, S.A. *Farm Subsidies and Obesity in the United States*; University of California: Berkeley, CA, USA, 2007; Available online: http://giannini.ucop.edu/media/are-update/files/articles/v11n2_1.pdf (accessed on 27 September 2020).

185. Menzel, P. Hungry Planet: What the World Eats—In pictures. *The Guardian*. 6 May 2019. Available online: https://www.theguardian.com/lifeandstyle/gallery/2013/may/06/hungry-planet-what-world-eats (accessed on 27 September 2020).
186. Crossley, D. 10 Reasons to Take "Our Future in the Land" Seriously. Available online: https://www.foodethicscouncil.org/10-reasons-to-take-our-future-in-the-land-seriously/ (accessed on 27 September 2020).
187. Schmidt, L.A.; Patel, A.; Brindis, C.D.; Lustig, R.H. Towards evidence-based policies for reduction of dietary sugars: Lessons from the alcohol experience. In *Dietary Sugars and Health*; Goran, M.I., Tappy, L., Le, K.A., Eds.; Taylor and Francis: Milton Park, UK, 2014; pp. 371–390.
188. Room, R. *The Effects of Nordic Alcohol Policies: What Happens to Drinking and Harm When Alcohol Controls Change?* Nordic Council for Alcohol and Drug Research: Helsinki, Finland, 2002.
189. Lima, J.M.; Galea, S. Corporate practices and health: A framework and mechanisms. *Glob. Health* **2018**, *14*, 21. [CrossRef]

5

Temperament and Character Traits of Female Eating Disorder Patients with(out) Non-Suicidal Self-Injury

Tinne Buelens [1,*], Koen Luyckx [1,2], Margaux Verschueren [1], Katrien Schoevaerts [3], Eva Dierckx [3,4], Lies Depestele [1,3] and Laurence Claes [1,5]

1 Faculty of Psychology and Educational Sciences, KU Leuven, 3000 Leuven, Belgium; koen.luyckx@kuleuven.be (K.L.); margaux.verschueren@kuleuven.be (M V.); lies.depestele@azt.broedersvanliefde.be (L.D.); laurence.claes@kuleuven.be (L.C.)
2 UNIBS, University of the Free State, 9300 Bloemfontein, South Africa
3 Psychiatric Hospital Alexianen Zorggroep Tienen, 3300 Tienen, Belgium; katrien.schoevaerts@azt.broedersvanliefde.be (K.S.); eva.dierckx@vub.be (E.D.)
4 Department of Psychology and Educational Sciences, Vrije Universiteit Brussel, 1050 Elsene, Belgium
5 Faculty of Medicine and Health Sciences, Universiteit Antwerpen, 2610 Wilrijk, Belgium
* Correspondence: tinne.buelens@kuleuven.be

Abstract: Eating disorder (ED) patients show alarmingly high prevalence rates of Non-Suicidal Self-Injury (NSSI). Adolescents seem to be particularly at risk, as EDs and NSSI both have their onset in mid-adolescence. It has been suggested that personality could be a transdiagnostic mechanism underlying both EDs and NSSI. However, little attention has been given to adolescent clinical samples compared to adult and/or community samples. Therefore, the current study investigated the role of personality in a sample of 189 female inpatients with an ED (M = 15.93, SD = 0.98). Our results confirmed the high prevalence of NSSI in EDs, specifically in patients with bingeing/purging behaviours (ED-BP). Temperamental differences were found between ED-BP and the restrictive ED subtype (ED-R). Namely, ED-BP patients showed more harm avoidance and less self-directedness compared to ED-R. Temperamental differences were found in NSSI as well, regardless of ED subtype: ED patients who had engaged in NSSI during their lifetime reported less self-directedness and more harm avoidance. Interestingly, only ED patients who recently engaged in NSSI showed less novelty seeking. These temperamental profiles should be recognised as key mechanisms in the treatment of adolescent ED patients with and without NSSI.

Keywords: non-suicidal self-injury; temperament; eating disorder; adolescence

---

1. Introduction

Non-Suicidal Self-Injury (NSSI) is defined as any socially unaccepted behaviour through which individuals deliberately and directly injure their own body [1]. NSSI can serve a wide variety of functions to the individual, but the most common self-reported function is to regulate negative emotions [2]. Typical methods of engaging in NSSI are cutting, scratching, burning, or bruising one's own skin [3]. NSSI is strongly associated with internal distress, rejection by peers, rumination, and psychopathology in general, both internalising and externalising symptoms [4–6]. Adolescents seem to be most vulnerable, as NSSI onset peaks in mid-adolescence, around the ages of 14 and 15 [7]. The vulnerability of adolescents is also reflected in NSSI prevalence rates; epidemiological research consistently indicates that as many as 17% of adolescents in non-clinical samples have engaged in NSSI at least once [8–10]. Prevalence rates rise even higher in clinical samples, with young patients with an eating disorder being particularly at risk as up to 60% of this adolescent population engages in NSSI throughout their lifetime [11–14].

Eating disorder (ED) symptomatology, just like NSSI, can be considered a dysfunctional coping strategy to regulate negative affect [15,16]. Both in NSSI and EDs, the body is often perceived as negative and can become the target of emotional dysregulation [17]. EDs include Bulimia Nervosa (BN), characterised by recurrent binge-eating and compensatory behaviours (e.g., purging), and Anorexia Nervosa (AN), characterised by an irrational fear of gaining weight and restricting food intake. By definition, BN patients are at a healthy weight or slightly overweight, whereas AN patients are underweight [18]. However, some underweight patients do show bulimia-like symptoms, such as binge eating and purging. Consequently, AN is further divided into two subtypes: the binge-eating/purging subtype (AN-BP) and the restrictive subtype (AN-R).

A 2007 review [16] reported that AN-BP patients were most likely to engage in self-harming behaviour, with prevalence rates between 27.8% and 68.1% for this subtype. AN-R patients showed the lowest occurrence with prevalence rates between 13.6% and 42.1%. BN patients were in between the two AN subtypes, with self-harm prevalence rates ranging from 26% to 55.2%. However, this review investigated self-harm, which typically includes suicidal behaviour, in contrast to NSSI, which explicitly excludes suicidal thoughts and behaviours. Yet, several other studies have affirmed that AN-BP patients are engaging more frequently in NSSI compared to AN-R patients [19–21]. For instance, in a sample of 226 female ED patients, the lifetime prevalence of NSSI was significantly higher in AN-BP patients compared to AN-R patients [22]. Some uncertainty remains, however, as a handful of studies did not find any significant differences between AN-BP and AN-R [16,23]. Furthermore, research is lacking regarding the NSSI methods that are used by subtypes of ED patients. To the best of our knowledge, only four studies investigated differences in NSSI methods by subtypes of ED patients. Three of these studies did not find any significant difference [19,24,25], whereas one study by Claes et al. [26] reported that cutting was more common in female ED patients with binge/purge behaviour (AN-BP, BN) as compared to those with restrictive behaviour.

To improve understanding regarding the interplay between EDs and NSSI, researchers have been looking for transdiagnostic mechanisms. It has been suggested that personality could be such a transdiagnostic mechanism, underlying both EDs and NSSI [20,27,28]. According to the psychobiological theory of Cloninger et al. [29,30], there are seven dimensions of personality: four genetically determined temperamental dimensions and three learned character dimensions. Novelty seeking (NS) is the first temperamental dimension and refers to curiosity, impulsivity, enthusiasm regarding new experiences, and rash decision-making. Second, harm avoidance (HA) is characterised by shyness, fearfulness and inhibition in social situations. For example, one HA item reads: "When I have to meet a group of strangers, I am more shy than most people" [31]. Moreover, HA is characterised by excessive worrying, insecurity, and pessimism, even in situations where others would not worry or fear. Third, reward dependence (RD) describes seeking out social approval and support, openness to others, and a tendency to respond to signals of reward. Fourth, persistence (PS) refers to a competitive spirit, being inclined towards perfectionism, and showing perseverance in spite of repeated setbacks, frustration, or fatigue. Self-directedness (SD), the first of three character dimensions, is the strong desire to achieve a set of goals and values and the ability to regulate and adapt one's own behaviour to reach these goals. Cloninger described SD as "willpower" [32], more recent literature linked SD to effortful control [33]. Second, cooperativeness (CO) concerns empathy, tolerance, agreeableness, and identification with others. Low CO is associated with a wide range of personality disorders [30]. Third and finally, self-transcendence (ST) involves spirituality and the idea of a transcendental union with nature and the universe.

Several studies used Cloninger's model to trace temperament and character dimensions in psychopathology. For instance, adolescents engaging in NSSI, both patients and non-clinical controls, are characterised by high novelty seeking and low persistence [20,34–36]. High NS and low PS both indicate high impulsivity, which could partially explain why those who engage in NSSI struggle with resisting the urge to self-injure [37]. Nock and Prinstein [38] corroborated the impulsive nature of NSSI and found that many individuals contemplated the act of self-injury for less than five minutes before committing it. High NS and impulsivity are linked to low self-directedness, which is also part of the personality profile of NSSI [39,40]. Those with low SD are more likely to experience emotion regulation difficulties and end up losing executive functions when they encounter a negative affect [40]. These individuals tend to have lower emotional clarity and are less likely to accept their own emotions [41]. The lack of adaptive emotion regulation strategies might push individuals with low SD towards NSSI once they are confronted with an overwhelming negative affect [42]. Contributing to these emotion regulation difficulties are the high harm avoidance levels in the personality profile of NSSI [34]. According to Cloninger, the combination of high NS and high HA results in an approach-avoidance conflict that can cause further affective instability [29]. Results are less clear regarding levels of cooperativeness in those engaging in NSSI: the scores seem to be dependent on the absence or presence of suicidal thoughts and behaviours (STBs) [43]. Specifically, female adolescents who engaged in self-injury and experienced STBs showed higher CO scores compared to those without STBs [43]. So far, no associations have been found between reward dependence and NSSI [34,36].

The temperament and character dimensions of EDs are similar to those of NSSI in terms of self-directedness and harm avoidance. Namely, like NSSI, all ED types are characterised by high harm avoidance [44–47] and low self-directedness when compared to healthy controls [44,45,47]. Within ED subtypes, it was found that individuals with bingeing and purging behaviour (i.e., AN-BP and BN patients) reached even lower SD levels compared to those restricting their food intake (i.e., AN-R patients [46]). Similar to those engaging in NSSI, individuals with bingeing and purging behaviour show high novelty seeking [44–47] and low persistence [44,46,47]. Thus, the tendency for impulsivity and excitableness is common in both NSSI and binge/purge EDs. However, those with restrictive eating behaviour show the exact opposite pattern: low novelty seeking and high persistence. This combination of characteristics is associated with perfectionism, obsessiveness, and rigidity, which may maintain restrictive, calculated eating behaviour [44–47]. In contrast to NSSI, low cooperativeness is generally found in all ED types [44–47]. Finally, although high reward dependence was hypothesised to be a core characteristic of EDs [48], no associations have been found between reward dependence and ED [49,50].

The vast majority of research on EDs and NSSI has been conducted in adult and/or community samples [9,21]. However, the onset of EDs and NSSI occurs during adolescence and prevalence rates peak during these teenage years, particularly so in clinical samples [7,12,13]. Furthermore, little attention has been given to temperament and character traits in adolescent ED patients, be it with or without NSSI, even though previous research has suggested temperament to be a potential transdiagnostic mechanism in EDs and NSSI [20,28]. Therefore, the current study will investigate temperament and character traits in a large sample of young patients diagnosed with an ED and with(out) NSSI. Our first aim is to investigate the frequency and methods of lifetime and recent NSSI across ED subtypes in this sample. Based on previous literature, we expect higher frequencies of lifetime and recent NSSI in ED patients of the bingeing/purging subtype, compared to the restrictive subtype [19–21]. Research is lacking regarding NSSI methods, which leaves us unable to make strong hypotheses on frequencies of NSSI methods across ED subtypes. As a second aim, we will examine temperament and character dimensions in the adolescent ED patients with and without NSSI. Based on the literature summarised above, we hypothesise both ED types to show high harm avoidance, low self-directedness and low cooperativeness. Furthermore, we hypothesise a combination of high novelty seeking and low persistence in patients with a bingeing/purging ED and the opposite combination, low novelty seeking and high persistence, in patients with a restrictive ED [44–47]. If patients are engaging in NSSI, we hypothesise those individuals to be characterised by high novelty seeking, low persistence, low self-directedness, and high harm avoidance [20,34–36].

2. Materials and Methods

2.1. Procedure and Participants.

Between 2011 and 2018, data was collected in female patients who were hospitalised at a specialised inpatient eating disorder ward in Belgium. Shortly after admission, all patients were invited to participate in the study. Those willing to participate provided written informed consent and completed a series of online questionnaires. All patients under 18 years old provided additional parental consent. The procedure of the current study was approved by both the ethical committee of the psychiatric hospital as well as the ethical committee of the faculty of Psychology and Educational Sciences of the first author to use the data retrospectively for research purposes.

The present study included only minor patients who filled out the Eating Disorder Evaluation Scale [51], the Self-Injury Questionnaire-Treatment Related (SIQ-TR [52]) and the brief Dutch version of Cloninger's Temperament and Character Inventory (VTCI [31]). In total, our sample consisted of 189 female patients with an ED, with a mean age of 15.93 years (SD = 0.98, range 14–17 years).

ED diagnoses, as specified in the DSM-5, were diagnosed by means of an interview conducted by experienced psychiatrists or psychologists and further validated with the Eating Disorder Evaluation Scale [51]. AN-R diagnosis was assigned to 87 participants (46%, M_{adjBMI} = 71.91, SD = 7.32), while 56 participants (29.6%, M_{adjBMI} = 74.32, SD = 6.28) were diagnosed with AN-BP, and 46 (24.3%, M_{adjBMI} = 94.67, SD = 8.16) were diagnosed with BN. Subsequently, data of patients with binge-eating/purging behaviours (AN-BP and BN) were merged, given that these patients show similar temperamental profiles [47]. Thus, we performed our analyses on a group of restrictive ED patients (ED-R; n = 87, 46%, M_{age} = 15.91, SD = 0.97) and a group of patients with binge-eating/purging behaviours (ED-BP; n = 102, 54%, M_{age} = 15.95, SD = 0.99), with no significant age difference between them ($F(1, 187) = 0.090$, *ns*). Additionally, we used the 13-item depression subscale of the Symptom Checklist-90 (SCL-90-D, [53]) to further describe our sample. Patients with recent NSSI presented with significantly higher depression scores compared to patients without recent NSSI (F (1, 188) = 13.957, $p < 0.000$, $\eta_p{}^2 = 0.070$). Similarly, patients with lifetime NSSI presented with significantly higher depression scores compared to patients without lifetime NSSI ($F(1, 188) = 9.983$, $p = 0.002$, $\eta_p{}^2 = 0.051$). ED-BP patients reported significantly higher depression scores compared to ED-R patients when lifetime NSSI was included ($F(1, 188) = 4.094$, $p = 0.044$, $\eta_p{}^2 = 0.022$), but not when recent NSSI was included in the analysis ($F(1, 188) = 2.265$, $p = 0.134$, $\eta_p{}^2 = 0.012$). There was no significant interaction between ED subtype and lifetime/recent NSSI in the prediction of mean depression scores.

2.2. Adjusted Body Mass Index (BMI).

We calculated BMI as weight/height^2 using the weight and height measures provided by the adolescents. Subsequently, we compared the BMI to representative values of adolescent girls in Belgium [54] and computed the adjusted BMI as [(BMI/Percentile 50 of BMI for age and gender) × 100]. The adjusted BMI results in a more accurate determination of the weight status of underaged adolescents and was therefore used throughout this study. In the current sample, 75.1% of the participating patients were underweight (n = 142, adjusted BMI ≤ 85) and 24.9% had a normal weight (n = 47, 85 < adjusted BMI < 120).

2.3. Non-Suicidal Self-Injury

NSSI was assessed using the Self-Injury Questionnaire-Treatment Related (SIQ-TR [55]), a self-report questionnaire that has been proven valid and reliable in female ED patient populations [52]. Patients responded to five yes/no items regarding the absence or presence of scratching, bruising, cutting, burning, and biting oneself. For each self-injurious behaviour, they were asked to complete a number of multiple-choice questions regarding the last time they engaged in that behaviour, how often it happened in certain timeframes, whether they experienced any pain during the behaviour, and which thoughts and feelings preceded and followed the NSSI. Based on these responses, recent NSSI (i.e., any form of NSSI within the last month) and lifetime NSSI (i.e., any form of NSSI throughout their life) were calculated. The Kuder–Richardson reliability coefficient for lifetime NSSI and recent NSSI was 0.673 and 0.489, respectively.

2.4. Temperament

The brief Dutch version of Cloninger's Temperament and Character Inventory (VTCI [31]) was administered to assess Cloninger's seven temperament scales; novelty seeking (NS), harm avoidance (HA), reward dependence (RD), persistence (PS), self-directedness (SD), cooperativeness (CO), and self-transcendence (ST) [29], [56]. Each of the seven scales contains 15 yes/no items, resulting in a total of 105 items. The VTCI was found to be a reliable and valid instrument in adolescent patient populations [57]. In the present study, Cronbach's alphas for these seven scales were, respectively, 0.702, 0.763, 0.609, 0.685, 0.806, 0.750, and 0.764.

2.5. Statistical Analyses

To analyse the frequency of the different lifetime/recent NSSI behaviours, descriptive statistics were calculated. The associations between the presence/absence of lifetime/recent NSSI and ED subtype (ED-R, ED-BP), were investigated with cross-tabulations and the Chi-square test statistic. Finally, to investigate temperamental differences between ED-R/ED-BP patients with and without lifetime/recent NSSI we performed two separate MANOVAs, both with the VTCI temperament scales as dependent variables and the ED subtype (ED-R, ED-BP) as an independent variable. In the first MANOVA, we included lifetime NSSI as an additional independent variable. In the second MANOVA, we included recent NSSI as an additional independent variable. In both MANOVAs, the interaction between ED and NSSI was included as the third and final independent variable. Partial eta squared (η^2) was used as a measure of effect size.

3. Results

3.1. Frequency of Lifetime and Recent NSSI

Overall, 59.8% of the patients (n = 113) engaged in at least one act of NSSI during their lifetime whereas 40.2% (n = 76) had never engaged in NSSI. The frequency of the reported lifetime NSSI behaviours, when ED-BP and ED-R were examined together, was distributed as follows: cutting (41.8%, n = 79), scratching (39.7%, n = 75), bruising (27%, n = 51), biting (16.9%, n = 32), and burning (7.9%, n = 15). Table 1 shows the number of different NSSI behaviours (NSSI versatility score) reported by the two ED subtypes. Patients with ED-R reported an average of 2.03 different lifetime NSSI behaviours (SD = 1.13), which was not significantly different from the average of 2.32 different lifetime NSSI behaviours (SD = 1.11) as reported by patients with ED-BP ($F(1, 112) = 1.741$, $p = 0.190$, partial $\eta^2 = 0.015$). However, on the level of individual NSSI behaviours, patients with ED-BP reported significantly more lifetime scratching, bruising, cutting, burning, and biting behaviours compared to patients with ED-R (see Table 2).

With respect to recent NSSI, 41.3% of patients (n = 78) reported at least one act of NSSI during the last week or the last month. The frequency of the recent NSSI behaviours, when ED-BP and ED-R were examined together, was distributed as follows: 25.4% (n = 48) reported scratching, 19.6% (n = 37) cutting, 12.7% (n = 24) bruising, 7.4% (n = 14) biting, and 2.6% (n = 5) burning oneself during the last week or month. The number of days one engaged in each of the five NSSI behaviours can be found in Supplementary Table S1. Patients with ED-R reported an average of 1.41 different recent NSSI behaviours (SD = 0.73), which was not significantly different from the average of 1.73 different recent NSSI behaviours (SD = 0.80) reported by patients with ED-BP ($F(1, 77) = 2.706$, $p = 0.104$, partial $\eta^2 = 0.034$, see Table 1). However, on the level of individual NSSI behaviours, patients with ED-BP reported significantly more recent scratching, bruising, cutting, and burning behaviours compared to ED-R patients (see Table 2).

Table 1. The number of different lifetime and recent NSSI behaviours ED-R and ED-BP engaged in.

	Lifetime NSSI $n = 113$				Recent NSSI $n = 78$			
	ED-R $n = 36$		ED-BP $n = 77$		ED-R $n = 22$		ED-BP $n = 56$	
	% [a]	n	% [a]	n	% [a]	n	% [a]	n
1 behaviour	38.9%	14	28.6%	22	68.2%	15	44.6%	25
2 behaviours	36.1%	13	29.9%	23	27.3%	6	41.1%	23
3 behaviours	13.9%	5	23.4%	18	0%	0	10.7%	6
4 behaviours	5.6%	2	16.9%	13	4.5%	1	3.6%	2
5 behaviours	5.6%	2	1.3%	1	0%	0	0%	0

Note. [a] Percentages of NSSI behaviours within ED category; NSSI = Non-Suicidal Self-Injury; ED-R = eating disorder of the restrictive type; ED-BP = eating disorder of the bingeing/purging type.

Table 2. Presence and absence of five NSSI behaviours in two ED subtypes.

	ED-R $n = 87$				ED-BP $n = 102$				
	Present		Absent		Present		Absent		
	% [a]	n	% [a]	n	% [a]	n	% [a]	n	$X^2_{(1)}$
Lifetime									
Scratch	28.7%	25	71.3%	62	49.0%	50	51.0%	52	8.071 **
Cut	24.1%	21	75.9%	66	56.9%	58	43.1%	44	20.669 ***
Bruise	17.2%	15	82.8%	72	35.3%	36	64.7%	66	7.766 **
Bite	10.3%	9	89.7%	78	22.5%	23	77.5%	79	4.972 *
Burn	3.4%	3	96.6%	84	11.8%	12	88.2%	90	4.444 *
Recent									
Scratch	12.6%	11	87.4%	76	36.3%	37	63.7%	65	13.838 ***
Cut	11.5%	10	88.5%	77	26.5%	27	73.5%	75	6.689 **
Bruise	4.6%	4	95.4%	83	19.6%	20	80.4%	82	9.542 **
Bite	6.9%	6	93.1%	81	7.8%	8	92.2%	94	0.061
Burn	0%	0	100%	87	4.9%	5	95.1%	97	4.381 *

Note. * $p < 0.05$, ** $p < 0.01$, *** $p < .001$; ED-R = Eating Disorder, Restrictive Subtype; ED-BP = Eating Disorder, Binge Eating/Purging Subtype, NSSI = Non-Suicidal Self-Injury. [a] Percentages of absent/present NSSI behaviour within each ED subtype.

The Pearson correlation coefficients between recent/lifetime NSSI and each of the seven temperament and character dimensions can be found in Table 3.

Table 3. Correlation coefficients between study variables.

	Lifetime NSSI	Recent NSSI	NS	HA	RD	PS	SD	CO
Recent NSSI	**0.687** ***							
NS	−0.016	−0.118						
HA	**0.205** **	**0.252** ***	**−0.370** ***					
RD	−0.098	−0.065	0.118	**−0.203** **				
PS	−0.049	0.084	**−0.345** ***	−0.024	0.121			
SD	**−0.225** **	**−0.204** **	0.108	**−0.488** ***	0.130	0.089		
CO	0.043	0.103	**−0.242** **	0.026	**−0.214** **	**−0.232** **	**−0.213** **	
ST	0.093	0.087	0.089	−0.060	0.102	−0.095	**−0.185** *	−0.071

Note. * $p < .05$, ** $p < .01$, *** $p < .001$; Significant correlation coefficients are marked in bold; NS = Novelty Seeking, HA = Harm Avoidance, RD = Reward Dependence, PS = Persistence, SD = Self-Directedness, CO = Cooperativeness, ST = Self-Transcendence.

3.2. *Temperamental Differences between R/BP Patients with(out) Recent NSSI*

With temperamental dimensions as the dependent variables, we included ED type, recent NSSI, and the ED × NSSI interaction as the three independent variables in our first MANOVA. Our results showed a main effect of ED subtype, indicating that there was a significant overall difference in temperamental dimensions, based on ED subtype (Wilks' Lambda = 0.903, $F(7, 179) = 2.733$, $p = 0.01$, partial $\eta^2 = 0.097$). As reported in Table 4, the univariate results further clarified that ED-BP patients reported significantly more novelty seeking and less persistence compared to ED-R patients. Second, our results showed a main effect of recent NSSI, indicating a significant overall difference in temperamental dimensions based on presence or absence of recent NSSI (Wilks' Lambda = 0.88, $F(7, 179) = 3.478$, $p = 0.002$, partial $\eta^2 = 0.12$). Namely, the univariate results in Table 4 show how those engaging in recent NSSI reported significantly less novelty seeking, more harm avoidance, and less self-directedness. Finally, there was no significant interaction between ED subtype and recent NSSI (Wilks' Lambda = 0.985, $F(7, 179) = 0.392$, $p = 0.906$, partial $\eta^2 = 0.015$) in the prediction of temperamental differences. To control for age, we conducted an additional MANCOVA with temperamental dimensions as the dependent variables, ED subtype, recent NSSI and the ED × NSSI interaction as independent variables, and age as a control variable. Age did not reach significance: Wilks' Lambda = 0.974, $F(7, 179) = 0.682$, $p = 0.687$, partial $\eta^2 = 0.026$ and all other results remained the same (i.e., main effect of ED subtype, main effect of recent NSSI, no interaction effect of ED subtype × NSSI).

Table 4. Means and standard deviations of the *z*-scores of the brief Dutch version of Cloninger's Temperament and Character Inventory for ED-R/BP patients with(out) recent NSSI (last week/last month).

	Main Effect ED Subtype					**Main Effect Absence/Presence of $NSSI_R$**				
	ED-R *n = 87*		**ED-BP** *n = 102*			**$NSSI_R = 0$** *n = 111*		**$NSSI_R = 1$** *n = 78*		
	M	***SD***	***M***	***SD***	***F*(1, 185)**	***M***	***SD***	***M***	***SD***	***F*(1, 185)**
NS	−0.25	(0.91)	0.24	(1.04)	18.47 ***	0.11	(1.02)	−0.13	(0.98)	9.04 **
HA	−0.00	(0.96)	−0.00	(1.02)	1.54	−0.21	(1.03)	0.29	(0.85)	14.23 ***
RD	0.02	(1.04)	−0.01	(0.95)	0.02	0.06	(1.07)	−0.07	(0.86)	0.78
PS	0.14	(.78)	−0.12	(1.15)	4.45 *	−0.07	(1.04)	0.10	(0.95)	2.94
SD	0.09	(1.12)	−0.11	(0.90)	0.03	0.16	(1.11)	−0.26	(0.78)	7.70 **
CO	0.07	(1.09)	−0.07	(0.92)	1.76	−0.09	(1.06)	0.12	(0.91)	2.75
ST	−0.12	(1.01)	0.08	(1.01)	1.08	−0.08	(0.93)	0.09	(1.11)	0.57

Note. * $p < 0.05$, ** $p < 0.01$, *** $p < 0.001$; ED-R = Eating Disorder, Restrictive Subtype; ED-BP = Eating Disorder, Binge Eating/Purging Subtype, $NSSI_R$ = Recent Non-Suicidal Self-Injury; NS = Novelty Seeking, HA = Harm Avoidance, RD = Reward Dependence, PS = Persistence, SD = Self-Directedness, CO = Cooperativeness, ST = Self-Transcendence.

3.3. *Temperamental Differences between R/BP Patients with(out) Lifetime NSSI*

In a second MANOVA, we substituted recent NSSI for lifetime NSSI while the other variables remained the same as in the first MANOVA. Thus, temperamental dimensions remained included as the dependent variables, and ED subtype, recent NSSI, and the ED × NSSI interaction term were included as the three independent variables. First, the main effect of ED subtype did not reach significance (Wilks' Lambda = 0.93, $F(7, 179) = 1.89$, $p = 0.073$, partial $\eta^2 = 0.069$). This lack of significance could potentially be ascribed to a statistical artefact. Specifically, by substituting one independent variable with another, the degrees of freedom and the level of explained variance might deviate slightly, which can result in a different main effect. For completeness, we did still include the univariate level in Table 5. Second, our results showed a main effect of NSSI, indicating a significant overall difference in temperamental dimensions based on the presence or absence of lifetime NSSI (Wilks' Lambda = 0.921, $F(7, 179) = 2.198$, $p = 0.036$, partial $\eta^2 = 0.079$). As described in Table 5, the univariate results clarified that those who engaged in lifetime NSSI reported significantly more harm avoidance and less self-directedness compared to those without lifetime NSSI. Contrasting our findings with recent NSSI, there was no significant difference in the level of novelty seeking between those with and without lifetime NSSI. Finally, the results did not show a significant interaction between ED subtype and lifetime NSSI (Wilks' Lambda = 0.98, $F(7, 179) = 0.49$, $p = 0.838$, partial $\eta^2 = 0.019$), indicating that the association between temperament and NSSI is similar in both ED subtypes. To control for age, we conducted an additional MANCOVA with temperamental dimensions as the dependent variables, ED subtype, lifetime NSSI and the ED × NSSI interaction as independent variables, and age as a control variable. Age did not reach significance: Wilks' Lambda = 0.974, $F(7, 179) = 0.667$, $p = 0.700$, partial $\eta^2 = 0.026$ and all other results remained the same (i.e., main effect of ED subtype, main effect of lifetime NSSI, no interaction effect of ED subtype × NSSI).

Table 5. Means and standard deviations of the *z*-scores of the brief Dutch version of Cloninger's Temperament and Character Inventory for ED-R/BP patients with(out) lifetime NSSI.

	Main Effect ED Subtype					**Main Effect Absence/Presence of $NSSI_L$**				
	ED-R *n = 87*		**ED-BP** *n = 102*			**$NSSI_L = 0$** *n = 76*		**$NSSI_L = 1$** *n = 113*		
	M	*SD*	*M*	*SD*	*F(1, 185)1*	*M*	*SD*	*M*	*SD*	*F(1, 185)*
NS	−0.25	(0.91)	0.24	(1.04)	12.68 ***	0.03	(0.99)	0.00	(1.03)	2.16
HA	0.00	(0.96)	0.00	(1.02)	0.97	−0.25	(0.97)	0.16	(0.98)	9.19 **
RD	0.02	(1.04)	−0.01	(0.95)	0.07	0.12	(1.01)	−0.07	(0.97)	1.82
PS	0.14	(0.78)	−0.12	(115)	1.87	0.06	(0.87)	−0.04	(1.09)	0.02
SD	0.09	(1.12)	−0.11	(0.90)	0.20	0.26	(1.16)	−0.20	(0.84)	7.82 **
CO	0.08	(1.08)	−0.08	(0.92)	1.92	−0.06	(1.05)	0.03	(0.98)	1.06
ST	−0.12	(1.01)	0.08	(1.01)	0.63	−0.12	(0.93)	0.07	(1.06)	0.82

Note. ** $p < 0.01$, *** $p < 0.001$; ED-R = Eating Disorder, Restrictive Subtype; ED-BP = Eating Disorder, Binge Eating/Purging Subtype, $NSSI_L$ = Lifetime Non-Suicidal Self-Injury; NS = Novelty Seeking, HA = Harm Avoidance, RD = Reward Dependence, PS = Persistence, SD = Self-Directedness, CO = Cooperativeness, ST = Self-Transcendence.

4. Discussion

The prevalence rates of NSSI in patients with any ED are alarmingly high. Both EDs and NSSI are driven by certain temperamental vulnerabilities, which, in their turn, increase the risk for later personality disorders [58,59]. To improve intervention of EDs and NSSI and prevention of later personality disorders, it is crucial to develop a thorough understanding of transdiagnostic temperamental vulnerabilities in adolescents. The vast majority of research on temperamental dimensions in EDs and NSSI has been conducted in adult samples [9,21]. Therefore, the current study examined temperament and character dimensions in a sample of adolescent ED patients with and without NSSI.

As a first aim, the present study investigated the prevalence of NSSI as well as the methods used to engage in NSSI. Our results confirmed the alarmingly high prevalence rates of NSSI previously found in young ED patients [16]. Namely, 60% of the current sample reported lifetime NSSI (i.e., having ever engaged in NSSI) and 40% of the sample reported recent NSSI (i.e., having engaged in NSSI in the past month). Thus, as this information was collected shortly after admission to an inpatient treatment facility, the latter indicates that 40% of the adolescents engaged in NSSI right before and/or during their ED treatment at the hospital ward. Interestingly, previous phenomenological qualitative research described how, during treatment, individuals with an ED experienced a loss of control when they were pressured to eat [60]. To lose control in one domain, be it due to treatment or due to pressure by parents or peers, often requires compensation in another domain [61]. Indeed, the participants in the phenomenological study reported how NSSI functioned as a means of control over anorectic thoughts and overwhelming emotions when they felt pressured to eat [60]. Future systematic research could investigate whether the high prevalence rates of NSSI found in the current study could be due to patients attempting to regain a sense of control.

Our results confirmed cutting and scratching to be the most common forms of NSSI, with, respectively, 42% and 40% of ED patients having engaged in these behaviours [16]. Moreover, each of the five assessed NSSI behaviours was significantly more common in patients of the ED-BP subtype, compared to the ED-R subtype. This ED-R/ED-BP distinction remained unchanged whether lifetime NSSI behaviours or recent NSSI behaviours were assessed. These findings align with previous research, which indicated that ED patients with bingeing/purging symptomatology engaged more often in NSSI overall [19–21]. Only for "biting oneself in the last month" the difference between ED-R and ED-BP did not reach significance, possibly due to the very low prevalence rate of "biting oneself" in both groups. Previously, research was lacking in how the specific NSSI behaviours compared between ED subtypes. With only four previous studies available, our results innovate by providing evidence for higher lifetime prevalence of cutting, scratching, bruising, biting, and burning in ED-BP compared to ED-R patients.

In search of a transdiagnostic mechanism in the ED–NSSI interplay, the current study investigated temperament and character dimensions as a second aim. First, our results showed significant differences in temperament and character based on ED subtype. Namely, patients with ED-BP showed significantly more novelty seeking and less persistence compared to patients with ED-R. Thus, the ED-BP patients had a greater tendency to seek out new, exciting experiences, possibly making impulsive decisions while doing so (high novelty seeking). Additionally, they were less likely than the ED-R patients to persevere and overcome setbacks or frustration, but rather felt frustrated or overwhelmed (low persistence). The differences between ED-BP and ED-R patients as found in the present study are consistent with ED literature [62–65]. Furthermore, both high novelty seeking and low persistence indicate impulse dysregulation, which previous research indeed attributed to bingeing and purging behaviours in ED patients [38]. Importantly, because NSSI too is characterised by high novelty seeking and low persistence [20,34–36], this temperamental profile might function as a transdiagnostic mechanism explaining the high comorbidity between NSSI and ED-BP specifically.

Second, our results showed significant differences in temperament and character based on the presence or absence of NSSI, regardless of the ED subtype. Specifically, ED patients with recent and/or lifetime NSSI reported less self-directedness and more harm avoidance compared to patients who were not engaging in NSSI. Thus, ED patients engaging in NSSI experience less control over their own emotions, they struggle to regulate themselves to set and reach goals (low self-directedness). They lack emotion regulation skills in comparison to adolescent ED patients who do not engage in NSSI. Moreover, NSSI in ED patients was associated with high harm avoidance, which indicates shyness and anxiety in social situations as well as excessive worrying and insecurity regarding interactions with others. These findings align with previous research indicating that emotion dysregulation and an increased amount of negative thoughts and feelings are common in those engaging in NSSI [5,61,66]. Specifically in ED patient populations, high harm avoidance can be related to self-punishment and rumination for those who self-injure. Patients with an ED who additionally engage in NSSI tend to be more concerned about meeting expectations of themselves and others, compared to patients with and ED who do not engage in NSSI [67]. In a qualitative study, ED patients in treatment facilities described how they would use NSSI to punish themselves when they failed to meet their own standards or felt that they had disappointed healthcare workers [60]. In conclusion, the temperamental profile of low self-directedness and high harm avoidance characterises patients with any ED who engage in NSSI.

Interestingly, when studying temperament in ED patients with recent NSSI, one more dimension besides low self-directedness and high harm avoidance showed up as significantly different in those with and without recent NSSI, regardless of ED subtype. Namely, ED patients engaging in recent NSSI reported significantly less novelty seeking. This stands for less curiosity and less impulsivity in those with recent NSSI, as they were less likely to seek out or be interested in new experiences, compared to ED patients without recent NSSI. Previous research, however, typically reported high levels of novelty seeking in adolescent patients engaging in NSSI [20,34–36]. Remarkably, these studies generally assessed lifetime, rather than recent, NSSI. A tentative suggestion as to why we found low novelty seeking in those with recent NSSI, could be the comorbidity of NSSI with depression at the time of assessment.

Depression is typified by high harm avoidance and low self-directedness and, importantly, low novelty seeking; a lack of interest, enthusiasm, and curiosity in one's surroundings [68]. At the time of assessment, those engaging in recent NSSI might have presented with more outspoken depressive symptoms, resulting in lower levels of novelty seeking compared to those without recent NSSI. Previous studies have indeed shown that at NSSI onset, impulsivity and high novelty seeking are common [34,69]. When individuals first start engaging in NSSI, often by experimenting once or twice with a certain method of self-injury, they are more likely to be looking for sensation or a new experience. Consequently, studies investigating lifetime NSSI report high novelty seeking [20,34–36]. However, research on various addictive behaviours suggested that, once the behaviour goes beyond mere experimenting and becomes a coping strategy in response to psychiatric distress, the impulsive, sensation-seeking function loses ground [70]. Rather, the emotion regulation function might become more salient as those with severe, persistent addiction(s) and comorbid psychopathology report engaging in the behaviour to avoid and regulate overwhelming negative affect [70]. Although future research should assess if this parallel with research on addiction is justified, our results on NSSI in ED patients do suggest a similar pattern. Namely, ED patients who present at a treatment facility with recent NSSI show temperamental and character dimensions resembling depression: low self-directedness, high harm avoidance, and, contrasting previous research, low novelty seeking.

The results of the current study support the focus on emotion and impulse dysregulation in evidence-based treatment of NSSI in ED patients. For instance, Dialectical Behavioural Therapy [71] and the Cutting Down treatment programme [72] have been proven effective in this specific patient population. High levels of harm avoidance could be related to serotonergic dysfunction [73] and could, therefore, be targeted by pharmacological treatments, for instance by the use of SSRI to focus on binge eating and self-harm in depressed ED patients [73]. Low levels of self-directedness could be treated by executive function training (e.g., by means of the "Playmancer" computer game [74]).

Although the present study contributes to the understanding of temperament ED patients with and without NSSI, our research is not without limitations. First, our findings are based solely on adolescent self-report questionnaires. Collecting self-report data from a single piece of information could result in reporting bias [75]. However, while we could have assessed peers, parents, or teachers about NSSI and its correlates, research has shown that people do not always observe internalising behaviours accurately in others [76], making NSSI and temperament often difficult to assess by other informants. Additionally, NSSI is often secretive [77] and people close to the adolescent who engages in NSSI, such as parents, are often unaware of the presence or severity of the NSSI [78]. Future research could embrace a multi-method approach and include structured or semi-structured interviews with the adolescents and/or use behavioural measures. Second, because the present study sample solely consists of adolescent girls in an eating disorder treatment facility, we cannot generalise the reported findings to male populations, younger or older individuals, or those receiving ambulatory care. Third, our conclusions are restricted by the cross-sectional nature of our study. As the field moves forward, longitudinal studies will be necessary to examine the developmental course and directionality of effects of temperament in ED patients with and without NSSI.

Author Contributions: Conceptualisation, K.L., K.S., L.D. and L.C.; data curation, E.D.; formal analysis, T.B. and L.C.; funding acquisition, K.L. and L.C.; investigation, K.S., E.D. and L.D.; methodology, K.L. and L.C.; project administration, T.B., K.L., M.V., K.S., E.D., L.D. and L.C.; resources, K.L. and L.C.; software, E.D.; supervision, K.L. and L.C.; validation, T.B., K.L., M.V., K.S., E.D., L.D. and L.C.; writing—original draft, T.B. and L.C.; writing—review and editing, T.B., K.L., M.V., L.D. and L.C. All authors have read and agreed to the published version of the manuscript.

References

1. Favazza, A.R. Nonsuicidal self-injury: Definition and classification. In *Understanding Nonsuicidal Self-Injury: Origins, Assessment, and Treatment*; American Psychological Association (APA): Washington, DC, USA, 2009; pp. 9–18.
2. Nock, M.K.; Cha, C. Psychological models of non-suicidal self-injury. In *Understanding Nonsuicidal Self-Injury: Origins, Assessment, and Treatment*; American Psychological Association (APA): Washington, DC, USA, 2009.
3. Nock, M.K. Why Do People Hurt Themselves? *Curr. Dir. Psychol. Sci.* **2009**, *18*, 78–83. [CrossRef]
4. Wilkinson, P.O.; Qiu, T.; Neufeld, S.; Jones, P.M.; Goodyer, I.M. Sporadic and recurrent non-suicidal self-injury before age 14 and incident onset of psychiatric disorders by 17 years: Prospective cohort study. *Br. J. Psychiatry* **2018**, *212*, 222–226. [CrossRef] [PubMed]
5. Buelens, T.; Luyckx, K.; Gandhi, A.; Kiekens, G.; Claes, L. Non-Suicidal Self-Injury in Adolescence: Longitudinal Associations with Psychological Distress and Rumination. *J. Abnorm. Child Psychol.* **2019**, *47*, 1569–1581. [CrossRef] [PubMed]
6. Crouch, W.; Wright, J. Deliberate Self-Harm at an Adolescent Unit: A Qualitative Investigation. *Clin. Child Psychol. Psychiatry* **2004**, *9*, 185–204. [CrossRef]
7. Gandhi, A.; Luyckx, K.; Baetens, I.; Kiekens, G.; Sleuwaegen, E.; Berens, A.; Maitra, S.; Claes, L. Age of onset of non-suicidal self-injury in Dutch-speaking adolescents and emerging adults: An event history analysis of pooled data. *Compr. Psychiatry* **2018**, *80*, 170–178. [CrossRef]
8. Muehlenkamp, J.J.; Claes, L.; Havertape, L.; Plener, P.L. International prevalence of adolescent non-suicidal self-injury and deliberate self-harm. *Child Adolesc. Psychiatry Ment. Health* **2012**, *6*, 10. [CrossRef]
9. Swannell, S.; Martin, G.; Page, A.N.; Hasking, P.; John, N.J.S. Prevalence of Nonsuicidal Self-Injury in Nonclinical Samples: Systematic Review, Meta-Analysis and Meta-Regression. *Suicide Life-Threat. Behav.* **2014**, *44*, 273–303. [CrossRef]
10. Buelens, T.; Luyckx, K.; Kiekens, G.; Gandhi, A.; Muehlenkamp, J.J.; Claes, L. Investigating the DSM-5 criteria for non-suicidal self-injury disorder in a community sample of adolescents. *J. Affect. Disord.* **2019**, *260*, 314–322. [CrossRef]
11. Muehlenkamp, J.J.; Claes, L.; Smits, D.; Peat, C.M.; Vandereycken, W. Non-suicidal self-injury in eating disordered patients: A test of a conceptual model. *Psychiatry Res.* **2011**, *188*, 102–108. [CrossRef]
12. Volpe, U.; Tortorella, A.; Manchia, M.; Monteleone, A.M.; Albert, U.; Monteleone, P. Eating disorders: What age at onset ? *Psychiatry Research* **2016**, *238*, 225–227. [CrossRef]
13. Kostro, K.; Lerman, J.B.; Attia, E. The current status of suicide and self-injury in eating disorders: A narrative review. *J. Eat. Disord.* **2014**, *2*, 19. [CrossRef]
14. Peebles, R.; Wilson, J.L.; Lock, J.D. Self-Injury in Adolescents With Eating Disorders: Correlates and Provider Bias. *J. Adolesc. Health* **2010**, *48*, 310–313. [CrossRef] [PubMed]
15. Claes, L.; Luyckx, K.; Bijttebier, P.; Turner, B.J.; Ghandi, A.; Smets, J.; Norré, J.; Van Assche, L.; Verheyen, E.; Goris, Y.; et al. Non-Suicidal Self-Injury in Patients with Eating Disorder: Associations with Identity Formation Above and Beyond Anxiety and Depression. *Eur. Eat. Disord. Rev.* **2014**, *23*, 119–125. [CrossRef] [PubMed]
16. Svirko, E.; Hawton, K. Self-Injurious Behavior and Eating Disorders: The Extent and Nature of the Association. *Suicide Life-Threat. Behav.* **2007**, *37*, 409–421. [CrossRef] [PubMed]
17. Sansone, R.A.; Sansone, L.A. Personality Disorders as Risk Factors for Eating Disorders. *Nutr. Clin. Pract.* **2010**, *25*, 116–121. [CrossRef] [PubMed]
18. McElroy, S.L.; Frye, M.A.; Hellemann, G.; Altshuler, L.; Leverich, G.S.; Suppes, T.; Keck, P.E.; Nolen, W.A.; Kupka, R.; Post, R.M. Prevalence and correlates of eating disorders in 875 patients with bipolar disorder. *J. Affect. Disord.* **2011**, *128*, 191–198. [CrossRef]
19. Favaro, A.; Santonastaso, P. Self-injurious behaviour in anorexia nervosa. *J. Nerv. Ment. Dis.* **2000**, *188*, 537–543. [CrossRef]
20. Davico, C.; Amianto, F.; Gaiotti, F.; Lasorsa, C.; Peloso, A.; Bosia, C.; Vesco, S.; Arletti, L.; Reale, L.; Vitiello, B. Clinical and personality characteristics of adolescents with anorexia nervosa with or without non-suicidal self-injurious behavior. *Compr. Psychiatry* **2019**, *94*, 152115. [CrossRef]

21. Bühren, K.; Schwarte, R.; Fluck, F.; Timmesfeld, N.; Krei, M.; Egberts, K.; Pfeiffer, E.; Fleischhaker, C.; Wewetzer, C.; Herpertz-Dahlmann, B. Comorbid Psychiatric Disorders in Female Adolescents with First-Onset Anorexia Nervosa. *Eur. Eat. Disord. Rev.* **2013**, *22*, 39–44. [CrossRef]
22. Perez, S.; Marco, J.H.; Cañabate, M. Non-suicidal self-injury in patients with eating disorders: Prevalence, forms, functions, and body image correlates. *Compr. Psychiatry* **2018**, *84*, 32–38. [CrossRef]
23. Claes, L.; Vandereycken, W.; Vertommen, H. Personality traits in eating disordered patients with and without self-injurious behaviours. *J. Personal. Disord.* **2004**, *18*, 399–404. [CrossRef]
24. Favaro, A.; Santonastaso, P. Different types of self-injurious behavior in bulimia nervosa. *Compr. Psychiatry* **1999**, *40*, 57–60. [CrossRef]
25. Claes, L.; Vandereycken, W.; Vertommen, H. Eating-disordered patients with and without self-injurious behaviours: A comparison of psychopathological features. *Eur. Eat. Disord. Rev.* **2003**, *11*, 379–396. [CrossRef]
26. Claes, L.; Vandereycken, W.; Vertommen, H. Self-injurious behaviors in eating-disordered patients. *Eat. Behav.* **2001**, *2*, 263–272. [CrossRef]
27. Baetens, I.; Claes, L.; Willem, L.; Muehlenkamp, J.; Bijttebier, P. The relationship between non-suicidal self-injury and temperament in male and female adolescents based on child- and parent-report. *Pers. Individ. Differ.* **2011**, *50*, 527–530. [CrossRef]
28. Claes, L.; Norré, J.; Van Assche, L.; Bijttebier, P. Non-suicidal self-injury (functions) in eating disorders: Associations with reactive and regulative temperament. *Personal. Individ. Differ.* **2014**, *57*, 65–69. [CrossRef]
29. Cloninger, C.R.; Przybeck, T.R.; Svrakic, D.M.; Wetzel, R.D. *The Temperament and Character Inventory (TCI): A Guide to Its Development and Use*; Center for Psychobiology of Personality: St. Louis, MI, USA, 1994.
30. De Fruyt, F.; Van De Wiele, L.; Van Heeringen, C. Cloninger's Psychobiological Model of Temperament and Character and the Five-Factor Model of Personality. *Personal. Individ. Differ.* **2000**, *29*, 441–452. [CrossRef]
31. Duijsens, I.J.; Spinhoven, P. *Handleiding Van De Nederlandse Verkorte Temperament En Karakter Vragenlijst*; Datec: Leiderdorp, The Netherlands, 2001.
32. Cloninger, C.R.; Svrakic, D.M.; Przybeck, T.R. A Psychobiological Model of Temperament and Character. *Arch. Gen. Psychiatry* **1993**, *50*, 975. [CrossRef]
33. Evans, D.E.; Rothbart, M.K. Developing a model for adult temperament. *J. Res. Personal.* **2007**, *41*, 868–888. [CrossRef]
34. Tschan, T.; Peter-Ruf, C.; Schmid, M.; In-Albon, T. Temperament and character traits in female adolescents with nonsuicidal self-injury disorder with and without comorbid borderline personality disorder. *Child Adolesc. Psychiatry Ment. Health* **2017**, *11*, 4. [CrossRef]
35. Joyce, P.R.; Light, K.J.; Rowe, S.; Cloninger, C.R.; Kennedy, M.A. Self-Mutilation and Suicide Attempts: Relationships to Bipolar Disorder, Borderline Personality Disorder, Temperament and Character. *Aust. N. Z. J. Psychiatry* **2010**, *44*, 250–257. [CrossRef] [PubMed]
36. Hefti, S.; In-Albon, T.; Schmeck, K.; Schmid, M. Temperaments- und Charaktereigenschaften und selbstverletzendes Verhalten bei Jugendlichen. *Nervenheilkd* **2013**, *32*, 45–53. [CrossRef]
37. Bresin, K.; Carter, D.L.; Gordon, K.H. The relationship between trait impulsivity, negative affective states, and urge for nonsuicidal self-injury: A daily diary study. *Psychiatry Res.* **2013**, *205*, 227–231. [CrossRef] [PubMed]
38. Nock, M.K.; Prinstein, M.J. Contextual Features and Behavioral Functions of Self-Mutilation Among Adolescents. *J. Abnorm. Psychol.* **2005**, *114*, 140–146. [CrossRef] [PubMed]
39. Doran, N.; McChargue, D.; Cohen, L. Impulsivity and the reinforcing value of cigarette smoking. *Addict. Behav.* **2007**, *32*, 90–98. [CrossRef]
40. Lüdtke, J.; Weizenegger, B.; Rauber, R.; Contin, B.; In-Albon, T.; Schmid, M. The influence of personality traits and emotional and behavioral problems on repetitive nonsuicidal self-injury in a school sample. *Compr. Psychiatry* **2017**, *74*, 214–223. [CrossRef]
41. Wolz, I.; Agüera, Z.; Granero, R.; Jiménez-Murcia, S.; Gratz, K.L.; Menchón, J.M.; Fernández-Aranda, F. Emotion regulation in disordered eating: Psychometric properties of the Difficulties in Emotion Regulation Scale among Spanish adults and its interrelations with personality and clinical severity. *Front. Psychol.* **2015**, *6*. [CrossRef]
42. Andover, M.S.; Morris, B.W. Expanding and Clarifying the Role of Emotion Regulation in Nonsuicidal Self-Injury. *Can. J. Psychiatry* **2014**, *59*, 569–575. [CrossRef]

43. Ohmann, S.; Schuch, B.; König, M.; Blaas, S.; Fliri, C.; Popow, C. Self-Injurious Behavior in Adolescent Girls. *Psychopathol.* **2008**, *41*, 226–235. [CrossRef]
44. Fassino, S.; Abbate-Daga, G.; Amianto, F.; Leombruni, P.; Boggio, S.; Rovera, G.G. Temperament and character profile of eating disorders: A controlled study with the Temperament and Character Inventory. *Int. J. Eat. Disord.* **2002**, *32*, 412–425. [CrossRef]
45. Fassino, S.; Abbate-Daga, G.; Pierò, A.; Leombruni, P.; Rovera, G.G. Anger and personality in eating disorders. *J. Psychosom. Res.* **2001**, *51*, 757–764. [CrossRef] [PubMed]
46. Klump, K.L.; Bulik, C.M.; Pollice, C.; A Halmi, K.; Fichter, M.; Berrettini, W.H.; Devlin, B.; Strober, M.; Kaplan, A.; Woodside, D.B.; et al. Temperament and Character in Women with Anorexia Nervosa. *J. Nerv. Ment. Dis.* **2000**, *188*, 559–567. [CrossRef] [PubMed]
47. Cassin, S.E.; Von Ranson, K.M. Personality and eating disorders: A decade in review. *Clin. Psychol. Rev.* **2005**, *25*, 895–916. [CrossRef] [PubMed]
48. Strober, M. Disorders of the self in anorexia nervosa: An organismic-developmental perspective. In *Psychodynamic Theory and Treatment of Anorexia Nervosa and Bulimia*; Guildford Press: New York, NY, USA, 1992; pp. 354–373.
49. Brewerton, T.D.; Hand, L.D.; Bishop, E.R. The tridimensional personality questionnaire in eating disorder patients. *Int. J. Eat. Disord.* **1993**, *14*, 213–218. [CrossRef] [PubMed]
50. Bulik, C.M.; Sullivan, P.F.; Fear, J.L.; Pickering, A. Outcome of anorexia nervosa: Eating attitudes, personality, and parental bonding. *Int. J. Eat. Disord.* **2000**, *28*, 139–147. [PubMed]
51. Vandereycken, W. The eating disorder evaluation scale (EDES). *Eat. Disord.* **1993**, *1*, 115–122. [CrossRef]
52. Claes, L.; Vandereycken, W. The Self-Injury Questionnaire-Treatment Related (SIQ-TR): Construction, reliability, and validity in a sample of female eating disorder patients. In *Psychological Tests*; Goldfarb, M., Ed.; Nova Science: New York, NY, USA, 2007.
53. Jorgenson, J. Symptom Checklist-90-Revised. *Encycl. Personal. Individ. Differ.* **2017**, 1–4. [CrossRef]
54. Roelants, M.; Hauspie, R. Groeicurven 2-20 jaar, Vlaanderen 2004 [Growth Charts 2–20 Years, Flanders 2004]. 2004. Available online: http://www.vub.ac.be/groeicurven (accessed on 11 March 2020).
55. Claes, L.; Vandereycken, W. The Self-Injury Questionnaire-Treatment Related. In *Psychological Tests and Testing Research Trends*; Goldfarb, P.M., Ed.; Nova Science: New York, NY, USA, 2007; pp. 111–139.
56. Svrakic, D.M.; Whitehead, C.; Przybeck, T.R.; Cloninger, C.R. Differential Diagnosis of Personality Disorders by the Seven-Factor Model of Temperament and Character. *Arch. Gen. Psychiatry* **1993**, *50*, 991. [CrossRef]
57. Duijsens, I.J.; Spinhoven, P.; Verschuur, M.; Eurelings-Bontekoe, E.H.M. De ontwikkeling van de nederlandse verkorte temperament en karakter vragenlijst (TCI-105). *Ned. Tijdschr. Psychol.* **1999**, *54*, 276–283.
58. Cloninger, C.R. A practical way to diagnosis personality disorder: A proposal. *J. Personal. Disord.* **2000**, *14*, 99–108. [CrossRef]
59. Mervielde, I.; De Clercq, B.; De Fruyt, F.; Van Leeuwen, K. Temperament, Personality, and Developmental Psychopathology as Childhood Antecedents of Personality Disorders. *J. Personal. Disord.* **2005**, *19*, 171–201. [CrossRef] [PubMed]
60. Verschueren, S.; Berends, T.; Kool-Goudzwaard, N.; Van Huigenbosch, E.; Gamel, C.; Dingemans, A.; Van Elburg, A.; Van Meijel, B. Patients With Anorexia Nervosa Who Self-Injure: A Phenomenological Study. *Perspect. Psychiatr. Care* **2014**, *51*, 63–70. [CrossRef] [PubMed]
61. Muehlenkamp, J.J.; Engel, S.G.; Wadeson, A.; Crosby, R.D.; Wonderlich, S.A.; Simonich, H.; Mitchell, J.E. Emotional states preceding and following acts of non-suicidal self-injury in bulimia nervosa patients. *Behav. Res. Ther.* **2008**, *47*, 83–87. [CrossRef] [PubMed]
62. Claes, L.; Vandereycken, W. Is There a Link between Traumatic Experiences and Self-Injurious Behaviors in Eating-Disordered Patients? *Eat. Disord.* **2007**, *15*, 305–315. [CrossRef] [PubMed]
63. DeJong, H.; Oldershaw, A.; Sternheim, L.; Samarawickrema, N.; Kenyon, M.; Broadbent, H.; Lavender, A.; Startup, H.; Treasure, J.; Schmidt, U. Quality of life in anorexia nervosa, bulimia nervosa and eating disorder not-otherwise-specified. *J. Eat. Disord.* **2013**, *1*, 43. [CrossRef]
64. Sanci, L.; Coffey, C.; Olsson, C.; Reid, S.; Carlin, J.; Patton, G. Childhood Sexual Abuse and Eating Disorders in Females. *Arch. Pediatr. Adolesc. Med.* **2008**, *162*, 261. [CrossRef]

65. Vanderlinden, J.; Schoevaerts, K.; Simons, A.; Eede, U.V.D.; Bruffaerts, R.; Serra, R.; Van Roie, E.; Vervaet, M.; Janssens, N.; Vrieze, E. Sociodemographic and clinical characteristics of eating disorder patients treated in the specialized residential settings in Belgium. *Eat. Weight. Disord.—Stud. Anorexia, Bulim. Obes.* **2020**, 1–7. [CrossRef]
66. Klonsky, E.D.; Victor, S.; Saffer, B.Y. Nonsuicidal self-injury: What we know, and what we need to know. *Can. J. Psychiatry* **2014**, *59*, 565–568. [CrossRef]
67. Claes, L.; Soenens, B.; Vansteenkiste, M.; Vandereycken, W. The Scars of the Inner Critic: Perfectionism and Nonsuicidal Self-Injury in Eating Disorders. *Eur. Eat. Disord. Rev.* **2011**, *20*, 196–202. [CrossRef]
68. Bijttebier, P.; Beck, I.; Claes, L.; Vandereycken, W. Gray's Reinforcement Sensitivity Theory as a framework for research on personality–psychopathology associations. *Clin. Psychol. Rev.* **2009**, *29*, 421–430. [CrossRef]
69. Riley, E.N.; Combs, J.L.; Jordan, C.E.; Smith, G.T. Negative Urgency and Lack of Perseverance: Identification of Differential Pathways of Onset and Maintenance Risk in the Longitudinal Prediction of Nonsuicidal Self-Injury. *Behav. Ther.* **2015**, *46*, 439–448. [CrossRef] [PubMed]
70. Brand, M.; Wegmann, E.; Stark, R.; Müller, A.; Wölfling, K.; Robbins, T.W.; Potenza, M.N. The Interaction of Person-Affect-Cognition-Execution (I-PACE) model for addictive behaviors: Update, generalization to addictive behaviors beyond internet-use disorders, and specification of the process character of addictive behaviors. *Neurosci. Biobehav. Rev.* **2019**, *104*, 1–10. [CrossRef] [PubMed]
71. Linehan, M.M. *Skills Training Manual for Treating Borderline Personality Disorder*; Guildford Press: New York, NY, USA, 1993.
72. Taylor, L. *Cutting Down: A CBT Workbook for Treating Young People who Self-Harm*; Informa UK Limited: Colchester, UK, 2015.
73. Claes, L.; Muehlenkamp, J.J. Non-suicidal self-injury and eating disorders: Dimensions of self-harm. In *Non-Suicidal Self-Injury in Eating Disorders*; Claes, L., Muehlenkamp, J.J., Eds.; Springer: Berlin/Heidelberg, Germany, 2014; pp. 3–18.
74. Giner-Bartolomé, C.; Fagundo, A.B.; Sanchez, I.; Jiménez-Murcia, S.; Santamaría, J.J.; Ladouceur, R.; Menchón, J.M.; Fernández-Aranda, F. Can an intervention based on a serious videogame prior to cognitive behavioral therapy be helpful in bulimia nervosa? A clinical case study. *Front. Psychol.* **2015**, *6*, 1–9. [CrossRef] [PubMed]
75. Podsakoff, P.M.; MacKenzie, S.B.; Lee, J.-Y.; Podsakoff, N.P. Common method biases in behavioral research: A critical review of the literature and recommended remedies. *J. Appl. Psychol.* **2003**, *88*, 879–903. [CrossRef]
76. Achenbach, T.M.; Mcconaughy, S.H.; Howell, C.T. Child/adolescent behavioral and emotional problems: Implications of cross-informant correlations for situational specificity. *Psychol. Bull.* **1987**, *101*, 213–232. [CrossRef]
77. Baetens, I.; Claes, L.; Muehlenkamp, J.; Grietens, H.; Onghena, P. Non-Suicidal and Suicidal Self-Injurious Behavior among Flemish Adolescents: A Web-Survey. *Arch. Suicide Res.* **2011**, *15*, 56–67. [CrossRef]
78. Baetens, I.; Claes, L.; Onghena, P.; Grietens, H.; Van Leeuwen, K.; Pieters, C.; Wiersema, J.R.; Griffith, J.W. The effects of nonsuicidal self-injury on parenting behaviors: A longitudinal analyses of the perspective of the parent. *Child Adolesc. Psychiatry Ment. Health* **2015**, *9*, 24. [CrossRef]

6

Food Addiction is Associated with Irrational Beliefs via Trait Anxiety and Emotional Eating

Laurence J. Nolan * and Steve M. Jenkins

Department of Psychology, Wagner College, 1 Campus Rd., Staten Island, NY 10301, USA
* Correspondence: LNolan@wagner.edu

Abstract: Irrational beliefs (IB) are believed, in cognitive behavioral therapies, to be a prime cause of psychopathologies including anxiety, depression, problem eating, and alcohol misuse. "Food addiction" (FA), which has been modeled on diagnostic criteria for substance use disorder, and emotional eating (EE) have both been implicated in the rise in overweight and obesity. Both FA and EE are associated with anxiety. Thus, in the present study, the hypothesis that IB is associated with FA and with EE was tested. Furthermore, possible mediation of these relationships by trait anxiety and depression (and EE for IB and FA) was examined. The responses of 239 adult participants to questionnaires measuring FA, IB, EE, depression, trait anxiety, and anthropometrics were recorded. The results revealed that IB was significantly positively correlated with FA and EE (and depression and trait anxiety). Furthermore, only EE mediated the effect of IB on FA and this was not moderated by BMI. Finally, trait anxiety (but not depression) mediated the effect of IB on EE. Exploratory analysis revealed a significant serial mediation such that IB predicted higher FA via elevated trait anxiety and emotional eating in that order. The results of this study suggest that IB may be a source of the anxiety that is associated with EE and FA and suggest that clinicians may find IB a target for treatment of those persons who report experiences of EE and FA. IB may play a role in food misuse that leads to elevated BMI.

Keywords: food addiction; irrational beliefs; emotional eating; anxiety; food misuse

1. Introduction

"Food addiction" (FA) has been suggested as a factor in the increased prevalence of overweight and obesity. Proponents of FA suggest that some energy-dense highly palatable foods (or specific additives to foods such as salt or refined sugar) generate addiction-like behaviors in those who consume them [1]. FA, as measured by the Yale Food Addiction Scale (YFAS), is associated with binge eating behavior (BED) [2–4], bulimia nervosa [5], night eating syndrome [6], and with elevated BMI even in the absence of BED [4,7,8]. The FA concept is not without controversy. Some critics prefer an alternate description that focuses on the behavior (i.e., "eating addiction") and suggest there is little evidence for an addicting substance in food. They instead suggest that overeating may be a form of habitual food "abuse" [9] or represent a possible food use disorder [10]. Others have suggested that there is not enough evidence yet to conclude that FA is a distinct entity that explains overeating [11]. Nonetheless, there has been significant interest in FA in the scientific community in recent years [12]. The YFAS, which was based on DSM IV substance dependence criteria, has now been updated to reflect the substance use disorder criteria described in the DSM-5 and dubbed the YFAS2 (which has since been provided in a shortened form [13]).

In cognitive behavioral therapies (CBT), irrational beliefs are believed to be a prime cause of psychopathologies including problem eating and addictive behavior. Ellis [14] and Beck [15] proposed that individuals often have habitual affect-eliciting thought patterns (referred to as irrational beliefs by

Ellis) that can lead to dysfunctional emotional and/or behavioral responses. These irrational beliefs originate from a core process of perfectionism [14] or absolutist thinking [16] and the idea that one should be extremely upset when things go wrong and that it is crucial to be successful and approved of by everyone [15]. This absolutist thinking inevitably leads to anxiety and, in turn, may lead to irrational coping strategies such as substance use and uncontrolled eating typified by emotional eating and FA.

In a meta-analysis of 100 independent samples, irrational beliefs were found to be moderately correlated with psychological distress [17]. More specifically, irrational beliefs were associated with trait anxiety [18,19]. While Rohsenow and Smith [18] did not find a connection between irrational beliefs and depression (as measured by Minnesota Multiphasic Personality Inventory), in daily reports of mood over several months, there was an association of irrational beliefs and reports of depression. Others reported that irrational beliefs were related to depression as measured by the Beck Depression Inventory in a sample of women [20]. Mayhew and Edeleman [21] found that irrational beliefs were predictive of poor coping strategies and low self-esteem. Irrational beliefs have been associated with addictive behaviors such as drug misuse [22–25] and problem gambling (see [26] for review) although, in the gambling studies, irrational beliefs are often assessed using different measures than they are in studies of depression and anxiety.

Several studies (mostly involving samples of undergraduate women without eating disorder diagnoses) have reported a link between irrational beliefs and problem eating. Ruderman [27] reported that irrational beliefs were associated with dietary restraint (the cognitive control of food consumption as measured by the Revised Restraint Scale or RRS), particularly the concern with dieting subscale. Studies examining the relationship between irrational beliefs and subclinical eating disorder symptoms are more common. Irrational beliefs predicted a number of bulimia symptoms in undergraduate women [20,28,29]. In addition, irrational beliefs were found to be predictive of drive for thinness, body dissatisfaction, ineffectiveness, and poor interceptive awareness as measured by the Eating Disorders Inventory [21]. More recently, Tomotaki et al. [30] reported that obsession with eating, dieting, and obese-phobia were predicted by irrational beliefs. Irrational beliefs were found to be higher in women with high body dissatisfaction when compared to a group diagnosed with eating disorders and a group with low body dissatisfaction [31].

While irrational beliefs have been associated with dietary restraint, it has not been examined in relation to emotional eating. Emotional eating is generally viewed as a response to negative emotion or distress [32,33] or ego-threat [34], and has been associated with overeating, binge eating, bulimia nervosa, and obesity (see [32]). There is a positive association between emotional eating and anxiety in persons with obesity (but not in persons with a BMI between 18 and 25) [35] and in a sample of children and adolescents [36]. Irrational beliefs and depression were positively correlated in a sample of women [37]. Thus, irrational beliefs may be associated with emotional eating, possibly as the source of anxiety and/or depression.

The research findings described above suggest that irrational beliefs could predict FA and emotional eating. If they do, it is likely that there would be mediating variables. FA is positively correlated to depression in persons with obesity. Furthermore, FA has been associated with depression in persons with obesity [2,3] and in students and the general population [6,38]. FA has also previously been associated with emotional eating [1,2] and with anxiety [39]. The present study was conducted to determine whether the presence of irrational beliefs predicts higher FA symptoms. Furthermore, if such a relationship exists, it may be mediated by depression, trait anxiety, and/or emotional eating, and may depend on BMI. Absolutist irrational beliefs are predicted to produce psychological distress via activation of anxiety. Maladaptive responses such as emotional or uncontrolled eating (e.g., FA) may occur in response to this anxiety. Thus, the following hypotheses (H) were tested. Irrational beliefs and FA are positively correlated (H1). Furthermore, the effect of irrational beliefs on FA is mediated by trait anxiety, depression, and/or emotional eating (H1a). It was also hypothesized that there would be a positive relationship between irrational beliefs and emotional eating (H2) and that the effect of irrational beliefs on emotional eating is mediated by trait anxiety and/or depression (H2a). Finally, it was hypothesized that there would be a moderation of these relationships by BMI; that the effect of irrational beliefs would depend on the value of BMI (H3). Moderation by gender was also hypothesized but not examined in the present study due to the relatively low number of men in the sample.

2. Materials and Methods

2.1. Participants

The participants were 239 adults; the sample included individuals who identified as women ($n = 176$), men ($n = 60$), or as having non-binary gender ($n = 3$). The sample was mostly composed of undergraduate students. The mean age of participants was 20.72 years (SEM = 0.42; range = 18–57) and their mean BMI was 24.07 kg/m^2 (SEM = 0.32; 5.4% had a BMI less than 18.5; 62.3% between 18.5 and 24.9; 20.9% were between 25 and 29.9; 11.3% $\geq$ 30). When asked in an open-ended question to describe their ethnic or racial background, participants described themselves as having Arab (1.3%), African (6.3%), Asian (4.2%), European (73.2%), South Asian (3.8%), or more than one primary (4.6%) ancestry. In addition, some of the participants (6.7%) also indicated Hispanic ancestry. In total, 17.8% of the participants met the criteria for FA. In total, 20.9% of the sample had a depression score of 50 or higher suggesting the presence of depression. See Table 1 for mean scores on questionnaires.

2.2. Measures

2.2.1. Food Addiction

FA was assessed by the Modified Yale Food Addiction Scale 2.0 (mYFAS2) which is designed to evaluate indications of "addiction" toward foods according to the DSM-5 criteria for substance use disorder but with fewer questions than the YFAS 2.0 [13]. The mYFAS2 has been validated against questionnaires that measure related constructs, and has a Kuder–Richardson's alpha of 0.86. In the present study, Kuder–Richardson's alpha was 0.77. The mYFAS2 has 13 items (11 for FA symptoms and 2 for distress) and is scored by counting the number of diagnostic criteria that are met. A person is considered to have FA when 3 or more of the criteria are met, and there is impairment or distress present. In analyses presented below, the mYFAS2 was entered as a continuous variable (number of symptoms).

2.2.2. Irrational Beliefs

Irrational beliefs were measured by the Shortened General Attitude and Belief Scale (SGABS) [40]. The SGABS is a 26-item scale that uses Likert-type ratings with responses ranging from 1 (strongly disagree) to 5 (strongly agree). The SGABS has one rational beliefs subscale and six irrationality subscales (need for achievement, need for approval, need for comfort, demand for fairness, self-downing, and other downing) that are summed to create a total irrationality score (higher scores indicate stronger irrational beliefs). Several instruments are available to measure irrational beliefs, some of which may be more sensitive to affect than to cognitions (for a review see [41]). The SGABS is based on the Ellis model of psychopathology [41] and its score has been shown to be less affected by mood than some previous measures [40]. The reliability for this sample was very good (Cronbach's $\alpha = 0.86$).

2.2.3. Eating Styles

Eating styles were measured by the Dutch Eating Behavior Questionnaire (DEBQ) which contains three subscales: restrained eating (DEBQr), emotional eating (DEBQe), and external eating (DEBQx) [42]. All 33 questions are rated on a 5-point Likert-type scale with "never" and "very often" as the anchors. The restraint (cognitive restraint of eating) and external eating (eating in the presence of external cues) scales each have 10 items while the DEBQe contains 13 items. Score for each subscale is the mean rating. In the present sample, the Cronbach's α for the DEBQe, DEBQr, and DEBQx were 0.94, 0.79, and 0.94 respectively.

2.2.4. Trait Anxiety

Trait anxiety was measured using the State-Trait Anxiety Inventory for Adults (STAI) [43]. The STAI differentiates between trait anxiety and state anxiety with 40 items (4-point Likert-type scale) regarding how participants generally feel (trait) and how they feel at this moment (state). Only the trait measure was used in the statistical analysis. In the present study, the Cronbach's α was 0.93.

2.2.5. Depression

Depression was assessed using the Self-report Depression Scale (SDS) [44]. The SDS score is the sum of responses to 20 questions to which the participant responds on a 4-point Likert-type scale. The total score can range from 20 to 80 with most depressed persons scoring between 50 and 69 [45]. The Cronbach's α for the SDS was 0.87 for this sample.

2.3. Procedure

The hypotheses were pre-registered with the Open Science Framework after data collection had commenced but prior to examination of the data (doi: 10.17605/OSF.IO/QWSRD). The procedure was approved by the Wagner College Human Experimentation Review Board (code F18–10).

All participants completed questionnaires using an online platform (Qualtrics, Provo, UT, USA). Questionnaires were presented in randomized order after informed consent was obtained. Questions regarding age, height and weight, gender, and ethnicity were presented after questionnaires. All participants were debriefed as to the purpose of the study after the survey was completed. In the debriefing, none of the participants appeared to be aware of the study's purpose. Students participated in groups at scheduled times in a computer laboratory as one way to complete a research requirement for an introductory psychology course ($n = 174$). Other participants were recruited via the university daily email bulletin and via a link (which took them to the same website on the university server as that used by the students) posted on Facebook. These participants were entered into a lottery to win one of four $25 gift cards if they wished.

2.4. Data Analysis

To ensure quality of data, records were screened for inappropriate responses to open-ended questions, lack of response variation (e.g., giving the same answer to all questions), and unusually short survey completion times.

Statistical analysis was performed using IBM SPSS (version 24). The variables were first correlated to establish whether there was a relationship between irrational beliefs and FA and whether each was correlated to trait anxiety, depression, eating styles, and BMI. Then, mediation multiple regression analysis was conducted using the PROCESS plug-in for SPSS (release 2.16.3) [46] using 5000 bootstrap samples. Variables were mean-centered and heteroscedasticity-consistent standard errors were used. Residuals were checked for stochasticity prior to the analysis. The unstandardized beta coefficients (B), confidence intervals (CI) and adjusted R^2 are reported. Planned analysis included testing whether the relationship between irrational beliefs and FA was mediated by emotional eating, trait anxiety, and/or depression and whether these would be moderated by BMI. That is, the causal hypothesis was that irrational beliefs produce an elevation in FA by increasing trait anxiety, depression, and/or emotional eating. Furthermore, the mediation of the effect of irrational beliefs on emotional eating by trait anxiety and/or depression was also examined (the hypothesis that irrational beliefs cause elevated emotional eating by increasing trait anxiety and/or depression). The results of these analyses led to an exploratory analysis of the indirect pathway between irrational beliefs, trait anxiety, depression, emotional eating, and FA in that order (serial mediation). This final analysis tested the hypothesis that irrational beliefs increase FA symptoms via a pathway from higher trait anxiety and/or depression to higher emotional eating.

3. Results

3.1. Confirmatory Analyses

3.1.1. Correlations

To examine the relationships among the questionnaire variables and test hypotheses H1 and H2, Pearson correlation coefficients were performed. The results indicated that irrational beliefs were positively correlated with all measures (most strongly with depression and trait anxiety; see Table 1). Correlation coefficients indicated that body mass index was significantly positively correlated only with dietary restraint and FA and not with irrational beliefs or other measures (see Table 2).

Table 1. Pearson correlation coefficients among and descriptive statistics for the questionnaire measures.

Measure	SGABS	DEBQe	DEBQx	DEBQr	SDS	mYFAS2	STAI
SGABS		0.298 [4]	0.166 [1]	0.242 [2]	0.498 [4]	0.282 [3]	0.601 [4]
DEBQe			0.530 [4]	0.388 [4]	0.338 [4]	0.485 [4]	0.422 [4]
DEBQx				0.219 [2]	0.039	0.409 [4]	0.057
DEBQr					0.182 [1]	0.328 [4]	0.240 [2]
SDS						0.342 [4]	0.800 [4]
mYFAS2							0.362 [4]
Mean	59.09	2.38	3.06	2.81	40.91	1.62	43.87
SEM	0.79	0.06	0.04	1.01	0.66	0.14	0.79

[1] $p \leq 0.01$, [2] $p \leq 0.001$, [3] $p < 0.0001$, [4] $p < 0.00001$. SGABS: Shortened General Attitude Belief Scale. DEBQe: Dutch Eating Behavior Questionnaire Emotional Eating. DEBQx: Dutch Eating Behavior Questionnaire External Eating. DEBQr: Dutch Eating Behavior Questionnaire Restrained Eating. SDS: Self-report Depression Scale. mYFAS2: Modified Food Addiction Scale 2.0. STAI: State-Trait Anxiety Inventory.

Table 2. Pearson correlation coefficients among the questionnaire measures and body mass index (BMI).

Measure	SGABS	DEBQe	DEBQx	DEBQr	SDS	mYFAS2	STAI
BMI	−0.020	0.082	0.037	0.161 [1]	−0.024	0.269 [2]	0.032

[1] $p < 0.05$, [2] $p < 0.0001$. SGABS: Shortened General Attitude Belief Scale. DEBQe: Dutch Eating Behavior Questionnaire Emotional Eating. DEBQx: Dutch Eating Behavior Questionnaire External Eating. DEBQr: Dutch Eating Behavior Questionnaire Restrained Eating. SDS: Self-report Depression Scale. mYFAS2: Modified Food Addiction Scale 2.0. STAI: State-Trait Anxiety Inventory.

3.1.2. Multiple Regression Mediation Analysis

Multiple Mediation of the Effect of Irrational Beliefs on FA

Multiple mediation analysis (PROCESS model 4) was used to determine whether the effect of irrational beliefs on FA was mediated by depression, trait anxiety, and/or emotional eating (H1a). BMI was included as a covariate because of its correlation with the criterion variable, FA. The results (see Figure 1) indicated that, although irrational beliefs significantly predicted elevated scores on depression, trait anxiety, and emotional eating measures, only emotional eating mediated the effect; there was a significant indirect effect of irrational beliefs on FA through emotional eating ($B = 0.02$; 95%CI: 0.010–0.034) but not though trait anxiety ($B = 0.00$; 95%CI: −0.021–0.021) or depression ($B = 0.02$; 95%CI: −0.001–0.035). In the mediation model, there was no significant direct effect of irrational beliefs on FA ($B = 0.02$, $t = 1.17$, $p = 0.242$; 95%CI: −0.010–0.040). The total effect was statistically significant ($B = 0.05$, $t = 4.20$, $p < 0.001$; 95%CI: 0.027–0.074).

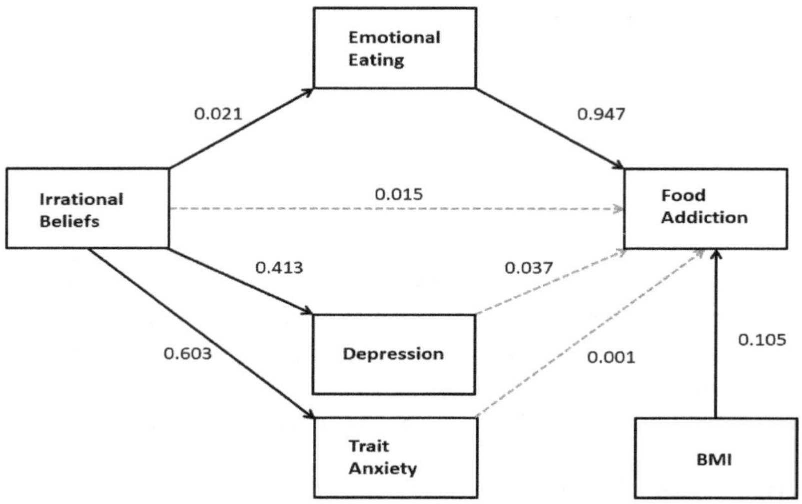

Figure 1. The relationship between irrational beliefs and food addiction (FA) is mediated by emotional eating but not depression or trait anxiety. Solid arrows indicate statistically significant regression coefficients. Nonsignificant BMI effects on mediators are not included for simplicity.

Moderated Mediation by BMI of the Effect of Irrational Beliefs on FA

In order to examine whether BMI moderated the direct and indirect (e.g., through emotional eating) effects of irrational beliefs on FA (H3), BMI was added to the model presented above as a moderator (a moderated mediation model, PROCESS model 15). The results of this analysis again showed emotional eating to be the only significant mediator of the effect of irrational beliefs on FA and indicated that there were no significant interactions between BMI and other effects on FA (see Figure 2). There was no significant conditional direct effect of irrational beliefs on FA at mean-1SD, mean, and mean+1SD values of BMI. In addition, there was a statistically significant conditional indirect effect of irrational beliefs on FA at mean-1SD BMI (95%CI: 0.008–0.037), mean BMI (95%CI: 0.009–0.034) and mean+1SD BMI (95%CI: 0.007–0.038); each coefficient was virtually identical ($B = 0.019$). The index for moderated mediation was not statistically significant (95%CI: −0.0017–0.0017). Finally, there was no moderation of the nonsignificant mediated effects of depression and trait anxiety on FA.

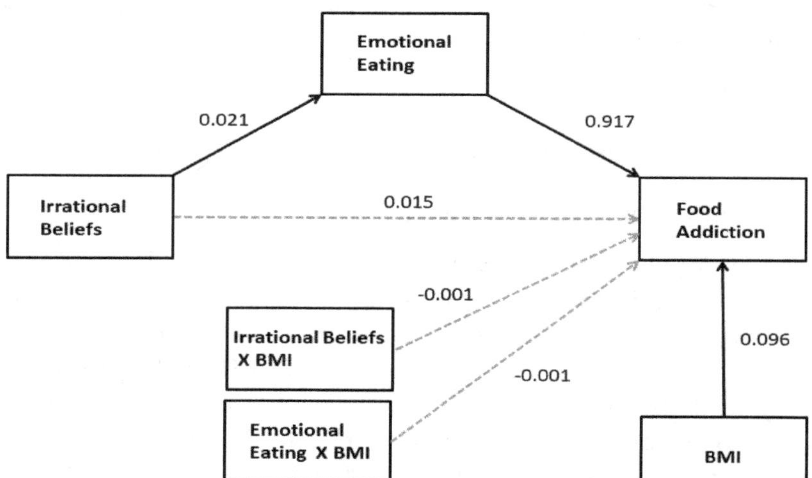

Figure 2. The statistical model for the moderated mediation of the effect of irrational beliefs on FA with BMI as moderator. Solid arrows indicate statistically significant regression coefficients. Nonsignificant mediator variables and BMI effects on mediators are not shown for simplicity.

Multiple Mediation of the Effect of Irrational Beliefs on Emotional Eating

Mediation analysis (PROCESS model 4) was used to determine whether the effect of irrational beliefs on emotional eating was mediated by depression and/or trait anxiety (H2a). The results indicated that, although irrational beliefs significantly predicted elevated scores on depression and trait anxiety, only the latter mediated the effect of irrational beliefs on FA (see Table 3). There was a significant indirect effect of irrational beliefs on emotional eating through trait anxiety ($B = 0.02$; 95%CI: 0.006–0.027) but not through depression ($B = 0.00$; 95%CI: −0.007–0.007; see Figure 3). In the mediation model, there was no significant direct effect of irrational beliefs on emotional eating ($B = 0.01$, $t = 0.83$, $p = 0.406$; 95%CI: −0.007–0.016). The total effect was statistically significant ($B = 0.02$, $t = 4.69$, $p < 0.001$, 95%CI: 0.012–0.030).

Table 3. Multiple mediation model predicting DEBQe from SGABS. Total effect: $R^2 = 0.181$, $F(3,235) = 15.98$, $p < 0.0001$.

Predictor	Mediator: STAI $R^2 = 0.362$, $F(1,237) = 148.52$, $p < 0.0001$			95% Confidence Interval	
	Coeff.	**SE**	***p***	**Lower**	**Upper**
SGABS	0.602	0.049	<0.0001	0.505	0.670
	Mediator: SDS $R^2 = 0.248$, $F(1,237) = 75.85$, $p < 0.0001$				
SGABS	0.413	0.048	<0.0001	0.320	0.507
	Criterion: DEBQe $R^2 = 0.182$, $F(3,235) = 15.98$, $p < 0.0001$				
SGABS	0.005	0.006	0.406	−0.007	0.016
STAI	0.027	0.009	0.002	0.010	0.044
SDS	0.000	0.008	0.989	−0.017	0.016

STAI: State-Trait Anxiety Inventory. SDS: Self-report Depression Scale. DEBQe: Dutch Eating Behavior Questionnaire Emotional Eating. SGABS: Shortened General Attitude Belief Scale.

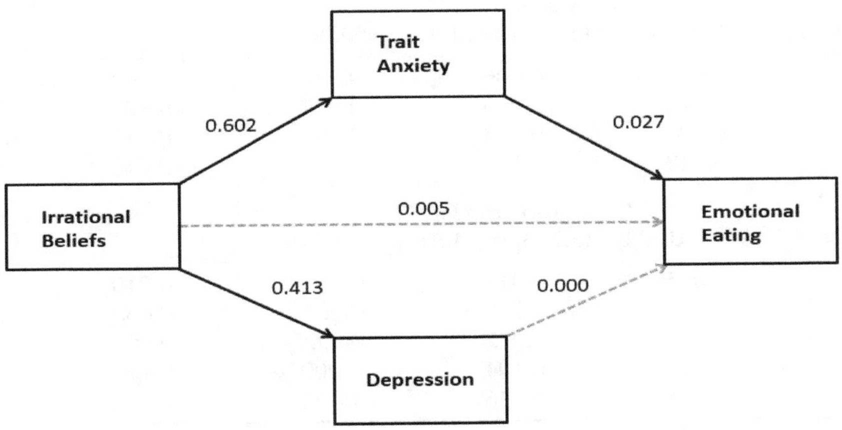

Figure 3. The relationship between irrational beliefs and emotional eating is mediated by trait anxiety but not depression. Solid arrows indicate statistically significant regression coefficients.

3.2. *Exploratory Analyses: Serial Mediation of the Effect of Irrational Beliefs on FA*

The results presented above indicate a strong relationship between irrational beliefs and depression and trait anxiety but neither predicted FA. Because irrational beliefs are associated with emotional eating via trait anxiety and anxiety and depressed mood have been associated with emotional eating, an additional serial mediation analysis was conducted. Based on the results of the planned correlational and mediation analyses presented above, the hypothesis that the indirect pathway between irrational beliefs and FA would include trait anxiety and depression was examined. Specifically, it was proposed that irrational beliefs would increase trait anxiety which, in turn, would increase depression. Depression and/or trait anxiety was expected to increase emotional eating which, in turn, would increase higher food addiction. BMI was included as a covariate in the model because of its correlation with FA. The results of this analysis (PROCESS model 6; see Table 4) largely supported this hypothesis with the exception that depression was not associated with elevated emotional eating. As depicted in Figure 4, there was a significant indirect effect of irrational beliefs on food addiction through trait anxiety and emotional eating ($B = 0.02$; 95%CI: 0.007–0.028). While trait anxiety was a significant predictor of higher depression score ($B = 0.65$, $t = 15.56$, $p < 0.001$; 95%CI: 0.568–0.732), the indirect path including depression was not statistically significant ($B = 0.00$; 95%CI: −0.006–0.007).

Table 4. Serial mediation analysis predicting mYFAS2 from SGABS. Total effect: $R^2 = 0.155$, $F(2,236) = 16.93$, $p < 0.0001$.

Predictor	Mediator: STAI $R^2 = 0.363$, $F(2,236) = 72.58$, $p < 0.0001$			95% Confidence Interval	
	Coeff.	**SE**	***p***	**Lower**	**Upper**
SGABS	0.603	0.050	<0.0001	0.504	0.702
BMI	0.109	0.171	0.525	−0.227	0.445
	Mediator: SDS $R^2 = 0.643$, $F(3,235) = 180.88$, $p < 0.0001$				
SGABS	0.020	0.044	0.656	−0.067	0.106
STAI	0.653	0.042	<0.0001	0.570	0.735
BMI	−0.100	0.083	0.229	−0.263	0.063
	Mediator: DEBQe $R^2 = 0.186$, $F(4,234) = 13.03$, $p < 0.0001$				
SGABS	0.005	0.006	0.387	−0.007	0.017
STAI	0.026	0.009	0.004	0.008	0.043
SDS	0.001	0.008	0.933	−0.016	0.017
BMI	0.013	0.120	0.299	−0.011	0.036
	Criterion: mYFAS2 $R^2 = 0.334$, $F(5,233) = 14.51$, $p < 0.0001$				
SGABS	0.015	0.013	0.242	−0.010	0.040
STAI	0.001	0.018	0.964	−0.035	0.037
SDS	0.037	0.022	0.092	−0.006	0.079
DEBQe	0.947	0.194	<0.0001	0.565	1.328
BMI	0.105	0.026	.0001	0.054	0.157

STAI: State-Trait Anxiety Inventory. SGABS: Shortened General Attitude Belief Scale. SDS: Self-report Depression Scale. DEBQe: Dutch Eating Behavior Questionnaire Emotional Eating. mYFAS2: Modified Food Addiction Scale 2.0.

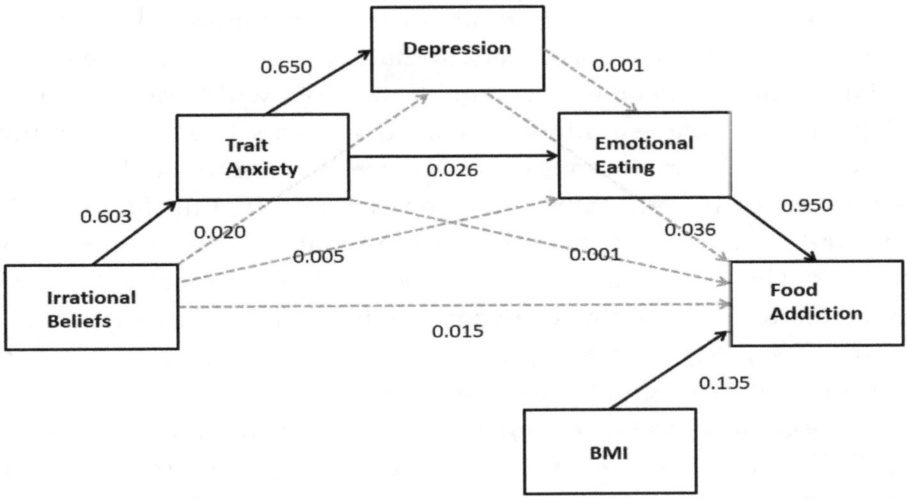

Figure 4. The relationship between irrational beliefs and FA is mediated by the serial pathway through trait anxiety and emotional eating. Solid arrows indicate statistically significant regression coefficients. Nonsignificant BMI effects on mediators are not included for simplicity.

4. Discussion

The results show that, as hypothesized, FA and emotional eating were each positively associated with irrational beliefs. The results of this study are consistent with cognitive behavioral theory and confirm previous findings using different measures of both irrational beliefs and psychopathology that irrational beliefs are associated with elevated trait anxiety and depression. While irrational beliefs did predict higher trait anxiety, depression, and emotional eating, only emotional eating mediated the effect of irrational beliefs on FA. This mediated effect was the same across values of BMI; thus, contrary to prediction, we were unable to show that BMI moderated the mediation of the effect of irrational beliefs on FA by emotional eating. The results also confirmed that the effect of irrational beliefs on emotional eating was mediated by trait anxiety. These findings suggested examination of a serial mediation which found that the indirect effect of irrational beliefs on FA also included trait anxiety. That is, the only significant pathway indicated that irrational beliefs increased trait anxiety which, in turn, increased emotional eating, which finally led to higher number of FA symptoms. The findings that trait anxiety and not depression mediated the associations between irrational beliefs and FA and emotional eating are consistent with the suggestion that anxiety is more important than depression of symptoms of problem eating [see 29]. Finally, we have confirmed that irrational beliefs were positively associated with restrained eating (using a measure other than the RRS) and have found that irrational beliefs were positively correlated with external eating (eating in the presence of food) both of which have been implicated in problem eating and control of body weight. The role of irrational beliefs in restraint and external eating warrants additional exploration as these relationships may be mediated by anxiety or depression.

The research method employed does not allow for causal relationships to be determined with certainty. However, mediation analysis depends upon a theory of causality in order to determine the order of placement of variables in statistical models. In the present analysis, the assumptions were that irrational beliefs are the cause of the psychopathologies and coping behaviors measured because, in CBT, irrational beliefs are considered prime sources of psychopathology. In traditional psychotherapy, it was often believed that activating events (i.e., negative occurrences) result in emotional consequences (i.e., psychological distress). However, according to Ellis [47], this theory is inaccurate or at best incomplete. In the research that led to the development of Rational Emotive Behavior Therapy (REBT), Ellis found that the emotional consequences of an activating event were primarily dictated by the belief a person holds about the activating event. For example, if an employee is reprimanded by an employer for a minor mistake, she or he could think "I am incompetent and will surely be fired from my job, and then no one will ever want to hire me!" The emotional consequence of such a belief would most likely be a significant level of anxiety. If that same person had the more rational thought "It is unfortunate that I made a mistake, but I am human so it will happen sometimes. It is highly unlikely that I will be fired if I make a minor mistake once in a while.", the emotional consequence would likely be one of mild concern or annoyance. Hence, one's emotional state is usually the result of how he or she interprets an event, rather than the event itself. Ellis [47] found that individuals who frequently interpret reality from a distorted, or irrational, perspective are likely to have anxiety or depressive disorders. He also found that when people are emotionally disturbed, they seek out ways to cope with the distress. Coping mechanisms can be adaptive (i.e., make appropriate changes, practice acceptance, exercise, etc.) or maladaptive (i.e., substance use, self-harm, uncontrolled eating). Indeed, some persons may eat to regulate mood and escape anxiety [48,49].

Irrational beliefs-based uncontrolled eating may not necessarily lead to weight gain; in the present study, irrational beliefs were not correlated with BMI. The research on the relationship between irrational beliefs and alcohol consumption indicates that irrational beliefs are associated with problems with alcohol use and not amount of alcohol used [22,23] or frequency of use or getting drunk [24]. Furthermore, perceived lack of control over alcohol use is correlated with irrational beliefs [24]. This is interesting in relation to FA as, unlike alcohol consumption, everyone needs to eat food but those with FA constitute a subset of people who have problem eating who often feel that they cannot control eating. Indeed, lack of control over eating is the most commonly reported FA symptom [50]. Irrational beliefs may lead to FA; FA is common in those with high BMI [7]. It is important to determine whether irrational beliefs are associated with energy consumption from food which may lead to higher BMI in some people. Recent findings suggest that psychological distress is associated with elevated BMI via higher FA and emotional eating [51]. Irrational beliefs may be a source of that psychological distress.

This study has several limitations. While mediation models often use causal wording (i.e., direct and indirect "effects"), the results are correlational and the direction of effect speculative. The sample is composed mostly of students who report having normal body weight. While students are of interest in the study of anxiety and other psychopathology due to high rates of anxiety, depression [52,53] and problem eating [54], their overrepresentation in the present study may limit the generalizability of the findings. Furthermore, while significant, the conditional effects are somewhat weak which may be due to the relatively low percentage of people with BMI greater than 25. In addition, while nearly a fifth of the sample meets the criterion for FA, the number of symptoms is rather low in the sample as a whole. Given the association of emotional eating and FA in persons with high BMI, the relationships reported here would be expected to be higher in those with high BMI.

5. Conclusions

In conclusion, these results suggest for the first time that irrational beliefs may underlie problem eating such as emotional eating and FA via trait anxiety. Additional research may consider whether anxiety sensitivity, the fear that somatic arousal leads to catastrophic consequences, more strongly mediates the relationship between irrational beliefs and FA than trait anxiety. Anxiety sensitivity is distinct from trait anxiety and has been related to substance misuse and emotional eating, particularly in those with high BMI [55]. The results of the present study also suggest that irrational beliefs may be an appropriate target for clinicians when treating problem eating; CBT is an effective approach in treatment of addictive behaviors and problem eating [56].

Author Contributions: Conceptualization, L.J.N. and S.M.J.; Formal analysis, L.J.N.; Investigation, L.J.N.; Methodology, L.J.N. and S.M.J.; Project administration, L.J.N.; Visualization, L.J.N.; Writing—original draft, L.J.N.; Writing—review and editing, L.J.N. and S.M.J.

References

1. Gearhardt, A.N.; Corbin, W.R.; Brownell, K.D. Preliminary validation of the Yale food addiction scale. *Appetite* **2009**, *52*, 430–436. [CrossRef] [PubMed]
2. Davis, C.; Curtis, C.; Levitan, R.D.; Carter, J.C.; Kaplan, A.S.; Kennedy, J.L. Evidence that 'food addiction' is a valid phenotype of obesity. *Appetite* **2011**, *57*, 711–717. [CrossRef] [PubMed]
3. Gearhardt, A.N.; White, M.A.; Masheb, R.M.; Morgan, P.T.; Crosby, R.D.; Grilo, C.M. An examination of the food addiction construct in obese patients with binge eating disorder. *Int. J. Eat. Disord.* **2012**, *45*, 657–663. [CrossRef] [PubMed]
4. Gearhardt, A.N.; Boswell, R.G.; White, M.A. The association of "food addiction" with disordered eating and body mass index. *Eat. Behav.* **2014**, *15*, 427–433. [CrossRef] [PubMed]
5. De Vries, S.K.; Meule, A. Food addiction and bulimia nervosa: New data based on the Yale Food Addiction Scale 2.0. *Eur. Eat. Disord. Rev.* **2016**, *24*, 518–522. [CrossRef] [PubMed]
6. Nolan, L.J.; Geliebter, A. "Food addiction" is associated with night eating severity. *Appetite* **2016**, *98*, 89–94. [CrossRef] [PubMed]
7. Meule, A. How prevalent is "food addiction"? *Front. Psychiatry* **2011**, *2*, 61. [CrossRef] [PubMed]
8. Pedram, P.; Wadden, D.; Amini, P.; Gulliver, W.; Randell, E.; Cahill, F.; Vasdev, S.; Goodridge, A.; Carter, J.C.; Zhai, G.; et al. Food addiction: Its prevalence and significant association with obesity in the general population. *PLoS ONE* **2013**, *8*, e74832. [CrossRef]
9. Hebebrand, J.; Albayrak, Ö.; Adan, R.; Antel, J.; Dieguez, C.; de Jong, J.; Leng, G.; Menzies, J.; Mercer, J.G.; Murphy, M.; et al. "Eating addiction", rather than "food addiction", better captures addictive-like eating behavior. *Neurosci. Biobehav. Rev.* **2014**, *47*, 295–306. [CrossRef]
10. Nolan, L.J. Is it time to consider the "food use disorder"? *Appetite* **2017**, *115*, 16–18. [CrossRef]
11. Long, C.G.; Blundell, J.E.; Finlayson, G. A systematic review of the application and correlates of YFAS-diagnosed 'food addiction' in humans: Are eating-related 'addictions' a cause for concern or empty concepts? *Obes. Facts* **2015**, *8*, 386–401. [CrossRef] [PubMed]
12. Meule, A. Back by popular demand: A narrative review on the history of food addiction research. *Yale J. Biol. Med.* **2015**, *88*, 295–302. [PubMed]
13. Schulte, E.M.; Gearhardt, A.N. Development of the modified Yale food addiction scale version 2.0. *Eur. Eat. Disord. Rev.* **2017**, *25*, 302–308. [CrossRef] [PubMed]
14. Ellis, A. *Reason and Emotion in Psychotherapy*; Lyle Stuart: New York, NY, USA, 1962.
15. Beck, A.T. *Cognitive Therapy and the Emotional Disorders*; International Universities Press: New York, NY, USA, 1976.
16. Ellis, A. The essence of RET—1984. *J. Ration. Emot. Cogn. Behav. Ther.* **1984**, *2*, 19–25. [CrossRef]
17. Vîslă, A.; Flückiger, C.; Grosse Holtforth, M.; David, D. Irrational beliefs and psychological distress: A meta-analysis. *Psychother. Psychosom.* **2016**, *85*, 8–15. [CrossRef] [PubMed]
18. Rohsenow, D.J.; Smith, R.E. Irrational beliefs and predictors of negative affective states. *Motiv. Emot.* **1982**, *6*, 299–314. [CrossRef]
19. Deffenbacher, J.L.; Zwemer, W.A.; Whisman, M.A.; Hill, R.A.; Sloan, R.D. Irrational beliefs and anxiety. *Cognit. Ther. Res.* **1986**, *10*, 281–291. [CrossRef]
20. Wertheim, E.H.; Poulakis, Z. The relationship among the General Attitude and Belief Scale, other dysfunctional cognition measures, and depressive or bulimic tendencies. *J. Ration. Emot. Cogn. Behav. Ther.* **1993**, *10*, 219–233. [CrossRef]
21. Mayhew, R.; Edelmann, R.J. Self-esteem, irrational beliefs and coping strategies in relation to eating problems in a non-clinical population. *Person. Individ. Differ.* **1989**, *10*, 581–584. [CrossRef]
22. Camatta, C.D.; Nagoshi, C.T. Stress, depression, irrational beliefs, and alcohol use and problems in a college student sample. *Alcohol. Clin. Exp. Res.* **1995**, *19*, 142–146. [CrossRef]
23. Hutchinson, G.T.; Patock-Peckham, J.A.; Cheong, J.; Nagoshi, C.T. Irrational beliefs and behavioral misregulation in the role of alcohol abuse among college students. *J. Ration. Emot. Cogn. Behav.* **1998**, *16*, 61–74. [CrossRef]
24. Nagoshi, C.T. Perceived control of drinking and other predictors of alcohol use and problems in a college student sample. *Addict. Res.* **1999**, *7*, 291–306. [CrossRef]

25. Denoff, M.S. Irrational beliefs as predictors of adolescent drug abuse and running away. *J. Clin. Psychol.* **1987**, *43*, 412–423. [CrossRef]
26. Jacobsen, L.H.; Knudsen, A.K.; Krogh, E.; Pallesen, S.; Molde, H. An overview of cognitive mechanisms in pathological gambling. *Nordic Psychol.* **2007**, *59*, 347–361. [CrossRef]
27. Ruderman, A.J. Restraint and irrational cognitions. *Behav. Res. Ther.* **1985**, *23*, 557–561. [CrossRef]
28. Ruderman, A.J. Bulimia and irrational beliefs. *Behav. Res. Ther.* **1986**, *24*, 193–197. [CrossRef]
29. Lohr, J.M.; Parkinson, D.L. Irrational beliefs and bulimia symptoms. *J. Ration. Emot. Cogn. Behav. Ther.* **1989**, *4*, 253–262. [CrossRef]
30. Tomotake, M.; Okura, M.; Taniguchi, T.; Ishimoto, Y. Traits of irrational beliefs related to eating problems in Japanese college women. *J. Med. Investig.* **2002**, *49*, 51–55.
31. Möller, A.T.; Bothma, M.E. Body dissatisfaction and irrational beliefs. *Psychol. Rep.* **2001**, *88*, 423–430. [CrossRef]
32. Lindeman, M.; Stark, K. Emotional eating and eating disorder psychopathology. *Eat. Disord.* **2001**, *9*, 251–259. [CrossRef]
33. Van Strien, T.; Ouwens, M.A. Effects of distress, alexithymia and impulsivity on eating. *Eat. Behav.* **2007**, *8*, 251–257. [CrossRef] [PubMed]
34. Wallis, D.J.; Hetherington, M.M. Stress and eating: The effects of ego-threat and cognitive demand on food intake in restrained and emotional eaters. *Appetite* **2004**, *43*, 39–46. [CrossRef] [PubMed]
35. Schneider, K.L.; Appelhans, B.M.; Whited, M.C.; Oleski, J.; Pagoto, S.L. Trait anxiety, but not trait anger, predisposes obese individuals to emotional eating. *Appetite* **2010**, *55*, 701–706. [CrossRef] [PubMed]
36. Goossens, L.; Braet, C.; Van Vlierberghe, L.; Mels, S. Loss of control over eating in overweight youngsters: The role of anxiety, depression and emotional eating. *Eur. Eat. Disord. Rev.* **2009**, *17*, 68–78. [CrossRef] [PubMed]
37. Ouwens, M.A.; van Strien, T.; van Leeuwe, J.F. Possible pathways between depression, emotional and external eating. A structural equation model. *Appetite* **2009**, *53*, 245–248. [CrossRef]
38. Meadows, A.; Nolan, L.J.; Higgs, S. Self-perceived food addiction: Prevalence, predictors, and prognosis. *Appetite* **2017**, *114*, 282–298. [CrossRef] [PubMed]
39. Parylak, S.L.; Koob, G.F.; Zorrilla, E.P. The dark side of food addiction. *Physiol. Behav.* **2011**, *104*, 149–156. [CrossRef]
40. Lindner, H.; Kirkby, R.; Wertheim, E.; Birch, P.A. brief assessment of irrational thinking: The Shortened General Attitudes and Belief Scale. *Cognit. Ther. Res.* **1999**, *23*, 651–663. [CrossRef]
41. Bridges, K.R.; Harnish, R.J. Role of irrational beliefs in depression and anxiety: A review. *Health* **2010**, *2*, 862–877. [CrossRef]
42. Van Strien, T.; Frijters, J.E.R.; Bergers, G.P.A.; Defares, P.B. The Dutch Eating Behavior Questionnaire (DEBQ) for assessment of restrained, emotional, and external eating behavior. *Int. J. Eat. Disord.* **1986**, *5*, 295–315. [CrossRef]
43. Spielberger, C.D.; Gorsuch, R.L.; Lushene, R.; Vagg, P.R.; Jacobs, G.A. *Manual for the State-Trait Anxiety Inventory*; Consulting Psychologists: Palo Alto, CA, USA, 1983.
44. Zung, W.W. A self-rating depression scale. *Arch. Gen. Psychiatry* **1965**, *12*, 63–70. [CrossRef] [PubMed]
45. Carroll, B.J.; Fielding, J.M.; Blashki, T.G. Depression rating scales: A critical review. *Arch. Gen. Psychiatry* **1973**, *28*, 361–366. [CrossRef]
46. Hayes, A.F. *Introduction to Mediation, Moderation, and Conditional Process Analysis: A Regression-Based Approach*; Guilford: New York, NY, USA, 2017.
47. Ellis, A. *Overcoming Destructive Beliefs, Feelings, and Behaviors: New Directions for Rational Emotive Behavior Therapy*; Prometheus Books: Amherst, NY, USA, 2001.
48. Greeno, C.G.; Wing, R.R. Stress-induced eating. *Psychol. Bull.* **1994**, *115*, 444–464. [CrossRef] [PubMed]
49. Heatherton, T.F.; Baumeister, R.F. Binge eating as escape from self-awareness. *Psychol. Bull.* **1991**, *110*, 86–108. [CrossRef] [PubMed]
50. Meule, A.; Gearhardt, A. Food addiction in the light of DSM-5. *Nutrients* **2014**, *6*, 3653–3671. [CrossRef] [PubMed]
51. Bourdier, L.; Orri, M.; Carre, A.; Gearhardt, A.N.; Romo, L.; Dantzer, C.; Berthoz, S. Are emotionally driven and addictive-like eating behaviors the missing links between psychological distress and greater body weight? *Appetite* **2018**, *120*, 536–546. [CrossRef] [PubMed]

52. Eisenberg, D.; Gollust, S.E.; Golberstein, E.; Hefner, J.L. Prevalence and correlates of depression, anxiety, and suicidality among university students. *Am. J. Orthopsychiatry* **2007**, *77*, 534–542. [CrossRef]
53. Beiter, R.; Nash, R.; McCrady, M.; Rhoades, D.; Linscomb, M.; Clarahan, M.; Sammut, S. The prevalence and correlates of depression, anxiety, and stress in a sample of college students. *J. Affect. Disord.* **2015**, *173*, 90–96. [CrossRef]
54. Zivin, K.; Eisenberg, D.; Gollust, S.E.; Golberstein, E. Persistence of mental health problems and needs in a college student population. *J. Affect. Disord.* **2009**, *117*, 180–185. [CrossRef]
55. Hearon, B.A.; Utschig, A.C.; Smits, J.A.; Moshier, S.J.; Otto, M.W. The role of anxiety sensitivity and eating expectancy in maladaptive eating behavior. *Cogn. Ther. Res.* **2013**, *37*, 923–933. [CrossRef]
56. Schulte, E.M.; Joyner, M.A.; Potenza, M.N.; Grilo, C.M.; Gearhardt, A.N. Current considerations regarding food addiction. *Curr. Psychiatry Rep.* **2015**, *17*, 563. [CrossRef] [PubMed]

7

Food Addiction and Psychosocial Adversity: Biological Embedding, Contextual Factors and Public Health Implications

David A. Wiss [1], Nicole Avena [2,3] and Mark Gold [4,*]

[1] Fielding School of Public Health, University of California Los Angeles, Los Angeles, CA 90095, USA; dwiss@ucla.edu
[2] Department of Neuroscience, Icahn School of Medicine at Mount Sinai, New York, NY 10029, USA; nicoleavena@gmail.com
[3] Department of Psychology, Princeton University, Princeton, NJ 08540, USA
[4] School of Medicine, Washington University in St. Louis, St. Louis, MO 63130, USA
* Correspondence: drmarkgold@gmail.com

Abstract: The role of stress, trauma, and adversity particularly early in life has been identified as a contributing factor in both drug and food addictions. While links between traumatic stress and substance use disorders are well documented, the pathways to food addiction and obesity are less established. This review focuses on psychosocial and neurobiological factors that may increase risk for addiction-like behaviors and ultimately increase BMI over the lifespan. Early childhood and adolescent adversity can induce long-lasting alterations in the glucocorticoid and dopamine systems that lead to increased addiction vulnerability later in life. Allostatic load, the hypothalamic-pituitary-adrenal axis, and emerging data on epigenetics in the context of biological embedding are highlighted. A conceptual model for food addiction is proposed, which integrates data on the biological embedding of adversity as well as upstream psychological, social, and environmental factors. Dietary restraint as a feature of disordered eating is discussed as an important contextual factor related to food addiction. Discussion of various public health and policy considerations are based on the concept that improved knowledge of biopsychosocial mechanisms contributing to food addiction may decrease stigma associated with obesity and disordered eating behavior.

Keywords: food addiction; eating disorder; obesity; stress; trauma; early life adversity; adverse childhood experience; dopamine; epigenetics; biopsychosocial

---

1. Background

The quest to discover the precise mechanisms of hedonic overeating began decades ago. While many theories have been proposed, none have been widely accepted, and the obesity epidemic continues to grow. The *Nutrition Transition* theory describes a global trend toward consumption of processed foods that are low in fiber and high in added sugars and fats [1]. The changing global food landscape in the past four decades have increased access to convenient "snack" foods and decreased time spent preparing foods at home [2]. Several lines of research have explored the idea that highly palatable foods can alter brain reward pathways. For example, a landmark study showed that dopamine (DA) receptors were significantly lower in individuals with obesity [3]. Soon after, investigators documented overlapping neuroimaging characteristics in humans with obesity and those with substance use disorders (SUDs), showing reductions in DA-D2 receptors [4]. It was then suggested that individuals may overeat to compensate for DA-D2 receptor dysfunction [5]. To date, it is not clear whether these neurochemical associations are a cause of addiction-like overeating or a consequence [6]. However, similar to other addictions, changes that occur in obesity show that food reinforcement adapts, strongly implicating biological underpinnings. Given the limited success in reversing the obesity trends, a better understanding of the various biopsychosocial mechanisms may help inform public health efforts.

Bart Hoebel pioneered the concept of food addiction (FA) research using animal models, showing evidence of bingeing, withdrawal, craving, and concomitant changes in dopaminergic and opioidergic systems in response to overeating sugar [7–14]. In rodent studies, early life adversity (ELA) has been shown to induce alterations in DA neuronal activity and synaptic function [15], impacting reward-directed behavior and partially accounting for individual variation along the mesolimbic DA projection [16]. More recently it has been shown that chronic stress dysregulates the reward system, promotes addiction-like eating, and contributes to the development of obesity [17]. Furthermore, palatable diets buffer against the negative impact of social stressors in juvenile rats [18]. Interestingly, environmental enrichment (larger space with conspecifics and novel objects) reduced sugar seeking and consumption [19]. Other rodent studies documented early and persistent alterations in amygdala circuitry and function following exposure to ELA, which were not diminished when the stressor was removed [20]. This suggests that ELA is not always redeemable by subsequent experience. At present, there is a gap in our understanding of how various forms of stress, trauma, and adversity link to addiction-like eating in real-world settings, particularly when viewed in social context, as well as over the lifespan.

In humans, various forms of ELA are associated with illicit drug use later in life [21–23]. In addition, there are established links between ELA and obesity [21,24], however, the exact mechanisms are not understood. A recent systematic review on childhood obesity implicated stress as a midstream factor that can lead to "junk food" self-medication and subtle addiction, in order to alleviate uncomfortable emotional states [25]. In a nationally representative sample of young adults (n = 10,813) exposure to multiple types of child maltreatment predicted excessive sugary beverage consumption [26]. In a Brazilian sample (n = 7639) FA was independently associated with early life physical and sexual abuse [27]. A positron emission tomography (PET) study also found that long-term exposure to adversity is associated with reduced striatal DA synthesis capacity [28]. Functional magnetic resonance imaging (fMRI) studies have linked ELA to blunted subjective responses to reward-predicting cues [29], and to altered connectivity in the extended reward network, leading to increased vulnerability to FA and obesity later in life [30]. While there are sufficient data that describes life course associations between ELA and adult weight outcomes [24], the actual biological mechanisms are less understood, which is a primary focus of this review. Another aim is to integrate psychologically relevant contextual factors such as weight stigma and pathological dieting.

The purpose of this review is to focus on literature from FA as well as obesity in the context of exposure to trauma, stress, and adversity, in an effort to answer three questions: (1) is FA a biologically plausible explanation for a life course association between ELA and obesity? (2) how might other relevant psychological, social, and environmental factors contribute to FA and to obesity? (see Figure 1) and finally, (3) what does it mean for public health? For simplicity, we have conceptually merged stress/trauma/adversity (STA) at several points throughout, particularly when reviewed outside of the context of early life, however we acknowledge these are not identical concepts. We also acknowledge that FA does not always lead to obesity, and that obesity can occur in the absence of FA. Additionally, ELA is used synonymously with adverse childhood experience (ACE) to describe exposures in the first 18 years of life. This review draws from literature across multiple disciplines in order to consider both individual and population health perspectives, and to describe contextual factors related to the neurobiology of FA. It is important to translate obesity science into a relevant social context, in order to identify achievable intervention targets which may have a meaningful impact upstream.

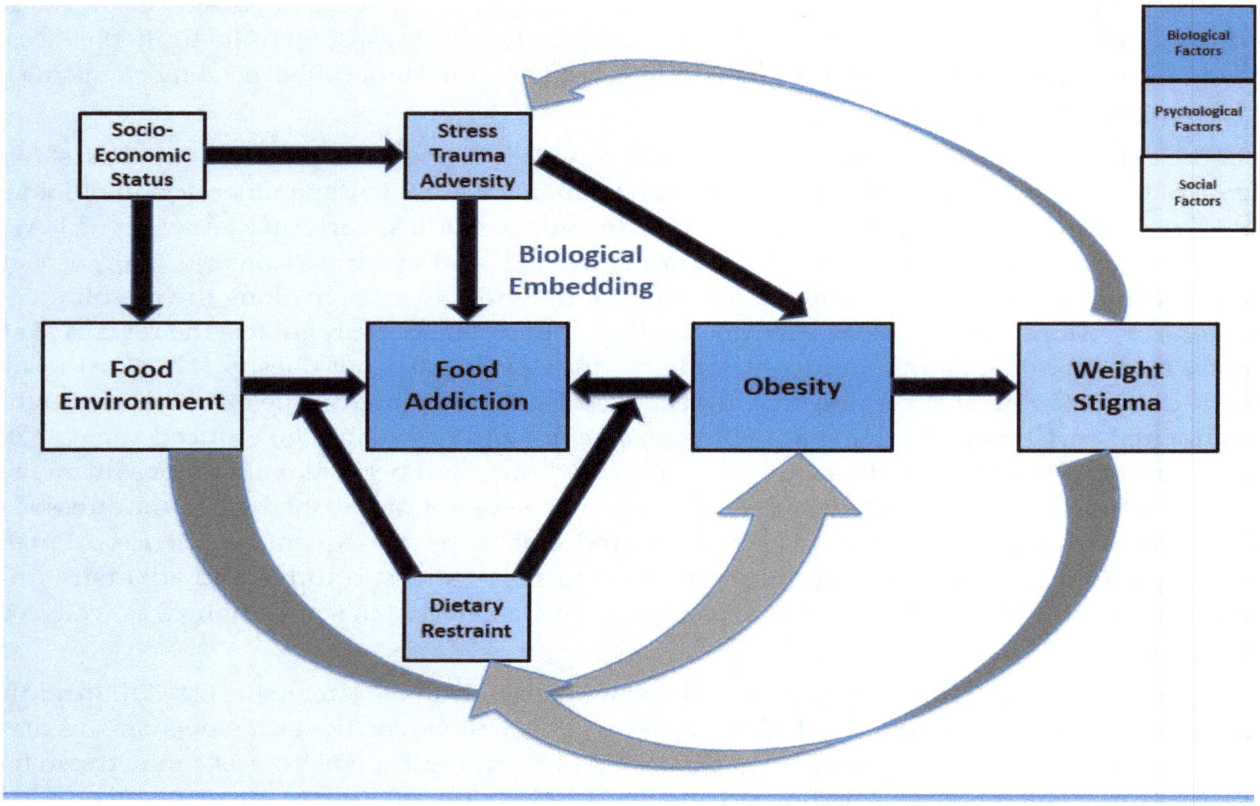

Figure 1. Food addiction and obesity following exposure to stress, trauma, and adversity: A biopsychosocial perspective of contextual factors.

1.1. The Biopsychosocial Model & Other Foundational Theories

Social and biological processes overlap and are inextricably linked. However, research methods are often incapable of capturing all features of an observed phenomenon, such as the various drivers of obesity (see Figure 1). Another example is how addiction neuroscience overlooks key social factors such as exclusion and marginalization which would make these findings more clinically relevant [31]. Biopsychosocial models were originally proposed by Engel as a new way to understand health and disease, by considering influence from various domains [32]. Biopsychosocial obesity research has found that lower educational attainment is associated with higher BMI, after adjusting for biological (energy intake and expenditure), psychological (decisional balance) and social (support) factors [33]. A biopsychosocial approach to childhood obesity should consider the (1) biology of the child (2) family environment and immediate psychosocial influences and (3) wider environmental, social, and cultural influences [34]. This creates opportunity for collaboration across multiple academic and clinically-focused disciplines. The current review employs a biopsychosocial perspective on FA, considering obesity as one possible outcome. This manuscript also incorporates Krieger's *Ecosocial Theory* which emphasizes the social production of disease over biomedical individualism, describing "embodiment" as the biological incorporation of social and ecological circumstances into everyday life [35]. A *Life Course Perspective* is used to link ELA to adult health [36–38]. Finally, a *Developmental Psychology* perspective views human development as relational, pertaining to dynamics (e.g., community features) which require individuals to be contextually situated into multidirectional and reciprocating ecological systems [39–41].

1.2. *Food Addiction & Eating Disorders*

With the validation of the *Yale Food Addiction Scale* (YFAS) in 2009 [42] and the updated YFAS 2.0 in 2016 [43], FA in humans has been operationalized across hundreds of studies. At the present time, FA has not been recognized as an official eating disorder (ED) in the Diagnostic and Statistical Manual (DSM) of Mental Disorders. Unique aspects of addictions include the importance of the substance, withdrawal, and tolerance, whereas unique aspects of EDs include restraint/rules, and shape/weight concerns [44]. It is well-established that dietary restraint/restriction can lead to rebound bingeing [45] yet it remains unclear if this is a cause or consequence of FA symptoms (discussed in Section 5.1). Thus, disordered eating characterized by dietary restraint provides important context for FA data. It has been recently suggested that the presence of dieting behavior must be carefully evaluated in order to separate the FA "signal" from the "noise" [46]. For example, ED research has identified significant overlap between FA and bulimia nervosa (BN), with FA symptoms improving when BN symptoms remit [47]. FA prevalence is the highest in BN [48] compared with other EDs, suggesting that FA treatment models should consider symptom contribution from dietary restraint and other compensatory behaviors. It has been proposed that FA is a transdiagnostic disorder associated with neurobiological vulnerability in certain people, who are more susceptible to using food as a coping mechanism [49]. It has also been shown that FA predicts a worse treatment outcome in patients with binge eating disorder (BED) [50].

Among those with an ED diagnosis, Brewerton (2017) proposed that the presence of FA be conceptualized as a meaningful correlate of post-traumatic stress disorder (PTSD) severity and symptoms [51]. For example, data from the Nurses' Health Study II has shown that severe physical and sexual abuse are associated with a 90% increase in FA risk [52]. The same dataset also suggested that symptoms of PTSD are associated with an increased prevalence of FA [53]. In a sample of 301 overweight and obese women, the association between FA and childhood trauma remained significant after adjusting for potential confounders such as socioeconomic status (SES) [54]. In a sample of bariatric surgery seeking patients (n = 1586), elevated ACE scores correlated with an increased likelihood of screening positive for FA [55]. A recent meta-analysis showed that multiple ACEs increased the odds of adult obesity by 46% (95% CI: 28–64%) [24] but several unmeasured confounders likely influence this estimate, such as the presence of EDs and SUDs, which frequently cluster, co-occur, and lead to weight fluctuations [56,57]. Therefore, risk estimates between childhood adversity and adult obesity would likely be higher after adjusting for these diagnoses often associated with dietary restriction and weight control, however this has not been formally tested. While data linking ELA to EDs are robust, only recently has it been shown that FA symptoms can mediate this pathway, as well as exacerbate ED symptoms significantly across all forms of childhood maltreatment [58]. Although EDs are not directly featured in Figure 1, the constructs of dietary restraint and weight stigma are used to contextualize important associations between EDs and FA. Notwithstanding, there are likely paths from ELA to obesity that are better captured by more classic ED pathology (e.g., BED) rather than FA, which are not directly featured by the model.

2. Food Addiction Neuroscience & Social Context

A frequent criticism of FA data in clinical settings is that the measure itself does not account for restrained eating [46] (discussed in Section 5.1). Another criticism is that it remains unclear how to intervene once FA has been detected. A recent systematic review of mostly pilot and feasibility studies concluded that currently there are no empirically supported psychosocial interventions for FA [59]. The authors recommend that clinicians assess for comorbid ED, and if present, provide evidence-based treatments (e.g., cognitive behavioral therapy) for those conditions. There is growing support for the FA construct in studies using the YFAS as well as neuroimaging studies on obesity that do not use "food addiction" terminology, with several examples provided below. It is worth noting that many authors reject the FA term in favor of other language such as eating addiction [60], or with additional qualifiers such as refined or processed food addiction [61,62], and even food use disorder [63]. Figure 1 proposes that FA is one driver of obesity, although there are several others, including some not captured by the model (discussed further in Section 2.1).

Neurobiological overlaps between obesity and addiction have been described within the mesolimbic pathway between the ventral tegmental area (VTA) and the ventral striatum, with further projection to limbic (amygdala and hippocampus) and cortical regions (prefrontal cortex [PFC] and cingulate gyrus) [64]. Recent data suggests that among 110 healthy lean adults, exposure to a Western-style diet for one week led to rapid declines in hippocampal-dependent learning and memory, as well as appetitive control [65]. Research has shown that obesity (similar to SUD) is associated with deficits in executive functioning, an umbrella term encompassing the higher-order cognitive processes that help people take goal-directed action [66]. In a sample of women with obesity (n = 36), FA severity has been associated with impaired decision-making, compared to controls [67]. Resting-state fMRI data has shown decreased functional connectivity in the frontal gyrus in adults with obesity (n = 20) compared to controls [68]. A large cross-sectional study of children ages 9–11 (n = 2700) showed that increased BMI is associated with a reduced mean cortical thickness as well as lower executive functioning [69]. A follow-up report from the same study (n = 3190) suggested that BMI is associated with PFC development as well as diminished working memory [70]. Interestingly, a nationally representative sample of US adults (n = 4769 mean age 29) found that obesity is associated with poor working memory in women, but not men [71]. While tempting to consider that biological sex differences explain these findings, social context would suggest that the experience of weight stigma (discussed in Section 5.2), which is higher in women than men [72] may be a contributing factor. Recent data on school-age children (n = 176) suggests that weight-related stereotype threat (fear of confirming a negative stereotype) may explain working memory deficits more so than excess body weight [73].

Among patients with obesity (n = 224), FA is more closely correlated with psychological factors (depressive symptoms, quality of life) than with metabolic parameters (BMI, fat percentage, waist circumference) [74]. In a small sample of adult community members (n = 52), individuals with FA had significantly higher scores on depressive symptoms, emotion dysregulation, emotional eating, demand characteristics, motives, impulsivity, and family history of mental health problems and addiction [75]. Impulsivity can be defined as decision-making with limited forethought (rash-spontaneous behavior), having strong associations with FA [76–79]. Impulsivity hinders inhibitory control and is associated with increased intake of food [80] and drugs [81], often heightened in response to novel stimuli [82]. Delay discounting (preference for "smaller sooner" rather than "larger later" rewards) is closely associated with impulsivity and has been correlated with YFAS scores [83]. These authors believe it to be a predisposing factor rather than a consequence, although bidirectionality is likely. It has been suggested that impulsivity-related domains such as lower self-control, higher reward sensitivity, and negative affect help explain some similarities between addiction and obesity [84]. While impulsivity has heritable components linked to the mesocorticolimbic system [85] as well as serotonin-related candidate genes (e.g., HTR2A) [86], the potential for these traits to be influenced by epigenetic modification following psychosocial adversity will be explored in Section 3.1.

2.1. Food Environment as a Driver of Food Addiction & Obesity

The proposed pathways in Figure 1 suggest that FA may partially mediate the relationship between the food environment and obesity. Other pathways also exist. For example, census tract data have been used to show that wealthier neighborhoods (using median income) have better access (physical availability) to markets with healthier foods compared to poor neighborhoods [87]. Considering the importance of the built environment, neighborhood features (e.g., crime) that discourage outdoor physical activity are consistently linked to higher BMIs [88]. Recognizing that built, socioeconomic, and social characteristics co-occur [89], several investigators have advocated for a better understanding of theory-driven mediators and moderators in the relationship between neighborhood context and obesity [90,91]. Given the link between STA and FA, unsafe environments associated with lower SES neighborhoods are likely to impact BMI through increases in reward-based eating. It has been established that diet quality tends to follow a SES gradient [92]. It has also been shown that parental fruit/vegetable consumption is linked to adolescent fruit/vegetable consumption [93], suggesting that the home food environment is important. Not eating dinner as a family has also been linked with increased BMI in kindergarten age children, regardless of SES [94]. It has been proposed that the maltreatment-obesity association is spurious, driven by confounding through the home food environment. However, after testing, researchers have found limited confounding influence [95] which supports arguments in favor of biological mechanisms.

Innovative methods that assess food environments include examining the (1) ratio of fast-food to full-service restaurants (2) ratio of bars/pubs to liquor stores and (3) presence of markets [96]. Multilevel models typically adjust for individual factors (education, hours of walking per week) as well as neighborhood factors (deprivation, walkability score). Perhaps the combination of food environment features matters more than individual components [96]. While several studies have described neighborhood "food swamps" (high density of high-calorie junk food) as predictive of obesity [97], few studies have looked at the potential roles of psychosocial pathways (mental health and wellbeing) [98]. A recent systematic review found that overall psychological resources (i.e., stress) had more consistent evidence of mediation than external neighborhood in the relationship between SES and BMI [91]. One study (n = 1112 adults) showed that paths from neighborhood characteristics to BMI could be partially explained by psychological distress and measures of inflammation [99] (discussed in Section 3). Taken together, FA is one potential pathway linking the food environment to obesity, however there is a "backdoor path" [100] through SES to STA, as well as a pathway that may not include FA (i.e., through the built environment). Comprehensive biopsychosocial frameworks cannot be tested or explained by any single study. There is conceptual support for the theory that the external environment (quick, cheap, highly palatable foods) is an upstream driver of EDs however this not been thoroughly investigated (discussed in Section 6.1). Figure 1 represents a synthesis of literature reviewed so far, as well as a roadmap for subsequent sections.

2.2. Socioeconomic Status

Given the inverse relationship between SES and BMI [101,102], obesity can also be viewed as a social phenomenon. This negative relationship has been shown in numerous countries outside of the US (e.g., Netherlands, Turkey, Morocco, South Asia) [103]. Hot-spot analysis in the US shows that higher BMI clusters are more likely in socioeconomically disadvantaged minority neighborhoods [104]. Meanwhile, large datasets (n = 43,864) have shown that obesity risk is decreased when positive contextual factors (maternal mental health, school safety, and child resilience) are present [105]. A large population-based cohort from the UK (n = 18,733) found that home-based deprivation was more closely associated with changes in child BMI than school-based deprivation [106]. On the other hand, some authors believe that the root cause of ACEs are largely based in the community, originating from an accumulation of contextual risk factors beyond a child's control, including family history, failed attachment, safety/security, and neighborhood risks [107]. While models of addiction and obesity are incomplete without psychosocial context, current research methods cannot adequately contextualize risk. Hence, literature from multiple disciplines was used to synthesize our conceptual model, which could be expanded with additional constructs such as resilience.

To illustrate further, a recent study showed that individuals with higher ACE scores were more likely to report not finishing high school, unemployment, and living below the poverty level [108]. Sustained activation and loss of capacity to respond to chronic stress might lead to a higher risk of illness and disease among people in lower SES categories [109]. It has been recognized that the processes which mediate the relationship between ELA and adult obesity might differ between men and women [110–112]. For example, a recent systematic review found that perceived stress from structural racism and weight stigma among black women creates negative emotions which predict emotional eating [113]. These stressors may then increase metabolic disturbance. Obesity itself can be a stressful state due to high prevalence of weight stigma [114] (discussed in Section 5.2), as highlighted by the feedback loop in Figure 1. Obesity may be driving changes in stress biology rather than stress biology driving obesity [115]. Next, we consider the impact of ELA (as well as STA more broadly) from a life course perspective, describing precise (as well as candidate) mechanisms by which social factors impact health, seen primarily through recent SUD and obesity research.

3. Biological Embedding of Stress, Trauma, & Adversity

The fetal and infant origins of adult disease was proposed by Barker in 1990 [116]. This focus on the biological basis of disease gave rise to concepts such as allostatic load (AL), defined as the "cost of chronic exposure to fluctuating or heightened neural or neuroendocrine response resulting from repeated or chronic environmental challenge" [117]. This can be operationalized using a range of biomarkers that indicate inflammation and long-term "weathering." A simpler definition of AL is the price of adaption that leads to disease states over time. It has been suggested that frequent activation of the stress response and the failure to shut off allostatic activity creates "wear and tear" [118]. A landmark study showed that higher AL scores were associated with poorer cognitive and physical functioning, increasing the risk of cardiovascular diseases independent of sociodemographic risk factors [119]. Higher levels of AL (indexed by measures of blood pressure, C-reactive protein, fibrinogen, cholesterol ratio, triglycerides, and cortisol) have been observed in higher weight individuals [120]. This research suggested that these cumulatively elevated biomarkers link to decreased inhibitory control, highlighting the potential for disordered eating to become very difficult to overcome, similar to drug addiction.

It has been suggested that inflammatory mediators act on cortico-amygdala (threat) and cortico-basal ganglia (reward) circuits in a manner which predisposes individuals to "self-medicating" behaviors such as drug use, smoking, and the excess consumption of highly palatable foods [121]. Such behaviors further propagate inflammation and create a self-sustaining feedback loop. The "neuroimmune network hypothesis" proposes that ELA amplifies the communication between the brain and the immune system, promoting low grade peripheral inflammation [122]. The "glucocorticoid cascade hypothesis" posits that stress hormones impair brain function which further increases cortisol levels [123]. Adolescents exposed to childhood adversity have larger pituitary gland volume, associated with lower cortisol awakening response [124]. These authors propose that attenuation of hypothalamic-pituitary-adrenal (HPA) axis function may derive from stress-induced chronic hyperactivation during childhood. Heightened susceptibility may be due to differences in corticotrophin-releasing hormone (CRH) within the HPA axis, responsible for the output of cortisol [125]. Individual differences in inflammatory reactivity might explain why people have differing susceptibility to the consequences of stress, which may include neuroinflammation from stress-induced pro-inflammatory cytokines [126]. A recent cohort study of nine- and ten-year-old children showed that pro-inflammatory diets (i.e., high in saturated fats) increase neuroinflammation in reward-related brain regions, which in turn lead to further unhealthy eating and obesity [127].

A meta-analysis of 1781 people documented significantly decreased hippocampal volumes following ELA, with weaker evidence of increased amygdala volumes [128]. Alterations in corticolimbic circuitry following exposure to trauma make adolescents (n = 64) less able to relax and more vulnerable to risky behavior [129]. Other observable neural changes following ELA include (1) structural variation in gray and white matter (2) functional variation in brain activity and functional connectivity and (3) altered neurotransmitter metabolism [130]. In line with what has been observed in rodent studies [131], these effects might not be restricted to one's own lifespan but may also be transmitted to offspring [132]. It is well established that paternal drug exposure has long-lasting consequences including altered drug sensitivity in subsequent generations [133] but only recently has intergenerational transmission of trauma consistent with epigenetic explanations been described [134]. In animal models, the effects of maternal care on developing DA pathways and reward-directed behavior may account for individual differences in the mesolimbic DA system [16]. In social context, addictions may promote compromised parenting increasing the possibility that suboptimal care may be provided to the next generation. There is a timely need for longitudinal studies that capture the precise biological mechanisms that link ELA to addictions over time, as well as their consequences.

3.1. *Epigenetic Mechanisms of Biological Embedding*

Epigenetics is the study of how the environment regulates the genome, best described as changes in gene function without changes in gene sequence. DNA methylation is an enzymatically-catalyzed modification of DNA and is one plausible mechanism through which early life exposures (low SES, nutritional patterns) become biologically embedded [135]. Methylation changes are apparent even years after the exposure but can be reversible in some cases. Epigenetic processes may be a key mediator between social environments during childhood and disease risk throughout life. Both DNA methylation and demethylation mechanisms are likely recruited during early life unfavorable experiences [136]. Other forms of epigenetic modification include histone modification and noncoding ribonucleic acids [137].

A milestone study confirmed what had been previously shown in animal models: human parental care impacts epigenetic regulation of hippocampal glucocorticoid receptor gene (NR3C1) expression [138]. Such epigenetic marks that persist into adulthood may influence vulnerability for psychopathology through its impact on HPA axis function. However, it is difficult to determine if DNA methylation changes are the immediate results of ELA or a consequence of the phenotypes associated with such adversity [139]. Notwithstanding, NR3C1 has been linked to prenatal stress [140] and is the most studied gene to date related to abuse and neglect [141]. Other genes involved in HPA axis regulation such as corticotrophin-releasing factor (CRF) have been investigated [142]. It is not implausible that developmental programming of the HPA axis and subsequent regulation of the stress response might impact addiction susceptibility, thereby increasing intake of substances known to activate reward pathways, including highly palatable food.

Epigenetic control of the expression of opioid receptor genes (mu-, delta-, and kappa-) has been reviewed in the context of SUDs [143]. While methylation at the mu-opioid receptor (MOR) gene is most strongly associated with drug addiction [144] as well as incentive motivation for processed food [145,146], decreased methylation at the kappa-opioid receptor (KOR) in the anterior insula has been shown in child abuse [147] (discussed further in Section 4.1). In this study of postmortem brain structures, the investigators were unable to detect a change in MOR expression, suggesting different epigenetic signatures associated with addictions and ELA. It is worth noting that different drugs have impacts at different brain regions and many include histone modifications in the nucleus accumbens (NAc) [148]. Other potentially relevant epigenetic modifications include the serotonin transporters [149–151] and proopiomelanocortin (POMC) [152]. Additional research is needed to determine how various epigenetic modifications associate with various forms of disordered eating, including FA.

In a sample of 206 women with bulimic symptomatology, there was evidence of increased methylation of the DA-D2 gene promoter, compared to controls [153]. Taq1A polymorphisms at the D2 receptor has been well-studied and known to influence impulsive behavior [154]. Recent data shows that DNA methylation in obesity-related genes may relate to obesity risk in adolescents [155]. Increased obesity susceptibility genes (e.g., FTO) have been found in the insula and substantia nigra (brain regions involved in addiction and reward) [156]. It has been shown that the methylation status on DA signaling genes (SLC18A1 and SLC6A3) might underlie epigenetic mechanisms contributing to carbohydrate and calorie consumption, as well as fat deposition [157]. Recently authors have linked specific dietary components with the gut microbiome in an effort to determine epigenetic factors on offspring susceptibility to obesity [158]. Expression levels of candidate genes implicated in glucose and energy homeostasis (e.g., HDAC7 and IGF2BP2) could be epigenetically regulated by gut bacterial populations [159]. The link between epigenetic marks and gut microbes appear to be mediated by host-microbial metabolites acting as substrates and cofactors for key epigenetic enzymes in the host [160]. More research linking epigenetics to the microbiome is timely and warranted, particularly in the context of dysfunctional eating behavior (including both under- and overeating).

4. Stress & Obesity

While a PTSD diagnosis is associated with an altered stress response, chronic stress can exist in the absence of PTSD, and has been the focus of several investigations related to eating behavior. Multiple pathways have been described which link stress to obesity, including (1) interference with cognitive processes (executive function, self-regulation) (2) behavior (eating, physical activity, sleep) (3) physiological changes (HPA axis, reward processing, gut microbiome) and (4) production of biochemical hormones and peptides (leptin, ghrelin, neuropeptide Y) [114]. At a basic level, stress may lead to food consumption in the absence of hunger. It is established that poor executive functioning is associated with consumption of palatable food, leading to inflammation and metabolic changes promoting weight gain [161–163]. Other pathways which have been identified include the autonomic nervous system (cardiovascular functioning), the epigenome (intergenerational transmission), and the metabolome (profile of metabolites in body) [164]. The vagus nerve (part of the autonomic nervous system) has been identified as an important physiological stress pathway linked to gut microbiota [165]. With rising interest in the gut-brain axis, novel pathways which include FA are being explored [166]. FA can be considered as a partial mediator in the stress-obesity pathway, likely resulting from one or many of the biologically embedded pathways described herein.

To illustrate further, individual differences in neural response to food cues under stress have been observed in human neuroimaging studies [167], lending support to differential susceptibility. It is well established that amygdala function is moderated by stress-induced glucocorticoid (GC) release [20], and a less efficient HPA axis negative feedback loop may represent a deficiency in emotion and stress regulation [168]. Highly palatable foods stimulate stress hormones that alter the limbic system (emotions) and striatal (motivational) pathways, promoting further food craving and excessive intake [169]. Rewarding foods upregulate CRF in the amygdala and related limbic striatal pathways. The most direct physiological pathway is dominated by cortisol, which stimulates fat storage and changes dietary behavior through increased reward sensitivity (DA and opioid systems) and increased appetite (arcuate nucleus in the hypothalamus) [165]. Future research should attempt to clarify the biological embedding of chronic stress both in the absence and presence of diagnosed PTSD, specifically impacting reward-related pathways associated with consumption behavior. Additionally, more research is needed on biopsychosocial factors of resilience in the context of both FA and obesity.

4.1. Stress & Addictions

Given the established links between stress and obesity, these links can be used to conceptualize relationships between stress and FA. The phenomenon of stress-induced reinstatement of drug-seeking is generalizable to other substances, including food [170]. To illustrate, the DA and GC systems are both highly involved in substance addictions, and ELA may induce long-lasting alterations in these systems. One of the most profound effects of stress is the activation of the HPA axis with release of CRF from the paraventricular nucleus. Human studies have shown stress exposure increases alcohol craving [171]. Both chronic stress and long-standing alcohol use promote PFC dysfunction [172]. Changes in CRF activity that result from chronic alcohol exposure within the extended amygdala network is thought to be key factor in withdrawal symptoms [173]. It has been proposed that repeated altered activity in the DA system and sustained activation of the CRF system leads to AL and negative emotional states [174]. The central thesis in Koob's allostatic view of stress and addiction is that stress leads to changes in brain CRF that have a direct impact on addiction [175]. Withdrawal can produce elevated levels of GCs and increase release of CRF in the central nucleus of the amygdala [175].

It has also been suggested that increased CRF alters serotonin release in the brain which facilitates DA in the accumbens [176]. Prolonged exposure to stress can lead to irregular changes in GC receptor density (epigenetics) which may increase the reinforcing effects of alcohol and drugs [177,178].

Interestingly, a higher salivary cortisol level in response to stress has been associated with higher drop-out rates in treatment [179]. It has also been suggested that variability in stress-related genes may contribute to the ability of certain individuals to remain abstinent from heroin, possibly due to higher stress resilience [180]. Importantly, not only does STA increase addiction behaviors, some authors have suggested this association also exists in the opposite direction [181,182]. With illicit drugs, their procurement and use can predispose individuals to traumatic stress [183,184]. In animal models, chronic opioid pretreatment is able to robustly augment associative fear learning [185]. These changes were not observed when opioids were given after the traumatic event, and potentiation lasted beyond discontinuation of drug exposure. This concept has been thoroughly described as part of the withdrawal process in widely accepted addiction models [186–188]. However, more research is needed to understand how long-term exposure to highly palatable foods may alter one's long-term response to stressful life experiences, and how this dynamic can play out in reciprocal and bidirectional ways, for example in the presence of weight stigma and dietary restraint (and cumulatively over time).

A recent review of preclinical data suggests three mechanisms by which DA and GCs interact: (1) GCs upregulate tyrosine hydroxylase (rate-limiting enzyme in DA synthesis) (2) GCs down-regulate monoamine oxidase (enzyme responsible for DA removal) and (3) GCs are hypothesized to decrease DA uptake subsequently increasing synaptic DA [189]. Clearly stress enhances substance abuse-related effects at multiple points along the mesolimbic projection. The KOR system plays an important role in behavioral stress responses and has been implicated in stress-induced maladaptive responses [190]. While MOR activation produces euphoria, KOR is generally aversive and may contribute to negative affect states in withdrawal. According to some authors, it is possible that a stress-induced increase in KOR function promotes drug seeking by reducing DA transmission [190]. Meanwhile, reduced MOR has been observed in comorbid binge eating disorder and obesity [191] and across SUDs [144] which strongly suggest neurochemical overlap in these conditions, and which can persist despite weight loss or periods of drug abstinence. Any change in stress neurobiology is likely to influence reward. Based on observed deficits in the ventral striatum, reward responsiveness and processing may be a primary mediator of the effects of ELA [192]. Taken together, FA is a biologically plausible explanation for the life course association between ELA and obesity, however important contextual factors from the psychological domain deserve further consideration.

5. Psychological Correlates of Food Addiction & Obesity

Thus far we have highlighted several social and environmental factors associated with STA and addiction-like eating. We have reviewed emerging data on the biological embedding of adversity, which may increase an individual's susceptibility to FA, and potentially lead to obesity over time. Based on the overlap between FA and EDs as well as SUDs, we have recommended including these variables into statistical models which investigate weight outcomes. Finally, we have proposed a comprehensive conceptual framework to further contextualize these relationships by including two psychological (as well as socially constructed) correlates of FA, EDs, and obesity: dietary restraint and weight stigma.

5.1. Dietary Restraint

Restrained eating is generally defined as a cognitive effort to eat less in order to lose weight [193], which has been viewed both as the problem and solution to obesity [194]. More recently it has become clear that theories of weight loss based on low-calorie dieting are failing, likely due to neurochemical, endocrine, and gastrointestinal factors which are not adequately captured by simple models of energy balance. While the concept of dietary restraint has been linked to some positive outcomes (e.g., weight management, prevention efforts) [195], it is included in our model as a risk factor for eating pathology, often associated with EDs (sometimes referred to as restriction). A classic study conducted by Ancel Keys in the 1940s examined the link between starvation and changes in human biology and behavior [196]. The study showed that significant (intentional) weight loss produced the onset of binge eating in 30% of participants (n = 36). Many of the individuals who were reduced to 50% of their baseline caloric intake for extended periods of time (months) began collecting recipes and cookbooks. The finding that caloric restriction leads to preoccupation with food has been widely cited in the ED literature. Meanwhile, it is less clear if deliberate efforts to eat differently (focusing on dietary quality rather than quantity) should be classified as pathological restraint. Extreme diets intended for health reasons which impair daily function have been described as "orthorexia nervosa" which appears to be growing problem [197]. Research linking FA recovery to orthorexia is timely and warranted.

A dieting intervention on 121 females which included monitoring and restricting showed that monitoring increases perceived stress, while restricting increases the cortisol output [198]. Dieting is stressful, which may explain why engaging in dieting behaviors aimed at losing weight can actually have the opposite effect. Future iterations of Figure 1 may include an arrow directly from dietary restraint to STA, whereas in the current model there is only a backdoor path through weight stigma. A twin study from Finland (n = 4129) showed that dieters are prone to future weight gain independent of genetic factors [199]. A recent fMRI study showed that "successful" restrained eaters had stronger activation in the middle frontal gyrus and cerebellum (associated with executive function and inhibition) suggesting that food temptations may trigger processes of positive inhibition in some, but not others [200]. It is likely that altered neurochemistry from SUD and/or ELA/STA will impact the degree of success with dietary restraint. More research is needed on the impact of trauma on various eating behaviors, including restriction. It will prove important to better define dietary restraint in the context of FA recovery.

There is considerable debate on how to approach FA from a nutritional standpoint, including incorporating FA data into the traditional ED landscape [201]. Meule has stated that "dietary restraint does not have to be dysfunctional as long as flexible elements are added" [202]. Based on available data linking FA and EDs (Section 1.2), it is proposed that restrained eating moderates the link between food environment and FA, as well as the link between FA and obesity (Figure 1). In other words, individuals engaging in dietary restraint are predicted to display higher levels of FA severity. Future research should examine the directionality as well as cumulative interplay of this relationship. Furthermore, it is proposed that individuals who meet criteria for FA and engage in dietary restraint may experience different effects on their weight status, depending on whether or not the restraint is successful, unsuccessful, pathological, or part of a restrictive ED. These theories need to be tested in both observational and experimental studies in an effort to better develop the emerging field of behavioral health nutrition. Recently, an 8-step process has been proposed to help clinicians discern FA from dietary restraint in order to inform inclusive vs. exclusive nutrition strategies [46]. The key discerning factors include the presence of SUD, PTSD, and ELA, which, if all present, can provide more confidence in the strength of an FA signal, particularly in the absence of dieting behaviors.

5.2. Weight Stigma

Weight stigma has been described as a "vicious cycle" where weight stigma begets weight gain [203]. Similar to dieting, the experience of stigmatization increases cortisol, which may drive food consumption by sensitizing the reward system [203]. In addition to increased cortisol, weight stigma also increases oxidative stress [204] providing further evidence of biological embedding. In a large sample of adolescents (n = 115,180), perceiving one's body as overweight increases risk of suicidality [205]. Conceptually, weight stigma is similar to other forms of STA, which we consider as midstream drivers of eating behavior and subsequent weight outcomes, both through biological and psychosocial pathways. While unproven, it is possible that body dissatisfaction and self-stigma drives avoidance behaviors (e.g., weight loss to avoid adiposity) which is similar to the avoidance experience in PTSD. This may be one reason why efforts to lose weight can be persistent (or even relentless) for so many, despite the fact that weight loss efforts have been unsuccessful (or unsustainable) in the past.

In a large national sample (n = 5129), weight discrimination was associated with overeating (specifically convenience foods) and less regular meal timing [206]. Individuals who are the target of weight stigma have been shown to decrease self-control and perceived capacity for weight management [207]. In a large sample of adolescents (n = 1497), FA and psychological distress mediated the association between weight-related self-stigma and binge eating [208]. It is worth acknowledging differences between externalized (others) and internalized (self) weight bias. It has also been shown that some people will experience longer term distress from weight stigma than others [209]. Perceptions and/or experiences of weight bias in primary care settings have been shown to negatively influence patient engagement with health care services [210]. In summary, weight stigma has emerged as an important component of obesity context, with strong arguments in favor of adopting weight-inclusive health policy [211]. While the FA explanation for weight control has been shown to decrease weight stigma among groups [212,213] it has been suggested that FA can increase internalized weight stigma among individuals [214]. More research is needed on the role of weight stigma driving dietary restraint, both as a cause and consequence of addiction-like eating.

6. What Does It Mean for Public Health?

Research on biological programming attempts to identify the most critical and sensitive periods that underlie the developmental origins of later childhood and adult disease [215]. It has been suggested that the timing of adversity explains more variability in DNA methylation than the accumulation or recency of exposure [216]. It has also been observed that different dimensions of adversity have distinct influences on neurodevelopment [217]. The exact mechanisms which link human DNA methylation with psychological disorders have not been elucidated [151]. What we do know is that the cumulative effects of STA can impact neural function with significant implications for substance-seeking behaviors. All addictions share a common neurobiology and have known relationships to STA in both directions. Sugar, salt, and fat added to foods make them more palatable and reinforce "drug-like" behavior with loss of control, continued use despite consequences, binge episodes, and other similarities with traditional drugs of abuse. It is clear that obesity causes changes in opioid and DA signaling which alter reward processing [218]. Given the established links between ELA and the propensity for behavioral health disorders including SUD, ED, and FA, prevention efforts might have a meaningful impact upstream. Addressing clusters of disorders with shared underpinnings jointly may be more fruitful than a one-disorder-at-a-time approach [122].

A recent study of New Orleans children showed that neighborhood stress exerts a direct influence on obesity, after adjusting for diet and activity [219]. Such findings support the need to improve social conditions rather than efforts to address obesity at the individual level. It will be important to identify positive contextual factors such as neighborhood and school safety, as well as resilience [105] and develop community-based programs that promote these protective factors. Resiliency-building programs that reduce delay discounting may decrease addictive behaviors [220]. Meanwhile, socioeconomic differences in the quality of early life create "cumulative disadvantage" that contribute to gradients in health status [37]. SES indicators are upstream determinants of health while biological factors are more proximate determinants [221]. Neighborhood disadvantage creates social context which may become biologically embedded [222]. The impact of low SES can become embedded into inflammatory processes, the HPA axis, and neural function/structure, all of which are epigenetically controlled [135]. It is not unreasonable to assume that normalizing/improving HPA axis function may be beneficial in the treatment and relapse of addiction-related disorders. Given that epigenetic patterns are sculpted during early life [137], reducing stressors appears crucial to the long-term management of FA.

A "systems thinking" multilevel approach will be critical to reverse obesity trends. For example, trauma-informed treatment and stress management curriculum should be made available in underserved communities, starting with schools [107]. Mobilizing cross-sector interdisciplinary partnerships to connect ELA to later life health outcomes will be critical. It has been stated that "fostering increased societal awareness about toxic stress exposures that are often hidden, stigmatized, and attached to shame needs to occur across generations" [223]. Greater awareness of the biological mechanisms discussed herein are likely to reduce weight stigma, which is a known barrier for individual help-seeking behaviors in those with obesity [224] as well as SUDs [225]. Feelings of rejection associated with weight stigma and disordered eating are additional stressors which may further perpetuate a negative cycle [114,168]. A recent study showed that the FA model explanation for obesity resulted in lower stigma than the traditional "diet and exercise" explanation that attributes obesity to personal responsibility [213]. Given that weight stigma is a psychosocial contributor to maladaptive eating behavior, interventions targeting stigma (at the individual and societal levels) are warranted.

6.1. Food Policy

This paper has reviewed evidence to suggest that improving the early childhood environment might impact obesity risk and therefore should be a public health priority. Meanwhile, if reward-related neuroadaptations associated with addiction persist over time, addressing only the underlying factors may fail to create lasting changes in eating behavior, suggesting that policies targeting the food environment will also be important. Given that the food environment in the US promotes easy access to foods with addictive potential [226] it is not unreasonable to hypothesize that highly palatable foods leave a biological imprint which may perpetuate FA symptoms across the lifespan and into subsequent generations, as has been shown in animal models [131]. Western-style diets rapidly impair appetitive control, compared to those on their habitual diet [65]. Combined with heightened susceptibility to STA stemming from ELA, efforts to address the obesity epidemic may be futile without strategic multilevel interventions targeting corporate responsibility (i.e., "Big Food") [227].

There is mounting evidence of the harmful effects of processed foods in contemporary diets. A recent trial comparing the caloric intake of those on ultra-processed foods (containing minimal whole foods) compared to unprocessed/whole foods for two weeks found ad libitum intake was increased by approximately 500 kcal/day on the ultra-processed diet [228]. Not surprisingly, people gained weight on the ultra-processed diet and lost weight on the unprocessed. Cross-sectional data (NHANES 2005–2014) has shown that higher consumption of ultra-processed foods is associated with excess weight and is more pronounced in females [229]. A study from Spain showed that four or more servings per day of ultra-processed foods is associated with a 62% increased hazard for all-cause mortality, where each additional serving increased all-cause mortality by 18% [230]. It remains unclear if the negative health effects are due to the direct impact of the processed foods, or the displacement of nutrient-dense high-fiber foods protective against oxidative stress and associated inflammation.

Public health interventions to increase access to healthy foods in lower SES communities have been unsuccessful in reducing obesity, therefore new approaches are needed. Identifying certain foods to be addictive may encourage collective efforts to avoid them [231] and is associated with support for policies to curb their use [232] similar to how public health officials addressed Big Tobacco. Only recently have researchers and policy makers begun to explore targeting the food environment in universal ED prevention efforts [233]. It has been suggested that "processed food addiction is the result of an intentional epidemic of addiction not an incidental by-product of Western environments" [62]. The term "processed food addiction" implicates the food industry rather than the individual. There is a critical need for increased awareness of FA and the role played by multinational food corporations in promoting processed foods with addictive qualities [214]. Evidence suggests that aggressive marketing of these foods to children, adolescents, and young adults disproportionately affects vulnerable groups [234–238]. While it is highly unlikely that food companies will re-formulate their products based on self-regulation, it also unrealistic to expect food-addicted individuals to regularly avoid food-related temptations. Policy support should include warning labels, industry reductions on sugar, and product bans (e.g., energy drinks) [232] while legal tools include advertising restrictions and class-action litigation [239]. Several authors have recommended policies restricting fast food advertising to adolescents [240,241]. Based on growing evidence for FA, this may be indicated

7. Conclusions

The biological underpinnings of addictions strongly imply a role for ELA in the development of FA and obesity. Importantly, ELA can alter the physiological response to various forms of psychosocial STA across multiple body systems, which can have a cumulative impact on health behaviors over the lifespan. FA research which began in animal models has since been described in human neuroimaging studies which capture neurobiological and behavioral overlap between FA and SUDs. A biopsychosocial perspective on FA considers biomarkers such as inflammatory markers and other measures of AL, the HPA axis including the output of cortisol, epigenetic mechanisms including those that influence the HPA axis, and various structural, functional, and morphological brain changes, following exposure to ELA and STA. In order to contextualize risk, a biopsychosocial model considers the upstream drivers and fundamental causes of health disparities, such as SES and environmental (e.g., neighborhood) factors that impact food access and food choices. Furthermore, obesity frameworks should incorporate weight stigma as an important cause and consequence of the epidemic, suggested herein as a form of STA that can also become biological embedded. Finally, the role of dietary restraint has been included as an important psychological factor that should be accounted for when conceptualizing FA and obesity, particularly given the strong relationship between ELA and EDs, as recently reviewed elsewhere [46].

Stress proliferates over the life course and across generations, widening health disparities between advantaged and disadvantaged groups [242]. This might explain why public health nutrition interventions in low SES communities have had limited success. Consumption of highly palatable foods to "self-medicate" the long-term biological impact of chronic stress may be a critical factor in understanding the obesity crisis. This is particularly true for marginalized groups with less access (e.g., affordability) to unprocessed foods. Higher SES groups are more likely to have success in reducing addiction-like eating compared to lower SES groups who are constrained by access and resources. Public health interventions should account for the growing inequities in health outcomes. Biopsychosocial approaches that consider the cumulative interplay between social and biological factors are helpful when conceptualizing multiple systems driving substance-related disorders, whether it be alcohol, drugs, nicotine, or food [243]. A biopsychosocial model may contribute to conceptual and methodological advances in our understanding and treatment of obesity. Meanwhile, separating constructs into biological, psychological, and social factors (as in Figure 1) can be contraindicated by ecological models that emphasize the dynamic reciprocity between these levels. However, our conceptual model has discerned between these factors in order to encourage further contextual analysis of FA.

Based on the biological plausibility of FA as a consequence of psychosocial STA, potential solutions to the obesity epidemic may include: (1) improve social conditions in order to reduce exposure to ELA, as well develop community-based programs for early intervention (2) decrease weight stigma based on FA data implying that body weight is not simply a "choice" (3) mind-body approaches (e.g., yoga, meditation) designed to improve the human stress response and (4) policy proposals aimed at the food industry to reduce exposure to highly palatable foods. More information is needed about the role of nutrition in the reversibility of unfavorable gene expression. More research is needed to investigate whether long-term dietary changes such as abstaining from highly palatable foods is even feasible. If so, will this improve the microbiome and stimulate/reverse epigenetic change and/or lead to altered reward pathways in the brain? At a minimum, it is reasonable to predict that reducing exposure to addiction-like eating can improve executive functioning. Since dietary restraint is a known risk factor for the development of EDs, drastic individual nutrition changes should be implemented in consultation with a qualified professional such as a registered dietitian nutritionist, particularly when there is underlying trauma and/or SUD. Treatment models should be trauma-informed and include staff trainings.

FA and SUD share multiple predisposing factors including ELA which can become biologically embedded. These findings may link social determinants to specific health outcomes and elucidate pathway effects of risk across the life course. Epigenetic processes may be a key mediator between social environments during childhood and disease risk in adulthood. Mediating mechanisms such as

AL, the HPA axis, DNA methylation, and altered reward sensitivity (i.e., dopamine systems) have scientific merit, however the fundamental causes of health inequalities present in society should not be overlooked. Low SES and neighborhood disadvantage remain important drivers of ELA, particularly within the context of the obesity epidemic. The cumulative effects of STA that impact neural function and heighten threat vigilance have significant implications for substance-seeking behaviors, including eating. The FA construct has gained credibility from animal and human studies reviewed herein, which may help reduce stigma associated with addiction-like behaviors, including obesity. More research is needed to understand the differential impact of inflammatory signaling markers on the brain, including assessment of blood brain barrier integrity. The study of neuroinflammation is likely to add explanatory power to our conceptual model and guide future research questions.

If the DSM accepts FA, it will lead to better treatment and eventually public health efforts to improve the national food environment and global nutrition landscape. More resources should be allocated for nutrition education during pregnancy and lactation, particularly in underserved communities where stress and adversity are high, and the food environment is suboptimal. Applying the FA framework has the potential to influence the way people view food, and to ultimately decrease addiction in future generations. FA treatment does not always require specific "food abstinence" but it does warrant reduced exposure and harm reduction strategies. Given the strong evidence that neurobiological responses to food differ among people, personalized precision nutrition interventions are warranted. In order for these strategies to be successful, cultural shifts around food norms will be necessary. Furthermore, FA is both an individual and collective health problem, and should be addressed at the societal level with broad policy interventions. We propose that unregulated promotion of addictive foods by the food industry are major contributors of obesity, particularly in the face of disadvantage and distress. Government interdiction may be required to reduce the epidemic of obesity and the growing problem of food addiction. Multidisciplinary efforts using trauma-informed integrated biopsychosocial frameworks will be necessary to reverse obesity trends.

Author Contributions: Conceptual model, literature review, and first draft preparation (D.A.W.). Draft revisions (N.A. & M.G.). All authors have read and agreed to the published version of the manuscript.

References

1. Popkin, B.M. Nutritional Patterns and Transitions. *Popul. Dev. Rev.* **1993**, *19*, 138–157. [CrossRef]
2. Hall, K.D. Did the Food Environment Cause the Obesity Epidemic? *Obesity* **2018**, *26*, 11–13. [CrossRef] [PubMed]
3. Wang, G.-J.; Volkow, N.D.; Logan, J.; Pappas, N.R.; Wong, C.T.; Zhu, W.; Netusll, N.; Fowler, J.S. Brain dopamine and obesity. *Lancet* **2001**, *357*, 354–357. [CrossRef]
4. Volkow, N.D.; Wise, R.A. How can drug addiction help us understand obesity? *Nat. Neurosci.* **2005**, *8*, 555–560. [CrossRef] [PubMed]
5. Stice, E.; Spoor, S.; Bohon, C.; Small, D. Relation Between Obesity and Blunted Striatal Response to Food Is Moderated by TaqIA A1 Allele. *Science* **2008**, *322*, 449–452. [CrossRef]
6. Saules, K.K.; Carr, M.M.; Herb, K.M. Overeating, Overweight, and Substance Use: What Is the Connection? *Curr. Addict. Rep.* **2018**, *5*, 232–242. [CrossRef]
7. Gold, M.S. From bedside to bench and back again: A 30-year saga. *Physiol. Behav.* **2011**, *104*, 157–161. [CrossRef]
8. Avena, N.M.; Hoebel, B.G. A diet promoting sugar dependency causes behavioral cross-sensitization to a low dose of amphetamine. *Neuroscience* **2003**, *122*, 17–20. [CrossRef]
9. Hoebel, B.G.; Avena, N.M.; Rada, P. Accumbens dopamine-acetylcholine balance in approach and avoidance. *Curr. Opin. Pharmacol.* **2007**, *7*, 617–627. [CrossRef]
10. Hoebel, B.G. Brain neurotransmitters in food and drug reward. *Am. J. Clin. Nutr.* **1985**, *42*, 1133–1150. [CrossRef] [PubMed]

11. Rada, P.; Avena, N.M.; Hoebel, B.G. Daily bingeing on sugar repeatedly releases dopamine in the accumbens shell. *Neuroscience* **2005**, *134*, 737–744. [CrossRef] [PubMed]
12. Avena, N.M.; Rada, P.; Hoebel, B.G. Underweight rats have enhanced dopamine release and blunted acetylcholine response in the nucleus accumbens while bingeing on sucrose. *Neuroscience* **2008**, *156*, 865–871. [CrossRef] [PubMed]
13. Avena, N.M.; Rada, P.; Hoebel, B.G. Evidence for sugar addiction: Behavioral and neurochemical effects of intermittent, excessive sugar intake. *Neurosci. Biobehav. Rev.* **2008**, *32*, 20–39. [CrossRef] [PubMed]
14. Wiss, D.A.; Avena, N.; Rada, P. Sugar Addiction: From Evolution to Revolution. *Front. Psychiatry* **2018**, *9*, 545. [CrossRef]
15. Kim, S.; Kwok, S.; Mayes, L.C.; Potenza, M.N.; Rutherford, H.J.; Strathearn, L. Early adverse experience and substance addiction: Dopamine, oxytocin, and glucocorticoid pathways. *Ann. N. Y. Acad. Sci.* **2017**, *1394*, 74–91. [CrossRef]
16. Peña, C.; Neugut, Y.D.; Calarco, C.A.; Champagne, F.A. Effects of maternal care on the development of midbrain dopamine pathways and reward-directed behavior in female offspring. *Eur. J. Neurosci.* **2014**, *39*, 946–956. [CrossRef]
17. Wei, N.-L.; Quan, Z.-F.; Zhao, T.; Yu, X.-D.; Xie, Q.; Zeng, J.; Ma, F.-K.; Wang, F.; Tang, Q.-S.; Wu, H.; et al. Chronic stress increases susceptibility to food addiction by increasing the levels of DR2 and MOR in the nucleus accumbens. *Neuropsychiatr. Dis. Treat.* **2019**, *15*, 1211–1229. [CrossRef]
18. MacKay, J.C.; Kent, P.; James, J.S.; Cayer, C.; Merali, Z. Ability of palatable food consumption to buffer against the short- and long-term behavioral consequences of social defeat exposure during juvenility in rats. *Physiol. Behav.* **2017**, *177*, 113–121. [CrossRef]
19. Grimm, J.W.; Hyde, J.; Glueck, E.; North, K.; Ginder, D.; Jiganti, K.; Hopkins, M.; Sauter, F.; MacDougall, D.; Hovander, D. Examining persistence of acute environmental enrichment-induced anti-sucrose craving effects in rats. *Appetite* **2019**, *139*, 50–58. [CrossRef]
20. Cohen, M.; Jing, D.; Yang, R.R.; Tottenham, N.; Lee, F.S.; Casey, B. Early-life stress has persistent effects on amygdala function and development in mice and humans. *Proc. Natl. Acad. Sci. USA* **2013**, *110*, 18274–18278. [CrossRef]
21. Felitti, V.J.; Anda, R.F.; Nordenberg, D.; Williamson, D.F.; Spitz, A.M.; Edwards, V.; Koss, M.P.; Marks, J.S. Relationship of Childhood Abuse and Household Dysfunction to Many of the Leading Causes of Death in Adults The Adverse Childhood Experiences (ACE) Study. *Am. J. Prev. Med.* **1998**, *14*, 245–258. [CrossRef]
22. Levis, S.C.; Bentzley, B.S.; Molet, J.; Bolton, J.L.; Perrone, C.R.; Baram, T.Z.; Mahler, S.V. On the early life origins of vulnerability to opioid addiction. *Mol. Psychiatr.* **2019**, 1–8. [CrossRef] [PubMed]
23. Al'Absi, M. The influence of stress and early life adversity on addiction: Psychobiological mechanisms of risk and resilience. *Int. Rev. Neurobiol.* **2020**, *152*, 71–100. [CrossRef] [PubMed]
24. Wiss, D.A.; Brewerton, T.D. Adverse Childhood Experiences and Adult Obesity: A Systematic Review of Plausible Mechanisms and Meta-Analysis of Cross-Sectional Studies. *Physiol. Behav.* **2020**, *223*, 112964. [CrossRef]
25. Hemmingsson, E. Early Childhood Obesity Risk Factors: Socioeconomic Adversity, Family Dysfunction, Offspring Distress, and Junk Food Self-Medication. *Curr. Obes. Rep.* **2018**, *7*, 204–209. [CrossRef]
26. Cammack, A.L.; Gazmararian, J.A.; Suglia, S.F. History of child maltreatment and excessive dietary and screen time behaviors in young adults: Results from a nationally representative study. *Prev. Med.* **2020**, *139*, 106176. [CrossRef]
27. Nunes-Neto, P.R.; Köhler, C.A.; Schuch, F.B.; Solmi, M.; Quevedo, J.; Maes, M.; Murru, A.; Vieta, E.; McIntyre, R.S.; McElroy, S.L.; et al. Food addiction: Prevalence, psychopathological correlates and associations with quality of life in a large sample. *J. Psychiatr. Res.* **2018**, *96*, 145–152. [CrossRef]
28. Bloomfield, M.A.; McCutcheon, R.A.; Kempton, M.; Freeman, T.P.; Howes, O. The effects of psychosocial stress on dopaminergic function and the acute stress response. *Elife* **2019**, *8*, e46797. [CrossRef]
29. Dillon, D.G.; Holmes, A.J.; Birk, J.L.; Brooks, N.; Lyons-Ruth, K.; Pizzagalli, D.A. Childhood Adversity Is Associated with Left Basal Ganglia Dysfunction During Reward Anticipation in Adulthood. *Biol. Psychiat.* **2009**, *66*, 206–213. [CrossRef]
30. Osadchiy, V.; Mayer, E.A.; Bhatt, R.; Labus, J.S.; Gao, L.; Kilpatrick, L.A.; Liu, C.; Tillisch, K.; Naliboff, B.; Chang, L.; et al. History of early life adversity is associated with increased food addiction and sex-specific alterations in reward network connectivity in obesity. *Obes. Sci. Pract.* **2019**, *5*, 416–436. [CrossRef]

31. Heilig, M.; Epstein, D.H.; Nader, M.A.; Shaham, Y. Time to connect: Bringing social context into addiction neuroscience. *Nat. Rev. Neurosci.* **2016**, *17*, 592–599. [CrossRef] [PubMed]
32. Engel, G.L. The need for a new medical model: A challenge for biomedicine. *Science* **1977**, *196*, 129–136. [CrossRef] [PubMed]
33. Baughman, K.; Logue, E.; Sutton, K.; Capers, C.; Jarjoura, D.; Smucker, W. Biopsychosocial characteristics of overweight and obese primary care patients: Do psychosocial and behavior factors mediate sociodemographic effects? *Prev. Med.* **2003**, *37*, 129–137. [CrossRef]
34. Qu, Y.; Galván, A.; Fuligni, A.J.; Telzer, E.H. A Biopsychosocial Approach to Examine Mexican American Adolescents' Academic Achievement and Substance Use. *RSF Russell Sage Found. J. Sci.* **2018**, *4*, 84–97. [CrossRef]
35. Krieger, N. Theories for social epidemiology in the 21st century: An ecosocial perspective. *Int. J. Epidemiol.* **2001**, *30*, 668–677. [CrossRef] [PubMed]
36. Elder, G.H., Jr. The Life Course as Developmental Theory. *Child. Dev.* **1998**, *69*, 1–12. [CrossRef]
37. Hertzman, C. The biological embedding of early experience and its effects on health in adulthood. *Ann. N. Y. Acad. Sci.* **1999**, *896*, 85–95. [CrossRef]
38. Ben-Shlomo, Y.; Kuh, D. A life course approach to chronic disease epidemiology: Conceptual models, empirical challenges and interdisciplinary perspectives. *Int. J. Epidemiol.* **2002**, *31*, 285–293. [CrossRef]
39. Lerner, R.M. The Place of Learning within the Human Development System: A Developmental Contextual Perspective. *Hum. Dev.* **1995**, *38*, 361–366. [CrossRef]
40. Overton, W.F.; Lerner, R.M. Fundamental Concepts and Methods in Developmental Science: A Relational Perspective. *Res. Hum. Dev.* **2014**, *11*, 63–73. [CrossRef]
41. Lerner, R.M.; Johnson, S.K.; Buckingham, M.H. Relational Developmental Systems-Based Theories and the Study of Children and Families: Lerner and Spanier (1978) Revisited. *J. Fam. Theor. Rev.* **2015**, *7*, 83–104. [CrossRef]
42. Gearhardt, A.N.; Corbin, W.R.; Brownell, K.D. Preliminary validation of the Yale Food Addiction Scale. *Appetite* **2009**, *52*, 430–436. [CrossRef] [PubMed]
43. Gearhardt, A.N.; Corbin, W.R.; Brownell, K.D. Development of the Yale Food Addiction Scale Version 2.0. *Psychol. Addict. Behav.* **2016**, *30*, 113–121. [CrossRef] [PubMed]
44. Schulte, E.M.; Grilo, C.M.; Gearhardt, A.N. Shared and unique mechanisms underlying binge eating disorder and addictive disorders. *Clin. Psychol. Rev.* **2016**, *44*, 125–139. [CrossRef] [PubMed]
45. Racine, S.E.; Burt, A.S.; Iacono, W.G.; McGue, M.; Klump, K.L. Dietary restraint moderates genetic risk for binge eating. *J. Abnorm. Psychol.* **2011**, *120*, 119–128. [CrossRef] [PubMed]
46. Wiss, D.; Brewerton, T. Separating the Signal from the Noise: How Psychiatric Diagnoses Can Help Discern Food Addiction from Dietary Restraint. *Nutrients* **2020**, *12*, 2937. [CrossRef]
47. Meule, A.; von Rezori, V.; Blechert, J. Food Addiction and Bulimia Nervosa. *Eur. Eat. Disord. Rev.* **2014**, *22*, 331–337. [CrossRef]
48. Meule, A.; Gearhardt, A.N. Ten Years of the Yale Food Addiction Scale: A Review of Version 2.0. *Curr. Addict. Rep.* **2019**, *6*, 218–228. [CrossRef]
49. Fernandez-Aranda, F.; Karwautz, A.; Treasure, J. Food addiction: A transdiagnostic construct of increasing interest. *Eur. Eat. Disord. Rev.* **2018**, *26*, 536–540. [CrossRef]
50. Romero, X.; Agüera, Z.; Granero, R.; Sánchez, I.; Riesco, N.; Jiménez-Murcia, S.; Gisbert-Rodriguez, M.; Sánchez-González, J.; Casalé, G.; Baenas, I.; et al. Is food addiction a predictor of treatment outcome among patients with eating disorder? *Eur Eat. Disord Rev.* **2019**, *27*, 700–711. [CrossRef]
51. Brewerton, T.D. Food addiction as a proxy for eating disorder and obesity severity, trauma history, PTSD symptoms, and comorbidity. *Eat. Weight. Disord. Stud. Anorex. Bulim. Obes.* **2017**, *22*, 241–247. [CrossRef] [PubMed]
52. Mason, S.M.; Flint, A.J.; Field, A.E.; Austin, B.S.; Rich-Edwards, J.W. Abuse victimization in childhood or adolescence and risk of food addiction in adult women. *Obesity* **2013**, *21*, E775–E781. [CrossRef] [PubMed]
53. Mason, S.M.; Flint, A.J.; Roberts, A.L.; Agnew-Blais, J.; Koenen, K.C.; Rich-Edwards, J.W. Posttraumatic Stress Disorder Symptoms and Food Addiction in Women by Timing and Type of Trauma Exposure. *JAMA Psychiatry* **2014**, *71*, 1271–1278. [CrossRef] [PubMed]

54. Imperatori, C.; Innamorati, M.; Lamis, D.A.; Farina, B.; Pompili, M.; Contardi, A.; Fabbricatore, M. Childhood trauma in obese and overweight women with food addiction and clinical-level of binge eating. *Child. Abus. Negl.* **2016**, *58*, 180–190. [CrossRef]
55. Holgerson, A.A.; Clark, M.M.; Ames, G.E.; Collazo-Clavell, M.L.; Kellogg, T.A.; Graszer, K.M.; Kalsy, S.A.; Grothe, K. Association of Adverse Childhood Experiences and Food Addiction to Bariatric Surgery Completion and Weight Loss Outcome. *Obes. Surg.* **2018**, *28*, 3386–3392. [CrossRef]
56. Warren, C.S.; Lindsay, A.R.; White, E.K.; Claudat, K.; Velasquez, S.C. Weight-related concerns related to drug use for women in substance abuse treatment: Prevalence and relationships with eating pathology. *J. Subst. Abus. Treat.* **2013**, *44*, 494–501. [CrossRef]
57. Wiss, D.A.; Waterhous, T.S. Nutrition Therapy for Eating Disorders, Substance Use Disorders, and Addictions. In *Eating Disorders, Addictions and Substance Use Disorders, Research, Clinical and Treatment Perspectives*; Springer: Berlin/Heidelberg, Germany, 2014; pp. 509–532. ISBN 9783642453779.
58. Khalil, R.B.; Sleilaty, G.; Richa, S.; Seneque, M.; Iceta, S.; Rodgers, R.; Alacreu-Crespo, A.; Maimoun, L.; Lefebvre, P.; Renard, E.; et al. The Impact of Retrospective Childhood Maltreatment on Eating Disorders as Mediated by Food Addiction: A Cross-Sectional Study. *Nutrients* **2020**, *12*, 2969. [CrossRef]
59. Cassin, S.E.; Sijercic, I.; Montemarano, V. Psychosocial Interventions for Food Addiction: A Systematic Review. *Curr. Addict. Rep.* **2020**, *7*, 9–19. [CrossRef]
60. Hebebrand, J.; Albayrak, Ö.; Adan, R.; Antel, J.; Dieguez, C.; de Jong, J.; Leng, G.; Menzies, J.; Mercer, J.G.; Murphy, M.; et al. "Eating addiction", rather than "food addiction", better captures addictive-like eating behavior. *Neurosci. Biobehav. Rev.* **2014**, *47*, 295–306. [CrossRef]
61. Ifland, J.R.; Preuss, H.G.; Marcus, M.T.; Rourke, K.M.; Taylor, W.C.; Burau, K.; Jacobs, W.S.; Kadish, W.; Manso, G. Refined food addiction: A classic substance use disorder. *Med. Hypotheses* **2009**, *72*, 518–526. [CrossRef]
62. Ifland, J.; Preuss, H.G.; Marcus, M.T.; Rourke, K.M.; Taylor, W.; Wright, T.H. Clearing the Confusion around Processed Food Addiction. *J. Am. Coll. Nutr.* **2015**, *34*, 240–243. [CrossRef] [PubMed]
63. Nolan, L.J. Is it time to consider the "food use disorder? " *Appetite* **2017**, *115*, 16–18. [CrossRef] [PubMed]
64. Volkow, N.D.; Wang, G.-J.; Tomasi, D.; Baler, R.D. Obesity and addiction: Neurobiological overlaps. *Obes. Rev.* **2013**, *14*, 2–18. [CrossRef] [PubMed]
65. Stevenson, R.J.; Francis, H.M.; Attuquayefio, T.; Gupta, D.; Yeomans, M.R.; Oaten, M.J.; Davidson, T. Hippocampal-dependent appetitive control is impaired by experimental exposure to a Western-style diet. *R. Soc. Open Sci.* **2020**, *7*, 191338. [CrossRef]
66. Dohle, S.; Diel, K.; Hofmann, W. Executive functions and the self-regulation of eating behavior: A review. *Appetite* **2018**, *124*, 4–9. [CrossRef]
67. Steward, T.; Mestre-Bach, G.; Vintró-Alcaraz, C.; Lozano-Madrid, M.; Agüera, Z.; Fernández-Formoso, J.A.; Granero, R.; Jiménez-Murcia, S.; Vilarrasa, N.; García-Ruiz-de-Gordejuela, A.; et al. Food addiction and impaired executive functions in women with obesity. *Eur. Eat. Disord. Rev.* **2018**, *26*, 574–584. [CrossRef]
68. Chao, S.-H.; Liao, Y.-T.; Chen, V.C.-H.; Li, C.-J.; McIntyre, R.S.; Lee, Y.; Weng, J.-C. Correlation between brain circuit segregation and obesity. *Behav. Brain Res.* **2018**, *337*, 218–227. [CrossRef]
69. Ronan, L.; Alexander-Bloch, A.; Fletcher, P.C. Childhood Obesity, Cortical Structure, and Executive Function in Healthy Children. *Cereb. Cortex* **2019**, *30*, 2519–2528. [CrossRef]
70. Laurent, J.S.; Watts, R.; Adise, S.; Allgaier, N.; Chaarani, B.; Garavan, H.; Potter, A.; Mackey, S. Associations Among Body Mass Index, Cortical Thickness, and Executive Function in Children. *JAMA Pediatr.* **2020**, *174*, 170. [CrossRef]
71. Yang, Y.; Shields, G.S.; Wu, Q.; Liu, Y.; Guo, C. Obesity is associated with poor working memory in women, not men: Findings from a nationally representative dataset of U.S. adults. *Eat. Behav.* **2019**, *35*, 101338. [CrossRef]
72. Sattler, K.M.; Deane, F.P.; Tapsell, L.; Kelly, P.J. Gender differences in the relationship of weight-based stigmatisation with motivation to exercise and physical activity in overweight individuals. *Health Psychol. Open* **2018**, *5*, 205510291875969. [CrossRef] [PubMed]
73. Guardabassi, V.; Tomasetto, C. Weight status or weight stigma? Obesity stereotypes—Not excess weight—Reduce working memory in school-aged children. *J. Exp. Child. Psychol.* **2019**, *189*, 104706. [CrossRef] [PubMed]

74. Kiyici, S.; Koca, N.; Sigirli, D.; Aslan, B.B.; Guclu, M.; Kisakol, G. Food Addiction Correlates with Psychosocial Functioning More Than Metabolic Parameters in Patients with Obesity. *Metab. Syndr. Relat. Disord.* **2020**, *18*, 161–167. [CrossRef] [PubMed]
75. Wenzel, K.R.; Weinstock, J.; McGrath, A.B. The Clinical Significance of Food Addiction. *J. Addict. Med.* **2020**, *14*, e153–e159. [CrossRef] [PubMed]
76. VanderBroek-Stice, L.; Stojek, M.K.; Beach, S.; vanDellen, M.R.; MacKillop, J. Multidimensional assessment of impulsivity in relation to obesity and food addiction. *Appetite* **2017**, *112*, 59–68. [CrossRef]
77. Wolz, I.; Granero, R.; Fernández-Aranda, F. A comprehensive model of food addiction in patients with binge-eating symptomatology: The essential role of negative urgency. *Compr. Psychiatry* **2017**, *74*, 118–124. [CrossRef]
78. Meule, A.; de Zwaan, M.; Müller, A. Attentional and motor impulsivity interactively predict 'food addiction' in obese individuals. *Compr. Psychiatry* **2017**, *72*, 83–87. [CrossRef]
79. Maxwell, A.L.; Gardiner, E.; Loxton, N.J. Investigating the relationship between reward sensitivity, impulsivity, and food addiction: A systematic review. *Eur. Eat. Disord. Rev. J. Eat. Disord. Assoc.* **2020**, *28*, 368–384. [CrossRef]
80. Nederkoorn, C.; Guerrieri, R.; Havermans, R.; Roefs, A.; Jansen, A. The interactive effect of hunger and impulsivity on food intake and purchase in a virtual supermarket. *Int. J. Obes.* **2009**, *33*, 905–912. [CrossRef]
81. Trifilieff, P.; Martinez, D. Imaging addiction: D2 receptors and dopamine signaling in the striatum as biomarkers for impulsivity. *Neuropharmacology* **2014**, *76*, 498–509. [CrossRef]
82. Savage, S.W.; Zald, D.H.; Cowan, R.L.; Volkow, N.D.; Marks-Shulman, P.A.; Kessler, R.M.; Abumrad, N.N.; Dunn, J.P. Regulation of novelty seeking by midbrain dopamine D2/D3 signaling and ghrelin is altered in obesity. *Obesity* **2014**, *22*, 1452–1457. [CrossRef] [PubMed]
83. Kekic, M.; McClelland, J.; Bartholdy, S.; Chamali, R.; Campbell, I.C.; Schmidt, U. Bad Things Come to Those Who Do Not Wait: Temporal Discounting Is Associated with Compulsive Overeating, Eating Disorder Psychopathology and Food Addiction. *Front. Psychiatry* **2019**, *10*, 978. [CrossRef] [PubMed]
84. Michaud, A.; Vainik, U.; Garcia-Garcia, I.; Dagher, A. Overlapping Neural Endophenotypes in Addiction and Obesity. *Front. Endocrinol.* **2017**, *8*, 127. [CrossRef] [PubMed]
85. Moloney, G.M.; van Oeffelen, W.E.P.A.; Ryan, F.J.; van de Wouw, M.; Cowan, C.; Claesson, M.J.; Schellekens, H.; Dinan, T.G.; Cryan, J.F. Differential gene expression in the mesocorticolimbic system of innately high- and low-impulsive rats. *Behav. Brain Res.* **2019**, *364*, 193–204. [CrossRef] [PubMed]
86. Gray, J.C.; MacKillop, J.; Weafer, J.; Hernandez, K.M.; Gao, J.; Palmer, A.A.; Wit, H. de Genetic analysis of impulsive personality traits: Examination of a priori candidates and genome-wide variation. *Psychiatry Res.* **2018**, *259*, 398–404. [CrossRef]
87. Morland, K.; Wing, S.; Roux, A.; Poole, C. Neighborhood characteristics associated with the location of food stores and food service places. *Am. J. Prev. Med.* **2002**, *22*, 23–29. [CrossRef]
88. Black, J.L.; Macinko, J. Neighborhoods and obesity. *Nutr. Rev.* **2008**, *66*, 2–20. [CrossRef]
89. Carroll-Scott, A.; Gilstad-Hayden, K.; Rosenthal, L.; Peters, S.M.; McCaslin, C.; Joyce, R.; Ickovics, J.R. Disentangling neighborhood contextual associations with child body mass index, diet, and physical activity: The role of built, socioeconomic, and social environments. *Soc. Sci. Med.* **2013**, *95*, 106–114. [CrossRef]
90. Kim, Y.; Cubbin, C.; Oh, S. A systematic review of neighbourhood economic context on child obesity and obesity-related behaviours. *Obes. Rev.* **2019**, *20*, 420–431. [CrossRef]
91. Claassen, M.; Klein, O.; Bratanova, B.; Claes, N.; Corneille, O. A systematic review of psychosocial explanations for the relationship between socioeconomic status and body mass index. *Appetite* **2019**, *132*, 208–221. [CrossRef]
92. Darmon, N.; Drewnowski, A. Does social class predict diet quality? *Am. J. Clin. Nutr.* **2008**, *87*, 1107–1117. [CrossRef] [PubMed]
93. Fleary, S.A.; Ettienne, R. The relationship between food parenting practices, parental diet and their adolescents' diet. *Appetite* **2019**, *135*, 79–85. [CrossRef] [PubMed]
94. Williams, A.S.; Ge, B.; Petroski, G.; Kruse, R.L.; McElroy, J.A.; Koopman, R.J. Socioeconomic Status and Other Factors Associated with Childhood Obesity. *J. Am. Board Fam. Med.* **2018**, *31*, 514–521. [CrossRef] [PubMed]
95. Mason, S.; Santaularia, N.; Berge, J.; Larson, N.; Neumark-Sztainer, D. Is the childhood home food environment a confounder of the association between child maltreatment exposure and adult body mass index? *Prev. Med.* **2018**, *110*, 86–92. [CrossRef] [PubMed]

96. Walker, B.B.; Shashank, A.; Gasevic, D.; Schuurman, N.; Poirier, P.; Teo, K.; Rangarajan, S.; Yusuf, S.; Lear, S.A. The Local Food Environment and Obesity: Evidence from Three Cities. *Obesity* **2019**, *28*, 40–45. [CrossRef]
97. Cooksey-Stowers, K.; Schwartz, M.B.; Brownell, K.D. Food Swamps Predict Obesity Rates Better Than Food Deserts in the United States. *Int. J. Environ. Res. Public Health* **2017**, *14*, 1366. [CrossRef]
98. Drewnowski, A.; Buszkiewicz, J.; Aggarwal, A.; Rose, C.; Gupta, S.; Bradshaw, A. Obesity and the Built Environment: A Reappraisal. *Obesity* **2019**, *28*, 22–30. [CrossRef]
99. Chirinos, D.A.; Garcini, L.M.; Seiler, A.; Murdock, K.W.; Peek, K.; Stowe, R.P.; Fagundes, C. Psychological and Biological Pathways Linking Perceived Neighborhood Characteristics and Body Mass Index. *Ann. Behav. Med.* **2018**, *53*, 827–838. [CrossRef]
100. Greenland, S.; Pearl, J.; Robins, J.M. Causal Diagrams for Epidemiologic Research. *Epidemiology* **1999**, *10*, 37–48. [CrossRef]
101. Sobal, J.; Stunkard, A.J. Socioeconomic Status and Obesity: A Review of the Literature. *Psychol. Bull.* **1989**, *105*, 260–275. [CrossRef]
102. McLaren, L. Socioeconomic Status and Obesity. *Epidemiol Rev.* **2007**, *29*, 29–48. [CrossRef] [PubMed]
103. De Wilde, J.; Eilander, M.; Middelkoop, B. Effect of neighbourhood socioeconomic status on overweight and obesity in children 2–15 years of different ethnic groups. *Eur. J. Public Health* **2019**, *29*, 796–801. [CrossRef] [PubMed]
104. Chen, M.; Creger, T.; Howard, V.; Judd, S.E.; Harrington, K.F.; Fontaine, K.R. Association of community food environment and obesity among US adults: A geographical information system analysis. *J. Epidemiol. Community Health* **2018**, *73*, 148–155. [CrossRef] [PubMed]
105. Lynch, B.A.; Rutten, L.J.; Wilson, P.M.; Kumar, S.; Phelan, S.; Jacobson, R.M.; Fan, C.; Agunwamba, A. The impact of positive contextual factors on the association between adverse family experiences and obesity in a National Survey of Children. *Prev. Med.* **2018**, *116*, 81–86. [CrossRef] [PubMed]
106. Twaits, A.; Alwan, N.A. The association between area-based deprivation and change in body-mass index over time in primary school children: A population-based cohort study in Hampshire, UK. *Int. J. Obes.* **2019**, *44*, 628–636. [CrossRef]
107. Ford, D.E. The Community and Public Well-being Model: A New Framework and Graduate Curriculum for Addressing Adverse Childhood Experiences. *Acad. Pediatrics* **2017**, *17*, S9–S11. [CrossRef]
108. Metzler, M.; Merrick, M.T.; Klevens, J.; Ports, K.A.; Ford, D.C. Adverse childhood experiences and life opportunities: Shifting the narrative. *Child. Youth Serv. Rev.* **2017**, *72*, 141–149. [CrossRef]
109. Kristenson, M.; Eriksen, H.R.; Sluiter, J.K.; Starke, D.; Ursin, H. Psychobiological mechanisms of socioeconomic differences in health. *Soc. Sci. Med.* **2004**, *58*, 1511–1522. [CrossRef]
110. Gunstad, J.; Paul, R.H.; Spitznagel, M.; Cohen, R.A.; Williams, L.M.; Kohn, M.; Gordon, E. Exposure to early life trauma is associated with adult obesity. *Psychiatry Res.* **2006**, *142*, 31–37. [CrossRef]
111. Friedman, E.M.; Montez, J.K.; Sheehan, C.M.; Guenewald, T.L.; Seeman, T.E. Childhood Adversities and Adult Cardiometabolic Health: Does the Quantity, Timing, and Type of Adversity Matter? *J. Aging Health* **2015**, *27*, 1311–1338. [CrossRef]
112. Mhamdi, S.E.; Lemieux, A.; Abroug, H.; Salah, A.B.; Bouanene, I.; Salem, K.B.; al'Absi, M. Childhood exposure to violence is associated with risk for mental disorders and adult's weight status: A community-based study in Tunisia. *J. Public Health* **2018**, *41*, 502–510. [CrossRef] [PubMed]
113. Pickett, S.; Burchenal, C.A.; Haber, L.; Batten, K.; Phillips, E. Understanding and effectively addressing disparities in obesity: A systematic review of the psychological determinants of emotional eating behaviours among Black women. *Obes. Rev.* **2020**, *21*, e13010. [CrossRef] [PubMed]
114. Tomiyama, A. Stress and Obesity. *Annu. Rev. Psychol.* **2019**, *70*, 703–718. [CrossRef] [PubMed]
115. Doom, J.R.; Lumeng, J.C.; Sturza, J.; Kaciroti, N.; Vazquez, D.M.; Miller, A.L. Longitudinal associations between overweight/obesity and stress biology in low-income children. *Int. J. Obes.* **2019**, *44*, 646–655. [CrossRef] [PubMed]
116. Barker, D. The fetal and infant origins of adult disease. *Br. Med. J.* **1990**, *301*, 1111. [CrossRef]
117. McEwen, B.S.; Stellar, E. Stress and the Individual: Mechanisms Leading to Disease. *Arch. Intern. Med.* **1993**, *153*, 2093–2101. [CrossRef]
118. McEwen, B.S. Stress, Adaption, and Disease. *Ann. N. Y. Acad. Sci.* **1998**, *840*, 33–44. [CrossRef]
119. Seeman, T.; Singer, B.; Rowe, J.; Horwitz, R.; McEwen, B. Price of adaptation—Allostatic load and its health consequences. MacArthur studies of successful aging. *Arch. Intern. Med.* **1997**, *157*, 2259–2268. [CrossRef]

120. Ottino-González, J.; Jurado, M.A.; García-García, I.; Caldú, X.; Prats-Soteras, X.; Tor, E.; Sender-Palacios, M.J.; Garolera, M. Allostatic load and executive functions in overweight adults. *Psychoneuroendocrinology* **2019**, *106*, 165–170. [CrossRef]
121. Nusslock, R.; Miller, G.E. Early-Life Adversity and Physical and Emotional Health Across the Lifespan: A Neuroimmune Network Hypothesis. *Biol. Psychiatry* **2016**, *80*, 23–32. [CrossRef]
122. Hostinar, C.E.; Nusslock, R.; Miller, G.E. Future Directions in the Study of Early-Life Stress and Physical and Emotional Health: Implications of the Neuroimmune Network Hypothesis. *J. Clin. Child. Adolesc. Psychol.* **2018**, *47*, 142–156. [CrossRef] [PubMed]
123. Sapolsky, R.; Krey, L.; McEwen, B. The neuroendocrinology of stress and aging: The glucocorticoid cascade hypothesis. *Endocr. Rev.* **1986**, *7*, 284–301. [CrossRef] [PubMed]
124. Kaess, M.; Whittle, S.; O'Brien-Simpson, L.; Allen, N.B.; Simmons, J.G. Childhood maltreatment, pituitary volume and adolescent hypothalamic-pituitary-adrenal axis—Evidence for a maltreatment-related attenuation. *Psychoneuroendocrinology* **2018**, *98*, 39–45. [CrossRef] [PubMed]
125. Boyce, T.W. Differential Susceptibility of the Developing Brain to Contextual Adversity and Stress. *Neuropsychopharmacology* **2015**, *41*, 142–162. [CrossRef] [PubMed]
126. Finnell, J.E.; Wood, S.K. Putative Inflammatory Sensitive Mechanisms Underlying Risk or Resilience to Social Stress. *Front. Behav. Neurosci.* **2018**, *12*, 240. [CrossRef] [PubMed]
127. Rapuano, K.M.; Laurent, J.S.; Hagler, D.J.; Hatton, S.N.; Thompson, W.K.; Jernigan, T.L.; Dale, A.M.; Casey, B.J.; Watts, R. Nucleus accumbens cytoarchitecture predicts weight gain in children. *Proc. Natl. Acad. Sci. USA* **2020**, *117*, 26977–26984. [CrossRef] [PubMed]
128. Calem, M.; Bromis, K.; McGuire, P.; Morgan, C.; Kempton, M.J. Meta-analysis of associations between childhood adversity and hippocampus and amygdala volume in non-clinical and general population samples. *Neuroimage Clin.* **2017**, *14*, 471–479. [CrossRef]
129. Elsey, J.; Coates, A.; Lacadie, C.M.; McCrory, E.J.; Sinha, R.; Mayes, L.C.; Potenza, M.N. Childhood Trauma and Neural Responses to Personalized Stress, Favorite-Food and Neutral-Relaxing Cues in Adolescents. *Neuropsychopharmacology* **2015**, *40*, 1580–1589. [CrossRef]
130. Berens, A.E.; Jensen, S.K.; Nelson, C.A. Biological embedding of childhood adversity: From physiological mechanisms to clinical implications. *BMC Med.* **2017**, *15*, 135. [CrossRef] [PubMed]
131. Wiss, D.A.; Criscitelli, K.; Gold, M.; Avena, N. Preclinical evidence for the addiction potential of highly palatable foods: Current developments related to maternal influence. *Appetite* **2017**, *115*, 19–27. [CrossRef] [PubMed]
132. Buss, C.; Entringer, S.; Moog, N.K.; Toepfer, P.; Fair, D.A.; Simhan, H.N.; Heim, C.M.; Wadhwa, P.D. Intergenerational Transmission of Maternal Childhood Maltreatment Exposure: Implications for Fetal Brain Development. *J. Am. Acad. Child. Adolesc. Psychiatry* **2017**, *56*, 373–382. [CrossRef]
133. Nieto, S.J.; Kosten, T.A. Who's your daddy? Behavioral and epigenetic consequences of paternal drug exposure. *Int. J. Dev. Neurosci.* **2019**, *78*, 109–121. [CrossRef]
134. Costa, D.L.; Yetter, N.; DeSomer, H. Intergenerational transmission of paternal trauma among US Civil War ex-POWs. *Proc. Natl. Acad. Sci. USA* **2018**, *115*, 11215–11220. [CrossRef] [PubMed]
135. Demetriou, C.A.; Veldhoven, K.; Relton, C.; Stringhini, S.; Kyriacou, K.; Vineis, P. Biological embedding of early-life exposures and disease risk in humans: A role for DNA methylation. *Eur. J. Clin. Investig.* **2015**, *45*, 303–332. [CrossRef] [PubMed]
136. Lutz, P.-E.; Turecki, G. DNA methylation and childhood maltreatment: From animal models to human studies. *Neuroscience* **2014**, *264*, 142–156. [CrossRef]
137. McGowan, P.O.; Szyf, M. The epigenetics of social adversity in early life: Implications for mental health outcomes. *Neurobiol. Dis.* **2010**, *39*, 66–72. [CrossRef] [PubMed]
138. McGowan, P.O.; Sasaki, A.; D'Alessio, A.C.; Dymov, S.; Labonté, B.; Szyf, M.; Turecki, G.; Meaney, M.J. Epigenetic regulation of the glucocorticoid receptor in human brain associates with childhood abuse. *Nat. Neurosci.* **2009**, *12*, 342–348. [CrossRef]
139. Szyf, M. DNA Methylation, Behavior and Early Life Adversity. *J. Genet. Genom.* **2013**, *40*, 331–338. [CrossRef]
140. Palma-Gudiel, H.; Córdova-Palomera, A.; Eixarch, E.; Deuschle, M.; Fañanás, L. Maternal psychosocial stress during pregnancy alters the epigenetic signature of the glucocorticoid receptor gene promoter in their offspring: A meta-analysis. *Epigenetics* **2015**, *10*, 893–902. [CrossRef]

141. Mitchell, C.; Schneper, L.M.; Notterman, D.A. DNA methylation, early life environment, and health outcomes. *Pediatric Res.* **2015**, *79*, 212–219. [CrossRef]
142. Bakusic, J.; Schaufeli, W.; Claes, S.; Godderis, L. Stress, burnout and depression: A systematic review on DNA methylation mechanisms. *J. Psychosom. Res.* **2017**, *92*, 34–44. [CrossRef] [PubMed]
143. Wei, L.-N. Epigenetic control of the expression of opioid receptor genes. *Epigenetics* **2008**, *3*, 119–121. [CrossRef] [PubMed]
144. Belzeaux, R.; Lalanne, L.; Kieffer, B.L.; Lutz, P.-E. Focusing on the Opioid System for Addiction Biomarker Discovery. *Trends Mol. Med.* **2018**, *24*, 206–220. [CrossRef] [PubMed]
145. Giuliano, C.; Cottone, P. The role of the opioid system in binge eating disorder. *CNS Spectr.* **2015**, *20*, 537–545. [CrossRef] [PubMed]
146. Pucci, M.; Bonaventura, M.; Vezzoli, V.; Zaplatic, E.; Massimini, M.; Mai, S.; Sartorio, A.; Scacchi, M.; Persani, L.; Maccarrone, M.; et al. Preclinical and Clinical Evidence for a Distinct Regulation of Mu Opioid and Type 1 Cannabinoid Receptor Genes Expression in Obesity. *Front. Genet.* **2019**, *10*, 523. [CrossRef]
147. Lutz, P.-E.; Gross, J.A.; Dhir, S.K.; Maussion, G.; Yang, J.; Bramoulle, A.; Meaney, M.J.; Turecki, G. Epigenetic Regulation of the Kappa Opioid Receptor by Child Abuse. *Biol. Psychiatry* **2018**, *84*, 751–761. [CrossRef] [PubMed]
148. Walker, D.M.; Nestler, E.J. Neuroepigenetics and addiction. *Sci. Direct* **2018**, *148*, 747–765. [CrossRef]
149. Denhardt, D.T. Effect of stress on human biology: Epigenetics, adaptation, inheritance, and social significance. *J. Cell. Physiol.* **2018**, *233*, 1975–1984. [CrossRef]
150. Seo, D.; Patrick, C.J.; Kennealy, P.J. Role of serotonin and dopamine system interactions in the neurobiology of impulsive aggression and its comorbidity with other clinical disorders. *Aggress. Violent Behav.* **2008**, *13*, 383–395. [CrossRef]
151. Kader, F.; Ghai, M.; Maharaj, L. The effects of DNA methylation on human psychology. *Behav Brain Res.* **2018**, *346*, 47–65. [CrossRef]
152. Candler, T.; Kühnen, P.; Prentice, A.M.; Silver, M. Epigenetic regulation of POMC; implications for nutritional programming, obesity and metabolic disease. *Front. Neuroendocrinol.* **2019**, *54*, 100773. [CrossRef] [PubMed]
153. Groleau, P.; Joober, R.; Israel, M.; Zeramdini, N.; DeGuzman, R.; Steiger, H. Methylation of the dopamine D2 receptor (DRD2) gene promoter in women with a bulimia-spectrum disorder: Associations with borderline personality disorder and exposure to childhood abuse. *J. Psychiatr. Res.* **2014**, *48*, 121–127. [CrossRef] [PubMed]
154. Jentsch, D.J.; Ashenhurst, J.R.; Cervantes, C.M.; Groman, S.M.; James, A.S.; Pennington, Z.T. Dissecting impulsivity and its relationships to drug addictions. *Ann. N. Y. Acad. Sci.* **2014**, *1327*, 1–26. [CrossRef] [PubMed]
155. He, F.; Berg, A.; Kawasawa, Y.; Bixler, E.O.; Fernandez-Mendoza, J.; Whitsel, E.A.; Liao, D. Association between DNA methylation in obesity-related genes and body mass index percentile in adolescents. *Sci. Rep.* **2019**, *9*, 1–8. [CrossRef] [PubMed]
156. Ndiaye, F.K.; Huyvaert, M.; Ortalli, A.; Canouil, M.; Lecoeur, C.; Verbanck, M.; Lobbens, S.; Khamis, A.; Marselli, L.; Marchetti, P.; et al. The expression of genes in top obesity-associated loci is enriched in insula and substantia nigra brain regions involved in addiction and reward. *Int. J. Obes.* **2020**, *44*, 539–543. [CrossRef] [PubMed]
157. Ramos-Lopez, O.; Riezu-Boj, J.I.; Milagro, F.I.; Martinez, A.J.; Project, M. Dopamine gene methylation patterns are associated with obesity markers and carbohydrate intake. *Brain Behav.* **2018**, *8*, e01017. [CrossRef] [PubMed]
158. Li, Y. Epigenetic Mechanisms Link Maternal Diets and Gut Microbiome to Obesity in the Offspring. *Front. Genet.* **2018**, *9*, 342. [CrossRef]
159. Ramos-Molina, B.; Sánchez-Alcoholado, L.; Cabrera-Mulero, A.; Lopez-Dominguez, R.; Carmona-Saez, P.; Garcia-Fuentes, E.; Moreno-Indias, I.; Tinahones, F.J. Gut Microbiota Composition Is Associated with the Global DNA Methylation Pattern in Obesity. *Front. Genet.* **2019**, *10*, 613. [CrossRef]
160. Miro-Blanch, J.; Yanes, O. Epigenetic Regulation at the Interplay Between Gut Microbiota and Host Metabolism. *Front. Genet.* **2019**, *10*, 638. [CrossRef]
161. Miller, A.L.; Lee, H.J.; Lumeng, J.C. Obesity-associated biomarkers and executive function in children. *Pediatr Res.* **2015**, *77*, 143–147. [CrossRef]

162. Favieri, F.; Forte, G.; Casagrande, M. The Executive Functions in Overweight and Obesity: A Systematic Review of Neuropsychological Cross-Sectional and Longitudinal Studies. *Front. Psychol* **2019**, *10*, 2126. [CrossRef] [PubMed]
163. Bourassa, K.; Sbarra, D.A. Body mass and cognitive decline are indirectly associated via inflammation among aging adults. *Brain Behav Immun* **2017**, *60*, 63–70. [CrossRef] [PubMed]
164. Miller, A.L.; Lumeng, J.C. Pathways of Association from Stress to Obesity in Early Childhood. *Obesity* **2016**. [CrossRef] [PubMed]
165. Michels, N. Biological underpinnings from psychosocial stress towards appetite and obesity during youth: Research implications towards metagenomics, epigenomics and metabolomics. *Nutr. Res. Rev.* **2019**, 282–293. [CrossRef]
166. Gupta, A.; Osadchiy, V.; Mayer, E.A. Brain–gut–microbiome interactions in obesity and food addiction. *Nat. Rev. Gastroentero* **2020**, 1–18. [CrossRef]
167. Wonderlich, J.A.; Breithaupt, L.; Thompson, J.C.; Crosby, R.D.; Engel, S.G.; Fischer, S. The impact of neural responses to food cues following stress on trajectories of negative and positive affect and binge eating in daily life. *J. Psychiatr. Res.* **2018**, *102*, 14–22. [CrossRef]
168. Chami, R.; Monteleone, A.; Treasure, J.; Monteleone, P. Stress hormones and eating disorders. *Mol. Cell. Endocrinol.* **2019**, *497*, 110349. [CrossRef]
169. Sinha, R. Role of addiction and stress neurobiology on food intake and obesity. *Biol. Psychol.* **2018**, *131*, 5–13. [CrossRef]
170. Mantsch, J.R.; Baker, D.A.; Funk, D.; Lê, A.D.; Shaham, Y. Stress-Induced Reinstatement of Drug Seeking: 20 Years of Progress. *Neuropsychopharmacol* **2016**, *41*, 335–356. [CrossRef]
171. McCaul, M.E.; Wand, G.S.; Weerts, E.M.; Xu, X. A paradigm for examining stress effects on alcohol-motivated behaviors in participants with alcohol use disorder. *Addict. Biol.* **2017**, *23*, 836–845. [CrossRef]
172. Blaine, S.K. Alcohol, stress, and glucocorticoids: From risk to dependence and relapse in alcohol use disorders. *Neuropharmacology* **2017**, *122*, 115–126. [CrossRef] [PubMed]
173. Becker, H.C. Influence of stress associated with chronic alcohol exposure on drinking. *Neuropharmacology* **2018**, *122*. [CrossRef] [PubMed]
174. George, O.; Moal, M.; Koob, G.F. Allostasis and addiction: Role of the dopamine and corticotropin-releasing factor systems. *Physiol. Behav.* **2012**, *106*, 58–64. [CrossRef] [PubMed]
175. Koob, G.F.; Schulkin, J. Addiction and Stress: An Allostatic View. *Neurosci. Biobehav. Rev.* **2019**, *106*, 245–262. [CrossRef] [PubMed]
176. Forster, G.L.; Anderson, E.M.; Scholl, J.L.; Lukkes, J.L.; Watt, M.J. Negative consequences of early-life adversity on substance use as mediated by corticotropin-releasing factor modulation of serotonin activity. *Neurobiol. Stress* **2018**, *9*, 29–39. [CrossRef] [PubMed]
177. Moustafa, A.A.; Parkes, D.; Fitzgerald, L.; Underhill, D.; Garami, J.; Levy-Gigi, E.; Stramecki, F.; Valikhani, A.; Frydecka, D.; Misiak, B. The relationship between childhood trauma, early-life stress, and alcohol and drug use, abuse, and addiction: An integrative review. *Curr. Psychol.* **2018**, 1–6. [CrossRef]
178. Kreek, M.; Nielsen, D.A.; Butelman, E.R.; LaForge, S.K. Genetic influences on impulsivity, risk taking, stress responsivity and vulnerability to drug abuse and addiction. *Nat. Neurosci.* **2005**, *8*, 1450–1457. [CrossRef]
179. Daughters, S.B.; Richards, J.M.; Gorka, S.M.; Sinha, R. HPA axis response to psychological stress and treatment retention in residential substance abuse treatment: A prospective study. *Drug Alcohol Depend.* **2009**, *105*, 202–208. [CrossRef]
180. Levran, O.; Peles, E.; Randesi, M.; da Rosa, J.; Shen, P.-H.; Rotrosen, J.; Adelson, M.; Kreek, M. Genetic variations in genes of the stress response pathway are associated with prolonged abstinence from heroin. *Pharmacogenomics* **2018**, *19*, 333–341. [CrossRef]
181. Jacques, A.; Chaaya, N.; Beecher, K.; Ali, S.A.; Belmer, A.; Bartlett, S. The impact of sugar consumption on stress driven, emotional and addictive behaviors. *Neurosci. Biobehav. Rev.* **2019**, *103*, 178–199. [CrossRef]
182. Evans, C.; Cahill, C. Neurobiology of opioid dependence in creating addiction vulnerability. *F1000Research* **2016**, *5*. [CrossRef]
183. Brady, K.T.; Dansky, B.S.; Sonne, S.C.; Saladin, M.E. Posttraumatic Stress Disorder and Cocaine Dependence: Order of Onset. *Am. J. Addict.* **1998**, *7*, 128–135. [CrossRef] [PubMed]
184. Cottler, L.B.; Compton, W.M.; Mager, D.; Spitznagel, E.L.; Janca, A. Posttraumatic stress disorder among substance users from the general population. *Am. J. Psychiatry* **1992**, *149*, 664–670. [CrossRef] [PubMed]

185. Pennington, Z.T.; Trott, J.M.; Rajbhandari, A.K.; Li, K.; Walwyn, W.M.; Evans, C.J.; Fanselow, M.S. Chronic opioid pretreatment potentiates the sensitization of fear learning by trauma. *Neuropsychopharmacol* **2019**, *45*, 482–490. [CrossRef] [PubMed]
186. Longo, D.L.; Volkow, N.D.; Koob, G.F.; McLellan, T.A. Neurobiologic Advances from the Brain Disease Model of Addiction. *N. Engl. J. Med.* **2016**, *374*, 363–371. [CrossRef]
187. Koob, G.F.; Volkow, N.D. Neurobiology of addiction: A neurocircuitry analysis. *Lancet Psychiatry* **2016**, *3*, 760–773. [CrossRef]
188. Volkow, N.D.; Koob, G. Brain disease model of addiction: Why is it so controversial? *Lancet Psychiatry* **2015**, *2*, 677–679. [CrossRef]
189. Mukhara, D.; Banks, M.L.; Neigh, G.N. Stress as a Risk Factor for Substance Use Disorders: A Mini-Review of Molecular Mediators. *Front. Behav. Neurosci.* **2018**, *12*, 309. [CrossRef]
190. Karkhanis, A.; Holleran, K.M.; Jones, S.R. International Review of Neurobiology. *Int. Rev. Neurobiol.* **2017**, *136*, 53–88. [CrossRef]
191. Joutsa, J.; Karlsson, H.K.; Majuri, J.; Nuutila, P.; Helin, S.; Kaasinen, V; Nummenmaa, L. Binge eating disorder and morbid obesity are associated with lowered mu-opioid receptor availability in the brain. *Psychiatry Res. Neuroimaging* **2018**, *276*, 41–45. [CrossRef]
192. Novick, A.M.; Levandowski, M.L.; Laumann, L.; Philip, N.S.; Price, L.H.; Tyrka, A.R. The effects of early life stress on reward processing. *J. Psychiatr. Res.* **2018**, *101*, 80–103. [CrossRef] [PubMed]
193. Meule, A. Chapter 16 An Addiction Perspective on Eating Disorders and Obesity. *Eat. Disord. Obes. Child. Adolesc.* **2019**, 99–104. [CrossRef]
194. Monnier, L.; Schlienger, J.-L.; Colette, C.; Bonnet, F. The obesity treatment dilemma: Why dieting is both the answer and the problem? A mechanistic overview. *Diabetes Metab.* **2020**. [CrossRef] [PubMed]
195. Schaumberg, K.; Anderson, D.A.; Anderson, L.M.; Reilly, E.E.; Gorrell, S. Dietary restraint: What's the harm? A review of the relationship between dietary restraint, weight trajectory and the development of eating pathology. *Clin. Obes.* **2016**, *6*, 89–100. [CrossRef]
196. Keys, A.; Brožek, J.; Henschel, A.; Mickelsen, O.; Taylor, H.L. *The Biology of Human Starvation, Vols. 1 & 2*; University of Minnesota Press: Minneapolis, MN, USA, 1950.
197. Dunn, T.M.; Bratman, S. On orthorexia nervosa: A review of the literature and proposed diagnostic criteria. *Eat. Behav.* **2016**, *21*, 11–17. [CrossRef]
198. Tomiyama, A.J.; Mann, T.; Vinas, D.; Hunger, J.M.; Dejager, J.; Taylor, S.E. Low calorie dieting increases cortisol. *Psychosom Med.* **2010**, *72*, 357. [CrossRef]
199. Pietiläinen, K.H.; Saarni, S.E.; Kaprio, J.; Rissanen, A. Does dieting make you fat? A twin study. *Int. J. Obes.* **2011**, *36*, 456–464. [CrossRef]
200. Su, Y.; Bi, T.; Gong, G.; Jiang, Q.; Chen, H. Why Do Most Restrained Eaters Fail in Losing Weight?: Evidence from an fMRI Study. *Psychol. Res. Behav Manag.* **2019**, *12*, 1127–1136. [CrossRef]
201. Wiss, D.A.; Brewerton, T.D. Incorporating food addiction into disordered eating: The disordered eating food addiction nutrition guide (DEFANG). *Eat. Weight Disord. Stud. Anorex. Bulim. Obes.* **2017**, *22*, 49–59. [CrossRef]
202. Meule, A. A Critical Examination of the Practical Implications Derived from the Food Addiction Concept. *Curr. Obes. Rep.* **2019**, *8*, 11–17. [CrossRef]
203. Tomiyama, A.J. Weight stigma is stressful. A review of evidence for the Cyclic Obesity/Weight-Based Stigma model. *Appetite* **2014**, *82*, 8–15. [CrossRef] [PubMed]
204. Tomiyama, A.J.; Epel, E.S.; McClatchey, T.M.; Poelke, G.; Kemeny, M.E.; McCoy, S.K.; Daubenmier, J. Associations of Weight Stigma with Cortisol and Oxidative Stress Independent of Adiposity. *Health Psychol.* **2014**, *33*, 862–867. [CrossRef] [PubMed]
205. Daly, M.; Robinson, E.; Sutin, A.R. Perceived overweight and suicidality among US adolescents from 1999 to 2017. *Int. J. Obes.* **2020**, *44*, 2075–2079. [CrossRef] [PubMed]
206. Sutin, A.; Robinson, E.; Daly, M.; Terracciano, A. Weight discrimination and unhealthy eating-related behaviors. *Appetite* **2016**, *102*, 83–89. [CrossRef]
207. Major, B.; Rathbone, J.A.; Blodorn, A.; Hunger, J.M. The Countervailing Effects of Weight Stigma on Weight-Loss Motivation and Perceived Capacity for Weight Control. *Personal. Soc. Psychol. Bull.* **2020**, 146167220903184. [CrossRef]

208. Ahorsu, D.K.; Lin, C.-Y.; Imani, V.; Griffiths, M.D.; Su, J.-A.; Latner, J.D.; Marshall, R.D.; Pakpour, A.H. A prospective study on the link between weight-related self-stigma and binge eating: Role of food addiction and psychological distress. *Int. J. Eat. Disord.* **2020**, *53*, 442–450. [CrossRef]
209. Pudney, E.V.; Himmelstein, M.S.; Puhl, R.M.; Foster, G.D. Distressed or not distressed? A mixed methods examination of reactions to weight stigma and implications for emotional wellbeing and internalized weight bias. *Soc. Sci. Med.* **2020**, *249*, 112854. [CrossRef]
210. Alberga, A.S.; Edache, I.Y.; Forhan, M.; Russell-Mayhew, S. Weight bias and health care utilization: A scoping review. *Prim. Heal. Care Res. Dev.* **2019**, *20*, e116. [CrossRef]
211. Hunger, J.M.; Smith, J.P.; Tomiyama, A.J. An Evidence-Based Rationale for Adopting Weight-Inclusive Health Policy. *Soc. Issues Policy Rev.* **2020**, *14*, 73–107. [CrossRef]
212. Latner, J.D.; Puhl, R.M.; Murakami, J.M.; O'Brien, K.S. Food addiction as a causal model of obesity. Effects on stigma, blame, and perceived psychopathology. *Appetite* **2014**, *77*, 79–84. [CrossRef]
213. O'Brien, K.S.; Puhl, R.M.; Latner, J.D.; Lynott, D.; Reid, J.D.; Vakhitova, Z.; Hunter, J.A.; Scarf, D.; Jeanes, R.; Bouguettaya, A.; et al. The Effect of a Food Addiction Explanation Model for Weight Control and Obesity on Weight Stigma. *Nutrients* **2020**, *12*, 294. [CrossRef] [PubMed]
214. Cassin, S.E.; Buchman, D.Z.; Leung, S.E.; Kantarovich, K.; Hawa, A.; Carter, A.; Sockalingam, S. Ethical, Stigma, and Policy Implications of Food Addiction: A Scoping Review. *Nutrients* **2019**, *11*, 710. [CrossRef]
215. Rubin, L.P. Maternal and Pediatric Health and Disease: Integrating Biopsychosocial Models and Epigenetics. *Pediatric Res.* **2015**, *79*, 127–135. [CrossRef] [PubMed]
216. Dunn, E.C.; Soare, T.W.; Zhu, Y.; Simpkin, A.J.; Suderman, M.J.; Klengel, T.; Smith, A.; Ressler, K.; Relton, C.L. Sensitive periods for the effect of childhood adversity on DNA methylation: Results from a prospective, longitudinal study. *Biol. Psychiatry* **2019**, *85*, 838–849. [CrossRef] [PubMed]
217. Gabard-Durnam, L.J.; McLaughlin, K.A. Do Sensitive Periods Exist for Exposure to Adversity? *Biol. Psychiatry* **2019**, *85*, 789–791. [CrossRef]
218. Matikainen-Ankney, B.A.; Kravitz, A.V. Persistent effects of obesity: A neuroplasticity hypothesis. *Ann. N. Y. Acad. Sci.* **2018**, *1428*, 221–239. [CrossRef]
219. Theall, K.P.; Chaparro, P.M.; Denstel, K.; Bilfield, A.; Drury, S.S. Childhood obesity and the associated roles of neighborhood and biologic stress. *Prev. Med. Rep.* **2019**, *14*, 100849. [CrossRef]
220. Rung, J.M.; Peck, S.; Hinnenkamp, J.E.; Preston, E.; Madden, G.J. Changing Delay Discounting and Impulsive Choice: Implications for Addictions, Prevention, and Human Health. *Perspect. Behav Sci.* **2019**, *42*, 397–417. [CrossRef]
221. Bortz, W.M. Biological basis of determinants of health. *Am. J. Public Health* **2005**, *95*, 389–392. [CrossRef]
222. Lei, M.-K.; Beach, S.R.; Simons, R.L. Biological embedding of neighborhood disadvantage and collective efficacy: Influences on chronic illness via accelerated cardiometabolic age. *Dev. Psychopathol.* **2018**, *30*, 1797–1815. [CrossRef]
223. Dube, S.R. Continuing conversations about adverse childhood experiences (ACEs) screening: A public health perspective. *Child. Abus. Neglect.* **2018**, *85*, 180–184. [CrossRef] [PubMed]
224. Tomiyama, A.J.; Carr, D.; Granberg, E.M.; Major, B.; Robinson, E.; Sutin, A.R.; Brewis, A. How and why weight stigma drives the obesity 'epidemic' and harms health. *BMC Med.* **2018**, *16*, 123. [CrossRef]
225. Yang, L.; Wong, L.Y.; Grivel, M.M.; Hasin, D.S. Stigma and substance use disorders. *Curr. Opin. Psychiatry* **2017**, *30*, 378. [CrossRef] [PubMed]
226. Schulte, E.M.; Avena, N.M.; Gearhardt, A.N. Which foods may be addictive? The roles of processing, fat content, and glycemic load. *PLoS ONE* **2015**, *10*, e0117959. [CrossRef] [PubMed]
227. Ayaz, A.; Nergiz-Unal, R.; Dedebayraktar, D.; Akyol, A.; Pekcan, A.G.; Besler, H.T.; Buyuktuncer, Z. How does food addiction influence dietary intake profile? *PLoS ONE* **2018**, *13*, e0195541. [CrossRef] [PubMed]
228. Hall, K.D.; Ayuketah, A.; Brychta, R.; Cai, H.; Cassimatis, T.; Chen, K.Y.; Chung, S.T.; Costa, E.; Courville, A.; Darcey, V.; et al. Ultra-Processed Diets Cause Excess Calorie Intake and Weight Gain: An Inpatient Randomized Controlled Trial of Ad Libitum Food Intake. *Cell Metab.* **2019**, *30*, 67–77. [CrossRef] [PubMed]
229. Juul, F.; Martinez-Steele, E.; Parekh, N.; Monteiro, C.A.; Chang, V.W. Ultra-processed food consumption and excess weight among US adults. *Br. J. Nutr.* **2018**, *120*, 90–100. [CrossRef]
230. Rico-Campà, A.; Martínez-González, M.A.; Alvarez-Alvarez, I.; de Mendonça, R.; de la Fuente-Arrillaga, C.; Gómez-Donoso, C.; Bes-Rastrollo, M. Association between consumption of ultra-processed foods and all cause mortality: SUN prospective cohort study. *BMJ* **2019**, *365*, l1949. [CrossRef]

231. Ruddock, H.K.; Hardman, C.A. Food Addiction Beliefs Amongst the Lay Public: What Are the Consequences for Eating Behaviour? *Curr. Addict. Rep.* **2017**, *4*, 110–115. [CrossRef]
232. Moran, A.; Musicus, A.; Soo, J.; Gearhardt, A.N.; Gollust, S.E.; Roberto, C.A. Believing that certain foods are addictive is associated with support for obesity-related public policies. *Prev. Med.* **2016**, *90*, 39–46. [CrossRef]
233. Rodgers, R.F.; Sonneville, K. Research for leveraging food policy in universal eating disorder prevention. *Int. J. Eat. Disord.* **2018**, *51*, 503–506. [CrossRef] [PubMed]
234. Mallarino, C.; Gómez, L.F.; González-Zapata, L.; Cadena, Y.; Parra, D.C. Advertising of ultra-processed foods and beverages: Children as a vulnerable population. *Rev. Saúde Pública* **2013**, *47*, 1006–1010. [CrossRef] [PubMed]
235. Freeman, B.; Kelly, B.; Vandevijvere, S.; Baur, L. Young adults: Beloved by food and drink marketers and forgotten by public health? *Health Promot. Int.* **2016**, *31*, 954–961. [CrossRef] [PubMed]
236. Story, M.; French, S. Food Advertising and Marketing Directed at Children and Adolescents in the US. *Int. J. Behav. Nutr. Phys.* **2004**, *1*, 3. [CrossRef] [PubMed]
237. Grier, S.A.; Kumanyika, S.K. The Context for Choice: Health Implications of Targeted Food and Beverage Marketing to African Americans. *Am. J. Public Health* **2008**, *98*, 1616–1629. [CrossRef]
238. Grier, S.; Kumanyika, S.K. Targeting Interventions for Ethnic Minority and Low-Income Populations. *Future Child.* **2006**, *16*, 187–207. [CrossRef]
239. Gearhardt, A.; Roberts, M.; Ashe, M. If Sugar is Addictive ... What Does it Mean for the Law? *J. Law Med. Ethics* **2013**, *41*, 46–49. [CrossRef]
240. Bragg, M.A.; Pageot, Y.K.; Amico, A.; Miller, A.N.; Gasbarre, A.; Rummo, P.E.; Elbel, B. Fast food, beverage, and snack brands on social media in the United States: An examination of marketing techniques utilized in 2000 brand posts. *Pediatr. Obes.* **2019**, *15*, e12606. [CrossRef]
241. Gearhardt, A.N.; Yokum, S.; Harris, J.L.; Epstein, L.H.; Lumeng, J.C. Neural response to fast food commercials in adolescents predicts intake. *Am. J. Clin. Nutr.* **2020**, *111*, 493–502. [CrossRef]
242. Thoits, P.A. Stress and Health: Major Findings and Policy Implications. *J. Health Soc. Behav* **2010**, *51*, S41–S53. [CrossRef]
243. Wiss, D.A. A Biopsychosocial Overview of the Opioid Crisis: Considering Nutrition and Gastrointestinal Health. *Front. Public Health* **2019**, *7*, 193. [CrossRef] [PubMed]

8

Cortical Complexity in Anorexia Nervosa: A Fractal Dimension Analysis

Enrico Collantoni [1,*], Christopher R. Madan [2], Paolo Meneguzzo [1], Iolanna Chiappini [1], Elena Tenconi [1,3], Renzo Manara [1] and Angela Favaro [1,3]

1 Department of Neurosciences, University of Padua, Via Giustiniani, 2-35128 Padova, Italy; meneguzzo.p@gmail.com (P.M.); iolanna.chiappini@gmail.com (I.C.); elena.tenconi@unipd.it (E.T.); renzo.manara@unipd.it (R.M.); angela.favaro@unipd.it (A.F.)
2 School of Psychology, University of Nottingham, Nottingham NG7 2QL, UK; Christopher.Madan@nottingham.ac.uk
3 Padua Neuroscience Center, University of Padua, 35128 Padova, Italy
* Correspondence: enrico.collantoni@unipd.it

Abstract: Fractal Dimension (FD) has shown to be a promising means to describe the morphology of cortical structures across different neurologic and psychiatric conditions, displaying a good sensitivity in capturing atrophy processes. In this study, we aimed at exploring the morphology of cortical areas by means of FD in 58 female patients with Anorexia Nervosa (AN) (38 currently underweight and 20 fully recovered) and 38 healthy controls (HC). All participants underwent high-resolution MRI. Surface extraction was completed using FreeSurfer, FD was computed using the calcFD toolbox. The whole cortex mean FD value was lower in acute AN patients compared to HC ($p < 0.001$). Recovered AN patients did not show differences in the global FD when compared to HC. However, some brain areas showed higher FD in patients than controls, while others showed the opposite pattern. Parietal regions showed lower FD in both AN groups. In acute AN patients, the FD correlated with age ($p < 0.001$), body mass index ($p = 0.019$) and duration of illness ($p = 0.011$). FD seems to represent a feasible method to explore cortical complexity in patients with AN since it demonstrated to be sensitive to the effects of both severity and duration of malnutrition.

Keywords: eating disorders; anorexia nervosa; malnutrition; neuroimaging; fractal dimension; cortical complexity

---

1. Introduction

Anorexia Nervosa (AN) is a severe psychiatric disorder with a typical onset during adolescence [1], characterized by severe and prolonged alterations of energy intake and high levels of mortality. Although there is a notable interest in understanding the effects of starvation on the brain, a full characterization of brain changes in patients with AN is still at its first stages [2]. The onset of AN typically occurs when neurodevelopment is still ongoing [3] and it is possible that the effects of malnutrition have a different impact in brain areas that are in a sensitive period of growth at the time of AN onset [4]. Moreover, evidence suggests that prenatal and perinatal factors are involved in the pathogenesis of AN and, for this reason, it is not easy to distinguish the structural brain alterations preceding the AN onset from the ones that might be a consequence of the disorder.

Most studies to date employed a Voxel-Based Morphometry approach and found a globally reduced GM volume, but inconsistent results emerged in the identification of specific regional changes in AN [2]. In addition, only few studies found a significant correlation with body weight or amount of weight loss, and almost none with age of onset or duration of illness [5]. The use of a Surface-Based Morphometry approach did not result in more consistent findings. In fact, while some studies reported a correlation between cortical thickness and BMI, others failed in evidencing a relationship between these two parameters [6–9]. Generally, a reduction of cortical thickness is described in different studies, but the extent of the reduction varies from almost the whole cortex to about a quarter or one third [6,9].

Other surface-based methods, such as the local gyrification index and cortical folding, have been employed to describe brain cortical changes in patients with AN [10–12]. Both measures displayed significant alterations in acute patients, but the interpretation of these findings is not clear, since gyrification tends to develop early in childhood and its alteration is usually attributed to prenatal or very early insults [13].

A novel way to quantify and analyze the cortex from a morphological and structural point of view has been offered by fractal geometry [14], which is specifically designed for the analysis of complex structural and morphological patterns [15]. The application of fractal geometry to neuroscience is consistent with the evidence, already highlighted by the increasing application of complex network science to neuroimaging data, that the central nervous system is organized in nested and hierarchical organization patterns that need to balance both regularity and randomness [16]. This multi-level structural organization of the brain seems to be well-described by fractal geometry, which is based on the concept of "self-similarity" [17]. Since the fractal properties of the cerebral cortex arise secondarily to folding [18], structural MRI studies used fractal dimension to quantify the morphological complexity of the cortex and its convolutional properties both in clinical and non-clinical samples [19–22].

Two types of fractal dimension can be considered, depending on whether the volume of the gray matter is included in the computation. Incorporating the volume of the gray matter into the computation ensures that changes in cortical thickness are directly integrated within the fractal dimension estimation. Thus, interestingly, fractal dimension appears to co-vary with both cortical thickness and gyrification [22]. Furthermore, it also appears to demonstrate a great sensitivity to detect cortical atrophy and to describe age-related effects [15,23]. Prior studies have suggested that FD may provide distinct information from the ones that are provided by conventional cortical structural indices such as gyrification, cortical thickness and sulcal morphology, and evidenced the presence of global and regional FD alterations in different psychiatric disorders such as ADHD, schizophrenia, bipolar and obsessive-compulsive disorders [20,21,24–27]. The use of FD to identify unique characteristics of cortical morphology could be particularly useful in the evaluation of AN, since this disorder has been shown to be characterized by complex (and not entirely determined) patterns of brain morphological alterations. Consistently with this, the first study investigating FD in AN [28] highlighted different patterns of absolute mean curvature and FD alterations in acute AN patients when compared to healthy subjects. More specifically, this research evidenced the presence of a higher FD in the left precentral gyrus as well as a trend toward a lower FD in frontal and occipital areas in patients with AN [28].

In the present study, we used a surface-based approach to explore the use of FD to describe cortical complexity in patients with AN. We hypothesize a reduction of cortical complexity in acute underweight patients and an improvement of this feature after remission.

2. Methods

Fifty-eight patients with AN (38 with acute AN and 20 in full remission) and 38 HC were included in the study. The sample included was the same as in a previous study [29]. Mean age of the patients was 26.1 years (SD = 7.2) ranging from 15.5 to 40.5 years old. Patients with AN were recruited from the Padova Hospital Eating Disorders Unit. AN was defined according to DSM-5 criteria. All patients fulfilling the inclusion criteria who were in treatment or referred to the Unit while the study was being carried out were asked to participate. A sample of HC similar to the patient group in age, ethnicity, educational level and hand lateralization was recruited from the same geographical area.

Patients who recovered from AN had full AN in their lifetime but have been asymptomatic for at least 6 months prior to the time of scanning [mean remission time: 38.5 months (SD = 33.2); range = 6–96 months]. The main clinical characteristics of the sample are reported in Table 1. Exclusion criteria for the recovered group were bingeing, food restriction, excessive exercise, amenorrhea, fasting and purging in the last 6 months. In the year following the study, none of the recovered patients relapsed. Moreover, recovered patients were within the normal weight range at the time of the scan (BMI ≥ 18.5). Exclusion criteria for all subjects were male gender, history of head trauma or injury with loss of consciousness, history of any serious neurological or medical illness, active use of systemic steroids, pregnancy, active suicidality or major depression, history of substance/alcohol abuse or dependence, bipolar disorder or schizophrenia spectrum disorder, moderate mental impairment (IQ < 60) or learning disabilities, use of medications other than antidepressants and known contraindications to conventional MRI. For healthy women, additional exclusion criteria were a history of any psychiatric disorder and the presence of first-degree relatives with an eating disorder.

At the time of recruitment, some individuals were excluded from the study: five AN patients were under antipsychotic medication and/or reported severe comorbidity; one AN patient and one healthy subject reported a previous head trauma; one AN patient, three recovered AN and two healthy subjects were not available to undergo MRI scanning when scheduled. The final sample comprised of 96 women (38 with AN, 20 recovered from AN and 38 HC). No further subject was excluded due to problems with scan acquisition, gross brain alterations or motion artifacts.

Ethical permission was obtained from the ethics committee of the Padova Hospital on 10 June 2008 (ID 1598P). After completely describing the study to the subjects, written informed consent was obtained.

Table 1. Socio-demographic and clinical characteristics of the sample.

	AN		AN-REC		HC		AN vs. HC	AN-REC. vs. HC
	(*n* = 38)		(*n* = 20)		(*n* = 38)			
	Mean	SD	Mean	SD	Mean	SD	Z (*p*)	Z (*p*)
Age (years)	26.1	7.2	26.3	7.0	25.2	6.7	0.38 (0.701)	0.44 (0.659)
Baseline BMI (kg/m^2)	16.0	1.8	19.6	1.6	21.6	3.0	7.42 (0.000)	3.09 (0.002)
Lowest BMI (kg/m^2)	14.0	1.8	15.7	1.4	19.8	2.5	7.17 (0.000)	5.35 (0.000)
Weight loss (kg)	7.1	2.8	5.2	3.1	3.4	1.7	-	-
Age of onset (years)	18.3	5.0	17.7	3.2	-	-	-	-
Duration of illness (months)	78.6	81.2	45.7	65.0	-	-	-	-
Duration of recovery (months)			45.4	47.0	-	-	-	-
Edinburgh laterality index	57.1	37.5	60.0	35.2	55.0	42.0	0.52 (0.603)	0.32 (0.749)
Education (years)	14.2	2.2	14.1	2.6	15.4	2.3	2.63 (0.009)	1.94 (0.053)
Drive to thinness	9.9	6.1	-	-	2.3	4.2	5.492 (0.000)	-
Depression	1.4	0.8	-	-	0.7	0.6	3.844 (0.000)	-
Trait anxiety	56.6	9.7	-	-	39.3	9.6	5.883 (0.000)	-
Cortex volume (mm^3)	440,936	38,526	456,932	36,916	458,753	31,225	9.55 (0.003)	0.07 (0.80)
Gyrification Index	2.85	0.09	2.90	0.09	2.90	0.11	2.09 (0.04)	0.08 (0.93)
Surface area (mm^2)	160,640	13,527	157,348	9381	165,082	12,113	2.20 (0.142)	6.11 (0.017)
Cortical Thickness (mm)	2.49	0.12	2.51	0.11	2.48	0.12	0.52 (0.14)	1.05 (0.30)

GLM, including Total Intracranial Volume as a covariate of no interest; BMI = body mass index Clinical assessment and Follow-up.

A diagnostic interview according to the Eating Disorders Section of the Structured Clinical Interview for DSM-5 [30] was performed in all subjects. A semi-structured interview was also used to collect socio-demographic and clinical variables [29,31]. Depressive and obsessive-compulsive symptoms were assessed by means of the Hopkins Symptoms Checklist [32]. Eating psychopathology was assessed by the Eating Disorders Inventory [33]. The Edinburgh Handedness Inventory [34] was also administered.

All subjects were recruited at the Eating Disorder Unit of the Hospital of Padova, fulfilled the diagnosis for AN according to DSM-IV criteria and were medically stable at the time of scanning. AN diagnosis was established by experienced senior consultants. Different diagnostic subtypes were observed at the time of scanning: 32 AN patients (84%) were restrictive, six AN patients were of the binge-eating/purging subtype and seven patients who were restrictive at the time of the present study reported previous recurrent binge eating and/or purging. Fourteen AN patients and four recovered women were under treatment with antidepressant drugs at the time the study was conducted (acute AN: one case mirtazapine, two paroxetine, two escitalopram, one fluoxetine, eight sertraline; recovered AN: four sertraline).

2.1. MRI Data Acquisition

Data were collected on a Philips Achieva 1.5 Tesla MRI scanner equipped with an eight-channel standard quadrature head coil equipped for echo-planar imaging. A high-resolution three-dimensional (3D) T1-weighted anatomical image was also acquired, in a gradient-echo sequence (repetition-time = 20 s, echo time = 3.78 ms, flip angle = 20°, 160 sagittal slices, acquisition voxel size = $1 \times 0.66 \times 0.66$ mm, field of view 21–22 cm).

2.2. Data Processing and Statistics

Data processing was performed using the FreeSurfer package (Martinos Center for Biomedical Imaging, Massachusetts General Hospital, Boston) version 5.3.0 [35]. The preprocessing was carried out according to the standard description using the following steps: skull-stripping and intensity correction, gray matter–white matter boundary determination for each cortical hemisphere using tissue intensity and neighborhood constraints, and finally, tessellation of the resulting surface boundary to generate multiple vertices across the whole brain before inflating.

Surface reconstruction and segmentation were inspected, and minor manual intervention was performed according to FreeSurfer guidelines. After cortical reconstruction, the cortex was parcellated based on individual gyral and sulcal structures [36]. Cortical thickness and local gyrification index were calculated as described in our previous work [10].

A freely available MATLAB toolbox, calcFD [15] (http://cmadan.github.io/calcFD/), was used to compute the fractal dimension of the cortical ribbon and of parcellated regions of the cortex. The toolbox uses intermediate files generated as part of the standard FreeSurfer analysis pipeline to perform the calculation. Fractal dimension has been shown to be more robust to alignment variability [37] and head motion [38]. We calculated FD of the cortical ribbon (i.e., FD of the filled volume) [15] using the dilation algorithm implemented in the calcFD toolbox and box sizes of 1, 2, and 4. Figure 1 illustrates the fractal dimension calculation for a representative parcellated cortical surface Correlation was performed using Spearmen's ρ (rho), while group comparisons were performed by means of GLM with age and hand-lateralization as covariates of no interest when appropriate. Given that FD values in the different areas of the brain cannot be considered as independent, in order to control for multiple tests, we adjusted for the False Discovery Rate (FDR) [39].

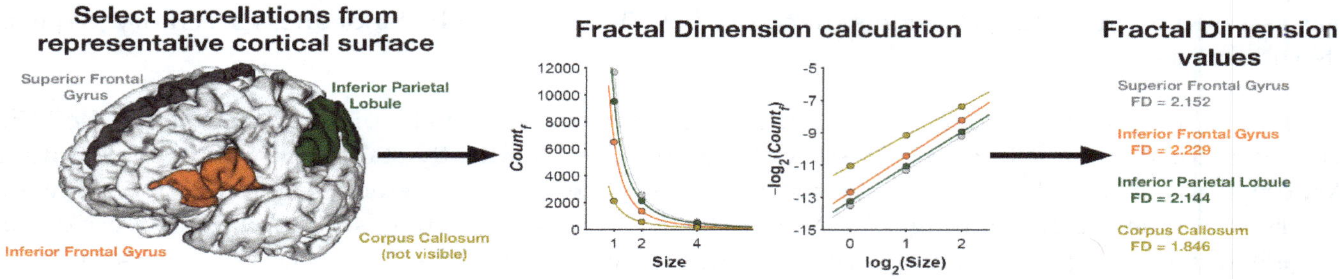

Figure 1. Illustration of the fractal dimension calculation. Individual parcellated regions (or the entire cortical ribbon) are isolated. For each region, the number of voxels at each respective box size is across different spatial resolutions, adjusting for alignment of the 'boxes' to the structure using the dilation algorithm. The counts and box sizes are then log-log transformed and the slope calculated. The slope in log-log space is taken as the fractal dimension of the region.

3. Results

Table 2 shows the average FD values of the three groups in the whole brain and in the frontal, parietal, temporal and occipital lobes.

Table 2. Cortical structures FD differences analysis between AN, REC-AN, and HC groups.

	AN	AN-REC	HC	AN vs. HC	AN-REC vs. HC
	Mean (SD)	Mean (SD)	Mean (SD)	F* (*p*)	F* (*p*)
Whole Brain (Cortical Ribbon)	2.49 (0.02)	2.52 (0.02)	2.51 (0.01)	**16.36 (0.000)**	0.32 (0.573)
Frontal Lobe	2.43 (0.02)	2.44 (0.02)	2.44 (0.01)	**13.07 (0.001)**	0.05 (0.829)
Parietal Lobe	2.30 (0.02)	2.32 (0.02)	2.32 (0.01)	**19.75 (0.000)**	0.72 (0.400)
Temporal Lobe	2.34 (0.02)	2.36 (0.01)	2.35 (0.01)	**5.40 (0.023)**	3.46 (0.068)
Occipital Lobe	2.30 (0.02)	2.32 (0.02)	2.32 (0.01)	**15.31 (0.000)**	0.55 (0.462)
Left Superior Parietal Lobule	2.13 (0.06)	2.16 (0.03)	2.19 (0.04)	**26.956 (0.000)**	**8.711 (0.005)**
Right Superior Parietal Lobule	2.11 (0.06)	2.13 (0.04)	2.16 (0.03)	**23.580 (0.000)**	**9.600 (0.003)**
Left Postcentral Gyrus	2.06 (0.06)	2.07 (0.04)	2.10 (0.04)	**9.851 (0.002)**	**5.689 (0.021)**
Right Intraparietal Sulcus	2.11 (0.05)	2.12 (0.04)	2.15 (0.03)	**18.715 (0.000)**	**8.170 (0.006)**
Left Parieto-Occipital Sulcus	2.13 (0.04)	2.13 (0.04)	2.16 (0.02)	**12.640 (0.001)**	**10.339 (0.002)**
Right Parieto-Occipital Sulcus	2.15 (0.04)	2.16 (0.04)	2.18 (0.03)	**17.123 (0.000)**	**7.250 (0.009)**

* F (GLM with age and hand lateralization as covariates of no interest; degrees of freedom = 3), *p* threshold determined based on FDR < 0.025. Significant effects are highlighted in **bold**.

Since the fractal dimension is not sensitive to smaller structures [37,40], we combined small regions with nearby anatomical regions for regions that were insufficient in size. Figure 2 illustrates the area of the original Destrieux parcellations as well as the combined regions. Figure 2 also shows the average surface area for each cortical region and the relationship between area and FD, similar to previous work [37]. As shown in the figure, relatively larger regions have a weak relationship between size and FD, allowing for the shape-related properties of FD to be sensitive to potential group differences (all FD values are included in Tables S1 and S2). Figure 3C shows these regions on the inflated cortical surface for the combined regions.

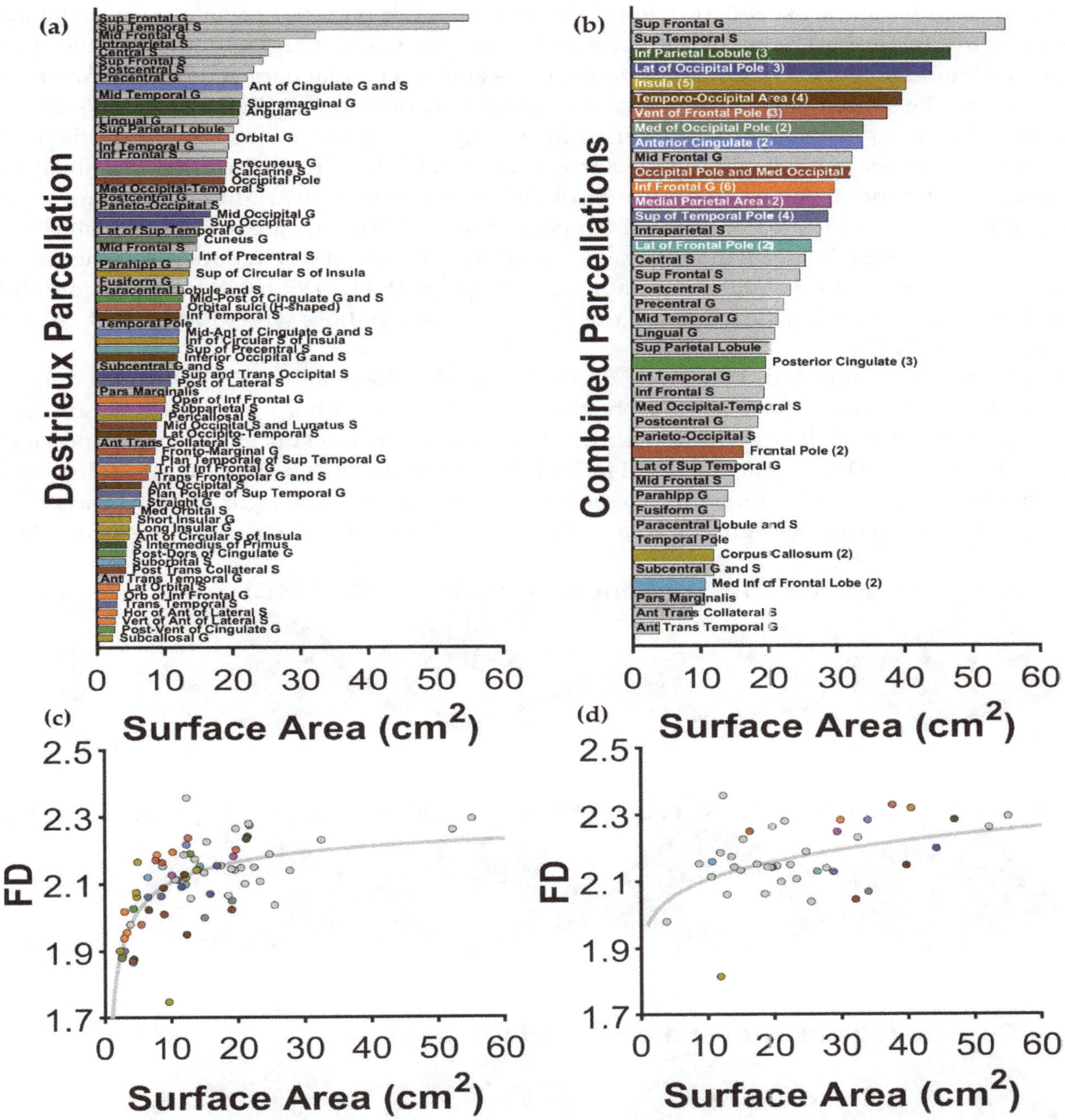

Figure 2. Mean surface area for all parcellation regions using the Destrieux atlas. Figures (**a**,**c**) show the surface area for parcellations in the original Destrieux atlas; Figures (**b**,**d**) show areas for combined regions—where the original regions were considered too small for reliable FD calculations. Regions maintained (not combined) in all plots are shown in gray. Regions that were combined to form larger regions are shown in distinct colors, matched between the panels and in Figure 3C. For Figure (**b**), after each combined region's name, the number of Destrieux regions combined is included in parentheses. Figures (**c**,**d**) show the relationship between surface area and FD (across all participants), showing that FD becomes increasingly distinct from size for larger regions and that the combined regions increased this property. As above, Figure c corresponds to the original Destrieux atlas, whereas figure d uses the recombined regions.

Patients with acute AN displayed significantly lower FD values in comparison to HC in 22 of the considered cortical areas, as shown in Figure 3A. In both hemispheres, the mean FD value of the cortical ribbon was significantly lower in in inferior frontal, middle frontal, superior frontal, postcentral and superior temporal (lateral aspect) gyri, in paracentral, superior parietal and inferior parietal lobules, in superior frontal, intraparietal, parieto-occipital, postcentral and marginal branch of the cingulate sulci, in the lateral aspect of occipital and frontal poles and in a medial parietal area encompassing the precuneus and the subparietal sulcus. In the left hemisphere only, we additionally found significantly decreased FD values in the precentral gyrus, in the superior aspect of the temporal pole and in a temporal-occipital area encompassing the anterior occipital sulcus, the inferior temporal sulcus, the lateral occipito-temporal sulcus and the inferior occipital gyrus. In the right hemisphere, we found decreased FD values in the medial occipital-temporal sulcus. (FD values are reported in Table S1 in the Supplementary Materials). No differences in FD values were observed in patients of the restricting type in comparison to those of the binge-eating/purging type (F (3, 34) = 0.005, $p = 0.946$ for total FD), nor in those who were taking antidepressants in comparison to those who did not (F (3, 34) = 0.478, $p = 0.494$, for total FD).

Recovered AN patients did not show differences in the global and lobar FD when compared to HC. The mean FD value of the cortical ribbon was significantly higher in the AN-REC group when compared to HC in the left superior temporal sulcus and in the left subcentral gyrus and sulcus as shown in Figure 3B (FD values are reported in Table S1). Some areas showed reduced FD in both acute and recovered AN patients in comparison to healthy women: the left and right superior parietal lobule, the left postcentral gyrus, the right intraparietal sulcus and the left and right parieto-occipital sulcus.

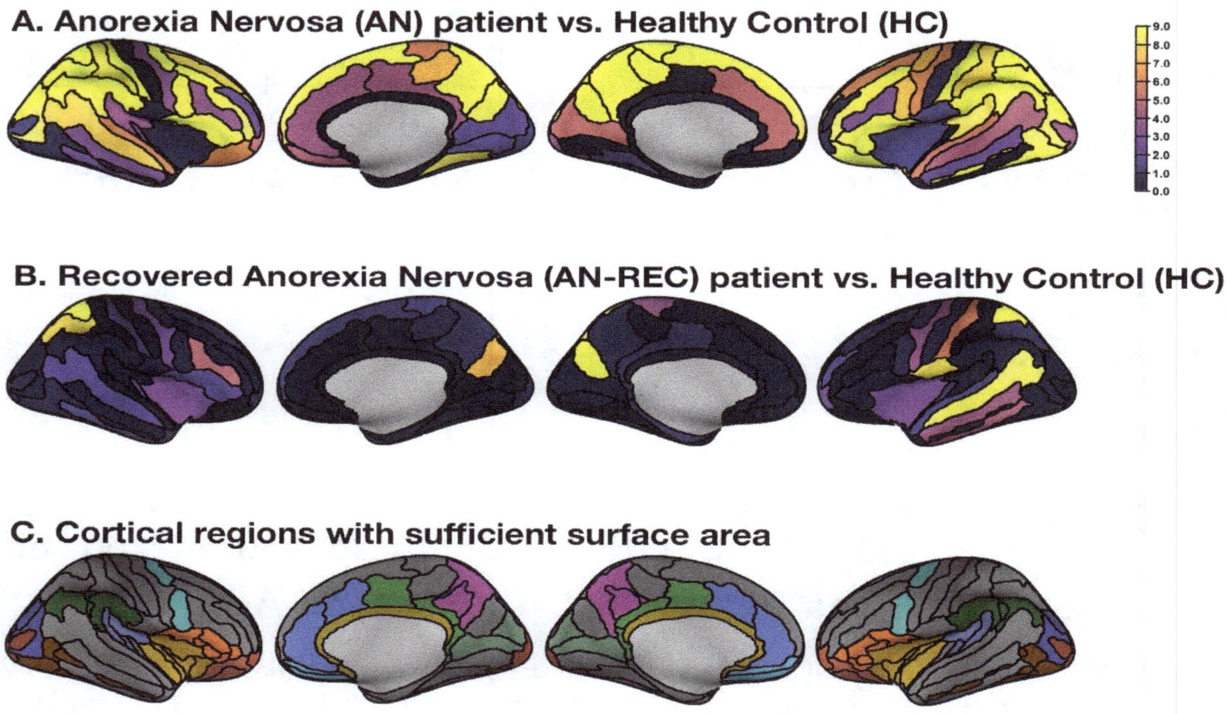

Figure 3. Unthresholded group comparison (F-statistics) plotted on the inflated cortical surface for the combined regions. (**A**) Regional F-statistics comparing Anorexia Nervosa (AN) patients and Healthy Controls (HC). (**B**) Regional F-statistics comparing recovered Anorexia Nervosa (AN-REC) patients with Healthy Controls (HC). (**C**) All cortical regions were included in the analysis. Regions shown in color were recombined with respect to the original Destrieux atlas to yield sufficiently large surfaces areas; colors match the labels and areas shown in Figure 2.

As expected, FD values were significantly negatively correlated with age in all three groups (Table 3) (compare with [15,38,40]). However, the decline of FD along with age tended to be stronger in the acute AN patients than in the other two groups, especially for the frontal and parietal lobes (Figure 4). In all three groups, no differences were observed in left-handed or mixed-handed (Edinburgh scores between −70 to +70) individuals in comparison to right-handed ones. Table 3 shows the correlations (Spearman's ρ [rho] rank correlation) between FD values and clinical variables in the three groups. Significant positive correlations emerged between whole-brain FD and BMI in acute AN, but not in the recovered group (see also [38] for a normative comparison). The FD value was also significantly negatively correlated with the duration of illness in the acute AN group. A significant negative correlation between the age of onset of the disorder and FD emerged in the recovered group. In this last group, the duration of the recovered status showed a negative nonsignificant correlation with FD (rho = −0.386, $p = 0.093$).

The whole-brain FD positively correlates with the volume of the cortex in all the three groups and with overall local gyrification index in HC, but not in the two AN groups.

Table 3. Correlation between whole-brain (cortical ribbon) FD and clinical variables within each group.

	AN ($n = 38$) **Rho** (p)	**AN-REC** ($n = 20$) **Rho** (p)	**Healthy Controls** ($n = 38$) **Rho** (p)
		Whole-brain FD	
Age	−0.608 (0.000) *	−0.617 (0.004) *	−0.527 (0.001) *
Body mass index (BMI)	0.380 (0.019) *	−0.351 (0.130)	−0.209 (0.207)
Duration of illness	−0.406 (0.011) *	−0.111 (0.642)	
Age of AN onset	−0.265 (0.108)	−0.586 (0.007) *	
Cortical volume	0.638 (0.000) *	0.537 (0.015) *	0.496 (0.002) *
Cortical gyrification	0.258 (0.118)	0.376 (0.102)	0.514 (0.001) *
Cortical thickness	0.000 (0.998)	0.65 (0.787)	0.025 (0.883)

FD: Fractal Dimension; Spearman's ρ(*rho*); * FDR < 0.025.

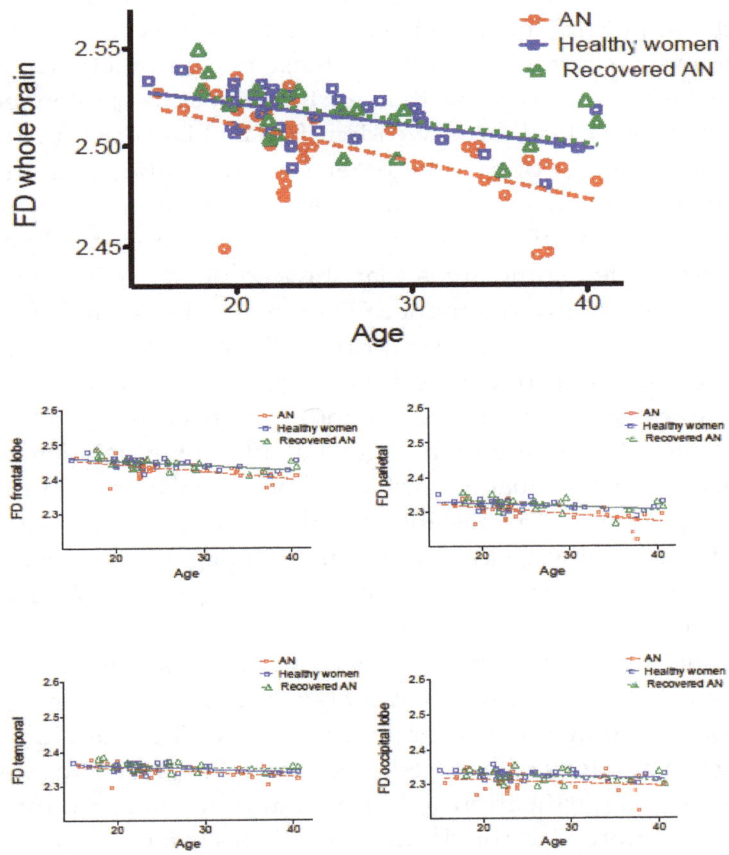

Figure 4. Correlations between whole-brain (cortical ribbon) and lobar FD and age in the three groups.

4. Discussion

In this paper, we explored the morphological complexity of cortical and subcortical brain structures by means of FD and investigated the relationship between FD with clinical variables. Our results showed the presence of a globally reduced cortical FD in patients with acute AN, while patients who recovered from the disorder did not show alterations in global FD values. This observation, together with the correlation between FD and BMI in the acute AN group, allowed us to hypothesize that a global reduction in cortical complexity may be an effect of malnutrition that can be recovered along with weight recovery. FD has been described in the literature as a sensitive measure to describe cortical atrophy and the effects of aging [15,22,23] and our data show that it also seems to describe the complex patterns of cortical morphology that are secondary to the effects of malnutrition in AN. The cortical structural modifications in AN are likely to depend on many factors, such as malnutrition, dehydration and endocrinological factors, but they could also reflect the alterations of neurodevelopmental trajectories that are hypothesized to precede the onset of the disorder [3]. The hypothesized developmental origin of AN [41] and the effects of its onset in critical developmental phases make it important to consider the relationship between any cortical alterations, the duration of the disorder and the patient's age and age of onset in the evaluation of structural MRI findings. Our results indicated that both the patient's age and the duration of the disorder correlate inversely with FD, suggesting an impact of AN on the reduction of cortical complexity. Since cortical complexity, measured by FD, is likely to reduce from adolescence to adulthood as a result of the cortical modeling mechanisms that physiologically occur with aging [42], we hypothesize an impact of the disorder in accelerating this process.

The observed correlation between FD and gyrification in HC, but not in patients with AN, suggests a sensitivity of FD to the effect of malnutrition. A direct correlation between FD and gyrification has been emphasized by previous studies in healthy as well as in neurological populations, indicating the sensitivity of FD in capturing the role of cortical folding in determining cortical complexity [15,22]. Gyrification appears to be largely determined during the earlier neurodevelopmental phases [13] and alterations in this structural parameter have been already pointed out by previous studies on AN patients [10,12]. The absence of a correlation between these two parameters in AN suggests that, in this group, FD could probably be more susceptible than gyrification to the prolonged effects of malnutrition.

From a regional analysis of cortical areas, we identified an FD reduction in various parietal regions that are crucial for the integration of body-image perception abilities both in acute and in recovered AN patients. These results suggest that these areas may be particularly susceptible to disorder-specific alterations and require to be specifically investigated by further research. Except for these regions, in the recovered group we identified some areas that showed no statistically significant differences in cortical complexity, while others showed a higher FD than HC. These findings could reflect reshaping processes induced by re-nutrition, therefore supporting the role of FD in describing how nutritional processes can influence the brain morphology. It is not clear why in the recovered patients the values of FD displayed different patterns in different brain regions. The negative trend we observed between FD and duration of recovery in this group might indicate that after an initial increase of cortical complexity following weight recovery—which probably implies the occurrence of reparative processes—FD tends to decrease towards average values. It is possible that this process occurs with different trajectories in different areas of the brain. In addition, since we observed a negative correlation between FD and age of onset in the recovered group, it seems that these reparative processes are more evident in patients with an earlier age of onset.

The present study has several strengths, as well as important limitations. It explores cortical complexity in AN by means of FD, a novel parameter that has been demonstrated to have a good sensitivity to cortical atrophy and age-related brain differences. The evaluation of cortical morphology with FD allows widening the horizons of surface-based cortical analysis, by integrating the information given by cortical thickness and gyrification with novel and non-redundant data. Furthermore, the correlation between FD alterations and the duration of illness is a new and interesting finding about MRI surface-based analysis in AN, hinting at the potentialities of this morphological index in capturing the effects of prolonged starvation on the cortical structure. A limitation of this study is represented by its cross-sectional design. In fact, longitudinal data could be particularly useful to understand how cortical complexity varies with the clinical course of the disorder and with weight recovery. Another limitation can be found in the absence of male patients in the sample. Any inference about alterations in cortical complexity in male patients with AN cannot be made and would be an interesting topic to explore in future studies.

In conclusion, the present study evidences that FD should be considered particularly useful to investigate the morpho-structural properties of brain cortex in AN, since it demonstrated to be suitable for identifying the negative effects of different clinical variables on cortical structure and giving non-redundant information with respect to other surface-based indexes.

Author Contributions: Conceptualization, E.C. and A.F.; methodology, E.C., C.R.M. and A.F.; formal analysis, E.C., C.R.M., A.F.; data curation, E.C., A.F., R.M., I.C., E.T. and P.M.; writing—original draft preparation, E.C.; writing—review and editing, C.R.M., P.M., A.F. All authors have read and agreed to the published version of the manuscript

References

1. Favaro, A.; Caregaro, L.; Tenconi, E.; Bosello, R.; Santonastaso, P. Time trends in age at onset of anorexia nervosa and bulimia nervosa. *J. Clin. Psychiatry* **2009**, *70*, 1715–1721. [CrossRef]
2. Seitz, J.; Bühren, K.; Von Polier, G.G.; Heussen, N.; Herpertz-Dahlmann, B.; Konrad, K. Morphological Changes in the Brain of Acutely Ill and Weight-Recovered Patients with Anorexia Nervosa a Meta-Analysis and Qualitative Review. *J. Child Adolesc. Psychiatry Psychother.* **2014**, *42*, 7–18.
3. Connan, F.; Campbell, I.C.; Katzman, M.; Lightman, S.L.; Treasure, J. A neurodevelopmental model for anorexia nervosa. *Physiol. Behav.* **2003**, *79*, 13–24. [CrossRef]
4. Andersen, S.L. Trajectories of brain development: Point of vulnerability or window of opportunity? *Neurosci. Biobehav. Rev.* **2003**, *27*, 3–18. [CrossRef]
5. Seitz, J.; Herpertz-Dahlmann, B.; Konrad, K. Brain morphological changes in adolescent and adult patients with anorexia nervosa. *J. Neural Transm.* **2016**, *123*, 949–959. [CrossRef] [PubMed]
6. Bernardoni, F.; King, J.A.; Geisler, D.; Stein, E.; Jaite, C.; Nätsch, D.; Tam, F.I.; Boehm, I.; Seidel, M.; Roessner, V.; et al. Weight restoration therapy rapidly reverses cortical thinning in anorexia nervosa: A longitudinal study. *Neuroimage* **2016**, *130*, 214–222. [CrossRef] [PubMed]
7. Lavagnino, L.; Amianto, F.; Mwangi, B.; D'Agata, F.; Spalatro, A.; Zunta Soares, G.B.; Daga, G.A.; Mortara, P.; Fassino, S.; Soares, J.C. The relationship between cortical thickness and body mass index differs between women with anorexia nervosa and healthy controls. *Psychiatry Res. Neuroimaging* **2016**, *248*, 105–109. [CrossRef]
8. Collantoni, E.; Meneguzzo, P.; Tenconi, E.; Manara, R.; Favaro, A. Small-world properties of brain morphological characteristics in Anorexia Nervosa. *PLoS ONE* **2019**, *14*, e0216154. [CrossRef] [PubMed]
9. Fuglset, T.S.; Endestad, T.; Hilland, E.; Bang, L.; Tamnes, C.K.; Landrø, N.I.; Rø, Ø. Brain volumes and regional cortical thickness in young females with anorexia nervosa. *BMC Psychiatry* **2016**, *16*, 404. [CrossRef] [PubMed]
10. Favaro, A.; Tenconi, E.; Degortes, D.; Manara, R.; Santonastaso, P. Gyrification brain abnormalities as predictors of outcome in anorexia nervosa. *Hum. Brain Mapp.* **2015**, *36*, 5113–5122. [CrossRef] [PubMed]
11. Schultz, C.C.; Wagner, G.; de la Cruz, F.; Berger, S.; Reichenbach, J.R.; Sauer, H.; Bär, K.J. Evidence for alterations of cortical folding in anorexia nervosa. *Eur. Arch. Psychiatry Clin. Neurosci.* **2017**, *267*, 41–49. [CrossRef] [PubMed]
12. Bernardoni, F.; King, J.A.; Geisler, D.; Birkenstock, J.; Tam, F.I.; Weidner, K.; Roessner, V.; White, T.; Ehrlich, S. Nutritional status affects cortical folding: Lessons learned from anorexia nervosa. *Biol. Psychiatry* **2018**, *84*, 692–701. [CrossRef] [PubMed]
13. White, T.; Su, S.; Schmidt, M.; Kao, C.Y.; Sapiro, G. The development of gyrification in childhood and adolescence. *Brain Cogn.* **2010**, *72*, 36–45. [CrossRef] [PubMed]
14. Kiselev, V.G.; Hahn, K.R.; Auer, D.P. Is the brain cortex a fractal? *Neuroimage* **2003**, *20*, 1765–1774. [CrossRef]
15. Madan, C.R.; Kensinger, E.A. Cortical complexity as a measure of age-related brain atrophy. *Neuroimage* **2016**, *134*, 617–629. [CrossRef]

16. Di Ieva, A. *The Fractal Geometry of the Brain: An Overview*; Springer: New York, NY, USA, 2016; ISBN 9781493939954.
17. Mandelbrot, B. How long is the coast of Britain? Statistical self-similarity and fractional dimension. *Science* **1967**, *156*, 636–638. [CrossRef]
18. Hofman, M.A. The fractal geometry of convoluted brains. *J. Hirnforsch.* **1991**, *32*, 103–111.
19. Cook, M.J.; Free, S.L.; Manford, M.R.A.; Fish, D.R.; Shorvon, S.D.; Stevens, J.M. Fractal Description of Cerebral Cortical Patterns in Frontal Lobe Epilepsy. *Eur. Neurol.* **1995**, *35*, 327–335. [CrossRef]
20. Nenadic, I.; Yotter, R.A.; Sauer, H.; Gaser, C. Cortical surface complexity in frontal and temporal areas varies across subgroups of schizophrenia. *Hum. Brain Mapp.* **2014**, *35*, 1691–1699. [CrossRef]
21. Sandu, A.-L.; Rasmussen, I.-A.; Lundervold, A.; Kreuder, F.; Neckelmann, G.; Hugdahl, K.; Specht, K. Fractal dimension analysis of MR images reveals grey matter structure irregularities in schizophrenia. *Comput. Med. Imaging Graph.* **2008**, *32*, 150–158. [CrossRef]
22. King, R.D.; Brown, B.; Hwang, M.; Jeon, T.; George, A.T. Fractal dimension analysis of the cortical ribbon in mild Alzheimer's disease. *Neuroimage* **2010**, *53*, 471–479. [CrossRef] [PubMed]
23. Madan, C.R.; Kensinger, E.A. Age-related differences in the structural complexity of subcortical and ventricular structures. *Neurobiol. Aging* **2017**, *50*, 87–95. [CrossRef] [PubMed]
24. Ha, T.H.; Yoon, U.; Lee, K.J.; Shin, Y.W.; Lee, J.-M.; Kim, I.Y.; Ha, K.S.; Kim, S.I.; Kwon, J.S. Fractal dimension of cerebral cortical surface in schizophrenia and obsessive–compulsive disorder. *Neurosci. Lett.* **2005**, *384*, 172–176. [CrossRef] [PubMed]
25. Li, X.; Jiang, J.; Zhu, W.; Yu, C.; Sui, M.; Wang, Y.; Jiang, T. Asymmetry of prefrontal cortical convolution complexity in males with attention-deficit/hyperactivity disorder using fractal information dimension. *Brain Dev.* **2007**, *29*, 649–655. [CrossRef] [PubMed]
26. Squarcina, L.; De Luca, A.; Bellani, M.; Brambilla, P.; Turkheimer, F.E.; Bertoldo, A. Fractal analysis of MRI data for the characterization of patients with schizophrenia and bipolar disorder. *Phys. Med. Biol.* **2015**, *60*, 1697–1716. [CrossRef] [PubMed]
27. Zhao, G.; Denisova, K.; Sehatpour, P.; Long, J.; Gui, W.; Qiao, J.; Javitt, D.C.; Wang, Z. Fractal dimension analysis of subcortical gray matter structures in schizophrenia. *PLoS ONE* **2016**, *11*, 1–23. [CrossRef]
28. Nickel, K.; Joos, A.; Tebartz van Elst, L.; Holovics, L.; Endres, D.; Zeeck, A.; Maier, S. Altered cortical folding and reduced sulcal depth in adults with anorexia nervosa. *Eur. Eat. Disord. Rev.* **2019**, *27*, 655–670. [CrossRef]
29. Favaro, A.; Clementi, M.; Manara, R.; Bosello, R.; Forzan, M.; Bruson, A.; Tenconi, E.; Degortes, D.; Titton, F.; Di Salle, F.; et al. Catechol-O-methyltransferase genotype modifies executive functioning and prefrontal functional connectivity in women with anorexia nervosa. *J. Psychiatry Neurosci.* **2013**, *38*, 241–248. [CrossRef]
30. American Psychiatric Association. *Diagnostic and Statistical Manual of Mental Disorders*; American Psychiatric Association: Virginia, VA, USA, 2013; ISBN 0-89042-555-8.
31. Favaro, A.; Santonastaso, P.; Manara, R.; Bosello, R.; Bommarito, G.; Tenconi, E.; Di Salle, F. Disruption of visuospatial and somatosensory functional connectivity in anorexia nervosa. *Biol. Psychiatry* **2012**, *72*, 864–870. [CrossRef]
32. Derogatis, L.R.; Lipman, R.S.; Rickels, K.; Uhlenhuth, E.H.; Covi, L. The Hopkins Symptom Checklist (HSCL): A Self Report Symptom Inventory. *Behav. Sci.* **1974**, *19*, 1–15. [CrossRef]
33. Garner, D.M.; Olmstead, M.P.; Polivy, J. Development and validation of a multidimensional eating disorder inventory for anorexia nervosa and bulimia. *Int. J. Eat. Disord.* **1983**, *2*, 15–34. [CrossRef]
34. Oldfield, R.C. The assessment and analysis of handedness: The Edinburgh inventory. *Neuropsychologia* **1971**, *9*, 97–113. [CrossRef]
35. Fischl, B. FreeSurfer. *Neuroimage* **2012**, *62*, 774–781. [CrossRef] [PubMed]
36. Destrieux, C.; Fischl, B.; Dale, A.; Halgren, E. Automatic parcellation of human cortical gyri and sulci using standard anatomical nomenclature. *Neuroimage* **2010**, *53*, 1–15. [CrossRef]
37. Madan, C.R.; Kensinger, E.A. Test–retest reliability of brain morphology estimates. *Brain Inform.* **2017**, *4*, 107–121. [CrossRef]
38. Madan, C.R. Age differences in head motion and estimates of cortical morphology. *PeerJ* **2018**, *6*, e5176. [CrossRef]
39. Benjamini, Y.; Hochberg, Y. Controlling the False Discovery Rate—A Practical and Powerful Approach to Multiple Testing. *J. R. Stat. Soc. Ser. B* **1995**, *57*, 289–300. [CrossRef]

40. Madan, C.R.; Kensinger, E.A. Predicting age from cortical structure across the lifespan. *Eur. J. Neurosci.* **2018**, *47*, 399–416. [CrossRef]

41. Favaro, A. Brain development and neurocircuit modeling are the interface between genetic/environmental risk factors and eating disorders. A commentary on keel & forney and friederich et al. *Int. J. Eat. Disord.* **2013**, *46*, 443–446.

42. Sandu, A.-L.; Izard, E.; Specht, K.; Beneventi, H.; Lundervold, A.; Ystad, M. Post-adolescent developmental changes in cortical complexity. *Behav. Brain Funct.* **2014**, *10*, 44. [CrossRef]

9

Ethical, Stigma and Policy Implications of Food Addiction

Stephanie E. Cassin [1,2,3], Daniel Z. Buchman [4,5,6], Samantha E. Leung [2,7], Karin Kantarovich [2,7], Aceel Hawa [8], Adrian Carter [9,10] and Sanjeev Sockalingam [2,3,7,8,*]

1 Department of Psychology, Ryerson University, 350 Victoria St., Toronto, ON M5B 2K3, Canada; stephanie.cassin@psych.ryerson.ca
2 Centre for Mental Health, University Health Network, Network - Toronto General Hospital, 200 Elizabeth Street, 8th Floor, Toronto, ON M5G 2C4, Canada; samantha.leung@uhn.ca (S.E.L.); kar.kantarovich@gmail.com (K.K.)
3 Department of Psychiatry, University of Toronto, 250 College Street, Toronto, ON M5T 1R8, Canada
4 University of Toronto Joint Centre of Bioethics, 155 College Street, Suite 754, Toronto, ON M5T 1P8, Canada; daniel.buchman@uhn.ca
5 Bioethics Program and Krembil Brain Institute, Toronto Western Hospital, University Health Network, 399 Bathurst Street, Toronto, ON M5T 1P8, Canada
6 Dalla Lana School of Public Health, University of Toronto, 155 College Street, 6th Floor, Toronto, ON M5T 1R8, Canada
7 Bariatric Surgery Program, University Health Network - Toronto Western Hospital, 399 Bathurst Street, East Wing – 4th Floor, Toronto, ON M5T 2S8, Canada
8 Department of Education, Centre for Addiction and Mental Health, 33 Russell Street, Toronto, ON M5S 2S1, Canada; aceel.hawa@gmail.com
9 School of Psychological Sciences, Monash University, Melbourne, VIC 3181, Australia; adrian.carter@monash.edu
10 UQ Centre for Clinical Research, University of Queensland, Herston, QLD 4029, Australia
* Correspondence: sanjeev.sockalingam@camh.ca

Abstract: The concept of food addiction has generated much controversy. In comparison to research examining the construct of food addiction and its validity, relatively little research has examined the broader implications of food addiction. The purpose of the current scoping review was to examine the potential ethical, stigma, and health policy implications of food addiction. Major themes were identified in the literature, and extensive overlap was identified between several of the themes. Ethics sub-themes related primarily to individual responsibility and included: (i) personal control, will power, and choice; and (ii) blame and weight bias. Stigma sub-themes included: (i) the impact on self-stigma and stigma from others, (ii) the differential impact of substance use disorder versus behavioral addiction on stigma, and (iii) the additive stigma of addiction plus obesity and/or eating disorder. Policy implications were broadly derived from comparisons to the tobacco industry and focused on addictive foods as opposed to food addiction. This scoping review underscored the need for increased awareness of food addiction and the role of the food industry, empirical research to identify specific hyperpalatable food substances, and policy interventions that are not simply extrapolated from tobacco.

Keywords: ethics; food addiction; health policy; stigma

1. Introduction

The average weight of Americans increased dramatically in the 1980s, and this trend did not discriminate based on age, gender, or race [1]. Kessler notes that one remarkable change that coincided with the dramatic weight increase was the availability of "hyperpalatable" foods, specifically those engineered to combine optimal amounts of sugar, fat, and salt [2]. Some authors likened these hyperpalatable foods to addictive drugs, such as cocaine [3]. Though obesity only began garnering serious medical and public attention in recent years, the idea that obesity is a result of a food addiction was, in fact, first posited during the 1940s and 1950s [4,5]. However, this early conceptualization of food addiction resulted in much societal debate as it intensified weight stigma and contributed to ineffective policy changes around obesity and its consequences [5]. Since then, views on obesity and food addiction have been evolving, though the concept of food addiction is still highly debated today.

Food addiction is not an official diagnosis in the Diagnostic and Statistical Manual of Mental Disorders (DSM-5) [6]; however, health care professionals, researchers, patients, and the general public use the term, and a questionnaire (Yale Food Addiction Scale; YFAS) has been developed to diagnose its purported core features [7]. Many similarities have been noted between substance use disorders (e.g., alcohol, nicotine) and food addiction, including consuming more of the substance than intended or over a longer period of time, preoccupation with the substance, craving or strong urge to use the substance, and continued consumption despite knowledge of adverse effects [8].

Food addiction can have negative impacts on individuals living with obesity. Several studies have found that individuals with obesity who meet criteria for food addiction (as measured by the YFAS) demonstrate greater levels of eating disorder psychopathology, poorer general and health-related quality of life, greater depressive symptoms, and higher scores on impulsivity and self-control measures [9–11]. Together, this underscores the importance of studying the relationship between food addiction and obesity.

A food addiction model proposes that some individuals are addicted to certain foods and feel driven to engage in weight promoting eating behaviors, such as binge eating or compulsive overeating, when exposed to "addictive" food substances [7,12,13]. Foods with added fat and refined carbohydrates have been shown to be consumed in a more addictive manner [13,14] and craved more intensely [15] than less refined foods. This is thought to be, in part, a result of such hyperpalatable foods activating the mesolimbic reward-related pathway of the brain, which connects the ventral tegmental area of the midbrain to the nucleus accumbens in the ventral striatum via dopaminergic neurons [16,17]. Neuroimaging studies on individuals meeting the cut-off for food addiction according to the YFAS have been shown to have dysfunctional patterns of reward-related neural activation [12,18], and studies employing the use of genotyping have demonstrated higher multi-locus genetic profile scores in this group, which is associated with enhanced dopamine signaling [19].

Despite mounting evidence for the compulsive consumption of highly palatable foods, food addiction has continued to generate much controversy [20]. Discourses have centered around several issues, including diagnostic challenges of food addiction; arguments that food addiction is not distinct from binge eating disorder [21,22]; debates as to whether food addiction is akin to a behavioral addiction versus a substance use disorder [23]; and the notion that food (albeit not hyperpalatable foods), unlike other substances, is necessary for survival [24]. With respect to the diagnostic challenges, there is emerging evidence that food addiction is distinct from binge eating disorder [25] and may be best classified as a substance (food) use disorder as opposed to a behavioral (eating) addiction [8,26]. A recent systematic review examining the validity of food addiction concluded that the existing research supports food addiction as a unique construct [8]. Amongst the 35 articles (52 studies), the largest number of studies found evidence for brain reward dysfunction and impaired control, followed by studies on tolerance and withdrawal for foods with the greater addictive potential, specifically added sugars and fats.

In comparison to research examining the construct of food addiction and its validity, relatively little research has examined the potential ethical, stigma, and health policy implications of food addiction. Other addictions to substances, such as tobacco, cannabis, or alcohol, have seen an increase in the use of stigmatization as a policy tool in order to promote public health [27]. As a result, ethical issues have arisen surrounding public health communication and its effect on individuals and on society as a whole [28]. Bayer has argued that the use of stigma may reduce the prevalence of behaviors linked to disease and mortality [29]. People who identify as "fat" or "obese" have long received stigmatizing "fat-shaming" messages from healthcare providers and public health officials. Stigmatization of people with obesity often has the opposite effect and is ethically indivisible given the stress and emotional and dignitary harms it causes [30]. This further emphasizes the importance of developing a nuanced understanding of the potential impact of a food addiction model on stigma, particularly given that it could have divergent effects on externalized stigma towards others and internalized stigma towards the self.

A recent systematic review of nine empirical studies examining the link between food addiction and weight stigma concluded that limited evidence suggests that food addiction explanations may reduce self-blame and stigma from others, but these benefits may be offset by the adverse impact on self-efficacy and eating behaviors [31]. However, the authors also noted that the existing empirical research is sparse and inconsistent. To our knowledge, no scoping reviews have been conducted to examine the ethical and health policy implications of food addiction, or the implications on stigma more broadly beyond weight stigma. The purpose of this scoping review was to highlight what has been published in the food addiction literature and to address these current gaps to help inform current perceptions by identifying the potential ethical, stigma, and health policy implications of food addiction.

2. Materials and Methods

This review was conducted as per the Arksey and O'Malley methodological framework for scoping reviews [32]. As part of the development of our research questions and approach, a stakeholder summit was organized in collaboration with the Canadian Obesity Network (CON) involving a broad and diverse group of 18 stakeholders including local knowledge users (i.e., people with experience with obesity-related treatment and food addiction), representatives from national obesity organizations and patient advocacy groups, primary care physicians, and interprofessional research leaders nationally and internationally in food addiction and/or obesity management. Data from a pre-summit online questionnaire exploring perceptions related to the ethical and policy issues of food addiction in obesity informed summit discussions aimed at identifying key themes related to food addiction. The pre-summit online questionnaire was derived from previous studies on food addiction in obesity [33,34] and included open-ended questions regarding the potential implications of food addiction on stigma, ethics, and health policy. The following five stages were completed as part of the scoping review methodology.

Stage 1: Identifying the Research Questions

Based on the analysis of themes resulting from the stakeholder summit, this scoping review was conducted to address the following question: What are the potential ethical, stigma and policy implications of food addiction in obesity?

Inclusion/exclusion criteria

We included peer- and non-peer reviewed articles, editorials, commentaries, letters, and replies to authors that met the following criteria:

1. Were published in English;
2. Were human studies;
3. Established a link between obesity or binge eating and addiction or substance use;
4. Presented a conceptual or mechanistic model of food addiction (i.e., had to include terms such as "reward," "reward pathway," "compulsion," "substance use," or "pleasurable" somewhere in the article); and
5. Presented the issue of food addiction using a key concept (rather than quoting a prevalence).

We excluded book chapters, dissertations, and policy documents. Papers were also excluded if they only focused on obesity and did not relate to food addiction.

Stage 2: Identifying Relevant Studies

We searched for relevant articles published up until January 26, 2017, for each question using the following databases: Medline and PsycINFO from the OvidSP platform and CINAHL from the EBSCO platform. Each of the OvidSP databases was searched individually. The searches were conducted with assistance from a research librarian from an academic health sciences center. The searches were run with the limits of human studies and English language studies only. When appropriate, controlled vocabulary terms and/or text words were used in the subject component blocks. For example, obesity/bariatric terms included one block, food addiction terms included a second block, and ethics/stigma/policy terms included a third block. Lastly, we reviewed key special issues on food addiction in prominent eating disorder and obesity periodicals to identify additional articles that may have met our inclusion criteria and were missed by our initial search. A total of 410 articles were identified from these search strategies.

Stage 3: Selecting Studies

All references resulting from the literature search were reviewed and 46 duplicates were removed. Preliminary screening was conducted by titles and abstracts by two independent reviewers. Seventeen references were missing and were excluded from screening. Screened abstracts were separated into three categories: articles to include, unsure articles, and non-relevant articles to exclude. A secondary screening was then conducted by two additional independent reviewers on the articles that were deemed unsure from the first round of screening. This screening procedure resulted in 296 articles being excluded. Full text articles for the remaining 60 abstracts were then retrieved for data collection (see Figure 1 for PRISMA diagram).

Stage 4: Charting the Data

Data were extracted from all included full-text articles by one reviewer into a spreadsheet that included authors, year of publication, and article type and relevant excerpts, themes, and quotes. Each domain was then separated into individual spreadsheets with the relevant articles and their respective identifiers and variables for coding and analysis.

Stage 5: Collating, Summarizing, and Reporting the Results

Three independent reviewers completed this step. Each of the three main domains of ethics, stigma, and policy had two reviewers who independently reviewed the full text articles and coded the data. A thematic analysis approach was used to critically analyze the articles and generate open codes. All reviewers then came together to discuss, compare, and organize the relevant excerpts, themes, and quotes that were extracted for each of the three main domains. These iterative discussions allowed for a higher level of thematic analysis, generating broad categories and higher-level themes. Reviewers met nine times at 1- to 2-month intervals for a total of 18 h to review codes and to generate domains summarized below.

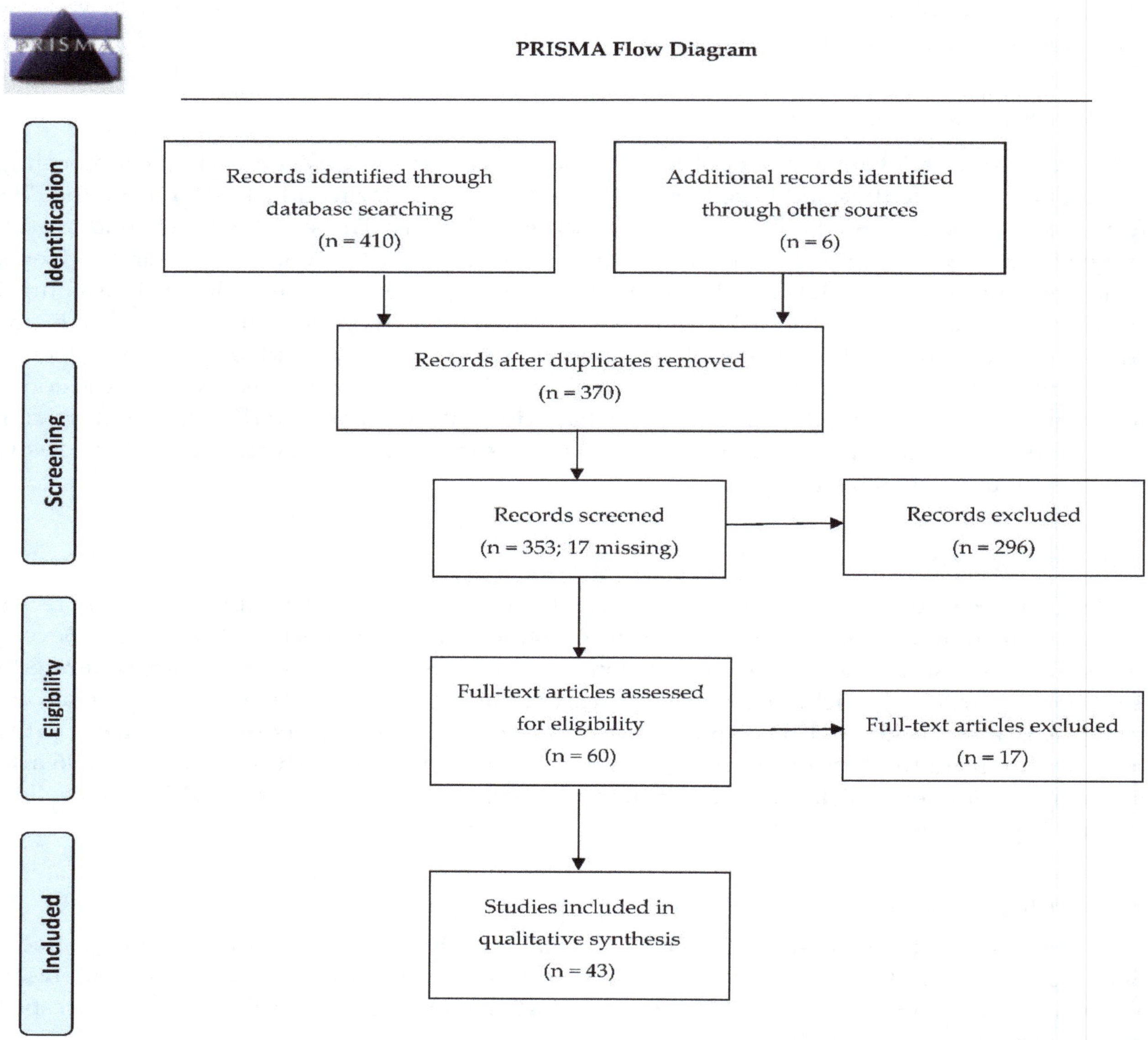

Figure 1. PRISMA flow diagram depicting the flow of information through the different phases of this scoping review. From: [35].

3. Results

Each of the three domains of ethics, stigma, and policy implications related to food addiction are described below. All articles included from the search strategy for each of the three domains are listed in Table S1. Of the 43 studies included in the analysis, 10 were reviews, 25 were original research articles, 5 were commentaries, 2 were opinions, and 1 was a brief. Table 1 provides a summary of themes and subthemes with sample quotes extracted from articles.

Table 1. Scoping review themes, subthemes, and representative quotes.

Themes and Sub-Themes	Authors	Sample Quote
ETHICS		
Personal control, will power, and choice	Foddy (2011) [36]	"The disease label implies a reduction in the autonomy of the addicted and obese. If their strong preferences for consuming food or drugs are merely the symptoms of disease, then these preferences should be viewed as irrelevant in assessing whether their behaviour is willful or not" (p. 86).
	Lee et al. (2014) [33]	"Equating obesity with food addiction could even justify the use of coercive treatments if obese individuals are seen to suffer from a form of addiction over which they have limited control" (pp. 5313–5314).
Blame and weight bias	Thibodeau et al. (2015) [37]	"The narrative of 'addiction' attributed relatively more blame to the behavior of an [obese] individual, evoking comparisons to alcoholism or drug abuse" (p. 29).
	Gearhardt et al. (2012) [38]	"[I]n addition to causing individual suffering weight bias creates personal and societal injustices for obese persons" (p. 409).
STIGMA		
Impact on self-stigma and stigma from others	Burmeister et al. (2013) [39]	"Food addiction symptoms were related to self-reports of internalized weight bias as well as a form of explicit weight bias in which participants indicated dislike of people who carry excess weight and fears related to becoming or remaining overweight. Given our culture's traditional views of addiction being a blameworthy illness, it may come as no surprise that obese food 'addicts' might tend to internalize these stigmatizing beliefs (p. 108)."
Differential impact of substance use disorder versus behavioral addiction	DePierre et al. (2013) [40]	"From the perspective of attribution theory, applying a food addict label to an obese individual could either ameliorate or exacerbate weight stigma. Attribution theory posits that the more a person is seen as responsible for his or her condition, the more people will blame and react to him or her negatively. Indeed, ascribing the cause of obesity to behavioral factors within personal control has been demonstrated to increase stigma, whereas people display fewer negative attitudes toward an individual whose overweight is attributed to biogenetic or physiological factors outside of personal control. Food addiction could be perceived as an external explanation for obesity, reducing blame and stigma. Alternatively, a food addict label could instead act as a behavioral causal attribution, leading obesity to be perceived simply as a result of overeating, potentially increasing weight bias (p. 11)."
	DePierre et al. (2014) [41]	"Food addiction was perceived as a problem of the mind more than either smoking or alcoholism, and received high endorsement as a behaviour resulting from personal unhappiness, indicating that food addiction is viewed as a mental or behavioural problem rather than a physical addiction. Such a perception may detract from beliefs that certain foods can be addictive, with food addiction instead being seen as rooted in an individual's psychological make-up. Additionally, given that mental illnesses elicit more stigma and blame than physical ailments, it is possible that food addiction may increase bias towards overweight/obese individuals with this disorder (p. 5)."
Additive stigma of addiction plus obesity and/or eating disorder	DePierre et al. (2013) [40]	"In the context of attribution theory, the food addict label may have increased blame toward obese individuals by attributing weight to eating behavior, where food addiction may be interpreted as a euphemism for overeating. Or perhaps, in line with Goffman's (1963) framework, categorizing obesity as the result of an addiction added to this 'abomination of the body' the stigma of a 'blemish of character'. Perceiving obesity as the result of a personal failing such as addiction may extend the domains in which it is stigmatized from the immediate social interaction to perceptions of competency for more solitary tasks (or, obesity may extend the otherwise concealable stigma of food addiction to social interactions), potentially explaining why an obese food addict was more negatively perceived than a food addict alone (p. 18)."

Table 1. *Cont.*

Themes and Sub-Themes	Authors	Sample Quote
POLICY		
Comparison to "Big Tobacco"	Allen et al. (2012) [42]	"It is also vital to consider the numerous elements unique to the obesity epidemic that may require novel policy strategies. Most evident is the fact that food is essential for survival, whereas tobacco use is viewed as a dispensable, or even recreational, activity."
Reducing access to addictive foods through regulation	Cullen et al. (2017) [43]	"[Restrictions] would probably help but if the person really wants a Coke every day, they would probably find the means to get it."
Food taxation	Pretlow RA. 2011 [44]	"Taxation of sugar-sweetened beverages, and possibly junk food and fast food, and restriction of such outlets to children, would seem warranted and even embraced by some children."
Limiting advertising for addictive foods	Gearhardt et al. (2012) [38]	"[The food industry] has pledged to remove its unhealthy products from schools and to market fewer unhealthy foods to children, in addition to a variety of other promises. Whether the public and elected officials find the industry trustworthy will determine in part how aggressive government will be in regulating industry practices."
Limited information on food addiction in obesity guidelines	Allen et al. (2012) [42]	"In these guidelines, nothing is said about the potential that an unhealthy diet may not be easily changed due to addictive aspects of hyperphagia. Furthermore, while they do recommend using interventions like taxation on high-energy food, they do not discuss more strict strategies like limiting the access of children to such food."

3.1. The Intersection of Ethics and Food Addiction

Our search yielded 20 articles related to ethics and food addiction. We identified individual responsibility as the primary theme of this section, with the following sub-themes: (i) personal control, will power, and choice; and (ii) blame and weight bias.

3.1.1. Personal Control, Will Power, and Choice

We found a tension in the literature between the traditional framings of addiction that emphasized personal control over food consumption, with medicalized, neuroscientific accounts of food addiction that emphasized reduced personal control. For example, Appelhans, Whited, Schneider, and Pagoto suggested, "[d]ietary lapses or failures should be conceptualized as the result of brain systems interacting with a toxic food environment, and not as a reflection of poor personal choices or lack of willpower" [45] (p. 1135). Some scholars argue that framing food addiction within a disease model may reduce individual blame [46] as the impairment in the person's autonomy and capacity for control reflects dysfunction in the brain's reward circuitry [36,44,47]. However, some scholars are skeptical that a food addiction label or a disease model will reduce responsibility or obviate perceptions that obesity is self-inflicted [5,48]. Others worry about the potential negative influence a brain disease model of food addiction might have on people with obesity. For example, Lee and colleagues suggest that a (brain) disease model could potentially justify coercive practices on a population that is thought to have reduced autonomy and limited control over their behavior [33].

A study by Lee and colleagues found that public support for a food addiction model of obesity was associated with the view that the individual had to overcome their condition through willpower and personal choice [34]. Other studies have reported that the public considers food addiction more of a personal choice than an addiction to other substances such as alcohol [41]. Green suggests that the free autonomous behavior to consume highly palatable foods could be deterred potentially by the implementation of sin taxes (or excise taxes) on said foods [49], but others, such as Franck, Grandi, and Eisenberg, question the evidence to support this recommendation [50]. Scholars have argued that the focus on individual-level factors, such as free will and personal choice, have failed to address the public health impact of high levels of highly palatable food consumption [51,52]. Some authors have argued that this narrow focus on individual-level factors "lets the food industry off the hook" for its contributions [53] (p. 2).

3.1.2. Blame and Weight Bias

Given the emphasis on personal responsibility in the literature, perspectives on who or what is to blame for food addiction are also far from stable. The literature reflects tensions between attributing blame for food addiction to the individual, the environment (including government and industry), or both, but seldom the alleged addictive properties of the food itself [5,41]. For instance, Thibodeau, Perko, and Flusberg found that participants who agreed with narratives that blamed the individual for their obesity (i.e., due to an addiction, a problem of individual behavior) were likely to support interventions that were penalizing, whereas support for narratives that blamed the environment were likely to support policy interventions that sought to protect people with obesity [37]. These tensions exist in a Western culture that values and legitimizes the over-consumption of foods and other material goods [51,54].

Weight bias is an ethically important concept in terms of its relevance to respect for persons, discrimination, and social justice, among others [38]. For example, entrenched harmful stereotypes that describe people with obesity as lazy and lacking in willpower underpins the moral view that they make poor choices with respect to food consumption and their health [38]. "Fat" people are considered "addict[ed] to inappropriate pleasures," which serves to further stigmatize and blame "fat" people [55] (p. 17).

3.2. Potential Implications of Food Addiction on Stigma

Our search yielded 19 articles related to stigma and food addiction. Identified themes included the following: (i) the impact on self-stigma and stigma from others, (ii) the differential impact of substance use disorder versus behavioral addiction on stigma, and (iii) the additive stigma of addiction plus obesity and/or eating disorder. As noted below, there was extensive overlap between several of the stigma and ethics themes.

3.2.1. The Impact on Self-Stigma and Stigma from Others

Related to the concepts of personal control, willpower, and choice, as well as blame and weight bias described above, several authors discussed potential implications of food addiction on self-stigma (internalized stigma) and stigma from others (externalized stigma). Similar to people who use substances, people with obesity receive messages from individuals and society that their obesity is a character flaw [56]. Empirical research using hypothetical case vignettes has found some evidence to suggest that a food addiction model may have a beneficial impact on stigma towards others who are overweight. Latner, Puhl, Murakami, and O'Brien randomly assigned participants to one of four conditions in which they read about either an addiction or non-addiction explanatory model of obesity, and subsequently read a vignette about a woman that was either obese or of normal weight [46]. Regardless of the participant's weight status, a food addiction explanatory model of obesity was found to result in less stigma, less blame, and less perceived psychopathology attributed to the woman in the vignette [46]. Moreover, a food addiction model resulted in less blame towards individuals with obesity in general, leading the authors to conclude that this explanatory model of obesity could have a beneficial impact on the pervasive prejudice against individuals with obesity.

Lee et al. conducted a large survey regarding public views of food addiction [34]. They found substantial support for the concept of food addiction, particularly among individuals with obesity [34]. They were less likely to agree that obesity is caused by overeating and they reported greater support for external causes of obesity. The authors speculated that a diagnosis of food addiction may reduce some of the guilt and self-blame associated with obesity. However, a correlational study by Burmeister, Hinman, Koball, Hoffman, and Carels found that weight-loss-seeking participants with a greater severity of food addiction, as measured by the YFAS, reported greater anti-fat attitudes (e.g., dislike of other people with excess weight), internalized weight bias (e.g., internalization of anti-fat attitudes), and body shame [39].

3.2.2. Differential Impact of Substance Use Disorder Versus Behavioral Addiction on Stigma

Despite evidence of shared neurobiological processes in substance use disorders and behavioral addictions, a false dichotomy permeates much of the discourse whereby substance use disorders are perceived as a neurobiological disease and behavioral addictions are perceived as a mental/psychological condition. Whether food addiction is considered a substance use disorder versus behavioral addiction may impact factors such as personal responsibility, autonomy, and blame attribution, which in turn have implications for internalized and externalized stigma. Stigma may decrease if food addiction is considered a substance use disorder because it provides an explanatory model for obesity "without invoking character flaws, such as lack of willpower" [45] (p. 1133), and shifts responsibility from the individual to the food substance and food industry. For example, Appelhans et al. state: "by emphasizing genetically-influenced neurobiological processes that confer vulnerability to overeating in a toxic food environment, the model enables dietetics practitioners to more effectively address obesity without promoting stigma" [45] (p. 1133). However, Rasmussen points out that the "neurochemical concept of obesity, as with drug addiction and eating disorders, can coexist with attribution of personal responsibility for the condition, and thus with blaming the impaired, addicted consumer rather than the supplier" (p. 217), and goes on to say that "it cannot be ruled out that attribution of addiction (as a chronic brain disease) will hurt more than it helps" [5] (p. 223).

Whereas opinions were mixed regarding whether considering food addiction as a substance use disorder would reduce internalized and externalized stigma, it was generally believed that considering food addiction as a behavioral addiction would either have little effect on stigma or actually increase stigma because it is perceived as a choice that is under personal control. DePierre, Puhl, and Luedicke conducted an empirical study to examine public perceptions of food addiction compared to nicotine and alcohol addiction. Food addiction was considered to be a disease to a greater extent than smoking and to be the product of personal choice to a greater extent than alcohol addiction, leading the authors to conclude that food addiction may be perceived as a behavioral addiction that is vulnerable to stigmatization rather than a substance addiction [41].

3.2.3. Additive Stigma of Addiction Plus Obesity/Eating Disorder

We found a tension in the literature regarding whether food addiction would reduce the stigma directed towards individuals with obesity or create an additional stigmatized identity. Several authors pointed out that substance-related disorders, such as nicotine, alcohol, and cocaine use disorders, are stigmatized to an even greater extent than obesity, a finding that may be due to the fact that everyone must eat food for survival, whereas a person must choose to seek out and use psychoactive substances of abuse [40,41,45]. It has also been suggested that food may be a less stigmatizing substance of abuse because it has less impact on others compared to nicotine (e.g., second-hand smoke) and alcohol (e.g., driving under the influence, impulsive behaviors) [40,41].

Several authors raised concerns that a diagnosis of food addiction could result in a double or additive stigma because the types of stigma associated with obesity and addiction differ [5,40,42,57]. For example, applying the types of stigma described by Goffman in this context, obesity could be considered a visible "abomination of the body," whereas addiction could be considered a "blemish of character" [40,58]. Foddy states: "I have said nothing about the myriad social dimensions in which we stigmatize and disadvantage addicts [sic] differently from the obese. It is hard to say exactly which group has the worse lot in this sense, since the stigma and discrimination takes different forms in each case" [36] (p. 87).

Rather than food addiction reducing stigma by providing an explanatory model for compulsive/binge eating and obesity that reduces blame and personal responsibility, several authors noted that food addiction may actually amplify the harms of stigma because obesity, eating disorders, and addictions are all stigmatized conditions, and neurobiological explanations do not necessarily modify attributions of personal responsibility. Allen et al. raised concerns about the "dietary obese being stigmatized as addicts [sic]" (p. 134) [42]. Rasmussen noted that "the stigmatizing attribution of addiction to people already stigmatized as obese may amplify the social harms that they suffer" (p. 217), "raising the risk that their combination might prove reinforcing" [5] (p. 223).

A few experimental studies have been conducted to examine the impact of food addiction on externalized stigma. Bannon, Hunter-Reel, Wilson, and Karlin randomly assigned participants to one of six conditions in which they read a vignette about a woman with obesity [59]. The independent variables were her binge eating status (present vs. absent) and the cause of her obesity (biological addiction vs. psychological vs. ambiguous). Unfortunately, the manipulation regarding the cause of her obesity was not successful, which prevented interpretation of the specific impact of food addiction on externalized stigma. However, the presence of binge eating increased externalized stigma such that participants rated individuals with obesity as less attractive and more blameworthy for their weight, and they desired greater social distance from them [59]. DePierre et al. directly examined the additive effect of food addiction on externalized stigma [40]. They found that labelling an individual as an "obese food addict" was more stigmatizing than either label on its own ("food addict" or "obese") and concluded that food addiction may increase the externalized stigma associated with obesity, but be less susceptible to stigma than other forms of addiction [40].

3.3. Potential Policy Implications of Food Addiction

Our search yielded 31 articles related to policy themes for addictive foods that were extrapolated to the construct of food addiction. Policy themes related to addictive foods were generally derived from comparisons to the tobacco industry. Articles identified specific policy interventions from "Big Tobacco" that could be applied to food addiction included the following: (i) reducing access to addictive foods, (ii) food taxation, and (iii) limiting advertising for addictive foods.

3.3.1. Comparisons to "Big Tobacco"

Many articles made parallels between the policy issues related to the food industry and the tobacco industry. The role of food taxation, reducing access to potentially addictive foods, litigation against the food industry, and limiting food advertising in addressing food addiction and obesity arise from this comparison to "Big Tobacco" and highlight a prominent theme amongst most articles focusing on policy issues of food addiction [38,52,53]. The association between the food industry and tobacco industry is contingent on a clear link between certain foods and their addictive potential. Authors argued that if certain foods are conceptualized as "a potentially disease-causing agent such as tobacco and alcohol then policy changes to encourage the intake of healthy food and decrease the intake of unhealthy foods are in order" [60] (p. 762). Furthermore, Schulte and colleagues argue that if the concept of food addiction is embraced by the public as it was for nicotine addiction, the shift in public perception of the substance (in this case, addictive foods) could generate enough support for change in public policies for obesity [61]. This argument has been supported by an online survey of 999 individuals from the U.S., including 52% of individuals who were overweight or obese, which showed that believing food is addictive increased support for obesity-related policies [62].

3.3.2. Reducing Access to Addictive Foods Through Regulation

In comparison to policies in the tobacco industry, the overall evidence for the effect of government regulations on limiting access to highly pleasurable food is still emerging and requires further exploration [63]. Current papers identified the role of government regulations on the food industry to support legislation, litigation, and regulation efforts to influence access to healthy as opposed to high fat or sugar foods [60,64]. Reports suggest that if food is deemed addictive, then governments need to establish clear policies to limit, restrict, or even ban addictive foods [52], such as limiting the number and location of fast food restaurants and soft drink vending machines in an area.

The support for policies focused on addictive food restriction for children and youth as opposed to adults. For example, in a survey of youth who were unable to lose weight using an online open-access website for obesity, participants felt that restriction of junk food and fast food outlets would be beneficial [36]. Additional articles supported early intervention efforts through increased regulation of pleasurable foods in children and youth settings such as schools, implementation of programs promoting healthy eating and food choices, and engagement of pediatricians and family physicians [65,66]. In contrast, a recent qualitative study with 23 individuals with obesity showed that individuals were skeptical about the effectiveness of restrictions on highly pleasurable foods, although they supported addictive food restrictions for children [43]. Nonetheless, reviews generally supported external control of addictive foods based on examples where cigarette smokers perceived external control as being influential or effective compared to individual motivating factors (e.g., willpower, personal choice) [67,68].

Despite this support for policy interventions focused on increased food regulation, concerns were expressed in articles around the lack of clarity around "addictive," or "good" and "bad," ingredients and foods [69]. The lack of clear evidence about foods categorized as "addictive" and the unique challenges with food being a necessary part of living (in contrast to alcohol) have complicated abstinence arguments and approaches thus far. Nonetheless, authors have used the comparison to the tobacco industry for informing food addiction policy interventions focused on restriction [56]. Empirical evidence has demonstrated that narratives where obesity was considered an addiction or a disorder led to increased public support for a protective approach to policy interventions for obesity; however, implications for obesity treatment are not fully understood [37].

Studies reiterated the importance of obesity experts being more explicit about food engineering and the need for greater public awareness of this issue beyond the traditional "obesogenic environment" discourses [44]. A greater focus on increasing public awareness about food engineering could lead to greater support for policy interventions focused on regulation and addictive food restriction. One article noted that a potential consequence of identifying and regulating specific "addictive" foods could be litigation and banning of the food industry for purposefully engineering foods to be more addictive [52].

3.3.3. Food Taxation

Themes related to food taxation also emerged predominantly from comparisons between the food and tobacco industries, as highlighted above [42,44]. The rationale stems from evidence for the taxation of tobacco products, which has estimated that a 10% increase in soft drink prices could result in approximately an 8–10% reduction in soft drink consumption by individuals [70,71]. Moreover, several countries, including France and Hungary, have implemented tax levies on high caloric density foods [41]. These national policy initiatives will be beneficial in evaluating the effects of these interventions longitudinally on mitigating food addiction.

Despite this early evidence, several factors complicate food taxation as a policy intervention to reduce access to caloric dense foods. In contrast to tobacco products, caloric dense foods are already cheaper than healthier food options [42]. Therefore, food taxation efforts would affect children and the poor disproportionately given the current low cost of caloric dense foods, although food taxes may potentially be used to offset costs for healthier foods in this population [42]. In addition, it is unclear what food ingredients are highly addictive and as a result, conclusive recommendations on specific ingredients warranting taxation remains a challenge [53].

3.3.4. Limiting Advertising for Addictive Foods

Studies have also articulated concerns about the early introduction of food advertising to young children and adolescents. Gearhardt and colleagues identified the need to limit food advertising to children to limit the potential long-term effects, such as food addiction [38]. Restriction of food marketing to youth has involved both government policies but also voluntary pledges by the food industry [38]. These initiatives have attempted to correct the default food industry messaging that has been inoculating children and youth for decades [71]. As a result, authors argue that voluntary self-regulatory efforts by the food industry are likely to be insufficient, and government protective policies are needed to counteract these trends in early childhood food marketing strategies by the food industry [38].

3.3.5. Limited Information on Food Addiction in Obesity Guidelines

Several papers focused on the limited discussion of food addiction within key obesity related guidelines and resources such as the World Health Organization (WHO) and Centre for Disease Control (CDC) [42]. Despite increasing public dialogue on food addiction, obesity guidelines have not included information on the controversies related to food addiction. This is complicated by the inability to differentiate specific addictive food ingredients and limited evidence for food addiction related interventions [72]. As a result, papers highlighted the need for an improved mechanistic understanding and the development and testing of new treatments for managing addictive foods.

Furthermore, there have been questions regarding the evidence for policy interventions for preventing and managing addictive foods in patients with obesity. Gostin and colleagues believe that the "lack of science" argument for food addiction policy interventions is a faulty argument given that no single intervention resulted in a substantial reduction in nicotine use and there is a need for a multi-level intervention approach [73]. Thus, further research is needed to clarify the construct of food addiction, risk factors and effectiveness of policy interventions to facilitate integration within obesity-related guidelines and resources.

4. Discussion

The current scoping review examined the potential ethical, stigma, and health policy implications of food addiction, identified the major themes in the literature, and provided insights into key challenges in these areas.

4.1. Potential Ethical Implications of Food Addiction

While various disease models of alcohol use disorders have circulated within the popular discourse since the early 19th century [74,75], more recently scholars have adopted the language of neuroscience to characterize addiction more generally as a chronic, relapsing brain disease [76,77]. We found that discussions in the literature lend themselves to moral debates over personal control, individual responsibility, and blame for the consequences of food consumption. Indeed, these moral framings are common in the obesity discourse [44,78]. However, the neurobiological theory of food addiction may place a disproportionate burden on the individual to treat their food addiction, which may provide less incentive for governments to scale up public health approaches, such as holding the food industry accountable for their food engineering practices as well as the social conditions that harm people who are defined as food addicted.

The focus of individual blame in the literature may be reflective of a culture of healthism, defined as the individual desire for health and well-being achieved primarily through lifestyle modification [79]. The moral assumptions underlying healthism is that individuals are responsible for making good choices as opposed to bad choices about their health. Our results suggest that healthism describes good choices as health-promoting and reflects self-control over eating while bad choices lead to food addiction or obesity. For instance, some dietary counselling recommendations include empowering the patient to take responsibility for their behaviors in the context of what they consider to be a toxic food environment [45]. Our results suggest that some authors were concerned about a culture that emphasizes healthism and individualism when the social conditions make the ability to make healthy eating choices near impossible [51]. Future research can build on the burgeoning literature in this area and provide deeper insights into the moral attitudes about food addiction held by diverse publics.

It will also be important for future research to explore if the empirical findings related to moral concepts align with the concerns raised in the conceptual philosophical and bioethics literatures.

4.2. Potential Stigma Implications of Food Addiction

Our review also examined the complex relationship between food addiction and stigma. Stigma is a multidimensional construct including many related concepts (e.g., labels, stereotypes, prejudice, discrimination), sources (e.g., self-stigma, public stigma, provider-based stigma [e.g., from healthcare providers], institutional stigma), characteristics (e.g., stigma of the physical body, stigma of character), and dimensions (e.g., social distance, perceptions of dangerousness) that can complicate analyses [80]. The limited empirical research conducted to date, much of which has experimentally manipulated the information provided in case vignettes, has generated mixed results regarding the impact of a food addiction model on externalized stigma. Whereas a food addiction explanation for obesity was found to reduce externalized stigma and blame towards a target in one study [45], another study found that labeling an individual as an "obese food addict" created an additive stigma that exceeded the stigma associated with either label on its own [40]. This finding is consistent with a recent qualitative study of individuals with obesity, which noted that some individuals who personally identified with the concept of food addiction felt reluctant to be described as an "addict" because they believed the label would increase self-stigma and stigma from others [43]. Interestingly, the one study identified through our scoping review that examined the association between food addiction and externalized stigma in a clinical sample found that patients with greater severity of food addiction reported greater anti-fat attitudes towards other individuals with excess weight [39]. The impact of food addiction on externalized stigma has been examined in student samples, community samples, and a clinical sample, and additional research is warranted to examine the impact of a food addiction model on externalized stigma among healthcare professionals.

In contrast to the mixed findings regarding the impact of a food addiction model on externalized stigma, the association between food addiction and internalized stigma has been fairly consistent. The aforementioned study conducted in a clinical sample found that patients with greater severity of food addiction reported greater internalized weight bias and body shame, as well as lower eating self-efficacy [39]. This finding is consistent with a recent study comparing three groups that varied with respect to food addiction (i.e., non-food-addicted, self-perceived food addicted, and food-addicted according to the YFAS) and found that internalized weight bias increased across the groups despite no differences in body mass index, whereas eating self-efficacy decreased across the groups [81]. Similarly, a recent systematic review examining the association between internalized weight bias and health-related variables reported that the published studies conducted to date have consistently found a positive association between food addiction and internalized weight bias [82]. Moreover, internalized weight bias was associated with a variety of negative mental and physical health outcomes including depression, anxiety, low self-esteem, poor body image, disordered eating, severity of obesity, reduced dietary adherence, and reduced motivation and self-efficacy to engage in health-promoting behaviors. Although much of the research conducted to date has been cross-sectional, which precludes conclusions regarding the direction of causality, if replicated in prospective research, such findings would lend support to concerns voiced by some authors that food addiction could have an adverse impact on internalized stigma and reduce the self-efficacy needed to improve eating behaviors [29]. Although the treatment implications of food addiction were beyond the scope of the current review, this important topic is recently receiving more attention in the literature [83,84] and the findings of the current review suggest that treatment approaches that reduce internalized weight bias and bolster self-efficacy would be advised.

Whether food addiction is best characterized as a behavioral addiction or a substance use disorder has been a topic of debate [26]. The results of the current review suggest that characterizing food addiction as a behavioral addiction likely has an adverse impact on externalized stigma compared to characterizing it as a substance use disorder. Despite evidence that behavioral addictions and substance use disorders have many shared features, including neurobiological mechanisms and genetic contributions [85,86], behavioral addictions are still commonly perceived as being more under personal control. The general public perceives food addiction as being less of a disease and more under personal control than alcoholism [41]. Increasing public awareness regarding the engineering of hyperpalatable foods and the validity of food addiction as a diagnostic construct that shares similarities with other substance use disorders [8] may be helpful as both a public health and stigma reduction intervention.

4.3. Potential Policy Implications of Food Addiction

Across reviewed articles, we found that the tobacco industry served as an example for many of the policy recommendations for managing food addiction in obesity. The challenges with these policy interventions were related to the lack of research on addictive food substances, specifically the current inability to classify foods more broadly in their addictive potential. Despite authors drawing parallels to "Big Tobacco," we identified a dearth of evidence for the effectiveness of food addiction as a driver for policy change in obesity. Therefore, many of the recommendations, such as food taxation, reducing advertising to children, and reducing access to addictive foods (especially in children and youth), were extrapolated from policy interventions observed in the tobacco industry as opposed to being specific to food addiction.

4.4. Limitations

Our results are subject to the following limitations associated with scoping review. Unlike a systematic review, we are unable to grade the quality of the studies or make any specific recommendations related to level of evidence. The articles included in this scoping review included commentaries and empirical research (e.g., experimental and correlational studies). Further, although our search used multiple methods to identify potential articles, it is possible that some studies were missed. This scoping review underscored the need for future research on the effectiveness of policy interventions to mitigate the effect of addictive foods on the obesity epidemic. The inclusion of food addiction within obesity guidelines was a notable omission in the literature that was identified in our review. It is possible that the absence of food addiction in obesity guidelines reflects the need for greater research on the role of food addiction on obesity management, including questions about its benefit for healthcare professionals and patients in obesity care.

5. Conclusions

This review is the first to explore the ethical, stigma, and policy issues related to food addiction using a scoping review methodology. The gaps in the evidence related to this scoping review underscore the need for additional research and increased clarity regarding the ethical and stigma related impact of a food addiction model. In addition, more rigorous studies are needed to move beyond policy interventions generated predominantly from past experiences in the tobacco industry.

Author Contributions: S.E.C., D.Z.B., and S.S. contributed to the conception and design of the study. S.E.L., K.K., and A.H. conducted literature searches and provided summaries of previous research studies. All authors contributed equally to the analysis and interpretation of the data and the writing of the manuscript. All authors have approved the final manuscript.

Acknowledgments: This project was funded by a Planning and Dissemination Grant from the Canadian Institutes of Health Research. We would like to thank Ashley Farrell for assisting with the scoping review methodology and literature search, as well as the individuals who participated in our food addiction retreat.

References

1. Kuczmarski, R.J.; Flegal, K.M.; Campbell, S.M.; Johnson, C.L. Increasing prevalence of overweight among US adults. The National Health and Nutrition Examination Surveys, 1960 to 1991. *JAMA* **1994**, *272*, 205–211. [PubMed]

2. Kessler, D.A. *The End of Overeating: Taking Control of the Insatiable American Appetite*; Rodale: New York, NY, USA, 2009.
3. Johnson, P.M.; Kenny, P.J. Dopamine D2 receptors in addiction-like reward dysfunction and compulsive eating in obese rats. *Nat. Neurosci.* **2010**, *13*, 635–641.
4. Parr, J.; Rasmussen, N. Making addicts of the fat: Obesity, psychiatry and the 'Fatties Anonymous' Model of Self-Help Weight Loss in the Post-War United States. In *Critical Perspectives on Addiction (Advances in Medical Sociology, Volume 14)*; Netherland, J., Ed.; Emerald Group Publishing Limited: Bingley, UK, 2012; pp. 181–200.
5. Rasmussen, N. Stigma and the addiction paradigm for obesity: Lessons from 1950s America. *Addiction* **2014**, *110*, 217–225.
6. American Psychiatric Association. *Diagnostic and Statistical Manual of Mental Disorders*, 5th ed.; American Psychiatric Association: Washington, DC, USA, 2013.
7. Gearhardt, A.N.; Corbin, W.R.; Brownell, K.D. Preliminary validation of the Yale food addiction Scale. *Appetite* **2009**, *52*, 430–436.
8. Gordon, E.L.; Ariel-Donges, A.H.; Bauman, V.; Merlo, L.J. What is the evidence for "food addiction"? A systematic review. *Nutrients* **2018**, *12*, 477.
9. Ivezaj, V.; White, M.A.; Grilo, C.M. Examining binge-eating disorder and food addiction in adults with overweight and obesity. *Obesity* **2016**, *24*, 2064–2069.
10. Chao, A.M.; Shaw, J.A.; Pearl, R.L.; Alamuddin, N.; Hopkins, C.M.; Bakizada, Z.M.; Berkowitz, R.I.; Wadden, T.A. Prevalence and psychosocial correlated of food addiction in persons with obesity seeking weight reduction. *Compr. Psychiatry* **2016**, *73*, 97–104. [PubMed]
11. Gearhardt, A.N.; White, M.A.; Masheb, R.M.; Morgan, P.T.; Crosby, R.D.; Grilo, C.M. An examination of the food addiction construct in obese patients with binge eating disorder. *Int. J. Eat. Disord.* **2012**, *45*, 657–663. [PubMed]
12. Gearhardt, A.N.; Davis, C.; Kuschner, R.; Brownell, K.D. The addiction potential of hyperpalatable foods. *Curr. Drug Abuse Rev.* **2011**, *4*, 140–145.
13. Schulte, E.M.; Avena, N.M.; Gearhardt, A.N. Which foods may be addictive? The roles of processing, fat content, and glycemic load. *PLoS ONE* **2015**, *10*, e0117959.
14. Curtis, C.; Davis, C. A qualitative study of binge eating and obesity from an addiction perspective. *Eat. Disord.* **2014**, *22*, 19–32.
15. Gihooly, C.H.; Das, S.K.; Golden, J.K.; McCrory, M.A.; Dallal, G.E.; Saltzman, E.; Kramer, F.M.; Roberts, S.B. Food cravings and energy regulation: The characteristics of craved foods and their relationship with eating behaviors and weight change during 6 months of dietary energy restriction. *Int. J. Obes.* **2007**, *31*, 1849–1858.
16. Smith, D.G.; Robbins, T.W. The neurobiological underpinnings of obesity and being eating: A rationale for adopting the food addiction model. *Biol. Psychiatry* **2013**, *73*, 804–810.
17. Volkow, N.D.; Wang, G.J.; Fowler, J.S.; Tomais, D.; Baler, R. Food and drug reward: Overlapping circuits in human obesity and addiction. *Curr. Top. Behav. Neurosci.* **2012**, *11*, 1–24. [PubMed]
18. Gearhardt, A.N.; Yokum, S.; Orr, P.; Stice, E.; Corbin, W.; Brownell, K.D. The neural correlates of 'food addiction'. *Arch. Gen. Psychiatry* **2011**, *68*, 808–816. [PubMed]
19. Davis, C.; Loxton, N.J.; Levitan, R.D.; Kaplan, A.S.; Carter, J.C.; Kennedy, J.L. 'Food addiction' and its association with a dopaminergic multilocus genetic profile. *Physiol. Behav.* **2013**, *118*, 63–69. [PubMed]
20. Fletcher, P.C.; Kenny, P.J. Food addiction: A valid concept? *Neuropsychopharmacology* **2018**, *43*, 2506–2513.
21. Burrows, T.; Skinner, J.; McKenna, R.; Rollo, M. Food addiction, binge eating disorder, and obesity: Is there a relationship? *Behav. Sci.* **2017**, *7*, 54.
22. Leigh, S.J.; Morris, M.J. The role of reward circuitry and food addiction in the obesity epidemic: An update. *Biol. Psychol.* **2018**, *131*, 31–42.
23. Muele, A.; Gearhardt, A.N. Food addiction in the light of DSM-5. *Nutrients* **2014**, *6*, 2652–2671.
24. Corwin, R.L.; Grigson, P.S. Symposium overview - food addiction: Fact or fiction? *J. Nutr.* **2009**, *139*, 617–619.
25. Davis, C. A commentary on the associations among 'food addiction', binge eating disorder, and obesity: Overlapping conditions with idiosyncratic clinical features. *Appetite* **2017**, *115*, 3–8. [PubMed]
26. Schulte, E.M.; Potenza, M.N.; Gearhardt, A.N. A commentary on the "eating addiction" versus "food addiction" perspectives on addictive-like food consumption. *Appetite* **2017**, *115*, 9–15.

27. Bell, K.; Salmon, A.; Bowers, M.; Bell, J.; McCullough, L. Smoking, stigma and tobacco 'denormalization': Further reflections on the use of stigma as a public health tool. *Soc. Sci. Med.* **2010**, *70*, 795–799.
28. Guttman, N.; Salmon, C.T. Guilt, fear, stigma and knowledge gaps: Ethical issues in public health communication interventions. *Bioethics* **2004**, *18*, 531–552. [PubMed]
29. Bayer, R. Stigma and the ethics of public health: Not can we but should we. *Soc. Sci. Med.* **2008**, *67*, 463–472.
30. Goldberg, D.S.; Puhl, R.M. Obesity stigma: A failed and ethically dubious strategy. *Hastings Cent. Rep.* **2013**, *43*, 5–6. [PubMed]
31. Reid, J.; O'Brien, K.S.; Puhl, R.; Hardman, C.A.; Carter, A. Food addiction and its potential links with weight stigma. *Curr. Addict. Rep.* **2018**, *5*, 192–201.
32. Arksey, H.; O'Malley, L. Scoping studies: Towards a methodological framework. *Int. J. Soc. Res. Methodol.* **2005**, *8*, 19–32.
33. Lee, N.M.; Hall, W.D.; Lucke, J.; Forlini, C.; Carter, A. Food Addiction and Its Impact on Weight-Based Stigma and the Treatment of Obese Individuals in the U.S. and Australia. *Nutrients* **2014**, *6*, 5312–5326.
34. Lee, N.M.; Lucke, J.; Hall, W.D.; Meurk, C.; Boyle, F.M.; Carter, A. Public Views on Food Addiction and Obesity: Implications for Policy and Treatment. *PLoS ONE* **2013**, *8*, e74836.
35. Moher, D.; Liberati, A.; Tetzlaff, J.; Altman, D.G. The PRISMA Group (2009). Preferred Reporting Items for Systematic Reviews and Meta-Analyses: The PRISMA Statement. *PLoS Med.* **2009**, *6*, e1000097. [CrossRef]
36. Foddy, B. Addicted to Food, Hungry for Drugs. *Neuroethics* **2011**, *4*, 79–89.
37. Thibodeau, P.H.; Perko, V.L.; Flusberg, S.J. The relationship between narrative classification of obesity and support for public policy interventions. *Soc. Sci. Med.* **2015**, *141*, 27–35. [PubMed]
38. Gearhardt, A.N.; Bragg, M.A.; Pearl, R.L.; Schvey, N.A.; Roberto, C.A.; Brownell, K.D. Obesity and public policy. *Annu. Rev. Clin. Psychol.* **2012**, *8*, 405–430. [PubMed]
39. Burmeister, J.M.; Hinman, N.; Koball, A.; Hoffmann, D.A.; Carels, R.A. Food addiction in adults seeking weight loss treatment. Implications for psychosocial health and weight loss. *Appetite* **2013**, *60*, 103–110. [PubMed]
40. DePierre, J.A.; Puhl, R.; Luedicke, J. A new stigmatized identity? Comparisons of a 'food addict' label with other stigmatized health conditions. *Basic Appl. Soc. Psych.* **2013**, *35*, 10–21.
41. DePierre, J.A.; Puhl, R.; Luedicke, J. Public perceptions of food addiction: A comparison with alcohol and tobacco. *J. Subst. Use* **2014**, *19*, 1–6.
42. Allen, P.J.; Batra, P.; Geiger, B.M.; Wommack, T.; Gilhooly, C.; Pothos, E.N. Rationale and consequences of reclassifying obesity as an addictive disorder: Neurobiology, food environment and social policy perspectives. *Physiol. Behav.* **2012**, *107*, 126–137.
43. Cullen, A.J.; Barnett, A.; Komesaroff, P.A.; Brown, W.; O'Brien, K.S.O.; Hall, W.; Carter, A. A qualitative study of overweight and obese Australians' views of food addiction. *Appetite* **2017**, *115*, 62–70. [PubMed]
44. Pretlow, R.A. Addiction to highly pleasurable food as a cause of the childhood obesity epidemic: A qualitative Internet study. *Eat. Disord.* **2011**, *19*, 295–307.
45. Appelhans, B.M.; Whited, M.C.; Schneider, K.L.; Pagoto, S.L. Time to abandon the notion of personal choice in dietary counseling for obesity? *J. Am. Diet. Assoc.* **2011**, *111*, 1130–1136. [PubMed]
46. Latner, J.D.; Puhl, R.M.; Murakami, J.M.; O'Brien, K.S. Food addiction as a causal model of obesity. Effects on stigma, blame, and perceived psychopathology. *Appetite* **2014**, *77*, 77–82. [PubMed]
47. Ho, A.L.; Sussman, E.S.; Pendharkar, A.V.; Azagury, D.E.; Bohon, C.; Halpern, C.H. Deep brain stimulation for obesity: Rationale and approach to trial design. *Neurosurg. Focus* **2015**, *38*, E8.
48. Ortiz, S.E.; Zimmerman, F.J.; Gilliam, F.D., Jr. Weighing in: The taste-engineering frame in obesity expert discourse. *Am. J. Public Health* **2015**, *105*, 554–559. [PubMed]
49. Green, R. The Ethics of Sin Taxes. *Public Health Nurs.* **2011**, *28*, 68–77. [PubMed]
50. Franck, C.; Grandi, S.M.; Eisenberg, M.J. Taxing Junk Food to Counter Obesity. *Am. J. Public Health* **2013**, *103*, 1949–1953.
51. Brownell, K.D.; Schwartz, M.B.; Puhl, R.M.; Henderson, K.E.; Harris, J.L. The need for bold action to prevent adolescent obesity. *J. Adolesc. Health* **2009**, *45*, S8–S17.
52. Pomeranz, J.L.; Teret, S.P.; Sugarman, S.D.; Rutkow, L.; Brownell, K.D. Innovative Legal Approaches to Address Obesity. *Milbank Q* **2009**, *87*, 185–213.
53. Hebebrand, J. Obesity prevention: Moving beyond the food addiction debate. *J. Neuroendocrinol.* **2015**, *27*, 737–738. [PubMed]

54. Blundell, J.E.; Finlayson, G. Food addiction not helpful: The hedonic component—Implicit wanting—Is important. *Addiction* **2011**, *106*, 1216–1218. [PubMed]
55. Mackenzie, R. Don't Let Them Eat Cake! A View from Across the Pond. *Am. J. Bioeth.* **2010**, *10*, 16–18. [PubMed]
56. deShazo, R.D.; Hall, J.E.; Skipworth, L.B. Obesity bias, medical technology, and the hormonal hypothesis: Should we stop demonizing fat people? *Am. J. Med.* **2015**, *128*, 456–460. [PubMed]
57. Rasmussen, N. Weight stigma, addiction, science, and the medication of fatness in mid-twentieth century America. *Sociol. Health Illn.* **2012**, *34*, 880–895.
58. Goffman, E. *Stigma: Notes on the Management of Spoiled Identity*; Simon & Schuster: New York, NY, USA, 1963.
59. Bannon, K.L.; Hunter-Reel, D.; Wilson, G.T.; Karlin, R.A. The effects of casual beliefs and binge eating on the stigmatization of obesity. *Int. J. Eat. Disord.* **2009**, *42*, 118–124.
60. Battle, E.K.; Brownell, K.D. Confronting a rising tide of eating disorders and obesity: Treatment vs. prevention and policy. *Addict. Behav.* **1996**, *21*, 755–765.
61. Schulte, E.M.; Tuttle, H.M.; Gearhardt, A.N. Belief in Food Addiction and Obesity-Related Policy Support. *PLoS ONE* **2016**, *11*, e0147557.
62. Moran, A.; Musicus, A.; Soo, J.; Gearhardt, A.N.; Gollust, S.E.; Roberto, C.A. Believing that certain foods are addictive is associated with support for obesity-related public policies. *Prev. Med.* **2016**, *90*, 39–46. [PubMed]
63. Alonso-Alonso, M.; Woods, S.C.; Pelchat, M.; Grigson, P.S.; Stice, E.; Faroogi, S.; Khoo, C.S.; Mattes, R.D.; Beauchamp, G.K. Food reward system: Current perspectives and future research needs. *Nutr. Rev.* **2015**, *73*, 296–307. [PubMed]
64. Gearhardt, A.N.; Corbin, W.R.; Brownell, K.D. Food addiction: An examination of the diagnostic criteria for dependence. *J. Addict. Med.* **2009**, *3*, 1–7.
65. Volkow, N.D.; Wise, R.A. How can drug addiction help us understand obesity? *Nat. Neurosci.* **2005**, *8*, 555–560. [PubMed]
66. Willette, A.L. Where have all the parents gone? Do efforts to regulate food advertising to curb childhood obesity pass constitutional muster? *J. Leg. Med.* **2007**, *28*, 561–577.
67. Morphett, K.; Partridge, B.; Gartner, C.; Carter, A.; Hall, W. Why Don't Smokers Want Help to Quit? A Qualitative Study of Smokers' Attitudes towards Assisted vs. Unassisted Quitting. *Int. J. Environ. Res. Public Health* **2015**, *12*, 6591–6607.
68. Uppal, N.; Shahab, L.; Britton, J.; Ratschen, E. The forgotten smoker: A qualitative study of attitudes towards smoking, quitting, and tobacco control policies among continuing smokers. *BMC Public Health* **2013**, *13*, 432.
69. Smith, T.G. All foods are habit-forming—What I want to know is which will kill me! *Addiction* **2011**, *106*, 1218–1220.
70. Andreyeva, T.; Long, M.W.; Brownell, K.D. The impact of food prices on consumption: A systematic review of research on the price elasticity of demand for food. *Am. J. Public Health* **2010**, *100*, 216–222.
71. Brownell, K.D.; Frieden, T.R. Ounces of prevention—The public policy case for taxes on sugared beverages. *N. Engl. J. Med.* **2009**, *360*, 1805–1808. [PubMed]
72. Gearhardt, A.N.; Grilo, C.M.; DiLeone, R.J.; Brownell, K.D.; Potenza, M.N. Can food be addictive? Public health and policy implications. *Addiction* **2011**, *106*, 1208–1212.
73. Gostin, L.O. Limiting what we can eat: A bridge too far? *Milbank Q.* **2014**, *92*, 173–176.
74. Rush, B. *An Inquiry into the Effects of Ardent Spirits Upon the Human Body and Mind: With an Account of the Means of Preventing, and of the Remedies for Curing Them*; James Loring: Boston, NY, USA, 1823.
75. Jellinek, E.M. *The Disease Concept of Alcoholism*; Hillhouse: New Haven, CT, USA, 1960.
76. Leshner, A.I. Addiction is a brain disease, and it matters. *Science* **1997**, *278*, 45–47. [PubMed]
77. Barnett, A.I.; Hall, W.; Fry, C.L.; Dilkes-Frayne, E.; Carter, A. Drug and alcohol treatment providers' views about the disease model of addiction and its impact on clinical practice: A systematic review. *Drug Alcohol Rev.* **2018**, *37*, 697–720.
78. Rich, E.; Evans, J. 'Fat ethics'—The obesity discourse and body politics. *Soc. Theory Health* **2005**, *3*, 341–358.
79. Crawford, R. Healthism and the medicalization of everyday life. *Int. J. Health Serv.* **1980**, *10*, 365–388. [PubMed]
80. Pescosolido, B.A.; Martin, J.K. The stigma complex. *Annu. Rev. Sociol.* **2015**, *41*, 87–116. [PubMed]

81. Meadows, A.; Nolan, L.J.; Higgs, S. Self-perceived food addiction: Prevalence, predictors, and prognosis. *Appetite* **2017**, *114*, 282–298. [PubMed]
82. Pearl, R.L.; Puhl, R.M. Weight bias internalization and health: A systematic review. *Obes. Rev.* **2018**, *19*, 1141–1163. [PubMed]
83. Schulte, E.M.; Joyner, M.A.; Schiestl, E.T.; Gearhardt, A.N. Future directions in "food addiction": Next steps and treatment implications. *Curr. Addict. Rep.* **2017**, *4*, 165–171.
84. Vella, S.C.; Pai, N.B. A narrative review of potential treatment strategies for food addiction. *Eat. Weight Disord.* **2017**, *22*, 387–393. [PubMed]
85. Grant, J.E.; Potenza, M.N.; Weinstein, A.; Gorelick, D.A. Introduction to behavioral addictions. *Am. J. Drug Alcohol Abuse* **2010**, *36*, 233–241.
86. Leeman, R.F.; Potenza, M.N. A targeted review of the neurobiology and genetics of behavioral additions: An emerging area of research. *Can. J. Psychiatry* **2014**, *58*, 260–273.

10

Food Addiction and Tobacco Use Disorder: Common Liability and Shared Mechanisms

Laurie Zawertailo [1,2,*,†], Sophia Attwells [2,†], Wayne K. deRuiter [2], Thao Lan Le [2], Danielle Dawson [2] and Peter Selby [2,3,4,5]

1 Department of Pharmacology and Toxicology, University of Toronto, 1 King's College Circle, Toronto, ON M5S 1A8, Canada
2 Centre for Addiction and Mental Health, 1025 Queen Street West, Toronto, ON M6J 1H4, Canada; sophia.attwells@camh.ca (S.A.); wayne.deruiter@camh.ca (W.K.d.); thaolan.le@gmail.com (T.L.L.); danielle.dawson@camh.ca (D.D.); peter.selby@camh.ca (P.S.)
3 Department of Family and Community Medicine, University of Toronto, 500 University Ave., Toronto, ON M5G 1V7, Canada
4 Department of Psychiatry, University of Toronto, 250 College St., Toronto, ON M5T 1L8, Canada
5 Dalla Lana School of Public Health, University of Toronto, 155 College St, Toronto, ON M5T 3M7, Canada
* Correspondence: laurie.zawertailo@camh.ca
† These authors contributed equally to this work.

Abstract: As food addiction is being more commonly recognized within the scientific community, parallels can be drawn between it and other addictive substance use disorders, including tobacco use disorder. Given that both unhealthy diets and smoking are leading risk factors for disability and death, a greater understanding of how food addiction and tobacco use disorder overlap with one another is necessary. This narrative review aimed to highlight literature that investigated prevalence, biology, psychology, and treatment options of food addiction and tobacco use disorder. Published studies up to August 2020 and written in English were included. Using a biopsychosocial lens, each disorder was assessed together and separately, as there is emerging evidence that the two disorders can develop concurrently or sequentially within individuals. Commonalities include but are not limited to the dopaminergic neurocircuitry, gut microbiota, childhood adversity, and attachment insecurity. In addition, the authors conducted a feasibility study with the purpose of examining the association between food addiction symptoms and tobacco use disorder among individuals seeking tobacco use disorder treatment. To inform future treatment approaches, more research is necessary to identify and understand the overlap between the two disorders.

Keywords: food addiction; nicotine; tobacco use disorder; comorbidity

1. Introduction

Smoking and obesity are the two most prevalent causes of preventable chronic disease morbidity and mortality worldwide [1,2]. Smoking and food addiction are both maladaptive behaviors in which an individual experiences loss of control and compulsive engagement in the behavior despite known harmful consequences. We have reached a pivotal time for understanding food addiction, similar to a time when tobacco use disorder was perceived as habit forming and not addictive. While food addiction does meet several of the American Psychiatric Association's diagnostic criteria outlining substance use disorder [3], more research is necessary to determine if certain foods are addictive and how to prevent and treat this condition.

The concept of food addiction represents a relatively new domain of research [4]. Food addiction refers to an "eating behavior involving the overconsumption of specific foods in an addiction-like manner". While the term "food addiction" was introduced to scientific literature in 1956 [5], research investigating the mechanisms, neurobiology, and genetics of food addiction was not pursued until the early 2000s. Food addiction in relation to certain foods has not been widely accepted or studied. As such, the diagnostic criteria of food addiction are not well established and are not formally recognized by the American Psychiatric Association as either a substance use disorder or a behavioral disorder in the Diagnosis and Statistical Manual of Mental Disorders 5 (DSM 5) [3]. Regardless, the criteria for food addiction have been modeled from substance use disorder criteria outlined in the DSM 5 [6].

In the DSM 5, substance use disorder is defined as a complex condition manifested by compulsive substance use despite harmful consequences. Furthermore, regular substance use may develop dependence and tolerance. The DSM 5 currently lists nine distinct disorders (e.g., tobacco use disorder and alcohol use disorder), but nearly all substances are diagnosed on the basis of the same overarching criteria [3]. Hallmark symptoms of food addiction include loss of control and frequent overconsumption, desire or repeated failed attempts to reduce or stop consumption, increased time spent in activities necessary to obtain and eat food, giving up on important activities such as physical exercise, continued consumption despite physical or psychological problems, and clinically significant impairment or distress [7].

Currently, limited research exists pertaining to food addiction and how it relates to other substance use disorders. Given that both unhealthy diets and smoking are among the leading risk factors for all-cause disability-adjusted life years, total deaths, and years lived with disability [8], a greater understanding of how food addiction and tobacco use disorder overlap with one another is necessary [9]. Furthermore, the role of food addiction in the common but understudied phenomenon of post-cessation weight gain among smokers trying to quit has not been researched. The purpose of this narrative review is to present and summarize the most up-to-date research findings on the prevalence, biology, psychology, and treatment of tobacco use disorder and food addiction as individual disorders, identifying overlap and commonalities that may help inform treatment approaches. It is important to understand each individual disorder in the context of the other since there is emerging evidence that the two disorders can develop concurrently or sequentially within individuals. To provide background on food addiction and tobacco use disorder, this review first discusses the prevalence of these disorders, measurements that assess severity, and theories of food addiction. This review then covers various subtopics such as biology, gut microbiome, psychosocial factors, and treatment options. The studies examined for this review mainly focus on food addiction rather than obesity and eating disorders, as these are two separate and complex conditions.

2. Methods

To locate relevant publications on the relationship between food addiction and tobacco use disorder, the following databases were searched: Ovid Medline, PsycInfo, and Embase. The Medline search strategy included both relevant medical subject headings (MESH) and keywords for the concepts of food addiction and tobacco use disorder/cessation. Food addiction-related terms included "food adj3 addict", "eat adj3 addict", "food adj3 dependence", "food use disorder", "compulsive eating", "Yale Food Addiction Scale", "obes", "diabetes", and "binge eating disorder". Smoking terms included "tobacco use disorder", "tobacco depend", "nicotine", "((nicotine or tobacco or smoking) adj3 (cessation or quit or quitting or quits or give up or giving up or stop or stopping or stopped or stops))", "((nicotine or tobacco or smoking) adj3 withdraw)", and "smoking cessation/or tobacco use cessation". The Medline search strategy was adapted for the controlled vocabulary of the other databases searched. All of the search results were limited to English language publications, but no date or study type limitations were applied. Furthermore, the database search was complemented by a manual review of reference lists from the retrieved articles. Articles related to the purpose of this narrative were retrieved from the database search. Studies examining eating disorders and obesity in the absence of food addiction were not reviewed as this was outside of the scope of this review.

3. Discussion

3.1. Prevalence

3.1.1. Prevalence and Severity Measurement of Tobacco Use Disorder

In 2017, 15% of the Canadian population (about 4.6 million people) were current smokers. Within that population, 11% and 4% reported being daily smokers and occasional smokers, respectively [10]. Daily smokers averaged approximately 14 cigarettes per day, with a higher percentage of smokers being male (17%) than female (13%) [10]. Furthermore, in 2018, nearly 34% of Canadian youth reported trying an electronic cigarette (e-cigarette) at least once in their lifetime [11]. Evidence suggests that e-cigarette use in youth increases the risk of developing tobacco use disorder later in life [12]. Similar statistics are reported in the United States, where approximately 12% of the population (or 40 million people) are daily smokers [13].

The DSM 5 replaced the DSM-IV's categories of nicotine abuse and dependence with tobacco use disorder. Within this context, problematic patterns of tobacco use must cause significant impairment and distress for at least two symptoms within a 1 year period to be considered a disorder. Other common measures of nicotine dependence severity include the Fagerstrom Test for Nicotine Dependence (FTND), Heaviness of Smoking Index (HSI), and time to first cigarette (TTFC). The FTND contains six questions scored 0–3 for a total possible score of 0–10. Higher scores indicate greater the physical dependence on nicotine. Similarly, HSI contains two measures: TTFC of the day and daily consumption of cigarettes. These metrics have been used to predict behavioral and biochemical indices of smoking, including ability to quit and cancer incidence and mortality [14]. Both measures are reliable over time and are important predictors of quitting [15,16].

3.1.2. Prevalence and Severity Measurement of Food Addiction

Food addiction is commonly measured using the Yale Food Addiction Scale (YFAS) [17], a 25-item tool developed in accordance with the substance dependence criteria of the DSM-IV [7,18]. The YFAS applies these criteria to the concept of food addiction for the purpose of identifying individuals who possess a predisposition toward the overconsumption of highly palatable foods within the previous 12 months [7,19]. The YFAS is capable of providing two scoring measures: (i) a cutoff score (yes/no) is achieved when an individual fulfills a minimum of three criteria and satisfies a clinical significant impairment or distress criterion, and (ii) a symptom count (0–7) in which the total number of endorsed criteria, with the exception of clinically significant impairment or distress criteria, is added together [7,18]. The YFAS represents a valid and reliable tool in identifying individuals who meet criteria for food addiction [7,20]; however, a major limitation of the YFAS is the reliance on self-reporting of symptoms. To date, there are no biological measurements to confirm the presence or absence of food addiction. Therefore, in conjunction with the lack of formal recognition by the DSM 5, a clinical diagnosis for food addiction does not exist at this time.

With the release of the DSM 5, criteria for diagnosing substance-related and addiction disorders have changed. Consequently, the 35-item YFAS 2.0 was developed to accurately align the concept of food addiction with the new DSM 5 substance use disorder criteria [21]. Another adaptation, the modified version of the YFAS (mYFAS), is an abbreviated nine-item version of the YFAS. Within the mYFAS, each of the seven DSM-4 substance dependence criteria is represented by one question [18]. The remaining two items of the mYFAS pertain to whether food or eating causes an individual clinically significant impairment or distress [18]. Both YFAS 2.0 and mYFAS have demonstrated marginal to good psychometric properties [20,22].

The observed prevalence rate of food addiction in a meta-analysis of 20 studies from North American and European countries was 19.9% (range: 16.3% to 24.0%) [23]. In a more recent meta-analysis of 36 articles, Burrows et al. (2018) concluded that the prevalence of individuals with mental health symptoms who met the cutoff for food addiction was 16.2% (range: 13.6% to 19.3%) [22]. A sex difference was also observed, where higher prevalence of food addiction appeared among females (12.2%) compared to males (6.4%) [23].

Although many individuals may not meet the threshold for food addiction, it is not uncommon for individuals to report specific symptoms. On average, individuals with mental health symptoms endorse approximately three symptoms for food addiction [22,23]. Of the seven YFAS symptoms for food addiction, "persistent desire or unsuccessful attempts to cut down or control eating" is one of the most frequently endorsed symptoms of food addiction [19,23,24].

3.1.3. Theories of Food Addiction

Several theories link specific high-caloric and palatable foods to food addiction. Similar to addictive substances, these foods exist on a spectrum of addiction [7]. For example, individuals meeting the cutoff for food addiction convey significant problems with highly palatable foods such as chocolate, doughnuts, cookies, cake, candy, white bread, pasta, rice, crackers, French fries, and hamburgers compared to their counterparts without food addiction [25,26]. In addition, more frequent consumption of hamburgers, candy bar, milk chocolate, butter, pizza, and low-calorie beverages was associated with meeting the cutoff for food addiction [26]. Conversely, more frequent consumption of dark chocolate, homemade cookies, white rice, and sugar-sweetened beverages was negatively associated with food addiction [26]. Other theories suggest that food itself is not addictive, but the manner in which the food is consumed is an addictive behavior. Specifically, the repetitive behavior of food restriction and dieting leads to periods of overeating and binging. While controversy surrounds the addictive properties of foods, it is important to consider that tobacco took several decades before it was declared an addictive substance [27]. Addictive substances including alcohol, tobacco, and cannabis have gained acceptance at some point and it was not until these substances were recognized as being addictive that society implemented changes that would provide opportunities for individuals to receive treatment [27].

3.2. *Biology*

3.2.1. Neurobiological Parallels between Food Addiction and Tobacco Use Disorder

Within the past several decades, neuroimaging has allowed the quantification of specific proteins and neurotransmitter receptors, the investigation of food and tobacco cues and their effects on neural activation, and the investigation of the integrity of gray and white matter, using positron emission tomography (PET), functional magnetic resonance imaging (fMRI), and structural MRI, respectively. Although no specific neuroimaging study has investigated the neural correlates of tobacco use disorder with comorbid food addiction, when investigated separately, the effects of food addiction on the brain often resemble those of tobacco use disorder. Specifically, highly palatable foods, such as those with high fat and sugar content, can activate the dopaminergic (DAergic) reward pathways [7,28–30], and specific conditioned food cues such as its sight, smell, and taste may trigger the desire or craving of eating [31]. This suggests that common neural substrates exist for both food and tobacco use disorder, both of which depend on DAergic pathways.

To date, no PET studies have investigated dopamine (DA) receptor availability in individuals with food addiction. Although obesity and food addiction are distinct disorders, most neurobiological literature surrounding food addiction is derived from obesity studies since the two conditions often co-occur. The first human neuroimaging study to examine striatal DA D2 receptor availability in relation to obesity was Wang et al. 2001 [32]. Measured by [^{11}C]raclopride PET, striatal DA D2 receptor availability was significantly lower in obese individuals compared to healthy controls, and body mass index (BMI) was negatively correlated with D2 receptor availability. Similarly, low levels of DA are often reported in individuals addicted to drugs including cocaine [33], alcohol [34], opiates [35], and nicotine [36], and low DA receptor levels are associated with addictive behaviors irrespective of food or addictive drugs [32]. DA deficiency may perpetuate pathological eating to replenish the mesolimbic DAergic pathway, and feeding has been shown to increase extracellular DA levels in the nucleus accumbens (NAcc) [37], a region thought to contribute to the reinforcing effects of euphoria [38]. It is possible that chronic overconsumption of food leads to increases in DA, resulting in DA D2 receptor downregulation. This produces a feed-forward cyclical pattern where overconsumption of food must then be sustained to replenish DA levels to avoid food cravings and withdrawal symptoms [39].

DA receptor availability in individuals with tobacco use disorder has been extensively investigated with [^{11}C]raclopride PET. For example, a 26% to 37% reduction in binding potential, indicative of greater DA release, was observed in the left ventral caudate, NAcc, and left ventral putamen in cigarette smokers compared to nonsmokers [40]. In contrast, several other PET studies using tobacco cigarettes and alternative methods of nicotine administration, such as nicotine nasal sprays and nicotine gum, found no significant changes in binding potential within smokers [41–44]. More recent nonhuman primate PET studies found [^{11}C]PHNO ([^{11}C]-(+)-propyl-hexahydro-naphtho-oxazin) to be more sensitive to nicotine-induced DA release compared to [^{11}C]raclopride [45]. To date, three studies have utilized [^{11}C]PHNO PET in relation to nicotine administration and smoking-associated cues in humans. Specifically, following cigarette smoking, a 12% to 15% reduction in D2 and D3 receptor binding potential was observed compared to control conditions [46]. These findings are likely influenced by genetics, where, during abstinence, slow metabolizers of nicotine had lower [^{11}C]PHNO-binding potential compared to fast metabolizers within the D2 regions of the striatum [47]. Interestingly, there was no change in [^{11}C]PHNO-binding potential in the striatum of nicotine-dependent individuals following the presentation of tobacco-associated cues [48].

The effects of food cues and craving on neural activity and DA receptor binding have been widely investigated. fMRI studies demonstrated that food cues activate the amygdala, insula, orbitofrontal cortex, and striatum brain regions compared to neutral cues [49,50]. These cues of highly palatable foods activate similar reward neurocircuitry to tobacco use disorder [51]. Furthermore, food cravings are associated with increased bold-oxygen-level-dependent (BOLD) signals in the hippocampus, insula, and caudate [50], regions involved in craving, motivation, and memory [52]. PET studies demonstrated a positive association of food cravings and increased dorsal caudate and putamen regional cerebral blood flow [53], as well as an association of DA ligand binding within the dorsal striatum and feeding [54]. In summary, molecular imaging studies food cues provide supportive evidence of DAergic pathway activation.

Similar to food addiction, fMRI studies have examined the neuronal activation patterns produced by nicotine. For example, dose- and time-dependent BOLD signal increases were observed within the anterior cingulate cortex, dorsolateral prefrontal cortex, and medial prefrontal cortex brain regions in cigarette smokers [55]. This pattern of brain activation is consistent with DAergic pathways innervating the frontal cortex, as well as evidence supporting acute nicotine's role in positively enhancing reaction time, short-term memory, working memory, and attention [56]. Furthermore, smoking-cue fMRI studies demonstrated that nicotine-dependent smokers exhibited more BOLD signal activation than nonsmokers in the prefrontal cortex, ventral striatum, and NAcc brain regions [57,58]. In addition, contextual factors such as cigarette availability can affect neural activity, and variation in tobacco use disorder severity and genotype can modulate cue-induced activity [59].

3.2.2. Neurobiology Unique to Tobacco Use Disorder

Nicotine is the main psychoactive component of tobacco, and it specifically acts as an agonist of nicotinic acetylcholine receptors (nAChRs) in the brain. nAChRs containing the $\alpha4$ and $\beta2$ subunits are critical for mediating nicotine reinforcement, nicotine sensitivity, reward motivation, and DA release [60–65]. nAChRs are located throughout the brain, with highest density within the thalamus, basal ganglia, frontal cortex, cingulate cortex, occipital cortex, and insula [66,67]. Most importantly, nicotine stimulates the release of DA in the mesolimbic area, the corpus striatum, and the frontal cortex [68,69]. These DAergic pathways are critical in nicotine-induced rewarding behaviors [70], as well as in regulating reward, motivation, decision-making, learning, and memory [71].

Several preclinical and clinical studies of tobacco use disorder examined the effects of cigarette smoking and smoking-related behaviors on brain function, specifically β2-nAChR desensitization and subsequent upregulation [72]. Preclinical studies assessing nicotine administration in animals and postmortem human studies of smokers demonstrated β2-nAChR upregulation throughout the striatum, frontal cortex, anterior cingulate cortex, temporal cortex, occipital cortex, and cerebellum [73], suggesting greater levels of β2-nAChR desensitization and inactivation produced by long-term smoking or nicotine administration [74]. Brain imaging studies examining β2-nAChR availability in human smokers mimicked these preclinical finding [74–77]. Dysregulation of these brain regions following drug use is commonly associated with processing of drug cues and loss of inhibitory control, the primary contributing factor to relapse [78–80]. Furthermore, human postmortem studies of smokers with variable lifelong smoking histories and former smokers demonstrated that nAChR upregulation was reversible following abstinence [81]. Taken together, many preclinical and clinical brain imaging studies support the theory that long-term nicotine administration or chronic smoking can lead to nAChR desensitization and upregulation in smokers [82], but this upregulation is reversible following extended periods of smoking abstinence [81,83].

3.2.3. Neurobiology Unique to Food Addiction

With the exception of the DAergic system, the literature on other neurocircuits implicated in food addiction is limited. To date, only a few fMRI studies have been conducted in individuals who met the YFAS cutoff threshold for food addiction. The first study by Gearhardt et al. (2011) found a positive correlation between food addiction scores and neural activation in the anterior cingulate cortex, medial orbitofrontal cortex, and amygdala when participants anticipated highly palatable foods [84]. Furthermore, upon tasteless food cue presentation, a negative correlation was observed between food addiction scores and activation in the caudate, a region implicated in reward motivation [84]. In a more recent fMRI study, Schulte et al. (2019) investigated food-cue effects on neural activity in obese women who either met the YFAS 2.0 threshold cutoff or did not [85]. When presented with highly palatable foods, participants with food addiction exhibited moderate, elevated activation in the superior frontal gyrus. Decreased activations were observed when minimally processed food cues were presented. Interestingly, participants in the control group had opposite responses in this region [85]. Most of the literature on the neurobiology of food addiction is derived from studies examining obesity; however, the findings from Schulte et al. (2019) presented food addiction as a unique phenotype within obesity.

Provided the limited neuroimaging research, it is theorized that dysregulation in the hypothalamus may also contribute to food addiction given its role as the main homeostatic regulation center for feeding behaviors. The hypothalamus integrates different hormonal and neuronal signals to control appetite and energy. This regulation system monitors body adiposity by using hormones such as leptin, insulin, and ghrelin [86]. Ghrelin, the "hunger peptide", stimulates DAergic reward pathways, whereas leptin and insulin inhibit these circuits [49]. Several brain regions, such as the amygdala, hippocampus, insula, orbitofrontal cortex, and striatum, are also involved with the regulation of feeding and appetite [49]. These brain structures are involved in learning about food, allocating attention and effort towards food, conditioning reward with specific food cues in the environment, and integrating homeostatic information such as hunger with availability of food in the environment [49,71]. For a recent review of potential mechanisms for food addiction (in the presence of obesity) using a systems approach, see [87].

3.3. *Role of the Gut Microbiome*

3.3.1. Parallels in the Role of Gut Microbiome in Both Tobacco Use Disorder and Food Addiction

As discussed in the section above, both food addiction and tobacco use disorder reflect an imbalance in the extended reward system in response to environmental stimuli. Peptides that regulate appetite such as glucagon-like peptide 1 (GLP-1), ghrelin, leptin, peptide YY, and neuromedin U are expressed throughout the brain reward circuitry, providing strong evidence that food addiction and tobacco use disorder share overlapping gut–brain axis mechanisms [88]. Endocrine signals play a significant role in reward regulation and dysregulation, which is a hallmark feature of all addictive disorders. The neuropeptides that have been studied most extensively are ghrelin and GLP-1.

There were only a few studies exploring the mechanism via which the gut microbiome affects the behavioral response to drugs of abuse [89–91]. Nonetheless, there is preliminary clinical and preclinical evidence of bacterial dysbiosis in response to drugs of abuse, which requires further investigation [92–96].

3.3.2. Tobacco Use Disorder and the Gut Microbiome

The effect of smoking on the brain–gut axis and its behavioral implications has been largely unexplored. However, it has been shown that smoking induces specific changes in the microbiome. Furthermore, evidence suggests that smoking cessation induces an increase in microbial diversity [97,98], thereby reversing the negative effects of smoking and tobacco dependence on gut microbiota. A study by Biedermann et al. (2013) examined the association between smoking and gut microbiota in smokers without specific diseases [98] and showed that smoking cessation induced an increase in Firmicutes and Actinobacteria and a decrease in Bacteroidetes and Proteobacteria [98]. However, this study was conducted in only 10 subjects, and most of the participants developed an increased BMI following smoking cessation [98]. Previous studies showed that higher BMI is associated with increased Firmicutes and decreased Bacteroidetes in the gut compared to normal BMI [99,100]. Therefore, changes in gut microbiota following smoking cessation [98] might be associated with cessation-induced weight gain, as well as with smoking itself.

In a more recent large-scale cross-sectional study that included current, former, and never male smokers, smoking status influenced gut microbiota composition. Specifically, current smokers had a higher proportion of Bacteroidetes compared to never and former smokers, as well as lower proportions of Firmicutes and Proteobacteria compared with never smokers [89]. There were no observed differences in the composition of gut microbiota between never and former smokers, suggesting that smoking cessation allows gut microbiota composition to recover to pre-smoking status. The three groups did not differ significantly in terms of BMI or nutrient intake, thereby providing stronger evidence for the reversal of gut microbiota changes to normal upon smoking cessation.

Furthermore, a recent study compared the oral and gut microbiota in current smokers, current e-cigarette users, and healthy controls [101]. Tobacco smoking was associated with significant differences in the bacterial profiles in fecal, buccal, and saliva samples, while the e-cigarette users were no different to healthy controls. In keeping with previous studies, tobacco smokers had higher relative abundance of *Prevotella* and lower relative abundance of *Bacteroides* in their gut microbiota. This is in accordance with existing data demonstrating gut microbiotal changes following smoking cessation [98,102]

3.3.3. Food Addiction and the Gut Microbiome

Eating behavior is regulated by both homeostatic and hedonic mechanisms in the central nervous system (CNS). These mechanisms involve orchestrated signaling from several sources including gut peptides, endocrine signals, and neuronal impulses, as well as signals from the gut microbiota. For example, ghrelin signals hunger and craving, putatively via amplification of DA signaling [103]. On the other hand, satiety is signaled by other intestinal hormones such as glucagon-like peptide 1 (GLP-1) and peptide YY [104]. Insulin also triggers hunger and increases the palatability of sugar. There is evidence that the gut microbiota can regulate insulin sensitivity through various mechanisms [105]. As discussed in the previous section, normal eating behavior is under the control of the extended reward network, which is involved in the processing of all rewarding stimuli including but not limited to food-related behaviors. These processes become maladaptive when the salience of a specific type of reward such as highly palatable food is greater than that of other stimuli and becomes preferred at the expense of other rewards, thereby leading to addiction-type behavior. At this point, the hedonic system becomes more prominent than the homeostatic system in the regulation of food intake. Therefore, eating behavior becomes driven predominantly by activation of the salience network of the brain, whereby food cues activate this network leading to increased attentional bias to the food cues at the expense of other cues. This in turn results in the uncontrolled overconsumption of highly palatable food.

While there is currently no evidence in humans that food addiction is caused by an altered gut microbiome or that it is driven by particular gut microbes or microbial metabolites, there is substantial evidence from rodent models that point to a role of the gut microbiome in food addiction-like behaviors. However, there is overwhelming evidence that a high-sugar, high-fat diet results in changes to the gut microbiome, which further "supports" addictive-like eating behaviors [87].

The few studies that examined the relationship between the gut microbiome and its metabolites with addictive-like eating behaviors have shown that tryptophan metabolites are implicated in modulating brain–gut–microbiome interactions [106]. In a recent study [107], the association between microbial profiles and tryptophan metabolites with food addiction was examined in a sample of human females with high BMI. The study found that there was a difference in the gut microbiome of females with food addiction versus those without, whereby levels of *Bacteroides* and *Akkermansia* were negatively associated with food addiction.

3.4. *Psychological*

3.4.1. Childhood Adversity

Adverse childhood experiences (ACEs) have been shown to have deleterious effects on adult health [108–110]. To standardize the operationalization of childhood adversity within studies, Felitti et al. (1998) developed the ACE Survey, which quantifies an individual's reports of exposure to abuse, neglect, and household dysfunction before the age of 18 [111]. These questions surveyed ACEs by asking about behaviors rather than subjective experiences of trauma. This survey originally encompassed seven categories including three of abuse and four of household dysfunction. More recent versions of the ACE study capture two additional categories of neglect and parental separation or divorce [112]. Cronholm et al. proposed the expansion of the concept of ACEs to include experiences such as witnessing violence, feeling discrimination, living in an unsafe neighborhood, experiencing bullying, and living in foster care to fully understand the influence of childhood adversity on adult substance use [113].

3.4.2. Overlap in Childhood Adversity of Tobacco Use Disorder and Food Addiction

Childhood adversity influences various physiological and behavioral mechanisms that contribute to adult addictive behaviors. Studies demonstrate that chronic stress in childhood may cause changes in the nervous, endocrine, and immune systems. Alterations in these systems may lead to impairments in cognitive, social, and emotional development that predispose individuals with ACEs to adopt addictive behaviors [114–116]. The original ACE study reported that individuals who experienced four or more categories of adversity were 2.2 times more likely to be a current smoker and 1.6 times more likely to have a BMI $\geq$ 35 (severe obesity) [111]. This study did not evaluate food addiction. While the focus here is on tobacco use disorder and food addiction, individuals who report ACEs also engage in other addictive behaviors including alcohol abuse and drug use [111]. This suggests that childhood adversity may have significant and varying downstream effects on numerous adult health behaviors. While there is research on the relationships between childhood adversity and food addiction and between childhood adversity and tobacco use disorder, research is needed to better understand the overlap of food addiction and tobacco use disorder.

3.4.3. Childhood Adversity and Tobacco Use Disorder

Using the ACE Survey, Felitti et al. (1998) produced a landmark paper describing the gradient relationships between the number of categories of childhood adversity and the prevalence of current smoking. Specifically, 6.8% of participants who reported no adversity (zero categories) and 16.5% of participants who reported four or more categories of adversity were current smokers. Participants who reported four or more categories of adversity were 2.2 times more likely to smoke than those who reported no adversity (odds ratio (OR) adjusted for age, gender, race, and educational attainment) [111]. Since then, a systematic review and a meta-analysis of 37 studies found that individuals who reported at least four categories of ACEs were more than twice as likely to be current smokers. Furthermore, there was a moderate association between childhood adversity and smoking [113].

3.4.4. Childhood Adversity and Food Addiction

There is limited research into food addiction. One study identified childhood abuse as a risk factor for food addiction. This study of 57,321 adult women examined the association between child abuse (specifically, physical and sexual child abuse) and food addiction (defined as three or more clinically significant symptoms on the mYFAS). In this sample, over 8% of participants reported severe physical abuse in childhood, 5.3% reported severe sexual abuse, and 8% met the criteria for food addiction. Findings indicated that women with food addiction had a higher BMI than women without food addiction. Furthermore, severe physical and severe sexual abuse was associated with about 90% increased risk for food addiction (physical abuse: relative risk (RR) 1.92, 95% confidence interval (CI) 1.76 to 2.09; sexual abuse: RR 1.87, 95% CI 1.69 to 2.05). The RR for combined severe physical abuse and sexual abuse was 2.40 (95% CI 2.16 to 2.67) demonstrating the additive effects of adversity [117]. Childhood adversity has also been linked to disordered eating, including food addiction, obesity, and binge eating, which has overlapping characteristics with food addiction [111,118–122].

3.4.5. Attachment Insecurity

Attachment theory describes how individuals internalize experiences with their caregivers to form mental representations of themselves and others. Individuals with high attachment anxiety tend to have negative self-views, are concerned about rejection, magnify their expressions of distress, and prefer close proximity to and support from a partner [123,124]. Individuals with high attachment avoidance tend to report positive self-views [123], suppress expressions of distress, and prefer emotional distance in relationships [124]. Individuals can be characterized by varying levels of attachment anxiety and avoidance, and both types of insecurity can co-occur [124]. The experience of childhood trauma is associated with both attachment anxiety and attachment avoidance in adulthood [125]. Attachment theory provides another framework to understand tobacco use disorder.

3.4.6. Overlap in Attachment Insecurity of Tobacco Use Disorder and Food Addiction

Attachment insecurity may influence several processes that may in turn contribute to tobacco use disorder and food addiction. While there is research on the relationships between attachment insecurity and food addiction and between attachment insecurity and tobacco use disorder, research is needed to better understand the overlap of food addiction and tobacco use disorder. Attachment insecurity is related to affect regulation [126], i.e., "the process by which individuals influence which emotions they have, when they have them, and how they experience and express these emotions" [127]. Emotional regulation involves efforts to up- and downregulate positive and negative emotions [127]. High levels of attachment insecurity are associated with a deficit in affect regulation [128]. Individuals with high attachment insecurity may feel less capable of disengaging from negative feelings and in turn attempt to calm themselves through food or other substances. Food or other substances (e.g., tobacco, alcohol, or drugs), when consumed in order to reduce feelings of insecurity, have been called "external regulators of affect" [129]. Individuals with high attachment insecurity are more likely to use these "external regulators of affect" instead of utilizing more adaptive emotional regulation strategies. Attachment insecurity has been studied in the context of disordered eating, eating disorders, and obesity, but there is still limited research on food addiction [130–132].

3.4.7. Attachment Insecurity and Tobacco Use Disorder

Insecure attachment patterns, specifically attachment anxiety, are associated with the use of tobacco and other drugs [133–136]. Attachment anxiety was associated with increased use of tobacco to reduce stress in college students [135]. In undergraduate and graduate students, significant differences in attachment patterns in tobacco users and nonusers were observed [122]. In a study of adults, findings suggested that attachment anxiety, but not attachment avoidance, was associated with current smoking [137]. In contrast, a study in adult women found that attachment avoidance was associated with being a current smoker [133]. It is currently unclear whether a particular dimension of attachment insecurity, such as attachment avoidance or attachment anxiety, is associated with tobacco use disorder.

3.4.8. Attachment Insecurity and Food Addiction

Few studies examined the association of attachment insecurity and food addiction. One study of a national nonclinical sample of 1841 respondents in the Czech Republic found that attachment insecurity was associated with increased scores of mYFAS 2.0 [138]. In a study of 195 adult women from an eating disorder treatment center, the prevalence of food addiction was 83.6%, and the most frequently reported food addiction criteria were "clinically significant impairment or distress in relation to food", "craving", and "persistent desire or repeated unsuccessful attempts to cut down". Within this sample, no differences in attachment insecurity were found between those meeting the criteria for food addiction and those who did not fulfill the criteria for food addiction [132]. As such, there may be a similarity between food addiction and eating disorders in terms of attachment patterns. The literature suggests that attachment insecurity is associated with unhealthy eating, including anorexia nervosa, bulimia nervosa, nonclinical levels of disordered eating, and obesity [130,131,139–148].

3.5. Treatment

3.5.1. Treating Tobacco Use Disorder

There is a wide array of smoking cessation interventions that are well-established by evidence from several systematic reviews. Individualized treatments such as nicotine replacement therapy (NRT), varenicline, bupropion, behavioral supports, e-cigarettes, and combination therapies have positive outcomes on cessation rates and sustained abstinence. In addition, community- or government-level efforts such as prohibiting smoking in public spaces, advertising restrictions, and health warning labels contribute to reductions in smoking.

NRT is a common first-line, over-the-counter cessation aid that is available in forms such as the patch, lozenge, inhaler, and gum. NRT has a >6.5% sustained abstinence rate after 6 months, more than double that of placebo [149,150]. Compared to placebo, NRT shows no statistically significant differences in adverse events, except nausea, which has been listed as a common side effect [150]. Using the NRT patch together with another type of NRT (e.g., gum, lozenge, mist, or inhaler), can increase that rate by an additional 15–36% [151]. NRT dose and duration also affect quit rate. Quit success is positively correlated with higher-dose NRT patches (25 mg worn over 16 h or 21 mg worn over 24 h) compared to smaller-dose patches (15 mg over 16 h or 14 mg over 24 h) [151].

Varenicline is well established as achieving the highest quit and sustained abstinence rate of all cessation aids, with minimal risk for adverse effects (see, for example, [149–151]). Varenicline more than doubles the chances of quit compared to placebo [152,153], helping approximately 50% more people to quit and have sustained abstinence than the NRT patch, tablets, spray, lozenge, and inhaler, and 70% more than NRT gum [152]. The antidepressant bupropion has similarly high quit success, making it 52–71% more likely that a person will quit [154]. There have been concerns surrounding varenicline and bupropion's linkage to psychiatric adverse events. A systematic review did not support this for varenicline, where the most frequently reported adverse event was nausea [153]. However, there is high-certainty evidence that unwanted mental health side-effects and adverse events linked to taking bupropion lead to lower medication adherence [154]. Furthermore, highest quit and sustained abstinence rates occur when pharmacotherapies are used in combination with behavioral supports. Behavioral therapy has been shown to increase effectiveness of pharmacotherapies by 83% to 97% across different care settings [155]. One systematic review compared the effects of brief physician advice to quit with offering assistance in the form of behavioral support or medication [156]. Physicians who offered assistance generated more quit attempts than those who gave advice to quit on medical grounds. Furthermore, when assistance was delivered in the form of motivational interviewing, a goal-oriented and patient-centered counseling approach that elicits motivation for change, abstinence rates were statistically significant and demonstrated up to 45% greater odds of smoking abstinence than control groups [157].

In recent years, e-cigarettes have become commonly used smoking cessation aids. While evidence is currently limited, the literature suggests the promise of e-cigarettes being an effective smoking cessation aid [158,159]. There is moderate-certainty evidence [using Grading of Recommendations Assessment, Development and Evaluation (GRADE)] from Cochrane systematic review that e-cigarettes with nicotine are more effective at helping people stop smoking for at least 6 months than NRT (three studies; 1498 participants), nicotine-free e-cigarettes (three studies; 802 participants), and no support or behavioral support alone (four studies; 2312 participants) [158]. Of the adverse events reported for e-cigarettes, throat and/or mouth irritation was the most commonly reported. Moderate-certainty evidence indicates the potential for results to change when more evidence becomes available. More research is needed to determine if e-cigarettes with nicotine are the preferred option for smoking cessation.

In summary, combination therapies that include either pharmacotherapy and behavioral support or a lower-risk nicotine product such as NRT or e-cigarettes with behavioral support increased quit attempts and boosted the level of sustained abstinence after one year. Organizational interventions also played a role in the sale and ease of promoting healthier smoking behaviors.

3.5.2. Treatment Options for Food Addiction

There is currently no well-established treatment model for intervening on food addiction. This is unsurprising given that there is no formal recognition of food addiction as a neurological or behavioral disease within the DSM 5 due to the debate of perceiving food addiction as a (non)substance use disorder or as a behavioral addiction. Furthermore, the heterogeneity of addiction makes it difficult to translate addiction into a working treatment model.

In its contextualization along the spectrum of eating disorders within the scientific literature, there are notable behavioral treatment options. Psychosocial interventions for food addiction include reducing access to processed foods, reducing habit-based eating, removing restrictions on eating healthy foods, and behavioral therapies to improve emotional regulation and to help combat submission to cravings and emotional eating [160]. Furthermore, participation in an integrative and psychological weight management group demonstrated promise in treatment efficacy [161]. Learning about mindful eating, keeping a food diary and keeping track of body weight, creating and maintaining an exercise plan, and planning for social eating are tactics that are taught to enable the maintenance of healthy body weight [161]. A systematic review revealed that additional research is needed to develop and test the efficacy of these types of interventions within the context of food addiction [162].

Noninvasive brain stimulation has been used most frequently for the treatment of addictions such as tobacco use disorder [163]. Transcranial direct current stimulation (tDCS) in particular, is a safe, economical, and accessible means of modifying neural activity [163]. A systematic review highlighted that tDCS significantly improved the symptoms of food addiction by reducing food cravings brought on by visual stimuli [164]. Craving was measured before and after stimulation using visual analogue scales, eye tracking, or the Food Craving Questionnaire—State, and tDCS was found to significantly repress the desire to eat, leading to less food consumption [164]. However, due to underpowered studies and the complexity of addiction, more research is necessary to make any definitive comments about the success of tDCS on food addiction. Tailoring neuromodulating interventions to individuals or subgroups, on the basis of cognitive and neural profiling, might prove to be useful [163]. Since food addiction often presents with comorbidities, current research suggests using evidence-based interventions to address other conditions first [162].

4. Current and Future Research Directions

Evidence demonstrates that individuals can expect to gain an average of 4 to 5 kg of weight after successfully achieving smoking cessation [165,166]. For many tobacco users, this potential increase in weight can be a substantial obstacle when attempting smoking cessation [167,168], thereby leading to continued tobacco use. One possible explanation for post-smoking cessation weight gain is that quitting smoking increases the desire to consume highly palatable, high-calorie foods. Consequently, the authors of this review developed a feasibility study with the purpose of examining the association between food addiction symptoms and smoking behavior among individuals seeking treatment for tobacco use disorder. This feasibility study recruited individuals from the Nicotine Dependence Clinic at the Centre for Addiction and Mental Health (CAMH) who had yet to begin their smoking cessation treatment. Those individuals who provided consent to participate in the study were asked to complete a survey which included the FTND and mYFAS questionnaires.

The sample of this feasibility study included 51 participants seeking treatment for tobacco use disorder. The majority of participants in this convenience sample were male (58.8%). Two-thirds of the sample consumed <20 cigarettes per day (CPD). The prevalence of individuals meeting the cutoff for food addiction was 11.8%. The average symptom count for food addiction was 1.5 ± 1.8 (standard deviation (SD)) symptoms.

Spearman rank correlation coefficients were conducted to examine the association between tobacco use disorder, specifically CPD, and food addiction symptom count, as measured by the mYFAS. No significant association was observed between CPD and food addiction symptom count for the overall sample ($r_s = 0.21$, $p = 0.14$) or by sex (male: $r_s = 0.20$, $p = 0.28$; female: $r_s = 0.24$, $p = 0.31$).

The results of this feasibility study, even though underpowered, represent an important initial step in developing future research. Using a cross-sectional study design, we were unable to observe a significant association between food addiction symptom count and CPD. The findings from another cross-sectional study examining the association between smoking and food addiction found that male smokers report twice as many YFAS symptoms compared to male nonsmokers [169]. However, among females, no relationship was observed between food addiction symptoms and smoking [169]. While this study provides some evidence of an association between smoking and food addiction, more research is needed. Applying a longitudinal study design and examining how changes in smoking behavior relate to changes food addiction symptoms could provide greater insight into the relationship between smoking cessation and weight gain. Furthermore, the feasibility study also revealed that the prevalence of food addiction may be lower among individuals seeking smoking cessation treatment compared to the general population, suggesting, perhaps, that food addiction may have a minor role in post-cessation weight gain. Therefore, examining other concepts such as the role that the gut microbiome may have on smoking cessation weight gain could be promising. However, it is also plausible that achieving smoking cessation could result in the adoption of an addictive behavior involving the overconsumption of highly palatable foods, a process known as addiction transfer [170].

E-cigarettes have been demonstrated to be effective smoking cessation aids [158]. As outlined above, e-cigarette users have gut and oral microbiomes that are more similar to healthy controls than to tobacco smokers [103]. Given that *Bacteriodes*, the bacterium that is most commonly significantly decreased in smokers compared to healthy controls and e-cigarette users, is also implicated in obesity [171], there is the potential that switching smokers to e-cigarettes may decrease their risk of cessation-related weight gain. This hypothesis has not yet been tested, and there is no clear evidence that smokers who switch to e-cigarettes avoid weight gain. As such, these are important research gaps to address.

5. Limitations

This was a narrative review; thus, limitations with respect to the scope of literature covered are present. The authors made every attempt to be systematic in their initial literature search, but they may have missed some important publications. Narrative reviews are also subject to bias, but the authors did their best to mitigate this by using systematic approaches to their literature search.

6. Conclusions

Food addiction and tobacco use disorder share similar but not identical neurological, physiological, and behavioral abnormalities. We attempted to summarize these similarities between the two disorders where there is evidence of their existence. Differences between the two disorders should not lead one to conclude that food addiction is not a "real" disorder. As argued in a recent perspective [172], core features of addiction can differ dramatically depending on which substance is being used, reflecting different underlying neurobiological processes at play. For example, the pattern of consumption and symptoms of withdrawal exhibited in cocaine use disorder completely different to what is seen in tobacco use disorder.

Addiction is a complex disorder that we are only beginning to understand at a system level. The role of the gut–brain axis in brain reward mechanisms related to addiction needs to be further researched. In addition, more attention needs to be paid to the role that early life events have on the risk of developing an addictive disorder. Taking learnings from different types of addictive behaviors such as food addiction, as well as newer "behavioral addictions" such as internet gaming, will help to further our understanding of the underlying mechanisms common to all addictive disorders. This will in turn pave the road toward effective treatment options. Exploring the commonalities between tobacco use disorder and food addiction is a step in this direction.

Author Contributions: L.Z. conceptualized the basis and structure of the review. L.Z., S.A., T.L.L., W.K.d., and D.D. wrote the initial drafts and subsequent drafts of the paper. L.Z., S.A., T.L.L., W.K.d., D.D., and P.S. approved the final version. All authors have read and agreed to the published version of the manuscript.

References

1. Abdelaal, M.; Le Roux, C.W.; Docherty, N.G. Morbidity and mortality associated with obesity. *Ann. Transl. Med.* **2017**, *5*, 161. [CrossRef]
2. Jamal, A.; Phillips, E.; Gentzke, A.S.; Homa, D.M.; Babb, S.D.; King, B.A.; Neff, L.J. Current Cigarette Smoking Among Adults — United States, 2016. *MMWR. Morb. Mortal. Wkly. Rep.* **2018**, *67*, 53–59. [CrossRef]
3. American Psychiatric Association. *Diagnostic and Statistical Manual of Mental Disorders*, 5th ed.; American Psychiatric Press: Washington, DC, USA, 2013.
4. Schulte, E.M.; Joyner, M.A.; Potenza, M.N.; Grilo, C.M.; Gearhardt, A.N. Current Considerations Regarding Food Addiction. *Curr. Psychiatry Rep.* **2015**, *17*, 1–8. [CrossRef]
5. Randolph, T.G. The Descriptive Features of Food Addiction. Addictive Eating and Drinking. *Q. J. Stud. Alcohol* **1956**, *17*, 198–224. [CrossRef]
6. Meule, A.; Gearhardt, A.N. Food Addiction in the Light of DSM-5. *Nutrients* **2014**, *6*, 3653–3671. [CrossRef]
7. Gearhardt, A.N.; Corbin, W.R.; Brownell, K.D. Preliminary validation of the Yale Food Addiction Scale. *Appetite* **2009**, *52*, 430–436. [CrossRef]
8. Alam, S.; Lang, J.J.; Drucker, A.M.; Gotay, C.; Kozloff, N.; Mate, K.; Patten, S.; Orpana, H.M.; Afshin, A.; Cahill, L.E. Assessment of the burden of diseases and injuries attributable to risk factors in Canada from 1990 to 2016: An analysis of the Global Burden of Disease Study. *CMAJ Open* **2019**, *7*, E140–E148. [CrossRef] [PubMed]

9. Criscitelli, K.; Avena, N.M. The neurobiological and behavioral overlaps of nicotine and food addiction. *Prev. Med.* **2016**, *92*, 82–89. [CrossRef] [PubMed]
10. Government of Canada. Canadian Tobacco, Alcohol and Drugs Survey (CTADS): Summary of Results for 2017. 2018. Available online: https://www.canada.ca/en/health-canada/services/canadian-tobacco-alcohol-drugs-survey/2017-summary.html (accessed on 4 September 2020).
11. Government of Canada. Summary of Results for the Canadian Student Tobacco, Alcohol and Drugs Survey 2018–2019. Available online: https://www.canada.ca/en/health-canada/services/canadian-student-tobacco-alcohol-drugs-survey/2018-2019-summary.html (accessed on 4 September 2020).
12. Spindle, T.R.; Hiler, M.M.; Cooke, M.E.; Eissenberg, T.; Kendler, K.S.; Dick, D.M. Electronic cigarette use and uptake of cigarette smoking: A longitudinal examination of U.S. college students. *Addict. Behav.* **2017**, *67*, 66–72. [CrossRef] [PubMed]
13. Centers for Disease Control and Prevention. Tobacco-Related Mortality. 2020. Available online: https://www.cdc.gov/tobacco/data_statistics/fact_sheets/health_effects/tobacco_related_mortality/index.htm (accessed on 4 September 2020).
14. Ward, R.C.; Tanner, N.T.; A Silvestri, G.; Gebregziabher, M. Impact of Tobacco Dependence in Risk Prediction Models for Lung Cancer Diagnoses and Deaths. *JNCI Cancer Spectr.* **2019**, *3*, pkz014. [CrossRef]
15. Pomerleau, C.S.; Carton, S.M.; Lutzke, M.L.; Flessland, K.A.; Pomerleau, O.F. Reliability of the fagerstrom tolerance questionnaire and the fagerstrom test for nicotine dependence. *Addict. Behav.* **1994**, *19*, 33–39. [CrossRef]
16. Borland, R.; Yong, H.-H.; O'Connor, R.J.; Hyland, A.; Thompson, M.E. The reliability and predictive validity of the Heaviness of Smoking Index and its two components: Findings from the International Tobacco Control Four Country study. *Nicotine Tob. Res.* **2010**, *12*, S45–S50. [CrossRef]
17. Penzenstadler, L.; Soares, C.; Karila, L.; Khazaal, Y. Systematic Review of Food Addiction as Measured with the Yale Food Addiction Scale: Implications for the Food Addiction Construct. *Curr. Neuropharmacol.* **2019**, *17*, 526–538. [CrossRef] [PubMed]
18. Meule, A.; Gearhardt, A.N. Five years of the Yale Food Addiction Scale: Taking stock and moving forward. *Curr. Addict. Rep.* **2014**, *1*, 193–205. [CrossRef]
19. Mies, G.W.; Treur, J.L.; Larsen, J.K.; Halberstadt, J.; Pasman, J.A.; Vink, J.M. The prevalence of food addiction in a large sample of adolescents and its association with addictive substances. *Appetite* **2017**, *118*, 97–105. [CrossRef] [PubMed]
20. Lemeshow, A.R.; Gearhardt, A.N.; Genkinger, J.M.; Corbin, W.R. Assessing the psychometric properties of two food addiction scales. *Eat. Behav.* **2016**, *23*, 110–114. [CrossRef]
21. Supplemental Material for Development of the Yale Food Addiction Scale Version 2.0. *Psychol. Addict. Behav.* **2016**, *30*, 113–121. [CrossRef]
22. Burrows, T.L.; Kay-Lambkin, F.; Pursey, K.; Skinner, J.; Dayas, C. Food addiction and associations with mental health symptoms: A systematic review with meta-analysis. *J. Hum. Nutr. Diet.* **2018**, *31*, 544–572. [CrossRef]
23. Pursey, K.M.; Stanwell, P.; Gearhardt, A.N.; Collins, C.; Burrows, T. The Prevalence of Food Addiction as Assessed by the Yale Food Addiction Scale: A Systematic Review. *Nutr.* **2014**, *6*, 4552–4590. [CrossRef]
24. Goluza, I.; Borchard, J.P.; Kiarie, E.; Mullan, J.; Pai, N. Exploration of food addiction in people living with schizophrenia. *Asian J. Psychiatry* **2017**, *27*, 81–84. [CrossRef]
25. Ayaz, A.; Nergiz-Unal, R.; Dedebayraktar, D.; Akyol, A.; Pekcan, A.G.; Besler, H.T.; Büyüktuncer, Z. How does food addiction influence dietary intake profile? *PLoS ONE* **2018**, *13*, e0195541. [CrossRef] [PubMed]
26. Lemeshow, A.R.; Rimm, E.B.; Hasin, D.S.; Gearhardt, A.N.; Flint, A.J.; Field, A.E.; Genkinger, J.M. Food and beverage consumption and food addiction among women in the Nurses' Health Studies. *Appetite* **2018**, *121*, 186–197. [CrossRef] [PubMed]
27. Ifland, J.; Preuss, H.; Marcus, M.; Rourke, K.; Taylor, W.; Burau, K.; Jacobs, W.; Kadish, W.; Manso, G. Refined food addiction: A classic substance use disorder. *Med Hypotheses* **2009**, *72*, 518–526. [CrossRef] [PubMed]
28. Bassareo, V.; Di Chiara, G. Differential Influence of Associative and Nonassociative Learning Mechanisms on the Responsiveness of Prefrontal and Accumbal Dopamine Transmission to Food Stimuli in Rats FedAd Libitum. *J. Neurosci.* **1997**, *17*, 851–861. [CrossRef]

29. Hernandez, L.; Hoebel, B.G. Food reward and cocaine increase extracellular dopamine in the nucleus accumbens as measured by microdialysis. *Life Sci.* **1988**, *42*, 1705–1712. [CrossRef]
30. Roitman, M.F.; Stuber, G.D.; Phillips, P.E.M.; Wightman, R.M.; Carelli, R.M. Dopamine Operates as a Subsecond Modulator of Food Seeking. *J. Neurosci.* **2004**, *24*, 1265–1271. [CrossRef]
31. Baik, J.-H. Dopamine signaling in food addiction: Role of dopamine D2 receptors. *BMB Rep.* **2013**, *46*, 519–526. [CrossRef]
32. Wang, G.-J.; Volkow, N.D.; Logan, J.; Pappas, N.R.; Wong, C.T.; Zhu, W.; Netusll, N.; Fowler, J.S. Brain dopamine and obesity. *Lancet* **2001**, *357*, 354–357. [CrossRef]
33. Martinez, D.; Broft, A.; Foltin, R.W.; Slifstein, M.; Hwang, D.-R.; Huang, Y.; Perez, A.; Frankel, W.G.; Cooper, T.; Kleber, H.D.; et al. Cocaine Dependence and D2 Receptor Availability in the Functional Subdivisions of the Striatum: Relationship with Cocaine-Seeking Behavior. *Neuropsychopharmacol.* **2004**, *29*, 1190–1202. [CrossRef]
34. Martinez, D.; Gil, R.; Slifstein, M.; Hwang, D.-R.; Huang, Y.; Perez, A.; Kegeles, L.; Talbot, P.; Evans, S.; Krystal, J.; et al. Alcohol Dependence Is Associated with Blunted Dopamine Transmission in the Ventral Striatum. *Biol. Psychiatry* **2005**, *58*, 779–786. [CrossRef]
35. Martinez, D.; Saccone, P.A.; Liu, F.; Slifstein, M.; Orlowska, D.; Grassetti, A.; Cook, S.H.; Broft, A.; Van Heertum, R.; Comer, S.D. Deficits in Dopamine D2 Receptors and Presynaptic Dopamine in Heroin Dependence: Commonalities and Differences with Other Types of Addiction. *Biol. Psychiatry* **2012**, *71*, 192–198. [CrossRef]
36. Fehr, C.; Yakushev, I.; Hohmann, D.P.N.; Buchholz, H.-G.; Landvogt, M.D.C.; Deckers, H.; Eberhardt, A.; Kläger, M.; Smolka, M.D.M.N.; Scheurich, A.; et al. Association of Low Striatal Dopamine D2Receptor Availability With Nicotine Dependence Similar to That Seen with Other Drugs of Abuse. *Am. J. Psychiatry* **2008**, *165*, 507–514. [CrossRef]
37. Bassareo, V.; Di Chiara, G. Differential responsiveness of dopamine transmission to food-stimuli in nucleus accumbens shell/core compartments. *Neurosci.* **1999**, *89*, 637–641. [CrossRef]
38. Pontieri, F.E.; Tanda, G.; Orzi, F.; Di Chiara, G. Effects of nicotine on the nucleus accumbens and similarity to those of addictive drugs. *Nat. Cell Biol.* **1996**, *382*, 255–257. [CrossRef]
39. Wang, G.J.; Volkow, N.D.; Thanos, P.K.; Fowler, J.S. Similarity between obesity and drug addiction as assessed by neurofunctional imaging: A concept review. *J. Addict. Dis.* **2004**, *23*, 39–53. [CrossRef]
40. Brody, A.L.; Olmstead, R.E.; London, E.D.; Farahi, J.; Meyer, J.H.; Grossman, P.; Lee, G.S.; Huang, J.; Hahn, E.L.; Mandelkern, M.A. Smoking-Induced Ventral Striatum Dopamine Release. *Am. J. Psychiatry* **2004**, *161*, 1211–1218. [CrossRef]
41. Barrett, S.P.; Boileau, I.; Okker, J.; Pihl, R.; Dagher, A. The hedonic response to cigarette smoking is proportional to dopamine release in the human striatum as measured by positron emission tomography and [^{11}C]raclopride. *Synapse* **2004**, *54*, 65–71. [CrossRef]
42. Scott, D.J.; Domino, E.F.; Heitzeg, M.M.; Koeppe, R.A.; Ni, L.; Guthrie, S.; Zubieta, J. Smoking modulation of mu-opioid and dopamine D2 receptor-mediated neurotransmission in humans. *Neuropsychopharmacology* **2007**, *32*, 450–457. [CrossRef]
43. Montgomery, A.J.; Lingford-Hughes, A.R.; Egerton, A.; Nutt, D.; Grasby, P.M. The effect of nicotine on striatal dopamine release in man: A [^{11}C]raclopride PET study. *Synapse* **2007**, *61*, 637–645. [CrossRef]
44. Takahashi, H.; Fujimura, Y.; Hayashi, M.; Takano, H.; Kato, M.; Okubo, Y.; Kanno, I.; Ito, H.; Suhara, T. Enhanced dopamine release by nicotine in cigarette smokers: A double-blind, randomized, placebo-controlled pilot study. *Int. J. Neuropsychopharmacol.* **2007**, *11*, 413–417. [CrossRef]
45. Gallezot, J.-D.; Kloczynski, T.; Weinzimmer, D.; Labaree, D.; Zheng, M.-Q.; Lim, K.; Rabiner, E.A.; Ridler, K.; Pittman, B.; Huang, Y.; et al. Imaging Nicotine- and Amphetamine-Induced Dopamine Release in Rhesus Monkeys with [^{11}C]PHNO vs [^{11}C]raclopride PET. *Neuropsychopharmacology* **2014**, *39*, 866–874. [CrossRef]
46. Le Foll, B.; Guranda, M.; A Wilson, A.; Houle, S.; Rusjan, P.M.; Wing, V.C.; Zawertailo, L.; E Busto, U.; Selby, P.; Brody, A.L.; et al. Elevation of Dopamine Induced by Cigarette Smoking: Novel Insights from a [^{11}C]-(+)-PHNO PET Study in Humans. *Neuropsychopharmacology* **2014**, *39*, 415–424. [CrossRef]
47. Di Ciano, P.; Tyndale, R.F.; Mansouri, E.; Hendershot, C.S.; A Wilson, A.; Lagzdins, D.; Houle, S.; Boileau, I.; Le Foll, B. Influence of Nicotine Metabolism Ratio on [^{11}C]-(+)-PHNO PET Binding in Tobacco Smokers. *Int. J. Neuropsychopharmacol.* **2018**, *21*, 503–512. [CrossRef]

48. Chiuccariello, L.; Boileau, I.; Guranda, M.; Rusjan, P.M.; Wilson, A.A.; Zawertailo, L.; Houle, S.; Busto, U.; Le Foll, B. Presentation of Smoking-Associated Cues Does Not Elicit Dopamine Release after One-Hour Smoking Abstinence: A [^{11}C]-(+)-PHNO PET Study. *PLoS ONE* **2013**, *8*, e60382. [CrossRef]
49. Dagher, A. The neurobiology of appetite: Hunger as addiction. *Int. J. Obes.* **2009**, *33*, S30–S33. [CrossRef]
50. Pelchat, M.L. Food Addiction in Humans. *J. Nutr.* **2009**, *139*, 620–622. [CrossRef]
51. Tang, D.; Fellows, L.K.; Small, D.M.; Dagher, A. Food and drug cues activate similar brain regions: A meta-analysis of functional MRI studies. *Physiol. Behav.* **2012**, *106*, 317–324. [CrossRef]
52. Blumenthal, D.M.; Gold, M.S. Neurobiology of food addiction. *Curr. Opin. Clin. Nutr. Metab. Care* **2010**, *13*, 359–365. [CrossRef]
53. Small, D.M.; Zatorre, R.J.; Dagher, A.; Evans, A.C.; Jones-Gotman, M. Changes in brain activity related to eating chocolate: From pleasure to aversion. *Brain* **2001**, *124*, 1720–1733. [CrossRef]
54. Small, D.M.; Jones-Gotman, M.; Daghera, A. Feeding-induced dopamine release in dorsal striatum correlates with meal pleasantness ratings in healthy human volunteers. *NeuroImage* **2003**, *19*, 1709–1715. [CrossRef]
55. Stein, E.A.; Pankiewicz, J.; Harsch, H.H.; Cho, J.-K.; Fuller, S.A.; Hoffmann, R.G.; Hawkins, M.; Rao, S.M.; Bandettini, P.A.; Bloom, A.S. Nicotine-Induced Limbic Cortical Activation in the Human Brain: A Functional MRI Study. *Am. J. Psychiatry* **1998**, *155*, 1009–1015. [CrossRef]
56. Heishman, S.J.; Kleykamp, B.A.; Singleton, E.G. Meta-analysis of the acute effects of nicotine and smoking on human performance. *Psychopharmacology* **2010**, *210*, 453–469. [CrossRef]
57. Due, D.L.; Huettel, S.A.; Hall, W.G.; Rubin, D.C. Activation in Mesolimbic and Visuospatial Neural Circuits Elicited by Smoking Cues: Evidence from Functional Magnetic Resonance Imaging. *Am. J. Psychiatry* **2002**, *159*, 954–960. [CrossRef]
58. David, S.P.; Munafò, M.R.; Johansen-Berg, H.; Smith, S.; Rogers, R.D.; Matthews, P.M.; Walton, R. Ventral Striatum/Nucleus Accumbens Activation to Smoking-Related Pictorial Cues in Smokers and Nonsmokers: A Functional Magnetic Resonance Imaging Study. *Biol. Psychiatry* **2005**, *58*, 488–494. [CrossRef]
59. Azizian, A.; Monterosso, J.; O'Neill, J.; London, E.D. Magnetic Resonance Imaging Studies of Cigarette Smoking. *Bone Regul. Osteoporos. Ther.* **2009**, *192*, 113–143. [CrossRef]
60. Picciotto, M.R.; Zoli, M.; Rimondini, R.; Léna, C.; Marubio, L.M.; Pich, E.M.; Fuxe, K.; Changeux, J.P. Acetylcholine receptors containing the beta2 subunit are involved in the reinforcing properties of nicotine. *Nature* **1998**, *391*, 173–177. [CrossRef]
61. Epping-Jordan, M.P.; Picciotto, M.R.; Changeux, J.-P.; Pich, E.M. Assessment of nicotinic acetylcholine receptor subunit contributions to nicotine self-administration in mutant mice. *Psychopharmacology* **1999**, *147*, 25–26. [CrossRef]
62. Koranda, J.L.; Cone, J.J.; McGehee, D.S.; Roitman, M.F.; Beeler, J.A.; Zhuang, X. Nicotinic receptors regulate the dynamic range of dopamine release in vivo. *J. Neurophysiol.* **2013**, *111*, 103–111. [CrossRef]
63. Cosgrove, K.P.; Esterlis, I.; McKee, S.; Bois, F.; Alagille, D.; Tamagnan, G.D.; Seibyl, J.P.; Krishnan-Sarin, S.; Staley, J.K. Beta2* nicotinic acetylcholine receptors modulate pain sensitivity in acutely abstinent tobacco smokers. *Nicotine Tob. Res.* **2010**, *12*, 535–539. [CrossRef]
64. Brunzell, D.H.; Boschen, K.E.; Hendrick, E.S.; Beardsley, P.M.; McIntosh, J.M. Alpha-conotoxin MII-sensitive nicotinic acetylcholine receptors in the nucleus accumbens shell regulate progressive ratio responding maintained by nicotine. *Neuropsychopharmacology* **2010**, *35*, 665–673. [CrossRef]
65. Perry, D.C.; Xiao, Y.; Nguyen, H.N.; Musachio, J.L.; Dávila-García, M.I.; Kellar, K.J. Measuring nicotinic receptors with characteristics of alpha4beta2, alpha3beta2 and alpha3beta4 subtypes in rat tissues by autoradiography. *J. Neurochem.* **2002**, *82*, 468–481. [CrossRef] [PubMed]
66. Mamede, M.; Ishizu, K.; Ueda, M.; Mukai, T.; Iida, Y.; Fukuyama, H.; Saga, T.; Saji, H. Quantification of human nicotinic acetylcholine receptors with 123I-5IA SPECT. *J. Nucl. Med.* **2004**, *45*, 1458–1470. [PubMed]
67. Ding, Y.S.; Gatley, S.J.; Fowler, J.S.; Volkow, N.D.; Aggarwal, D.; Logan, J.; Dewey, S.L.; Liang, F.; Carroll, F.I.; Kuhar, M.J. Mapping nicotinic acetylcholine receptors with PET. *Synapse* **1996**, *24*, 403–407. [CrossRef]
68. Brody, A.L. Functional brain imaging of tobacco use and dependence. *J. Psychiatr. Res.* **2006**, *40*, 404–418. [CrossRef]
69. Imperato, A.; Mulas, A.; Di Chiara, G. Nicotine preferentially stimulates dopamine release in the limbic system of freely moving rats. *Eur. J. Pharmacol.* **1986**, *132*, 337–338. [CrossRef]
70. Dani, J.A.; De Biasi, M. Cellular mechanisms of nicotine addiction. *Pharmacol. Biochem. Behav.* **2001**, *70*, 439–446. [CrossRef]

71. Wang, G.J.; Volkow, N.D.; Thanos, P.K.; Fowler, J.S. Imaging of brain dopamine pathways: Implications for understanding obesity. *J. Addict. Med.* **2009**, *3*, 8–18. [CrossRef] [PubMed]
72. Sharma, A.; Brody, A.L. In vivo Brain Imaging of Human Exposure to Nicotine and Tobacco. *Handb. Exp. Pharmacol.* **2009**, 145–171. [CrossRef]
73. Cosgrove, K.P.; Esterlis, I.; Sandiego, C.; Petrulli, R.; Morris, E.D. Imaging Tobacco Smoking with PET and SPECT. *Behav. Neurobiol. Anxiety Treat.* **2015**, *24*, 1–17. [CrossRef]
74. Staley, J.K.; Krishnan-Sarin, S.; Cosgrove, K.P.; Krantzler, E.; Frohlich, E.; Perry, E.; Dubin, J.A.; Estok, K.; Brenner, E.; Baldwin, R.M.; et al. Human Tobacco Smokers in Early Abstinence Have Higher Levels of beta2* Nicotinic Acetylcholine Receptors than Nonsmokers. *J. Neurosci.* **2006**, *26*, 8707–8714. [CrossRef]
75. Rourke, S.B.; Dupont, R.M.; Grant, I.; Lehr, P.P.; Lamoureux, G.; Halpern, S.; Yeung, D.W. Reduction in cortical IMP-SPET tracer uptake with recent cigarette consumption in a young group of healthy males. San Diego HIV Neurobehavioral Research Center. *S. Diego HIV Neurobehav. Res. Cent. Eur. J. Nucl. Med.* **1997**, *24*, 422–427.
76. Yamamoto, Y.; Nishiyama, Y.; Monden, T.; Satoh, K.; Ohkawa, M. A study of the acute effect of smoking on cerebral blood flow using 99mTc-ECD SPET. *Eur. J. Nucl. Med. Mol. Imaging* **2003**, *30*, 612–614. [CrossRef] [PubMed]
77. Brašić, J.R.; Zhou, Y.; Musachio, J.L.; Hilton, J.; Fan, H.; Crabb, A.; Endres, C.J.; Reinhardt, M.J.; Dogan, A.S.; Alexander, M.; et al. Single photon emission computed tomography experience with (S)-5-[^{123}I]iodo-3-(2-azetidinylmethoxy)pyridine in the living human brain of smokers and nonsmokers. *Synapse* **2009**, *63*, 339–358. [CrossRef] [PubMed]
78. Goldstein, R.Z.; Volkow, N.D. Dysfunction of the prefrontal cortex in addiction: Neuroimaging findings and clinical implications. *Nat. Rev. Neurosci.* **2011**, *12*, 652–669. [CrossRef] [PubMed]
79. Goldstein, R.Z.; Tomasi, D.; Rajaram, S.; Cottone, L.A.; Zhang, L.; Maloney, T.; Telang, F.; Alia-Klein, N.; Volkow, N.D. Role of the anterior cingulate and medial orbitofrontal cortex in processing drug cues in cocaine addiction. *Neuroscience* **2007**, *144*, 1153–1159. [CrossRef] [PubMed]
80. Feil, J.; Sheppard, D.; Fitzgerald, P.B.; Yücel, M.; Lubman, D.I.; Bradshaw, J.L. Addiction, compulsive drug seeking, and the role of frontostriatal mechanisms in regulating inhibitory control. *Neurosci. Biobehav. Rev.* **2010**, *35*, 248–275. [CrossRef]
81. Breese, C.R.; Marks, M.J.; Logel, J.; Adams, C.E.; Sullivan, B.; Collins, A.C.; Leonard, S. Effect of smoking history on [3H]nicotine binding in human postmortem brain. *J. Pharmacol. Exp. Ther.* **1997**, *282*, 7–13.
82. Brody, A.L.; Mandelkern, M.A.; London, E.D.; Olmstead, R.E.; Farahi, J.; Scheibal, D.; Jou, J.; Allen, V.; Tiongson, E.; Chefer, S.I.; et al. Cigarette smoking saturates brain alpha 4 beta 2 nicotinic acetylcholine receptors. *Arch. Gen. Psychiatry* **2006**, *63*, 907–915. [CrossRef]
83. Jasinska, A.J.; Zorick, T.; Brody, A.L.; Stein, E.A. Dual role of nicotine in addiction and cognition: A review of neuroimaging studies in humans. *Neuropharmacology* **2014**, *84*, 111–122. [CrossRef]
84. Gearhardt, A.N. Neural Correlates of Food Addiction. *Arch. Gen. Psychiatry* **2011**, *68*, 808–816. [CrossRef]
85. Schulte, E.M.; Yokum, S.; Jahn, A.; Gearhardt, A.N. Food cue reactivity in food addiction: A functional magnetic resonance imaging study. *Physiol. Behav.* **2019**, *208*, 112574. [CrossRef] [PubMed]
86. Morton, G.J.; Cummings, D.E.; Baskin, D.G.; Barsh, G.S.; Schwartz, M.W. Central nervous system control of food intake and body weight. *Nat. Cell Biol.* **2006**, *443*, 289–295. [CrossRef] [PubMed]
87. Gupta, A.; Osadchiy, V.; Mayer, E.A. Brain-gut-microbiome interactions in obesity and food addiction. *Nat. Rev. Gastroenterol. Hepatol.* **2020**, *17*, 655–672. [CrossRef] [PubMed]
88. Morganstern, I.; Barson, J.R.; Leibowitz, S.F. Regulation of drug and palatable food overconsumption by similar peptide systems. *Curr. Drug Abus. Rev.* **2011**, *4*, 163–173. [CrossRef] [PubMed]
89. Lee, S.H.; Yun, Y.; Kim, S.J.; Lee, E.-J.; Chang, Y.; Ryu, S.; Shin, H.; Kim, H.-L.; Kim, H.-N.; Lee, J.H. Association between Cigarette Smoking Status and Composition of Gut Microbiota: Population-Based Cross-Sectional Study. *J. Clin. Med.* **2018**, *7*, 282. [CrossRef] [PubMed]
90. Kiraly, D.D.; Walker, D.M.; Calipari, E.S.; LaBonte, B.; Issler, O.; Pena, C.J.; Ribeiro, E.A.; Russo, S.J.; Nestler, E.J. Alterations of the Host Microbiome Affect Behavioral Responses to Cocaine. *Sci. Rep.* **2016**, *6*, 35455. [CrossRef]

91. Kang, M.; Mischel, R.A.; Bhave, S.; Komla, E.; Cho, A.; Huang, C.; Dewey, W.L.; Akbarali, H.I. The effect of gut microbiome on tolerance to morphine mediated antinociception in mice. *Sci. Rep.* **2017**, *7*, srep42658. [CrossRef]
92. E Volpe, G.; Ward, H.; Mwamburi, M.; Dinh, D.; Bhalchandra, S.; Wanke, C.; Kane, A.V. Associations of Cocaine Use and HIV Infection with the Intestinal Microbiota, Microbial Translocation, and Inflammation. *J. Stud. Alcohol Drugs* **2014**, *75*, 347–357. [CrossRef]
93. Temko, J.E.; Bouhlal, S.; Farokhnia, M.; Lee, M.R.; Cryan, J.F.; Leggio, L. The Microbiota, the Gut and the Brain in Eating and Alcohol Use Disorders: A 'Menage a Trois'? *Alcohol Alcohol.* **2017**, *52*, 403–413. [CrossRef]
94. Wang, F.; Roy, S. Gut Homeostasis, Microbial Dysbiosis, and Opioids. *Toxicol. Pathol.* **2016**, *45*, 150–156. [CrossRef]
95. Hillemacher, T.; Bachmann, O.; Kahl, K.G.; Frieling, H. Alcohol, microbiome, and their effect on psychiatric disorders. *Prog. Neuro Psychopharmacol. Biol. Psychiatry* **2018**, *85*, 105–115. [CrossRef] [PubMed]
96. Hofford, R.S.; Russo, S.J.; Kiraly, D.D. Neuroimmune mechanisms of psychostimulant and opioid use disorders. *Eur. J. Neurosci.* **2019**, *50*, 2562–2573. [CrossRef] [PubMed]
97. Cussotto, S.; Clarke, G.; Dinan, T.G.; Cryan, J.F. Psychotropics and the Microbiome: A Chamber of Secrets ... *Psychopharmacology* **2019**, *236*, 1411–1432. [CrossRef] [PubMed]
98. Biedermann, L.; Zeitz, J.; Mwinyi, J.; Sutter-Minder, E.; Rehman, A.; Ott, S.J.; Steurer-Stey, C.; Frei, A.; Frei, P.; Scharl, M.; et al. Smoking Cessation Induces Profound Changes in the Composition of the Intestinal Microbiota in Humans. *PLoS ONE* **2013**, *8*, e59260. [CrossRef]
99. Kaufmann, S. Faculty Opinions recommendation of Microbial ecology: Human gut microbes associated with obesity. *Fac. Opin. Post Publ. Peer Rev. Biomed. Lit.* **2007**, *444*, 1022–1023. [CrossRef]
100. Koliada, A.; Syzenko, G.; Moseiko, V.; Budovska, L.; Puchkov, K.; Perederiy, V.; Gavalko, Y.; Dorofeyev, A.; Romanenko, M.; Tkach, S.; et al. Association between body mass index and Firmicutes/Bacteroidetes ratio in an adult Ukrainian population. *BMC Microbiol.* **2017**, *17*, 120. [CrossRef]
101. Stewart, C.J.; Auchtung, T.A.; Ajami, N.J.; Velasquez, K.; Smith, D.P.; De La Garza, R., 2nd; Salas, R.; Petrosino, J.F. Effects of tobacco smoke and electronic cigarette vapor exposure on the oral and gut microbiota in humans: A pilot study. *PeerJ* **2018**, *6*, e4693. [CrossRef]
102. Biedermann, L.; Brülisauer, K.; Zeitz, J.; Frei, P.; Scharl, M.; Vavricka, S.R.; Fried, M.; Loessner, M.J.; Rogler, G.; Schuppler, M. Tu1771 Smoking Cessation Alters Intestinal Microbiota: Further Insights from Quantitative Investigations on Human Fecal Samples Using FISH and qPCR. *Gastroenterology* **2014**, *146*, 1496–1501. [CrossRef]
103. Skibicka, K.P.; Dickson, S.L. Ghrelin and food reward: The story of potential underlying substrates. *Peptides* **2011**, *32*, 2265–2273. [CrossRef]
104. Steinert, R.E.; Poller, B.; Castelli, M.C.; Drewe, J.; Beglinger, C. Oral administration of glucagon-like peptide 1 or peptide YY 3-36 affects food intake in healthy male subjects. *Am. J. Clin. Nutr.* **2010**, *92*, 810–817. [CrossRef]
105. Bagarolli, R.A.; Tobar, N.; Oliveira, A.G.; Araújo, T.G.; Carvalho, B.M.; Rocha, G.Z.; Vecina, J.F.; Calisto, K.; Guadagnini, D.; Prada, P.O.; et al. Probiotics modulate gut microbiota and improve insulin sensitivity in DIO mice. *J. Nutr. Biochem.* **2017**, *50*, 16–25. [CrossRef]
106. Osadchiy, V.; Labus, J.S.; Gupta, A.; Jacobs, J.; Ashe-McNalley, C.; Hsiao, E.Y.; Mayer, E.A. Correlation of tryptophan metabolites with connectivity of extended central reward network in healthy subjects. *PLoS ONE* **2018**, *13*, e0201772. [CrossRef] [PubMed]
107. Dong, T.S.; Mayer, E.A.; Osadchiy, V.; Chang, C.; Katzka, W.; Lagishetty, V.; Gonzalez, K.; Kalani, A.; Stains, J.; Jacobs, J.P.; et al. A Distinct Brain-Gut-Microbiome Profile Exists for Females with Obesity and Food Addiction. *Obesity* **2020**, *28*, 1477–1486. [CrossRef] [PubMed]
108. Dong, M.; Giles, W.H.; Felitti, V.J.; Dube, S.R.; Williams, J.E.; Chapman, D.P.; Anda, R.F. Insights into causal pathways for ischemic heart disease: Adverse childhood experiences study. *Circulation* **2004**, *110*, 1761–1766. [CrossRef] [PubMed]
109. Anda, R.F.; Brown, D.W.; Dube, S.R.; Bremner, J.D.; Felitti, V.J.; Giles, W.H. Adverse Childhood Experiences and Chronic Obstructive Pulmonary Disease in Adults. *Am. J. Prev. Med* **2008**, *34*, 396–403. [CrossRef]
110. Brown, D.W.; Anda, R.F.; Felitti, V.J.; Edwards, V.J.; Malarcher, A.; Croft, J.B.; Giles, W.H. Adverse childhood experiences are associated with the risk of lung cancer: A prospective cohort study. *BMC Public Heal.* **2010**, *10*, 20. [CrossRef]

111. Felitti, V.J.; Anda, R.F.; Nordenberg, D.; Williamson, D.F.; Spitz, A.M.; Edwards, V.; Koss, M.P.; Marks, J.S. REPRINT OF: Relationship of Childhood Abuse and Household Dysfunction to Many of the Leading Causes of Death in Adults: The Adverse Childhood Experiences (ACE) Study. *Am. J. Prev. Med.* **2019**, *56*, 774–786. [CrossRef]
112. Dube, S.R.; Felitti, V.J.; Dong, M.; Chapman, D.P.; Giles, W.H.; Anda, R.F. Childhood Abuse, Neglect, and Household Dysfunction and the Risk of Illicit Drug Use: The Adverse Childhood Experiences Study. *Pediatrics* **2003**, *111*, 564–572. [CrossRef]
113. Cronholm, P.F.; Fokre, C.M.; Wade, R.; Bair-Merritt, M.H.; Davis, M.; Harkins-Schwarz, M.; Pachter, L.M.; Fein, J.A. Adverse Childhood Experiences: Expanding the Concept of Adversity. *Am. J. Prev. Med.* **2015**, *49*, 354–361. [CrossRef]
114. Anda, R.F.; Croft, J.B.; Felitti, V.J.; Nordenberg, D.; Giles, W.H.; Williamson, D.F.; Giovino, G.A. Adverse Childhood Experiences and Smoking During Adolescence and Adulthood. *JAMA* **1999**, *282*, 1652–1658. [CrossRef]
115. Dube, S.R.; Anda, R.F.; Felitti, V.J.; Edwards, V.J.; Croft, J.B. Adverse childhood experiences and personal alcohol abuse as an adult. *Addict. Behav.* **2002**, *27*, 713–725. [CrossRef]
116. Dube, S.R.; Cook, M.L.; Edwards, V.J. Health-Related Outcomes of Adverse Childhood Experiences in Texas, 2002. *Prev. Chronic Dis.* **2010**, *7*, 52.
117. Mason, S.M.; Flint, A.J.; Field, A.E.; Austin, S.B.; Rich-Edwards, J.W. Abuse victimization in childhood or adolescence and risk of food addiction in adult women. *Obesity* **2013**, *21*, E775–E781. [CrossRef] [PubMed]
118. Smolak, L.; Murnen, S.K. A meta-analytic examination of the relationship between child sexual abuse and eating disorders. *Int. J. Eat. Disord.* **2002**, *31*, 136–150. [CrossRef]
119. Kinzl, J.F.; Traweger, C.; Guenther, V.; Biebl, W. Family background and sexual abuse associated with eating disorders. *Am. J. Psychiatry* **1994**, *151*, 1127–1131. [CrossRef]
120. Smyth, J.M.; Heron, K.E.; Wonderlich, S.A.; Crosby, R.D.; Thompson, K.M. The influence of reported trauma and adverse events on eating disturbance in young adults. *Int. J. Eat. Disord.* **2008**, *41*, 195–202. [CrossRef]
121. Johnson, J.G.; Cohen, P.; Kasen, S.; Brook, J.S. Eating Disorders During Adolescence and the Risk for Physical and Mental Disorders During Early Adulthood. *Arch. Gen. Psychiatry* **2002**, *59*, 545–552. [CrossRef]
122. Wise, M.H.; Weierbach, F.; Cao, Y.; Phillips, K. Tobacco Use and Attachment Style in Appalachia. *Issues Ment. Heal. Nurs.* **2017**, *38*, 562–569. [CrossRef]
123. Mikulincer, M. Adult attachment style and affect regulation: Strategic variations in self-appraisals. *J. Pers. Soc. Psychol.* **1998**, *75*, 420–435. [CrossRef]
124. Griffin, D.; Bartholomew, K. Models of the self and other: Fundamental dimensions underlying measures of adult attachment. *J. Personal. Soc. Psychol.* **1994**, *67*, 430–445. [CrossRef]
125. Fowler, J.C.; Allen, J.; Oldham, J.M.; Frueh, B.C. Exposure to interpersonal trauma, attachment insecurity, and depression severity. *J. Affect. Disord.* **2013**, *149*, 313–318. [CrossRef]
126. Mikulincer, M.; Shaver, P.R.; Pereg, D. Attachment Theory and Affect Regulation: The Dynamics, Development, and Cognitive Consequences of Attachment-Related Strategies. *Motiv. Emot.* **2003**, *27*, 77–102. [CrossRef]
127. Gross, J.J. The emerging field of emotion regulation: An integrative review. *Rev. Gen. Psychol.* **1998**, *2*, 271–299. [CrossRef]
128. Kobak, R.R.; Cole, H.E.; Ferenz-Gillies, R.; Fleming, W.S.; Gamble, W. Attachment and Emotion Regulation during Mother-Teen Problem Solving: A Control Theory Analysis. *Child Dev.* **1993**, *64*, 231. [CrossRef] [PubMed]
129. Maunder, R.G.; Hunter, J.J. Attachment and Psychosomatic Medicine: Developmental Contributions to Stress and Disease. *Psychosom. Med.* **2001**, *63*, 556–567. [CrossRef]
130. Faber, A.; Dubé, L.; Knäuper, B. Attachment and eating: A meta-analytic review of the relevance of attachment for unhealthy and healthy eating behaviors in the general population. *Appetite* **2018**, *123*, 410–438. [CrossRef]
131. Shakory, S.; Van Exan, J.; Mills, J.S.; Sockalingam, S.; Keating, L.; Taube-Schiff, M. Binge eating in bariatric surgery candidates: The role of insecure attachment and emotion regulation. *Appetite* **2015**, *91*, 69–75. [CrossRef]

132. Fauconnier, M.; Rousselet, M.; Brunault, P.; Thiabaud, E.; Lambert, S.; Rocher, B.; Challet-Bouju, G.; Grall-Bronnec, M. Food Addiction among Female Patients Seeking Treatment for an Eating Disorder: Prevalence and Associated Factors. *Nutrients* **2020**, *12*, 1897. [CrossRef]
133. Ahrens, K.R.; Ciechanowski, P.; Katon, W. Associations between adult attachment style and health risk behaviors in an adult female primary care population. *J. Psychosom. Res.* **2012**, *72*, 364–370. [CrossRef]
134. Cooper, M.L.; Shaver, P.R.; Collins, N.L. Attachment styles, emotion regulation, and adjustment in adolescence. *J. Pers. Soc. Psychol.* **1998**, *74*, 1380–1397. [CrossRef]
135. Kassel, J.D.; Wardle, M.; Roberts, J.E. Adult attachment security and college student substance use. *Addict. Behav.* **2007**, *32*, 1164–1176. [CrossRef] [PubMed]
136. McNally, A.M.; Palfai, T.P.; Levine, R.V.; Moore, B.M. Attachment dimensions and drinking-related problems among young adults: The mediational role of coping motives. *Addict. Behav.* **2003**, *28*, 1115–1127. [CrossRef]
137. Le, T.L.; Mann, R.E.; Levitan, R.D.; George, T.P.; Maunder, R.G. Sex differences in the relationships between childhood adversity, attachment anxiety and current smoking. *Addict. Res. Theory* **2017**, *25*, 146–153. [CrossRef]
138. Pipová, H.; Kaščáková, N.; Fürstová, J.; Tavel, P. Development of the Modified Yale Food Addiction Scale Version 2.0 summary version in a representative sample of Czech population. *J. Eat. Disord.* **2020**, *8*, 16. [CrossRef] [PubMed]
139. Armstrong, J.G.; Roth, D.M. Attachment and separation difficulties in eating disorders: A preliminary investigation. *Int. J. Eat. Disord.* **1989**, *8*, 141–155. [CrossRef]
140. Broberg, A.G.; Hjalmers, I.; Nevonen, L. Eating disorders, attachment and interpersonal difficulties: A comparison between 18- to 24-year-old patients and normal controls. *Eur. Eat. Disord. Rev.* **2001**, *9*, 381–396. [CrossRef]
141. Chassler, L. Understanding Anorexia Nervosa and Bulimia Nervosa from an Attachment Perspective. *Clin. Soc. Work. J.* **1997**, *25*, 407–423. [CrossRef]
142. Kenny, M.; Hart, K. Relationship between parental attachment and eating disorders in an inpatient and a college sample. *J. Couns. Psychol.* **1992**, *39*, 521–526. [CrossRef]
143. Latzer, Y.; Hochdorf, Z.; Bachar, E.; Canetti, L. Attachment Style and Family Functioning as Discriminating Factors in Eating Disorders. *Contemp. Fam. Ther.* **2002**, *24*, 581–599. [CrossRef]
144. Orzolek-Kronner, C. The Effect of Attachment Theory in the Development of Eating Disorders: Can Symptoms Be Proximity-Seeking? *Child Adolesc. Soc. Work. J.* **2002**, *19*, 421–435. [CrossRef]
145. Ward, A.; Ramsay, R.; Treasure, J. Attachment research in eating disorders. *Br. J. Med Psychol.* **2000**, *73*, 35–51. [CrossRef] [PubMed]
146. Illing, V.; Tasca, G.A.; Balfour, L.; Bissada, H. Attachment Insecurity Predicts Eating Disorder Symptoms and Treatment Outcomes in a Clinical Sample of Women. *J. Nerv. Ment. Dis.* **2010**, *198*, 653–659. [CrossRef] [PubMed]
147. Taube-Schiff, M.; Van Exan, J.; Tanaka, R.; Wnuk, S.; Hawa, R.; Sockalingam, S. Attachment style and emotional eating in bariatric surgery candidates: The mediating role of difficulties in emotion regulation. *Eat. Behav.* **2015**, *18*, 36–40. [CrossRef] [PubMed]
148. Wilkinson, L.L.; Rowe, A.C.; Sheldon, C.; Johnson, A.; Brunstrom, J.M. Disinhibited eating mediates differences in attachment insecurity between bariatric surgery candidates/recipients and lean controls. *Int. J. Obes.* **2017**, *41*, 1831–1834. [CrossRef] [PubMed]
149. Wang, D.; Connock, M.; Barton, P.; Fry-Smith, A.; Aveyard, P.; Moore, D. 'Cut down to quit' with nicotine replacement therapies in smoking cessation: A systematic review of effectiveness and economic analysis. *Heal. Technol. Assess.* **2008**, *12*. [CrossRef] [PubMed]
150. Moore, D.; Aveyard, P.; Connock, M.; Wang, D.; Fry-Smith, A.; Barton, P. Effectiveness and safety of nicotine replacement therapy assisted reduction to stop smoking: Systematic review and meta-analysis. *BMJ* **2009**, *338*, b1024. [CrossRef]
151. Lindson, N.; Chepkin, S.C.; Ye, W.; Fanshawe, T.R.; Bullen, C.; Hartmann-Boyce, J. Different doses, durations and modes of delivery of nicotine replacement therapy for smoking cessation. *Cochrane Database Syst. Rev.* **2019**, *4*, CD013308. [CrossRef]
152. Cahill, K.; Stevens, S.; Perera, R.; Lancaster, T. Pharmacological interventions for smoking cessation: An overview and network meta-analysis. *Cochrane Database Syst. Rev.* **2013**, *5*, CD009329. [CrossRef]
153. Cahill, K.; Lindson-Hawley, N.; Thomas, K.H.; Fanshawe, T.R.; Lancaster, T. Nicotine receptor partial agonists for smoking cessation. *Cochrane Database Syst. Rev.* **2016**, *2016*, CD006103. [CrossRef]

154. Howes, S.; Hartmann-Boyce, J.; Livingstone-Banks, J.; Hong, B.; Lindson, N. Antidepressants for smoking cessation. *Cochrane Database Syst. Rev.* **2020**, *4*, CD000031. [CrossRef]
155. Stead, L.F.; Perera, R.; Bullen, C.; Mant, D.; Hartmann-Boyce, J.; Cahill, K.; Lancaster, T. Nicotine replacement therapy for smoking cessation. *Cochrane Database Syst. Rev.* **2012**, *11*, CD000146. [CrossRef] [PubMed]
156. Aveyard, P.; Begh, R.; Parsons, A.; West, R. Brief opportunistic smoking cessation interventions: A systematic review and meta-analysis to compare advice to quit and offer of assistance. *Addiction* **2012**, *107*, 1066–1073. [CrossRef] [PubMed]
157. Heckman, C.J.; Egleston, B.L.; Hofmann, M.T. Efficacy of motivational interviewing for smoking cessation: A systematic review and meta-analysis. *Tob. Control.* **2010**, *19*, 410–416. [CrossRef] [PubMed]
158. Hartmann-Boyce, J.; McRobbie, H.; Lindson, N.; Bullen, C.; Begh, R.; Theodoulou, A.; Notley, C.; A Rigotti, N.; Turner, T.; Butler, A.R.; et al. Electronic cigarettes for smoking cessation. *Cochrane Database Syst. Rev.* **2020**, *10*, CD010216. [CrossRef] [PubMed]
159. Hajek, P.; Phillips-Waller, A.; Przulj, D.; Pesola, F.; Smith, K.M.; Bisal, N.; Li, J.; Parrott, S.; Sasieni, P.; Dawkins, L.; et al. A Randomized Trial of E-Cigarettes versus Nicotine-Replacement Therapy. *N. Engl. J. Med.* **2019**, *380*, 629–637. [CrossRef]
160. Treasure, J.; Leslie, M.; Chami, R.; Fernández-Aranda, F. Are trans diagnostic models of eating disorders fit for purpose? A consideration of the evidence for food addiction. *Eur. Eat. Disord. Rev.* **2018**, *26*, 83–91. [CrossRef]
161. Miller-Matero, L.R.; Brescacin, C.; Clark, S.M.; Troncone, C.L.; Tobin, E.T. Why WAIT? Preliminary evaluation of the weight assistance and intervention techniques (WAIT) group. *Psychol. Heal. Med.* **2019**, *24*, 1029–1037. [CrossRef]
162. Cassin, S.; Sijercic, I.; Montemarano, V. Psychosocial Interventions for Food Addiction: A Systematic Review. *Curr. Addict. Rep.* **2020**, *7*, 9–19. [CrossRef]
163. Luigjes, J.; Segrave, R.; De Joode, N.; Figee, M.; Denys, D. Efficacy of Invasive and Non-Invasive Brain Modulation Interventions for Addiction. *Neuropsychol. Rev.* **2019**, *29*, 116–138. [CrossRef]
164. Sauvaget, A.; Etrojak, B.; Ebulteau, S.; Ejiménez-Murcia, S.; Efernandez-Aranda, F.; Ewolz, I.; Menchón, J.M.; Eachab, S.; Evanelle, J.-M.; Egrall-Bronnec, M. Transcranial direct current stimulation (tDCS) in behavioral and food addiction: A systematic review of efficacy, technical, and methodological issues. *Front. Neurosci.* **2015**, *9*, 349. [CrossRef]
165. Aubin, H.-J.; Farley, A.; Lycett, D.; Lahmek, P.; Aveyard, P. Weight gain in smokers after quitting cigarettes: Meta-analysis. *BMJ* **2012**, *345*, e4439. [CrossRef] [PubMed]
166. Tian, J.; Venn, A.; Otahal, P.; Gall, S. The association between quitting smoking and weight gain: A systematic review and meta-analysis of prospective cohort studies. *Obes. Rev.* **2015**, *16*, 883–901. [CrossRef] [PubMed]
167. Clark, M.M.; Hurt, R.D.; Croghan, I.T.; A Patten, C.; Novotny, P.; Sloan, J.A.; Dakhil, S.R.; Croghan, G.A.; Wos, E.J.; Rowland, K.M.; et al. The prevalence of weight concerns in a smoking abstinence clinical trial. *Addict. Behav.* **2006**, *31*, 1144–1152. [CrossRef] [PubMed]
168. Clark, M.M.; Decker, P.A.; Offord, K.P.; A Patten, C.; Vickers, K.S.; Croghan, I.T.; Schaff, H.V.; Hurt, R.D.; Dale, L.C. Weight concerns among male smokers. *Addict. Behav.* **2004**, *29*, 1637–1641. [CrossRef]
169. Owari, Y.; Miyatake, N.; Suzuki, H. Relationship between Food Dependence and Nicotine Dependence in Smokers: A Cross-Sectional Study of Staff and Students at Medical Colleges. *Medicina* **2019**, *55*, 202. [CrossRef]
170. Blum, K.; Bailey, J.; Gonzalez, A.M.; Oscar-Berman, M.; Liu, Y.; Giordano, J.; Braverman, E.; Gold, M. Neuro-genetics of reward deficiency syndrome (RDS) as the root cause of "addiction transfer": A new phenomenon common after bariatric surgery. *J. Genet. Syndr. Gene Ther.* **2011**, S2-001. [CrossRef]
171. Turnbaugh, P.J.; Ley, R.E.; Mahowald, M.A.; Magrini, V.; Mardis, E.R.; Gordon, J.I. An obesity-associated gut microbiome with increased capacity for energy harvest. *Nat. Cell Biol.* **2006**, *444*, 1027–1031. [CrossRef]
172. Fletcher, P.C.; Kenny, P.J. Food addiction: A valid concept? *Neuropsychopharmacology* **2018**, *43*, 2506–2513. [CrossRef]

11

Insular Cell Integrity Markers Linked to Weight Concern in Anorexia Nervosa—An MR-Spectroscopy Study

Simon Maier [1,2,*], Kathrin Nickel [2], Evgeniy Perlov [2,3], Alina Kukies [1], Almut Zeeck [1], Ludger Tebartz van Elst [2], Dominique Endres [2], Derek Spieler [1], Lukas Holovics [1], Armin Hartmann [1], Michael Dacko [4], Thomas Lange [4] and Andreas Joos [1,5]

1. Department of Psychosomatic Medicine and Psychotherapy, Medical Center—University of Freiburg, Faculty of Medicine, University of Freiburg, 79104 Freiburg, Germany; alinakukies@hotmail.com (A.K.); almut.zeeck@uniklinik-freiburg.de (A.Z.); derek.spieler@uniklinik-freiburg.de (D.S.); lukas.holovics@uniklinik-freiburg.de (L.H.); armin.hartmann@uniklinik-freiburg.de (A.H.); andreas.joos@uniklinik-freiburg.de (A.J.)
2. Department of Psychiatry and Psychotherapy, Medical Center—University of Freiburg, Faculty of Medicine, University of Freiburg, 79104 Freiburg, Germany; kathrin.nickel@uniklinik-freiburg.de (K.N.); evgeniy.perlov@lups.ch (E.P.); tebartzvanelst@uniklinik-freiburg.de (L.T.v.E.); dominique.endres@uniklinik-freiburg.de (D.E.)
3. Luzerner Psychiatrie, Hospital St. Urban, 4915 St. Urban, Switzerland
4. Department of Radiology, Medical Physics, Medical Center—University of Freiburg, Faculty of Medicine, University of Freiburg, 79106 Freiburg, Germany; michael.dacko@uniklinik-freiburg.de (M.D.); thomas.lange@uniklinik-freiburg.de (T.L.)
5. Department of Psychosomatic Medicine and Psychotherapy, Ortenau Klinikum, Teaching Hospital of University of Freiburg, 77654 Offenburg, Germany

* Correspondence: simon.maier@uniklinik-freiburg.de

Abstract: Objective: An insular involvement in the pathogenesis of anorexia nervosa (AN) has been suggested in many structural and functional neuroimaging studies. This magnetic resonance spectroscopy (MRS) study is the first to investigate metabolic signals in the anterior insular cortex in patients with AN and recovered individuals (REC). Method: The MR spectra of 32 adult women with AN, 21 REC subjects and 33 healthy controls (HC) were quantified for absolute *N*-acetylaspartate (NAA), glutamate + glutamine (Glx), total choline, myo-inositol, creatine concentrations (mM/L). After adjusting the metabolite concentrations for age and partial gray/white matter volume, group differences were tested using one-way multivariate analyses of variance (MANOVA). Post-hoc analyses of variance were applied to identify those metabolites that showed significant group effects. Correlations were tested for associations with psychometric measures (eating disorder examination), duration of illness, and body mass index. Results: The MANOVA exhibited a significant group effect. The NAA signal was reduced in the AN group compared to the HC group. The REC and the HC groups did not differ in metabolite concentrations. In the AN group, lower NAA and Glx signals were related to increased weight concern. Discussion: We interpret the decreased NAA availability in the anterior insula as a signal of impaired neuronal integrity or density. The association of weight concern, which is a core feature of AN, with decreased NAA and Glx indicates that disturbances of glutamatergic neurotransmission might be related to core psychopathology in AN. The absence of significant metabolic differences between the REC and HC subjects suggests that metabolic alterations in AN represent a state rather than a trait phenomenon.

Keywords: anorexia nervosa; magnetic resonance spectroscopy; MRS; insula; glutamate; *N*-acetylaspartate; NAA

1. Introduction

Patients with anorexia nervosa (AN) persistently restricted their food intake because of severe weight concerns and body image disturbance. AN mainly affects young women [1–3] and has the highest mortality rate of all mental disorders [4,5], while only about half of such patients fully recover [1,2].

Two decades ago, the first magnetic resonance spectroscopy (MRS) studies searched for metabolic anomalies associated with AN. MRS is a non-invasive and nonradioactive method for the in vivo detection of several neurometabolites. MRS sequences that measure the ^{1}H chemical shift allow the simultaneous absolute quantification of the concentrations of *N*-acetylaspartate (NAA) + *N*-acetyl-aspartyl-glutamate (NAAG), glutamate (Glu) + glutamine (Gln), glycerophosphorylcholine + phosphocholine (total choline, t-Cho), myo-inositol (mI), phosphocreatine (PCre), and creatine (Cre).

NAA is relatively abundant in healthy neuronal tissue and is therefore often used as a marker for neuronal integrity and density [6]. However, it has also been detected in oligodendrocytes and myelin [7,8], and it is synthesized in the mitochondria. Decreased concentrations of NAA indicate a loss of neuronal cells. Although NAA signal differences have been reported in various studies on AN, the results were inconsistent regarding a diminished or elevated NAA level [9–13] (see Table 1).

Glu is the primary excitatory neurotransmitter in the human brain (~85% of all synapses in the central nervous system are glutamatergic) [14] and has been implicated in different psychiatric disorders associated with AN, including anxiety disorders, depression, and obsessive-compulsive disorder [15–18]. Elevated Glu has toxic effects on neurons as well as oligodendrocytes, astrocytes, and endothelial and immune cells [19]. The distinction of Glu from its precursor and the metabolite Gln is difficult because of a considerable overlap of the spectral peaks. Therefore, the combined Glu and Gln resonances are often denoted collectively as Glx [20]. Previous MRS studies have reported lower Glx [10,12,21] and Glu [22] in the AN group compared to HC subjects or in response to AN-related symptoms; while this has mainly been in frontal cortices, it has also been in the basal ganglia and occipital lobe [22]. Notably, one study reported higher Glx signals in AN [9].

The major part of the t-Cho signal results from glycerophosphorylcholine and phosphocholine, but it also comes from other choline-containing compounds. Glycerophosphorylcholine and phosphocholine are integral components of the cell membrane and are more highly concentrated in glial cells than they are in neurons [23]. Changes in the t-Cho signal have been associated with changes in cell proliferation or cell degeneration [24]. MRS studies that detected t-Cho differences in AN or in relation to anorectic symptoms reported increased concentrations [9,11–13,25].

Creatine and phosphocreatine are measured as combined resonances (Cre) and are involved in the creatine kinase cycle. Despite their important role in energy metabolism, the level of the Cre signal remains relatively constant, even under conditions of increased energy demand [26]. Therefore, the Cre signal is widely used as an internal reference in MRS studies. While MRS studies reporting Cre signal differences in AN mostly showed increased Cre [9,12,25] in the anterior cingulate and frontal cortices, lower Cre was observed in the dorsolateral prefrontal cortex (dlPFC) [21].

The concentration of the sugar mI is thought to be increased in glial cells compared to neurons, and it serves as an intracellular second messenger. For this reason, mI is used as a glial marker [27]. In AN, mI was found to be decreased [10,21,22,28] whenever mI differences were detected.

Table 1. Overview of previous magnetic resonance spectroscopy (MRS) studies in anorexia nervosa.

Author	Patient Collective	Age	Sex	Patients/Controls	MR Method	Target Region	Results
Kato et al. (1997) [29]	AN (3 comorbid BN)	18–32	female	4 (2 longitudinal)/13	Localized ^{31}P (TE = 20 ms) 1.5T	Frontal lobe	PDE/*P* total + decreasing after gaining weight
Schlemmer et al. (1998) [13] *	AN	16 ± 1.9	female	10/17	^{1}H SVS STEAM (TE = 50 ms) 1.5T	(1) Thalamus (2) parieto-occipital WM	(1) Cho/Cr+, NAA/Cho−
Möckel et al. (1999) [30] *	AN	15.7 ± 1.7	female	22/17 (11 longitudinal)	^{1}H SVS STEAM (TE = 50 ms) 1.5T	(1) Thalamus (2) parieto-occiptal WM	Both: Cho/Cr+ normalization with recovery
Hentschel et al. (1999) [11] *	AN	15.7 ± 1.7	female	15/17	^{1}H SVS STEAM (TE = 50 ms) 1.5T	(1) Thalamus (2) parieto-occiptal WM	(1) Cho/Cr+ NAA/Cr+
Roser et al. (1999) [28]	AN and BN	10–28	19 female 1 male	20/15	^{1}H SVS STEAM (TE = 20 ms) 1.5T	(1) Frontal white matter (2) occipital gray matter, (3) cerebellum	(1) mI/Cr− lipid/Cr− (2) lipid/Cr− (3) all metabolites + except lipids
Rzanny et al. (2003) [31]	AN	12–20	female	10/10	Localized ^{31}P (TE = 16 ms) 1.5T	Frontal lobe	PDE/*P* total−
Ohrmann et al. (2004) [21]	AN	22.7 ± 3.8	female	10/12	^{1}H SVS STEAM (TE = 20 ms) 1.5T	(1) Rostral ACC (2) dlPFC	(1) Glx− (2) Cr−, mI−
Grzelak et al. (2005) [32]	AN	16–22	female	10/10	^{1}H SVS STEAM (TE = 20 ms) 1.5T	Parietal WM, parietal GM	WM: lipid−
Castro-Fornieles et al. (2007) [10]	AN	11–17	female	12/12	^{1}H SVS PRESS (TE = 35 ms) 1.5T	Frontal grey matter	NAA−, Glx−, ml− 7 months follow-up NAA+
Castro-Fornieles et al. (2010) [25]	AN vs. short-term recovered	13–18	female	32/20	^{1}H SVS PRESS (TE = 35 ms) 1.5T	prefrontal	Cho+, Cr+
Joos et al. (2011) [12]	10 BN 7AN	24.8 ± 4.9	female	17/14	^{1}H SVS PRESS (TE = 30 ms) 3T	ACC	No difference: NAA, Cho, Cr, mI, Glu, Glx
Blasel et al. (2012) [9]	AN	14.4 ± 1.9	female	21/29	^{1}H SVS PRESS (TE = 30 ms) ^{31}P (TE = 2.3 ms) 3T	centrum semiovale (including ACC)	GM: Glx+, NAA+, Cr+, Cho+, lipid catabolites−
Godlewska et al. (2017) [22]	AN	18–41	female	13/12	^{1}H SVS STEAM (TE = 11 ms) 7T	ACC, occipital cortex and putamen	Glu− in all areas mI− in ACC and occipital lobe

Abbreviations: ACC = anterior cingulate cortex; AN = anorexia nervosa; BN = bulimia nervose; Cho = choline; re = creatine; dlPFC = dorsolateral prefrontal cortex; Glx = glutamate+glutamine; GM = grey matter; HC = healthy control; mI = myo-inositol; NAA = *N*-acetylaspartate; P total = total phosphate; PDE = phosphodiesters; SVS = single voxel spectroscopy; TE = echo time; WM = white matter; ^{1}H = proton spectroscopy; ^{31}P = phosphate spectroscopy. * overlapping samples.

Small sample sizes, low MR field strengths, and differences in voxel positioning are likely to be the main cause of the heterogeneous results of previous ^{1}H-MRS studies (Table 1). Given that higher field strengths are particularly recommended for the quantification of Glx, and considering that the Cre signal, which was often used as a reference in earlier studies [9,21,25], often reveals inconsistent results, older studies must be interpreted cautiously.

In conclusion, no metabolite was consistently altered across all studies, but increased t-Cho and Cre and decreased mI were the most consistent findings (Table 1). In general, the results of newer studies with higher field strengths and more advanced MRS protocols in combination with larger sample sizes are more reliable.

A longitudinal ^{1}H-MRS study reported a normalization of increased t-Cho/Cre ratios with recovery [29], while a small study of adolescent females with AN also indicated normalization, which was (in this case) decreased NAA in the frontal gray matter (GM) [10].

In terms of region of interest (ROI) localization, the anterior insular cortex appears to be of importance. The relevance of this region in AN has been emphasized in various brain structural [33–37] and functional [38–41] studies, and it even led to the postulation of the so-called *"insula hypothesis"* of AN [42,43]. This hypothesis states that early developmental damage in combination with socio-cultural and other stressors, such as dieting and hormonal changes, may lead to an impairment of insula function. The insula, as a central hub, conveys the information of numerous cortical and subcortical brain areas and therefore plays a central role in the interoceptional awareness and monitoring of the bodily state (somatic marker hypothesis) [44,45]. This includes, among other functions, the experience of physiological correlates of fear and anxiety [46] as well as taste [47,48], hunger [49], disgust [50], and visceral information [51]. Hence, altered insula functioning could explain the dysfunction of interoceptive awareness in AN in turn by not only biasing the experience of one's own bodily condition or the pleasantness/valence of consumed food but also the reward-related and motivational aspects of food intake [52]. Despite the high relevance of the insular lobe in AN pathomechanism, this area has never been targeted by previous MRS studies.

Rationale of our Study

This study examined female adults with AN, female adults who had recovered (REC) from AN, and healthy controls (HC) via MRS, which targeted the insular cortex. Considering the results of earlier studies, we expected to observe increased Cre and t-Cho signals in women with AN and decreased mI, while no clear hypothesis regarding NAA and Glx could be derived from previous studies. All hypothetical differences were expected to normalize in the REC subjects.

2. Methods and Materials

2.1. Participants

The MR spectra of 35 female patients with AN were acquired. Patients were recruited at the in- and outpatient units of the Department of Psychosomatic Medicine and Psychotherapy at the University of Freiburg as well as cooperating hospitals. Diagnoses were made by experienced and board-certified psychiatrists and psychologists and were confirmed by the structured clinical interviews SCID-I and SCID-II [53,54]. Diagnostic criteria according to the DSM-5 [55] were relevant for study inclusion. All AN patients met the weight criterion of a body mass index (BMI) < 18.5 kg/m^2. Three patients had to be excluded because of either data loss or corruption. Of the 32 remaining AN patients, 3 were of the binge eating/purging subtype, while all others were of the restrictive subtype.

Twenty-two REC were recruited for MRS acquisition and fulfilled the following recovery criteria [56]: No eating disorder symptomatology for at least 12 months with a conservative eating disorder examination total score (EDE) total score [57,58] within 1 standard deviation of normal. For study inclusion, a minimal BMI of >20 kg/m^2 was envisaged, which most REC participants met. However, the BMI of four REC subjects was slightly below 20 kg/m^2 (19.3–19.8 kg/m^2).

These participants were clinically completely recovered and had never exceeded a BMI >20 kg/m^2. In addition, 2 REC subjects had a BMI of 18.5–19.0 kg/m^2 with similar features, while 1 REC participant had to be excluded because of data loss or corruption, resulting in a final sample size of 21 individuals for the REC group. Finally, 1 REC participant was of the binge eating/purging subtype, while all others were of the restrictive subtype.

HC subjects were recruited via advertisements in local newspapers and announcements on the notice board of the participating hospital. The MR spectra of 40 age-matched female HC subjects were available. Mental disorders in HC subjects were ruled out by SCID-I and II interviews. After 7 HC participants were excluded because of either data loss or corruption, the final HC sample size was 33 individuals.

The general exclusion criteria included any history of head injury or surgery, neurological disorders, severe psychiatric comorbidities (psychosis, bipolar disorders, substance abuse), current regular psychotropic medication, and an inability to undergo MRI scans (e.g., metal implants, claustrophobia). In total, 7 AN, 17 HC, and 10 REC subjects took hormonal contraceptives. One woman with AN had only just started a minor dose of citalopram (10 mg/day; serum level of 31 ng/mL, which is below the therapeutic range) and was thus considered appropriate to be included.

The participants who took no hormonal contraceptives were studied in the luteal phase of the menstrual cycle. Regarding hormonal contraception, they had to be in the progesterone and estrogen phase (i.e., similar to the physiology of the luteal phase). Given that, the AN participants were mostly amenorrhoeic, the phase of their menstrual cycle could not be assessed.

2.2. Ethics Statement

All subjects gave written informed consent prior to participation, and the study was approved by the ethics committee of the University Medical Center Freiburg (Approval ID: EK-Freiburg 520/13 June 2013).

2.3. Psychometric Assessment

Apart from the SCID interviews [53,54] and the EDE interviews [57,58] mentioned above, the participants completed self-report questionnaires to assess their eating disorder pathology using the Eating Disorder Inventory–2 [59,60] and to assess any depression using the Beck Depression Inventory-II, BDI-II [61–63].

2.4. Procedure Before Scanning

Starting between 7:30 a.m. and 8:00 a.m., participants received a standardized breakfast, and their consumed calories were assessed. The participants read study-relevant information and completed an MR-safety questionnaire.

2.5. Data Acquisition and Processing

All measurements were performed at the University Medical Center of Freiburg using a 3T MAGNETOM Prisma scanner (Siemens Healthineers, Erlangen, Germany), which was equipped with a 20-channel head coil.

Before the MRS measurement was taken, a T1-weighted MPRAGE sequence (repetition time: 2000 ms, echo time: 4.11 ms, flip angle: 12°, field of view: 256 × 256 mm, 160 slices, voxel size: 1 × 1 × 1 mm) was performed and used for manual localization of spectroscopic voxels in the left insular cortex (size: 20 × 20 × 20 mm). A point resolved spectroscopy (PRESS) sequence with an echo time of 30 ms, a relaxation time of 3000 ms, 256 averages, and with water saturation was used. The water reference spectrum was obtained using 16 averages of the same PRESS sequence without water saturation. Shimming parameters were further manually adjusted to minimize the full-width at half maximum of the water peak. The established linear combination of model spectra (LCModel 6.3, Oakville, ON, Canada) software was used for spectra fitting and quantification [64]. The absolute metabolite concentrations of Cre, NAA, Cho, Glx, and mI were estimated [64–66]. All spectra were visually controlled to fulfill the internal criterion of quality (i.e., adequate visible peaks of main metabolites), and only spectra with Cramér-Rao lower bounds (CRLBs) for the main metabolites below 20% were included in further analyses. All voxels were segmented into GM, white matter (WM), and cerebrospinal fluid (CSF) using the statistical parametric mapping software SPM12 (Wellcome Trust Centre of Imaging Neuroscience, London, United Kingdom; for details, see [67]), according to the co-registered voxel position of the corresponding morphological T1-weighted image.

2.6. Statistical Analyses

The metabolite concentrations, as assessed in the LCModel, were transferred to a data table together with all clinical and psychometric data. All statistical analyses were performed using R statistical computing (version 3.4, R Foundation for Statistical Computing, Vienna, Austria [68]). All dependent variables of interest (metabolite concentrations) were first linearly adjusted for differences in age and partial GM+WM volume using the "predict" function of the R stats package. The resulting adjusted metabolite concentrations were then tested for normality of distribution using the Shapiro–Wilk test of normality. Subsequently, the Levene's test for homogeneity of variance across groups was computed for the adjusted metabolite concentrations.

Because the adjusted metabolite concentrations of NAA/NAAG, Cre/PCre and mI were not normally distributed, we tested group differences with a robust one-way MANOVA [69] using the rrcov package (version 1.4–3) in R [70]. In the robust MANOVA, a classical Wilk's Lambda statistic for testing the equality of the group means was modified into a robust one through substituting the classical estimates by the highly robust and efficiently reweighted minimum covariance determinant estimators for mean and variances. The procedure used 10,000 trials for the simulations to compute the multiplication factor for the approximate distribution of the robust Lambda statistic and the degrees of freedom.

To determine which metabolites significantly differed between groups, a post-hoc heteroscedastic one-way ANOVA for trimmed means was carried out with the WRS2 package [71,72]. A p-level of <0.05 was chosen as the criterion for significance. The explanatory power is reported using ξ as a robust measure of effect size [73]. A post-hoc Lincon test (with robustness equivalent to the Tukey-Kramer test) was carried out to assess the direction of the effects [71].

The robust MANOVA was repeated with adjusted metabolite concentrations after additionally correcting for the influence contraceptive use.

Finally, the adjusted metabolite concentrations were correlated with psychometric measures of AN (EDE scores, BMI, and duration of illness) using robust correlations (pbcor function of the WRS2 package [72]) independently for the AN group and across all groups (but not for duration of illness). The resulting p-values of the correlation analyses were corrected for multiple comparisons using the Benjamini and Hochberg False Discovery Rate [74].

3. Results

3.1. Demographic and Psychometric Data

The demographic and psychometric data of the participants are summarized in Table 2. For the final data analysis, 32 patients with AN, 21 REC participants, and 33 HCs were included in the study. The REC group was older than were both the AN and HC participants. As expected, there was a difference with respect to BMI between all three groups, with the lowest BMI in patients with AN (AN < REC < HC). The AN group showed more depressive symptoms in the BDI-II than did the REC and HC participants (HC > REC > AN). Diagnoses in the AN group included seven participants with depression, one with a specific phobia, one with obsessive-compulsive disorder, and two with generalized anxiety disorder. Two participants of the REC group had specific phobias. One participant of the AN, two of the HC, and none of the REC group were left-handed.

Table 2. Overview of demographic and psychometric data.

	Anorexia (n = 32)		Recovered (n = 21)		Healthy Controls (n = 33)		ANOVA	Post hoc t-Test Tukey-Kramer *
	Mean	SD	Mean	SD	Mean	SD	(d.f.; F; p)	
Age (Years)	23.7	4.2	27.6	5.2	23.2	3.4	2, 83; 5.8, 0.004 *	REC > AN, HC
Current BMI (kg/m^2)	16.2	1.3	20.6	1.3	22.1	2.4	2, 83; 91.0; <0.001 *	HC > REC > AN
Lowest-Lifetime BMI (kg/m^2)	14.8	1.4	15.1	2.2	-	-	2, 49; 0.5; 0.5	-
Calorie Intake at Breakfast (kcal)	135.9	161.9	297.7	128.1	399.3	86.4	2, 83; 23.7; <0.001 *	HC, RE > AN
EDE Total Score	3.2	1.2	0.6	0.4	0.4	0.3	2, 83; 119.9; <0.001 *	AN > REC, HC
EDE Restraint	3.4	1.4	0.5	0.7	0.4	0.5	2, 79; 90.2; <0.001 *	AN > REC, HC
EDE Eating Concern	2.6	1.5	0.1	0.2	0.0	0.1	2, 79; 76.3; <0.001 *	AN > REC, HC
EDE Weight Concern	3.1	1.4	0.7	0.5	0.4	0.3	2, 79; 76.4; <0.001 *	AN > REC, HC
EDE Shape Concern	3.5	1.4	0.8	0.7	0.6	0.5	2, 79; 88.1, <0.001 *	AN > REC, HC
EDI- Total Score	61.8	9.9	47.2	5.1	44.1	2.8	2, 83; 61.4; <0.001*	AN > REC, HC
Duration of Illness (Years)	6.4	3.9	6.1	5.4	-	-	2, 46; 0.6; 0.5	-
SIAB III	7.4	4.8	4.5	5.5	2.7	3.2	2, 83; 9.1; <0.001 *	AN > REC, HC
BDI-II	21.7	9.7	6.5	6.1	1.6	2.3	2, 83; 75.6; <0.001 *	AN > REC, HC
MWTB	27.9	5.2	29.2	4.8	28.3	4.8	2, 83; 0.5; 0.6	-
Partial GM Volume **	0.59	0.1	0.63	0.1	0.59	0.1	2,83; 2.3, 0.112	-
Partial WM Volume **	0.30	0.1	0.27	0.1	0.32	0.1	2,83; 2.1, 0.134	-
Partial CSF Volume **	0.11	0.0	0.11	0.1	0.10	0.0	2,83; 1.6, 0.202	-

Abbreviation: BMI = body mass index, d.f. = degrees of freedom, EDE = eating disorder examination, EDI = Eating Disorder Inventory–2, SIAB III = Structured Interview for Anorexic and Bulimic Syndromes, Subscale III, BDI-II = Beck Depression Inventory-II, MWT-B = Multiwortwahltest for IQ assessment, AN = anorexia nervosa; HC = healthy control; REC = recovered. * significant group effects, ** partial volume of the left insular MRS voxel.

3.2. MRS

After filtering all CRLBs above 20%, the Cho signal of one HC had to be removed from further analyses.

The robust one-way MANOVA model with the five metabolites as independent variables revealed a significant group effect ($\Lambda = 0.712$, χ^2 (8.41) = 17.1, $p = 0.036$). The robust one-way ANOVAs performed *post-hoc* were significant for the NAA peak (F (2,31.4) = 3.760; $p = 0.034$, $\xi = 0.35$), with the AN group showing lower NAA concentrations (Table 3, Figure 1). These differences remained significant after applying false discovery rate (FDR) correction for multiple comparisons. When comparing the AN group to the REC group the NAA peak differences reached the trend level, but this result failed to survive FDR correction. Both the REC and HC groups exhibited no significant differences in any metabolites. The robust one-way MANOVA model did still show a significant group effect after adjusting the data for the influence of contraceptive use ($\Lambda = 0.723$, χ^2 (8.41) = 16.3, $p = 0.047$).

Partial GM, WM, and CSF volumes of the left insular MRS voxel exhibited no significant group differences (Table 2).

Table 3. Robust one-way ANOVA results for the five metabolites compared across groups and *p*-value adjusted for multiple comparisons using false discovery rate (FDR) correction.

Metabolite	ANOVA	Post-Hoc Lincon
Cho	F (2.32) = 0.53; $p = 0.593$; $\xi = 0.17$	-
mI	F (2.31) = 1.06; $p = 0.360$; $\xi = 0.22$	-
NAA	F (2.31) = 3.76; $p = 0.034$ *; $\xi = 0.36$	AN < HC
Glx	F (2.28) = 0.39; $p = 0.678$; $\xi = 0.11$	-
Cre	F (2.33) = 0.04; $p = 0.963$; $\xi = 0.11$	-

Abbreviations: Cho = choline; mI = myo-inositol; NAA = *N*-acetylaspartate; lx = glutamate+glutamine; Cre = creatine. AN = anorexia nervosa; HC = healthy control; ξ = effect size. * significant group effects.

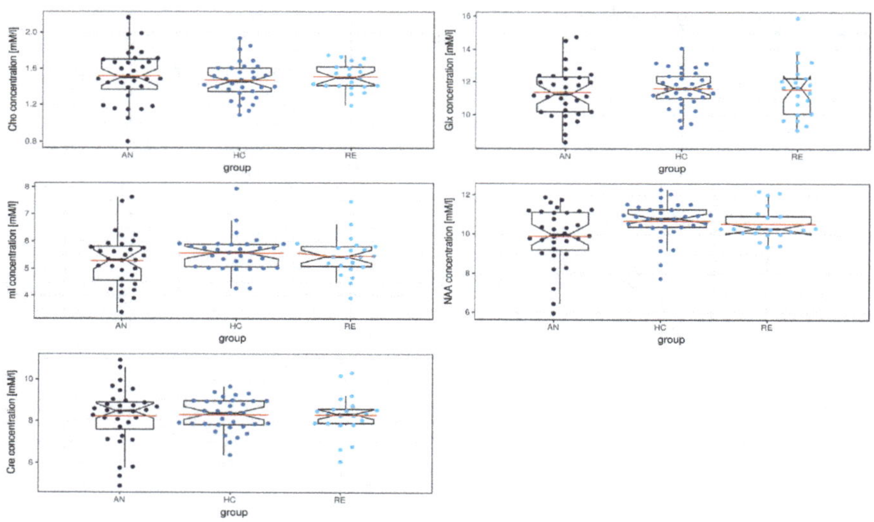

Figure 1. Boxplot of left insula metabolite concentrations across the anorexia nervosa (AN), healthy control (HC) and recovered group (RE). Red lines indicate mean metabolite concentrations. Abbreviations: Cho = choline; mI = myo-inositol; NAA = *N*-acetylaspartate; Glx = glutamate+glutamine; Cre = creatine.

In the AN group, correlation analyses with dimensional measures of AN severity showed a significant negative association of Glx concentrations with EDE shape concern as well as NAA and Glx concentrations with the EDE weight concern score (Table 4, Figure 2). There were no correlations with either the BMI (Cho: $p = 0.835$, Ins: $p = 0.361$, NAA: $p = 0.870$, Glx: $p = 0.557$, Cre: $p = 0.664$) or the duration of illness (Cho: $p = 0.397$, Ins: $p = 0.508$, NAA: $p = 0.275$, Glx: $p = 0.016$, Cre: $p = 0.223$). Only the correlation of NAA and Glx signals with the EDE weight concern score remained significant after FDR correction.

Table 4. Robust correlation results for the five metabolites with eating disorder symptom severity according to the eating disorder examination (EDE) scale in the AN group. p-values adjusted for multiple comparisons using FDR correction.

Metabolite	Total Score	Restrain	Eating Concern	Weight Concern	Shape Concern
Cho	r = −0.09 $p = 0.643$ $p_{FDR} = 0.804$	r = −0.18 $p = 0.315$ $p_{FDR} = 0.525$	r = −0.09 $p = 0.636$ $p_{FDR} = 0.655$	r = −0.17 $p = 0.365$ $p_{FDR} = 0.457$	r = −0.12 $p = 0.510$ $p_{FDR} = 0.616$
mI	r = 0.03 $p = 0.868$ $p_{FDR} = 0.868$	r = 0.31 $p = 0.080$ $p_{FDR} = 0.398$	r = 0.08 $p = 0.655$ $p_{FDR} = 0.655$	r = −0.06 $p = 0.733$ $p_{FDR} = 0.733$	r = −0.09 $p = 0.616$ $p_{FDR} = 0.616$
NAA	r = −0.28 $p = 0.120$ $p_{FDR} = 0.300$	r = −0.06 $p = 0.745$ $p_{FDR} = 0.849$	r = −0.25 $p = 0.174$ $p_{FDR} = 0.655$	r = −0.46 $p = 0.008$* $p_{FDR} = 0.020$	r = −0.25 $p = 0.171$ $p_{FDR} = 0.322$
Glx	r = −0.33 $p = 0.061$ $p_{FDR} = 0.300$	r = −0.04 $p = 0.849$ $p_{FDR} = 0.849$	r = −0.16 $p = 0.377$ $p_{FDR} = 0.655$	r = −0.48 $p = 0.005$ * $p_{FDR} = 0.020$	r = −0.40 $p = 0.025$ * $p_{FDR} = 0.126$
Cre	r = −0.15 $p = 0.423$ $p_{FDR} = 0.705$	r = −0.23 $p = 0.215$ $p_{FDR} = 0.525$	r = −0.13 $p = 0.489$ $p_{FDR} = 0.655$	r = −0.25 $p = 0.169$ $p_{FDR} = 0.281$	r = −0.23 $p = 0.193$ $p_{FDR} = 0.322$

Abbreviations: Cho = choline; mI = myo-inositol; NAA = *N*-acetylaspartate; Glx = glutamate+glutamine; Cre = creatine. AN = anorexia nervosa; FDR = false discovery rate. * significant correlations.

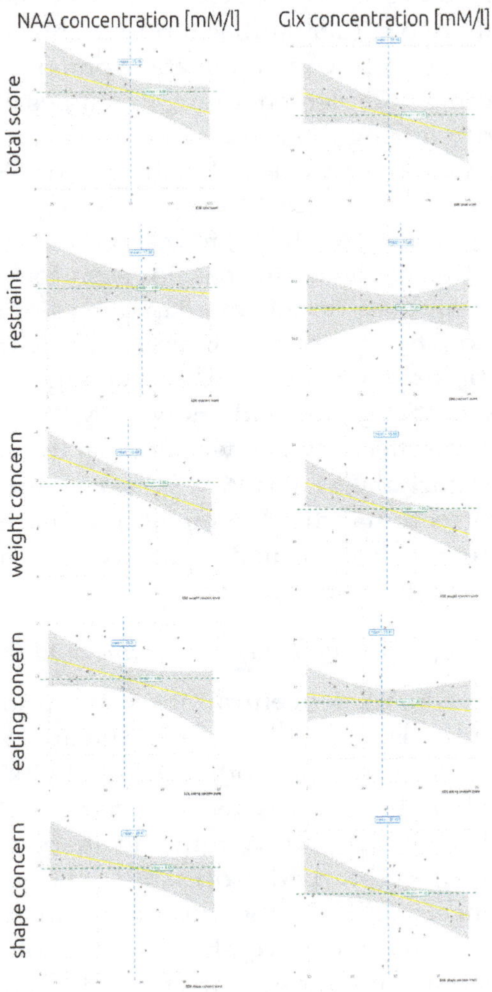

Figure 2. Scatterplot of eating disorder examination (EDE) total scores and subscores of the Anorexia group with left insular *N*-acetylaspartate (NAA) and glutamate + glutamine (Glx) concentrations, respectively. Blue lines indicate mean EDE scores. Green lines indicate mean metabolite concentrations. Regression lines are depicted in yellow with the 95% confidence interval as grey area. Significant correlations are NAA with weight concerns and Glx with weight and shape concerns.

Additional robust correlations between the five different metabolites showed a significant correlation across the concentration of all metabolites (Table S1).

4. Discussion

This MRS study is the largest to date to investigate insular metabolic alterations in women with acute AN and individuals who had recovered from AN. It was found that AN patients exhibited a significantly lower concentration of NAA in the anterior insular cortex in comparison to the REC and HC subjects, while the concentrations of all other investigated metabolites (t-Cho, mI, Glx, Cre) were unaltered. The REC and HC subjects showed no differences in the concentration of metabolites.

In the AN group, concerns about body weight (as measured with the EDE) were associated with lower NAA and Glx availability in the insular cortex. Prior to correction for multiple comparisons, shape concerns also showed a negative association with Glx concentration. It might be questioned whether this finding is due to a very low BMI or a long illness duration. Neither the BMI nor the duration of illness was associated with insular NAA concentrations.

4.1. Comparison to Earlier MRS Studies

A comparison to earlier MRS studies is complicated by the fact that this study is the first to target the anterior insular cortex in AN. Only two earlier studies reported lower NAA signals in WM and frontal GM [10,13], while one reported increased NAA in anorectic women in the anterior cingulate cortex and parieto-occipital WM [9]. Our findings complement previous studies that showed a reduction in the GM and WM volumes and the integrity during the acute stage of AN [35,75–77]. The detected decreased NAA signal as a marker of neuronal integrity and density [6] in AN might therefore support these earlier results. Structural changes during acute AN appear to be more pronounced in some cortical areas, including the insula [34,78]. Brooks et al. [34] found reduced GM in the right insular cortex in restrictive AN patients. Although the insular cortex has not been consistently affected across structural studies [35,79], in a study of our group with largely overlapping samples, reduced insular volumes and cortical thinning could be observed [78]. Regionally different concentrations of metabolites could thus, in principle, result from differently pronounced structural changes. To determine whether there are changes in metabolite concentration that go beyond known GM/WM volume changes in AN, one has to correct for partial GM/WM volume effects, which was done in the current study. Not all earlier MRS studies statistically controlled for partial GM and WM volume content of the MRS voxel. Metabolic differences that survive such a correction indicate a metabolic disturbance beyond the direct GM or WM volume effect and might therefore be associated with a loss of neuronal integrity, density, or other metabolic changes, some of which might not be known.

4.2. Possible Implications of the Findings: Beyond Density, Volume, and Integrity Effects

Our data indicated that lower NAA concentrations were associated with increased concerns about body weight (according to the EDE), which is a core feature of AN. The Glx signal showed a similar association with weight concerns and both NAA and Glx availability were important for glutamatergic neurotransmission [80,81]. Glx was also associated with shape concern, which did not survive the correction for multiple comparisons. Weight and shape concerns are central constructs of AN psychopathology and are part of a disturbed processing of body signals and integration of one's own body perception. Weight concern refers to the importance of body weight, dissatisfaction with one's own body weight, and the desire to lose weight as well as the preoccupation with shape and weight. Shape concerns imply feelings of fatness, fear of weight gain, and discomfort when looking at one's own body (for further details see: [57,58]). Therefore, the lower the Glx and NAA levels are, the more serious are these concerns.

Importantly, because there were no correlations of NAA and Glx with the BMI and we have corrected for the partial GM and WM volume, the correlation most likely does not simply reflect GM or body weight-related deficits. The associations of insular NAA and Glx availability with weight problems and, in the case of Glx, shape concerns, suggest that a lack of Glx or loss of neuronal density/integrity (which are predominantly glutamatergic in the neocortex) may be related to an exacerbation of AN symptoms, presumably because of a decreased glutamatergic effect.

Disturbed glutamatergic action in the insular cortex might therefore be related to AN's symptoms of "bodily awareness," such as perception of one's own body weight, state, and shape [43,82] and reflect dysregulation within the insular lobe (particularly in anterior parts), which serve to integrate multiple pieces of information. The insular cortex is highly connected and, according to Damasio's somatic marker hypothesis, the insula plays a central role in integrating various perceptions into a cognitive representational map. These perceptions include the information on the bodily state, the state of the autonomic nervous system, appetite, hunger, and disgust [43,44]. Although these are possible associations, no causal relationships can be deduced from these cross-sectional data (i.e., that cerebral dysfunction causes AN psychopathology). Conversely, aberrant perceptions and behavior in AN might lead to metabolic anomalies. A unifying explanation could be that both initially mild behavioral or perceptual abnormalities and initially minor cerebral aberrations reinforce each other in a kind of vicious circle until a full-blown psychopathology and pathophysiology manifests itself.

The absence of the NAA signal reductions in women who had recovered from AN compared to those with AN suggests that the apparent loss of neuronal density/integrity (apart from volume changes, e.g., due to dehydration effects) seem to be of particular importance in acute patients. This aligns with brain volumetric and other structural studies, which report a normalization of WM and GM changes after recovery [37,75,78,83]. Importantly, these patients also recovered with regard to psychopathology—as did our sample—which therefore does not allow any definite conclusions on causality between metabolic changes and psychopathology. At least in the AN group, a simple association with body weight seems unlikely.

However, we cannot completely rule out that the signal similarities of the REC and HC subjects can be attributed to a REC subgroup with a particularly good forecast; only long-term follow-up studies would be able to clarify this point [84].

A recent functional study on anxiety processing in AN showed marked dysfunction of key areas of the so-called "fear network," including the anterior insula cortex. [84]. Other studies have shown that functional abnormalities in the insula are not only in acute AN but also in REC subjects [38,39,41,85]. These observations suggest that NAA changes are likely to reflect anomalies of neurochemical processes beyond cell density or volume effects [37,75,78,83]. NAA is synthesized in neuronal mitochondria and finally absorbed and metabolized by glial cells. For example, in a longitudinal study on bipolar depression in which the NAA signal was regarded as a state marker for the disorder, the reduced NAA levels were interpreted as a dysregulation of the glial function [86].

4.3. Limitations

A longitudinal study design to test for the reversibility of the metabolic differences within the subjects would have been preferable and is envisaged for a subgroup of the AN patients of this study. Another problem was the presence of GM and WM volume effects after correcting for the volume of CSF in the LCModel. To the best of our knowledge there are no biological models available to adjust the concentrations of the different metabolites according to their abundance in GM or WM tissue, respectively. The overlap of the reported structural, functional, and metabolic alterations in the insular cortex in AN, which was investigated in the same subjects, should be confirmed in an independent sample.

5. Summary

In this study, we found decreased NAA signals in the anterior insular cortex of women with AN and lower NAA and Glx concentrations in patients with stronger AN symptoms. These changes cannot be explained by mere GM and WM volume changes, but they could be an expression of reduced neuronal and glial cell density, integrity, or function. These metabolic changes may reflect altered neurotransmission; thus, they may be related to anomalies of insula functioning that are known from functional MRI studies. This possible association should be further investigated in future combined MRS+fMRI studies. The REC and HC participants showed no differences in metabolite concentrations, which is encouraging for both patients and therapists. These data also improve our understanding of the pathophysiology of acute and recovered patients with AN, which can influence both our clinical thinking and psychoeducational interventions [87].

Author Contributions: Conceptualization, S.M., E.P., A.Z., L.T.v.E., and A.J.; data curation, S.M., A.K., L.H., and M.D.; formal analysis, A.H.; funding acquisition, A.Z. and A.J.; investigation, S.M., K.N., and A.K.; methodology, S.M., E.P., D.E., L.H., A.H., M.D., and T.L.; project administration, S.M. and A.J.; resources, A.J.; software, M.D. and T.L.; visualization, S.M.; writing—original draft, S.M. and A.K.; writing—review and editing, K.N., A.Z., L.T.v.E., D.E., D.S., and A.J. All authors have read and agreed to the published version of the manuscript.

Acknowledgments: This study was carried out as part of the study DFG (German Research Foundation) of DFG-Grant JO 744-2/1. D.E. and D.S. were supported by the Berta-Ottenstein-Program for Advanced Clinician Scientists, Faculty of Medicine, University of Freiburg. "The article processing charge was funded by the Baden-Wuerttemberg Ministry of Science, Research and Art and the University of Freiburg in the funding program Open Access Publishing.

References

1. Roux, H.; Chapelon, E.; Godart, N. Epidemiology of anorexia nervosa: A review. *Encephale* **2013**, *39*, 85–93. [CrossRef] [PubMed]
2. Smink, F.R.E.; van Hoeken, D.; Hoek, H.W. Epidemiology of Eating Disorders: Incidence, Prevalence and Mortality Rates. *Curr. Psychiatry Rep.* **2012**, *14*, 406–414. [CrossRef] [PubMed]
3. Swanson, S.A.; Crow, S.J.; Le Grange, D.; Swendsen, J.; Merikangas, K.R. Prevalence and correlates of eating disorders in adolescents. Results from the national comorbidity survey replication adolescent supplement. *Arch. Gen. Psychiatry* **2011**, *68*, 714–723. [CrossRef] [PubMed]
4. Arcelus, J.; Mitchell, A.J.; Wales, J.; Nielsen, S. Mortality rates in patients with anorexia nervosa and other eating disorders. A meta-analysis of 36 studies. *Arch. Gen. Psychiatry* **2011**, *68*, 724–731. [CrossRef]
5. Sullivan, P.F. Mortality in anorexia nervosa. *Am. J. Psychiatry* **1995**, *152*, 1073–1074.
6. Birken, D.L.; Oldendorf, W.H. N-Acetyl-L-Aspartic acid: A literature review of a compound prominent in 1H-NMR spectroscopic studies of brain. *Neurosci. Biobehav. Rev.* **1989**, *13*, 23–31. [CrossRef]
7. Baslow, M.H. Evidence supporting a role for N-acetyl-l-aspartate as a molecular water pump in myelinated neurons in the central nervous system: An analytical review. *Neurochem. Int.* **2002**, *40*, 295–300. [CrossRef]
8. Bhakoo, K.K.; Pearce, D. In Vitro Expression of N-Acetyl Aspartate by Oligodendrocytes. *J. Neurochem.* **2000**, *74*, 254–262. [CrossRef]
9. Blasel, S.; Pilatus, U.; Magerkurth, J.; Stauffenberg, M. von; Vronski, D.; Mueller, M.; Woeckel, L.; Hattingen, E. Metabolic gray matter changes of adolescents with anorexia nervosa in combined MR proton and phosphorus spectroscopy. *Neuroradiology* **2012**, *54*, 753–764. [CrossRef]
10. Castro-Fornieles, J.; Bargalló, N.; Lázaro, L.; Andrés, S.; Falcon, C.; Plana, M.T.; Junqué, C. Adolescent anorexia nervosa: Cross-sectional and follow-up frontal gray matter disturbances detected with proton magnetic resonance spectroscopy. *J. Psychiatr. Res.* **2007**, *41*, 952–958. [CrossRef]
11. Hentschel, J.; Möckel, R.; Schlemmer, H.P.; Markus, A.; Göpel, C.; Gückel, F.; Köpke, J.; Georgi, M.; Schmidt, M.H. 1H-MR spectroscopy in anorexia nervosa: The characteristic differences between patients and healthy subjects. *ROFO Fortschr. Geb. Rontgenstr. Nuklearmed.* **1999**, *170*, 284–289. [CrossRef] [PubMed]
12. Joos, A.A.B.; Perlov, E.; Büchert, M.; Hartmann, A.; Saum, B.; Glauche, V.; Freyer, T.; Weber-Fahr, W.; Zeeck, A.; Tebartz van Elst, L. Magnetic resonance spectroscopy of the anterior cingulate cortex in eating disorders. *Psychiatry Res. Neuroimag.* **2011**, *191*, 196–200. [CrossRef] [PubMed]
13. Schlemmer, H.P.; Möckel, R.; Marcus, A.; Hentschel, F.; Göpel, C.; Becker, G.; Köpke, J.; Gückel, F.; Schmidt, M.H.; Georgi, M. Proton magnetic resonance spectroscopy in acute, juvenile anorexia nervosa. *Psychiatry Res.* **1998**, *82*, 171–179. [CrossRef]
14. Braitenberg, V.; Schüz, A. Cortical Architectonics. In *Cortex: Statistics and Geometry of Neuronal Connectivity*; Springer: Berlin/Heidelberg, Germany, 1998; pp. 135–137. ISBN 978-3-662-03735-5.

15. Hasler, G.; Veen, J.W.; van der Tumonis, T.; Meyers, N.; Shen, J.; Drevets, W.C. Reduced Prefrontal Glutamate/Glutamine and γ-Aminobutyric Acid Levels in Major Depression Determined Using Proton Magnetic Resonance Spectroscopy. *Arch. Gen. Psychiatry* **2007**, *64*, 193–200. [CrossRef] [PubMed]
16. Naaijen, J.; Lythgoe, D.J.; Amiri, H.; Buitelaar, J.K.; Glennon, J.C. Fronto-striatal glutamatergic compounds in compulsive and impulsive syndromes: A review of magnetic resonance spectroscopy studies. *Neurosci. Biobehav. Rev.* **2015**, *52*, 74–88. [CrossRef]
17. Pollack, M.H.; Jensen, J.E.; Simon, N.M.; Kaufman, R.E.; Renshaw, P.F. High-field MRS study of GABA, glutamate and glutamine in social anxiety disorder: Response to treatment with levetiracetam. *Prog. Neuropsychopharmacol. Biol. Psychiatry* **2008**, *32*, 739–743. [CrossRef]
18. Yüksel, C.; Öngür, D. Magnetic resonance spectroscopy studies of glutamate-related abnormalities in mood disorders. *Biol. Psychiatry* **2010**, *68*, 785–794. [CrossRef]
19. Macrez, R.; Stys, P.K.; Vivien, D.; Lipton, S.A.; Docagne, F. Mechanisms of glutamate toxicity in multiple sclerosis: Biomarker and therapeutic opportunities. *Lancet Neurol.* **2016**, *15*, 1089–1102. [CrossRef]
20. Bartha, R.; Williamson, P.C.; Drost, D.J.; Malla, A.; Carr, T.J.; Cortese, L.; Canaran, G.; Rylett, R.J.; Neufeld, R.W.J. Measurement of Glutamate and Glutamine in the Medial Prefrontal Cortex of Never-Treated Schizophrenic Patients and Healthy Controls by Proton Magnetic Resonance Spectroscopy. *Arch. Gen. Psychiatry* **1997**, *54*, 959–965. [CrossRef]
21. Ohrmann, P.; Kersting, A.; Suslow, T.; Lalee-Mentzel, J.; Donges, U.-S.; Fiebich, M.; Arolt, V.; Heindel, W.; Pfleiderer, B. Proton magnetic resonance spectroscopy in anorexia nervosa: Correlations with cognition. *Neuroreport* **2004**, *15*, 549–553. [CrossRef]
22. Godlewska, B.R.; Pike, A.; Sharpley, A.L.; Ayton, A.; Park, R.J.; Cowen, P.J.; Emir, U.E. Brain glutamate in anorexia nervosa: A magnetic resonance spectroscopy case control study at 7 Tesla. *Psychopharmacology* **2017**, *234*, 421–426. [CrossRef] [PubMed]
23. Plitman, E.; de la Fuente-Sandoval, C.; Reyes-Madrigal, F.; Chavez, S.; Gómez-Cruz, G.; León-Ortiz, P.; Graff-Guerrero, A. Elevated Myo-Inositol, Choline, and Glutamate Levels in the Associative Striatum of Antipsychotic-Naive Patients With First-Episode Psychosis: A Proton Magnetic Resonance Spectroscopy Study With Implications for Glial Dysfunction. *Schizophr. Bull.* **2015**, *42*, 415–424. [CrossRef] [PubMed]
24. Baek, H.-M.; Chen, J.-H.; Nalcioglu, O.; Su, M.-Y. Choline as a Biomarker for Cell Proliferation: Do the Results from Proton MR Spectroscopy Show Difference between HER2/neu Positive and Negative Breast Cancers? *Int. J. Cancer J. Int. Cancer* **2008**, *123*, 1219–1221. [CrossRef]
25. Castro-Fornieles, J.; Garcia, A.I.; Lazaro, L.; Andrés-Perpiñá, S.; Falcón, C.; Plana, M.T.; Bargallo, N. Prefrontal brain metabolites in short-term weight-recovered adolescent anorexia nervosa patients. *Prog. Neuropsychopharmacol. Biol. Psychiatry* **2010**, *34*, 1049–1053. [CrossRef] [PubMed]
26. Wyss, M.; Kaddurah-Daouk, R. Creatine and Creatinine Metabolism. *Physiol. Rev.* **2000**, *80*, 1107–1213. [CrossRef]
27. Soares, D.P.; Law, M. Magnetic resonance spectroscopy of the brain: Review of metabolites and clinical applications. *Clin. Radiol.* **2009**, *64*, 12–21. [CrossRef]
28. Roser, W.; Bubl, R.; Buergin, D.; Seelig, J.; Radue, E.W.; Rost, B. Metabolic changes in the brain of patients with anorexia and bulimia nervosa as detected by proton magnetic resonance spectroscopy. *Int. J. Eat. Disord.* **1999**, *26*, 119–136. [CrossRef]
29. Kato, T.; Shioiri, T.; Murashita, J.; Inubushi, T. Phosphorus-31 magnetic resonance spectroscopic observations in 4 cases with anorexia nervosa. *Prog. Neuropsychopharmacol. Biol. Psychiatry* **1997**, *21*, 719–724. [CrossRef]
30. Möckel, R.; Schlemmer, H.P.; Gückel, F.; Göpel, C.; Becker, G.; Köpke, J.; Hentschel, F.; Schmidt, M.; Georgi, M. 1H-MR spectroscopy in anorexia nervosa: Reversible cerebral metabolic changes. *ROFO Fortschr. Geb. Rontgenstr. Nuklearmed.* **1999**, *170*, 371–377. [CrossRef]
31. Rzanny, R.; Freesmeyer, D.; Reichenbach, J.R.; Mentzel, H.J.; Pfleiderer, S.O.R.; Klemm, S.; Gerhard, U.J.; Blanz, B.; Kaiser, W.A. 31P-MR spectroscopy of the brain in patients with anorexia nervosa: Characteristic differences in the spectra between patients and healthy control subjects. *ROFO Fortschr. Geb. Rontgenstr. Nuklearmed.* **2003**, *175*, 75–82. [CrossRef]
32. Grzelak, P.; Gajewicz, W.; Wyszogrodzka-Kucharska, A.; Rotkiewicz, A.; Stefańczyk, L.; Góraj, B.; Rabe-Jabłońska, J. Brain metabolism alterations in patients with anorexia nervosa observed in 1H-MRS. *Psychiatr. Pol.* **2005**, *39*, 761–771. [PubMed]

33. Bomba, M.; Riva, A.; Morzenti, S.; Grimaldi, M.; Neri, F.; Nacinovich, R. Global and regional brain volumes normalization in weight-recovered adolescents with anorexia nervosa: Preliminary findings of a longitudinal voxel-based morphometry study. *Neuropsychiatr. Dis. Treat.* **2015**, *11*, 637–645. [CrossRef] [PubMed]
34. Brooks, S.J.; Barker, G.J.; O'Daly, O.G.; Brammer, M.; Williams, S.C.; Benedict, C.; Schiöth, H.B.; Treasure, J.; Campbell, I.C. Restraint of appetite and reduced regional brain volumes in anorexia nervosa: A voxel-based morphometric study. *BMC Psychiatry* **2011**, *11*, 179. [CrossRef] [PubMed]
35. Frank, G.K.W.; Shott, M.E.; Hagman, J.O.; Yang, T.T. Localized Brain Volume and White Matter Integrity Alterations in Adolescent Anorexia Nervosa. *J. Am. Acad. Child Adolesc. Psychiatry* **2013**, *52*, 1066–1075. [CrossRef] [PubMed]
36. Friederich, H.-C.; Walther, S.; Bendszus, M.; Biller, A.; Thomann, P.; Zeigermann, S.; Katus, T.; Brunner, R.; Zastrow, A.; Herzog, W. Grey matter abnormalities within cortico-limbic-striatal circuits in acute and weight-restored anorexia nervosa patients. *NeuroImage* **2012**, *59*, 1106–1113. [CrossRef] [PubMed]
37. Wagner, A.; Greer, P.; Bailer, U.F.; Frank, G.K.; Henry, S.E.; Putnam, K.; Meltzer, C.C.; Ziolko, S.K.; Hoge, J.; McConaha, C.; et al. Normal Brain Tissue Volumes after Long-Term Recovery in Anorexia and Bulimia Nervosa. *Biol. Psychiatry* **2006**, *59*, 291–293. [CrossRef] [PubMed]
38. Kerr, K.L.; Moseman, S.E.; Avery, J.A.; Bodurka, J.; Zucker, N.L.; Simmons, W.K. Altered Insula Activity during Visceral Interoception in Weight-Restored Patients with Anorexia Nervosa. *Neuropsychopharmacology* **2016**, *41*, 521–528. [CrossRef]
39. Kim, K.R.; Ku, J.; Lee, J.-H.; Lee, H.; Jung, Y.-C. Functional and effective connectivity of anterior insula in anorexia nervosa and bulimia nervosa. *Neurosci. Lett.* **2012**, *521*, 152–157. [CrossRef]
40. Oberndorfer, T.; Simmons, A.; McCurdy, D.; Strigo, I.; Matthews, S.; Yang, T.; Irvine, Z.; Kaye, W. Greater anterior insula activation during anticipation of food images in women recovered from anorexia nervosa versus controls. *Psychiatry Res. Neuroimag.* **2013**, *214*, 132–141. [CrossRef]
41. Strigo, I.A.; Matthews, S.C.; Simmons, A.N.; Oberndorfer, T.; Klabunde, M.; Reinhardt, L.E.; Kaye, W.H. Altered insula activation during pain anticipation in individuals recovered from anorexia nervosa: Evidence of interoceptive dysregulation. *Int. J. Eat. Disord.* **2013**, *46*, 23–33. [CrossRef]
42. Nunn, K.; Frampton, I.; Gordon, I.; Lask, B. The fault is not in her parents but in her insula—A neurobiological hypothesis of anorexia nervosa. *Eur. Eat. Disord. Rev. J. Eat. Disord. Assoc.* **2008**, *16*, 355–360. [CrossRef] [PubMed]
43. Nunn, K.; Frampton, I.; Fuglset, T.S.; Törzsök-Sonnevend, M.; Lask, B. Anorexia nervosa and the insula. *Med. Hypotheses* **2011**, *76*, 353–357. [CrossRef]
44. Craig, A.D.B. How do you feel now? The anterior insula and human awareness. *Nat. Rev. Neurosci.* **2009**, *10*, 59–70. [CrossRef] [PubMed]
45. Craig, A.D. Interoception: The sense of the physiological condition of the body. *Curr. Opin. Neurobiol.* **2003**, *13*, 500–505. [CrossRef]
46. Paulus, M.P.; Stein, M.B. An insular view of anxiety. *Biol. Psychiatry* **2006**, *60*, 383–387. [CrossRef]
47. Mazzola, L.; Royet, J.-P.; Catenoix, H.; Montavont, A.; Isnard, J.; Mauguière, F. Gustatory and olfactory responses to stimulation of the human insula. *Ann. Neurol.* **2017**, *82*, 360–370. [CrossRef]
48. Small, D.M. Taste representation in the human insula. *Brain Struct. Funct.* **2010**, *214*, 551–561. [CrossRef]
49. Haase, L.; Cerf-Ducastel, B.; Murphy, C. Cortical activation in response to pure taste stimuli during the physiological states of hunger and satiety. *NeuroImage* **2009**, *44*, 1008–1021. [CrossRef]
50. Pujol, J.; Blanco-Hinojo, L.; Coronas, R.; Esteba-Castillo, S.; Rigla, M.; Martínez-Vilavella, G.; Deus, J.; Novell, R.; Caixàs, A. Mapping the sequence of brain events in response to disgusting food: Brain Response to Disgusting Food. *Hum. Brain Mapp.* **2018**, *39*, 369–380. [CrossRef]
51. Critchley, H.D.; Harrison, N.A. Visceral Influences on Brain and Behavior. *Neuron* **2013**, *77*, 624–638. [CrossRef]
52. Kaye, W.H.; Fudge, J.L.; Paulus, M. New insights into symptoms and neurocircuit function of anorexia nervosa. *Nat. Rev. Neurosci.* **2009**, *10*, 573–584. [CrossRef] [PubMed]
53. Fydrich, T.; Renneberg, B.; Schmitz, B.; Wittchen, H.U. *SKID-II. Strukturiertes Klinisches Interview für DSM-IV. Achse II: Persönlichkeitsstörungen, Interviewheft*; Hogrefe: Gottingen, Germany, 1997.
54. Wittchen, H.U.; Zaudig, M.; Fydrich, T. *SKID. Strukturiertes Klinisches Interview für DSM-IV. Achse I und II, Handanweisung*; Hogrefe: Gottingen, Germany, 1997.

55. American Psychiatric Association. *The Diagnostic and Statistical Manual of Mental Disorders: DSM 5*; American Psychiatric Publishing: Arlington, TX, USA, 2013.
56. Couturier, J.; Lock, J. What is remission in adolescent anorexia nervosa? A review of various conceptualizations and quantitative analysis. *Int. J. Eat. Disord.* **2006**, *39*, 175–183. [CrossRef] [PubMed]
57. Hilbert, A.; Tuschen-Caffier, B.; Karwautz, A.; Niederhofer, H.; Munsch, S. Eating Disorder Examination-Questionnaire. *Diagnostica* **2007**, *53*, 144–154. [CrossRef]
58. Hilbert, A.; Tuschen-Caffier, B.; Ohms, M. Eating Disorder Examination: Deutschsprachige Version des strukturierten Essstörungsinterviews. *Diagnostica* **2004**, *50*, 98–106. [CrossRef]
59. Garner, D.M. *Eating Disorder Inventory-2*; Psychological Assessment Resources: Odessa, TX, USA, 1991.
60. Meermann, R.; Napierski, C.; Schulenkorf, E. *Eating Disorder Inventory (German Version)*; Walter de Gruyter: Berlin, Germany, 1987.
61. Hautzinger, M.; Keller, F.; Kühner, C. *Beck Depressions-Inventar (BDI-II)*; Harcourt Test Services: Frankfurt, Germany, 2006.
62. Beck, A.T.; Steer, R.A. *Beck Depression Inventory*; The Psychological Corporation: San Antonio, TX, USA, 1987.
63. Herzberg, P.; Goldschmidt, S.; Heinrichs, N. Beck Depressions-Inventar (BDI-II). *Revis. Rep. Psychol.* **2008**, *33*, 301–302.
64. Provencher, S.W. Estimation of metabolite concentrations from localized in vivo proton NMR spectra. *Magn. Reason. Med.* **1993**, *30*, 672–679. [CrossRef]
65. Provencher, S.W. Automatic quantitation of localized in vivo 1H spectra with LCModel. *NMR Biomed.* **2001**, *14*, 260–264. [CrossRef]
66. Endres, D.; Perlov, E.; Maier, S.; Feige, B.; Nickel, K.; Goll, P.; Bubl, E.; Lange, T.; Glauche, V.; Graf, E.; et al. Normal Neurochemistry in the Prefrontal and Cerebellar Brain of Adults with Attention-Deficit Hyperactivity Disorder. *Front. Behav. Neurosci.* **2015**, *9*, 242. [CrossRef]
67. Friston, K.J. *Statistical Parametric Mapping: The Analysis of Functional Brain Images*; Elsevier: Amsterdam, The Netherlands, 2008.
68. R Core Team. *R: A Language and Environment for Statistical Computing*; R Foundation for Statistical Computing: Vienna, Austria, 2016.
69. Todorov, V.; Filzmoser, P. Robust statistic for the one-way MANOVA. *Comput. Stat. Data Anal.* **2010**, *54*, 37–48. [CrossRef]
70. Todorov, V.; Filzmoser, P. An Object-Oriented Framework for Robust Multivariate Analysis. *J. Stat. Softw.* **2009**. [CrossRef]
71. Wilcox, R.R. *Introduction to Robust Estimation and Hypothesis Testing*; Academic Press: Cambridge, MA, USA, 2011.
72. Schoenbrodt, F.; Wilcox, R. *WRS2: Wilcox Robust Estimation and Testing*; Version 0.9; R Core Team: Vienna, Austria, 2017.
73. Wilcox, R.R.; Tian, T.S. Measuring effect size: A robust heteroscedastic approach for two or more groups. *J. Appl. Stat.* **2011**, *38*, 1359–1368. [CrossRef]
74. Benjamini, Y.; Hochberg, Y. Controlling the False Discovery Rate: A Practical and Powerful Approach to Multiple Testing. *J. R. Stat. Soc. Ser. B Methodol.* **1995**, *57*, 289–300. [CrossRef]
75. Bang, L.; Rø, Ø.; Endestad, T. Normal gray matter volumes in women recovered from anorexia nervosa: A voxel-based morphometry study. *BMC Psychiatry* **2016**, *16*, 144. [CrossRef] [PubMed]
76. Fuglset, T.S.; Endestad, T.; Hilland, E.; Bang, L.; Tamnes, C.K.; Landrø, N.I.; Rø, Ø. Brain volumes and regional cortical thickness in young females with anorexia nervosa. *BMC Psychiatry* **2016**, *16*, 404. [CrossRef] [PubMed]
77. King, J.A.; Geisler, D.; Ritschel, F.; Boehm, I.; Seidel, M.; Roschinski, B.; Soltwedel, L.; Zwipp, J.; Pfuhl, G.; Marxen, M.; et al. Global cortical thinning in acute anorexia nervosa normalizes following long-term weight restoration. *Biol. Psychiatry* **2015**, *77*, 624–632. [CrossRef]
78. Nickel, K.; Joos, A.; Elst, L.T.; van Matthis, J.; Holovics, L.; Endres, D.; Zeeck, A.; Hartmann, A.; Tüscher, O.; Maier, S. Recovery of cortical volume and thickness after remission from acute anorexia nervosa. *Int. J. Eat. Disord.* **2018**, *51*, 1056–1069. [CrossRef]
79. Lavagnino, L.; Amianto, F.; Mwangi, B.; D'Agata, F.; Spalatro, A.; Zunta Soares, G.B.; Daga, G.A.; Mortara, P.; Fassino, S.; Soares, J.C. The relationship between cortical thickness and body mass index differs between women with anorexia nervosa and healthy controls. *Psychiatry Res. Neuroimag.* **2016** *248*, 105–109. [CrossRef]

80. Yan, H.-D.; Ishihara, K.; Serikawa, T.; Sasa, M. Activation by N-Acetyl-l-Aspartate of Acutely Dissociated Hippocampal Neurons in Rats via Metabotropic Glutamate Receptors. *Epilepsia* **2003**, *44*, 1153–1159. [CrossRef]
81. Reiner, A.; Levitz, J. Glutamatergic Signaling in the Central Nervous System: Ionotropic and Metabotropic Receptors in Concert. *Neuron* **2018**, *98*, 1080–1098. [CrossRef]
82. Hogeveen, J.; Bird, G.; Chau, A.; Krueger, F.; Grafman, J. Acquired alexithymia following damage to the anterior insula. *Neuropsychologia* **2016**, *82*, 142–148. [CrossRef]
83. Lázaro, L.; Andrés, S.; Calvo, A.; Cullell, C.; Moreno, E.; Plana, M.T.; Falcón, C.; Bargalló, N.; Castro-Fornieles, J. Normal gray and white matter volume after weight restoration in adolescents with anorexia nervosa. *Int. J. Eat. Disord.* **2013**, *46*, 841–848. [CrossRef] [PubMed]
84. Maier, S.; Schneider, K.; Stark, C.; Zeeck, A.; Tebartz van Elst, L.; Holovics, L.; Hartmann, A.; Lahmann, C.; Domschke, K.; Nickel, K.; et al. Fear Network Unresponsiveness in Women with Anorexia Nervosa. *Psychother. Psychosom.* **2018**. [CrossRef] [PubMed]
85. Leppanen, J.; Cardi, V.; Paloyelis, Y.; Simmons, A.; Tchanturia, K.; Treasure, J. Blunted neural response to implicit negative facial affect in anorexia nervosa. *Biol. Psychol.* **2017**, *128*, 105–111. [CrossRef] [PubMed]
86. Croarkin, P.E.; Thomas, M.A.; Port, J.D.; Baruth, J.M.; Choi, D.-S.; Abulseoud, O.A.; Frye, M.A. N-acetylaspartate normalization in bipolar depression after lamotrigine treatment. *Bipolar Disord.* **2015**, *17*, 450–457. [CrossRef]
87. Bang, L.; Treasure, J.; Rø, Ø.; Joos, A. Advancing our understanding of the neurobiology of anorexia nervosa: Translation into treatment. *J. Eat. Disord.* **2017**, *5*, 38. [CrossRef]

12

Obesity Stigma: Is the 'Food Addiction' Label Feeding the Problem?

Helen K. Ruddock [1,2], Michael Orwin [1,3], Emma J. Boyland [1], Elizabeth H. Evans [3] and Charlotte A. Hardman [1,*]

1 Department of Psychological Sciences, University of Liverpool, Liverpool L69 7ZX, UK
2 School of Psychology, University of Birmingham, Birmingham B15 2TT, UK
3 School of Psychology, Newcastle University, Newcastle NE1 7RU, UK
* Correspondence: charlotte.hardman@liverpool.ac.uk

Abstract: Obesity is often attributed to an addiction to high-calorie foods. However, the effect of "food addiction" explanations on weight-related stigma remains unclear. In two online studies, participants (n = 439, n = 523, respectively, recruited from separate samples) read a vignette about a target female who was described as 'very overweight'. Participants were randomly allocated to one of three conditions which differed in the information provided in the vignette: (1) in the "medical condition", the target had been diagnosed with food addiction by her doctor; (2) in the "self-diagnosed condition", the target believed herself to be a food addict; (3) in the control condition, there was no reference to food addiction. Participants then completed questionnaires measuring target-specific stigma (i.e., stigma towards the female described in the vignette), general stigma towards obesity (both studies), addiction-like eating behavior and causal beliefs about addiction (Study 2 only). In Study 1, participants in the medical and self-diagnosed food addiction conditions demonstrated greater target-specific stigma relative to the control condition. In Study 2, participants in the medical condition had greater target-specific stigma than the control condition but only those with low levels of addiction-like eating behavior. There was no effect of condition on general weight-based stigma in either study. These findings suggest that the food addiction label may increase stigmatizing attitudes towards a person with obesity, particularly within individuals with low levels of addiction-like eating behavior.

Keywords: food addiction; obesity; stigma; eating behavior; attitudes

---

1. Introduction

According to recent statistics, more than one-third of the world's population is overweight or obesity. In the UK, these rates are even higher, with 64% of adults classed as having overweight or obesity [1]. Despite its prevalence, people with obesity frequently experience devaluation and discrimination (known as weight-related stigma) within educational, workplace, and healthcare settings [2]. Evidence also suggests that people may be more likely to face discrimination because of their weight than because of their ethnicity, gender, or sexual orientation [3]. Weight-related stigma has negative consequences for individuals' psychological and physical well-being [2,4,5] and may impede weight-loss by prompting maladaptive eating patterns and exercise avoidance [2].

Negative attitudes towards people with obesity can be exacerbated by beliefs about the *causes* of weight-gain. This is central to attribution theory, which suggests that people make judgements about the cause of a condition; in turn, these judgements determine their attitudes towards an individual [6,7]. For example, attributing obesity to factors that are within personal control (e.g., food choices) is thought to perpetuate obesity stigma [8]. Conversely, stigmatizing attitudes may be attenuated by the belief that weight-gain is caused by uncontrollable factors (e.g., genetics). In support of this, weight-related stigma was found to be most prevalent amongst individuals who believed that obesity was within personal control and caused by a lack of willpower, inactivity, and overeating [9,10]. Similar findings have been obtained from studies in which participants' causal beliefs about obesity were experimentally manipulated. Specifically, participants who read an article that stated that obesity is caused by overeating and a lack of exercise demonstrated more stigmatizing attitudes than participants in a 'no-prime' control condition or those who read a neutral article about research into memory skills [11,12]. Conversely, participants who were led to believe that obesity is caused by physiological factors (i.e., factors that are beyond personal control) demonstrated less weight-related stigma than those in a control condition [8,13].

One increasingly prevalent etiological theory is that obesity is caused by an addiction to high-calorie foods [14]. Proponents of this idea suggest that food and drugs have similar effects on the brain and argue that the clinical symptoms of substance abuse coincide with the behaviors and experiences of people who engage in compulsive overeating [15,16]. While this idea is widely debated throughout the scientific community (e.g., [17–19]), the concept of food addiction has been readily accepted by the general public [20]. Indeed, research suggests that the majority of people believe that obesity can be caused by food addiction [21], and up to half of people believe that they are themselves addicted to food [22–24]. In light of its popularity, it is important to establish how food addiction models of obesity might affect weight-related stigma.

A small number of studies have examined the effect of the food addiction label on obesity stigma. However, results to date have been inconsistent [25,26]. In one study [27], participants' attitudes towards a person with 'food addiction' were compared with attitudes towards persons with obesity, drug addiction, and disability. The study reported similarly high levels of stigma towards the "obese" and "food addict" labels and, when combined, these labels together elicited greater stigma than either label alone. These findings align with those obtained by Lee et al. [21] who found that, while the majority (72%) of survey respondents believed that obesity could be caused by a 'food addiction', more than half held the view that people with obesity are responsible for their condition (which would be expected to perpetuate obesity stigma). However, in contrast, Latner et al. [28] found that providing a food addiction explanation for obesity appeared to *reduce* weight-stigma. In this study, participants read one of two descriptions of a woman with obesity. In one condition (i.e., the 'food addiction' condition), the woman was described as fitting "the typical profile of someone who is addicted to food". In another condition (i.e., the 'non-addiction' condition), the woman was described as "someone who makes unhealthy food choices". The study found that participants in the food addiction condition displayed lower levels of stigma towards the woman, and towards people with obesity more generally, compared with those in the non-addiction condition.

Inconsistent findings in previous studies may be explained by differences in participants' causal beliefs about food addiction. Specifically, the effect of the "food addiction" label on obesity stigma may depend on the extent to which food addiction is perceived to be a legitimate medical condition. One qualitative study found that people with overweight and obesity were reluctant to label themselves as a food addict due to concerns that this would be viewed as an 'excuse' for overeating [29]. Indeed, providing excuses for weight gain may exacerbate negative attitudes towards those with obesity [30]. In contrast, attributing obesity to a medically diagnosed 'food addiction' may legitimize the condition and help to reduce weight-related stigma by removing personal responsibility from the individual [31,32].

To test these ideas, across two studies, we examined the effect of medically-diagnosed and self-diagnosed food addiction on weight-related stigma. Using a similar technique to Latner et al. [28], participants read one of three vignettes which described a woman with obesity. In the 'medical' condition, the vignette stated that the woman had been diagnosed with food addiction by her general practitioner (GP). In the 'self-diagnosed' condition, the vignette stated that the woman believed herself to be a food addict. There was no reference to food addiction in the control condition. Subsequent attitudes towards the woman (i.e., target-specific stigma) and obesity in general (i.e., general stigma) were then assessed. We hypothesized that weight-related stigma would be significantly lower in the medical condition, and higher in the self-diagnosed condition, relative to in the control condition. Based on previous findings [28], we predicted that the food addiction label would influence both target-specific and general weight-related stigma.

2. Study 1 Method

2.1. Participants

Female participants were invited to take part in a study into 'perceptions of employability among students'. Participants were recruited via social media advertisements and on internal webpages at the University of Liverpool, UK. Participants who were enrolled in the Psychology degree program at the University received course credits in exchange for taking part. A total of 440 participants completed the survey (533 participants started the study, but 93 did not complete all of the measures and so were excluded from analyses). To be eligible to take part, participants were required to be aged over 18 years old. The majority of participants were students (81%), and 90% of the sample were Caucasian. The mean age of participants was 21.2 y (SD = 7.1), and the mean self-reported body mass index (BMI) was 22.2 kg/m^2 (SD = 3.4). Participants with a self-reported BMI over 30 kg/m^2 (i.e., classified as having obesity) comprised 2.7% of the sample, 12.5% had a self-reported BMI between 25–29.9 kg/m^2 (i.e., 'overweight'), 76.8% had a self-reported BMI between 18.5–24.9 kg/m^2 (i.e., healthy weight), and 8.0% had a BMI below 18.5 kg/m^2 (i.e., 'underweight'). Participants provided informed consent prior to completing the study. Ethical approval was granted by the University of Liverpool's ethics committee (approval code: IPHS-1516-SMc-259-Generic RETH000619).

2.2. Procedure

The study was delivered via the online survey platform, Qualtrics (Qualtrics, Provo, UT, USA). Participants were asked to read an information sheet and, if they wished to continue with the study, were required to tick a consent box. On the first screen of the survey, a picture of a woman with obesity ("Paulina") was displayed, along with a short vignette which described her hobbies, family, and education (see online supplementary material). Paulina was also described as being 'very overweight'. Participants were randomly allocated to view one of three versions of the vignette: (1) In the 'medical' condition, the vignette stated that Paulina's "GP had recently diagnosed her as having a food addiction"; (2) in the 'self-diagnosed' condition, the vignette stated that Paulina "believes herself to be addicted to food"; (3) in the 'control' condition, there was no mention of food addiction. After reading the vignette, participants completed the measures in the following order: Modified Fat-Phobia Scale (M-FPS) (to assess target-specific stigma towards Paulina), employability questionnaire (included as part of the cover story), Anti-fat Attitudes (AFA; to assess general stigma towards people with obesity), and the Dutch Eating Behavior Questionnaire (DEBQ; to assess external, restrained, and emotional eating behavior). Participants were then asked to indicate their gender, age, ethnicity, occupation, and height and weight (which were used to calculate BMI). They then completed the item about self-perceived food addiction. After completing the study, participants read a debrief sheet which explained the true aim of the study.

2.3. Measures

2.3.1. Target Specific Stigma: Modified Fat-Phobia Scale (M-FPS)

The 14-item Fat Phobia Scale [33] was modified such that participants were asked to indicate their beliefs about a fictional individual named Paulina (Paulina was the name of the target female featured in the vignette. See Section 2.2). This scale consists of 14 pairs of antonyms which could be used to describe individuals with obesity (e.g., 'lazy' vs. 'industrious'). Higher scores on the M-FPS (i.e., indicative of more negative attitudes) have been positively associated with beliefs that obesity is within personal control [9]. Participants were required to indicate their perceptions of Paulina by selecting one of five points between each pair of words. A mean score was calculated for each participant. Higher scores on this measure indicated more negative attitudes towards Paulina. In the current sample, the internal reliability of the M-FPS was high (Cronbach's $\alpha = 0.834$).

2.3.2. General Stigma: Anti-fat Attitudes (AFA)

The AFA [8] consists of 13 items which assess stigmatizing attitudes toward individuals with obesity (e.g., "I dislike people who are overweight or obese"). Responses are provided on a 9-point scale ranging from 'Very strongly disagree' to 'Very strongly agree' (in Study 1, a 5-point Likert scale was used, but this was corrected to a 9-point scale in Study 2). Higher scores indicate stronger anti-fat attitudes. The scale comprises three subscales which assess dislike (i.e., obesity stigma), willpower (i.e., beliefs about weight controllability), and fear of fat (i.e., concerns about personal weight gain) (Cronbach's $\alpha = 0.796$).

2.3.3. Dutch Eating Behavior Scale (DEBQ)

The DEBQ [34] consists of 33 items which assess eating behavior. The scale comprises three subscales assessing Restrained Eating (DEBQ-R; 10 items), Emotional Eating (DEBQ-EM; 13 items), and External Eating (DEBQ-EX; 10-items). Previous research has demonstrated the ability of the DEBQ to predict restrictive eating tendencies [35], eating in response to external food-cues [36], and stress-induced eating [37]. Responses are recorded on a 5-point Likert-type scale ranging from 'Never' to 'Very often'. Higher scores indicate greater restrained, emotional, or external eating. The DEBQ was included to ensure that participants did not differ, between conditions, with regards to their eating behavior. The internal reliability for each of the subscales was high (DEBQ-R: Cronbach's $\alpha = 0.933$; DEBQ-EX: Cronbach's $\alpha = 0.869$; DEBQ-EM Cronbach's $\alpha = 0.932$).

2.3.4. Self-Perceived Food Addiction (SPFA)

To assess whether or not participants believed themselves to be a food addict, participants were presented with the statement "I believe myself to be a food addict" with response options "Yes" or "No". Similar measures have been used in previous research, and positive responses on this assessment have been associated with greater food reward, overeating [23,38], and fear of being stigmatized by others [22].

2.3.5. Employability Questions

For consistency with the study's cover story, seven items were included which assessed participants' beliefs about Paulina's employability (e.g., How likely would you be to employ Paulina?). Responses were recorded using Visual Analogue Scales (VAS) ranging from 0 (not at all) to 100 (extremely). Higher scores indicated more positive attitudes towards Paulina's employability. Analyses of the effect of condition on employability ratings are presented in the supplementary materials.

2.4. Data Analysis

A MANOVA was conducted to check whether participants differed between conditions on age, BMI, and DEBQ subscale scores. Chi-squared tests were conducted to check for any differences between the proportion of students/non-students and Caucasian/non-Caucasian participants allocated to each condition. To examine the effect of condition on target-specific and general stigma, two ANOVAs were conducted with the condition (i.e., control, medical, self-diagnosed) as the independent variable, and M-FPS (i.e., target specific stigma) and AFA (i.e., general stigma) scores as dependent variables. Where significant main effects were identified, these were followed up by inspecting pairwise comparisons.

We conducted exploratory analyses to examine whether self-reported BMI moderated the effect of condition on mean Modified Fat Phobia Scale (M-FPS) and Anti-Fat Attitudes (AFA) scores. To do this, we conducted two hierarchical multiple linear regression to examine the relative contributions of BMI (centered) and condition to mean M-FPS scores and AFA scores. All three conditions were dummy coded with the Control condition as the reference variable. To assign dummy codes, two dummy variables were created: D_1 (Medical) and D_2 (Self-diagnosed). Participants in the medical condition were assigned '1' to D_1, and '0' for D_2. Participants in the self-diagnosed condition were assigned '0' to D_1 and 1 to D_2. Participants in the control condition (i.e., the reference category) were assigned 0 to both D_1 and D_2. (see [39] for more information about dummy coding). Dummy-coded conditions were then entered into Step 1 of each regression model, along with BMI. The interaction terms (i.e., BMI × medical vs. control/self-diagnosed vs. control) were entered into Step 2 of the model.

Additional exploratory analyses were conducted to examine whether the effect of condition on target-specific and general stigma was moderated by participants' age or DEBQ subscales. Further details and results from these analyses are provided in the supplementary materials.

3. Results

3.1. Participant Characteristics

The MANOVA revealed that BMI differed significantly between conditions, $F(2,434) = 4.80$, $p = 0.009$, $\eta p^2 = 0.022$. This was due to a higher mean BMI in the medical condition relative to the self-diagnosed condition ($p = 0.002$). Participant characteristics as a function of condition are displayed in Table 1. Participants did not differ with regards to age or scores on DEBQ-subscales. Chi-squared tests (X^2) revealed no difference in the proportion of students/non-students and Caucasian/non-Caucasian participants in each condition.

Table 1. Participant characteristics as a function of condition.

Variable	Medical ($N = 148$)	Self-Diagnosed ($N = 144$)	Control ($N = 146$)	Between-Group Differences
Age (y)	21.09 (±6.44)	21.07 (±7.45)	21.38 (±7.32)	$F(2,435) = 0.09$, $p = 0.916$
BMI (kg/m^2)	22.60 (±3.22) *	21.60 (±2.95) *	22.04 (±2.93)	$F(2,432) = 3.64$, $p = 0.027$
DEBQ-Restraint	2.94 (±0.96)	2.72 (±0.90)	2.89 (±0.86)	$F(2,436) = 2.38$, $p = 0.094$
DEBQ-Emotion	2.97 (±0.90)	2.80 (±0.90)	2.84 (±0.86)	$F(2,436) = 1.43$, $p = 0.240$
DEBQ-External	3.34 (±0.69)	3.21 (±0.59)	3.35 (±0.71)	$F(2,436) = 1.95$, $p = 0.143$
Ethnicity (% Caucasian)	93.3	91.0	86.4	$X^2(2) = 4.12$, $p = 0.127$
Occupation (% students)	83.2	83.3	81.6	$X^2(2) = 0.186$, $p = 0.911$

Results are means (standard deviations) unless otherwise specified (* significant difference, $p < 0.05$).

3.2. Effect of Condition on Target-Specific and General Stigma

There was a main effect of condition on mean Modified Fat Phobia Scale (M-FPS) score (i.e., target-specific stigma), $F(2,437) = 9.07$, $p < 0.001$, $\eta p^2 = 0.040$. Pairwise comparisons revealed that, compared to those in the control condition, M-FPS scores were higher in the medical ($p < 0.001$) and self-diagnosed ($p = 0.001$) conditions (Figure 1) (Control condition: Mean = 3.47, SD = 0.47, range = 2.29–4.71; Self-diagnosed: Mean = 3.66, SD = 0.48, range = 2.71–4.93; Medical: Mean = 3.68, SD = 0.52, range = 1.00–5.00). There was no difference in mean M-FPS scores between those in the medical and self-diagnosed conditions ($p = 0.730$). There was no effect of condition on Anti-Fat Attitudes (AFA) total scores (i.e., general stigma), $F(2,437) = 0.754$, $p = 0.471$, (Control condition: Mean = 1.78, SD = 0.56, range = 0.31–3.46; Self-diagnosed: Mean = 1.71, SD = 0.56, range = 0.23–3.00; Medical: Mean = 1.72, SD = 0.56, range = 0.38–3.38).

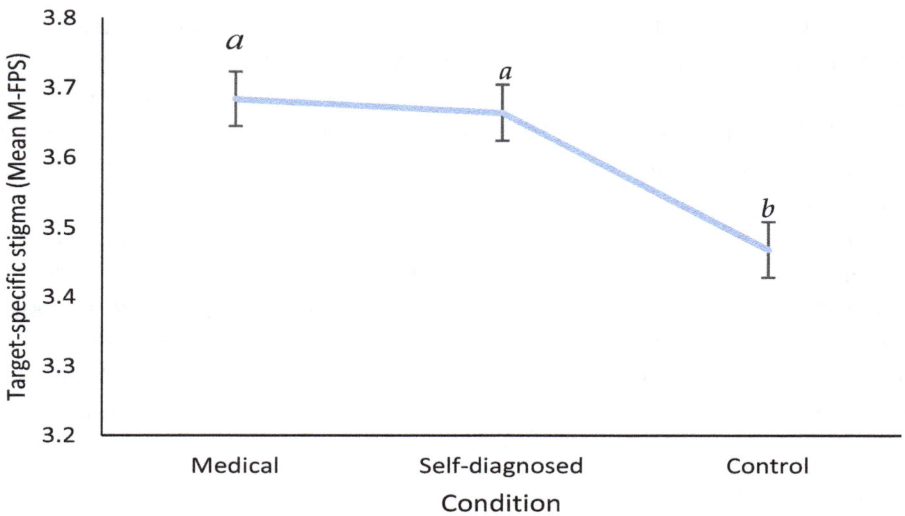

Figure 1. Mean Modified Fat Phobia Scale (M-FPS) scores (i.e., target specific stigma) as a function of condition. Different letters indicate significant differences. Higher scores indicate more negative attitudes towards Paulina (i.e., higher levels of target-specific stigma). Error bars denote standard error.

3.3. Moderating Effect of BMI

Hierarchical linear regression analyses were conducted to examine whether BMI moderated the effect of condition on target-specific (i.e., M-FPS scores) and general (AFA scores) stigma. Results from the exploratory analysis predicting M-FPS scores are provided in Table 2. In Step 1 and Step 2 of the model, M-FPS scores were significantly predicted by both condition (medical vs. control and self-diagnosed vs. control) and BMI; higher BMI was associated with lower M-FPS scores. However, M-FPS scores were not significantly predicted by the BMI × Condition interaction terms in Step 2 of the model.

Neither BMI nor condition predicted AFA scores in Step 1 of the model ($r^2 = 0.005$, $p = 0.510$), and the inclusion of interaction terms in Step 2 did significantly improve the fit of the model $r^2 = 0.015$, $p = 0.124$).

Table 2. Regression output with mean M-FPS (i.e., target-specific stigma) as the dependent variable.

Model	B	SE	*t*	*p*
Step 1				
BMI	−0.015 *	0.007	−2.119	0.035
Medical	0.230 **	0.056	4.109	<0.001
Self-diagnosed	0.189 **	0.056	3.360	0.001
Step 2				
BMI	−0.034 *	0.013	−2.547	0.011
Medical	0.223 **	0.056	3.992	<0.001
Self-diagnosed	0.190 **	0.056	3.360	0.001
BMI × Medical	0.031	0.017	1.816	0.070
BMI × Self-diagnosed	0.019	0.019	0.980	0.327

* $p < 0.05$, ** $p < 0.01$. Step 1: $r^2 = 0.051$, $p < 0.001$; Step 2: $r^2 = 0.058$, $p = 0.194$

4. Interim Discussion

Study 1 found that female participants who were exposed to medical and self-diagnosed food addiction vignettes exhibited more target-specific stigma towards a woman with obesity than those in the control condition. This is consistent with previous research in which the food addiction label was found to exacerbate stigmatizing attitudes towards an individual with obesity and 'food addiction' [27].

One possibility is that 'food addiction' stigma may be particularly high amongst those who perceive addiction to be within personal control [7]. This is supported by previous research in which perceiving addiction as a disease, rather than due to personal choice, was associated with reduced stigma towards people with addictive disorders [40,41]. Similarly, biogenetic explanations have been found to reduce stigma towards obesity, problematic eating, and substance abuse, relative to behavior-based explanations [10,31,42]. In Study 2, we examined whether the effect of food addiction condition on stigma would be moderated by the extent that addiction is viewed as a 'disease' relative to personal choice.

We also examined whether stigmatizing attitudes towards the target with food-addiction would be moderated by individuals' scores on a measure of addiction-like eating. Previous research has found that individuals with personal experience of addiction have less negative attitudes towards others with addiction [43]. Furthermore, social identity theory suggests that individuals view other 'in-group' members more favorably than out-group members [44]. Therefore, we predicted that the effect of condition on target-specific stigma would be attenuated in participants with greater levels of addiction-like eating behavior.

Finally, we examined whether the effect of condition on target-specific and general stigma would differ between males and females. Previous research has found that females demonstrate less obesity-related stigma and stigma towards the 'food addiction' label than males [27]. We, therefore, hypothesized that the exacerbating effect of the food addiction label on stigma would be most pronounced in males.

To summarize, Study 2 examined the following hypotheses: (1) The effect of condition on target-specific and general stigma would be attenuated in those with greater support for the disease model of addiction. (2) The effect of condition on stigma would be attenuated in those who score highly on a measure of addiction-like eating, relative to those who score lower on addiction-like eating. (3) The effect of condition on stigma would be attenuated in females, relative to males.

5. Study 2 Method

5.1. Participants

Male and female participants, aged over 18 years, were invited to take part in a study into 'employability perceptions'. A total of 523 (190 males; 314 females; 19 did not disclose their gender) participants completed the study. Six hundred and ten participants started the online survey, but 87 either did not complete it or were aged under 18 years old and were excluded from analyses. Participants were recruited from the University of Liverpool (n = 333) and Newcastle University (n = 190) in the UK. The mean age of participants was 27.1 (SD = 11.3) years, and the mean self-reported BMI was 23.6 kg/m^2 (SD = 4.1). Participants with self-reported BMI over 30 kg/m^2 (i.e., classified as having obesity) comprised 7.1% of the sample, 21.6% had a self-reported BMI between 25–29.9 kg/m^2 (i.e., 'overweight'), 64.4% had a self-reported BMI between 18.5–24.9 kg/m^2 (i.e., healthy weight), and 5.5% had a self-reported BMI below 18.5 kg/m^2 (i.e., 'underweight'). Just over half of the sample were university students (n = 275, 52.4%) and the majority were Caucasian (n = 465, 88.9%). Ethical approval was granted by the relevant ethics committee at each of the two sites (University of Liverpool approval code: IPHS-1516-SMc-259-Generic RETH000619; Newcastle University approval code 1485/4293).

5.2. Materials and Procedure

Study 2 used the same materials and procedure as Study 1 but with the following additional measures:

5.2.1. Addiction Belief Scale (ABS)

The ABS [39] was used to measure beliefs about addiction. Nine items assessed the belief that addiction is a disease (disease subscale, Cronbach's $\alpha = 0.590$), and nine items assessed the belief that addiction is within personal control (free will subscale, Cronbach's $\alpha = 0.546$). Items were rated on a 5-point Likert scale ranging from 'strongly disagree' to 'strongly agree'. Higher scores indicate greater support for the belief that addiction is akin to a disease (disease subscale), and a matter of personal choice (free will subscale).

5.2.2. Addiction-Like Eating Behaviour Scale (AEBS)

The AEBS [45] consists of 15 items which assess the presence of behaviors that are commonly associated with addiction-like eating (e.g., 'I continue to eat despite feeling full'). Responses are provided on 5-point Likert Scales ranging from 'Strongly disagree' to 'Strongly agree', and from 'Never' to 'Always'. The scale comprises two subscales: appetitive drive (9 items, Cronbach's $\alpha = 0.890$) and low dietary control (6 items, Cronbach's $\alpha = 0.806$). Higher scores indicate greater addiction-like eating behavior. Previous research suggests that this measure correlates positively with other measures of disinhibited eating (i.e., the Binge Eating Scale, [46]) and explains greater variance in BMI over and above other measures of 'food addiction' such as the Yale Food Addiction Scale [47].

5.2.3. Data Analysis

A MANOVA was conducted to check whether participants differed, between conditions, with regards to age, BMI, DEBQ subscales scores, and scores on the Addiction-like Eating Behaviour Scale (AEBS) and Addiction Belief Scale (ABS). Chi-squared tests were conducted to check for any differences between the proportion of students/non-students, Caucasian/non-Caucasian, and males/females allocated to each condition. As in Study 1, two univariate ANOVAs were conducted to examine the effect of condition on Anti-fat Attitudes (AFA; general stigma) and Modified-Fat Phobia Scale (M-FPS) scores (target-specific stigma). Gender was also included in the model as a between-subjects variable.

Hierarchical multiple linear regression analyses were conducted to examine whether any effects of condition on target-specific and general stigma were moderated by support for the 'disease' model of addiction (i.e., ABS-disease scores), and addiction-like eating behavior (i.e., AEBS scores). All three conditions were dummy coded with the Control condition as the reference variable. To assign dummy codes, two dummy variables were created: D_1 (Medical) and D_2 (Self-diagnosed). Participants in the medical condition were assigned '1' to D_1, and '0' for D_2. Participants in the self-diagnosed condition were assigned '0' to D_1 and 1 to D_2. Participants in the control condition (i.e., the reference category) were assigned 0 to both D_1 and D_2. (see [48] for more information about dummy coding). Dummy-coded conditions were then entered into Step 1 of each regression model, along with Addiction Belief Scale (disease subscale) or AEBS scores. The interaction terms (i.e., AEBS/Addiction Belief Scale (disease subscale) $\times$ medical vs. control/self-diagnosed vs. control) were entered into Step 2 of the model. Separate regression analyses were conducted to examine the ability of each interaction term to predict AFA scores (i.e., general stigma) and M-FPS scores (i.e., target-specific stigma). Addiction Belief Scale (disease subscale) and AEBS scores were centered prior to analyses.

6. Results

6.1. Participant Characteristics

Participants did not differ between conditions on any of the assessed characteristics (Table 3).

Table 3. Participant characteristics as a function of condition (Study 2).

Variable	Medical (*N* = 178)	Self-Diagnosed (*N* = 175)	Control (*N* = 170)	Between-Group Differences
Age (y)	26.6 (11.1)	26.9 (10.9)	27.8 (12.0)	F(2,511) = 0.34, p = 0.711
BMI (kg/m^2)	23.6 (4.5)	23.6 (4.2)	23.5 (3.7)	F(2,511) = 0.03, p = 0.974
DEBQ-Restraint	2.66 (0.91)	2.67 (.86)	2.76 (0.90)	F(2,511) = 0.47, p = 0.626
DEBQ-Emotion	2.67 (0.90)	2.64 (.98)	2.77 (0.99)	F(2,511) = 1.16, p = 0.314
DEBQ-External	3.29 (0.58)	3.26 (.57)	3.38 (0.55)	F(2,511) = 2.44, p = 0.088
AEBS	36.57 (9.65)	35.99 (9.87)	36.05 (8.70)	F(2,511) = 0.33, p = 0.720
ABS-disease	25.80 (3.75)	25.19 (3.92)	25.86 (4.41)	F(2,511) = 1.45, p = 0.236
ABS-Free Will	30.01 (3.29)	29.95 (3.72)	30.15 (4.04)	F(2,511) = 0.14, p = 0.873
Ethnicity (% Caucasian)	89%	89%	88%	$X^2(2)$ = 0.119, p=0.942
Occupation (% students)	57%	49%	52%	$X^2(2)$ = 2.08, p = 0.354
Gender (% male)	42%	31%	38%	$X^2(2)$ = 4.95, p = 0.084

Abbreviations: AEBS, Addiction-like Eating Behavior Scale; ABS, Addiction Beliefs Scale; DEBQ, Dutch Eating Behaviour Scale.

6.2. *Effect of Condition and Gender on Target Specific Stigma*

In contrast to Study 1, there was no main effect of condition on target-specific stigma, F(2,517) = 0.69, p = 0.501, (Control condition: Mean = 3.56, SD = 0.48, range = 2.43–5.00; Self-diagnosed: Mean = 3.63, SD = 0.47, range = 2.36–4.64; Medical: Mean = 3.63, SD = 0.47, range = 2.57–4.93). Contrary to hypothesis 3, there was no gender × condition interaction for target-specific stigma, F(2,517) = 1.18, p = 0.309. However, there was a main effect of gender, F(1,517) = 5.13, p = 0.024, ηp^2 = 0.010, such that males had significantly higher scores on the Modified Fat Phobia Scale (M-FPS) than females i.e., they showed higher levels of target-specific stigma (Males: M = 3.67, SE = 0.034; Females: M = 3.57, SE = 0.026).

6.3. *Effect of Condition and Gender on General Stigma*

As in Study 1, there was no effect of condition on Anti-fat Attitudes (AFA) scores (i.e., general stigma), F(2,517) = 1.18, p = 0.308, (Control: Mean = 4.34, SD = 1.00, range = 2.15–7.31; Self-diagnosed: Mean = 4.17, SD = 1.00, range = 1.54–7.15; Medical: Mean = 4.29, SD = 1.09, range = 1.31–7.85). Contrary to hypothesis 3, there was no gender × condition interaction, F(2,517) = 0.02, p = 0.978. There was also no main effect of gender on AFA scores, F(1,517) = 0.02, p = 0.978. For further analyses of gender differences on the AFA subscales, please see the supplementary materials (Figure S1).

6.4. *Effect of Disease Beliefs on Stigma*

Scores on the disease subscale of the Addiction Belief Scale (ABS) significantly predicted mean Modified-Fat Phobia Scale (M-FPS) scores in Step 1 and Step 2 of the model such that higher scores on the scale (i.e., greater belief that addiction is akin to a disease) were associated with greater target specific stigma (i.e., higher M-FPS scores) (Table 4). However, M-FPS scores were not significantly predicted by condition, and there was no condition × ABS-disease interaction, contrary to our hypothesis. Step 1: r = 0.204, r^2 = 0.042, $p < 0.001$; Step 2: r = 0.204, r^2 = 0.042, p = 0.972.

Table 4. Regression output for Addiction Belief Scale (ABS)-disease with M-FPS (target-specific stigma) as the dependent variable.

Model	B	SE	*t*	*p*
Step 1				
Medical	0.072	0.050	1.427	0.154
Self-diagnosed	0.091	0.051	1.797	0.073
ABS-disease	0.023 **	0.005	4.439	0.000
Step 2				
Medical	0.071	0.050	1.415	0.158
Self-diagnosed	0.090	0.051	1.781	0.076
ABS-disease	0.022 **	0.008	2.685	0.007
ABS-Disease × Medical	0.002	0.012	0.195	0.846
ABS-Disease × Self-diagnosed	0.000	0.012	−0.034	0.972

** $p < 0.01$. The control condition was used as the reference category against which medical and self-diagnosed conditions were compared. Abbreviations: ABS, Addiction Belief Scale. Step 1: $r^2 = 0.042$, $p < 0.001$; Step 2: $r^2 = 0.042$, $p = 0.972$).

Similarly, scores on the disease subscale of the ABS significantly predicted Anti Fat Attitude (AFA) scores (i.e., general stigma) in Step 1 and Step 2 of the model such that higher scores on the ABS-disease subscale predicted higher AFA scores (Table 5). Contrary to hypothesis 1, AFA scores were not significantly predicted by condition, and there was no interaction between condition and disease scores on AFA.

Table 5. Regression output for ABS-disease with Anti Fat Attitude (AFA; general stigma) as the dependent variable.

Model	B	SE	*t*	*p*
Step 1				
Medical	−0.056	0.109	−0.516	0.606
Self-diagnosed	−0.146	0.110	−1.331	0.184
ABS-disease	0.047 **	0.011	4.281	0.000
Step 2				
Medical	−0.053	0.109	−0.482	0.630
Self-diagnosed	−0.147	0.110	−1.337	0.182
ABS-disease	0.059 **	0.018	3.295	0.001
ABS-Disease × Medical	−0.016	0.027	−0.582	0.560
ABS-Disease × Self-diagnosed	−0.021	0.026	−0.791	0.429

** $p < 0.01$. The control condition was used as the reference category against which medical and self-diagnosed conditions were compared. Step 1: $r = 0.198$, $r^2 = 0.039$, $p < 0.001$; Step 2: $r = 0.201$, $r^2 = 0.040$, $p = 0.707$.

6.5. Addiction-Like Eating Behavior

Addiction-like Eating Behavior Scale (AEBS) scores and condition did not predict Modified Fat Phobia Scale (M-FPS) (target-specific stigma) scores in Step 1 of the model. However, the inclusion of the interaction terms in Step 2 significantly improved the fit of the model. Regression coefficients revealed a significant interaction between AEBS scores and medical (vs. control) condition on M-FPS scores (Table 6).

Table 6. Regression output for Addiction-like Eating Behavior Scale (AEBS) scores with M-FPS (target-specific stigma) as the dependent variable.

Model	B	SE	*t*	*p*
Step 1				
Medical	0.067	0.051	1.32	0.186
Self-diagnosed	0.071	0.051	1.38	0.168
AEBS	0.003	0.002	1.42	0.156
Step 2				
Medical	0.067	0.051	1.32	0.187
Self-diagnosed	0.071	0.051	1.39	0.165
AEBS	0.008	0.004	1.90	0.058
AEBS × Medical	−0.013 *	0.006	−2.35	0.019
AEBS × Self-diagnosed	0.000	0.006	−0.065	0.948

* $p < 0.05$. The control condition was used as the reference category against which medical and self-diagnosed conditions were compared. Abbreviations: AEBS, Addiction-like Eating Behavior Scale. Step 1: $r^2 = 0.009$, $p = 0.214$; Step 2: $r^2 = 0.023$, $p = 0.020$.

To further examine the interaction between AEBS scores and condition on M-FPS scores, we used the Johnson–Neyman technique [49] to identify the levels of addiction-like eating (i.e., AEBS scores) at which condition elicited a significant difference on M-FPS scores [50]. Using PROCESS (Version 3.1., [51]), the Medical (dummy-coded) condition was entered as the predictor variable, AEBS scores were entered as the moderator variable, and Self-diagnosed condition (dummy-coded) and the Self-diagnosed × AEBS interaction term were entered as covariates. Mean-FPS scores were entered as the dependent variable. This analysis showed that the Medical condition resulted in significantly greater M-FPS scores, relative to the Self-diagnosed and Control conditions (ps < 0.05), but only for those with low AEBS scores (centered AEBS score ≤ −2.81) (Figure 2). Findings are, therefore, consistent with our hypothesis that the effect of condition on stigma would be attenuated in those with higher levels of addiction-like eating behavior.

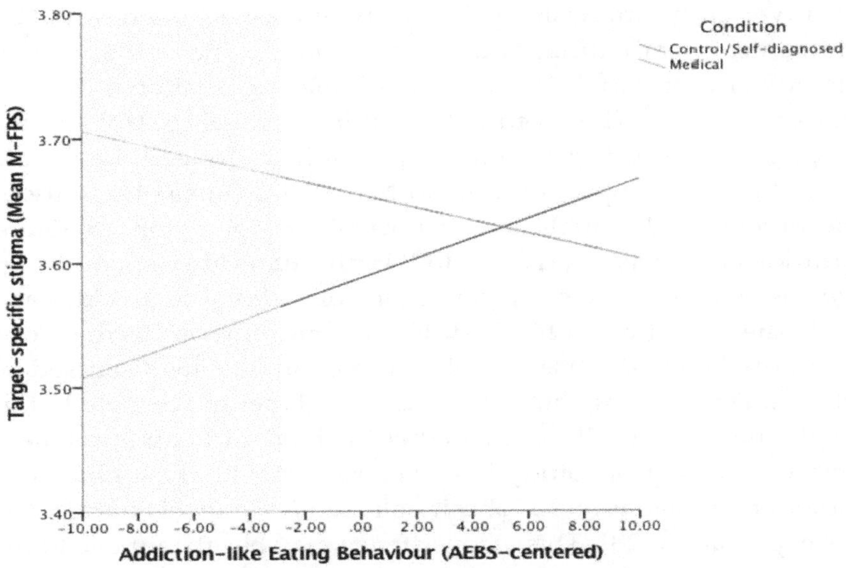

Figure 2. The effect of condition on M-FPS scores at different levels of addiction-like eating behavior (assessed using the AEBS). The shaded area represents the region of significance identified using the Johnson-Neyman technique.

The condition × AEBS scores model predicting (general stigma) AFA scores was not significant (Step 1: $r = 0.069$, $r^2 = 0.005$, $p = 0.484$; Step 2: $r = 0.084$, $r^2 = 0.007$, $p = 0.540$).

7. Discussion

Across two studies, we examined the effect of the food addiction label on stigmatizing attitudes towards an individual with obesity (i.e., target specific), and towards people with obesity more generally (i.e., general stigma). In Study 1, participants in both the medical and self-diagnosed food addiction conditions demonstrated greater target-specific stigma relative to the control condition. There was no effect of condition on general stigmatizing attitudes towards people with obesity. However, findings from Study 1 were not replicated in Study 2, in which we included both male and female participants. That is, we found no overall differences between the food addiction conditions and the control condition on target-specific stigma. The effect of condition on target-specific or general stigma was also not moderated by addiction disease beliefs (i.e., the extent to which addiction is perceived as a disease) or gender, in Study 2. However, there was a significant condition by addiction-like eating behavior interaction on target-specific stigma; participants who scored low on a measure of addiction-like eating demonstrated greater target-specific stigma in the Medical condition relative to Control and Self-diagnosed conditions. In contrast, target-specific stigma did not differ as a function of condition for those with high levels of addiction-like eating.

Findings from Study 1 are consistent with previous findings in which the food addiction label added to the stigma of obesity [27]. Higher levels of stigma towards the 'self-perceived' food-addicted target in the current study may reflect perceptions of food addiction as an 'excuse' for overeating. This is supported by qualitative evidence that individuals with overweight or obesity may be reluctant to label themselves as food addicts due to concerns that this would be perceived as an 'excuse' for their weight [29].

We predicted that the medical condition might legitimize the concept of food addiction and thereby reduce weight-related stigma (i.e., by removing personal responsibility from the individual). However, contrary to our hypothesis, in Study 1, we found that target-specific stigma was also higher in the medical condition compared to the control condition and did not differ from levels observed in the self-diagnosed condition. This finding is inconsistent with predictions from attribution theory [7] in which undesirable behaviors that are perceived as beyond personal control are thought to elicit less stigma than those that are perceived as controllable. One possibility is that food addiction explanations increase stigma by inadvertently emphasizing the behavioral aspect of obesity. That is, food addiction may imply a loss of control over eating, and previous studies have found that this may increase stigmatizing attitudes towards obesity [52]. Another possible explanation is that food addiction, unlike other biological causes of obesity, is believed to be within personal control and that medicalizing the term does not remove perceptions of personal responsibility. Indeed, Lee et al. [21] reported that almost three-quarters of people supported food addiction as a cause of obesity, and yet obesity was still viewed as a condition that individuals need to take responsibility for. Therefore, it may be the case that stigmatizing attitudes towards 'food addicted' individuals are dependent upon the extent that addiction is perceived as being outside of personal control and/or akin to a disease. In relation to this, Study 2 examined whether the effect of food addiction condition on stigma would be attenuated in those with greater support for the disease model of addiction (results discussed below).

Study 1 therefore suggests that the food addiction label exacerbated stigmatizing attitudes towards a woman with obesity, regardless of whether the food addiction was medically diagnosed or self-diagnosed. Notably, findings from Study 1 are inconsistent with those obtained in a previous study in which a 'food addiction' explanation for obesity elicited *lower* levels of target-specific and general stigma than a control explanation [28]. This inconsistency may be attributable to the control conditions used in ours and Latner et al.'s [28] study; in the current study, participants in the control condition were not provided with any explanation for the target's weight status. In contrast, participants in Latner et al.'s [28] study read that obesity is caused by repeatedly choosing to consume high-calorie foods. By emphasizing the role of personal choice, it is possible that the control condition used by Latner et al. [28] may have elicited greater stigma than a 'food addiction' explanation for obesity.

In Study 2, we found that greater support for the disease model of addiction was associated with greater target-specific and general stigma towards obesity. This finding was unexpected and is contrary to predictions derived from attribution theory. One possibility is that the perception of addiction as a 'disease' encourages the view that addicts are abnormal and perpetuates an 'us-them' distinction [53]. Holding disease views of addiction also suggests that the person's condition is irrevocable and permanent [54]. Another possibility is that causal beliefs about food addiction do not coincide with perceptions of other addictions. That is, individuals who support the 'disease' model for substance-based addictions may not necessarily attribute food addiction to a disease. Previous research supports this, indicating that addictions vary in the extent to which they are attributed to disease or personal choice. In particular, de Pierre et al. [40] found that food addiction was perceived as less of a disease and more within personal control compared with other addictions such as alcoholism. The measure of addiction beliefs (i.e., the ABS) used in the current study referred to addiction in general, and thus may not have reflected participants' beliefs about food addiction per se.

However, the moderating effect of addiction-like eating on target-specific stigma, observed in Study 2, suggest that medically diagnosed food addiction could exacerbate weight-related stigma but only for people with low levels of addiction-like eating tendencies. A possible explanation for this finding is that individuals with personal experience of problematic eating (i.e., high AEBS scores) may have identified more with the target in the vignette and thereby displayed less negative attitudes towards her food addiction (e.g., see [43,44]) as opposed to participants with low AEBS scores.

In Study 2, male participants demonstrated significantly higher target-specific stigma, relative to female participants. Males and females did not differ on a measure of general weight-related stigma. However, the lack of interaction between gender and condition is inconsistent with previous research [27] in which stigmatizing attitudes towards a 'food addicted' target were lower in females, relative to males. This null result may be explained by the fact that, in the current study, males had a significantly higher mean BMI than females (see Table S1). A previous study found that people with higher BMI hold less stigmatizing attitudes towards the 'food addict' label, relative to those with lower BMI [27]. Consistent with this, in Study 1, we found that higher BMI was associated with lower target-specific weight stigma. It is therefore possible that, in the current study, any moderating effect of gender on stigma may have been masked by the higher BMI of male, relative to female, participants. Future research should examine the moderating effect of gender on stigmatizing attitudes towards a food-addicted target in samples of males and females matched for BMI.

The inconsistent findings obtained across Studies 1 and 2 could not be attributable to the inclusion of males in Study 2 as the effect of condition on target-specific stigma was not moderated by gender. The sample tested in Study 2 comprised a larger proportion of older, non-students than the sample tested in Study 1. However, exploratory analyses revealed that the effect of condition on stigma was not moderated by student status or age (see online supplementary material). Differences between Studies 1 and 2 are, therefore, likely due to another (unknown) variable. Moreover, these findings suggest that the effects of the food addiction label on weight-related stigma may not be generalizable across populations.

There are several limitations to the current study that require consideration. Firstly, we note that the Addiction Belief Scale, used in Study 2, examined beliefs about the causes of addiction in general, and thus may not have captured individual differences in beliefs about the causes of food addiction. Future research could use an adapted version of the ABS (such as that used by de Pierre et al. [40]) to test whether food addiction stigma is attenuated in individuals who have greater support for a disease model of food addiction. Secondly, we did not examine whether participants believed the food addiction explanation for obesity, nor did we check whether participants had guessed the study aims. It is, therefore, possible that the effect of the food addiction label on stigma, observed in Study 1, could be due to demand characteristics that were not present in Study 2. Thirdly, the use of a female target in the current study precludes the generalizability of our findings to males. Previous research suggests that females are more likely than males to be stigmatized due to their weight [55], and so attitudes towards the food addiction label may similarly differ as a function of the target's gender. Finally, it is important to consider that the findings may have been affected by the order in which the questionnaires were presented. In particular, the significant effect of condition on target-specific stigma (M-FPS) (in Study 1), and lack of effect of general stigma (AFA), may be due to the fact that participants completed the M-FPS immediately after reading the vignette, while general stigma (i.e., AFA scores) were assessed later in the study.

Future research should aim to clarify the effect of the food addiction label on weight-related stigma. This may be achieved by considering possible moderating effects of pre-existing beliefs about food addiction (e.g., the extent that it is a legitimate condition, whether it is controllable, etc.). There has been much debate in the scientific literature about whether addiction-like eating should be considered a substance-based 'food addiction' or a behavioral 'eating addiction' (e.g., [11]). Therefore, it will also be important to compare attitudes elicited by a 'food addiction' label, with attitudes towards an 'eating addiction' label. It would also be interesting to compare the effect on the stigma of medically-diagnosed food addiction, with other medical causes of weight gain (e.g., hypothyroidism). Doing so would provide insight into whether the potential exacerbating effect of medicalization on stigma is specific to the food addiction label or whether it extends to the medical model per se. It is also possible that emphasizing the non-behavioral aspect of food addiction (e.g., brain differences to food) may reduce any deleterious effect of a medical diagnosis on stigma. More broadly, the clinical implications of food addiction labels on weight-related stigma must now be considered. In particular, it is important to consider whether the food addiction label may affect people's approaches to treatment (e.g., seeking pharmacological solutions rather than psychotherapy). It is also possible that, by perpetuating weight-related stigma, the food addiction label could be detrimental to psychological well-being and undermine people's attempts to lose weight.

8. Conclusions

The results indicate that the food addiction label may exacerbate stigmatizing attitudes towards an individual with obesity. Furthermore, there is preliminary evidence that this effect may be most pronounced in people with pre-existing low levels of addiction-like eating behavior. Further research is needed to determine the longer-term effects of the food addiction label on weight stigma and clinical implications.

Author Contributions: Conceptualization, E.J.B. and C.A.H.; Data curation, H.K.R. and M.O.; Formal analysis, H.K.R. and M.O.; Methodology, M.O., E.J.B. and C.A.H.; Supervision, E.H.E. and C.A.H.; Writing—original draft, H.K.R. and C.A.H.; Writing—review & editing, M.O., E.J.B., E.H.E. and C.A.H.

Acknowledgments: The authors thank Kerry Boult, Richard Ensell, Helena Leech, and Belen Valle-Metaxas for assistance with data collection.

References

1. NHS Digital. Available online: Digital.nhs.uk/data-and-information/publications/statistical/sand-diet/statistics-on-obesity-physical-activity-and-diet-england-2019 (accessed on 27 June 2019).
2. Puhl, R.M.; Heuer, C.A. The stigma of obesity: A review and update. *Obesity* **2009**, *17*, 941–964. [CrossRef] [PubMed]
3. Brinsden, H.; Coltman-Patel, T.; Sievert, K. Weight Stigma in the Media. Available online: https://www.britishlivertrust.org.uk/wp-content/up (accessed on 27 June 2019).
4. Pearl, R.L.; Wadden, T.A.; Hopkins, C.M.; Shaw, J.A.; Hayes, M.R.; Bakizada, Z.M.; Alfaris, N.; Chao, A.M.; Pinkasavage, E.; Berkowitz, R.I.; et al. Association between weight bias internalization and metabolic syndrome among treatment-seeking individuals with obesity. *Obesity* **2017**, *25*, 317–322. [CrossRef] [PubMed]
5. Nolan, L.J.; Eshleman, A. Paved with good intentions: Paradoxical eating responses to weight stigma. *Appetite* **2016**, *102*, 15–24. [CrossRef] [PubMed]

6. Rush, L.L. Affective reactions to multiple social stigmas. *J. Soc. Psychol.* **1998**, *138*, 421–430. [CrossRef]
7. Weiner, B. An attributional theory of achievement motivation and emotion. *Psychol. Rev.* **1985**, *92*, 548–573. [CrossRef] [PubMed]
8. Crandall, C.S. Prejudice against fat people: Ideology and self-interest. *J. Personal. Soc. Psychol.* **1994**, *66*, 882–894. [CrossRef]
9. Pearl, R.L.; Lebowitz, M.S. Beyond personal responsibility: Effects of causal attributions for overweight and obesity on weight-related beliefs, stigma, and policy support. *Psychol. Health* **2014**, *29*, 1176–1191. [CrossRef]
10. Hilbert, A.; Rief, W.; Braehler, E. Stigmatizing attitudes toward obesity in a representative population-based sample. *Obesity* **2008**, *16*, 1529–1534. [CrossRef]
11. Teachman, B.A.; Gapinski, K.D.; Brownell, K.D.; Rawlins, M.; Jeyaram, S. Demonstrations of implicit anti-fat bias: The impact of providing causal information and evoking empathy. *Health Psychol.* **2003**, *22*, 68–78. [CrossRef]
12. Lewis, R.J.; Cash, T.F.; Jacobi, L.; Bubb-Lewis, C. Prejudice toward fat people: The development and validation of the antifat attitudes test. *Obes. Res.* **1997**, *5*, 297–307. [CrossRef]
13. Dejong, W. The stigma of obesity: The consequences of naive assumptions concerning the causes of physical deviance. *J. Health Soc. Behav.* **1980**, *21*, 75–87. [CrossRef] [PubMed]
14. Lerma-Cabrera, J.M.; Carvajal, F.; Lopez-Legarrea, P. Food addiction as a new piece of the obesity framework. *Nutr. J.* **2016**, *15*, 5. [CrossRef]
15. Schulte, E.M.; Avena, N.M.; Gearhardt, A.N. Which foods may be addictive? The roles of processing, fat content, and glycemic load. *PLoS ONE* **2015**, *10*, e0117959. [CrossRef]
16. Schulte, E.M.; Grilo, C.M.; Gearhardt, A.N. Shared and unique mechanisms underlying binge eating disorder and addictive disorders. *Clin. Psychol. Rev.* **2016**, *44*, 125–139. [CrossRef] [PubMed]
17. Rogers, P.J. Food and drug addictions: Similarities and differences. *Pharmacol. Biochem. Behav.* **2017**, *153*, 182–190. [CrossRef]
18. Ziauddeen, H.; Farooqi, I.S.; Fletcher, P.C. Obesity and the brain: How convincing is the addiction model? *Nat. Rev. Neurosci.* **2012**, *13*, 279–286. [CrossRef] [PubMed]
19. Hebebrand, J.; Albayrak, Ö.; Adan, R.; Antel, J.; Dieguez, C.; de Jong, J.; Leng, G.; Menzies, J.; Mercer, J.G.; Murphy, M.; et al. "Eating addiction", rather than "food addiction", better captures addictive-like eating behavior. *Neurosci. Biobehav. Rev.* **2014**, *47*, 295–306. [CrossRef] [PubMed]
20. Ruddock, H.K.; Hardman, C.A. Food addiction beliefs amongst the lay public: What are the consequences for eating behaviour? *Curr. Addict. Rep.* **2017**, *4*, 110–115. [CrossRef]
21. Lee, N.M.; Lucke, J.; Hall, W.D.; Meurk, C.; Boyle, F.M.; Carter, A. Public views on food addiction and obesity: Implications for policy and treatment. *PLoS ONE* **2013**, *8*, e74836. [CrossRef]
22. Meadows, A.; Nolan, L.J.; Higgs, S. Self-perceived food addiction: Prevalence, predictors, and prognosis. *Appetite* **2017**, *114*, 282–298. [CrossRef]
23. Ruddock, H.K.; Dickson, J.M.; Field, M.; Hardman, C.A. Eating to live or living to eat? Exploring the causal attributions of self-perceived food addiction. *Appetite* **2015**, *95*, 262–268. [CrossRef] [PubMed]
24. Hardman, C.A.; Rogers, P.J.; Dallas, R.; Scott, J.; Ruddock, H.; Robinson, E. "Food addiction is real": The effects of exposure to this message on self-diagnosed food addiction and eating behaviour. *Appetite* **2015**, *91*, 179–184. [CrossRef] [PubMed]
25. Reid, J.; Brien, K.S.O.; Puhl, R.; Hardman, C.A.; Carter, A. Food addiction and its potential links with weight stigma. *Curr. Addict. Rep.* **2018**, *5*, 192–201. [CrossRef]
26. Cassin, S.E.; Buchman, D.Z.; Leung, S.E.; Kantarovich, K.; Hawa, A.; Carter, A.; Sockalingam, S. Ethical, stigma, and policy implications of food addiction: A scoping review. *Nutrients* **2019**, *11*, 710. [CrossRef] [PubMed]
27. DePierre, J.A.; Puhl, R.M.; Luedicke, J. A new stigmatized identity? Comparisons of a "food addict" label with other stigmatized health conditions. *Basic Appl. Soc. Psychol.* **2013**, *35*, 10–21. [CrossRef]
28. Latner, J.D.; Puhl, R.M.; Murakami, J.M.; O'Brien, K.S. Food addiction as a causal model of obesity. Effects on stigma, blame, and perceived psychopathology. *Appetite* **2014**, *77*, 77–82. [CrossRef] [PubMed]
29. Cullen, A.J.; Barnett, A.; Komesaroff, P.A.; Brown, W.; O'Brien, K.S.; Hall, W.; Carter, A. A qualitative study of overweight and obese Australians' views of food addiction. *Appetite* **2017**, *115*, 62–70. [CrossRef]

30. Epstein, L.; Ogden, J. A qualitative study of GPs' views of treating obesity. *Br. J. Gen. Pract.* **2005**, *55*, 750–754. [PubMed]
31. Kvaale, E.P.; Haslam, N.; Gottdiener, W.H. The "side effects" of medicalization: A meta-analytic review of how biogenetic explanations affect stigma. *Clin. Psychol. Rev.* **2013**, *33*, 782–794. [CrossRef] [PubMed]
32. Schulte, E.M.; Tuttle, H.M.; Gearhardt, A.N. Belief in food addiction and obesity-related policy support. *PLoS ONE* **2016**, *11*, e0147557. [CrossRef]
33. Bacon, J.; Scheltema, K.; Robinson, B. Fat phobia scale revisited: The short form. *Int. J. Obes.* **2001**, *25*, 252. [CrossRef] [PubMed]
34. Van Strien, T.; Frijters, J.E.R.; van Staveren, W.A.; Defares, P.B.; Deurenberg, P. The predictive validity of the Dutch restrained eating scale. *Int. J. Eat. Disord.* **1986**, *5*, 747–755. [CrossRef]
35. Van Strien, T.; Bergers, G.P.A.; Defares, P.B. The Dutch eating behavior questionnaire (DEBQ) for assessment of restrained, emotional, and external eating behavior. *Int. J. Eat. Disord.* **1986**, *5*, 295–315. [CrossRef]
36. Van Strien, T.; Peter Herman, C.; Anschutz, D. The predictive validity of the DEBQ-external eating scale for eating in response to food commercials while watching television. *Int. J. Eat. Disord.* **2012**, *45*, 257–262. [CrossRef] [PubMed]
37. Oliver Georgina, L.; Wardle Jane, L.; Gibson, E.L. Stress and food choice: A laboratory study. *Psychosom. Med.* **2000**, *62*, 853–865. [CrossRef] [PubMed]
38. Ruddock, H.K.; Field, M.; Hardman, C.A. Exploring food reward and calorie intake in self-perceived food addicts. *Appetite* **2017**, *115*, 36–44. [CrossRef] [PubMed]
39. Schaler, J.A. The addiction belief scale. *Int. J. Addict.* **1995**, *30*, 117–134. [CrossRef]
40. DePierre, J.A.; Puhl, R.M.; Luedicke, J. Public perceptions of food addiction: A comparison with alcohol and tobacco. *J. Subst. Use* **2014**, *19*, 1–6. [CrossRef]
41. Cunningham, J.A.; Sobell, L.C.; Freedman, J.L.; Sobell, M.B. Beliefs about the causes of substance abuse: A comparison of three drugs. *J. Subst. Abus.* **1994**, *6*, 219–226. [CrossRef]
42. O'Brien, K.S.; Puhl, R.M.; Latner, J.D.; Mir, A.S.; Hunter, J.A. Reducing anti-fat prejudice in preservice health students: A randomized trial. *Obesity* **2010**, *18*, 2138–2144. [CrossRef]
43. Meurk, C.; Carter, A.; Partridge, B.; Lucke, J.; Hall, W. How is acceptance of the brain disease model of addiction related to Australians' attitudes towards addicted individuals and treatments for addiction? *BMC Psychiatry* **2014**, *14*, 373. [CrossRef] [PubMed]
44. Tajfel, H.; Turner, J. *The Social Identity Theory of Intergroup Behaviour. U: Worchel S. i Austin WG (ur.) Psychology of Intergroup Relations*; Nelson Hall: Chicago, IL, USA, 1986.
45. Ruddock, H.K.; Christiansen, P.; Halford, J.C.G.; Hardman, C.A. The development and validation of the addiction-like eating behaviour scale. *Int. J. Obes.* **2017**, *41*, 1710. [CrossRef] [PubMed]
46. Gormally, J.; Black, S.; Daston, S.; Rardin, D. The assessment of binge eating severity among obese persons. *Addict. Behav.* **1982**, *7*, 47–55. [CrossRef]
47. Gearhardt, A.N.; Corbin, W.R.; Brownell, K.D. Preliminary validation of the Yale food addiction scale. *Appetite* **2009**, *52*, 430–436. [CrossRef] [PubMed]
48. Alkharusi, H. Categorical variables in regression analysis: A comparison of dummy and effect coding. *Int. J. Educ.* **2012**, *4*, 202–210. [CrossRef]
49. Johnson, P.O.; Neyman, J. Tests of certain linear hypotheses and their application to some educational problems. *Stat. Res. Mem.* **1936**, *1*, 57–93.
50. Hayes, A.F.; Montoya, A.K. A tutorial on testing, visualizing, and probing an interaction involving a multicategorical variable in linear regression analysis. *Commun. Methods Meas.* **2017**, *11*, 1–30. [CrossRef]
51. Hayes, A.F. *Introduction to Mediation, Moderation, and Conditional Process Analysis*; The Guildford Press: New York, NY, USA, 2017.
52. Bannon, K.L.; Hunter-Reel, D.; Wilson, G.T.; Karlin, R.A. The effects of causal beliefs and binge eating on the stigmatization of obesity. *Int. J. Eat. Disord.* **2009**, *42*, 118–124. [CrossRef]
53. Phelan, J.C. Genetic bases of mental illness—A cure for stigma? *Trends Neurosci.* **2002**, *25*, 430–431. [CrossRef]
54. Phelan, J.C. Geneticization of deviant behavior and consequences for stigma: The case of mental illness. *J. Health Soc. Behav.* **2005**, *46*, 307–322. [CrossRef]
55. Puhl, R.M.; Andreyeva, T.; Brownell, K.D. Perceptions of weight discrimination: Prevalence and comparison to race and gender discrimination in America. *Int. J. Obes.* **2008**, *32*, 992–1000. [CrossRef] [PubMed]

A Randomized Trial of Deep Brain Stimulation to the Subcallosal Cingulate and Nucleus Accumbens in Patients with Treatment-Refractory, Chronic and Severe Anorexia Nervosa: Initial Results at 6 Months of Follow Up

Gloria Villalba Martínez [1,2], Azucena Justicia [3,4,5], Purificación Salgado [4], José María Ginés [4], Rocío Guardiola [4], Carlos Cedrón [4], María Polo [4], Ignacio Delgado-Martínez [1], Santiago Medrano [6], Rosa María Manero [7], Gerardo Conesa [1,3,8], Gustavo Faus [9], Antoni Grau [9], Matilde Elices [3,5,*] and Víctor Pérez [2,3,4,5]

1 Department of Neurosurgery, Hospital del Mar, 08003 Barcelona, Spain; gloriavillabamartinez@gmail.com (G.V.M.); idelgadom@parcdesalutmar.cat (I.D.-M.); gconesa@parcdesalutmar.cat (G.C.)
2 Department of Psychiatry and Forensic Medicine, Universitat Autònoma de Barcelona, Cerdanyola del Vallès, 08193 Barcelona, Spain; vperezsola@parcdesalutmar.cat
3 Hospital del Mar Medical Research Institute (IMIM), 08003 Barcelona, Spain; ajusticia@imim.es
4 Institut de Neuropsiquiatria i Adiccions (INAD), Hospital del Mar, 08003 Barcelona, Spain; psalgado@parcdesalutmar.cat (P.S.); jgines@parcdesalutmar.cat (J.M.G.); rguardiola@parcdesalutmar.cat (R.G.); ccedron@parcdesalutmar.cat (C.C.); mpolo@parcdesalutmar.cat (M.P.)
5 Centro de Investigación Biomédica en Red de Salud Mental (CIBERSAM), 28029 Madrid, Spain
6 Department of Radiology, Hospital del Mar, 08003 Barcelona, Spain; santiago.medrano@upf.edu
7 Department of Neurology, Hospital del Mar, 08003 Barcelona, Spain; rmanero@parcdesalutmar.cat
8 Department of Surgery, Universitat Autònoma de Barcelona, Cerdanyola del Vallès, 08193 Barcelona, Spain
9 ITA, Mental Health Specialists, 08036 Barcelona, Spain; gfaus@ita.com (G.F.); agrau@ita.com (A.G.)
* Correspondence: melices@imim.es

Abstract: Background: The main objective of this study was to assess the safety and efficacy of deep brain stimulation (DBS) in patients with severe anorexia nervosa (AN). Methods: Eight participants received active DBS to the subcallosal cingulate (SCC) or nucleus accumbens (NAcc) depending on comorbidities (affective or anxiety disorders, respectively) and type of AN. The primary outcome measure was body mass index (BMI). Results: Overall, we found no significant difference ($p = 0.84$) between mean preoperative and postoperative (month 6) BMI. A BMI reference value (BMI-RV) was calculated. In patients that received preoperative inpatient care to raise the BMI, the BMI-RV was defined as the mean BMI value in the 12 months prior to surgery. In patients that did not require inpatient care, the BMI-RV was defined as the mean BMI in the 3-month period before surgery. This value was compared to the postoperative BMI (month 6), revealing a significant increase ($p = 0.02$). After 6 months of DBS, five participants showed an increase of ≥10% in the BMI-RV. Quality of life was improved ($p = 0.03$). Three cases presented cutaneous complications. Conclusion: DBS may be effective for some patients with severe AN. Cutaneous complications were observed. Longer term data are needed.

Keywords: anorexia nervosa; deep brain stimulation; psychosurgery; clinical trial; subcallosal cingulate; nucleus accumbens; body mass index

---

1. Introduction

Anorexia nervosa (AN) is a psychiatric disorder with an estimated prevalence of 0.7–3%. It primarily affects females and is usually diagnosed in adolescence and young adulthood [1,2]. AN is a life-threatening illness that can have a devastating impact on patients and their family [2,3]. The Diagnostic and Statistical Manual of Mental Disorders (DSM-5) criteria define two subtypes of AN: the restricting type and the binge-eating/purging type, with the latter type (purging) having a worse prognosis. Treatment of AN involves a combination of nutritional, pharmacological, psychological, and family interventions, all of which aim to restore normal weight, alter behavioural patterns, and address associated psychological issues. However, the optimal treatment for AN remains unclear and controversial [4,5].

Clear criteria to determine treatment refractoriness has not been fully established yet for this complex illness. Refractoriness in AN is currently defined as a failure to respond to repeated interventions over an extended time period (5–10 years), with recovery considered unlikely or, at best, limited in patients who have had AN for more than 10 years [3,6]. This condition is believed to be multifactorial, including neurobiological, environmental, and genetic factors, among others. Several studies seem to agree that AN is primarily caused by neurobiological alterations provoked by underlying dysfunction in the brain circuits. Although numerous models have been proposed to explain this dysfunction, most researchers agree that limbic system alterations are likely the main cause [7–13]. It has also been suggested that AN is, at least partially, maintained by dysfunctional activity in key neuroanatomic circuits [14–17], primarily those related to the modulation of reward and motivation, such as the mesolimbic cortex and the striatum [8,12].

Some authors have suggested that brain areas involved in the cognitive control of appetite (dorsolateral prefrontal and the parietal cortex) could also be involved in the pathophysiology of AN [10,13]. Morphological and functional studies in patients with AN have shown alterations in insular activity and in the prefrontal cortex, orbitofrontal, temporal, parietal, anterior cingulate, and ventral striatum (nucleus accumbens, NAcc) [18–20]. The available evidence suggests that the two most relevant targets for the surgical treatment of AN appear to be the NAcc [21] and the subcallosal cingulate (SCC), mainly due to the substantial involvement of these two structures in the reward circuits, but also because these two areas serve as communication links between the limbic and cortical systems [7,9].

Deep brain stimulation (DBS) is a surgical technique with a long history in the treatment of movement disorders such as Parkinson's disease, dystonia, and essential tremor, offering good outcomes with only minimal complications [10,22,23]. In recent decades, this technique has also been used to treat mental disorders such as obsessive-compulsive disorder (OCD), major depressive disorder (MDD), and schizophrenia [24,25]. However, OCD is the only mental disorder for which DBS is currently approved by both the United States Food and Drug Administration (FDA) and by the European Union (CE Marking certification) [24,26,27]. In other mental disorders, DBS has only been performed in the context of clinical trials or for compassionate use.

Although the precise mechanism of action of DBS remains unclear, several models and hypotheses have been proposed. Electrophysiological studies suggest that the effect of DBS depends on the type of stimulated brain tissue (e.g., grey or white matter) and on the type of fibers involved in the stimulation [13,28,29]. In addition, DBS is believed to alter neuronal discharge patterns in the target area (jamming effect). These different mechanisms may thus combine both inhibitory and excitatory processes, which could act simultaneously. Even though DBS is applied locally to a specific brain area, both focal and distal effects have been reported [29].

Experience with DBS in patients with AN is limited. To date, a total of 26 women with AN, with variable clinical characteristics (e.g., severity, chronicity) have participated in clinical studies. Moreover, those studies targeted different brain structures. McLaughlin et al. reported a case of a patient with comorbid AN and OCD (body mass index (BMI): 18.5) whose condition improved slightly after DBS to the ventral striatum [30]. Wang and colleagues described two cases of adolescent patients with AN who received bilateral DBS to the NAcc, with no complications; over the course of 12-month follow up, both patients in that study successfully reached a normal BMI and also showed improvements in psychopathological symptoms and quality of life. Wu et. al. [31] also reported results of a case series of four adolescents with AN in which DBS was applied to the NAcc. In all four cases, psychological symptoms improved and body weight increased by up to 65%, without complications over a follow-up period that ranged from 9 to 50 months. In that same year (2013), Lipsman et al. reported results from a phase 1 pilot trial in which DBS was applied to the subcallosal cingulate in 6 patients with AN [32]. At nine months of follow up, half of the patients showed a response to treatment (BMI above baseline values); in addition, four patients presented improved psychometric assessments. Israel et al. published a case report of a patient with MDD and comorbid AN, who received DBS to the SCC (unilateral, right side, intermittent). The results were good and the patient successfully maintained BMI = 19.6 for more than 30 months [33]. In 2017, the same research group reported the results of a 12-month clinical trial involving 16 patients with AN (including the six patients from the original study) who received DBS to the SCC. Mean BMI values and psychometric assessments improved in all 16 patients over time; moreover, a flurodeoxyglucose–positron-emission tomography (FDG-PET) scan showed metabolic changes in the brain after six months of DBS. However, several adverse events were reported, including one event of each of the following: air embolism, seizure, skin infection, worsening in mood, and intraoperative panic attack, and five of the patients also experienced pain [34]. Blomstedt and colleagues published a case report of a patient with MDD and comorbid AN in whom DBS was administered to the bed nucleus of the stria terminalis (BNST). Although the procedure did not significantly change the BMI, it did improve the patient's anxiety about food and eating [35]. Finally, the most recently published study was reported by Manuelli et al. (in 2019), who described the case of a patient with moderate AN who underwent DBS to the BNST. In that patient, BMI, core AN symptoms, and nutritional status all improved at six months of follow up [36].

Together, the limited evidence for DBS as a treatment for AN suggests that DBS appears to be a safe and effective treatment. However, due to the heterogeneity of this disorder, and the difficulty of recruiting patients to participate in clinical trials and studies, it is difficult to make definitive conclusions about the efficacy of DBS, the optimal target site, and the clinical and radiological variables that determine response. In this context, the main aim of the present clinical trial was to assess the efficacy and safety of DBS applied to two different targets (SCC and NAcc) to treat patients with chronic, severe, refractory AN. This study has been divided into three distinctive phases. Phase I involved the selection of participants and preoperative procedures. Phase II involved the surgical procedure itself, including a 6-month period of active stimulation. In phase III, patients considered responders to the DBS implant were randomized to one of two arms (ON/OFF or OFF/ON), while non-responders were not randomized, rather, they continued to be assessed monthly throughout the 12-month follow-up period. As phase III is currently ongoing, the current report presents data on phase I (preoperative) and phase II (6 months follow up).

2. Materials and Methods

2.1. Participants and Setting

A total of eight participants diagnosed with chronic, severe, refractory AN were included in this trial over a one-year period, which was conducted jointly by the Departments of Psychiatry and the Surgery Department of the Hospital del Mar in Barcelona, Spain, a tertiary care university hospital. Participants were recruited from collaborating sites around Spain, including the *Eating Disorders Institute, Mental Health Specialists* (in Spanish, *ITA Especialistas en Salud Mental)*, a national network of hospitals and treatment centers across Spain providing specialized care for patients with eating disorders.

The inclusion criteria were as follows: age: 18–60 years, clinical diagnosis of any type of AN (DSM-5 criteria), duration of AN > 10 years, treatment-resistant AN, defined as follows: (a) lack of response to ≥3 voluntary intensive treatments (full or partial hospitalization) or (b) clinical worsening and unwillingness to receive any further treatment, including ≥2 hospital admissions for involuntary feeding, preoperative BMI between 13 and 15.99 (patients with BMI values outside this range could be included on case-by-case basis), and capacity to fully understand the study and to provide informed consent. Exclusion criteria: current or past psychotic episode, comorbid neurological illness, drug abuse in the last year, contraindications to undergo magnetic resonance imaging (MRI) or DBS, any medical condition involving a risk for the surgical procedure, and pregnancy.

Written informed consent was obtained from all participants before proceeding with any intervention. The study was performed according to the ethical standards stated in the Declaration of Helsinki and subsequent updates. The study was approved by the Ethics Committee of the Parc de Salut (Barcelona, Spain, approval number: 2016/6813/I). Trial registration: Clinicaltrials.gov: NCT03168893.

2.2. *Design and Procedure*

This is a randomized, double-blind, controlled crossover clinical trial consisting of two consecutive 6-month phases (total duration: 12 months). Target selection was based on the presence of comorbidities with other psychiatric conditions and the type of AN. Patients whose predominant comorbidity was an affective disorder received DBS to the SCC, while patients whose predominant comorbidity was an anxiety disorder received DBS to the NAcc. The predominant comorbidity was determined by a clinical psychiatrist based on the MINI International Neuropsychiatric Interview scores and a comprehensive clinical interview. Each case was then reviewed by the other members of the clinical research team (a psychologist and a psychiatrist) to ensure their assessments for each comorbidity were consistent. For patients that did not show any clear predominant comorbidity, the target was selected based on the type of AN: patients with binge-eating/purgative AN received DBS to the NAcc, and patients with restrictive AN received DBS to the SCC. If a patient presented criteria for both targets, the target that corresponded to the most severe comorbidity was selected.

Phase I of the study consisted of the patient recruitment and selection. Potential candidates were interviewed by a member of the research team (psychiatrist). After this initial screening, an independent, external psychiatrist confirmed that the patient met all inclusion criteria. Patients were required to present normal results on all of the following preoperative tests: chest x-ray, electrocardiogram, and anesthesia tolerance test. Minimal alterations in blood test results were allowed, provided that these were normalized prior to surgery. The optimal pre-operative BMI was set at ≥13; in cases with a BMI < 13, the participant was admitted to the inpatient ward to raise the BMI to meet the minimum threshold. A 1.5 T MRI with diffusion tensor imaging (DTI) was performed pre-operatively. Before study inclusion, the participants' BMI data in the previous year was registered (lowest, highest, and mean).

Phase II involved the surgical procedure and six-month follow-up. The DBS system was implanted using robotic stereotactic assistance (ROSA; Zimmer Biomet, Inc. Montpellier, France). The surgical procedure was performed under general anesthesia and divided into three steps: (1) fiducial markers were inserted followed by an intraoperative computerized tomography (CT) scan, (2) the ROSA robotic arm was prepared and electrodes (Infinity; Abbott Inc., Saint Paul, MN, USA) were placed on the selected target through two trephine holes, at the frontal level, bilaterally. The Infinity electrodes (Abbott Inc., Saint Paul, MN, USA) are directional electrodes with four contacts, 1.5 mm in diameter, with 1.5 mm spacing between contacts, with an inactive distal part, and (3) finally, a pulse generator was implanted subfascially at the right abdominal area and connected to the electrodes. A postoperative cranial CT scan was performed and fused with the preoperative MRI CT scan. Correct placement of the electrode contact points was verified. Next, monopolar stimulation was performed. The stimulation started at 3.5 milliamperes (MA) and was increased according to patient response. The frequency (130 Hz), pulse amplitude (90 micros), and contact were set to remain constant throughout the trial.

Stimulation began 24 hours after surgery and participants were discharged 72 hours after the intervention. At 10 days, an initial postoperative assessment was performed by the psychiatrist and neurosurgeon at the outpatient clinic, and subsequent evaluations were scheduled to be performed monthly. All participants were provided with contact details (telephone/email) for the surgeon and co-primary investigator to communicate any adverse events over the course of the trial.

A third and final phase (phase III) of this trial is still ongoing. Consequently, the present report focuses on describing phase I and on presenting the data from phase II (6-months follow up). A flowchart of the complete study design is shown in Figure 1.

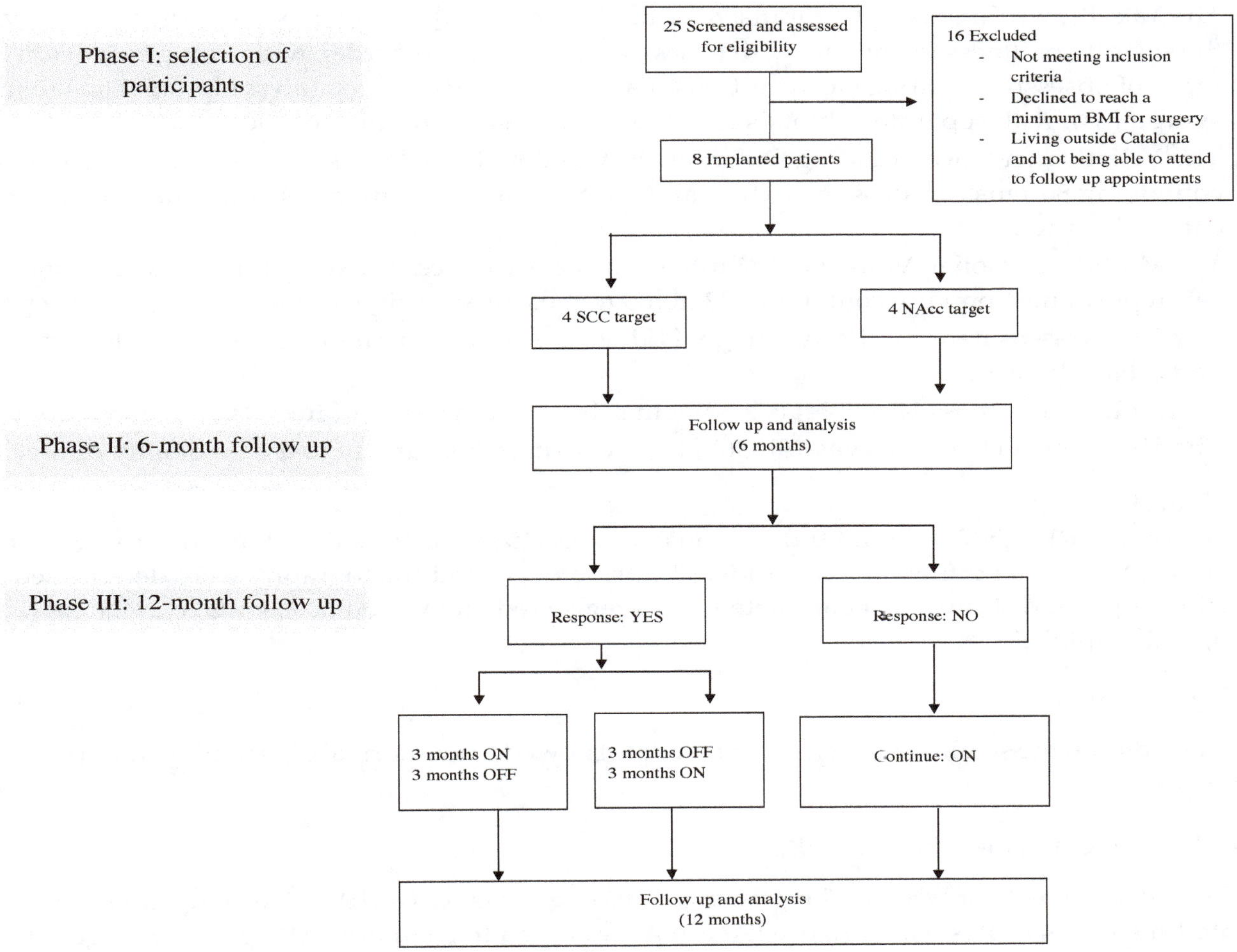

Figure 1. Participants' selection and pathway for the randomized crossover controlled clinical trial. Here, results are presented including the follow-up analysis at 6 months.

2.3. Measures

A wide range of variables were collected, including sociodemographic characteristics of the sample and a complete clinical history.

Primary outcome:

The primary outcome measure was BMI. Anthropometric measures (weight and BMI calculation) were collected at baseline, immediately before surgery, and monthly thereafter.

Secondary outcomes:

Secondary outcome measures include scores on a range of instruments described below.

Clinical outcome measures:

- The Mini-International Neuropsychiatric Interview (MINI) [37], a short diagnostic structured interview.

- The Hamilton Depression Rating Scale ($HAMD_{17}$) [38], designed to assess depressive symptoms. Each item on the questionnaire is scored on a 3- or 5-point scale, depending on the item. The original version contains 17 items ($HAMD_{17}$).
- Hamilton Anxiety Rating Scale (HAM-A) [39], a 14-item scale designed to rate the severity of anxiety symptoms. Each item contains a group of symptoms rated on a scale of 0–4, with 4 being the most severe.
- The Yale-Brown Obsessive Compulsive Scale (Y-BOCS) [40], a 10-item scale designed to measure the severity of illness in patients with obsessive-compulsive disorder, with a range of severity and types of obsessive-compulsive symptoms. Each item is rated from 0 (no symptoms) to 4 (extreme symptoms), with separate subtotals for severity of obsessions and compulsions.
- The Yale-Brown-Cornell Eating Disorders Scale (YBC-EDS) [41] is a semi-structured interview containing 8 items to assess the nature and severity of preoccupations and rituals related to the eating disorder.
- The Multidimensional Assessment of Interoceptive Awareness (MAIA) [42] is an 8-scale state-trait self-report questionnaire containing 32 items to measure multiple dimensions of interoception.
- Gardner Assessment of Body-Image [43] is a set of schematic contour scales to assess body disturbances.
- Barratt Impulsiveness Scale [44] is a 30-item self-report measure of impulsive personality traits.
- The Short Form Health Survey (SF-36) [45] is a 36-item instrument to assess quality of life.

Neuroimaging:

A brain MRI (1.5 T + DTI, 60 directions) was performed. Fractional anisotropy (FA), mean diffusivity (MD), axial diffusion (AD), radial diffusion (RD), and tractography were determined. The following target and stimulation parameters were registered: active contacts, voltage, frequency, pulse width, and amplitude.

2.4. Data Analyses

Considering the small sample size and that data showed a non-normal distribution, non-parametric tests were run.

2.4.1. Primary Outcome: change in BMI Value

To test the effects of DBS on the primary outcome measure (BMI), Friedman's non-parametric, repeated-measures analysis of variance (ANOVA) was used to compare BMI values at surgery to BMI values at each of the six-monthly postoperative determinations. As the main aim of the study was to evaluate treatment effects after 6 months of DBS, the Wilcoxon rank test was also used to compare two data points: pre-surgery BMI versus BMI at month 6.

Some participants required inpatient care before surgery to reach the minimum preoperative BMI value. Consequently, this preoperative BMI was not their "usual" BMI, but rather the result of inpatient treatment. To reflect this, we determined a BMI reference value (BMI-RV) for each patient, which was calculated differently depending on whether or not the patient required preoperative inpatient care. For patients who required preoperative inpatient care (patients 3, 4, 6 and 8), the BMI-RV was defined as the mean BMI achieved in the year prior to surgery (not including the BMI values obtained during inpatient care). For patients that did not require preoperative inpatient care (patients 1, 2, 5, 7), the BMI-RV was defined as the mean BMI achieved in the three-month period immediately prior to surgery. The same statistical analyses described above (Friedman's and Wilcoxon) were repeated, but this time based on the BMI-RV values. The BMI-RV value was used to determine treatment response, which was defined as an increase of $\geq$10% in the pre-treatment BMI-RV value.

For exploratory purposes, the sample was also divided into different subgroups (i.e., participants who received preoperative inpatient care versus those that did not and participants with SCC stimulation versus participants with NAcc stimulation) to test for possible changes in BMI values between those groups (Wilcoxon rank test).

2.4.2. Secondary Outcomes: Change in Anorexia Nervosa Behavior and Clinical Variables

Given the small sample size, the data on AN-related behaviors are given only as descriptive data. The Wilcoxon signed-rank test was used to compare scores obtained on the various instruments administered at baseline with the scores obtained at the end of month six of follow up. The results of this pre-post comparison were also used to determine whether participants who received DBS to the SCC or NAcc differed in terms of their relative improvement on depression and obsessive-compulsive scores (HAMD-17 and YBOCS, respectively).

3. Results

3.1. Participants Characteristics

The study sample included eight participants (7 female), with a mean age at surgery of 40.75 years (standard deviation (SD) = 15.49). Most patients (n = 6) had a primary diagnosis of AN-restrictive type. The mean time since disease onset was 25.25 years (SD = 11.25). Comorbidities with other psychiatric diagnoses were frequent, most commonly major depressive disorder (MDD, n = 7), followed by panic disorder (PD, n = 3), and obsessive-compulsive disorder (OCD, n = 3). Six of the eight patients (75%) were taking benzodiazepines, while three were under antidepressant treatment, and one was taking antipsychotic medication.

The minimum and maximum BMI values over the last five years were registered. We evaluated variability in the BMI values over the 15 months prior to DBS implantation. The patients presented three main BMI fluctuation patterns over this period, which we classified as pattern A, B, or C. Pattern A consisted of a stable BMI trajectory, observed in participants 1, 4, 5, 7, and 8. Pattern B was characterized by frequent hospital admissions and ascendant and descendent peaks in BMI (unstable BMI trajectory), which was observed in two patients (3 and 6). Finally, one patient (2) showed a stable but descendent weight trajectory, which was denominated pattern C. Preoperative inpatient care was required in four cases to achieve the minimum BMI (=13) level required for surgery. Of these four patients, only one (participant 4) did not achieve the minimum BMI; however, the patient's BMI (12.12) was considered acceptable and surgery was performed.

In participants 1, 2, 3, and 4, target selection was based on anatomical/stereotactic references; in participants 5, 6, 7, and 8, target selection was based on anatomical/stereotactic references as well as DTI data. Stimulation started at 3.5 MA for all patients and was maintained or increased accordingly to patient response, which was assessed monthly. The maximum stimulation was set at 8 MA.

Table 1 describes the demographic and clinical characteristics of the sample, with the active contacts and stimulation parameters. Figure 2 shows location of electrode active contacts.

Table 1. Participant's demographic and clinical characteristics, active contacts, and stimulating parameters.

Patient	Sex	Age	Type AN	AN Duration (Years)	Inpatient Care before Surgery	Minimum BMI	Maximum BMI	Reference BMI Value	Pharmacological Treatment	Main Comorbidity	Target	Active Contact (−), left	Active Contact (−), right	Maximum Intensity (MA)
1	Female	37	Restrictive	26	NO	14.64	16.22	16.22	Clonazepam	Affective Disorder	SCC	2	2	7
2	Male	45	Restrictive	32	NO	13.44	17.51	13.44	None	Anxiety Disorder	NAcc	1	1	8
3	Female	45	Restrictive	16	YES	10.06	11.72	10.94	Citalopram, Diazepam, Olanzapine, Lormetazepam	Affective Disorder	SCC	3	1	8
4	Female	39	Purgative	25	YES	11.47	12.55	11.83	Lorazepam	Anxiety Disorder	NAcc	2	1	8
5	Female	36	Restrictive	22	NO	13.07	15.18	13.07	Sertraline, Venlafaxine, Mirtazapine	Affective Disorder	SCC	2.3	2	7
6	Female	33	Restrictive	21	YES	9.64	12.73	11.57	Bromazepam	Affective Disorder	SCC	1.2	3.4	8
7	Female	57	Restrictive	41	NO	11.92	12.74	12.33	Venlafaxine, Mirtazapine, Bromazepam, Lormetazepam	Anxiety Disorder	NAcc	2	2.3	7.5
8	Female	34	Binge-Purge	19	YES	11.61	12.34	11.98	Lorazepam	Anxiety Disorder	NAcc	3.4	3.4	8

Note. AN = Anorexia Nervosa. MINI = International Psychiatric Interview for Mental Disorders. BMI = Body Mass Index. OCD = Obsessive Compulsive Disorder. MDD = Major Depressive Disorder. SCC = subcallosal cingulate. NAcc = Nucleus accumbens. MA = Milliampere. Minimum and maximum BMI refer to the last 5 years.

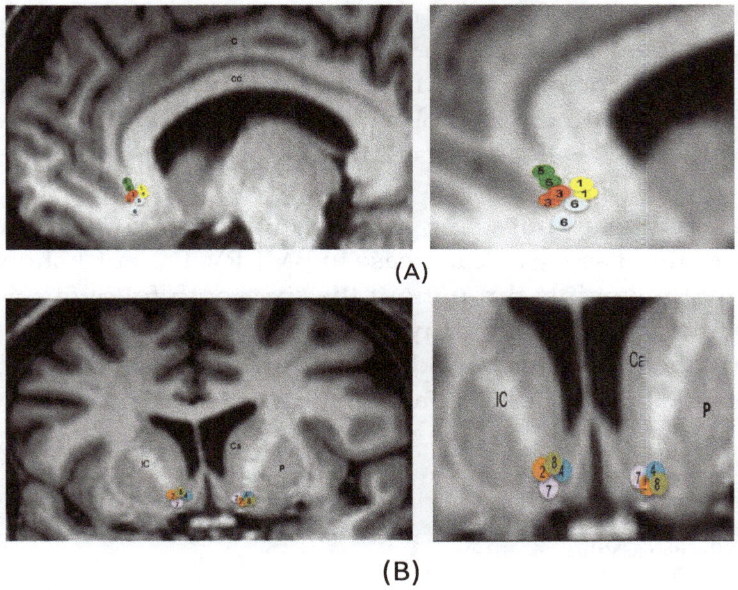

Figure 2. Location of electrode active contacts. (**A**) Location of electrode contacts on a sagittal view for patients with DBS on the subcallosal cingulate. Circles are schematic representations of electrode active contacts. Numbers within circles correspond to each patient. The figure at the right side is an enlargement. C = cingulate. CC = corpus callosum. (**B**) Location of electrode contacts on a coronal view for patients with DBS on the nucleus accumbens. Circles are schematic representations of electrode active contacts. Numbers within circles correspond to each patient. The figure at the right side is an enlargement. CA = caudate nucleus. CI = internal capsule. P = putamen. DBS = deep brain stimulation.

3.2. Primary Outcome: Change in Body Mass Index Values

To assess the effect of the DBS on BMI (the primary outcome measure), we compared the preoperative BMI for all patients (regardless of receiving inpatient care before surgery or not) to the BMI values measured at each postoperative time point (monthly). On this analysis, the Friedman repeated-measures ANOVA revealed no significant increase in BMI after surgery ($X^2 = 2.71$, $p = 0.84$). A Wilcoxon signed-rank test was performed to compare only two data points: preoperative BMI with BMI at month 6 of follow up, also revealing no significant changes ($Z = -0.28$, $p = 0.78$). Figure 3 shows the mean BMI scores for each patient over the six-month study period.

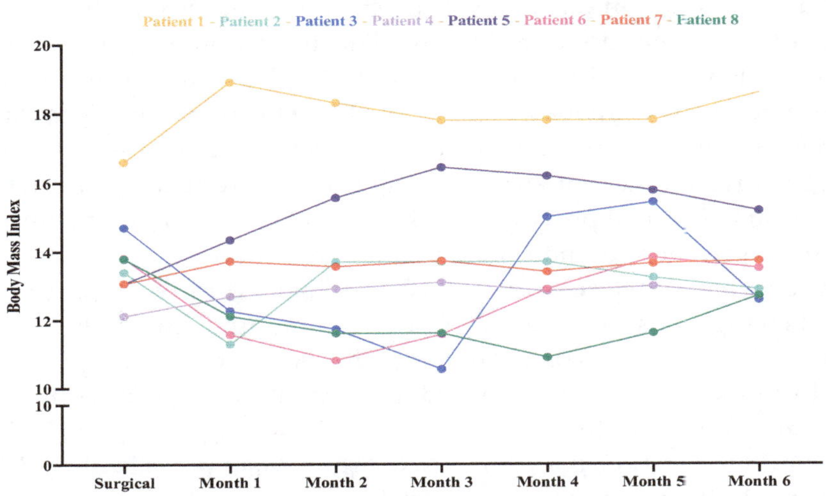

Figure 3. Individual changes in body mass index (BMI) during the six month follow-up period. BMI at surgery (criterion 1) was used as the reference value for this comparison.

These analyses were repeated using a BMI reference value (BMI-RV; see the Data Analyses Section for a description) for each patient as the pre-operative BMI measure. The Friedman repeated measures ANOVA showed no significant increase in BMI ($X^2 = 7.96$, $p = 0.24$). However, when we compared only two data points (BMI-RV with the BMI obtained at the six month follow up), the increase was significant (BMI-RV: M = 12.67, SD = 1.64 versus BMI value at month 6: M = 13.98, SD = 2.05, Z = −2.38, $p = 0.02$).

The data were analyzed again but using a different approach (as explained above), in which treatment response was defined as a ≥10% increase in BMI-RV. Patient 1 showed a sustained gain in BMI (10%) at all monthly time points throughout the six month follow up. By contrast, patients 2 and 8 did not achieve a 10% gain in BMI at any time point. Finally, the other three patients showed a variable pattern during the follow-up period. However, at month 6, five of the eight participants presented an increase of at least 10% in BMI. Table 2 shows the reference BMI values for each patient and their response.

Table 2. Participant response defined as a 10% increase in BMI during the six-month follow-up period.

Patient	Reference BMI Value	Response Value (10% Increase)	Months						Response to DBS (YES/NO)
			1	2	3	4	5	6	
1	16.22	17.842							YES
2	13.44	14.784							NO
3	10.94	12.034							YES
4	11.83	13.013							NO
5	13.07	14.377							YES
6	11.57	12.727							NO
7	12.33	13.563							YES
8	11.98	13.178							NO

Note. A green box indicates that the patient achieved a 10% increase in BMI at a given month while a red box means that the patient did not reach the 10% BMI gain threshold for that month. DBS = deep brain stimulation. BMI = body mass index.

Lastly, were performed other analyses (Wilcoxon rank test) to explore differences between the subgroups. No significant pre/post (6 months) differences in BMI were found for participants who received preoperative inpatient care (Z = −1.09, $p = 0.27$) versus those who did not (Z = −1.46, $p = 0.14$). Similarly, neither subgroup (SCC nor NAcc) showed a significant increase in BMI: SCC stimulation (Z = 0.00, $p = 1.00$) versus NAcc stimulation (Z = 0.00, $p = 1.0$).

3.3. Secondary Outcomes: Change in Anorexia Nervosa Behaviors and Clinical Variables

Patient 1 showed a reduction in daily physical activity (walking), which decreased from 6 hours per day to one hour/day at the one-month follow up. This reduction was maintained over the 6-month study period. Patient 2 also reduced the amount of daily physical activity from 6 hours to 3. Two patients (4 and 8) presented purging behavior prior to DBS. During the five years prior to DBS, patient 4 had maintained an exclusively liquid diet. After one month of DBS, the patient included two solid meals a day. Diuretic/laxative intake (patient 4) was significantly reduced from 40 tablets of furosemide a day to 5 tablets a day, and from 70 powder laxative sachets at baseline to complete abstinence. For patient 8, the purging frequency remained unchanged at month 6.

No significant improvement was observed (Wilcoxon signed-rank test) for most clinical variables. However, a significant change was found in SF-36 scores at month 6, indicating an improvement in the patients' quality of life (Z = 2.10, $p = 0.03$). Patients stimulated at the SCC (patients: 2, 4, 7, 8) whose predominant comorbidities were affective disorders presented larger improvements in depression scores (HAMD-17) than patients with SCC stimulation (SCC target: $M_{pre} = 13.50$, SD = 3.31 versus $M_{6months} = 4.75$, SD = 3.30, Z = −1.82, $p = 0.06$; NAcc target: $M_{pre} = 17.25$, SD = 7.13; $M_{6months} = 16.25$, SD = 11.32, Z = 0.00, $p = 1.00$); however, these differences were not statistically significant. In terms of YBOCs scores, no significant differences were found for patients with SCC stimulation or those who received NAcc stimulation (SCC target: $M_{pre} = 18.50$, SD = 6.60; $M_{6months} = 16.50$, SD = 11.61,

$Z = -0.55$, $p = 0.58$; NAcc target: $M_{pre} = 14.50$, SD = 9.14 versus $M_{6months} = 9.00$, SD = 12.27, $Z = 0.53$, $p = 0.59$). Table 3 shows the results of the secondary outcomes from baseline to the 6 months follow-up assessment. Figure 4A, B shows changes in depression (HAMD-17) and obsessive-compulsive (YBOCS) scores for each patient.

Table 3. Wilcoxon signed-rank test for secondary outcomes measured preoperatively (baseline) and at month 6 of follow up.

	Mean	Standard Deviation	Z	*p*
HAMD-17				
Pre-surgery	15.38	5.52	−1.47	0.14
Month 6	10.50	9.87		
YBOCS				
Pre-surgery	16.50	7.69	−0.85	0.39
Month 6	12.75	11.76		
HAM-A				
Pre-surgery	13.63	6.30	−1.26	0.21
Month 6	10.94	11.84		
YBC-EDS				
Pre-surgery	111.38	48.28	−1.54	0.12
Month 6	87.62	64.26		
MAIA				
Pre-surgery	15.53	7.11	0.42	0.67
Month 6	15.15	7.61		
Gardner—Distortion				
Pre-surgery	2.50	3.65	−0.70	0.48
Month 6	2.75	4.09		
Gardner—Dissatisfaction				
Pre-surgery	2.75	3.19	−0.32	0.74
Month 6	3.00	4.17		
SF36				
Pre-surgery	32.18	16.98	2.10	0.03
Month 6	60.56	22.40		
BIS-11				
Pre-surgery	43.88	19.66	−0.42	0.67
Month 6	42.25	10.06		

Note. HAMD-17 = Hamilton Depression Rating Scale. YBOCS = Yale-Brown Obsessive-Compulsive Scale. HAMA = Hamilton Anxiety Rating Scale. YBC-EDS = Yale-Brown-Cornell Eating Disorders Scale. MAIA = Multidimensional Assessment of Interoceptive Awareness. Gardner Assessment of Body-Image. SF36 = Short Form Health Survey. BIS-11 = Barrat Impulsivity Scale 11.

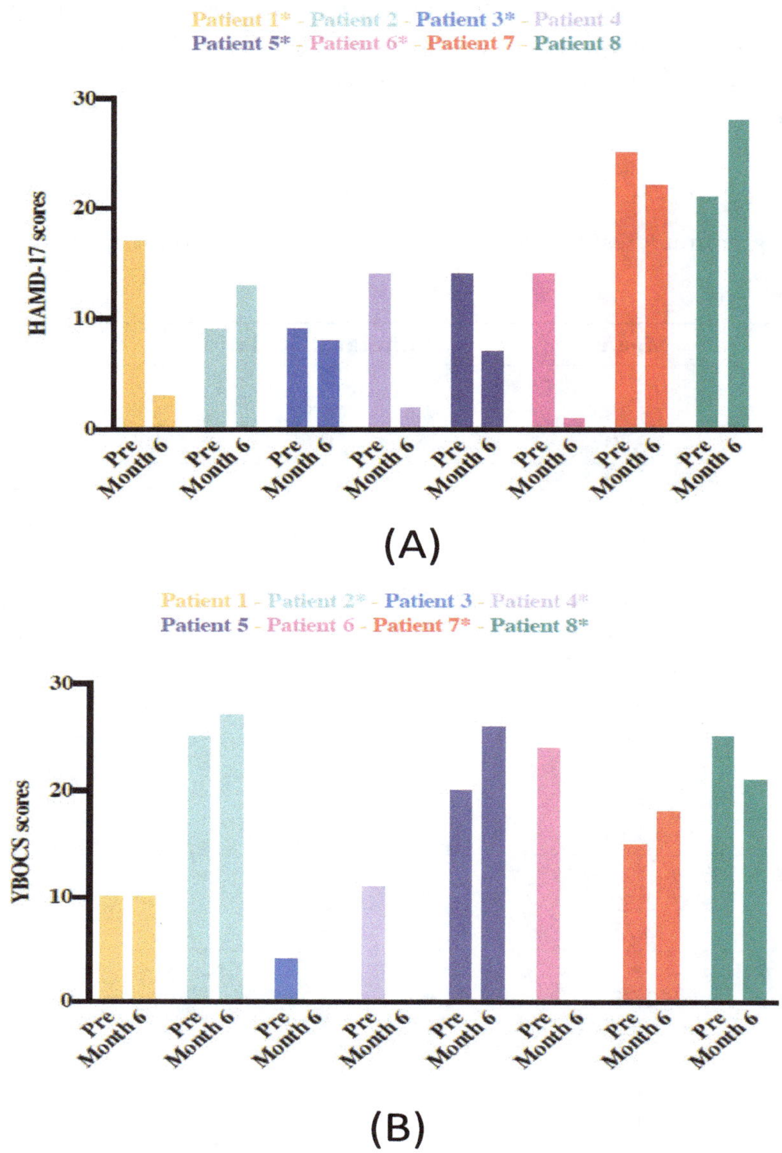

Figure 4. Changes in depression (HAMD-17) and obsessive-compulsive (YBOCS) scores for each patient. (**A**) Changes in depression scores based on the Hamilton Rating Scale for Depression (HAMD-17) from baseline to month 6 post-DBS. Patients identified with an asterisk (*) are those whose main comorbidity was an affective disorder, with SCC stimulation. (**B**) Changes in obsessive-compulsive symptoms based on the Yale-Brown Obsessive-Compulsive Scale (YBOCS) from baseline to month 6 post-DBS. Patients identified with an asterisk (*) are those whose main comorbidity was an anxiety disorder, with NAcc stimulation. HAMD-17 = Hamilton Depression Rating Scale. YBOCS = Yale-Brown Obsessive-Compulsive Scale.

3.4. Adverse Events

Cutaneous complications occurred in 3 patients (2, 5, and 6). Approximately 72 h after the procedure, patient 2 developed a greyish coloration in the area of the right electrode, potentially indicative of reduced blood flow; three days later (day 6), a necrotic eschar was observed, requiring skin flap surgery. Ten days after surgery, patient 5 developed skin dehiscence at the site of the incision for the surgical fiducial marker. The dehiscence did not respond to conservative treatment, and therefore the affected area was surgically cleaned to prevent infection. Patient 6 developed a chronic infection at the site of the skin incisions for surgical fiducial markers. The infection did not respond to antibiotic treatment and surgical cleaning was performed. No other intraoperative or postoperative complications or adverse events were registered.

4. Discussion

Overall, the initial results of this study of six months of DBS to the NAcc and SCC in patients with severe and chronic AN show that DBS did not produce a statistically significant increase in BMI. Five out of eight patients achieved an increase of ≥10% in BMI (at month 6), and three out of eight presented changes in AN behaviors, including reduced physical activity and use of laxatives and diuretics. At month 6, DBS was associated with improvements in a patient-reported measure of quality of life (SF-36). Almost 40% of the patients treated developed skin complications that required treatment, including surgery.

As indicate above (in the Methods Section), we used two different criteria to assess the primary outcome (change in BMI). First, we compared preoperative BMI to postoperative BMI values obtained at the monthly assessments, finding no significant increase in body mass in the overall sample. This lack of a significant difference in BMI could be attributed to the particular characteristics of our patient sample versus other studies that did find significant differences in BMI after DBS [29,30,32,34]. First, unlike many of those studies, we included treatment-resistant, chronic patients. Second, we required a minimal preoperative BMI (13), which meant that half of the patients (n = 4) required inpatient intensive treatment to gain weight before they could undergo DBS implantation. Although we managed to recruit the sample over a one-year period, many patients with a severe AN profile declined to participate in the study due to this criterion (i.e., they were unwilling to gain weight). For some patients with AN, the idea of participating in a clinical trial whose main aim is to restore weight can seem to contradict their personal objectives. Third, we used different stimulation targets (SCC or NAcc) depending on the comorbid psychopathology (affective predominance or anxious predominance, respectively). Previous studies [29,31–34] have also evaluated DBS for AN, using the same targets (SCC and NAcc). However, to our knowledge, none of those studies considered comorbidities or the type of AN when selecting the DBS target. This is relevant given that data obtained from studies using functional MRI reveal differences between AN subtype (restrictive versus bingeing/purging) in terms of brain activation [12,14]. Moreover, in contrast to our study, most patients included in previous studies were characterized by less severe AN with a shorter time from diagnosis and/or were willing to achieve a BMI > 15 before undergoing surgery [30,31,36].

Interestingly, when we calculated a preoperative reference BMI value (BMI-RV) for each patient, we found a significant increase in BMI at month 6 (versus the preoperative BMI-RV), although the mean BMI at this follow-up assessment was still quite low (M = 13.98). Although the use of this novel value (BMI-RV) could be questioned, we believe that it better captures the patients' true BMI before surgery, as it reflects the mean BMI over a longer time frame beyond just the immediate preoperative period.

When we performed another analysis in which treatment response was defined as an increase in BMI ≥ 10% (considered sufficient in this group of chronic, severe patients), five of the eight participants met this objective at month 6 and were thus considered responders (Table 2). Using the 10% gain in BMI as the cut-off to define treatment response, we observed different patterns. Of the four patients who met this criterion and were thus considered responders (patients 1, 3, 5, and 7), three received DBS stimulation to the SCC. In addition, most of these patients (1,5, and 7) presented a pattern A BMI trajectory before surgery, while only one patient (3) was characterized in the "unstable BMI trajectory" group (pattern B). Patient 2 showed a clear pattern of no-response that was consistent with the preoperative BMI pattern (sustained disease severity with clinical worsening). Together, these findings seem to suggest a link between the BMI pattern (i.e., illness trajectory) and the impact of DBS; however, more data are needed to corroborate this potential association. AN-specific behaviors in our sample were inverse, as some patients (1, 2, 4) presented a decrease in physical activity and diuretic/laxative use.

Of the various secondary clinical outcomes evaluated in this study, most did not show statistically significant improvements, which could be due to the short follow-up [34]. However, two findings were particularly noteworthy. First, we observed a significant increase in SF-36 scores, which indicates that the patients perceived a subjective improvement in quality of life after the intervention (month 6). Second, as we expected, patients whose predominant comorbidities were affective disorders and received stimulation to the SCC presented larger improvements in depression scores, while those with NAcc stimulation presented a greater improvement in the YBOCS (although none reached statistical significance). However, a positive impact on these measures related to features of AN (YBC-EDS; MAIA and Gardner) was not evidenced, in contrast to the findings of Lipsman et al. [34], who reported significant reductions on several subscales of the YBC-EDS. Nevertheless, the results of our study and those of Lipsman and colleagues [34] are not directly comparable, as that study had a much longer (12 months) follow-up period.

These results must be interpreted in the context of the study limitations. First, the small sample size and preliminary findings. Nevertheless, our data were obtained from a real-world sample of patients with chronic AN, a population in urgent need of novel treatment options such as DBS. Second, a recommended cut-off point for inclusion in this trial was BMI ≥ 13. To reach this cut-off point, some participants required inpatient intensive care, and therefore, the BMI reached at pre-surgery reflected this time under treatment. This cut-off point was established because excessively thin patients are more likely to develop pressure ulcers caused by the pulse generator implanted under the skin (due to the decreased skin thickness and greater fragility of the subcutaneous tissue). Although a higher BMI cut-off point would reduce this risk even further, doing so would likely require the exclusion of very severe patients (which is why we offered inpatient treatment to raise the BMI in selected patients). Indeed, even though we provided preoperative inpatient care, one patient still underwent surgery despite not reaching the minimum BMI. The decision to allow this patient to participate was made after careful consideration. The research team concluded that the patient's safety could be ensured and therefore we decided to proceed. The patient did not experience any adverse events and, despite a lack of response in terms of BMI, her use of diuretics/laxatives decreased significantly, which we consider a good outcome. A third limitation is that we only included one male. Consequently, it was not possible to assess differences between men and women in treatment response. Fourth, the relatively short follow-up (6 months) is a limitation; however, the longer-term stability of our findings will be reported when data from the phase III part of this trial (12 months of follow up) become available. In addition, we observed cutaneous complications, which might be related to lower BMI and to other differences in the patients' characteristics. In some patients, resolution of the cutaneous complications required surgery, as less invasive treatments were unsuccessful. However, and in contrast with other studies, no devices needed to be explanted.

5. Conclusions

After 6 months of DBS, some patients in this study with severe, chronic AN showed some benefits: increase in BMI, reduction in AN behavior, and improvement in quality of life (regardless of whether or not BMI improved). The percentage of patients developing cutaneous complications was high, but effectively resolved. Due to the short follow-up (6 months), we cannot reach any conclusions regarding the superiority of the target site (NAcc versus SCC) in terms of treatment outcomes. However, in the future, we will report longer term outcomes (12 months), which will provide a clearer picture of the long-term stability of BMI. Studies that include larger samples are needed to clarify whether DBS in patients with AN is associated with an improvement in comorbid symptoms (i.e., depression, anxiety). Finally, more research is needed to better characterize the relationship between BMI fluctuations, comorbid symptoms, and DBS targets.

Author Contributions: Conceptualization, G.V.M. and V.P.; Formal analysis, M.E.; Funding acquisition, V.P.; Investigation, G.V.M., P.S., J.M.G., R.G., C.C., M.P., I.D.-M., S.M., R.M.M., G.C., G.F., and A.G.; Methodology,

G.V.M. and V.P.; Supervision, V.P.; Writing—original draft, G.V.M. and A.J.; Writing—review and editing, M.E. All authors have read and agreed to the published version of the manuscript.

Acknowledgments: M.E. has a Juan de la Cierva research contract awarded by the ISCIII (FJCI-2017-31738). V.P. and M.E. want to thank unrestricted research funding from "Secretaria d'Universitats i Recerca del Departament d'Economia i Coneixement (2017 SGR 134 to "Mental Health Research Group"), Generalitat de Catalunya (Government of Catalonia). We thank Bradley Londres for professional English language editing.

References

1. Hoek, H.W. Incidence, prevalence and mortality of anorexia nervosa and other eating disorders. *Curr. Opin. Psychiatry* **2006**, *19*, 389–394. [CrossRef] [PubMed]
2. Machado, P.P.; Machado, B.C.; Gonçalves, S.; Hoek, H.W. The prevalence of eating disorders not otherwise specified. *Int. J. Eat. Disord.* **2007**, *40*, 7–212. [CrossRef] [PubMed]
3. Bulik, C.M.; Reba, L.; Siega-Riz, A.M.; Reichborn-Kjennerud, T. Anorexia nervosa: Definition, epidemiology, and cycle of risk. *Int. J. Eat. Disord.* **2005**, *37*, S2–S9. [CrossRef] [PubMed]
4. Lock, J.; Kraemer, H.C.; Jo, B.; Couturier, J. When meta-analyses get it wrong: Response to 'treatment outcomes for anorexia nervosa: A systematic review and meta-analysis of randomized controlled trials'. *Psychol. Med.* **2019**, *49*, 697–698. [CrossRef] [PubMed]
5. Hay, P.J.; Touyz, S.; Sud, R. Treatment for severe and enduring anorexia nervosa: A review. *Aust. N. Z. J. Psychiatry* **2012**, *46*, 44–1136. [CrossRef]
6. Steinhausen, H.C. The outcome of anorexia nervosa in the 20th century. *Am. J. Psychiatry* **2002**, *159*, 93–1284. [CrossRef]
7. Avena, N.M.; Bocarsly, M.E. Dysregulation of brain reward systems in eating disorders: Neurochemical information from animal models of binge eating, bulimia nervosa, and anorexia nervosa. *Neuropharmacology* **2012**, *63*, 87–96. [CrossRef]
8. Fladung, A.K.; Grön, G.; Grammer, K.; Herrnberger, B.; Schilly, E.; Grasteit, S.; Wolf, R.C.; Walter, H.; von Wietersheim, J. A neural signature of anorexia nervosa in the ventral striatal reward system. *Am. J. Psychiatry* **2010**, *167*, 12–206. [CrossRef]
9. Friederich, H.C.; Wu, M.; Simon, J.J.; Herzog, W. Neurocircuit function in eating disorders. *Int. J. Eat. Disord.* **2013**, *46*, 32–425. [CrossRef]
10. Jauregui-Lobera, I.; Martinez-Quinones, J.V. Neuromodulation in eating disorders and obesity: A promising way of treatment? *Neuropsychiatr. Dis. Treat.* **2018**, *14*, 2817–2835. [CrossRef]
11. Keating, C.; Tilbrook, A.J.; Rossell, S.L.; Enticott, P.G.; Fitzgerald, P.B. Reward processing in anorexia nervosa. *Neuropsychologia* **2012**, *50*, 75–567. [CrossRef] [PubMed]
12. Lipsman, N.; Woodside, D.B.; Lozano, A.M. Neurocircuitry of limbic dysfunction in anorexia nervosa. *Cortex* **2015**, *62*, 18–109. [CrossRef] [PubMed]
13. Whiting, A.C.; Oh, M.Y.; Whiting, D.M. Deep brain stimulation for appetite disorders: A review. *Neurosurg. Focus* **2018**, *45*, E9. [CrossRef] [PubMed]
14. Kaye, W.H.; Wagner, A.; Fudge, J.L.; Paulus, M. Neurocircuity of eating disorders. *Curr. Top. Behav. Neurosci.* **2011**, *6*, 37–57.
15. Van Kuyck, K.; Gérard, N.; Van Laere, K.; Casteels, C.; Pieters, G.; Gabriëls, L.; Nuttin, B. Towards a neurocircuitry in anorexia nervosa: Evidence from functional neuroimaging studies. *J. Psychiatr. Res.* **2009**, *43*, 45–1133. [CrossRef]
16. Sodersten, P.; Bergh, C.; Ammar, A. Anorexia nervosa: Towards a neurobiologically based therapy. *Eur. J. Pharmacol.* **2003**, *480*, 67–74. [CrossRef]
17. Lozano, A.M.; Lipsman, N.; Bergman, H.; Brown, P.; Chabardes, S.; Chang, J.W.; Matthews, K.; McIntyre, C.C.; Schlaepfer, T.E.; Schulder, M.; et al. Deep brain stimulation: Current challenges and future directions. *Nat. Rev. Neurol.* **2019**, *15*, 148–160. [CrossRef]
18. Bar, K.J.; de la Cruz, F.; Berger, S.; Schultz, C.C.; Wagner, G. Structural and functional differences in the cingulate cortex relate to disease severity in anorexia nervosa. *J. Psychiatry Neurosci.* **2015**, *40*, 79–269. [CrossRef]
19. Gaudio, S.; Wiemerslage, L.; Brooks, S.J.; Helgi, B. A systematic review of resting-state functional-MRI studies in anorexia nervosa: Evidence for functional connectivity impairment in cognitive control and visuospatial and body-signal integration. *Neurosci. Biobehav. Rev.* **2016** *71*, 578–589. [CrossRef]

20. Nico, D.; Claser, C.; Borja-Cabrera, G.P.; Travassos, L.R.; Palatnik, M.; da Silva Soares, I.; Rodrigues, M.M. Palatnik-de-Sousa, C.B. Adaptive immunity against Leishmania nucleoside hydrolase maps its c-terminal domain as the target of the CD4+ T cell-driven protective response. *PLoS Negl. Trop. Dis.* **2010**, *4*, e866. [CrossRef]
21. Blanchet, C.; Guillaume, S.; Bat-Pitault, F.; Carles, M.E.; Clarke, J.; Dodin, V.; Duriez, P.; Gerardin, P.; Hanachi-Guidoum, M.; Iceta, S.; et al. Medication in AN: A Multidisciplinary Overview of Meta-Analyses and Systematic Reviews. *J. Clin. Med.* **2019**, *8*. [CrossRef] [PubMed]
22. Pugh, J.; Maslen, H.; Savulescu, J. Deep Brain Stimulation, Authenticity and Value-CORRIGENDUM. *Camb. Q. Healthc. Ethics* **2018**, *27*, 179. [CrossRef] [PubMed]
23. Zrinzo, L.; Foltynie, T.; Limousin, P.; Hariz, M.I. Reducing hemorrhagic complications in functional neurosurgery: A large case series and systematic literature review. *J. Neurosurg.* **2012**, *116*, 84–94. [CrossRef]
24. Clair, A.H.; Haynes, W.; Mallet, L. Recent advances in deep brain stimulation in psychiatric disorders. *F1000Res* **2018**, *7*. [CrossRef]
25. Graat, I.; Figee, M.; Denys, D. The application of deep brain stimulation in the treatment of psychiatric disorders. *Int. Rev. Psychiatry* **2017**, *29*, 178–190. [CrossRef] [PubMed]
26. Arya, S.; Filkowski, M.M.; Nanda, P.; Sheth, S.A. Deep brain stimulation for obsessive-compulsive disorder. *Bull. Menn. Clin.* **2019**, *83*, 84–96. [CrossRef] [PubMed]
27. Naesstrom, M.; Blomstedt, P.; Bodlund, O. A systematic review of psychiatric indications for deep brain stimulation, with focus on major depressive and obsessive-compulsive disorder. *Nord. J. Psychiatry* **2016**, *70*, 91–483. [CrossRef]
28. Pugh, J.; Maslen, H.; Savulescu, J. Deep Brain Stimulation, Authenticity and Value. *Camb. Q. Healthc. Ethics* **2017**, *26*, 640–657. [CrossRef]
29. Wang, D.; Liu, X.; Zhou, B.; Kuang, W.; Guo, T. Advanced research on deep brain stimulation in treating mental disorders. *Exp. Ther. Med.* **2018**, *15*, 3–12. [CrossRef]
30. McLaughlin, N.C.; Didie, E.R.; Machado, A.G.; Haber, S.N.; Eskandar, E.N.; Greenberg, B.D. Improvements in anorexia symptoms after deep brain stimulation for intractable obsessive-compulsive disorder. *Biol. Psychiatry* **2013**, *73*, e29–31. [CrossRef]
31. Wu, H.; Van Dyck-Lippens, P.J.; Santegoeds, R.; van Kuyck, K.; Gabriëls, L.; Lin, G.; Pan, G.; Li, Y.; Li, D.; Zhan, S.; et al. Deep-brain stimulation for anorexia nervosa. *World Neurosurg.* **2013**, *80*, S29.e1-10. [CrossRef] [PubMed]
32. Lipsman, N.; Woodside, D.B.; Giacobbe, P.; Hamani, C.; Carter, J.C.; Norwood, S.J.; Sutandar, K.; Staab, R.; Elias, G.; Lyman, C.H.; et al. Subcallosal cingulate deep brain stimulation for treatment-refractory anorexia nervosa: A phase 1 pilot trial. *Lancet* **2013**, *381*, 1361–1370. [CrossRef]
33. Israel, M.; Steiger, H.; Kolivakis, T.; McGregor, L.; Sadikot, A.F. Deep brain stimulation in the subgenual cingulate cortex for an intractable eating disorder. *Biol. Psychiatry* **2010**, *67*, e4–53. [CrossRef] [PubMed]
34. Lipsman, N.; Lam, E.; Volpini, M.; Sutandar, K.; Twose, R.; Giacobbe, P.; Sodums, D.J.; Smith, G.S.; Woodside, D.B.; Lozano, A.M. Deep brain stimulation of the subcallosal cingulate for treatment-refractory anorexia nervosa: 1 year follow-up of an open-label trial. *Lancet. Psychiatry* **2017**, *4*, 285–294. [CrossRef]
35. Blomstedt, P.; Naesstrom, M.; Bodlund, O. Deep brain stimulation in the bed nucleus of the stria terminalis and medial forebrain bundle in a patient with major depressive disorder and anorexia nervosa. *Clin. Case Rep.* **2017**, *5*, 679–684. [CrossRef]
36. Manuelli, M.; Franzini, A.; Galentino, R.; Bidone, R.; Dell'Osso, B.; Porta, M.; Servello, D.; Cena, H. Changes in eating behavior after deep brain stimulation for anorexia nervosa. A case study. *Eat. Weight. Disord.* **2019**. [CrossRef]
37. Sheehan, D.V.; Lecrubier, Y.; Sheehan, K.H.; Amorim, P.; Janavs, J.; Weiller, E.; Hergueta, T.; Baker, R.; Dunbar, G.C. The Mini-International Neuropsychiatric Interview (M.I.N.I.): The development and validation of a structured diagnostic psychiatric interview for DSM-IV and ICD-10. *J. Clin. Psychiatry* **1998**, *59*, 22–33.
38. Hamilton, M. A rating scale for depression. *J. Neurol. Neurosurg. Psychiatry* **1960**, *23*, 56–62. [CrossRef]
39. Hamilton, M. The assessment of anxiety states by rating. *Br. J. Med Psychol.* **1959**, *32*, 5–50. [CrossRef]
40. Goodman, W.K.; Price, L.H.; Rasmussen, S.A.; Mazure, C.; Fleischmann, R.L.; Hill, C.L.; Heninger, G.R.; Charney, D.S. The Yale-Brown Obsessive Compulsive Scale. I. Development, use, and reliability. *Arch. Gen. Psychiatry* **1989**, *46*, 11–1006.

41. Mazure, C.M.; Halmi, K.A.; Sunday, S.R.; Romano, S.J.; Einhorn, A.M. The Yale-Brown-Cornell Eating Disorder Scale: Development, use, reliability and validity. *J. Psychiatr. Res.* **1994**, *28*, 45–425. [CrossRef]
42. Mehling, W.E.; Price, C.; Daubenmier, J.J.; Acree, M.; Bartmess, E.; Stewart, A. The Multidimensional Assessment of Interoceptive Awareness (MAIA). *PLoS ONE* **2012**, *7*, e48230. [CrossRef] [PubMed]
43. Gardner, R.M.; Stark, K.I.M.; Jackson, N.A.; Friedman, B.N. Development and validation of two new scales for assessment of body-image. *Percept. Mot. Ski.* **1999**, *89*, 93–981. [CrossRef] [PubMed]
44. Barratt, E.S. Violence and mental disorder: Developments in risk assessment. In *Impulsiveness and Aggression*; Monoham, J., Steadman, H.J., Eds.; University of Chicago Press: Chicago, IL, USA, 1994; pp. 61–79.
45. Ware, J.E.; Kosinski, M.; Gandek, B. *SF-36 Health Survey. Manual and Interpretation Guide*; The Health Institute, New England Medical Center: Boston, MA, USA, 1993.

Permissions

All chapters in this book were first published by MDPI; hereby published with permission under the Creative Commons Attribution License or equivalent. Every chapter published in this book has been scrutinized by our experts. Their significance has been extensively debated. The topics covered herein carry significant findings which will fuel the growth of the discipline. They may even be implemented as practical applications or may be referred to as a beginning point for another development.

The contributors of this book come from diverse backgrounds, making this book a truly international effort. This book will bring forth new frontiers with its revolutionizing research information and detailed analysis of the nascent developments around the world.

We would like to thank all the contributing authors for lending their expertise to make the book truly unique. They have played a crucial role in the development of this book. Without their invaluable contributions this book wouldn't have been possible. They have made vital efforts to compile up to date information on the varied aspects of this subject to make this book a valuable addition to the collection of many professionals and students.

This book was conceptualized with the vision of imparting up-to-date information and advanced data in this field. To ensure the same, a matchless editorial board was set up. Every individual on the board went through rigorous rounds of assessment to prove their worth. After which they invested a large part of their time researching and compiling the most relevant data for our readers.

The editorial board has been involved in producing this book since its inception. They have spent rigorous hours researching and exploring the diverse topics which have resulted in the successful publishing of this book. They have passed on their knowledge of decades through this book. To expedite this challenging task, the publisher supported the team at every step. A small team of assistant editors was also appointed to further simplify the editing procedure and attain best results for the readers.

Apart from the editorial board, the designing team has also invested a significant amount of their time in understanding the subject and creating the most relevant covers. They scrutinized every image to scout for the most suitable representation of the subject and create an appropriate cover for the book.

The publishing team has been an ardent support to the editorial, designing and production team. Their endless efforts to recruit the best for this project, has resulted in the accomplishment of this book. They are a veteran in the field of academics and their pool of knowledge is as vast as their experience in printing. Their expertise and guidance has proved useful at every step. Their uncompromising quality standards have made this book an exceptional effort. Their encouragement from time to time has been an inspiration for everyone.

The publisher and the editorial board hope that this book will prove to be a valuable piece of knowledge for researchers, students, practitioners and scholars across the globe.

List of Contributors

Patricia E. Durning and Michael G. Perri
Department of Clinical and Health Psychology, University of Florida, Gainesville, FL 32610, USA

Eliza L. Gordon
Department of Clinical and Health Psychology, University of Florida, Gainesville, FL 32610, USA
Division of Physical Medicine & Rehabilitation, University of Utah, 30 N 1900 E (Rm 1B620), Salt Lake City, UT 84132, USA

Lisa J. Merlo
Department of Psychiatry, McKnight Brain Institute, University of Florida College of Medicine, L4-100K, Gainesville, FL 32611, USA

Kentaro Matsui
Japan Somnology Center, Neuropsychiatric Research Institute, Tokyo 1510053, Japan
Department of Psychiatry, Tokyo Women's Medical University, Tokyo 1628666, Japan
Clinical Laboratory, National Institute of Mental Health, National Center of Neurology and Psychiatry, Tokyo 1878551, Japan
Department of Sleep-Wake Disorders, National Institute of Mental Health, National Center of Neurology and Psychiatry, Tokyo 1878551, Japan

Katsuji Nishimura
Department of Psychiatry, Tokyo Women's Medical University, Tokyo 1628666, Japan

Kenichi Kuriyama
Department of Sleep-Wake Disorders, National Institute of Mental Health, National Center of Neurology and Psychiatry, Tokyo 1878551, Japan

Yoko Komada
Liberal Arts, Meiji Pharmaceutical University, Tokyo 2048588, Japan

Yuichi Inoue
Japan Somnology Center, Neuropsychiatric Research Institute, Tokyo 1510053, Japan
Department of Somnology, Tokyo Medical University, Tokyo 1608402, Japan

Susana Jiménez-Murcia and Fernando Fernández-Aranda
Department of Psychiatry, University Hospital of Bellvitge-IDIBELL, L'Hospitalet de Llobregat, 08907 Barcelona, Spain
CIBER Fisiopatología Obesidad y Nutrición (CIBERobn), Instituto de Salud Carlos III, L'Hospitalet de Llobregat, 08907 Barcelona, Spain
Clinical Sciences Department, School of Medicine, University of Barcelona, 08907 L'Hospitalet de Llobregat, Spain

Jéssica Sánchez-González and Isabel Baenas
Department of Psychiatry, University Hospital of Bellvitge-IDIBELL, L'Hospitalet de Llobregat, 08907 Barcelona, Spain

Isabel Sánchez and Nadine Riesco
Department of Psychiatry, University Hospital of Bellvitge-IDIBELL, L'Hospitalet de Llobregat, 08907 Barcelona, Spain
CIBER Fisiopatología Obesidad y Nutrición (CIBERobn), Instituto de Salud Carlos III, L'Hospitalet de Llobregat, 08907 Barcelona, Spain

Zaida Agüera
Department of Psychiatry, University Hospital of Bellvitge-IDIBELL, L'Hospitalet de Llobregat, 08907 Barcelona, Spain
CIBER Fisiopatología Obesidad y Nutrición (CIBERobn), Instituto de Salud Carlos III, L'Hospitalet de Llobregat, 08907 Barcelona, Spain
Department of Public Health, Mental Health and Maternal-Child Nursing, School of Nursing, University of Barcelona, 08907 L'Hospitalet de Llobregat, Spain

Georgios Paslakis
Toronto General Hospital, University Health Network, Toronto, ON M5G 2C4, Canada
Department of Psychiatry, University of Toronto, Toronto, ON M5T 1R8, Canada

Lucero Munguia
Clinical Sciences Department, School of Medicine, University of Barcelona, 08907 L'Hospitalet de Llobregat, Spain

Roser Granero
CIBER Fisiopatología Obesidad y Nutrición (CIBERobn), Instituto de Salud Carlos III, L'Hospitalet de Llobregat, 08907 Barcelona, Spain
Department of Psychobiology and Methodology, Autonomous University of Barcelona, 08193 Barcelona, Spain

Ashley N Gearhardt
Department of Psychology, University of Michigan, Ann Arbor, MI 48109, USA

Carlos Dieguez
CIBER Fisiopatología Obesidad y Nutrición (CIBERobn), Instituto de Salud Carlos III, L'Hospitalet de Llobregat, 08907 Barcelona, Spain
Department of Physiology, Center for Research in Molecular Medicine and Chronic Diseases (CIMUS), Health Research Institute of Santiago USC-IDIS, University Santiago de Compostela, 15705 Santiago de Compostela, Spain

Gilda Fazia
Department of Health Sciences, University "Magna Graecia" of Catanzaro, Viale Europa, 88100 Catanzaro, Italy
Center for Clinical Research and Treatment of Eating Disorders, Azienda Ospedaliera Universitaria Mater Domini, 88100 Catanzaro, Italy

Cristina Segura-García
Center for Clinical Research and Treatment of Eating Disorders, Azienda Ospedaliera Universitaria Mater Domini, 88100 Catanzaro, Italy
Department of Medical and Surgical Sciences, University "Magna Graecia" of Catanzaro, 88100 Catanzaro, Italy

José M Menchón
Department of Psychiatry, University Hospital of Bellvitge-IDIBELL, L'Hospitalet de Llobregat, 08907 Barcelona, Spain
Clinical Sciences Department, School of Medicine, University of Barcelona, 08907 L'Hospitalet de Llobregat, Spain
CIBER de Salud Mental (CIBERSAM), Instituto de Salud Carlos III, L'Hospitalet de Llobregat, 08907 Barcelona, Spain

Robert H. Lustig
Department of Pediatrics, University of California, San Francisco, CA 94143, USA
Institute for Health Policy Studies, University of California, San Francisco, CA 94143, USA
Department of Research, Touro University-California, Vallejo, CA 94592, USA

Tinne Buelens and Margaux Verschueren
Faculty of Psychology and Educational Sciences, KU Leuven, 3000 Leuven, Belgium

Koen Luyckx
Faculty of Psychology and Educational Sciences, KU Leuven, 3000 Leuven, Belgium
UNIBS, University of the Free State, 9300 Bloemfontein, South Africa

Katrien Schoevaerts
Psychiatric Hospital Alexianen Zorggroep Tienen, 3300 Tienen, Belgium

Eva Dierckx
Psychiatric Hospital Alexianen Zorggroep Tienen, 3300 Tienen, Belgium
Department of Psychology and Educational Sciences, Vrije Universiteit Brussel, 1050 Elsene, Belgium

Lies Depestele
Faculty of Psychology and Educational Sciences, KU Leuven, 3000 Leuven, Belgium
Psychiatric Hospital Alexianen Zorggroep Tienen, 3300 Tienen, Belgium

Laurence Claes
Faculty of Medicine and Health Sciences, Universiteit Antwerpen, 2610 Wilrijk, Belgium

Laurence J. Nolan and Steve M. Jenkins
Department of Psychology, Wagner College, 1 Campus Rd., Staten Island, NY 10301, USA

David A. Wiss
Fielding School of Public Health, University of California Los Angeles, Los Angeles, CA 90095, USA

Nicole Avena
Department of Neuroscience, Icahn School of Medicine at Mount Sinai, New York, NY 10029, USA
Department of Psychology, Princeton University, Princeton, NJ 08540, USA

Mark Gold
School of Medicine, Washington University in St. Louis, St. Louis, MO 63130, USA

Enrico Collantoni, Paolo Meneguzzo, Iolanna Chiappini and Renzo Manara
Department of Neurosciences, University of Padua, Via Giustiniani, 2-35128 Padova, Italy

Christopher R. Madan
School of Psychology, University of Nottingham, Nottingham NG7 2QL, UK

Elena Tenconi and Angela Favaro
Padua Neuroscience Center, University of Padua, 35128 Padova, Italy

Elizabeth H. Evans
School of Psychology, Newcastle University, Newcastle NE1 7RU, UK

Stephanie E. Cassin
Department of Psychology, Ryerson University, 350 Victoria St., Toronto, ON M5B 2K3, Canada
Centre for Mental Health, University Health Network, Network - Toronto General Hospital, 200 Elizabeth Street, 8th Floor, Toronto, ON M5G 2C4, Canada
Department of Psychiatry, University of Toronto, 250 College Street, Toronto, ON M5T 1R8, Canada

Daniel Z. Buchman
University of Toronto Joint Centre of Bioethics, 155 College Street, Suite 754, Toronto, ON M5T 1P8, Canada
Bioethics Program and Krembil Brain Institute, Toronto Western Hospital, University Health Network, 399 Bathurst Street, Toronto, ON M5T 1P8, Canada
Dalla Lana School of Public Health, University of Toronto, 155 College Street, 6th Floor, Toronto, ON M5T 1R8, Canada

Samantha E. Leung and Karin Kantarovich
Centre for Mental Health, University Health Network, Network - Toronto General Hospital, 200 Elizabeth Street, 8th Floor, Toronto, ON M5G 2C4, Canada
Bariatric Surgery Program, University Health Network - Toronto Western Hospital, 399 Bathurst Street, East Wing - 4th Floor, Toronto, ON M5T 2S8, Canada

Aceel Hawa
Department of Education, Centre for Addiction and Mental Health, 33 Russell Street, Toronto, ON M5S 2S1, Canada

Adrian Carter
School of Psychological Sciences, Monash University, Melbourne, VIC 3181, Australia
UQ Centre for Clinical Research, University of Queensland, Herston, QLD 4029, Australia

Sanjeev Sockalingam
Centre for Mental Health, University Health Network, Network - Toronto General Hospital, 200 Elizabeth Street, 8th Floor, Toronto, ON M5G 2C4, Canada
Department of Psychiatry, University of Toronto, 250 College Street, Toronto, ON M5T 1R8, Canada
Bariatric Surgery Program, University Health Network - Toronto Western Hospital, 399 Bathurst Street, East Wing - 4th Floor, Toronto, ON M5T 2S8, Canada
Department of Education, Centre for Addiction and Mental Health, 33 Russell Street, Toronto, ON M5S 2S1, Canada

Laurie Zawertailo
Department of Pharmacology and Toxicology, University of Toronto, 1 King's College Circle, Toronto, ON M5S 1A8, Canada
Centre for Addiction and Mental Health, 1025 Queen Street West, Toronto, ON M6J 1H4, Canada

Sophia Attwells, Wayne K. deRuiter, Thao Lan Le and Danielle Dawson
Centre for Addiction and Mental Health, 1025 Queen Street West, Toronto, ON M6J 1H4, Canada

Peter Selby
Centre for Addiction and Mental Health, 1025 Queen Street West, Toronto, ON M6J 1H4, Canada
Department of Family and Community Medicine, University of Toronto, 500 University Ave., Toronto, ON M5G 1V7, Canada
Department of Psychiatry, University of Toronto, 250 College St., Toronto, ON M5T 1L8, Canada
Dalla Lana School of Public Health, University of Toronto, 155 College St, Toronto, ON M5T 3M7, Canada

Alina Kukies, Almut Zeeck, Derek Spieler, Lukas Holovics and Armin Hartmann
Department of Psychosomatic Medicine and Psychotherapy, Medical Center – University of Freiburg, Faculty of Medicine, University of Freiburg, 79104 Freiburg, Germany

Simon Maier
Department of Psychosomatic Medicine and Psychotherapy, Medical Center – University of Freiburg, Faculty of Medicine, University of Freiburg, 79104 Freiburg, Germany
Department of Psychiatry and Psychotherapy, Medical Center – University of Freiburg, Faculty of Medicine, University of Freiburg, 79104 Freiburg, Germany

Kathrin Nickel, Ludger Tebartz van Elst and Dominique Endres
Department of Psychiatry and Psychotherapy, Medical Center – University of Freiburg, Faculty of Medicine, University of Freiburg, 79104 Freiburg, Germany

Evgeniy Perlov
Department of Psychiatry and Psychotherapy, Medical Center – University of Freiburg, Faculty of Medicine, University of Freiburg, 79104 Freiburg, Germany
Luzerner Psychiatrie, Hospital St. Urban, 4915 St. Urban, Switzerland

Michael Dacko and Thomas Lange
Department of Radiology, Medical Physics, Medical Center – University of Freiburg, Faculty of Medicine, University of Freiburg, 79106 Freiburg, Germany

Emma J. Boyland and Charlotte A. Hardman
Department of Psychological Sciences, University of Liverpool, Liverpool L69 7ZX, UK

Andreas Joos
Department of Psychosomatic Medicine and Psychotherapy, Medical Center—University of Freiburg, Faculty of Medicine, University of Freiburg, 79104 Freiburg, Germany
Department of Psychosomatic Medicine and Psychotherapy, Ortenau Klinikum, Teaching Hospital of University of Freiburg, 77654 Offenburg, Germany

Helen K. Ruddock
Department of Psychological Sciences, University of Liverpool, Liverpool L69 7ZX, UK
School of Psychology, University of Birmingham, Birmingham B15 2TT, UK

Michael Orwin
Department of Psychological Sciences, University of Liverpool, Liverpool L69 7ZX, UK
School of Psychology, Newcastle University, Newcastle NE1 7RU, UK

Ignacio Delgado-Martínez
Department of Neurosurgery, Hospital del Mar, 08003 Barcelona, Spain

Gloria Villalba Martínez
Department of Neurosurgery, Hospital del Mar, 08003 Barcelona, Spain
Department of Psychiatry and Forensic Medicine, Universitat Autònoma de Barcelona, Cerdanyola del Vallès, 08193 Barcelona, Spain

Matilde Elices
Hospital del Mar Medical Research Institute (IMIM), 08003 Barcelona, Spain
Centro de Investigación Biomédica en Red de Salud Mental (CIBERSAM), 28029 Madrid, Spain

Víctor Pérez
Department of Psychiatry and Forensic Medicine, Universitat Autònoma de Barcelona, Cerdanyola del Vallès, 08193 Barcelona, Spain
Hospital del Mar Medical Research Institute (IMIM), 08003 Barcelona, Spain
Institut de Neuropsiquiatria i Adiccions (INAD), Hospital del Mar, 08003 Barcelona, Spain
Centro de Investigación Biomédica en Red de Salud Mental (CIBERSAM), 28029 Madrid, Spain

Azucena Justicia
Hospital del Mar Medical Research Institute (IMIM), 08003 Barcelona, Spain
Institut de Neuropsiquiatria i Adiccions (INAD), Hospital del Mar, 08003 Barcelona, Spain
Centro de Investigación Biomédica en Red de Salud Mental (CIBERSAM), 28029 Madrid, Spain

Purificación Salgado, José María Ginés, Rocío Guardiola, Carlos Cedrón and María Polo
Institut de Neuropsiquiatria i Adiccions (INAD), Hospital del Mar, 08003 Barcelona, Spain

Santiago Medrano
Department of Radiology, Hospital del Mar, 08003 Barcelona, Spain

Rosa María Manero
Department of Neurology, Hospital del Mar, 08003 Barcelona, Spain

Gerardo Conesa
Department of Neurosurgery, Hospital del Mar, 08003 Barcelona, Spain
Hospital del Mar Medical Research Institute (IMIM), 08003 Barcelona, Spain
Department of Surgery, Universitat Autònoma de Barcelona, Cerdanyola del Vallès, 08193 Barcelona, Spain

Gustavo Faus and Antoni Grau
ITA, Mental Health Specialists, 08036 Barcelona, Spain

Index

www.ingramcontent.com/pod-product-compliance
Lightning Source LLC
LaVergne TN
LVHW082215200926
848484LV00008B/2258